The Spanish Portrait

FROM EL GRECO TO PICASSO

First published in 2004 by
Scala Publishers Ltd
Northburgh House
10 Northburgh Street
London EC1V 0AT

ISBN 1 85759 374 X

PROJECT MANAGEMENT AND EDITORIAL
Museo Nacional del Prado:
Gabriele Finaldi, Raquel González, Alejandro Vergara, Lorena Casas
Ediciones El Viso: Santiago Saavedra, Lola Gómez, Isla Aguilar
Scala Publishers Ltd: Oliver Craske, Esme West, Emma Pattison

TRANSLATORS:
Phil Goddard, Paul Edson, Joanna Martinez, Gilla Evans, Isabel Varea, Isabel Del Rio, Shirley Brotherton-Pinniger, Mary Shovelin, Kim Eddy
COPY EDITOR: Julie Pickard
TYPESETTING & ADDITIONAL EDITING: Helen Robertson

Printed and bound in Spain

WITH THE SUPPORT
OF THE

BBVA

The Spanish Portrait

FROM EL GRECO TO PICASSO

Javier Portús

José Álvarez Lopera
Javier Barón
José Luis Díez
Miguel Falomir
Gabriele Finaldi
Nigel Glendinning
Manuela B. Mena Marqués
Alfonso E. Pérez Sánchez
Leticia Ruiz Gómez
Pilar Silva Maroto

20 October 2004 – 6 February 2005

MUSEO NACIONAL DEL PRADO

LENDERS AND DEPOSITARY INSTITUTIONS TO THE EXHIBITION

BARCELONA Private collection

BARCELONA Museu Picasso

BERLIN Staatliche Museen zu Berlin, Gemäldegalerie

BILBAO Museo de Bellas Artes

BOSTON Museum of Fine Arts

CHICAGO The Art Institute of Chicago

FORT WORTH Kimbell Art Museum

LONDON English Heritage (Apsley House)

LONDON The National Gallery

MADRID Colección Banco de España

MADRID Fundación Casa de Alba

MADRID Instituto Valencia de Don Juan

MADRID Museo Nacional Centro de Arte Reina Sofía

MADRID Museo de la Real Academia de Bellas Artes de San Fernando

MADRID Museo Thyssen-Bornemisza

MADRID Patrimonio Nacional, Real Monasterio de San Lorenzo de El Escorial

MILAN Museo Poldi Pezzoli

MINNEAPOLIS The Minneapolis Institute of Arts

NEW YORK The Hispanic Society of America

NEW YORK The Metropolitan Museum of Art

PAREDES DE NAVA Iglesia Museo Parroquial de Santa Eulalia

PARIS Musée d'Orsay

PARIS Musée du Louvre

PARIS Musée Picasso

PARMA Fondazione Magnani-Rocca

ROUEN Musée des Beaux-Arts

SEVILLE Seville Cathedral

SEVILLE Hermandad de la Santa Caridad

SEVILLE Museo de Bellas Artes

TOKYO Private collection, courtesy of Fuji Television Gallery

VALENCIA Museo de Bellas Artes

VIENNA Kunsthistorisches Museum, Gemäldegalerie

Colección Masaveu

The Lerma Bequest. Toledo, Palacio Tavera, Fundación Casa Ducal de Medinaceli

ACKNOWLEDGEMENTS

Duquesa de Alba, Juan Manuel Albendea, Rafael Alonso, Monseñor Carlos Amigo, Evaristo Arce, Stephanie D'Alessandro, Ronni Baer, Renato Barilli, Fernando Benito, Antonio Bonet Correa, Juan Manuel Bonet Planes, Julius Bryant, Marcus Burke, Marisa Caballero Infante, Francisco Calvo Serraller, Ignacio Cano, Isabel Carmona, Dawson Carr, Jaime Caruana Lacorte, Rosy Cinnamond, Mitchell A. Codding, José Luis Colomer, Roberto Contini, James Cuno, Margarita Cuyás, Stephanie D'Alessandro, Rosario Díez del Corral, Monseñor Antonio Domínguez Valverde, Marqués de Douro, Douglas Druick, Dominique Dupuis-Labbé, Larry Feinberg, Marta Finaldi, Lucia Fornari Schianchi, Juan Gaitán de Ayala y Maestre, Carmen García Frías, Rafael García Ormaechea, Gonzalo Gil, Nigel Glendinning, Ramón González de Amezúa, Jorge González, Duque de Huéscar, Tadao Ishizuka, David Jaffé, Jan Kelch, Teresa Laguna Paul, Serge Lemoine, Bernd Lindemann, Tomás Llorens, Henri Loyrette, Neil MacGregor, Beatriz Mariño, María Martín de Argila, Ana Martínez de Aguilar, Evan Maurer, Philippe de Montebello, Patrick Noon, María Teresa Ocaña, Reverendo Francisco Ortiz Gómez, Monseñor Rafael Palmero, Cristina Partearroyo, Reverendo Manuel Pérez Gallardo, Alfonso Pérez Sánchez, Christine Pinault, Joachim Pissarro, Vincent Pomarède, Timothy F. Potts, Wolfgang Prohaska, Miguel Ángel Recio Crespo, Gérard Regnier, Bernardo Riviere Cinamond, José María Rodríguez-Ponga, Malcolm Rogers, Bernard Ruiz-Picasso, Laurent Salomé, Duque de San Carlos, Monseñor Ángel Sancho Campo, Charles Saumarez Smith, Peter-Klaus Schuster, Karl Schütz, Duque de Segorbe, Wilfried Seipel, George T. M. Shackelford, Lisa Shakespeare, Simon Thurley, Baronesa Thyssen, Patrice Triboux, Simona Tosini Pizzetti, Cristina del Valle, Javier Viar, José María Viñuela, Duque de Wellington, James N. Wood, Susumu Yamamoto, Annalisa Zanni

The Spanish Portrait from El Greco to Picasso is a major cultural event, which brings together a large selection of outstanding paintings spanning several centuries. Through the works of such masters as El Greco, Velázquez, Goya and Picasso, it surveys the development of one of the most important artistic genres – the portait – from the late Middle Ages to the early twentieth century. The exhibition also affords visitors a fascinating overview of the evolution of Spanish painting over this period, since portraiture is a genre in which Spain's greatest painters have always excelled.

Though first and foremost a source of intense aesthetic pleasure, the exhibition also allows us to reflect upon our common past and find evidence of our collective identity – for the portrait is, after all, one of the main windows through which a society can examine its own history. As we study this chronological succession of kings, queens and princesses, court jesters, artists, politicians, professionals, intellectuals, family groups and outcasts, we learn not only about the physical appearance of our forebears but also about their social relationships, their expectations and the image they wished to project. The portrait, as a genre, has always been rich in meaning; through it, both artist and sitter have conveyed their ideas, their psychological make-up and their place in society.

Such an ambitious project would not have been possible without the sponsorship of BBVA, a Benefactor of the Museo Nacional del Prado. The relationship between the two institutions, which have been working together successfully for several years, is a fine example of fruitful cooperation between the public and private sectors. I should like to take this opportunity, on behalf of the Ministry of Culture, to thank the BBVA for its generosity as sponsor of this exhibition.

I should also like to thank the Comunidad de Madrid for their help and support in organising the exhibition.

The Museo Nacional del Prado sought the cooperation of a number of national and international institutions, all of which – aware of the significance of the event – responded promptly to loan requests. Key portraits by Spanish artists have been lent by museums and collections in France, Italy, Britain, Austria, the United States, Germany and Japan, as well as by various Spanish collections. My sincere thanks to all of them and, of course, to the Museum staff.

Carmen Calvo Poyato

SPANISH MINISTER OF CULTURE

This is the first comprehensive and detailed survey of the portrait as a genre to be held in Spain. Both the exhibition itself, *The Spanish Portrait from El Greco to Picasso*, and the accompanying catalogue will therefore be hailed as major events by students and lovers of Spanish art.

All of us at the Museo Nacional del Prado take pride in the skill and professionalism with which the Museum responds to challenging projects such as this, and I should like to congratulate the staff on such a splendid achievement.

As the chief repository of Spain's pictorial memory and home to the Royal Collections, the Museo del Prado is the perfect venue for an exhibition of this nature. Its permanent collection boasts a wealth of portraits, a favourite genre among Spain's royal collectors, and any survey of the Spanish portrait must necessarily include many of the portraits held by the Prado.

However, this exhibition would not have been possible without the support and sponsorship of various public and private institutions; in this context, special mention should be made of BBVA, Benefactor of the Museum and the principal sponsor of the exhibition. Moreover, numerous people and institutions, both in Spain and abroad, have lent works. To all of them, our sincere thanks.

Rodrigo Uría Meruéndano

CHAIRMAN, BOARD OF PATRONS OF THE
MUSEO NACIONAL DEL PRADO

BBVA is especially pleased to be involved in a new joint venture with the Museo Nacional del Prado, particularly one as remarkable as *The Spanish Portrait from El Greco to Picasso*.

This project forms part of an agreement signed last year between the two institutions, by which BBVA became Benefactor of the Museum and undertook to support its Programme of Major Exhibitions, thus ensuring not only a series of temporary exhibitions of the highest quality but also a wide range of concurrent activities.

The first of the exhibitions held under the agreement was last year's *Vermeer and the Dutch Interior*. There are no works by the Master of Delft in Spain and this exhibition brought together, for the first time in our country, nine paintings by Vermeer – of which few works survive – as well as works by other leading Dutch contemporaries.

Our participation in this present project is the latest in a long series of joint ventures between the companies that form Grupo BBVA and the Museo Nacional del Prado. Previous sponsorship successes include a number of major cultural events such as retrospectives dedicated to Zurbarán (1988), Ribera (1992) and Goya (1995), as well as the exhibition *Latest Acquisitions 1982–1995* (1995) and *The Five Senses and Art* (1997).

Through a series of over eighty paintings, some from the Museum's permanent collection and others lent by national and international institutions, the current exhibition offers, for the first time, a general survey of the history of the portrait in Spain, from its origins in the late Middle Ages to the first avant-garde movements in the early twentieth century.

The importance of portraiture as a genre in the history of Spanish painting relates partly to the sheer number of portraits produced, partly to the identity of the sitters, and partly to the opportunity portraits provide to reconstruct a historical and cultural image of ourselves. But its importance stems equally from the fact that most leading Spanish painters were famed for their portraits – some having been, indeed, portrait painters above all else. Velázquez springs immediately to mind, but so too do El Greco, Goya and Picasso, key figures in the history of Western art.

By taking part in this challenging project, BBVA hopes to support the Museo Nacional del Prado in enhancing its splendid permanent collection with a series of temporary exhibitions and thus to foster, on an ongoing basis, a deeper awareness of the great masters of European Art.

The project forms part of Grupo BBVA's social commitment, an essential element of our corporate culture. We feel that, as committed citizens, it is our duty to contribute to the development and general welfare of the society in which we operate. We firmly believe that, through art and culture, we can provide a powerful means of enhancing knowledge and improving society.

Finally, we would like to thank the Ministry of Culture and the Museo Nacional del Prado for giving us the chance to take part in this exhibition of the 'New Prado', an outstanding example of public and private partnership which highlights once again the key role of the private sector in supporting cultural events.

Francisco González Rodríguez
CHAIRMAN, BBVA

Since the nineteenth century, when awareness of Spain's great painting tradition spread throughout Europe and it became widely acknowledged that the country had provided some of the major names in the history of Western art, there has been a considerable increase in the study of leading Spanish painters and their best-known works, and of the genres and themes most representative of Spanish art. This growth in historiographical research has been matched, especially over the last fifty years, by a rise in the number of exhibitions of Spanish art. Today, as a result, people have a fairly clear idea of the history of Spanish painting, and know something of not only the personalities of the foremost painters but also the development of the various genres; both in Spain and abroad, art lovers are aware of a 'Spanish School' and can identify its main characteristics.

Surprisingly, however, one area of Spanish painting has received only cursory attention, in spite of – or perhaps because of – its undeniable importance. Indeed, there have been no monographs and no exhibitions tracing the overall development of the portrait as a genre in Spain. Countless studies have, of course, addressed the approach to portraiture adopted by the great Spanish painters, led by Velázquez, Goya, El Greco and Picasso, and there have been some, albeit few, exhibitions on the subject; but until now, no one has shown in detail how these painters link together to create a tradition, a chartable history of the subject.

This gap is all the more striking given the importance of the portrait in the history of Spanish painting; for not only did all of Spain's best artists work in this genre to a greater or lesser extent, but some were 'portrait painters' above all else. Velázquez and Picasso are outstanding examples. Indeed, among the masterpieces of Spanish art there are many portraits, such as the royal families depicted by Velázquez and Goya. But the portrait is also important as the main genre through which we can discern a 'tradition' in Spanish painting. An unbroken line can be traced from the sixteenth century to Picasso; its key feature being the portrait, and its primary setting the Court. The best artists (Spanish and foreign) of every period were appointed court painters to the Kings of Spain; and each took as his starting point the work and models of his predecessors. It is a history that begins with Titian, a Venetian, and with the Flemish painter Anthonis Mor, and continues through Sánchez Coello, Pantoja, Velázquez and Carreño, right up to Goya. When, in the nineteenth century, Spanish and occasionally foreign painters set out to trace the history of Spanish painting, they focused above all on that tradition of portraiture, a tradition they themselves continued by using it as a starting point for their own work. Closer to us in time, Picasso also reflected deeply on the Spanish portrait, evidence of which is to be found throughout his work. Although the influences that shaped these artists were clearly many and varied, one cannot understand Picasso fully unless one is familiar with El Greco and Velázquez; and Goya's work speaks of his debt to Velázquez, who in turn was influenced by the portraits by El Greco and Titian that he so admired.

Aware of the fact that there was such an interesting story to be told, and above all to be shown, the Museo Nacional del Prado sees this exhibition, *The Spanish Portrait from El Greco to Picasso*, not only as a great opportunity but also as a major responsibility. The Museum houses an incomparable collection of Spanish portraits, including many masterpieces, some of which could not conceivably be exhibited elsewhere. A tremendous effort was therefore made to organise an exhibition of paintings of the highest quality that would demonstrate the development of the portrait as a genre, from the late sixteenth century to the early twentieth, highlighting those elements which testify to a tradition and showing the influence of successive artists on the works of their predecessors.

An event of this magnitude requires immense input from everyone involved in the life of the Museum. The theoretical underpinning posed a considerable challenge, to which Javier Portús, of the Museum's curatorial staff, responded with zeal as the curator of the exhibition. In the arduous task of planning the exhibition and editing the catalogue, he was ably assisted by a large team of specialists, including many of the Museum's curators. This not only testifies to the team effort behind the exhibition but also illustrates the extent to which its subject matter overlaps with the expertise of the Museum itself. I should like to draw particular attention to the assistance provided by Alfonso Pérez Sánchez, Honorary Director of the Museum, and Professor Nigel Glendinning, of the University of London, both of whom have contributed with the inclusion of remarkable essays. Together, all these specialists have constructed the first overview of the historical development of the portrait in Spain and I should like to thank all of them for their splendid contributions.

Like any exhibition on this scale, the present project required the generous cooperation of museums, institutions and collections both in Spain and abroad, who readily agreed to lend works of art so that they might be seen and enjoyed by the visitors to this exhibition. Thanks to the temporary loan of these outstanding works, the Museo del Prado has been able to reconstruct – in the emblematic Central Gallery of the Villanueva building – a remarkable chapter in the history of painting. Our warmest thanks to all those institutions.

The programme of temporary exhibitions is undoubtedly a crucial means of furthering our scientific and research activity, and of implementing the Museum's cultural mission. The aim of this programme is to complement, extend and enrich our permanent collections. The Museum could not respond to this remarkable challenge without the special support of our Benefactors, among whom is BBVA. We are fortunate to enjoy once more their sponsorship of a project as extraordinary as this. I should like to express here our great pleasure at this new joint venture, which will strengthen the already exemplary partnership that exists between BBVA and the Museo del Prado. We are also grateful for the assistance of the Comunidad de Madrid, a contribution that falls into part of their ongoing support for the arts.

Finally, I should like to offer my warmest thanks to all the Museum staff for organising and mounting this exhibition, whose success is – as always – due to the joint efforts of everyone involved.

Miguel Zugaza Miranda
DIRECTOR OF THE MUSEO NACIONAL DEL PRADO

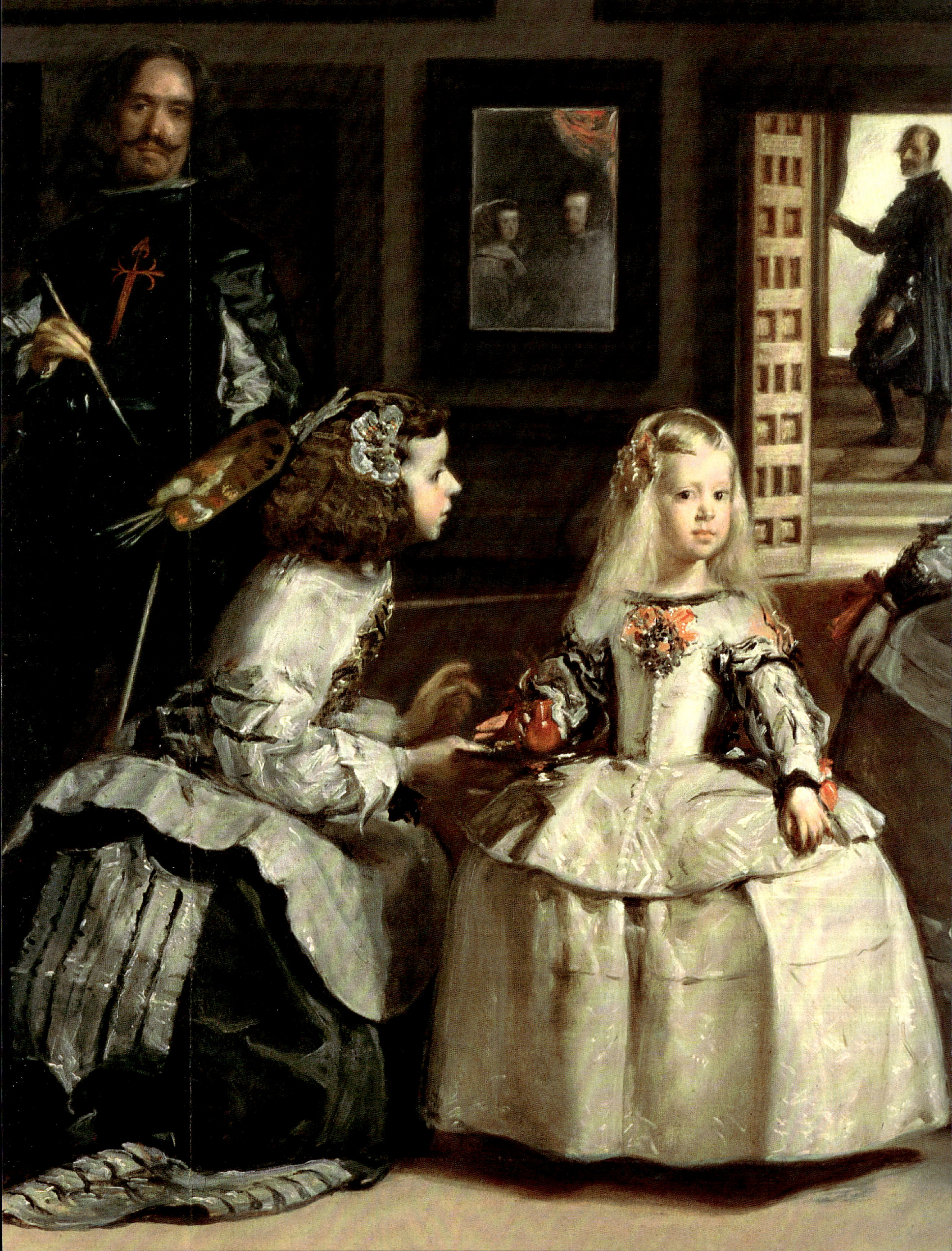

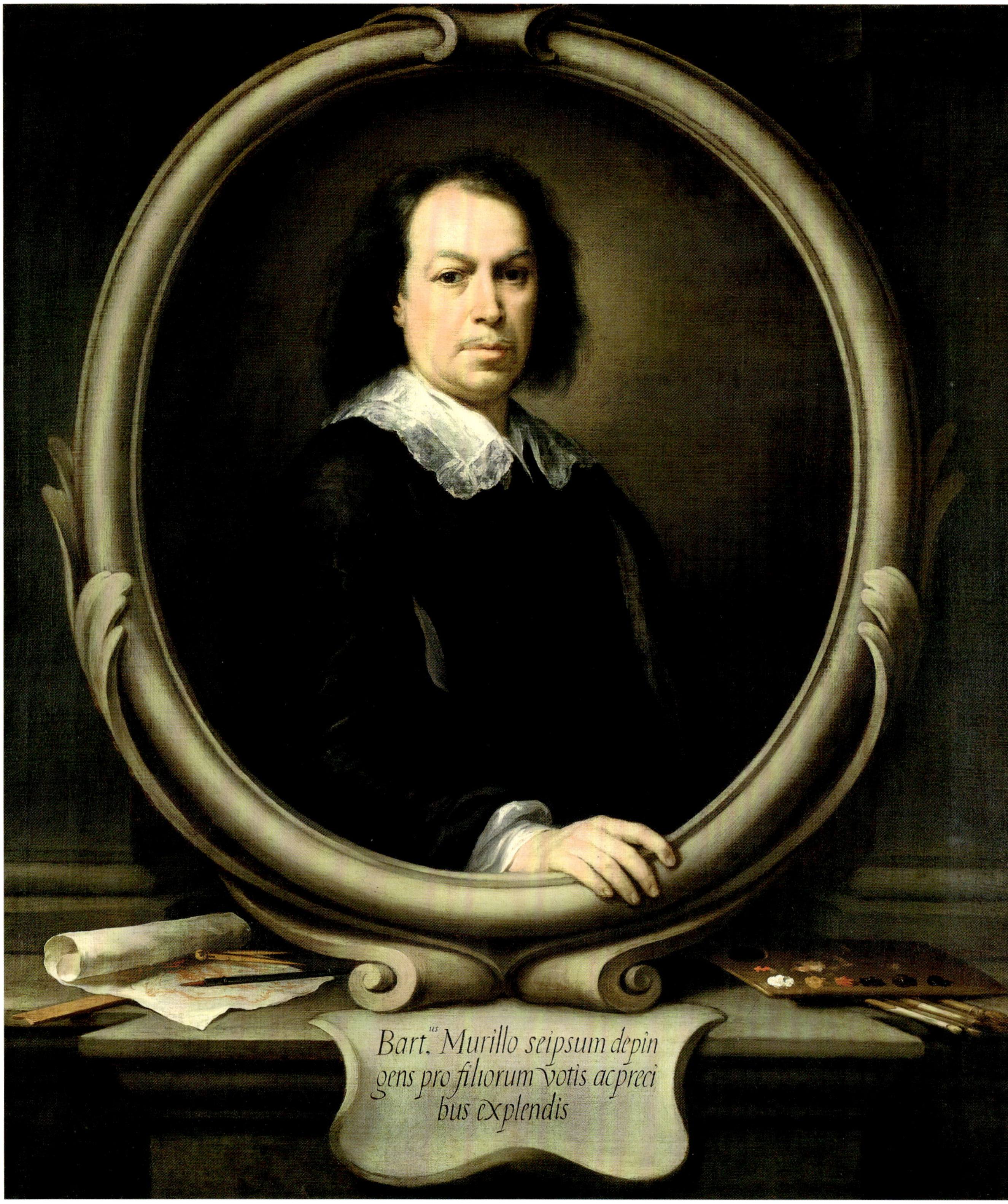

FIG. 1. Bartolomé Esteban Murillo, *Self Portrait*, *ca.* 1670. London, The National Gallery [6153]

The Varied Fortunes of the Portrait in Spain

Javier Portús

In a 1907 text on Spanish painting, the British critics Albert F. Calvert and C. Gasquoine Hartley concluded that Spain was very much a nation of portraitists. It was in portraiture that the country's artistic genius lay, and it had produced an almost continuous line of great masters in this genre. This, they believed, gave Spanish art its distinctive personality, which had its origin in Spain's individualism and desire to 'express its art as drama'.[1]

Of course this is very much a generalisation, and must be seen in the context of the quest by nineteenth- and twentieth-century artists and intellectuals, both in Spain and abroad, for signs and myths of Spanish identity. But while the two authors' assertions about this national personality may be open to question, there is still a great deal of truth in what they say. It reflects a widely held view among historians of Spanish painting that portraits have often been disproportionately influential, given the relatively small number of artists who worked in this genre and the limited number of portraits they painted.

The idea of a tradition of Spanish portraiture developed among essayists in the seventeenth century. The Aragonese author Jusepe Martínez wrote in around 1675: 'There have been many admirable [Spanish] portrait artists, as we can clearly see from the fact that their works are still greatly venerated today.'[2]

The vast majority of Spanish painting during this period was devoted to religious narrative.[3] This was partly because the church was still the main patron of artists, though large numbers of religious images were also bought by private collectors for reasons both of devotion and taste. Other genres were much less common, although their fortunes waxed and waned from one century to the next.

Portraits became more common as time passed, but remained relatively few in number until the early nineteenth century. Despite this, they played an undeniably important role in the history of Spanish painting, and any anthology inevitably contains a sizeable number of them. One of the main reasons for this is that although few artists specialised in portraits, those who did included some of Spain's finest painters, notably Velázquez and Goya. Other artists of similar calibre, such as El Greco, painted a significant number of portraits, and the list of specialist portraitists includes a number of lesser figures who nevertheless achieved high standards of excellence, such as Alonso Sánchez Coello, Juan Carreño and Claudio Coello.

The high quality of Spanish portraits during the Early Modern Period has much to do with the ways in which they were used and the kind of people who bought them. As we will see later on, the portrait was an urban genre. It was associated mainly with those who held the reins of power, and especially the monarchy and aristocracy, who used the greatest artists of their time to propagate their own image.

In the western artistic tradition, quality is frequently synonymous with originality, and art is seen as a continuous process of breaking with previous models. Spain's finest portrait painters were profoundly original, conveying a very personal vision of art and life: El Greco's portraits of gentlemen, Velázquez's kings, queens and buffoons, and the intellectuals and aristocrats immortalised by Goya, are among the greatest masterworks of their respective ages. But Ribera developed his own very personal style of portraiture, Murillo injected new life into the genre in Seville, Carreño made his unmistakable mark with portrayals of the court of Charles II, and Luis Meléndez and Luis Paret both saw portraiture through new eyes. The genre was adept at taking on new life, partly thanks to changing aesthetic tastes and partly because of its ability to keep pace with the constantly changing vagaries of fashion, which inevitably played a major part in the end result.

In evaluating the importance of portraiture in the history of Spanish painting, we must also take the concept of tradition into account. Portraiture as a genre was practised fairly continuously from the late Middle Ages (and in some cases even earlier) until the twentieth century. The main reason for its continuity from the mid-sixteenth century onwards was the existence of a fixed court. This drew on the services of specialist Spanish and foreign artists who had to live at the court (with some exceptions, such as Titian) and who developed their own tradition, in many cases building on that of earlier artists. The nineteenth and twentieth centuries saw a renewed awareness of this tradition, which made itself felt in the work of many painters. Federico de Madrazo, Rosales, Sorolla, Zuloaga and even Picasso all worked at a time when Spanish painting was engaged in a deep-rooted reflection on its own history.

The prominent role of portraits in the history of Spanish painting is not simply a reflection of their artistic quality. They were also the most obvious alternative to religious themes, and of all the genres traditionally practised in Spain they undoubtedly had the greatest documentary value. There was no real tradition of depicting local customs or important scenes from recent history, and Spanish and foreign artists therefore expressed the country's past using images of its kings, queens, princes, nobles and wealthy middle classes. These works of art were also valuable historical documents, and their versatility accounts for much of the popularity they enjoyed.

Art historians implicitly or explicitly agree on the importance of the portrait in Spanish painting, and there are numerous studies of the great portraitists. But there are no monographs that approach the history of portraiture from a broader perspective – unlike, say, still life, a more limited genre in many respects but one whose study has been revitalised in recent decades thanks to numerous exhibitions and publications.

The exhibition which this book accompanies is the first large-scale attempt to trace the development of the portrait in Spain from the late fifteenth to the early twentieth century.[4] Holding it at the Museo del Prado has made it possible to include key works such as Velázquez's and Goya's portraits of royal families which could not be shown elsewhere. The choice of pictures is an attempt to demonstrate the high standard achieved by the genre in Spain over the centuries, to trace the emergence of a tradition which inspired successive generations of artists, to bear witness to the originality with which the great painters drew on the example set by their forebears, and to show how the genre spread to include increasingly wide sections of society. Although El Greco, Velázquez, Goya and Picasso made more important contributions than other artists in terms of quality and originality, the exhibition is a representative selection of great Spanish portraitists and the different types of picture they painted.

The display is essentially chronological, but it also provides opportunities to compare artists who lived at different times. In addition, it focuses on the important contribution made by foreign artists to the genre's history, with works by Juan de Flandes, Titian, Pedro de Campaña, Anthonis Mor and Antón Rafael Mengs, reminding us that Spanish art is also European art.

Visitors to the exhibition and readers of this catalogue may be surprised to see some pictures that are not portraits in the obvious sense, since they do not show people with specific identities. These have been included throughout the display in the form of works by the likes of Bartolomé Bermejo, Ribera, Murillo, Velázquez and Picasso. They are an opportunity to reflect on the boundaries between portrait, reality and representation, and show how the deep-rooted tradition of Spanish portraiture was paralleled by a considerable flair for naturalistic description on the part of the country's painters.

The Museo del Prado is very much aware of its responsibility as the main organiser of this first historical overview of the Spanish portrait. In many respects this is an event which cannot be repeated. We have therefore sought to include works of very high quality, and to select and group them in a manner which, while respecting their individuality, also emphasises that they were part of a tradition.

The catalogue has been put together with similar aims in mind. It is the first monograph on the history of Spanish portraiture, and we have combined texts which offer a broad overview of the subject with others approaching it from specific perspectives. The introductions to the various sections trace the main milestones in the chronology of the genre in Spain.

In the pages that follow, I have explored some general issues in the history of the Spanish portrait: the various purposes it served, its content and meaning, and the careers of some of the most prolific portraitists. I have also analysed the way in which a tradition of portrait painting developed, partly in response to outside stimuli, resulting in the appearance of the distinguishing features which gave Spanish portraiture such a strong personality.

More than any other artistic theme (with the possible exception of the nude), the portrait is a point of convergence between many different ideas, meanings and experiences,[5] both artistic and otherwise. For example, it highlights the illusionistic aspirations that characterised western figurative art for many centuries, but it also requires us to confront the tensions between art and reality, in which the image transcends its purely narrative role and acquires a more complex significance. For example, the Spanish literature of the Golden Age teaches us that the portrait was considered as a 'representation' or duplication of the subject, who lost a part of his or her personality as a result of having his or her portrait painted. Likewise, for much of its history the genre had class connotations: owning a portrait of oneself, and being depicted in a particular way, were both indicators of social status.

This is therefore a genre with its own specific set of problems. Its multiple purposes and richness of content is widely documented, not only in official records and treatises on art but in literature of all kinds. In fact, any overview of the history, meaning and uses of portraiture in Spain would be incomplete without an examination of the observations contained in drama, novels and poetry. These tell us, for example, how the genre had many non-artistic associations.

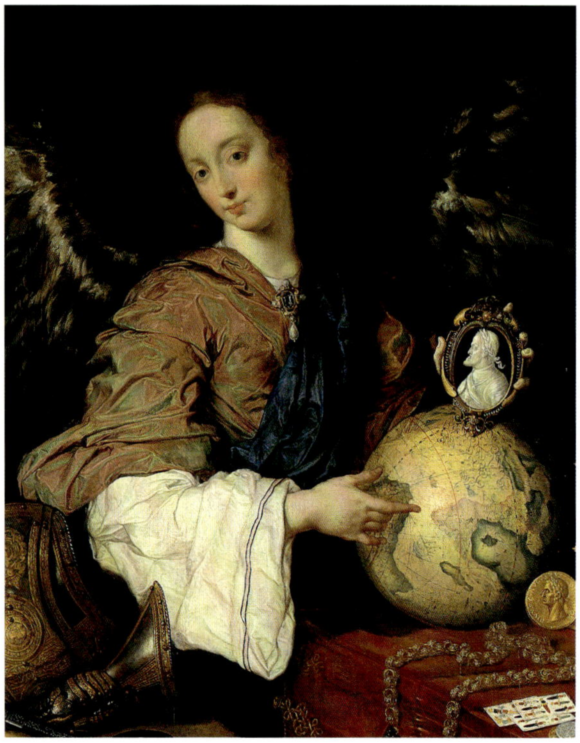

FIG. 2. Antonio Pereda, *Vanitas* (detail), *ca.* 1635. Vienna, Kunsthistorisches Museum

THE SEMANTICS OF THE PORTRAIT

These days most people would agree on what is meant by a portrait. But in past centuries there was a significant degree of ambiguity in the word's semantic content. It usually meant an accurate reproduction of a specific person's features; this is how it was used, for example, in the *Introducción al conocimiento de las bellas artes* (*Introduction to the Knowledge of the Fine Arts*) by the essayist Francisco Martínez (1788).[6] However, it was often used much more broadly in ways that tell us a great deal about how the genre was perceived. The concepts most commonly associated with it were 'description', 'faithful' and 'true'.

Antonio Palomino, in the dictionary at the end of volume 2 of his *El Museo pictórico o escala óptica* (*The Pictorial Museum or Optical Scale*), defines 'portray' as 'to copy or form the exact image of a subject'. His entry for the word 'portrait' refers the reader to the definition of 'image': 'an accurate semblance of any corporeal thing'.[7] Although Palomino is clearly well aware of the type of work generally referred to as a portrait, he is acknowledging the word's wide variety of meanings, which were considerably more diverse than they are today. Contemporary inventories used the term to describe works which we would now define as being of a different genre. For example, an inventory of the assets of the painter Juan de Arellano dated 20 October 1676 includes seventeen 'portraits of hunts' and 'eleven old canvases bearing portraits of angels and kings'.[8] The word was also often used to refer to detailed renditions of animals,[9] cities and other subjects.

The concept of 'exact description' is also linked with that of truthfulness, and the use of the latter term in religious contexts is very significant. The Catholic religion has made constant and effective use of figurative media both to inspire devotion and to promote a knowledge of its own history. For centuries institutions produced literary texts and figurative materials which they used to develop a tradition based on 'historic' documents. One of the best ways of guaranteeing a picture's historical veracity was to call it a 'portrait', and this word frequently appears on prints of Christ and the Virgin Mary, with the expression 'true portrait' being used to assure the believer that the image was only one step removed from the original and had similar powers.[10]

The term is also very often used in the context of miracles, as a way of lending them credibility. For example it is frequently used in the captions to *ex votos* or small pictures depicting miracles, confirming that the miraculous event actually happened and that the person depicted was its beneficiary. An *ex voto* from the hermitage of Nuestra Señora de los Nogales in Villanueva de Cameros (La Rioja), dating from 1783, tells how Rosa García was bedridden and her husband asked the Virgin to intercede for her recovery. In return he promised to have a 'portrait' made of the miracle.[11]

Although, as Palomino pointed out in his dictionary, the word 'portrait' was closely associated with pictures, it soon transcended this figurative meaning and was often used in purely literary contexts, which can be very helpful in understanding its connotations. Sometimes it appears in book titles, such as *Political Portrait of King Alfonso VII*,[12] *Portrait of the True Priest*,[13] *Affections Sold and Portrait of a Good Ministry*,[14] *First Part of the Portrait of the Happy Man and Human Felicity*,[15] *Portrait of the Perfect Doctor in Dialogues*,[16] *Portrait of the Good Vassal*[17] and *Portrait of the Private Political Christian*.[18] These show a curious association between the word 'portrait' and the idea of setting an example to others: in each case there is a didactic purpose, with the subjects being proffered as models of behaviour. The use of the word in the title of Francisco Delicado's famous novel of 1528, *Retrato de la lozana andaluza* (*Portrait of a Young Andalusian Woman*) is no exception: here again there is an underlying moralistic purpose.

These associations are deliberate, and they help us to understand the connotations of portrait painting which, while it gradually became accessible to all classes, originally dealt with persons of political, religious or social 'quality' who were worthy of imitation, as expressed in the definition offered by Covarrubias in his *Tesoro de la lengua castellana* (*Treasury of the Castilian language*).[19]

In literature, the term is also used to refer to descriptions of places and events.[20] There is even a genre of poetry known as *pintura* or *retrato*, describing real or imaginary people (mostly female) and inspired by the Petrarchan tradition. These works were highly popular during the Golden Age, and are of interest to art historians tracing the uses and connotations of the word in relation to paintings and to the tension between art and life.[21]

THE CONCEPT OF LIKENESS

Just as in literature the term *retrato* is semantically ambiguous, so its definition in art has changed a great deal over the centuries. Portraits have not always borne a sufficiently close resemblance to their subjects to be identified as such, and sometimes they are not true portraits at all but images based on a very precise verbal description of a person's facial features.

The former situation was particularly common during the Romanesque period, when artists were often unwilling or unable to produce the naturalistic depictions that subsequent eras took for granted. They were frequently more interested in telling stories using traditional, highly codified figures than in representing real living people. Portraits were therefore very rare, and artists developed forms of identification that did not involve a physical likeness. They did this mainly in two ways: by incorporating information about the subject's social or professional status, and using text to clarify his or her identity.

The range of subjects depicted during the Romanesque era was inevitably very limited: kings, queens and other secular figures of authority, the occasional church dignitary and artists themselves; although self-portraits and signatures were still very rare, they were starting to show the first halting signs of being aware of their professional identity. One example is 'Michaelis' [FIG. 3], the artist who sculpted the south portico of the church of Revilla de Santullán, a small village in the Palentina mountains of northern Spain. He depicted himself at the end of the archivolt, putting the finishing touches to a scene showing the Last Supper. We know his name thanks to an inscription which serves both as a signature and the identification of the sculptor.[22]

With the advent of the more naturalistic art of the Gothic period, the idea that a portrait should bear a physical or facial likeness to its subject became more widespread. However, the old ways were not abandoned, and survived for centuries afterwards. For a long time, most of the donors or other figures included in religious scenes had very little in the way of individual features, and inscriptions were widely used to immortalise their identities. We will return to this theme later on, since it is fundamentally important to any understanding of the genre's worth during the Early Modern Period in Spain. And for a long time portraits were more concerned with the attributes of social or professional status than with individual identity, and resemblance played an ambiguous and in some cases secondary role.

Until relatively recently, most Spanish portraits told viewers a great deal about their subjects' social status and occupations, and little if anything about their names and personalities. Much of this was because clothing was an important social marker, but it also showed how much of an individual's personality was predicated on belonging to particular geographical, social, occupational and other groups – as even the most perfunctory glance at the illustrations in this catalogue will show.

But as the Early Modern Period progressed, the idea of physical resemblance became increasingly important, not simply because western art sought to create the illusion of reality but also for its religious and magical connotations. When a portrait becomes a likeness of its subject, its role is no longer merely descriptive and it becomes something altogether more powerful.

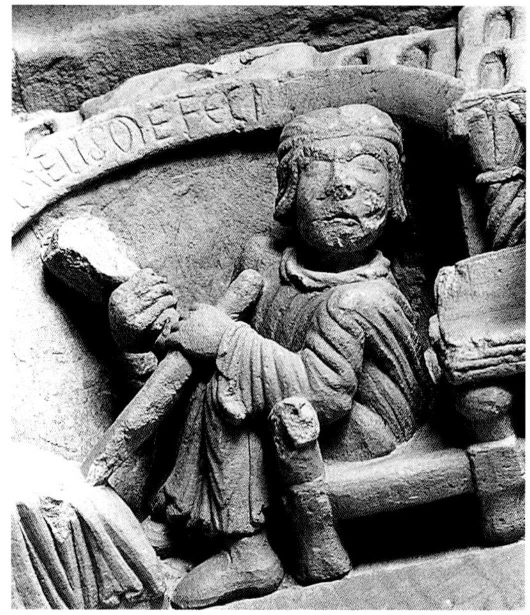

FIG. 3. Master Micaelis, *Self Portrait carving the Last Supper*, *ca.* 1200. Palencia, South portal of the Parish Church of Revilla de Santullán

THE PORTRAIT AS SUBSTITUTE

The increased emphasis on physical likeness had much to do with the notion of 'decorum', the desire to achieve a truthful pictorial representation. The contract commissioning Juan Fernández Navarrete to paint thirty-two pictures of saints for the basilica of the Escorial stated: 'If any saint has previously been portrayed from life, their picture shall be based on that portrait, and due diligence shall be shown in locating it.'[23] From a religious point of view, the concepts of history, truth and legitimation were closely linked, which is why this obligation was so important.

When looking at the significance of the portrait in a sacred context, it should also be borne in mind that Catholicism had established a whole network of spiritual and material benefits distributed by many intermediaries, who might be real people or devotional objects associated with them. This was the system that had created the concept of the relic, and so the portrait gained a very distinctive role. It was a way of showing what the religion's iconic figures looked like and encouraging viewers to follow their example,[24] but it also became an almost sacred object. It was in this context that the idea of the *vera efigies* or 'true portrait' developed, resulting in numerous tales of miracles occurring both while the pictures were being painted and after they were completed.[25]

One example is the story of Brother Juan de la Magdalena, whose exemplary life and death moved the brothers of his order to commission a painting of his dead body. The artist received supernatural assistance in this important task:

> His eyes were open, and everyone saw that they were beautifully clear and resplendent. But some of the monks said that since he was dead, it would be more appropriate to paint him with his eyes closed. He immediately closed his eyes. Then they decided that perhaps his eyes should be open, and he opened them again.[26]

This is obviously an extreme instance, but it shows the wide range of powers attributed to such images. It also demonstrates how the ways in which portraits are used, and people's expectations of them, have changed so much over the centuries.

One instance of miraculous powers being ascribed to a secular portrait relates to the *Recapture of Bahía* [FIG. 49], painted by Juan Bautista Maíno for the Salón de Reinos in the Palacio del Buen Retiro. This is an important piece in the history of the Spanish portrait, because it clearly shows how such an image could serve not only as the mediator of a message but also as a substitute or duplicate of the subject it portrays. The picture depicts Don Fadrique de Toledo pardoning the defeated Dutch, acting in his role as an intermediary for Philip IV. The picture is based on *El Brasil Restituido*, a play written by Lope de Vega in 1625, which provides important information about its significance. In the play, Don Fadrique states that he does not wish to accept 'conditions of peace or other compromises', and then addresses a portrait of Philip IV as follows:

> Great Philip, these people are asking pardon for their errors. Does your majesty wish us to forgive them this time?

He looks at the portrait, and then says: 'He appears to be saying yes'.[27] Although audiences would not have accepted the idea of a portrait coming to life as a literal truth, this scene provides further evidence of how such pictures embodied the tension between art and life. Only an audience familiar with this tension could accept such an episode.

This relationship is apparent in a large proportion of the many literary references to portraits during the Golden Age, not only in artistic treatises (which refer to the idea of a likeness solely in terms of representation), but in poems,[28] novels and plays. Portraits are often described as second selves, and artists as miracle workers who are capable of replicating reality. Significantly, one of the verbs most commonly used in this context is *hurtar*, which Palomino[29] defines as follows: 'In painting, to compose a history by taking figures and other elements from different sources.' But its meaning is usually broader than this; it most often refers to appropriating, in this case not just the form of the painting but also the personality of its subject.[30]

The act of painting a portrait as a form of interaction between painter and model which transcends pure mimesis appears fairly often in literary works. They include Pedro Calderón's *El pintor de su deshonra* (*The Painter of his own Dishonour*), one of the most important pieces of classical Spanish theatre, written *ca.* 1648–1650. Its protagonist, Juan Roca, is a Barcelona nobleman who paints in his spare time. In one scene he tries unsuccessfully to paint a life-like portrait of his wife, a subtle way of expressing the difficulties in their relationship which eventually brings about the tragedy.[31] There are many more such examples which help us understand the complex nexus of non-artistic connotations associated with portraits during the Early Modern Period.

LIKENESS AND ILLUSION

But the concept of likeness can also be seen from other perspectives. Some portraits were used for purely utilitarian purposes, to tell a person preparing for marriage what their future spouse looked like. This was common practice in the Spanish royal courts, as we can see from works by Juan de Flandes and Velázquez, and among the aristocracy and wealthy merchant classes. One famous anecdote tells how the artist Juan Bautista Maíno helped a friend to marry a woman from Granada by painting a portrait of him, but gained her enmity when she found out that the painting was much more attractive than the real thing.[32]

The theme of falling in love via a portrait appears in many Spanish plays and novels, such as *La garduña de Sevilla* (*The Thieving Woman of Seville*, 1642), by Alonso Castillo Solórzano, in which a man and a woman exchange portraits via the man's cousin. The artist is asked not flatter the woman by exaggerating her physical virtues.[33] Portraits were also often used to record the changing appearance of absent loved ones; for example, Don Sebastián of Portugal periodically sent portraits of himself from Portugal to his mother Doña Juana, who had lived in Spain since his infancy.[34]

Apart from these practical functions, a good likeness was essential from an artistic point of view. Western painting of the Early Modern Period sought to create the illusion of reality, and its ultimate aspiration was to create images which could be confused with reality. Artistic treatises abound with anecdotes in which the portrait is mistaken for its subject, such as the scene in *Juan de Pareja* and Palomino's story about the sixteenth-century artist Luis de Vargas:

> Among the many portraits he painted was one of the precentor of the time on the predella of the Adam and Eve altarpiece in Seville cathedral…where the precentor would say his hours, and the boys would surround him, looking at the portrait and the original and admiring their similarity and decorum.[35]

Similarity and decorum were long considered the two fundamental requirements of a portrait: it must faithfully record the subject's physical appearance and must also provide the viewer with basic information about them as a person. Over time, there was an increased emphasis on other requirements, described by the essayist Francisco Martínez as *aire y temperamento*, elegance and temperament.[36] This theme preoccupied growing numbers of painters, and in many cases displaced other considerations. Federico de Madrazo, one of Spain's most prolific portraitists, wrote: 'If a portrait is to be truthful, it must not only resemble the subject, but have character. That is to say, it is not about the portrait, but about the person portrayed.' He illustrates this assertion by comparing his own portrait of Alfonso XII with that painted by José Casado de Alisal. Although the latter is 'better executed', his own has 'more character' because 'a portrait does not simply involve copying the features and ensuring that every wart and scar is in the right place, but is principally about accentuating the whole of the person'.[37]

This is a curious statement for an artist known for his extremely detailed portraits, but it reflects a trend which has become increasingly evident in contemporary art. It reached a peak in the work of Picasso, who brilliantly substituted moral likeness for physical resemblance, as in the magnificent portrait of Gertrude Stein included in this exhibition [CAT. 83].

Velázquez provides another example of the complex implications of the concept of likeness, since his portraits are often structured differently, according to the subject's status and personality. For example, he often paints the king's face differently from those of other individuals, as we can see by comparing *Philip IV as a Hunter* (Madrid, Museo del Prado, P-1184) with any of his buffoons. Alternatively, in this exhibition, compare the bust-length portrait of a mature Philip IV [CAT. 12] with the *Portrait of a Man, 'The Pope's Barber'* [CAT. 35]. Although these are of very similar date, their style is quite different. The latter's face is strongly accentuated by the light, which brings out the rich unevenness of his skin and gives an extraordinary sense of vivacity, as though of a moment frozen in time. The technique of *Philip IV* is equally impressive, revealing an artist in full control of his resources but without the same emphasis on the topography of the skin. The result is a picture which, although highly expressive, is rather more distant and static, as one might expect from a royal portrait. What we have here is a 'likeness' which pertains not only to physical features, but to the subject's status as a person.[38]

NATURALISTIC DESCRIPTION

One theme which has been closely associated with that of likeness ever since the fifteenth century is that of naturalistic description. This has close parallels with portraiture, since it often achieves a very portrait-like quality. Over this period, there are many examples of figures which seem to have been taken from real life and have little of the stereotypical idealisation of the western figurative tradition during the Early Modern Period. There are many examples in this catalogue.

In Bermejo's panel of *Saint Dominic of Silos* [CAT. 1] the saint gazes solemnly and timelessly at us like a Christ Pantocrator, but his facial traits are extraordinarily individual. Berruguete's near-contemporary *Hezekiah*, from the *retable* of the parish church of Santa Eulalia in Paredes de Nava [CAT. 2], was for a long time considered to be a self-portrait.[39] The fact that this is no longer the case simply underlines the genre's ambiguity.

So does the oeuvre of Velázquez, in which many of the figures appear to have been painted from real life. The most dramatic examples are the Rouen *Democritus* [CAT. 32] and the Prado *Mars* [FIG. 4], which have sometimes been described as depicting buffoons.[40] It has been suggested that the *Sibyl* (Madrid, Museo del Prado, P-1197) is a specific woman, many critics (particularly during the nineteenth century) have asserted that *The Drunkards* are real people, and identifications have been advanced for other great paintings such as *The Surrender of Breda*, including the painter himself [FIG. 5]. This common desire to create ambiguity by blurring the boundaries between portrait and fiction were undoubtedly deliberate, forming part of the reflection on reality, representation and the artistic vision that is a common thread of Velázquez's oeuvre.

In *Democritus* and *Mars*, Velázquez makes us think about the relationship between what the picture represents and who it describes, and it is this ambiguity which accounts for much of their effectiveness as a form of communication. The figures look like real, recognisable people, probably of limited social standing but in the noble guises of a great ancient philosopher and the god of war. It is important not so much to decide whether these were real people as to appreciate how Velázquez used the techniques of portraiture to endow myth and ancient history with the semblance of reality. He uses the faces of himself and his relatives in *Adoration of the Magi* (Madrid, Museo del Prado, P-1166).[41] *Aesop* [CAT. 31], too, has sometimes been held to be inspired by a real face,[42] although it actually comes from an illustration in Giovan Battista Dalla Porta's *Della fisionomía dell'uomo*.

It is not surprising that the Rouen *Democritus* was until 1881 believed to be the work of Jusepe de Ribera. It was the naturalist school, with which Ribera was so closely associated, that most forcefully advocated the use of reality as the raw material of painting. But to Spanish painters during the Golden Age, the idea of realism had very different connotations from those of today, and the word 'reality' itself had very specific moral and religious overtones. This was brilliantly demonstrated by Julián Gállego,[43] who described as 'transcendent realism' the contemporary belief that everything had a meaning beyond mere appearances. Although naturalist painters were widely condemned by art critics for failing to idealise their depictions of humans, they played an important part in ennobling and dignifying reality.

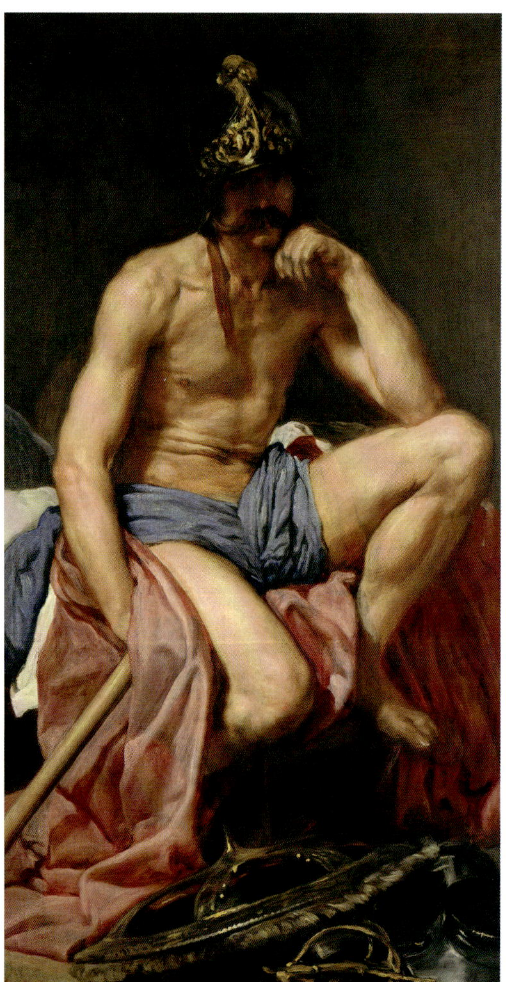

FIG. 4. Diego Velázquez, *Mars*, *ca.* 1640. Madrid, Museo del Prado [P-1208]

The portrait was one of the most commonly used ways of reasserting the primacy of reality and depicting people who appeared to have individual, concrete personalities. Ribera was among the artists to employ it to best effect, and many of his apostles, philosophers and other figures have ordinary, everyday faces. If we compare, for example, his *Maddalena Ventura with her Husband ('The Bearded Woman')* [CAT. 25] with his portrait of the philosopher Democritus [CAT. 26], we see clear similarities in the facial features; all the figures are bursting with life and individuality.

But we must not be deceived into thinking that all of Ribera's life-like figures are portraits. He may have taken some of his inspiration from classical statuary, and he also had a flair for creating the appearance of reality through such devices as very detailed, craggy complexions; hence his practice of using ordinary people as models.

In his use of portrait-like conventions, there is one thing that separates Ribera from his Italian, French and Flemish naturalist colleagues and brings him closer to painters like Velázquez and, to a lesser extent, Zurbarán. The extraordinary emphasis on individual expression, both in his 'portraits' and his stereotypical figures, inspires an empathy that is rare in other European painting of the time, with a few exceptions, such as Rembrandt. There is very little intermediation between ourselves and the subject, and although we are provided with information about their social and intellectual status, the idea of the individual is given primacy and expressed with extraordinary directness and intensity. Lafuente Ferrari described this as 'the salvation of the individual'.[44]

The fact is that, as any visitor to the exhibition will see, this idea runs through the entire history of Spanish portraiture, though of course it is not present in the work of all Spanish artists and neither is it absent from foreign art. It is also very much dependent on the degree of freedom the painters were given by their subjects, and therefore particularly evident in pictures of clowns and beggars and self-portraits, and where portrait-like features have been used to construct 'types'. For example, although these characteristics are common to a large part of Velázquez's output, nowhere are they more apparent than in his dwarfs and buffoons [CATS 31, 33 and 34] and in *Democritus* and *Mars*.

Even in royal portraits, the degree of communication with the viewer varies depending on the type of picture. Velázquez's *Queen Mariana of Austria* [CAT. 13] is artistically magnificent but aloof and distant, whereas the bust-length portrait of the mature Philip IV [CAT. 12] conveys a sense of both majesty and individual expression. Likewise, Goya was nowhere more intense than in his self-portraits [CATS 59, 65 and 66],[45] although other subjects, such as the family of Charles IV [CAT. 46] and the Condesa de Chinchón [CAT. 64], have a distinctly cadaverous air to them. In the latter, spatial and environmental references have been minimised so as to emphasise the subject's facial expression and pregnant body.

This emphasis on the sitter's individual character and his or her interaction with the viewer is also apparent in many works by Picasso. One example is his 1972 *Self Portrait* [CAT. 87], in which he distorts

FIG. 5. Diego Velázquez, *The Surrender of Breda* (detail), 1634–1635. Madrid, Museo del Prado [P-1172]

the face and enlarges the eyes, sacrificing naturalistic truth in favour of expressive intensity. Others include early works such as *Boy with a Pipe* [FIG. 6, private collection], which recalls Velázquez's buffoons such as *The Buffoon Calabacillas* [CAT. 33], in its framing, in aspects of its pose and expression, and even in its point of view. In both cases we are confronted face-to-face with a living being, emphasising the feeling of abandonment and destitution which, although specific to this figure, is also inseparable from its genre.

'RETRATOS A LO DIVINO'

Spanish painting contains plentiful examples of the boundaries between portrait and likeness being blurred, usually deliberately. One is the genre known as *retrato a lo divino*, or portrait in the guise of a divine figure. Variations on this theme also appeared in other countries, for example the French court's 'mythological portraits', but it had a distinctive presence of its own in Spain, in which a living person took on the attributes, and even the personality, of a holy person. It appears

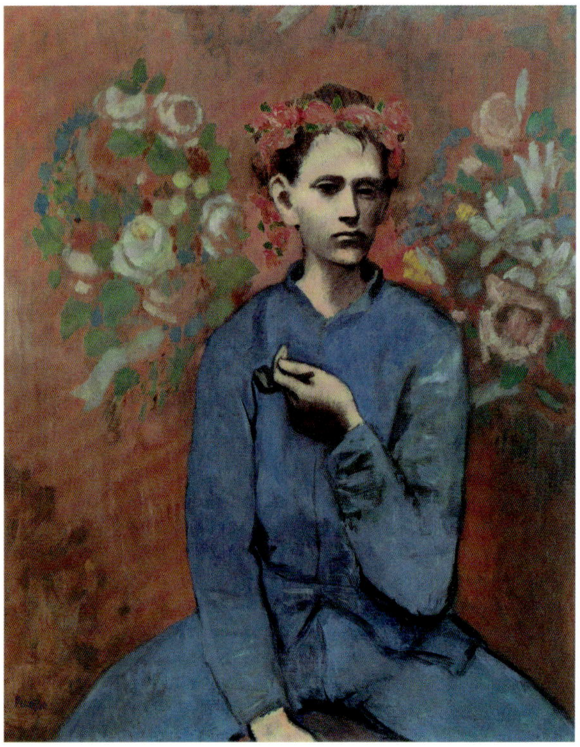

FIG. 6. Pablo Picasso, *Boy with a Pipe*, 1905. Private collection

in courtly contexts such as Michel Sittow's *Saint Catherine* (Vienna, Kunsthistorisches Museum), which bears the features of the infanta of the same name, and in works by Pantoja depicting various members of Philip III's family in episodes from the gospels such as *The Birth of the Virgin* and *The Adoration of the Shepherds* (both Madrid, Museo del Prado, nos P-1038 and P-1039).

In seventeenth-century Spain this custom spread to include portraits of subjects who were not members of royalty or the aristocracy. It is exemplified primarily by religious images with strongly defined portrait characteristics such as some of Zurbarán's pictures of saints, and particularly *Saint Isabel of Portugal* [FIG. 7], whose face has a much stronger degree of individuality than other similar paintings.[46] Further evidence of this practice in Spanish painting comes in a series of poems dedicated to the pictures themselves. These include one by Ulloa Pereira entitled *On the Occasion of having superimposed a Woman's Face onto an Image of Saint Lucy*;[47] an epigram by the Príncipe de Esquilache, *To a Woman portrayed with the Insignia and Costume of Saint Helen*;[48] Lope de Vega's sonnet *To a Picture of Saint Susanna into which was inserted a Portrait of a Lady*,[49] and Salcedo Coronel's composition *To the Portrait of a Woman dressed as the penitent Mary Magdalene*.[50] These and others have been studied in detail by Emilio Orozco.[51]

Most, if not all, of these poems are probably literary stratagems rather than references to real pictures, but they have no meaning unless they reflect a real practice. Either way, both the poems and the pictures are indications of an artistic culture which loved to exploit the possibilities of the portrait and blur the dividing lines between genres by confusing reality and fiction.

HOW A PORTRAIT BECAME A THEOLOGY OF PAINTING

As we have already noted, part of the reason why portraiture occupies such an important place in the history of Spanish painting is that so much of it is of exceptional quality. But its significance also derives from the fact that it received so much attention, more than in the rest of Europe, from so many distinguished writers and artists. One of the foundations of the classicist outlook on European painting in the Early Modern Period was a thematic hierarchy whereby different artistic genres were ranked in order of importance. The apex was so-called history painting, which took its motifs from the Christian tradition, myth and classical national histories. This was undoubtedly the most noble genre because it required both culture and inventiveness on the part of the artist, and was intended to convey a moral message.

Other genres were of lesser importance, and were partly dependent on the painter's imitative skills. The most noble of these was portraiture, because it depicted illustrious personages and deeds which were worthy of imitation. Because the divisions between genres were often not entirely clear-cut during the Early Modern Period, portraiture frequently overlapped with history painting, partly because elements of the former were often incorporated into the latter and partly because portraits of individuals had so much 'historic' significance in the broadest sense of the word.

Some of the most important debates on the boundaries and meanings of portraiture took place in Spain, particularly at the court, around the middle of the seventeenth century. It was during this period that Spain's first two great artistic treatises were published: one by Vicente Carducho, which appeared in 1633, and the other by Francisco Pacheco, printed in 1649, a year after the author's death. The first, *Diálogos de la pintura*, is a scrupulously classicist work which restates the traditional doctrine concerning pictorial genres and relegates the portrait to a secondary role. As evidence of its inferiority, the author writes: 'The great and eminent painters were not portraitists.'[52] He put this belief into practice in his own pictures, the vast majority of which were history paintings. With the exception of a single self-portrait (Glasgow, Pollok House), he used portraits only in passing, including them in paintings of contemporary battles.

Although Carducho's treatise was consistent in its disdain for portraits, this must be seen in the light of his own position at the court, where he was being displaced by a younger artist who had arrived from Seville. Although Diego Velázquez had produced some important history paintings, he preferred to devote himself to portraits, particularly of the royal family. The rivalry between the two artists is visible elsewhere in the treatise. It tells us a great deal about their specific working conditions, and also about the conflict between portraiture and history painting in Spain at the time.

Another prominent figure in this polemic was Francisco Pacheco. His *Arte de la pintura* is a spirited defence of the creativity of portraiture, a genre requiring both a flair for imitation and a considerable degree of inventiveness. He underpins his argument with historical examples such as that of Apelles, the most famous painter of ancient times, who mainly painted

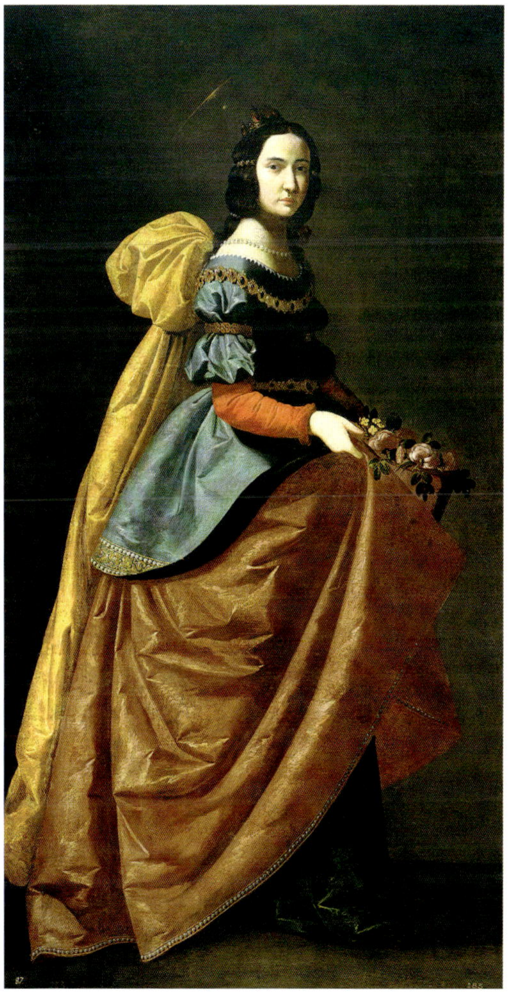

FIG. 7. Francisco de Zurbarán, *Saint Isabel of Portugal*, 1630–1635. Madrid, Museo del Prado, [P-1239]

pictures of Alexander the Great.[53] As Edouard Pommier has pointed out, Pacheco's receptiveness towards the genre is the exception to the rule within a European context.[54] But it was perpetuated in Spain by Palomino who, at the beginning of the eighteenth century, wrote:

> If a painting consists of one or two single, independent figures, but also contains other components such as a fragment of architecture, a landscape, a curtain or a desk, even though it is a portrait, in pictorial terms we also call it a history painting because, although there are only one or two figures, the harmonious combination of components results in a perfect whole. This can be seen as a history painting because its composition requires the same subtle moderation as such a painting, and because these components are a substitute for the placing of the figures.[55]

Pacheco's opinions were coloured by the fact that Velázquez was his son-in-law, and much of the treatise is concerned with defending him and publicising his achievements.

A PORTRAITIST BY PROFESSION

Of all the artists of his time, Velázquez probably made the biggest contribution to elevating the reputation of portraiture. He did this not only through the virtuosity of his works, but also in paintings which reflect explicitly on this theme, and through his own attitude to life.

It is very useful to compare what he did during his two trips to Italy, some twenty years apart. He began the first in the summer of 1629, returning early in 1631 after visiting Venice, Ferrara, Naples and other places and living in Rome for a long period.[56] The city was still the home of painting, the world's biggest repository of western art and a mecca for artists of all nationalities. It was also a hive of creativity,[57] with great masters such as Guercino, Reni, Pietro da Cortona, Poussin and Claude Lorrain at the height of their powers and engaging in intense and lively debate on classicism. This affected the way in which the different genres were perceived.

Velázquez probably went to Italy on the advice of Rubens, with the intention of learning from, and perhaps meeting, some of the most prominent artists who worked there. Most of the pieces he had painted for the court were portraits, but when he arrived in Rome, instead of displaying his exceptional prowess in this field, he preferred to work in other genres. The two biggest works he painted there were *Vulcan's Forge* (Madrid, Museo del Prado, P-1171) and *Joseph's Bloody Coat Presented to Jacob* (Monasterio de El Escorial). These are both history paintings in the broadest sense, partly because they are scenes from mythology and the Bible, but also because they emphasise one of the most specific features of the genre: the representation of emotions. At the time, this theme was preoccupying some of the finest artists working in Italy.[58]

During this first journey, Velázquez painted two superb views of the gardens of the Villa Medici in Rome (Madrid, Museo del Prado, nos. P-1210 and P-1211), a magnificent response to the efforts of Claude Lorrain and other artists in the city to revive the reputation of landscape painting. Pacheco and Palomino, who are still the main sources of information on this period of Velázquez's career, make no mention of any portraits painted in Rome, though they do refer to one painted in Naples: that of Mary of Austria, Queen of Hungary [FIG. 8].

Judging by this, Velázquez's main preoccupation when he arrived in Italy was history painting, which was generally considered the most important genre. *Vulcan's Forge* and *Joseph's Bloody Coat presented to Jacob* are testimony to his talent for confronting this theme in an innovative way. But after his return to Spain he continued to explore a great variety of subjects with astonishing originality and virtuosity. These include such masterpieces as *Christ on the Cross, The Surrender of Breda* and *Saint Anthony Abbot and Saint Paul the Hermit* (all Madrid, Museo del Prado; nos P-1167, P-1172 and P-1169, respectively).

But most of his efforts were dedicated to portraits, and in the 1630s and 1640s he confirmed himself to be one of the greatest portrait painters in the history of western art. We will discuss some of these works later on, but suffice it to say that he showed a huge degree of confidence and versatility, enjoying a privileged role as painter to Philip IV, who was still one of Europe's most important monarchs. Velázquez was not an indiscriminate portraitist, but a court painter who used his art and culture to glorify the king and his entourage and played an important part in propagating the image of the monarchy.

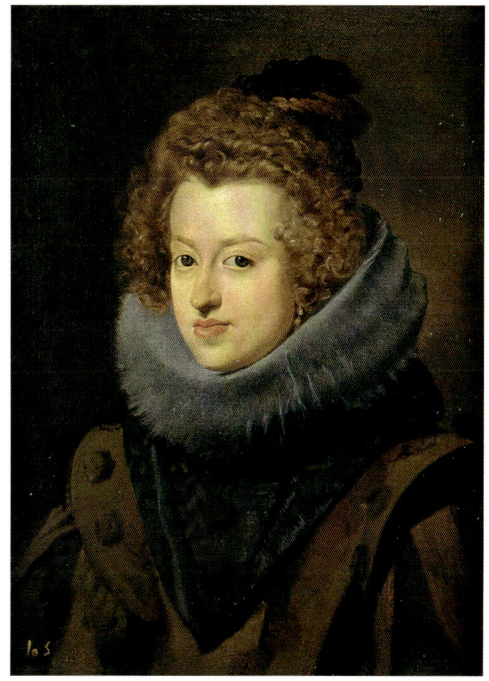

FIG. 8. Diego Velázquez, *Mary of Austria, Queen of Hungary*, 1630. Madrid, Museo del Prado [P-1187]

There are clear signs that Velázquez was becoming aware of his crucial role as a portraitist, though he occasionally worked in other genres. This is borne out by what we know about his second trip to Italy between 1648 and 1651.[59] He arrived there as a mature artist approaching fifty and with a confidence borne of three and a half decades of fruitful activity. This time the purpose of his journey was not to learn, but to serve his king by acquiring paintings, casts of ancient statues and other items. And this time, instead of seeking out the great painters of monumental history pictures who were active in Rome, he painted only portraits. Although he was in Italy on an official mission, he was there for so long that if he had been truly determined to paint religious or mythological scenes, he could have done.

In fact, his output was significant. Palomino lists twelve paintings and an indeterminate number of unfinished ones, and he was considerably more productive during his Rome years than he had been in Madrid. All the works were portraits, and most depicted members of the papal court from Pope Innocent X downwards [FIG. 9]. But all the paintings of the time which have been identified are pure portraits, devoid of any allegorical or rhetorical traits which might classify them as history pieces. They are primarily exercises in psychology, and as such are extremely important, constituting a peak in the development of European portraiture.

Velázquez had been given an opportunity to demonstrate his creativity to Rome's artistic community and the papal court, and he did this using portraits. Judging by contemporary sources his efforts met with a reasonably warm reception, and in January 1650 he was admitted as a member of the highly prestigious Academy of Saint Luke.

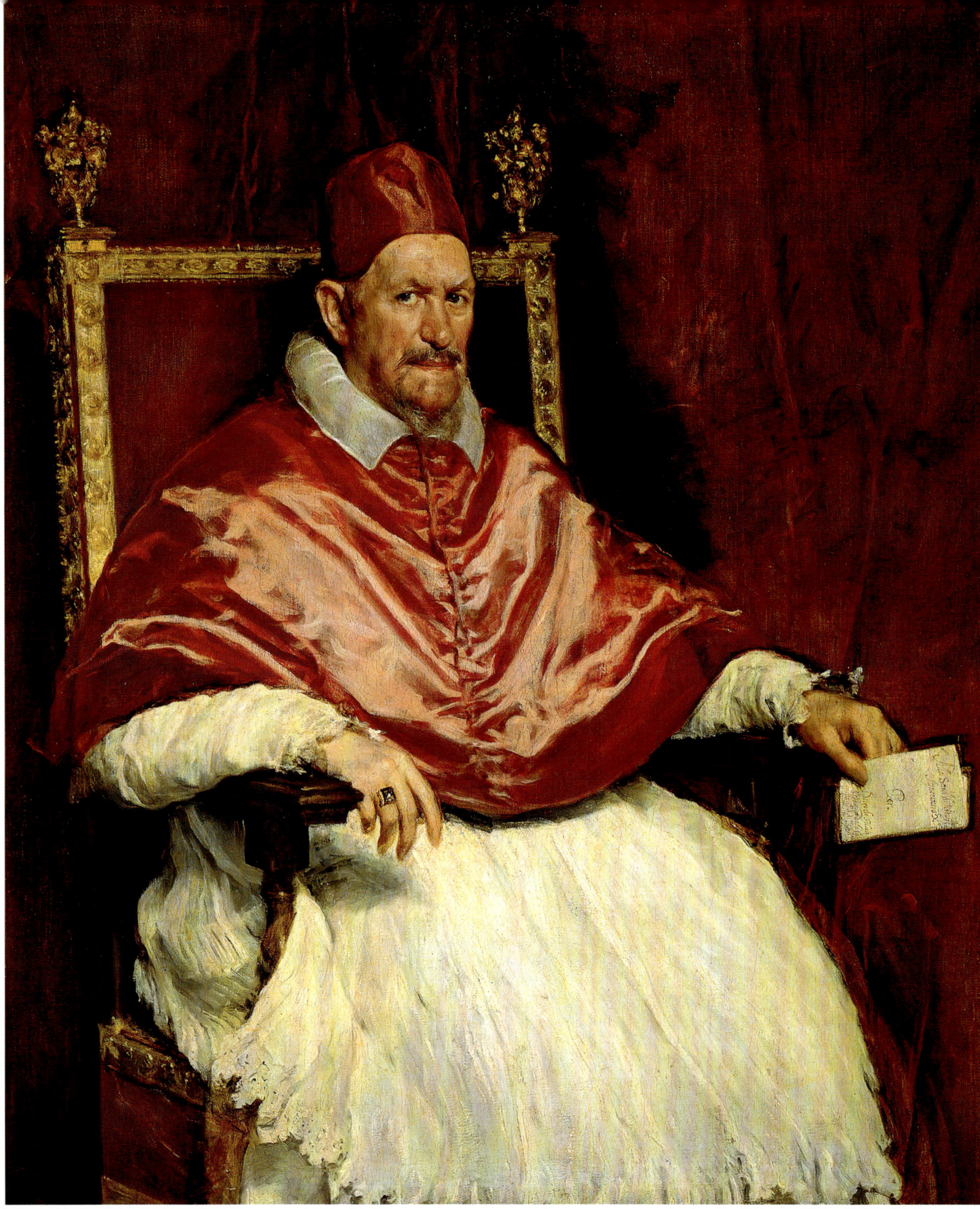

FIG. 9. Diego Velázquez, *Pope Innocent X*, 1650. Rome, Galleria Doria Pamphilj

THE 'THEOLOGY OF PAINTING'

Six years later, Velázquez painted what Palomino calls his 'most illustrious work', one of the most important pieces in the history of western art. *Las Meninas* [CAT. 43] is described by Luca Giordano as 'the theology of painting…by which I mean that just as theology is the most superior of the sciences, so that picture is the most superior in painting.'[60] It has been the subject of more questions and speculation than any other work of Spanish art, thanks not only to its extraordinary quality and compositional complexity but also to its deliberately ambiguous nature, designed to maximise the interaction between the viewer and the work.[61] Aside from the web of artistic and historical meanings that has been assigned to it, one thing is obvious and undisputed: this masterpiece of Spanish art is first and foremost a group portrait, although neither its size nor its complexity are typical of this genre.

Las Meninas is an explicit and implicit reflection on the genre to which it belongs and on Velázquez's personal status as a painter. In this respect, the painting's size is in itself highly significant; it is one of the largest canvases Velázquez ever produced, and he was undoubtedly aware that he was painting a masterpiece and one of the paintings for which he would be most remembered. Although art historians emphasise that it was painted primarily for the eyes of Philip IV, the artist would have been aware that the king was a fleeting figure on the European stage and that the painting would presumably outlive him. Even if it were lost, it would live on in literature, just as the great works of Apelles and other painters of antiquity had done. Velázquez had a strong historical awareness; he knew he was part of a tradition going back to antiquity and probably extending far into the future.

Las Meninas was intended to be one of the most ambitious works of his career, and Velázquez had no hesitation about including himself in it. This makes it a personal manifesto, and his is one of the most important presences in the composition. The painting contains many different points of view: those of the figures in the foreground, the king and queen further away from us, their presence revealed in the mirror in the background, and the viewer, a perplexed witness to this dialogue. But one person seems to control all these perspectives: Velázquez, on the left, dominates the scene by virtue of his position and size, and is also the only person to know the precise subject of the canvas he is painting. This canvas has been a source of endless conjecture. It has been thought of as a portrait of the royal couple, so that what we see in the mirror is a reflection of the surface of this enigmatic painting. But its size is completely inappropriate for a portrait of the king and queen. It has also been suggested that Velázquez actually portrayed himself painting *Las Meninas*, though this would contradict some of the fundamental laws of western composition because it undermines the whole concept of representation.

If we put both these possibilities to one side, the only other indication of the picture's possible content is its size. Judging by this, Velázquez intended it as a history painting; although large portraits were occasionally painted (including a number of equestrian scenes by the artist himself), they were usually much smaller. Later on, we will explore the relationships between the sizes, materials and meanings of portraits; for example, the function of a miniature was very different from that of a half-length picture, and that of an oil quite different from a bronze statue. For this reason, any contemporary viewer seeing the picture that the artist is working on would immediately have recognised it as a history painting.

But Velázquez's reassertion of himself as a history painter in *Las Meninas* is also made through other means. He has used a group portrait to create a very dense network of references which not only reveals the physical appearance of each subject and their status in the court, but also constructs a discourse in which he reflects on the nature and importance of painting, and also on political matters.[62]

There has been much discussion of the painting's specific historical message, which has to do with the situation of the monarchy at the time and the possible succession of the king and queen reflected in the mirror.[63] But whatever this content may have been, there can be no doubt that the purpose of *Las Meninas* was not simply to immortalise a group of people from the court of Philip IV. The pictures in the background, the choice of setting, the interplay of gazes between the infanta and her parents, and the nature and actions of the figures surrounding her are all part of a statement about the monarchy. Velázquez is also reflecting upon himself as a painter and courtier who has placed his art (in the sense of both manual dexterity and intelligence) at the service of his king. Within this exploration of the courtier's role, he reminds us that he had the important task of propagating the monarchs' images both during their lifetime and for posterity.[64]

In this masterpiece, Velázquez ponders the limits of portraiture as a genre and its revitalisation through the use of themes more generally associated with history painting. But we must also consider the structure of the composition. Contrary to classicist art theory, which denigrates portraiture as mere imitation, Velázquez shows how a portrait can be one of the most complex pictures in history from the point of view not only of its content, but also of the structure of its perspective. It displays a clear knowledge of the Renaissance laws of 'scientific' perspective, but these have been adjusted through the use of the more empirical aerial perspective. At the same time, the composition is very measured, and there is evidence of technical mastery everywhere we look on the canvas. In this group portrait, more than in any other work, the artist displays his complete mastery of the secrets of his art. We will return to *Las Meninas* later on, because as soon as it was painted it became a yardstick for later artists and a milestone in the development of the historical identity of Spanish painting.

GOD AS PORTRAITIST

At the same time as Pacheco and Velázquez were increasing the stature of the portrait as a genre, the writer Pedro Calderón de la Barca was doing the same in some of his dramatic works. One of these was an *auto sacramental* (an allegorical play performed on the feast of Corpus Christi) entitled *El pintor de su deshonra* (*The Painter of his Own Dishonour*). This is less highly regarded by critics than the *comedia* of the same name, but is nevertheless a valuable expression of its author's aesthetic ideas. It deals with such themes as the intellectual status of painting, the dignity of the painter, his divine genealogy, the tensions between matter and form and between art and life, and the role of the 'idea' or thematic hierarchy. Its vocabulary, too, is rich in artistic references.

The work's central theme is the history of man's creation, sin and redemption. It uses the image of God as the painter of the great canvas of creation who looked at his 'idea' and 'made a portrait' of man in its likeness.[65] This theme appears in other works by Calderón, such as his *Deposición a favor de los profesores de la pintura* (*Deposition in Favour of Painting Teachers*) of 1676, in which he states:

> God portrayed himself in man, making him in his own image and semblance by looking at his own idea. When God was man, because the world did not want to be without this glorious garment, he portrayed himself in the fine white silk of the pious Saint Veronica.[66]

These ennobling references to portraiture must also be seen in the wider context of the theory of genres, which are very subtly reflected on in Calderón's play. Here, once God has created man as a portrait of himself, he gives him free will, making possible the construction of 'history'.[67]

Spanish literature of the Golden Age, and drama in particular, deals repeatedly with the theme of portraits and portrait painters. Although it sometimes condemns them for their ability to falsify reality, it more often puts them in a very favourable light. The artist most commonly mentioned is Apelles, the portrayer of Alexander the Great, and the relationship between the king and his artist is the central theme of a number of plays, including Calderón's *Darlo todo y no dar nada*

(*Give Him Everything and Give Nothing*), Lope de Vega's *Las grandezas de Alejandro* (*The Greatness of Alexander, ca.* 1604–1610),[68] and the anonymous *La mayor hazaña de Alejandro Magno* (*The Greatest Achievement of Alexander the Great*). All emphasise the ingenuity of painters and their major role in embodying the splendour of state.[69] As Lope de Vega's play points out: 'Look at what painters are by nature / After the office of the king, the most important is that of the painter.'[70]

MORE ABOUT PORTRAITS AND HISTORY

The figures of Apelles and Alexander the Great are a reminder of the growing importance of portraits in Spain during and after the Golden Age. Much of this was a matter of historical perception: the majority of the artists most widely remembered from the seventeenth century onwards were portraitists, and Velázquez was regarded as the great national hero of painting. Palomino and subsequent generations of art historians had no choice but to analyse and describe his portraits and those of other important artists before and after him. In fact, the first Spanish monograph dedicated to a painting was that by Jovellanos on the presumed oil sketch for *Las Meninas* (Bankes Collection, Kingston Lacy).

As this painting demonstrates, portraits were becoming more important as a genre partly because of the way in which they served as exemplars of noble behaviour. They included important religious figures and the so-called state portrait, which is precisely what Apelles painted.

Many of the most important and respected European painters of the sixteenth and seventeenth centuries, including Titian, Rubens and Van Dyck, dedicated part of their work to portrayals of kings, princes and courtiers. They owed much of their fame to pictures of this kind, and the great court painters were at the height of their powers in terms of personal and professional respect and wealth.[71] In Spain, the artists most favoured by the authorities and the nobility included three prolific painters of royal portraits: Velázquez himself, Alonso Sánchez Coello and Juan Carreño de Miranda. All three were constantly cited by authors in support of the assertion that painting was a noble art.

By placing their talents at the service of the state and disseminating the image of the monarchy and aristocracy, these painters were fulfilling one of art's highest aspirations, which was to be useful to society and set an example to others. They were part of a chosen few; just as Alexander had allowed only Apelles to paint portraits of him, so in seventeenth-century Spain there were significant efforts to impose controls on royal images,[72] and the number of artists allowed to paint them from life was greatly restricted.

The prestige of the state portrait derived not only from its subjects, its political function and the personality of its painter, but also from its rhetorical content. Here, the concepts of portrait and history were often very similar. Many pictures showed only the face of one courtier, such as the figure in Juan de Flandes' *Portrait of an Infanta* [CAT. 3], who may be Catherine of Aragon but is more probably Joanna, and Velázquez's portrait of a mature Philip IV [CAT. 12], both of which are in this exhibition. But many others contain coded messages of varying degrees of sophistication about the subjects' political and historical identities.[73]

The work of some of the great court portraitists allows us to reconstruct contemporary theories of the state, and the rights and obligations of the king and

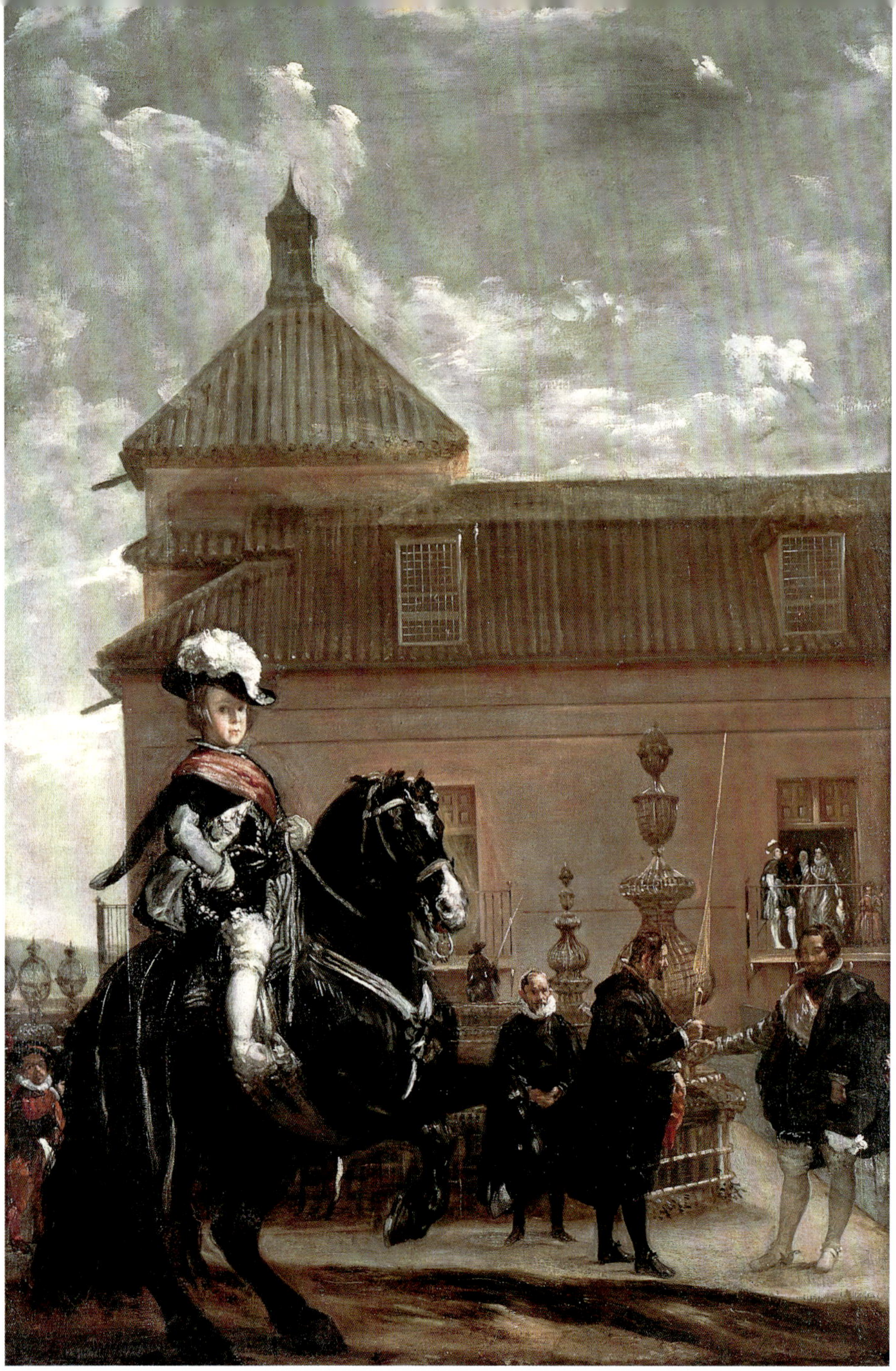

FIG. 10. Diego Velázquez, *Prince Baltasar Carlos's Riding Lesson*, *ca.* 1636. London, Collection of the Duke of Westminster

those closest to him. Once again, the example *par excellence* is Velázquez. The numerous surviving portraits of Philip IV by the artist or his studio tell us about much more than the subject's appearance and personality. There are full-length portraits of him holding a piece of paper or sitting at a desk, equestrian series of himself and members of his family, and depictions in hunting dress or kneeling in devotion. Each tells us something about his administrative and military responsibilities, his identity as a Catholic monarch or his membership of a dynastic line.[74]

Likewise, Velázquez's pictures of Philip's brothers, his wives Isabella of Bourbon and Mariana of Austria, his son Prince Baltasar Carlos, the infantas Margarita and Teresa, and his chief minister the Count-Duke of Olivares are all part of a reflection on the roles of members of the royal family and the system of intermediation on which state politics was based and which had Olivares at its apex.

One magnificent example of the way in which Velázquez's royal portraits shed light on the power of the state and the monarchy is *Prince Baltasar Carlos's*

Riding Lesson [FIG. 10].[75] The prince is shown close-up and mounted on a rearing horse, a pose laden with political connotations, symbolising the fact that the ruler must be able to control both himself and his subjects. Further in the distance we see the Count-Duke of Olivares, his master of the horse, responsible for teaching him to ride and by extension for his political education.

Alonso Martínez de Espinar, a palace official who wrote a treatise on the use of the crossbow, is holding out a lance to the prince, and beyond him is the master of the hunt, Juan Mateos. In the background, Philip IV and his wife Isabel of Bourbon supervise the activities. The setting is the Buen Retiro palace, built shortly before this canvas was painted, and the portrait highlights the Count-Duke's role in Spanish politics, with each of the main figures serving a specific political function. The picture transcends its purpose as an anecdote of a riding lesson, and becomes an allegory of the prince's political education and the system through which power is mediated. In this respect, it bears many similarities to Juan Bautista Maíno's *Recapture of Bahía* [FIG. 49]. Of all the paintings in his victory series for the Salón de Reinos in the Buen Retiro palace, this is the only one clearly to show that all these military successes had Philip IV as their focal point, and that he was assisted by the Count-Duke in the task of governing his dominions.

Velázquez was not the only court painter to create portraits conveying both the physical appearance of kings and princes and a specific concept of the monarchy. It was not enough simply to produce a good likeness, and these artists were required to demonstrate qualities more commonly associated with history painters. Anyone over the centuries who has contemplated Titian's *Charles V at Mühlberg* [FIG. 52] cannot fail to be astonished by the artist's virtuosity, sense of decorum and ability to synthesise ancient and contemporary traditions, creating an archetype of the Christian knight without abandoning the precision of portraiture. Another equestrian portrait of Philip IV, this time by Rubens and surviving only in the form of a copy (Florence, Galleria degli Uffizi), provides a further example of how, at the time it was painted (1628–1629), a portrait could have the connotations of a history painting. This is evinced by the two lengthy poems and a rather prolix verse description dedicated to the picture by Lope de Vega, López de Zárate and Juan de Piña, respectively, showing the density of political meanings such a portrait could embody.[76]

Of course, other examples abound. Juan Bautista Martínez del Mazo's portrait of the widowed Mariana of Austria, and Juan Carreño's of King Charles II, both display an obvious but complex symbolic content which to some extent is the heir to that of Velázquez.[77] The latter picture powerfully draws our attention to the contrast between the king's frail appearance and his sumptuous surroundings. The same is true of the full-length portraits of him in the Salón de los Espejos in the Alcázar, and particularly that showing him clad in a magnificent golden fleece [FIG. 11]. Although unforgettable in its richness, instead of lending elegance to its subject it simply emphasises his vulnerability. This contrast has sometimes been used to symbolise the decline of the Hapsburg dynasty in Spain. Here it merely shows how, in portrayals of monarchs and other royals during the Early Modern Period, there is a tension between individual and institutional personality, between the 'two bodies of the king'.[78]

The construction of a political rhetoric in royal portraits was largely independent of the subject's physical reality. Charles II's exalted surroundings are rich in symbolism, and would probably have been much the same if another monarch had been reigning. In fact a similar allegorical language was used for his stepbrother Juan José of Austria, who was a much more energetic figure.

The strong rhetorical connotations of royal portraits persisted throughout the eighteenth century, and they continued to bear many similarities to history painting. This was partly because the Bourbon dynasty's accession to the throne favoured the employment of French painters who had trained in the portrait tradition of the court of Louis XIV, where these traits were fully developed.[79] Later, the creation of the Academia de Bellas Artes de San Fernando served to codify and regulate this language, which was similar to that used by the painter Antón Rafael Mengs during his stays at the court in Madrid. These sources also influenced Goya, although he successfully combined the conventions of international court painting with the lessons he had learned from the Spanish tradition and which he so often used in his royal portraits.

Another factor in the overlap between portraiture and history painting was their shared relationship with the concept of biography. For centuries, the western model of history has been a biographical one,[80] with many political and religious chronicles being built around the lives of distinguished people.[81] Likewise, portraits tended to depict subjects who were important or worthy of imitation, and for a long time their purpose was to offer a snapshot, not of a specific person, but of their social or historical identity.

PORTRAIT GALLERIES

One of the best examples of portraits being used to make historical statements is the portrait gallery, containing a series of pictures of people linked by a common thread. These collections were amassed by institutions and individuals throughout Europe during the Early Modern and Modern Periods, but the persons considered worthy of being portrayed have broadened over time, reflecting changes in society.

The collections inevitably depict groups of people who share a common history. The most obvious subject, and that which appears in the greatest variety of collecting contexts, is the monarchy of the country concerned.[82] In Spain, as we might expect, these tend to be located in royal palaces. The collection of the Palace of El Pardo, on the outskirts of Madrid, was particularly famous for its portraits of kings, queens and other members of the royal family.[83] Other important collections were amassed by institutions with royal connections such as the Alcázar in Segovia, with its series of Castilian kings,[84] the regional government of Aragón, which has portraits of all the kingdom's monarchs from the Middle Ages to Charles II, and monastic buildings such as the Royal Monastery of the Descalzas Reales in Madrid, which has a very important collection depicting members of the Hapsburg dynasty.[85]

Other such galleries can be found in town halls and in the palaces of nobles or senior officials, who used them to flaunt their loyalty to their monarchs.[86] In some cases, such as the kings of Aragón, many of the paintings were not portraits in the strict sense of the word. They were not faithful reproductions of their subjects' physical appearance, partly because there were no contemporary portraits on which to base them, but this did not matter because they bore identifying inscriptions.[87] What mattered was to express the idea of succession and continuity, which served as a historic reminder of the legitimacy of power.

The Church also made use of portraits to display its history. That is why so many Spanish dioceses have

FIG. 11. Juan Carreño de Miranda, *Charles II as the Grand Master of the Order of the Golden Fleece*, 1677. Schloss Rohrau, Graf Harrach'sche Familiensammlung

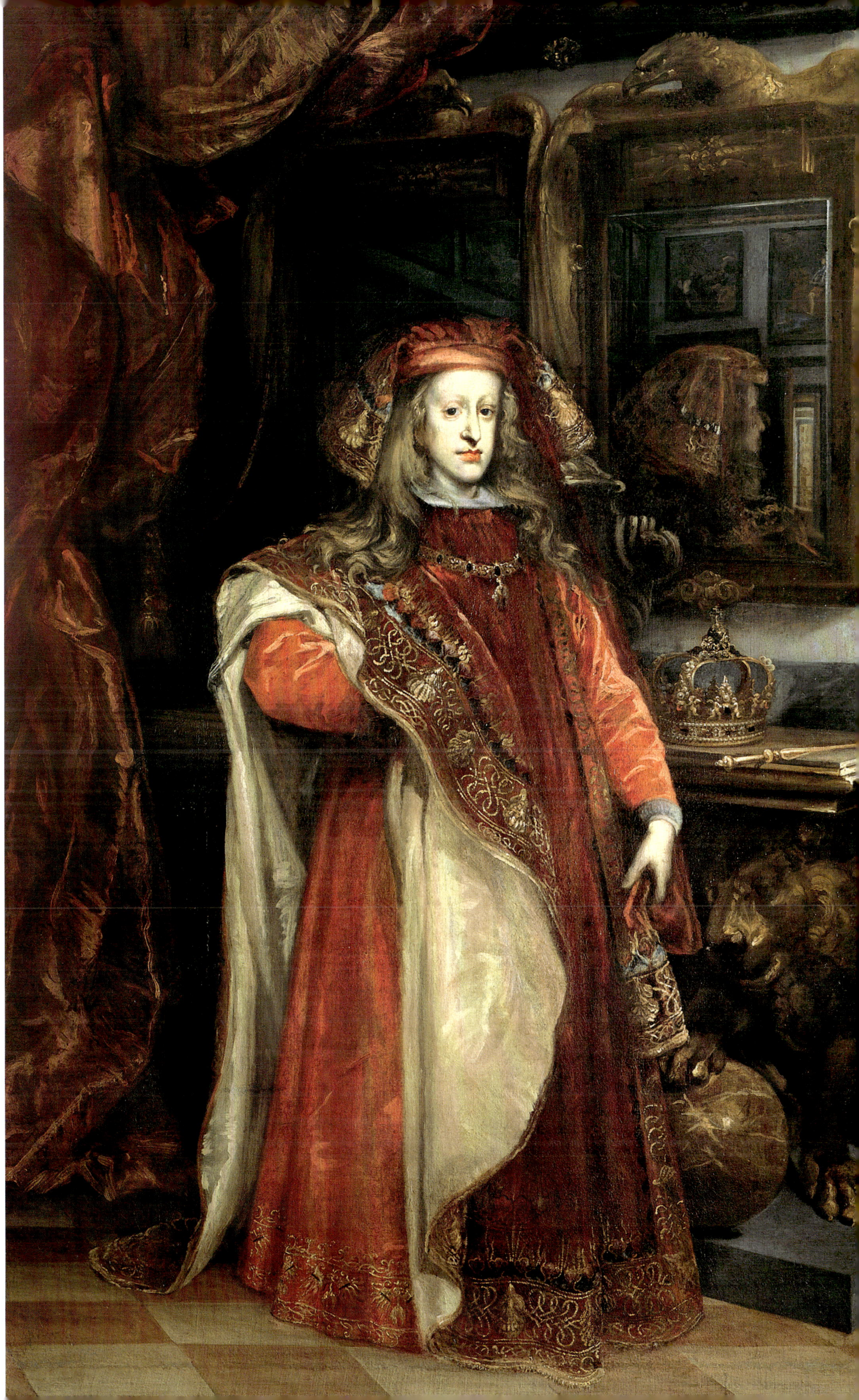

collections of pictures depicting previous bishops. Toledo Cathedral has a famous series of paintings showing all the Primates of Spain [FIG. 31]. Others exist only in printed form, such as that engraved by Francisco Heylan for González de Mendoza's book *Historia del monte Celia...* (Granada, 1616), which includes a list of all seventy-six bishops and archbishops of Granada since Saint Cecil.[88] The illustrations were a particularly important feature of this book, since it seeks to provide evidence of the historic origins of the church in Granada, which were contested by some people.

This desire to reclaim legitimacy by appealing to history was also deeply rooted among the religious orders, who frequently produced written and visual catalogues of members whose holy and exemplary lives demonstrated the order's importance. One famous example is the series commissioned from Zurbarán by the elders of the monastery of Guadalupe, depicting their order's most important friars.[89]

Some aristocratic dynasties owned their own family portrait galleries; one of the best known was that of the Dukes of Villahermosa at their palace in Pedrola, in Aragón. Other collections depicted military heroes and, as art and literature gained in prestige, poets and painters. The great precedent for these galleries was that established during the sixteenth century by Paolo Giovio at his villa on Lake Como. He also gave it literary expression by publishing a book of engraved portraits, each accompanied by a commentary on the life of the sitter.[90] This was a highly influential work, which contributed to establishing the whole idea of a gallery of illustrious figures, and it had important echoes in Spain, such as Francisco Pacheco's *Libro de descripción de verdaderos retratos de ilustres y memorables varones* (*Description of the True Portraits of Illustrious and Memorable Men*) [FIG. 12], which includes a selection of portraits of intellectuals.[91]

Spain also has many galleries of writers' and artists' portraits. One of these was located in the palace of Morata de Tajuña, owned by the Counts of Altamira. It was established in honour of painters and poets, and bore an inscription referring to the close relationship between practitioners of these two art forms.[92]

This idea of the portrait as a fundamental component of Spain's historical memory culminated in the late eighteenth century, with a renewed interest in the study of history and a change in attitudes towards this discipline. One outcome of this was a series of prints entitled *Retratos de los Españoles Ilustres*, begun in 1788 at the instigation of the Count of Floridablanca and printed by the recently established Calcografía Nacional.[93] By 1814, 114 prints had been published, each comprising a portrait and a cartouche identifying the subject and describing the main events in their life. This series is of great interest because it tells us who were regarded as the most important figures in Spanish history at the time and what achievements merited the description 'illustrious'. They include poets, novelists, philosophers, historians, soldiers, religious figures and artists, most of whom lived during the centuries we now describe as the Early Modern Period. Overall, the series is typical of such illustrated publications and has a strong secular bias, religious figures mostly being included for their literary or intellectual achievements. It was also during this period that the Banco de San Carlos portrait gallery was established. This still exists as part of the Banco de España collection, and shows how banks and other institutions have used portraits of senior officials as a means of chronicling their past [see CAT. 52].

Although the nineteenth century saw a revolution in the study of history, many writers continued to use the biographical model. In 1800 Juan Agustín Ceán Bermúdez published his monumental history of

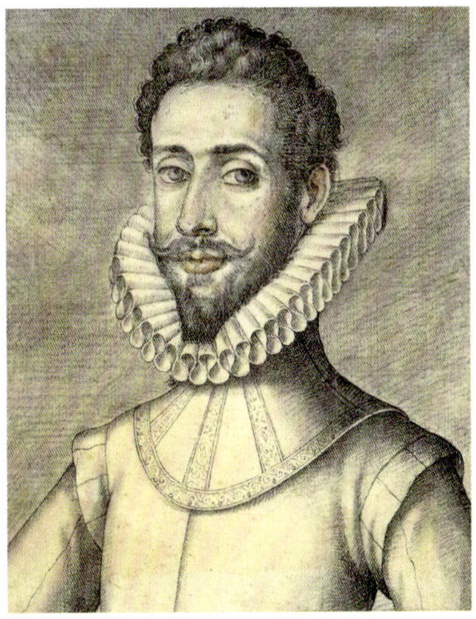

FIG. 12. Francisco Pacheco, *Lope de Vega (?), ca.* 1600, from the *Description of the True Portraits of Illustrious and Memorable Men.* Madrid, Museo Fundación Lázaro Galdiano

Spanish art based on an alphabetical series of artists' biographies. A few decades later came Valentin de Carderera's *Iconografía española*, one of the most ambitious historical undertakings of Spanish Romanticism, which took the format of a 'portrait gallery'.[94] At around the same time, the Museo del Prado was preparing its 'Galería Iconográfica' in which it endeavoured to include portraits of all of Spain's monarchs, and other public and private institutions were forming galleries of their own.

The painter José Moreno Carbonero, in his admission speech to the Academia de Bellas Artes de San Fernando in 1898, proposed that in future, new members should donate a picture instead of making a speech:

> If the works donated by new members were painted or sculpted portraits of previous academicians, the resulting collection would be of indisputable value and twofold historical interest. It would perpetuate the memory of distinguished academicians with works of real merit bearing the signatures of the most renowned artists of their time.[95]

Related to the Portrait Gallery are the ensembles of group portraits. In the 1590s, for example, the former Salón de Cortes in Valencia was painted with murals depicting 'the various members of the legislature in the kingdom of Valencia, personified by the regional government and the three arms or estates', meaning the church, the military or nobility, and the populace [FIG. 13].[96] The historical significance of this portrait collection would therefore have been apparent to anyone who saw it.

THEORY AND PRACTICE

The fortunes of the portrait in Spain are symptomatic of a common phenomenon during the Early Modern Period. The theory of art was highly codified, with each artistic theme and form occupying a specific place on the scale of values. But the reality was much more fluid, depending not so much on theoretical prejudices as on the day-to-day interaction between the artist and his public. This meant that the portrait genre sometimes enjoyed considerable prestige; we need only look at Palomino's treatise to see the favourable critical reception it could enjoy. The theoretical part of the book is ambiguous, an exaltation of history painting which gives rise to the concept of the *retrato historiador*, or historicising portrait. But the historical section, which consists of a series of artists' lives, contains many eulogies to portraits and portraitists.

Likewise, a very large proportion of the allusions to paintings in the literature of the Golden Age are references to portraits.[97] This is often the result of the persons they portray – either the writer himself, or people he wishes to praise such as kings, nobles and patrons – but it also reflects the relationships which sometimes existed between the writer and the artist.

This tension between theory and practice increased during the nineteenth century, when many believed that art had a moral purpose and could exert a positive influence on society.[98] José Galofre, for example, drew up a hierarchy of pictorial themes based on how they could benefit society,[99] and in 1867 José García relegated portraits to a secondary position behind history and even genre painting, which, he said, 'deal with the totality of man's relations with God and his peers'. Portraits, on the other hand, 'far from setting an example and inspiring great actions that help to make society more perfect, content themselves with other secondary and indirect goals.[100] It was not until the final decades of the nineteenth century that there was a more wide-ranging response to this state of affairs.[101] This theoretical context explains the dramatic growth of history painting and the strong literary bias of so much artistic activity.

But the reality was more complex than the theory, and nineteenth-century Spain saw a major revolution among artistic genres. Many of the themes previously considered secondary were taken up by a growing number of painters, including the most prominent ones. Portraits, and to a lesser extent landscapes, enjoyed a great popularity as the number of potential buyers expanded.

This contrast between theoretical ideals and the demands of the marketplace is evident in a letter from José de Madrazo to his brother Federico in Paris. In typically pragmatic style, he tells him about the possibilities of working as a painter in the Spanish capital:

> What you will be asked to paint in Madrid are portraits, and these will be your bread and butter. When there are none of these, or in between them, a hardworking painter like yourself who enjoys fame (and it is possible to gain fame by painting portraits) can occupy oneself with history paintings. If you cannot sell these here and they are not too large, you can send them to France or England, where people will certainly buy them. I am sure that as soon as you arrive here you will become the most fashionable painter on your own merit.[102]

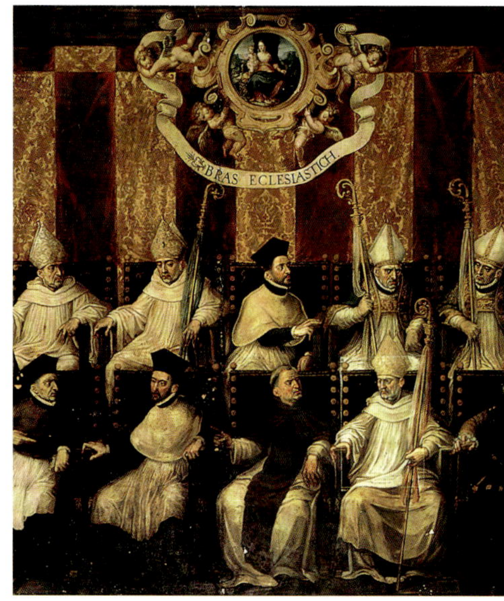

FIG. 13. Vicente Requena, *The Ecclesiastical Estate* (detail), 1592. Salón de Cortes de la Generalitat de Valencia

MODELS FOR A PORTRAIT

The history of the Spanish portrait since the Middle Ages is one of continual expansion in the range of social groups it depicted, the types of portraits that existed, and the content associated with them. These three variables were interrelated. New types of portrait developed partly in response to the expansion of the social groups most likely to have their portraits painted, and this also led to a gradual enrichment in their content. It is impossible to chronicle the genre's history without taking account of the social and political changes that took place in Spain. In the following pages we will briefly review the evolution of society's attitude to portraits.

While religious paintings were intended to convey a message to as many people as possible, portraits were more associated with the court and with city dwellers. These days we are all often portrayed, but for a long time the genre was restricted to certain sectors of society who were seen as having achieved a particular degree of sophistication. This idea is reflected in a number of literary pieces from the Golden Age, including the anonymous play *A pastoral Refuge*. In one scene, two peasants are walking through the countryside and see a portrait hanging from a tree. One asks what it is, and the other replies: 'You always talk such nonsense. It is sacred, because it is a painting.'[103]

A similar idea appears in Calderón's play *Darlo todo y no dar nada* (*Give Him Everything and Give Nothing*), where one of the characters, Campaspe, has always lived in the country and has never seen a town. He says that although he is familiar with all genres of painting directly or indirectly related to religion, he does not know what a portrait is.[104] These are extreme examples which do not reflect a specific reality, but they undoubtedly say a great deal about the deep-rooted social connotations of portraiture.

Other seventeenth-century writers insist that the genre's appeal is limited to a small part of society, as we see in the dismissive comment by Sebastián de Covarrubias cited earlier (see note 19). Here, we see another facet of the relationship between portrait and history which I mentioned earlier. The reality was much more complex and by now portraits had become the province of a relatively broad sector of the population. Significantly, some writers express disappointment at this gradual democratisation of the genre. There was Carducho's famous comment, cited elsewhere in this catalogue,[105] and three decades later Jacinto de Ayala confirmed: 'Having one's portrait has become a common practice.'[106]

It had taken a long time for the portrait to attain this degree of popularity, mirroring the country's transition from the strictly hierarchical and largely rural society of the Middle Ages to one of absolutist government, with a very powerful court and urban society playing an increasingly important role. During the medieval period the portrait was a comparatively rare genre in the Iberian peninsula, restricted to the more powerful social classes: the monarchy, the aristocracy and the senior clergy. Portraits were found in places that became much less widespread in subsequent centuries. The most obvious was the funerary monument, which from the Gothic period onwards frequently included images of the deceased, sometimes with the deliberate intention of creating a realistic portrait. These were obviously confined to the minority who had sufficient wealth and social status to have such tombs built.

DONORS

Another very important type of portrayal was the inclusion, in altarpieces and other paintings, of the figures of the donors who had commissioned and paid for the work of art. These generally comply with a hierarchy of sizes and positions;[107] their presence bears witness both to their devotion and generosity in financing the work, in a gesture combining religiosity with ostentation. This practice was very common from the fourteenth century onwards, and persisted throughout the Early Modern Period, albeit on a lesser scale. Sometimes the artist made no attempt to produce a realistic depiction of the donors but in many other cases he did.

Some of the most important Spanish portraits are donor figures. One example is Bartolomé Bermejo's *Pietà* [FIG. 33] in Barcelona Cathedral, where the donor, Canon Luis Desplá, is almost the principal figure thanks to his central position in the picture and minutely detailed features and expression. Another instance is Lluis Dalmau's *Our Lady of the Councillors* [FIG. 32]. One notable feature of such pictures is the social status of the donors and other figures included in religious scenes, which is similar to that of funerary sculpture. Apart from members of the royal family (such as Ferdinand and Isabella), they show church dignitaries such as Desplá, secular figures of authority such as the councillors, prominent aristocrats such as the Marquis of Santillana in his Buitrago retable (collection of the Duque del Infantado), and members of the local nobility such as the García de Burgos family (in the church of San Gil, Burgos) and the Alfaro family of Seville, who commissioned a Flemish painter (probably Van Hemessen) to paint a triptych including their likenesses (Seville, church of San Vicente).

Some of these works introduced an innovation not found in funerary sculptures: the family group portrait. These provide fascinating evidence of how the genre reflected changes in Spanish society; there was no better way of expressing the strict hierarchy of the family, confirming the superiority of man over woman. He invariably appears on the right of the main devotional motif (i.e. to the viewer's left), and the woman on the left. In addition, the size or position of the parents is used to indicate that they are in charge of the children [see CATS 4 and 5].[108]

COURT PORTRAITS

The types of image described above show the close relationship between the fortunes of the portrait and those of the various Spanish courts.[109] The growing prevalence of portraits of individual members of Spain's royal families marks the emergence of portraits in their own right. Although there were precedents in the court of Aragón, these began to make their mark in the late fifteenth century with the work of Juan de Flandes, who was summoned to Spain by Queen Isabella and painted a highly attractive series of portraits of her children.[110] Part of their purpose was to serve as expressions of the matrimonial policies of the various European courts.

From this point onwards, the quality and variety of court portraits expanded dramatically in Spain. Their variety was much greater than in portraits of other strata of society.[111] As this is the subject of another essay in this catalogue, I will confine myself to pointing out some of its general features, using a number of paintings typical of this sub-genre.

An anonymous portrait of Charles II [FIG. 14], sometimes attributed to the circle of Sebastián Herrera Barnuevo, tells us a great deal about the meanings of the different iconographies and materials. It shows the king as a child, full length, sumptuously dressed and wearing the Order of the Golden Fleece. He holds a staff of office in his right hand, and is surrounded by a rich variety of symbols. These include a lion subduing a globe (a symbol of the child's universal empire), a large vase bearing his name and coat of arms, a putto with a crown and sceptre flying overhead, and a large number of portraits. A portrait of his mother, Mariana of Austria, appears above him, the piece of paper in her hand and the writing materials beside her emphasising her role as regent.

Further towards the background, in a separate area of the picture, we see portraits of Charles' family, including one of his father Philip IV mounting a rearing horse, holding a staff of office and dressed in military uniform. The composition is a direct reference to the idea of control and governance. Two miniatures and an open book appear beside Charles on a table; these personal items probably represent his half-sister María Teresa and her husband. The book is a collection of portraits of kings and queens, presumably recounting the stories of the young king's forebears as an example to him. Apart from the paintings, the picture also includes a bronze sculpture of Charles V crowned with a laurel wreath above a double imperial eagle holding the insignia of the Order of the Golden Fleece. A group of military trophies appears on the base. The emperor was the most important member of the Hapsburg dynasty, and both the material used for his effigy and the classical-style iconography are powerful signals of his identity. The image serves to confer legitimacy upon the king based on such ideas as genealogy, history, political virtue and dynastic succession.[112] Its purpose and significance are different to those of a miniature in a book or portrait gallery, a bronze statue, an equestrian, full-length or bust-length portrait of a king, or a portrait of the king and queen or the whole royal family. Each medium and type had its own specific meaning, though in practice many could be used in a wide variety of ways.

One of the characteristics of the court portrait is that it frequently deals with the concepts of dependence and subordination. This is not surprising given the strict hierarchy of the court. For example, in the portrait which I have just discussed, Charles II is defined as a king in relation to his forebears. The portrait within a portrait was very common in the Spanish court, showing a series of people each displaying a portrait of another and highlighting their interdependence as a family and a political dynasty. One very interesting example is Philip II, whose picture appears in portraits of his sister Joanna, his wife Isabel de Valois, his daughters Isabel Clara Eugenia and Catalina Micaela, and even of artists such as Federico Zuccaro and Pompeo Leoni. The status of each of these figures was measured by reference to the king's dynastic or professional identity.[113] This practice continued until the eighteenth century; one particularly impressive example is Miguel Jacinto Meléndez's portrait of Isabella Farnese pointing to a print of Philip V [FIG. 15].[114]

This network of relationships based on dynastic roles is also apparent in two masterpieces of Spanish art: Velázquez's *Las Meninas* [CAT. 43] and Goya's *The Family of the Infante Don Luis* [CAT. 45]. In the former, Margarita is defined as the infanta not only by the presence of the king and queen, but also by the accompanying group of servants and the way in which the two maids of honour (*meninas*) are waiting upon her.[115] Much the same is true of Goya's painting, whose meaning is much closer to Velázquez than to Goya's own *The Family of Charles IV* [CAT. 46]. The painter could not have found a more effective way of indicating the

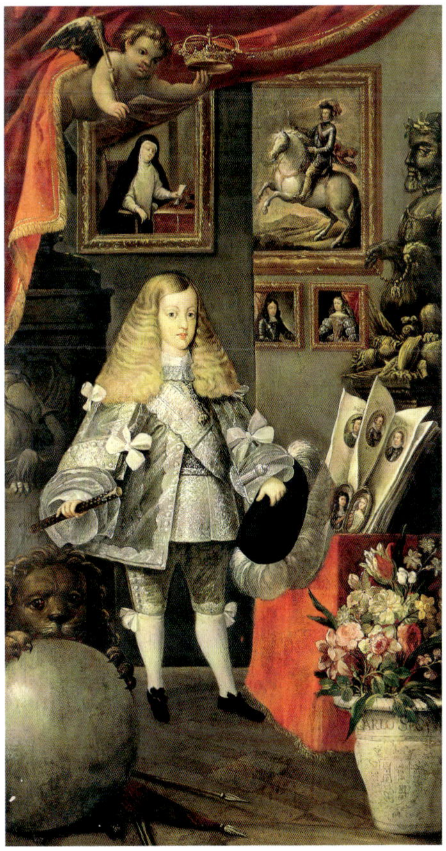

FIG. 14. Anonymous Spanish painter, *Charles II as a Child, with Portraits of his Ancestors, ca.* 1670. Madrid, Museo Fundación Lázaro Galdiano

infante's high status than this apparently simple scene, which is full of allusions to rank. Much of the action is centred on the noble couple, who are depicted very informally and engaged in very prosaic activities: she having her portrait painted and he apparently playing cards. But it is precisely this everyday simplicity and the presence of the retinue, that give the protagonists such emphasis, recalling pictures and written accounts of the Spanish and European courts with their highly significant mixture of intimacy and spectacle.

THE 'CIVIL PORTRAIT'

The culture of the portrait was gradually spreading far beyond kings, queens and their families. A few portraits of non-courtiers appeared during the initial decades of the sixteenth century, including Michel Sittow's resplendent *Diego de Guevara* [FIG. 16],[116] but it was not until the 1570s that this type of painting became more common and the custom of having one's portrait painted spread to the lesser nobility and affluent middle classes. This trend was closely linked

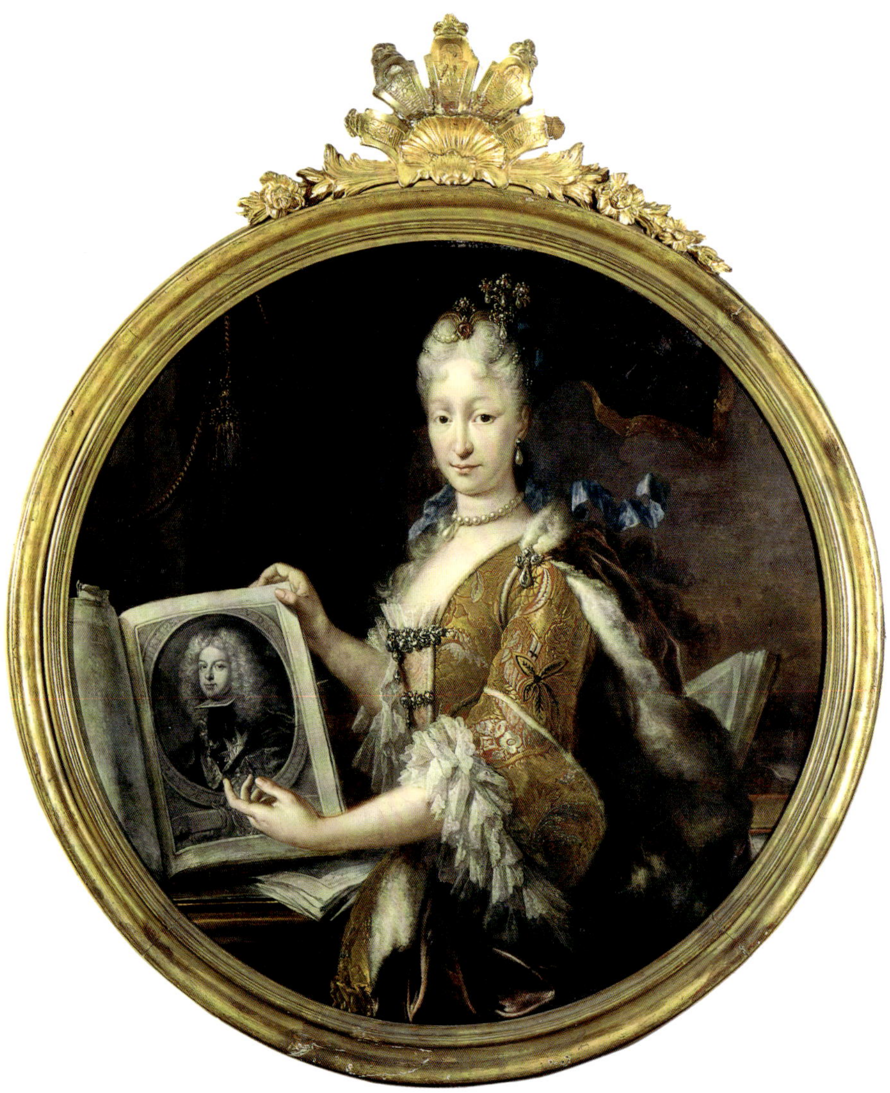

FIG. 15. Miguel Jacinto Meléndez, *Isabella Farnese*, 1727. Madrid, Biblioteca Nacional [519]

to the flowering of an urban culture, in which theatre, novels and other art forms reached their apex. One of its main focuses was Toledo, which was going through one of the most culturally fertile periods of its history.[117] Moreover, the city was fortunate to have El Greco among its inhabitants, and he left behind an extraordinary gallery of portraits of his contemporaries. A comparison with Seville shows that the history of the Spanish portrait was shaped not so much by a process of evolution as by the presence of influential personalities. Seville was richer and more powerful than Toledo, and its society much more varied and cosmopolitan, but the absence of an influential portraitist meant that the genre was much less developed there despite such exceptional works as Pacheco's *Libro de retratos*. It was not until the appearance of Murillo that Seville, a city then in decline, acquired its own great school of portrait painters.

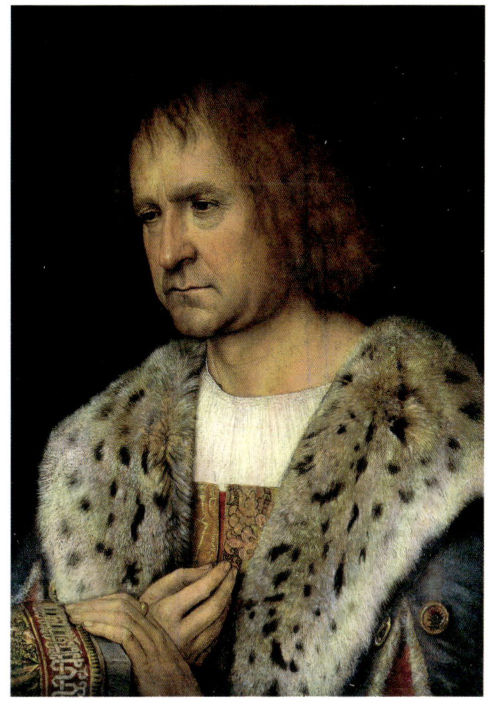

FIG. 16. Michel Sittow, *Diego de Guevara*, 1517. Washington, National Gallery of Art [Andrew Mellon Collection 1937.1.46]

Within the history of Spanish art, the gallery of figures painted by El Greco in Toledo was one of the cornerstones of the civil portrait. Many of these depicted Castilian gentlemen,[118] and each contains information about the subject's social identity, be it through his pose, hairstyle or dress. But the portraits are also often surprisingly relaxed and intimate, with considerable emphasis on individual expression. A large number of those which have been identified show members of El Greco's circle: family members such as his son Jorge Manuel [CAT. 17] or perhaps the subject of the emotive *Portrait of an Old Man* [FIG. 60]; intellectuals such as Covarrubias [FIG. 62], his doctor Rodrigo de la Fuente [FIG. 59], and so on.[119] Others are group portraits, such as that in the background of *The Burial of the Count of Orgaz* [FIG. 17] (Toledo, parish church of Santo Tomé), where leading figures in Toledo society are depicted in the manner of a frieze. One of El Greco's finest and most strikingly innovative portraits is *Fray Hortensio Félix Paravicino* [CAT. 19], probably not the result of a formal commission but of the relationship that developed between the elderly painter and the young, passionate and highly respected preacher, who dedicated a magnificent sonnet to the painting.

El Greco is one of the earliest examples of a 'civil portraitist' in Spain, using his art not only to depict religious scenes but also to immortalise members of the cultivated urban class to which he belonged. But he was not unique: literary sources also mention a number of other painters whose careers were partly driven by the demand for civil portraits in the late sixteenth century.

One of these was Felipe de Liaño, known as 'little Titian' for his mastery at producing small portraits. The only work known to be by him is a portrait of Cristóbal Mosquera de Figueroa included in a patent

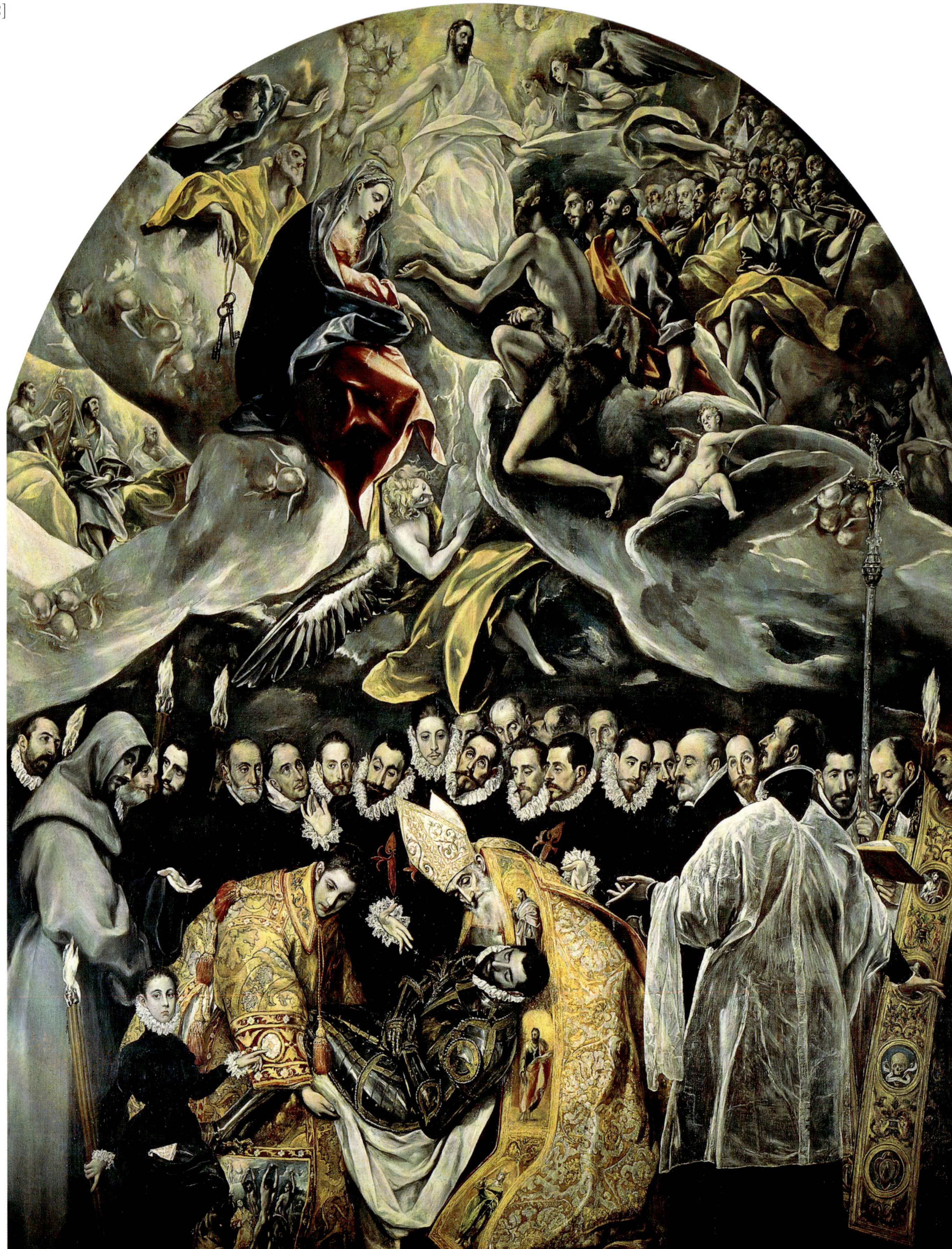

FIG. 17. El Greco, *The Burial of the Count of Orgaz*, 1588. Toledo, Parish Church of Santo Tomé

of nobility [FIG. 18],[120] and which in turn served as a model for Pacheco's *Libro de retratos*. Apart from this we know little about him,[121] other than he was a friend of Lope de Vega, who used him as the basis for one of the characters in *La Dorotea*, a play based on the writer's youthful love affair with Elena Osorio. Liaño's portraits were often exchanged between lovers as keepsakes, and the play shows they had become popular among the prosperous middle classes to which Lope and Elena belonged.[122]

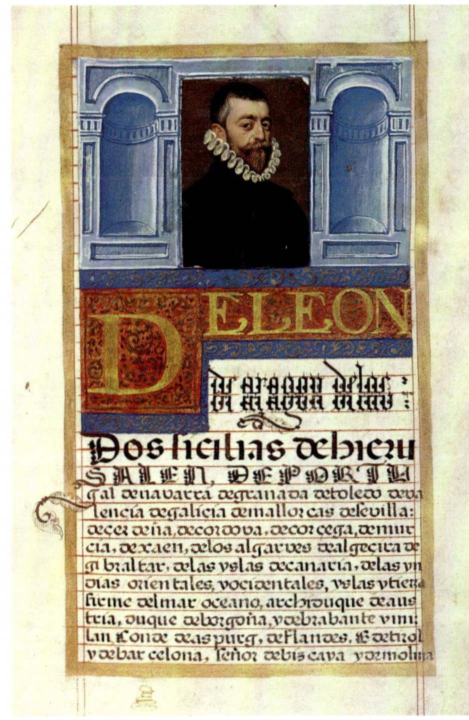

FIG. 18. Felipe de Liaño, *Cristóbal Mosquera de Figueroa*, from the 'Patent of Nobility of the Licenciado Cristóbal Mosquera de Figueroa', 1587. Madrid, private collection

PORTRAITS AND FAME

Lope de Vega's play also highlights another aspect of the rise of the Spanish portrait in Spain: its links with intellectual reputation. A very large proportion of Spanish non-royal portraits depict writers and appear at the beginning of their books. This practice became particularly common from the second half of the sixteenth century onwards, in parallel with the growth of the civil portrait; the pictures generally include attributes of the subject's profession or other themes, providing evidence of the writer's self-awareness. Of course, they are also intended to make the author more famous, although they are sometimes justified in some other way. For instance, Bernardino de Villegas explains the inclusion of his portrait in his book *Vitoria y triunfo de Jesu Christo* (1603) as a 'signature' with the purpose of indicating the edition has been authorised by the writer.[123]

But the relationship between portrait and fame was particularly close in the case of Lope de Vega, who was, when alive, the most famous Spanish writer of the Early Modern Period and thus the most often depicted in art. We know that there were some twenty-five different portraits made of him, of which nine have survived. These include prints used as illustrations for his literary works, paintings, and pictures included in portrait books. Although some of these were produced under his supervision or painted by friends such as Francisco Ribalta, many others bear witness to his desire that his admiring public should know what he looked like.[124] He had a flair for using the visual arts as a form of self-publicity, and when he died, his friend Pérez de Montalbán wrote: 'There is scarcely a curious man whose house does not contain a portrait of him on paper, canvas, or in the form of an engraving.'[125]

The idea of fame during the Early Modern Period, and the use of portraits to promote it, was not confined to writers. It was also closely associated with political and religious figures such as the bishop and viceroy Don Juan de Palafox, who was the subject of a promotional campaign both before and after his death in which portraits played a very prominent role.[126]

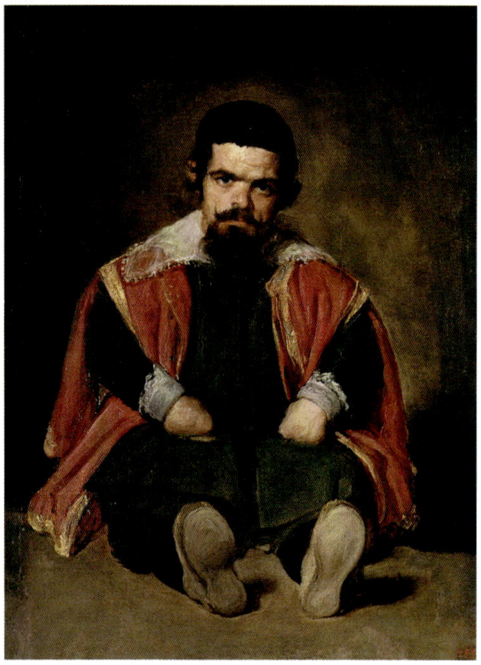

FIG. 19. Diego Velázquez, *Don Sebastián de Morra*, *ca.* 1643. Madrid, Museo del Prado [P-1202]

During the remainder of the seventeenth century and much of the eighteenth, there was little change in the social strata covered by the Spanish portrait, being primarily restricted to the court, the church authorities, the minor nobility, the liberal professions and wealthy merchants. But new types emerged, partly in the wake of changes in the court portrait. Compared to the time of El Greco there was now a greater variety of form and symbolic context, as evidenced by the work of artists such as Murillo.

Among the most obvious additions to the genre were buffoons, dwarfs and similar figures. These had occasionally appeared in the work of artists before Velázquez (such as Mor and Van der Hamen), but it was he who developed them to their full potential, leaving behind a gallery representing a high point in the history of western portraits. As I have noted previously, the unusual status of these figures, and the fact that they had not commissioned their own portraits, gave Velázquez greater freedom to exploit the expressive potential of the genre. He used them to explore character, mood and the human condition in general [CATS 33 and 34, and FIG. 19].

SELF-PORTRAITS

Another type of painting which developed in its own distinctive way in Spain was the self-portrait.[127] While all portraits during the Early Modern Period were painted for a purpose and could contain symbolic meaning, this was particularly true of self-portraits. These were intended to convey a particular image of the artist, especially at a time when the social and intellectual status of painting was ambiguous.

Sometimes artists used the format of the *retrato a lo divino*, as in Ribalta's portrait of himself as Saint Luke [CAT. 20], with its passing allusion to the concept of the sacred origin of painting. At other times the emphasis was on the intellectual component of art, as in Vicente Carducho's self-portrait (Glasgow, Pollok House), which shows him writing his *Diálogos de la pintura* with his painter's equipment beside him.[128] These also appear in Murillo's self-portrait [FIG. 1],[129] a dazzling display both of the painter's virtuosity and the tools he uses in the service of his art. His magnificent style, with its deliberate and highly effective use of a limited palette, is a eulogy to the possibilities of painting. It can even create the illusion of reality, as we see in the hand extending beyond the frame. A Latin inscription places the picture in a learned context, and the painting utensils on either side of the mantelpiece refer to this art form's two fundamental components: colour, represented by the palette and brushes on the right, and drawing, embodied by the ruler, compass, pencil and anatomy study on the left, all showing that painting is a scientific activity subject to rules and measurements.

But self-portraits can convey a much wider range of messages. Juan de Pareja includes one in his painting *The Vocation of Saint Matthew* (Madrid, Museo del Prado, P-1041), and uses it as a means of personal affirmation. He is dressed as a gentleman, carrying a sword and looking at the viewer with a very self-confident air. In his right hand he holds a piece of paper bearing his signature and the date, 1661. If we compare his face here with that in the picture by Velázquez [FIG. 76], we can see that Juan de Pareja has considerably toned down the features that reveal him to be of mixed-race descent.

FIG. 20. Juan de Pareja, *The Calling of Saint Matthew* (detail of presumed self-portrait of the artist), 1661. Madrid, Museo del Prado [P-1041]

AFFECTION

From the second half of the eighteenth century onwards, political and social upheaval in Spain and the rest of western Europe resulted in a new conception of humanity and history and new forms of social relations. There were also changes in the connection between art and society, though this was more true of some countries than others. All of this was very obviously mirrored in the portrait.

In Spain, this was the period in which Goya was active. He was the direct heir of Velázquez in terms of his ability to look on the portrait with new eyes, but it would be wrong to credit him with all the innovations in this genre; many are signs of a social reality which transcended his own life and work. One of the most obvious changes was the big increase in the number of portraits that were painted. In fact, Carducho's comment that all kinds of people were having their portraits painted is more appropriate to the last few decades of the eighteenth century than to his own period. A very large number of portraits have survived from this period, and this is only partly because it was relatively recent or the result of population growth. It was also simply a reflection of demand.

Many painters, including Goya, Vicente López, Esteve and Luis de la Cruz, devoted a significant part of their oeuvre to non-royal portraits. Goya's oeuvre, in particular, bears witness to the expansion in the kinds of social group that had their portraits painted. Of course there was still a direct correlation between affluence and the consumption of portraits, but the demand no longer came primarily from royalty and the aristocracy; there was increasing demand from politicians, senior officials and the aristocracy, and also from new patrons such as actors and bullfighters.[130]

There were also changes in the content of the portrait during this period. One of the most obvious was the appearance of warmth and affection. Until then, portraits of more than one person had usually expressed the relationships between them in terms of hierarchies of superior and inferior, even when depicting families. But from the late eighteenth century onwards, this gave way to a culture of emotion which also occurred in other media such as theatre. In *The Countess of Montijo with her Daughters* (collection of the Duchess of Alba), attributed to Esteve, the daughters are grouped lovingly around their mother in a circle of family intimacy. Here, the family is not simply a group of people linked by ties of parenthood; they are also bound together by mutual sympathy, love and affection. Much the same feeling is expressed by Goya's *The Duques de Osuna and their Children* of 1788 [FIG. 21], where the family group is isolated from any disruptive environmental reference in a vivid and enchanting image where the parents are very much the loving protectors of the children.

The transition was apparent even in the portrait-within-a-portrait. Goya's *María Tomasa Palafox, Marquesa de Villafranca* [FIG. 101], dating from 1804, shows the subject sitting in an armchair and painting her husband's portrait. This painting is one of tenderness rather than subjection, especially bearing in mind the long tradition that links portraits and love. This idea has classical and Christian antecedents[131] which we can see, for example, in Calderón's play *El pintor de su deshonra* (*The Painter of his Own Dishonour*).

The painting by Goya is not the only Spanish work of the time to subtly allude to marital love. Another is Agustín Esteve's *Portrait of María Terán de Amorós* (Oviedo, Museo de Bellas Artes de Asturias), where the subject is inscribing her husband's name on a tree. This theme has a close parallel in the words 'only Goya' written in the sand in the portrait *The Duchess of Alba* [CAT. 62], and had been used to embody love ever since Ariosto employed it in the story of Angelica and Medoro.[132]

SECULAR 'EX VOTOS'

Another example of the profound changes in the content of some traditional types of portrait is Goya's exquisite *Self Portrait with Dr Arrieta* [CAT. 66], showing the painter in bed being attended by his doctor and watched over by demons.[133] The cartouche at the bottom reads: 'Goya is grateful to his friend Arrieta for his skill and care in saving his life when he suffered an acute and dangerous illness late in 1819 when he was seventy-three years old. He painted this in 1820.'

The picture marks a turning point in the history of the Spanish portrait, and in this respect is comparable in importance to his 'black paintings'. It reflects the transition to the Modern Period and summarises very explicitly the secularisation of the portrait. To anyone at all familiar with Spanish popular iconography the painting will immediately recall a votive offering, and this is precisely how it is intended, though the offering is a secular one. It is very useful to compare it, for example, with a work of this type dated 1816 and belonging to the hermitage of Nuestra Señora de los Nogales, in Villanueva de Cameros [FIG. 22]. In the foreground we see two peasants and a priest attending a little girl, while in the background the Virgin of los Nogales appears in a tree. The inscription states that through her intercession, the girl was revived after being trapped in a millrace for twenty-five minutes.[134]

The essential elements are the same in both pictures: a sick person, another figure ministering to them, and an inscription expressing the beneficiary's gratitude. The difference is the person doing the tending: in the *ex voto* it is the Virgin, through the intermediation of the priest, and in Goya's work it is science, through the doctor. This picture not only recognises the benefits of medicine but uses typological precedents to point out its role as a substitute for religion, at least to the extent that in Catholic religious practice there was a tacit

FIG. 21. Francisco de Goya, *The Duques de Osuna and their Children*, 1788. Madrid, Museo del Prado [P-739]

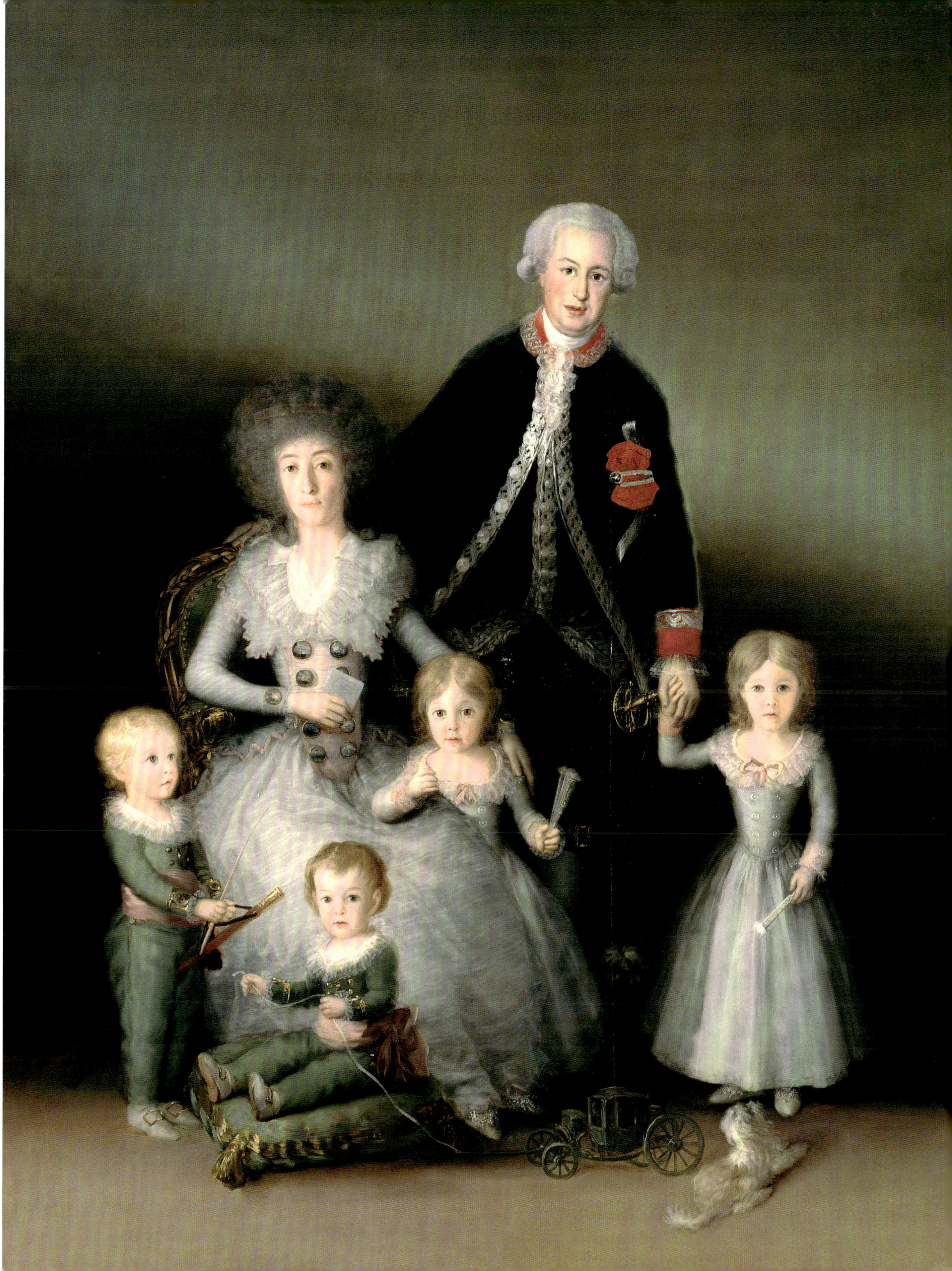

agreement between the faithful and God that temporal benefits could be obtained in exchange for spiritual devotion.

The development both of works like these and of portraits conveying affection marked a break with tradition. Paradoxically, and given that portraiture is the depiction of real human beings, we might expect this to be the genre most likely to be used to express the great variety of human emotions. But for centuries this potential went untapped, and the range of emotions remained very limited. The portrait was a highly codified straitjacket that sought to convey people's social identities and in some cases their character, rather than capture highly individual and expressive moments. All this changed during Goya's time, as the range of emotions broadened and became more spontaneous. They included love, and even, as the *Self Portrait with Dr Arrieta* shows, pain.

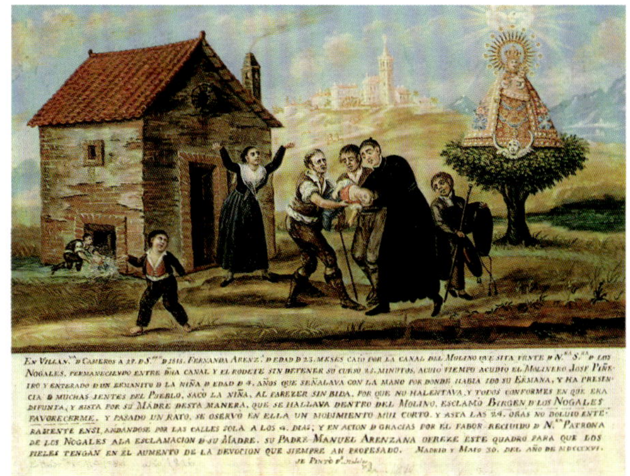

FIG. 22. Hidalgo, *Miracle of Nuestra Señora de los Nogales*, 1816. Villanueva de Cameros (Rioja), Hermitage of Nuestra Señora de los Nogales

MELANCHOLIA

This interest in a wider range of expression is also apparent in a type of portrait which was quite popular at this time, as this exhibition shows: depictions of introspective, melancholic artists and intellectuals. One example is Paret's *Self Portrait* [CAT. 58] with his head leaning on his left arm and surrounded by a fascinating variety of attributes that tell us about his interests and cultural background.[135] Another is Goya's portrait of Gaspar Melchor de Jovellanos [CAT. 63], who is shown in a similar pose and with allusions to his role as justice minister and (in the case of the statue of Minerva) to his status as an intellectual.[136] The front of the desk is decorated with a reproduction of the skull of a horned animal, probably a reference to Capricorn and to the saturnine personality associated with introspection and the intellectual life. The fact that a minister should choose to have himself portrayed displaying intellectual doubt is emblematic of the changes that had occurred in portraiture. It would have been unthinkable fifty or a hundred years earlier, when the focus would have been on the trappings of rank and dignity – as shown by Goya's portrait of the Count of Floridablanca [FIG. 106].

However, the latter picture also shows how changes in the meanings and typology of Spanish portraiture did not necessarily mean abandoning the old ones. The rigid, hierarchical formality of portraits during the Old Regime was maintained throughout the nineteenth century in the many official portraits of the royal family (including numerous pictures of Isabella II)[137] and politicians in institutional galleries such as those of the ministries and the Banco de España.

SPONTANEITY

While these vestiges remained, the appeal and content of portraiture expanded greatly over the course of the century. The invention and spread of photography put it within reach of most of the population, and painted portraits became increasingly common. This was the great century of portraiture in Spanish art, and its fortunes were boosted by the growth in the population as a whole and the middle classes in particular. Many leading painters specialised in the genre, and some sub-genres became much more widespread.

The group portrait reached its zenith, and featured not only royal and aristocratic families but the middle classes and professional groups such as Esquivel's famous *A Reading of Zorrilla in the Painter's Studio* [FIG. 23], which includes many of the most prominent members of the Madrid intelligentsia during the Romantic period. In the wake of such artists as Goya and Esteve, it acquired new meanings and values, one of them being spontaneity. This was one of the characteristics that distinguished portraits of this period from those of the Early Modern Period, and became increasingly prevalent as the nineteenth century progressed. It resulted in scenes in which the protagonists, far from posing, appear to have been surprised in an everyday situation, as in *Interior in the Open Air* (Madrid, Museo Thyssen-Bornemisza) by Ramón Casas. This strategy of representation developed in parallel with the dissemination of photography.

IN SEARCH OF A TRADITION

Spanish portraiture in the nineteenth and early twentieth centuries is the subject of separate essays in this catalogue. At this point, I would like to concentrate on one of its many facets, and one which is evident throughout the exhibition: the development of a tradition of portraiture and the ways in which different artists responded to it.

The history of painting in Spain and the western world is one of learning, borrowing and innovation. The prime source of inspiration for all artists has been the work of their predecessors, to which they have reacted in very different ways. Sometimes they were

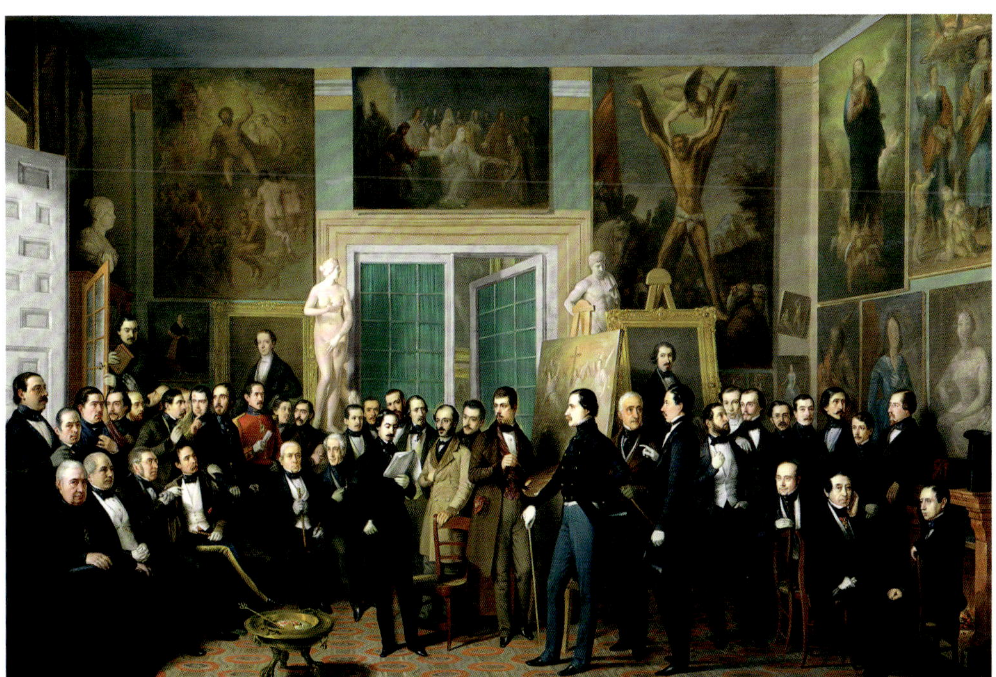

FIG. 23. Antonio María Esquivel, *A Reading of Zorilla in the Painter's Studio*, 1846. Madrid, Museo del Prado [P-4299]

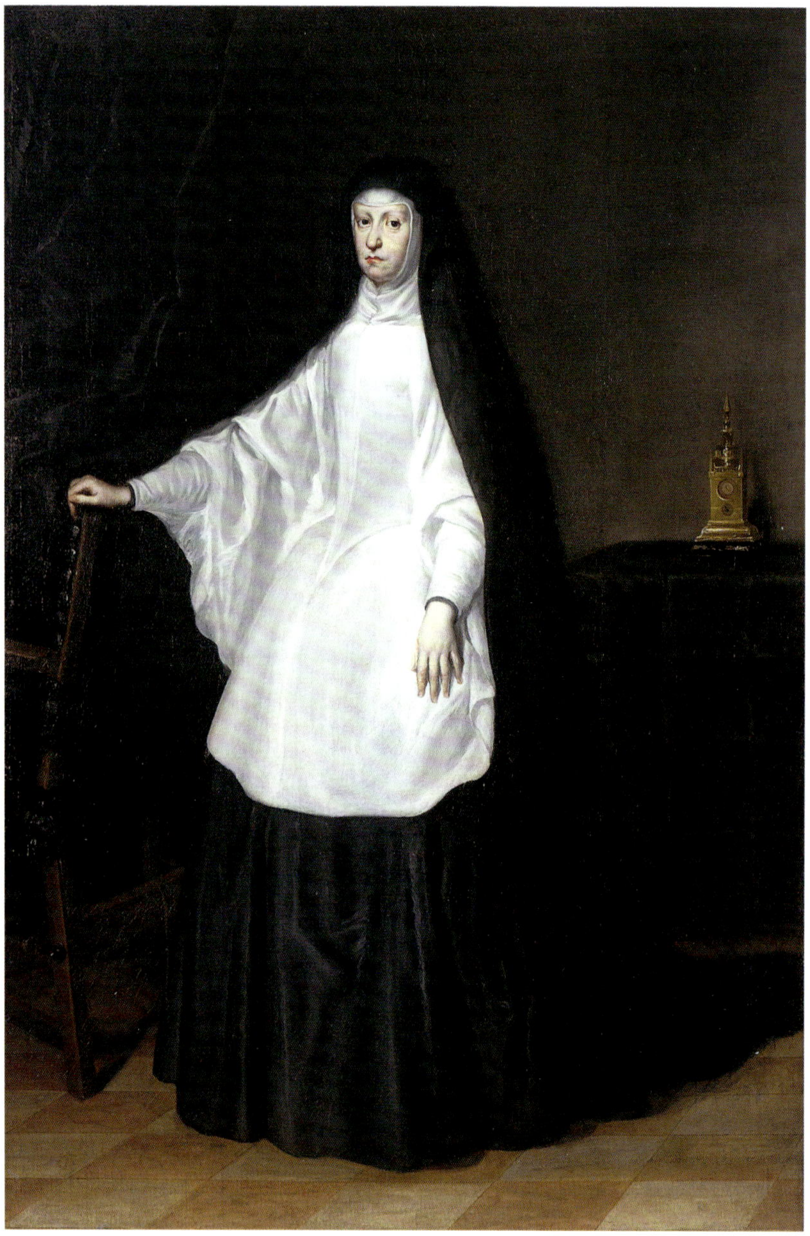

FIG. 24. Juan Carreño de Miranda, *Queen Mariana of Austria*, 1677. Schloss Rohrau, Graf Harrach'sche Familiensammlung

influenced by artists from the same region, but very often it was artists who had been born and worked in different countries. During the early centuries of the Early Modern Period, the main influences on Spanish artists were their counterparts in Italy and Flanders. Early critics were aware of this, and one of them, Palomino, considered Titian to be the initiator of the Spanish school.[138] The issue of traditions and influences is particularly pertinent to the Spanish portrait because from the late fifteenth century to the early twentieth it was significantly influenced by its own tradition. Between the second half of the sixteenth century and the time of Goya, this was mainly because so much portraiture derived from the court and therefore often involved foreign artists such as Titian, Mor, the French and Italian painters who worked there in the early eighteenth century, and the German artist Mengs. The court imposed a series of models and traditions on successive painters, who established a fruitful dialogue with their forebears.

As is so often the case, one of the best examples is Velázquez, in terms both of his debt to the past and his major influence on future generations. His royal portraits were very much inspired by earlier artists. For example, his early full-length portraits of Philip IV and some of his brothers owe much to Alonso Sánchez Coello,[139] whose work in turn was rooted in that of Titian and Mor. Likewise, his *Philip IV on Horseback* [CAT. 47] cannot be fully understood without reference to Titian's *Charles V at Mühlberg* [FIG. 52], which shares the same feeling of majestic calm.

At the same time, throughout his long career, Velázquez placed his own individual stamp on the royal portrait by employing new strategies of representation and an equally innovative technique. This set him apart from the trend in other European courts, where these was an increased emphasis on symbolic content.[140] He also developed new types of image, such as group portraits, hunters and buffoons.

VELAZQUEZ'S FOLLOWERS

Velázquez went on to become the most important source of inspiration in the history of Spanish portraiture; his influence was not confined only to the court, and we can even trace it in the work of Picasso. Of course, the first to fall under its spell were his disciples and his successors as royal portraitists. One was his son-in-law, Juan Bautista Martínez del Mazo, who was only six years younger than himself, and who lived in his shadow professionally.

The background in his portrait of Queen Mariana of Spain in mourning (London, National Gallery) contains a clear reference to the action centred on Margarita in *Las Meninas*, and the latter is also the point of reference for Mazo's *The Family of the Painter* [CAT. 44], one of the first Spanish paintings to show a non-royal, non-aristocratic family in a domestic setting, with the father's profession being used as a marker of identity. The artist's work bears close similarities to Velázquez both in theme and in the rendition of space, and as such pays homage to the master.

Juan Carreño de Miranda was another artist who, in his own way, owed much to the Velázquez tradition.[141] His court portraits of Charles II and others tend to display a greater rhetorical complexity, but he is sometimes extraordinarily close to his predecessor, as in the magnificent *Queen Mariana of Austria* [FIG. 24], which is a paraphrase of Velázquez's own portrait of the Queen [CAT. 13]. The pose and the surrounding elements, including the precious clock, are exactly the same. But the colour range is very different, and the richly hued clothing and surroundings in Velázquez's version are transformed into grey in Carreño's, partly to remind us that the subject is a widow.[142] Whatever Carreño's reasons for imitating Velázquez, this is his most explicit homage to his predecessor. However, his portraits reveal a wide variety of other influences, showing how the Spanish tradition cohabited peacefully with those of other countries. For example, one of the main influences in *The Duke of Pastrana* [CAT. 40] is Flemish painting, and especially that of Van Dyck,[143] which was also an important factor in Murillo's revival of the Sevillean portrait.[144]

Claudio Coello's *The Adoration of the Eucharistic Host of Gorkum* [FIG. 25] shows a similar aptitude for highly original forms of representation, but within the bounds of tradition. This is one of the most important group portraits of its time. Like *Las Meninas*, it contains a complex interplay of spatial and political references, placing it midway between portrait and history painting.[145]

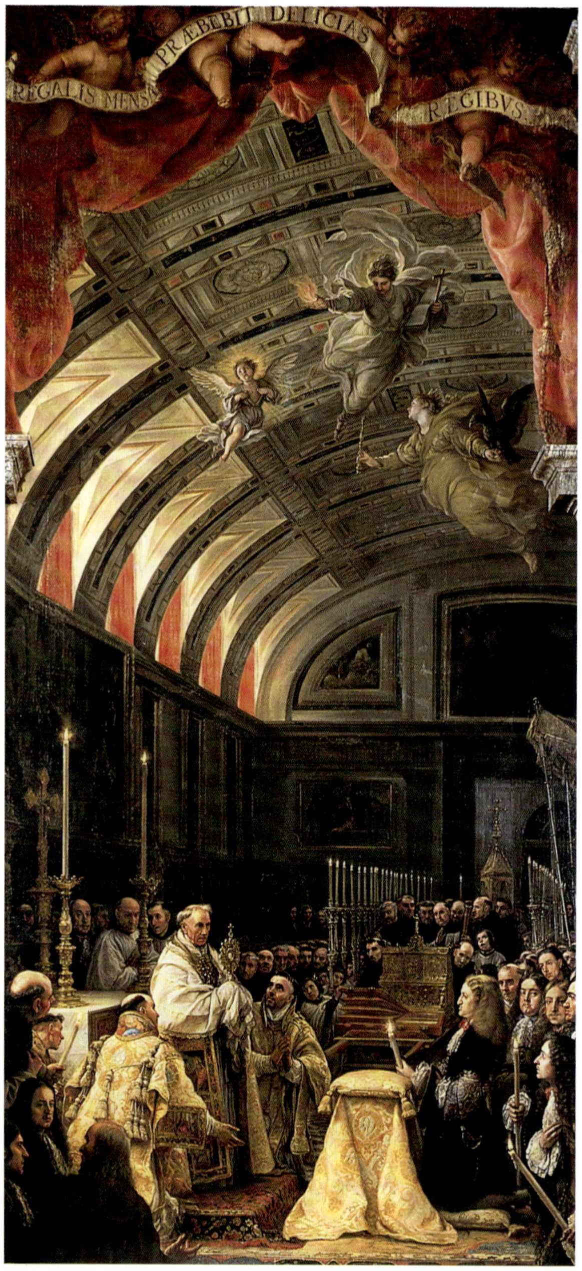

FIG. 25. Claudio Coello, *The Adoration of the Eucharistic Host of Gorkum*, 1690. Patrimonio Nacional, Real Monasterio de San Lorenzo del Escorial, Sacristy

VELÁZQUEZ AND THE EIGHTEENTH CENTURY

There are still distant echoes of Velázquez in some of the court portraits of the first half of the eighteenth century, such as Van Loo's *The Family of Philip V* and Houasse's *Luis I* (both Madrid, Museo del Prado, nos P-2283 and P-2387). Most court portraitists had been born and trained abroad, and pursued different interests when they arrived. French artists such as Van Loo, Rigaud and Ranc, and Italians like Amigoni and Procaccini, pushed the Spanish court portrait more towards the formal tradition codified during the reign of Louis XIV, an international language that remained in use for the rest of the century. Around the middle of the century this tradition remained alive in the work of the Bohemian painter Antón Rafael Mengs, who influenced many Spanish painters working for the court, including Francisco Bayeu and Mariano Salvador Maella.

The revival of Velázquez's reputation did not occur until the last three decades of the eighteenth century. Palomino had already published his treatise naming him as the greatest figure in the history of Spanish painting, and there were a number of other important initiatives aimed at restoring him to prominence, including the publication of a large number of prints based on his work by the Compañía para el Grabado de los Cuadros de los Reales Palacios (Company for the Engraving of Paintings in the Royal Palaces). A major critical debate was also instigated by, among others, Jovellanos, one of the most important figures of the Spanish Enlightenment. In his *Elogio de las bellas artes* (1782) as well as his essay on *Las Meninas* he praised Velázquez's paintings and held them up as the principal example for other artists to follow. This implied a defence of naturalism and a difference of opinion from the influential painter and writer Antón Rafael Mengs, who, although he admired Velázquez's naturalism and use of aerial perspective, regarded his style as undignified. It was not worthy of imitation by the aspiring artist, who would do better to take his inspiration from Correggio or Raphael.[146]

The rehabilitation of Velázquez by Jovellanos was motivated not only by a spirit of nationalism, but by the return to nature that he advocated in his writings.

Further evidence of Velázquez's growing reputation lies in Francisco Bayeu's frescoes for the Salón de los Espejos in Madrid's Palacio Real, where the art of painting is represented by a woman sitting beside an easel on which stands a study for Velázquez's *Aesop*.[147]

It was this latter painting that sparked some of the greatest interest among artists during the late eighteenth and nineteenth centuries. One of these was Goya, who reproduced it as one of his prints dedicated to Velázquez's works.[148] This was an early series which familiarised Goya with the painting and engraving techniques of Velázquez, who from then onwards became a major influence on his career. He borrowed Velázquez's subjects and techniques, and also learned from his very free and direct approach to painting.[149]

Significantly, one of the genres in which Goya displays the greatest dependence on Velázquez is royal portraiture. Instead of following the path marked out by his immediate predecessors in this area, such as Mengs and the Italian and French painters, he took his lead from Velázquez and breathed new life into the great tradition of Spanish court portraiture. His pictures of Charles III and Charles IV as hunters [CAT. 49 and Madrid, Palacio Real, respectively) clearly have as their precedent Velázquez's hunting portraits of Philip IV, the Cardinal Infante and Baltasar Carlos

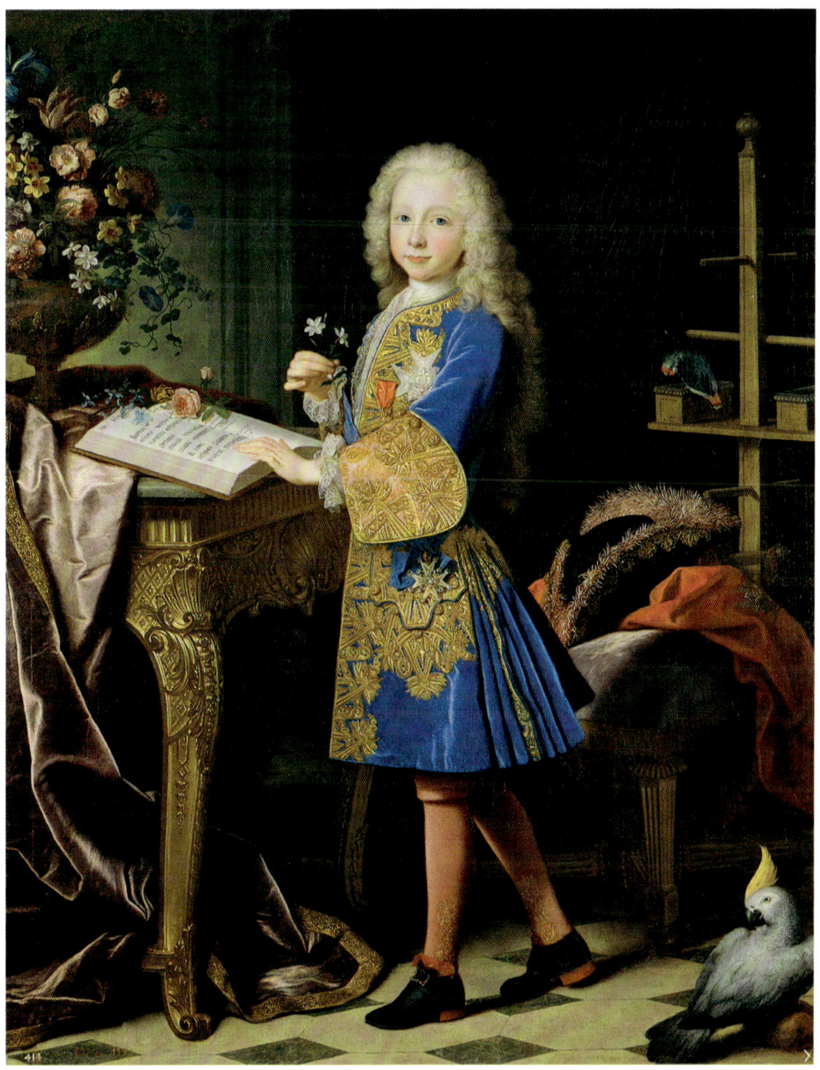

FIG. 26. Jean Ranc, *Charles III as a Child*, 1723. Madrid, Museo del Prado [P-2334]

[CAT. 50]. Goya's equestrian portrait of Charles IV [CAT. 48] can be fully understood only by reference to Velázquez's picture of Philip IV [CAT. 47], and his *Family of Charles IV* and *Family of the Infante don Luis* contain so many references to *Las Meninas* that they can be seen as a homage to Velázquez's masterpiece.

Like Velázquez, Goya included himself painting in both pictures, probably as a way of emphasising his connection with his predecessors, since his presence in them was strictly necessary. However, we do not know whether this revival of the Spanish court painting tradition was a personal initiative by Goya, or whether he was responding to efforts to reclaim the country's artistic past expressed in such writings as Antonio Ponz's *Viaje de España* and Ceán Bermúdez's famous dictionary of Spanish painters.

THE INVENTION OF THE 'SPANISH SCHOOL'

These eighteenth-century precedents contributed to the invention of the 'Spanish school' of painting during the nineteenth century, as Spanish and foreign artists and intellectuals realised that their country had its own continuous tradition which included some very important artists. Also, both the school as a whole and some of its most prominent representatives had distinguished themselves by their use of a naturalistic or realistic style, which struck a powerful chord with the more innovative artists of the nineteenth century. Following the example set by Goya, nearly all of the century's great portraitists drew, to varying degrees, on this tradition, which remained dominated by Velázquez, whose influence continued to make itself felt.

Even the painters who were most receptive to foreign trends regarded Velázquez as a precedent to follow and reflected his influence in some of their canvases. The style of Federico de Madrazo, for example, owed much to Ingres and the Nazarenes, and his conception of portraiture was quite different from that of Velázquez. But he believed that the latter's portraits were second to none in terms of 'character'; in other words, they were the highest to which a portraitist could aspire.[150] A number of his pictures bear the mark of Velázquez. One is *Federico Flórez as a Boy* (Madrid, Museo del Prado, P-4452), whose composition owes much to that of *Prince Baltasar Carlos as a Hunter* [CAT. 50]; another is *Segismundo Moret* (Madrid, Museo del Prado, P-4466), with its very limited palette but rich variety of greys.[151]

The influence of Velázquez is more apparent in the work of Eduardo Rosales, one of the finest and most original Spanish painters of the nineteenth century. His debt to Velázquez lies not just in his technique and use of space, but in his whole concept of painting. His works question some of the most widely held artistic views of the time, such as the notion of 'completion'. Some of them were highly polemical and, curiously, Velázquez's name crops up frequently in the critical debate about them, from both his defenders and his detractors. This was the case with his famous *Queen Isabella dictating her Will* (Madrid, Museo del Prado, P-4625). While attacking Rosales, Cruzada Villamil imagines a conversation with Velázquez, in which the latter advises Rosales to paint more slowly. Pi y Margall describes *Queen Isabella dictating her Will* as 'reminiscent of Velázquez'.[152] The debt to his portraits is very clear.

The Duke of Fernán Núñez (private collection, 1865) shows the subject standing against a brownish-grey background following Velázquez's full-length portrait of Philip IV [CAT. 11] and *The Infante Don Carlos* (Madrid, Museo del Prado, P-1188). The shadow he casts on the ground is also very similar, as is the position of the right hand holding a hat and a glove. There are more allusions to Velázquez in Rosales' *The*

Condesa de Santovenia [CAT. 73], particularly in the very full skirt, the combination of grey, silver and pink, and the way in which the light helps to create volume and bring the figure to life.[153]

Velázquez was so versatile and effective in his themes and styles that he influenced artists of many different schools. What they most appreciated about him in the nineteenth century was his seemingly natural relationship with his subjects, with its frank gaze and open technique. In Spain, he was the artist who best embodied the local tradition. His painting combined wisdom, spontaneity and technical mastery, and had a significant impact on painters such as Sorolla, who shared these characteristics, albeit on a lesser scale. He showed a profound and constant admiration for his predecessor,[154] greater than that which he felt for any other artist, Goya included. Again, the genre in which he expressed this most obviously was the portrait,[155] where he adopted Velázquez's more outward qualities such as grace, spontaneity and elegance.

One very fine example of this is Sorolla's *María Guerrero* [FIG. 27], where he transforms Velázquez's static portrait of the Infanta Margarita into a figure that is full of life. Another is *Aureliano de Beruete, Father* [CAT. 74], the painter and critic who wrote one of the most important monographs on Velázquez, who is shown seated in front of a picture which appears to depict Toledo. This painting consists mostly of a varied range of greys which further emphasise the subject's poise and elegance.[156]

With time, the list of Spanish artists who served as inspiration for their successors grew longer. The names of Velázquez and Goya were joined in the late nineteenth century by that of El Greco, whose was belatedly rehabilitated by critics, art historians and artists. Most prominent among the latter were Catalan artists such as Ramón Casas, whose work spanned the

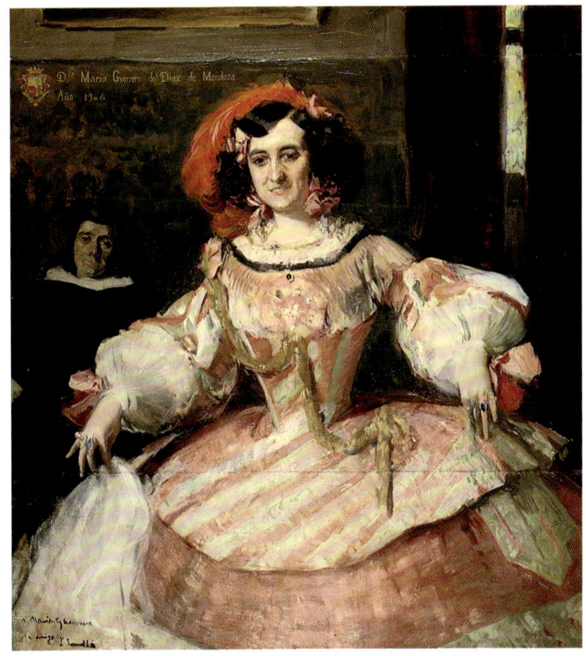

FIG. 27. Joaquín Sorolla, *The Actress María Guerrero as 'La Dama boba'*, painted in 1897, reworked in 1906. Madrid, Museo del Prado [P-4647]

two centuries. A drawing by Casas on a letter of 3 May 1904 shows him standing and copying El Greco's *Gentleman with a Hand on his Chest*.[157]

Casas also painted an interesting portrait of Santiago Rusiñol [CAT. 75], who was one of the principal forces in the revival of El Greco's reputation and owned a number of the latter's works. This is a casual portrait in an international style that owes much to Velázquez and includes a curious reference to him. On the wall, below a landscape signed by Rusiñol, we see part of a copy of *Las Meninas* showing the top of the Infanta Margarita's head.[158] Not surprisingly, this is not the only reference to Velázquez in Casas's oeuvre. His portrait of the actor Riquelme (Barcelona, Instituto del Teatro) is directly inspired by Velázquez's *Pablo de Valladolid* [CAT. 51]. The latter was one of Velázquez's most successful works, and the point of departure for paintings by a number of other leading artists such as Goya's *Francisco Cabarrús* [CAT. 52] and Manet's *The Tragic Actor* and *The Fife Player*.

TRADITION AND THE CONCEPT OF SPANISHNESS

The turn of the twentieth century was an extremely interesting period for Spanish painting. A great variety of artists were active, many of them were technically very distinctive, and the artistic panorama had never been more varied. Two particular trends made themselves felt in Spanish painting. One was a growing interest among intellectuals in reflecting on the collective identity and what it meant to be Spanish, an exploration personified in the group of writers known as the 'Generation of 98', but also shared by many other authors, politicians and artists. Much of it involved shedding new light not only on Spain's history, but also on its landscapes and people. The other trend was the rediscovery of key figures in Spanish art. The first major exhibition of Goya's work took place in 1900, and Manuel Bartolomé Cossío's highly influential monograph on El Greco was published in 1908. This completed the process of what might be called the hispanicisation, or perhaps castilianisation, of the Greek-born painter, even though the author takes pains to emphasise the foreign roots of his art.

Both trends made themselves felt in the work of most leading painters of the time, although not everyone responded in the same way. Sorolla, for example, portrayed the great variety of Spain's urban and natural landscapes and people in pictures that were full of light and optimism. Other painters took a more dramatic approach to reality.

One of these was Ignacio Zuloaga, whose pictures expressed many of the same themes as those expounded in writing by the 'Generation of 98'. He was an internationally successful artist, portraying both members of Spain's high society and peasants who served as archetypes of the country's more arcane aspects. For example, in *The Dwarf Gregorio el Botero* at Sepúlveda (St Petersburg, Hermitage Museum), the subject is shown outside a Castilian village, his diminutive stature made even more obvious by comparison with the wineskin at his side. In *The Dwarf Doña Mercedes* [CAT. 79], the subject is holding a ball in which we see a reflection of the painter at work.[159]

Zuloaga was popular among contemporary intellectuals, some of whose portraits he painted; for example that of Maurice Barrés, who is shown in front of a view of Toledo (Nancy, Musée Historique Lorrain). They appreciated his ability to express Spanishness not only through people and landscapes but also in his style. Miquel Utrillo, one of the key figures in turn-of-the-century Catalan art, wrote of a series of Zuloaga's paintings: 'They spoke to you in Spanish without your having to read the signature.'[160] But not everyone liked this very literary painting with its concentration on one particular theme. The writer Azorín accused him of looking at reality and reproducing it in the manner of a foreigner looking for clichés about Spain.[161]

In recreating his country on the canvas, Zuloaga sought inspiration not only in its people and landscapes, but also in previous generations of artists. This is acknowledged by Azorín, who mentions Velázquez, El Greco and Goya as being among his sources. The painter and writer Santiago Rusiñol lived in Paris at the same time as Zuloaga, and wrote of him in his *Impresiones de arte*: 'Mor, Coello and Ribera spoke to him of great and concise things. He was enthused by the great Velázquez, but most of all it was the energy, madness and incredible simplicity of El Greco that became his idol and sacred example.'[162]

There are constant references to Spanish artists in Zuloaga's portraits. His painting *The Dwarf Doña Mercedes* recalls Velázquez, as does the interplay of reflections in the picture. *The Cardinal* (Bilbao, Museo de Bellas Artes) is a reference to El Greco, and there are many allusions to Goya in his paintings, including *Doña Rosita Gutiérrez* (Bilbao, Museo de Bellas Artes), where the *Naked Maja* appears on the fan. But his realistic, broad-brush style also owes much to local tradition.

It is most instructive to compare *The Dwarf Doña Mercedes* with works by Isidre Nonell, showing how the contemporary vogue for transforming portraits into types or archetypes could be expressed in very different ways. While Zuloaga was an extroverted artist who appears to have used his painting to develop a theory of Spain and Spanishness, Nonell was more inward-looking, reflecting what he saw around him with a profound degree of personal involvement. Zuloaga maintains a distance from his subjects, whereas Nonell's relationship with them is one of emotional projection. The world of gypsies, which he knew very well, provided the inspiration for such highly original and emotional works as *La Paloma* [FIG. 28],[163] where the subject is shown very close up, from a low angle and standing out against the background, with a distant gaze and very prominent facial features. The limited colour range and broad brushstrokes radiate expressiveness, while the framing and viewpoint give her a monumentality and dignity whose only precedents are Velázquez's buffoons.

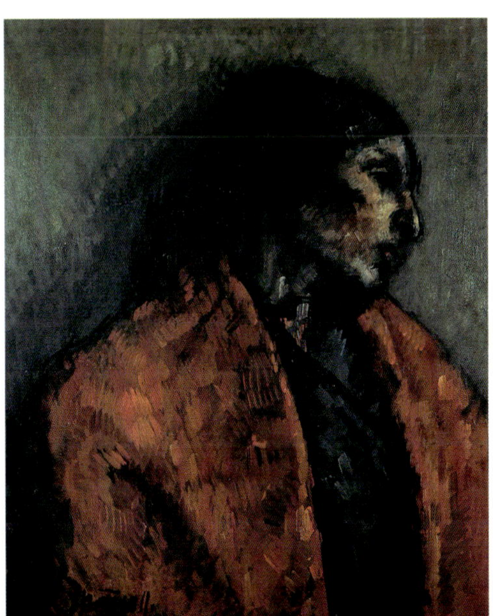

FIG. 28. Isidro Nonell, *La Paloma*, *ca.* 1904. Barcelona, Museu Nacional d'Art de Catalunya

Another painter to create an extraordinarily personal world of his own was José Gutiérrez Solana, who shared Zuloaga's penchant for rhetorical and literary references. The main difference between the two is the choice of literature, which in Solana's case results in exceptional originality. His organisation of themes and techniques is wholly unmistakable, and he uses these to explore reality in an expressionistic, unvarnished way, with a taste for paradox and a strong dose of humour and distance. His style and world view have often been associated with the Spanish tradition, and particularly with Goya, his main thematic and stylistic precedent.

One critic who drew attention to these parallels was Ramón Gómez de la Serna, whose outlook on life was similar to Solana's. He wrote: 'This bristly, acerbic, rebellious, tenacious, pigheaded and pent-up artistic talent grabs at, rather than caresses, everything it sees. It is common to some of our most brilliant Spanish painters: Mor, Carreño, Valdés Leal, Zurbarán, Alenza and, beneath the brightly coloured dresses and capes of his time, Goya himself.'[164]

Rather than being shown in isolation, the figures in Solana's paintings are part of a very distinctive environment. The image we take away with us is very much conditioned by the portrayal of the surroundings; he was also a writer, and this was equally true of his literary technique. The urban landscape plays an important part in the atmosphere of his painting of prostitutes, *Mujeres de la vida* [CAT. 80].[165] Another depiction of this theme in his book *La España negra* uses background detail to add emphasis to human figures:

> In one room a yellowish woman is having her hair combed, her back bare and white through lack of sunlight. A door opens, and through the dark doorway we see the brown arms and backs of many half-naked peasant girls. We see a room with a decrepit wardrobe and a very low ceiling. The window has a hole with a piece of string that you pull to open it. Something tells us that the window does not overlook some magnificent Zamora landscape.[166]

It is worth comparing Solana's painting with Picasso's *Les Demoiselles d'Avignon* [FIG. 129], a work similar in theme but different in content, its expressionism the very opposite of Solana's archetypal figures and containing nods to artists from a variety of artistic traditions, including Cézanne and El Greco.[167] Of course, this is nothing unusual: like Velázquez, Picasso consistently showed an acute awareness of historical tradition and engaged in a constant dialogue with the artists of the past.

Many of those artists were Spanish.[168] Two of the Picassos in this exhibition, *La Celestina* [CAT. 81] and *La Nana* [CAT. 77], are very much bound up with the Spanish literary and iconographic tradition, exemplifying the long history of blurred boundaries between archetypes and portraits that runs throughout Spanish art – though it is also very much of its time.

This confusion is also evident in the *Family of Saltimbanques*, dating from 1905 [FIG. 29], the last spectacular milestone in this genealogy of Spanish portraiture. The line of group and family portraits extends from El Greco's *The Burial of Count Orgaz* through Goya's *The Family of Charles IV* and Velazquez's *Las Meninas* to Van Loo's *The Family of Philip V*, all of them monumental works. Picasso's subjects are not Toledan aristocrats, kings or infantes, but a family of acrobats with himself as the father.[169] In this inclusion of a self-portrait, he is following in the footsteps of Velázquez and Goya.

NOTES

1 Calvert and Gasquoine Hartley 1907, pp. 38–39.
2 Martínez (*ca.* 1675) 1988, p. 203.
3 This can also be seen in studies on collecting, such as those of Agulló 1978, 1981 and 1994; Bravo Lozano 1981; Morán and Checa 1985; Martín Morales 1986; and Burke and Cherry 1998. Glendinning has some particularly interesting tables showing the presence of the different genres in twenty-eight collections dating from between 1646 and 1845. These show a very high proportion of religious painting until the last quarter of the eighteenth century and a gradual increase in other themes from then onwards. Glendinning 1999, pp. 234–36.
4 There is one precedent, held in Brussels in 1970 and covering the period up until the nineteenth century.
5 Of the general approaches to the portrait in western art, see especially Francastel 1978; and Brilliant 1991.
6 Martínez 1788, pp. 352 ff.
7 Palomino (1715–1724) 1944, vol. II, pp. 407 and 400.
8 Agulló 1998, p. 34.
9 For example, in the anonymous work entitled *Declaración de las prodigiosas señales del monstruoso pescado que se halló en un río de Polonia (…) cuyo retrato se embió a España* (*Account of the Prodigious and Monstruous Fish caught in a River in Poland… whose Portrait was sent to Spain*), Seville 1624.
10 See, on this subject, Cea 2004.
11 *Es un Voto* 1997, no. 55.
12 *Retrato político del señor rey D. Alfonso el VII*, Gaspar Mercader, Valencia, 1679.
13 *Retrato del verdadero sacerdote*, Felix de Alamín, Madrid, 1704.
14 *Afectos vendidos and retrato de un buen ministro*, Marqués de Salmerón, Madrid, ca. 1701.

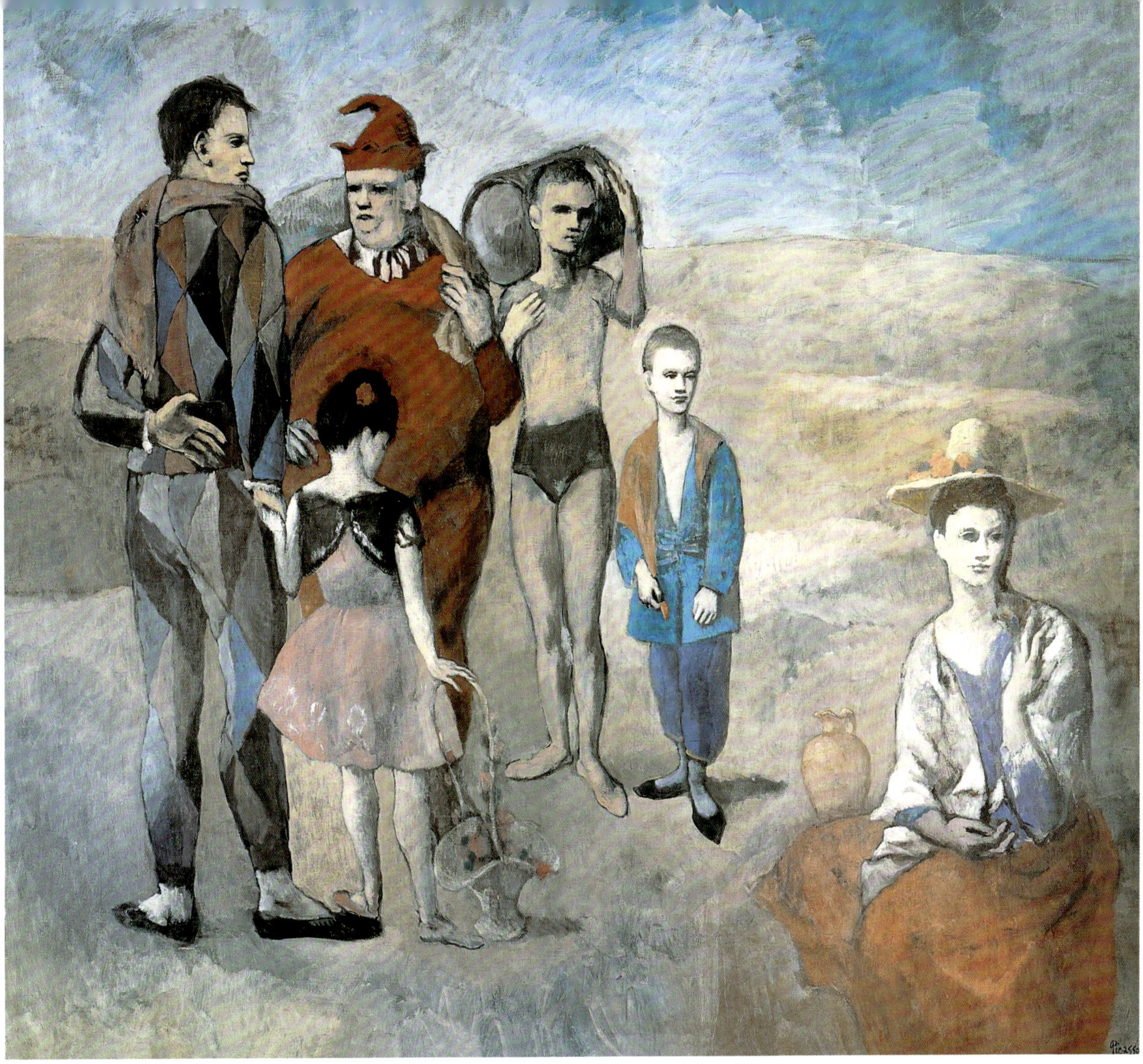

FIG. 29. Pablo Picasso, *Family of Saltimbanques*, 1905. Washington D.C., National Gallery of Art [Chester Dale Collection]

15 *Primera parte del retrato del hombre feliz and humana felicidad*, Fray Tomás de Mozábal, Pamplona, 1618.

16 *Retrato del perfeto médico en diálogos*, Anrrique Jorge Anrríquez, Salamanca, 1595.

17 *Retrato del buen vasallo*, Francisco Pinel, Madrid, 1677.

18 *Retrato del privado christiano político*, Francisco de Balboa y Paz, Naples, 1635.

19 Covarrubias (1611) 1987, in the entry for *retrato*: 'the counterfeit image of some person of account, intended to preserve their memory for centuries to come'. For a study of the moral connotations of the portrait at the time of Covarrubias, see Benito 1994, pp. 183–91.

20 For example, *Retrato del incendio que sucedió en la plaza de la Villa de Madrid* (*Portrait of the Fire which Occurred in the Plaza de la Villa in Madrid*), place of publication unknown, 1672.

21 This subject is studied in Davies 1975.

22 Mariño 1990, pp. 66–70 and 257–58.

23 Zarco 1931, p. 40.

24 For example, the biographer of the seventeenth-century writer Martín de Zayas states of him: 'many of those who confided in him, and disciples of his great teachings, wanted to have his portrait painted so they could preserve the memory of this distinguished and illustrious man by looking at his picture'. Zayas 1662, fol. 129v.

25 Portús 1999a, pp. 169–88.

26 San Esteban 1662, fol. 199r–v.

27 Brown and Elliott 1981, pp. 195–98.

28 On the presence of portraits in the poetry of the Golden Age, see Beamud 1985.

29 Palomino (1714–1724) 1944, vol. II, p. 400.

30 Bergmann 1979, pp. 84 ff.

31 On this subject, see the chapter entitled 'To possess her in paint: (pro)creative failure and crisis in *El pintor de su deshonra*', in Bass 2000b, pp. 194–275.

32 Martínez (*ca.* 1675) 1988, pp. 199–200.

33 Zamora Vicente (ed.) 1976, pp. 672–73.

34 Jordan 1994, pp. 116 ff.

35 Palomino (1724) 1986, pp. 58–59.

36 Martínez 1788, pp. 352 ff.

37 Madrazo 1994b, p. 110.

38 López-Rey 1963, pp. 52 ff.

39 On this subject, see Silva 1998, p. 162.

40 López-Rey 1963, pp. 72–75.

41 Serrera 1999, pp. 351–65.

42 Gerstenberg 1960, p. 202.

43 Gállego 1972.

44 Lafuente 1942.

45 Gállego 1978.

46 On this typology in the work of Zurbarán, see Vincent 2002, pp. 17–30.

47 *En ocasión de haber puesto una dama la copia de su rostro en una imagen de Santa Lucía*, 1674.

48 *A una dama retratada con la insignia and vestido de santa Elena*, 1654.

49 *A una tabla de Susana, en cuya figura se hizo retratar una dama*, undated.

50 *Al retrato de una dama en traje de Magdalena penitente*, undated.

51 Orozco 1977, pp. 199 ff.

52 Carducho (1633) 1979, p. 190.

53 Hellwig 1999, p. 266. ff.

54 Pommier 1998, p. 289 ff.

55 Palomino (1715–1724) 1944, I, p. 64.

56 The main source of information on the first voyage is still Palomino (1724) 1986, pp. 163–65.

57 Bonnefoy 1994.

58 Colomer 1999, pp. 39–49.

59 Palomino (1724) 1986, pp. 172–78.

60 Palomino (1724) 1986, p. 183.

61 There is a very large bibliography on this painting. Some of the most interesting contributions are assembled in Marías (ed.) 1995.

62 Concerning this debate, which takes the format of a dialogue between the painter and the king, see Calvo Serraller 1995.

63 On *Las Meninas* and its creative and political context, see Brown 1980, pp. 115–42; and Brown, Elliott and Garrido 1999, pp. 85–124.

64 Marías 1995, pp. 247–78.

65 See Bass 2000a, pp. 57 ff.

66 Calvo Serraller 1981, pp. 545–46.

67 Portús 2000a, pp. 53–54.

68 For a study of the role of the portrait in this play, see Civil 1999.

69 I have discussed these plays in Portús 1997, pp. 131 ff.

70 Armas 1981, pp. 730 ff.

71 Warnke 1993.

72 See, for example, Herrero García 1936, pp. 66–68; Lafuente 1941, pp. 55–58; and Serrera 1990, pp. 58–59.

73 Concerning the general characteristics of the genre, see Jenkins 1977 and, in relation to France, Marin 1981. Concerning Spain, see Gállego (1968) 1987, pp. 217 ff.

74 Brown 1988, pp. 137–54.

75 For a discussion of this painting and its interpretations see, among others, Harris 1976a, pp. 266–75; González de Zárate 1987, pp. 27–38; and Moffitt 1991, pp. 195–212.

76 Ligo 1970, pp. 345–54.

77 Sebastián 1991–1992, pp. 194–99; Rodríguez de Cevallos 2000, pp. 93–110; Morán 2003, pp. 63–72.

78 Kantorowicz 1985; and Lisón 1992, pp. 182–86.

79 On the portrait in the France of Louis XIV, see Marin 1981 and *Visages du Grand Siècle*, 1997. Concerning the portrait in the court of Philip V, see Morán 1990; Bottineau 1986; Luna 1975; Urrea 1994; and Úbeda 2002.

80 See, for example, Caro Baroja 1986.

81 Significantly, history books are often illustrated mainly with pictures of important personalities.

82 For a general study of this theme, see Tormo 1927.

83 Kusche 1991.

84 Collar de Cáceres 1983.

85 Tormo 1944; García Sainz and Ruiz 2000.

86 The spread of the royal portrait into private contexts is studied in detail in Varela 2000, pp. 99–134.

87 Egido 1983; Morte 1990 and 1991.

88 Moreno Garrido 1976, no. 61 ff.

89 Delenda 2004.

90 Giovio (ed.) 1999, with introductory study and bibliography.

91 This was dated 1599, but remained unpublished until the nineteenth century. The most recent edition is by Piñero and Reyes (Seville, 1985). Concerning the relationship between biography and portrait gallery in relation to Pacheco's *Libro...*, see Soria 1981.

92 The inventory was first published in Agulló 1994, pp. 150 ff.

93 *Memoria histórica...*, 1988.

94 Carderera 1855 and 1864.

95 Moreno Carbonero 1898, p. 19.

96 Tramoyers 1891, p. 33.

97 Surveys of such references are included in Herrero García 1943 and Sánchez Cantón 1941. For a general study of portrait poetry in the Golden Age, see Beamud 1985.

98 Gutiérrez Burón 1987, pp. 742–43.

99 Galofre 1851, p. 85: 'Another potential benefit of art is the use of painting, sculpture and architecture to encourage civic virtues and immortalise heroic deeds, and to create an avid thirst to imitate these among those who see them.' This idea is shared by many other critics, including Tubino 1872, p. 58.

100 García 1867, p. 131.

101 Pardo 1908, pp. 46 ff, calls for an end to the whole system of genres.

102 Letter dated 10 September 1841. Madrazo 1998, p. 477.

103 For a time, this was believed to be the work of Vega. Cited in

Vega Carpio 1963–1972, vol. XXXIX, p. 210b.

104 Calderón 1945, vol. III, p. 148.

105 Carducho 1633, pp. 110–12.

106 Ayala 1666, p. 24.

107 There are general discussions of this theme in Yarza 1994, pp. 67–98, and in Raquejo 1981–1982, pp 76–87.

108 Portús 2002, pp. 22–33.

109 Falomir 1996a, pp. 177–95.

110 Bermejo 1962.

111 The Spanish court portrait has given rise to a very large bibliography. General discussions of its history and some of its key moments include those of Sánchez Cantón 1948; Alonso Sánchez Coello 1990; Brown 1994; Brown (dir.) 1999; and Kusche 2003. Various works on the uses and functions of these pictures have appeared in recent years, including Checa 1987a; Serrera 1990; Bouza 1998 and 1999; Portús 2000b and 2000c; Davies 1998; Falomir 1998; and Mulcahy 2000. A large proportion of court portraits were engravings. See, among others, *Los Austrias* 1993 and Matilla 2000.

112 Mínguez 1991, pp. 71–81.

113 *El linaje del emperador*, 2000, pp. 363–80.

114 Santiago 1990, pp. 84–85.

115 Marías 1995.

116 *Reyes and Mecenas* 1992, no. 87.

117 Kagan 1982 and 2003.

118 This process reached its height in Cossío 1908, pp. 385 ff.

119 See, among others, Álvarez Lopera 2003.

120 Dated 1587. *El documento pintado* 2000, no. 35. The portrait is included in the letters patent of nobility of Cristóbal Mosquera de Figueroa.

121 These are included in Lassalle 1981, pp. 51–84.

122 Peyton 1962.

123 Balsinde and Portús 1997, p. 43. Concerning portraits of writers, see also Civil 1991.

124 See Lafuente 1935, and the chapter entitled 'Lope pintado' in Portús 1999b, pp. 161–70.

125 Pérez de Montalbán 1636.

126 See Fernández Gracia 2002.

127 For a discussion of the fortunes of this genre in Spanish art, see Gaya Nuño 1950.

128 Angulo and Pérez Sánchez 1969, pp. 181–82.

129 Angulo 1981, vol. II, no. 414.

130 Concerning Goya as a portraitist see, among others, Beruete 1916 and, most importantly, Glendinning 1992.

131 See, for example, Palomino (1715–1724) 1944, vol. I, p. 39.

132 See Lee 1977.

133 Ciofalo 2001, pp. 101–10; Moffitt 1981–1982, pp. 2–13.

134 *Es un voto* 1997, no. 60.

135 Calvo Serraller 1996.

136 Helman 1970.

137 For a discussion of these, see Reyero 2004, pp. 233–46.

138 Palomino (1715–1724) 1944, I, 23–25.

139 Mulcahy 1996, pp. 517–21.

140 Brown 1988, pp. 137–54.

141 Pérez Sánchez 1985, pp. 73–74.

142 *Cortes del barroco* 2003, p. 261.

143 Palomino (1724) 1986, p. 289. Díaz Padrón 1982, pp. 129–42 emphasises the importance of Flemish painting to seventeenth-century Spanish portraiture.

144 Pérez Sánchez 1994, p. 238.

145 There is a very penetrating study of this theme in Sullivan 1989, pp. 109–35.

146 Gaya Nuño 1976, p. 133; Portús 2000d, pp. 104–08.

147 Morales Marín 1979, pp. 83–84.

148 For a study of the series, see Vega 2000, pp. 45–93.

149 Agueda 1991; Glendinning 2000.

150 Madrazo 1994, p. 110.

151 Federico de Madrazo 1994, nos. 180 and 186.

152 Rubio 2000, p. 53.

153 Salas 1982.

154 Santa Ana 1999, pp. 435–40.

155 Juan Ramón Jiménez wrote: 'The shadow of the old masters never left Sorolla. He painted their portraits.' Jiménez 1904, p. 24.

156 Pérez Rojas 2000, pp. 112–13.

157 The letter is in a private collection. See Coll 1999, p. 171.

158 Ramón Casas 2001, no. 12.

159 Lafuente Ferrari 1950, pp. 50 and 219.

160 Utrillo 1907, p. 210.

161 Azorín 1970, pp. 143–45.

162 Rusiñol, year not specified, p. 22.

163 Coll 1999.

164 Gómez de la Serna 1972, p. 22.

165 Alonso Fernández 1979, p. 73.

166 Gutiérrez Solana 1975, p. 180.

167 Lubar 1999, pp. 39 ff.

168 Brown (ed.) 1999.

169 Vardenoe 1996.

I The Origin of Portrait Painting in Spain

FROM THE ABSENCE OF SPECIALISTS TO THE LARGE WORKSHOP

Miguel Falomir

In 1416, in one of his massively attended sermons, Saint Vincent Ferrer (1350–1419) used a pictorial simile to explain the doctrinal differences between the Old Testament and the New Testament. This Dominican from Valencia spoke about the Christian attitude to the Old Testament, suggesting it should be like that of a sovereign who wanted to marry a foreign princess he had never seen and so asked his ambassadors to find an artist to paint a portrait of her. Alone in his palace, the king would kiss and embrace the portrait and contemplate the beauty of his future wife, but once he had met her the portrait would have no further purpose and would be put away in a box. This, according to Saint Vincent, should be the attitude of Christians to the Old Testament, for its importance diminished with the arrival of Christ and the subsequent writing of the New Testament.[1] Saint Vincent's words are exceptional on account of their early date (they precede any similar testimony), their reliability (he was the brother-in-law of the painter Père Morlans and had been confessor to Queen Yolanda de Bar, wife of Juan I of Aragon), and also because, as part of a sermon in Catalan addressed to a vast audience, they suggested that the popularity of portraits extended beyond the palace walls.

This essay focuses upon these and other reflections provoked by the sermon, and in it I have opted for an approach to portraiture that comprises, on the one hand, its origins as a distinctive pictorial genre in the fourteenth century and its subsequent development up to the 1560s, and on the other hand, the inclusion of images of individuals in broader, generally religious contexts, which are usually known as donor portraits.[2] By limiting the notion of portraiture to these types of representations, I have to exclude others, particularly portraits of sovereigns, that were very widespread in the Middle Ages in the form of miniatures or wax seals.[3] These images – tangible symbols of royalty – merited the same respect as the person of the king himself, and as early as 1255 Alfonso X of Castile (1252–1284) imposed severe penalties on anyone who did not treat them as such.[4] However, they can hardly be classified as portraits, since the intention of those who produced and promoted them was to provide a convincing idea of majesty with its characteristic attributes rather than the physical features of any one particular monarch, as Alfonso X confirmed by equating painted and sculpted images to the more schematic royal seals.[5] The series of sculptural and pictorial images of sovereigns that decorated the royal palaces should not, strictly

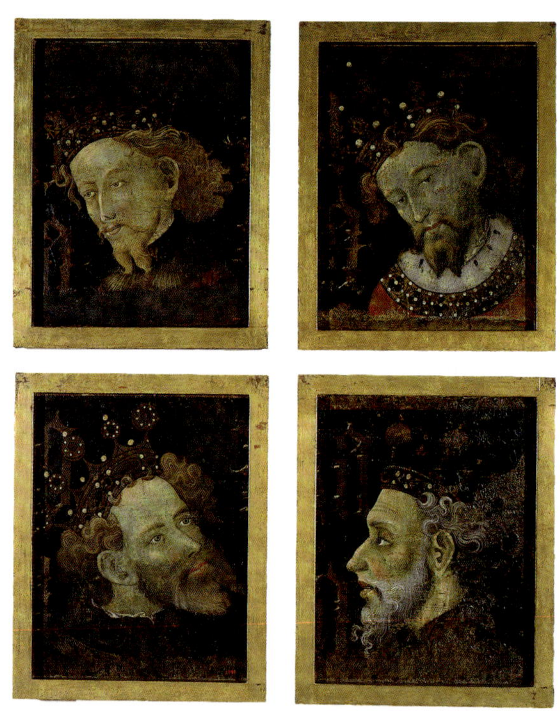

FIG. 30. Series attributed to Jaume Mateu and Gonçal Peris Sarrià, *Jaime I, Alfonso II, Pedro III and Alfonso V*, 1427–1428. Barcelona, Museu Nacional d'Art de Catalunya

speaking, be considered as portraits either, and Tormo had already noted that in the conception of these series the legitimation of the group was of more importance than the value attached to the individual,[6] whereas in Martindale's opinion these institutional, genealogical series that were popular in Europe as far back as the fourteenth century were more the closing stages of a long tradition than the early beginnings of modern portraiture.[7] There are various literary and documentary references to royal series, beginning with the one ordered by Alfonso X of Castile for the Alcázar in Segovia in 1258: thirty-eight polychrome statues of the kings of Oviedo, León and Castile and their wives, from their origins down to Fernando III, father of Alfonso.[8] The first similar series in the territories of the kingdom of Aragon is dated 1342, when Pedro IV (1336–1387) commissioned Master Aloy to produce twelve alabaster sculptures of his predecessors for the palace in Barcelona, while in Navarra the palace in Tudela was decorated on the orders of Carlos II and Carlos III with paintings of Christian sovereigns and emperors from 1382 to 1392.[9] Sculpted or painted in *fresco* or on panel, these images were produced for purposes of propaganda or legitimation, while at the same time they served as instructive 'mirrors' for the reigning monarch, encouraging him to emulate his predecessors.[10] By the middle of the fifteenth century they had become so widespread that they appeared in works of literature. In his *Laberinto de Fortuna* of 1451, Juan de Mena described the throne of Juan II of Castile as a receptacle for paintings with the names and deeds of his forebears, while Joanot Martorell (*ca.* 1414–1468) imagined a gallery of gold statues of Christian sovereigns in the great hall of the palace of the emperor of Byzantium in *Tirant lo Blanch*.[11] In addition, as in Paris, Venice, Haarlem or Leyden, Spanish towns housed royal paintings that were testimony to their connections with the sovereign, and four images of the kings of Aragon attributed to Gonçal Peris and Jaume Mateu, painted in 1427–28 [FIG. 30], have been identified as originally belonging to the City Hall in Valencia.

The fact that the dynastic series preceded what is known as 'modern portraiture' does not mean that they

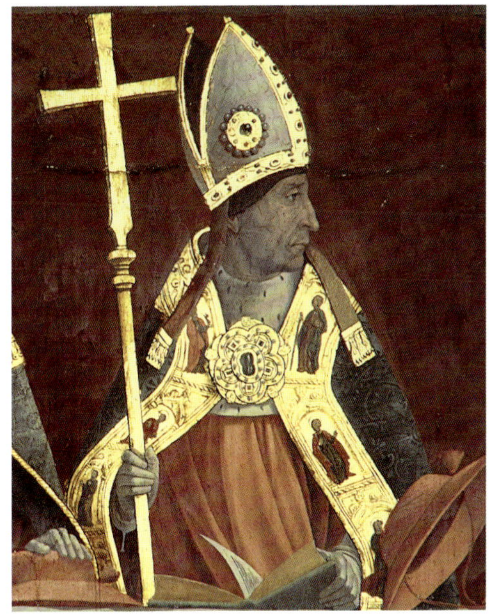

FIG. 31. Juan de Borgoña, *Cardinal Gonzalo Jiménez Cisneros* (detail from the 'Gallery of Archbishops'), 1509–1510. Toledo Cathedral, Chapter House

stopped being produced with its arrival; on the contrary, increasingly 'contaminated' in form, typology and concept by the modern portrait, they were to enjoy considerable favour until the present time.[12] In addition, in the fifteenth and sixteenth centuries other classes, such as the nobility and the clergy, emulated the monarchy in producing visual representations of their predecessors, although in the case of the clergy this was probably also influenced by the tradition of papal portraits that had existed uninterruptedly since the fifth century. Good examples both of the renewed vitality of these paintings and of their debt to the independent portrait are the series of the archbishops of Toledo and Valencia that were begun respectively by Juan de Borgoña (1470–1534) and Juan de Juanes (*ca.* 1510–1579). The former, painted in *fresco* in the chapter room of Toledo cathedral, must have been started between 1509 and 1511. Borgoña was to produce the series of portraits from Eugenio I (AD 96) to Cisneros, and according to Blas Ortiz in 1549 they were 'so perfectly painted that anyone glancing at them would consider them real rather than painted',[13] although only the portrait of Cisneros [FIG. 31] and perhaps that of his predecessor Pedro González de Mendoza were painted from life. The same observation can be made concerning the Valencian series, painted on leather from 1568 onwards, which together with imaginary pictures of the early prelates included other portraits from life of the promoters of the project.[14]

But what do we understand by 'modern portrait' and from when can it be considered to date? There is a certain consensus that the turning point was the portrait that Simone Martini painted of Laura for Petrarch in Avignon *ca.* 1335–1336 – an image in which Martindale distinguishes three features: emotiveness (it evoked an absent person), portability (it could be easily transported) and temporality (as its purpose was essentially to substitute, and it was no longer of any use once the person portrayed was present).[15] These characteristics also applied to the portrait referred to by Saint Vincent Ferrer: a portable object – it had been brought by ambassadors – that was able to excite the king who kissed it, but then lost its purpose when the princess appeared and so was put away. Even the status that Martindale accorded to Avignon as the birthplace of modern portraiture fits this scene, for Saint Vincent spent a long time at the papal court there. The genesis of modern portrait painting cannot be dissociated from the gradual appreciation of the individual that had been perceptible since the twelfth century and involved both philosophical factors (a different perception of Nature based on Aristotelian thought and Nominalism, where the emphasis on the specific encouraged a new 'realism' in the visual arts) and religious factors (the emergence of the mendicant orders, whose attitude to religion gave priority to the subjective and the sensorial over the abstract and speculative).[16] The phenomenon was not confined solely to the fine arts, and in the Iberian peninsula it became established earlier and to a greater extent in literature: from the fourteenth century onwards a growing interest can be noted in the characterisation of individuals, which was to crystallise in such explicit titles as *Generaciones y Semblazas* by Fernán Pérez de Guzmán (*ca.* 1450) and *Claros Varones de Castilla* by Hernando del Pulgar (1486). These contain numerous 'portraits' that are often more moral than physical,[17] although there are also others that are as explicit as that of himself by Pedro IV of Aragon in his *Crónica*.[18] This emphasis on biography had its visual counterpart in the interest in the representation of the individual in painting and sculpture, the epitome of which would be the independent portrait. However, it can also be seen in the diversification of the physiognomies in religious compositions, some of which are so strongly characterised that they make us think we are looking at 'crypto-portraits' or portraits of contemporaries in the likeness of figures of the past.[19] Examples of this can be found in *Saint Dominic of Silos* by Bartolomé Bermejo (doc. 1468–1501) [CAT. 1] or *Hezekiah* by Pedro Berruguete (*ca.* 1445/50–1503) [CAT. 2].

The interest in physical and historical accuracy in the representation of individuals goes back at least to Pedro IV of Aragon. On 20 October 1351 he commissioned a stone statue '*ad similitudem nostri factam*'. On 2 September 1358 he asked the Abbot of Ripoll about the garments and physical appearance of his predecessors in order to reproduce them properly, and in 1385 he ordered the sculptor working on the image of one of his ancestors to cover the legs with '*gamberes e sabates de ferro*' (iron greaves and shoes) since these, he maintained, were worn at the time.[20] However, we do not know whether these concerns applied to modern portraits, and I have only located one reference to an image of Pope Urban V, since lost, painted on canvas in 1373 by Llorens Saragossa (*ca.* 1340 to post-1405) for Queen Leonor's chapel,[21] which I am unable to comment on.

Various artistic practices must have contributed to this new 'realism', such as casting faces in plaster, described in detail by Cennino Cennini at the end of the fourteenth century,[22] or producing images in wax, sometimes but not always using moulds.[23] Although we can only speculate about the use of casting in mediaeval Spain, the presence of wax *ex votos* is widely documented. There were both those limited to the part of the body for which a cure was sought or obtained,[24] and entire figures, which are of more interest to us because, as Freedberg argued, their likeness ensured their effectiveness as *ex votos*.[25] Furthermore, *ex votos* of this type not only had pictorial connections but were usually produced by painters.

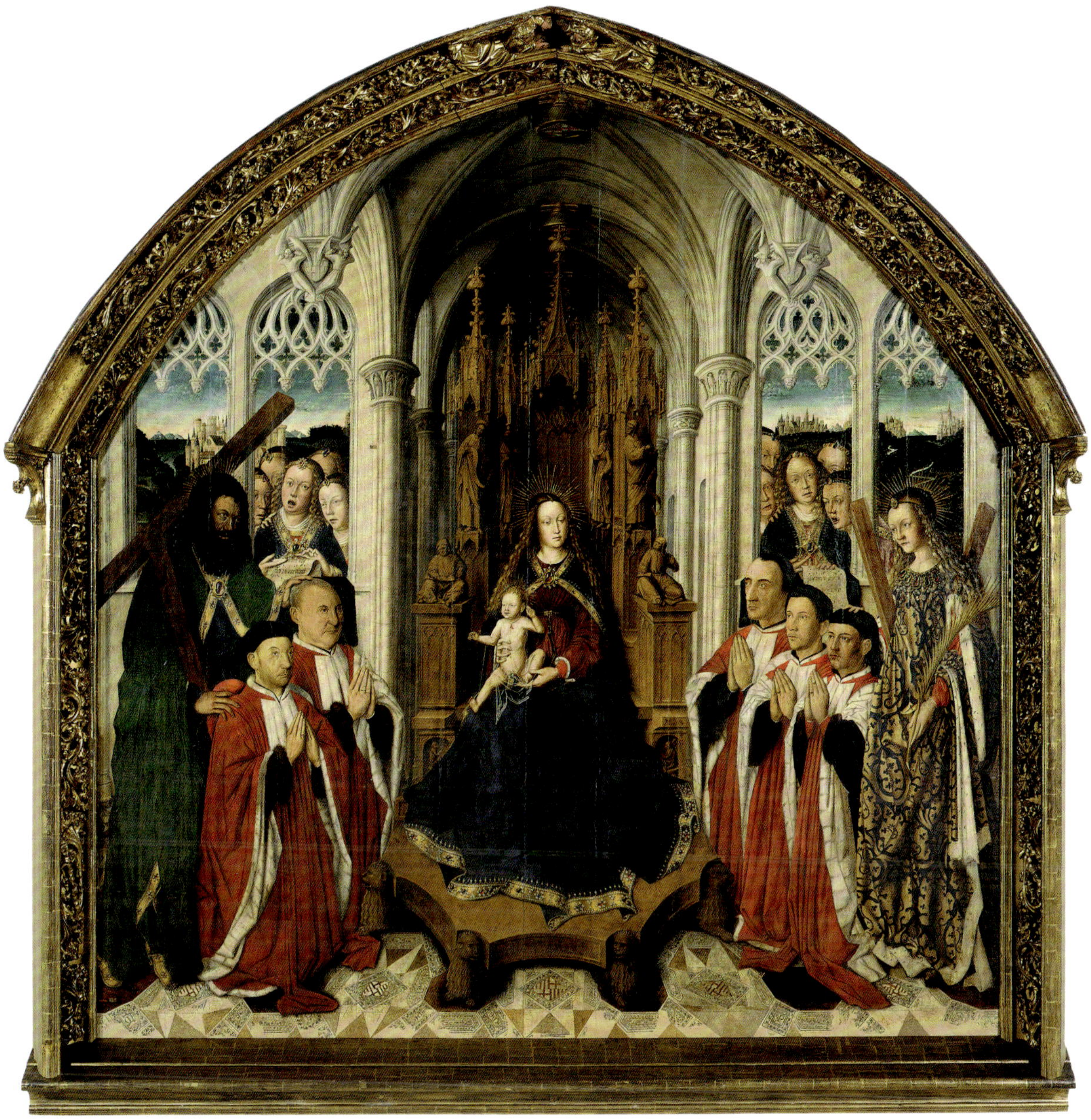

FIG. 32. Lluís Dalmau, *Our Lady of the Councillors*, 1443–1445. Barcelona, Museu Nacional d'Art de Catalunya [15938]

Although there is a record in 1273 of an *ex voto* image of Jaime I of Aragon,[26] they became widespread in the fourteenth century, especially in Aragon. In 1343, Leonor of Sicily (wife of Pedro IV) commissioned two wax images for the cathedral in Barcelona and the monastery of Montserrat to intercede for the health of the Infanta Constanza. In 1355 the Valencian painter Bernat Mercer produced 'an image in wood covered in wax…in the likeness of that lady [Leonor of Sicily]', and in 1377 Esteban de Burgos made a similar one of Pedro IV.[27] Compared with the relative abundance of these votive images, placed on tabernacles in front of the altar, the use of wax figures in royal funerals, as had been the custom in England since the funeral of Edward I in 1307, was rare in Spain.[28] Moreover – though it is the only such case recorded – for the funeral of Alfonso V of Aragon in Huesca in 1458 the painter Johan d'Uroc made a wax effigy with 'the likeness and face of the king',[29] which suggests that this was more an initiative by the municipal authorities than a practice fostered by the crown. There are, however, records of the inclusion of painted portraits in royal funerals, as in those held in Valencia cathedral for Alfonso V (1458) and his nephew Carlos de Viana (1461),[30] a practice that could be associated with the *repraesentatio*, consisting of the inclusion of a portrait of the deceased sovereign in order to symbolise the continuity of power until the coronation or proclamation of his successor.[31]

It was also in the time of Pedro IV that donors made their appearance in painting in Aragon. Although no images have survived of the sovereign in this guise, there are surviving images of figures such as the Dominican friar Martín de Alpartil on an altarpiece painted by Jaume Serra (fl. 1360–1375) in 1361–1362 for the church of the Holy Sepulchre in Zaragoza. The portrait of Enrique II with his family in the votive panel in Tobed (1373) is the first work showing a king as donor in Castile, although it was painted by an Aragonese artist (either Pedro or Jaume Serra). The reasons that led an individual to include his image in a religious picture are many and not mutually exclusive. It was often for the purpose of leaving a record of their patronage – and as such their images are on a par with other representative items, such as heraldic elements – or of their devotion to a particular saint, either individually (normally the saint of the namesake of the donor 'introducing' them to the Virgin and Child) or collectively, in the case of images commissioned by institutions, such as *Our Lady of the Councillors* by Lluís Dalmau [FIG. 32] or *Our Lady of the Sailors* by Alejo Fernández (ca. 1470–1543) in the Reales Alcázares in Seville, dated between 1531 and 1536. The presence of donors, though, is of greater interest for eschatological or strictly devotional reasons. With respect to the former, faith in the effectiveness of praying for the souls of the dead led many people to try and keep their memory alive through their image, trusting in the benefits this would

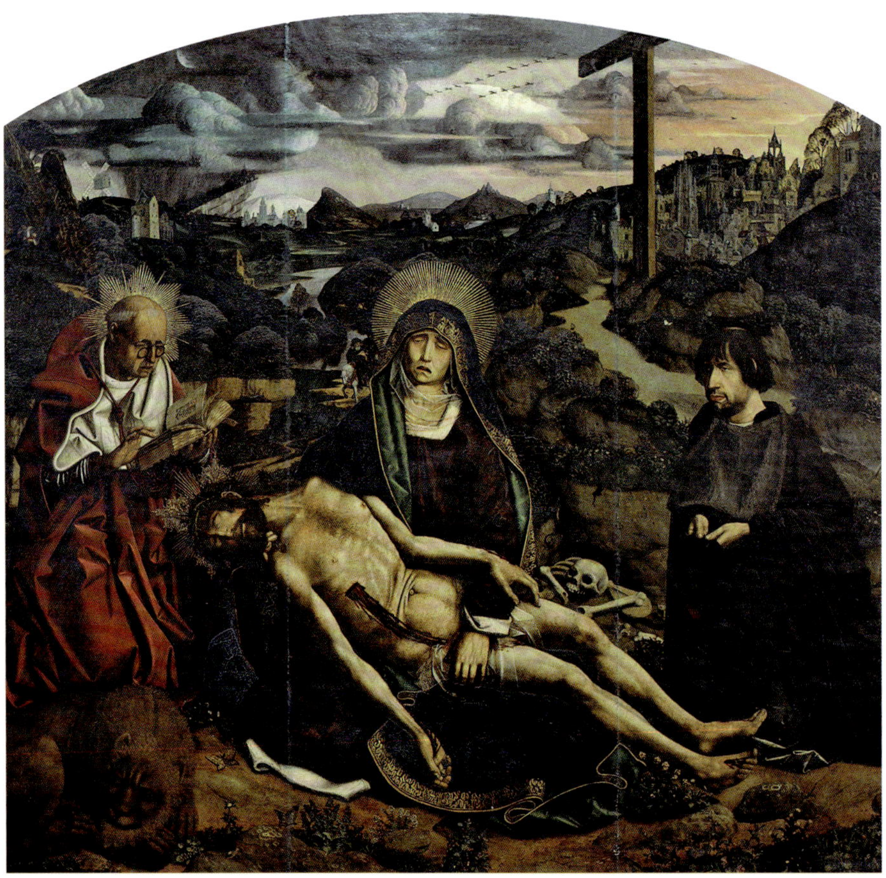

FIG. 33. Bartolomé Bermejo, *The Pietà with Canon Lluís Desplá*, 1490. Barcelona, Cathedral

bring for their spiritual salvation.[32] It is therefore not surprising to find a proliferation of donor portraits in altarpieces for funerary chapels, such as the one commissioned in 1488 for the Luna family chapel in Toledo cathedral – which also contains an underlying defence of the Condestable of Castile[33] – or in eschatological iconographies such as the Mass of Saint Gregory in a painting on the subject attributed to Pedro Berruguete in Segovia cathedral. Of greater interest is the inclusion of the donor in an *imago pietatis*, a kind of visual spiritual exercise in an indirect style where the subject appears both as viewer and donor. The empathy inherent in these devout images reached its apogee in the magnificent *Pietà with Canon Lluís Desplá* [FIG. 33], produced in 1490 by Bartolomé Bermejo, the only fifteenth-century Spanish painter who is comparable to the great Flemish masters in his treatment of donors. But over and above these formal aspects the *Pietà* is an exceptionally sophisticated work in which the donor, Desplá, is conducted to the strict *imago pietatis* (Our Lady with the Dead Christ) through the text read by Saint Jerome (the *Vulgata*),[34] thus setting up a representation of a *visio spiritualis* – which according to Saint Augustine evokes or imagines what is not present by means of verbal or textual descriptions – and in an effusive tribute to the visual experience.[35] The Desplá *Pietà* exhausts the treatment of the donor in Spanish painting, which was never again to achieve such spatial and emotional integration between private individuals and holy figures, even when the former are disguised as the latter, as often occurs in the works of Juan de Flandes (doc. 1496–1519). In fact, the sixteenth century scarcely added anything new to the representation of the donor, although it provided some fascinating examples of the adaptation of old models from the Late Middle Ages to the new requirements of the Counter-Reformation, thanks to the talents of artists such as Titian in *'La Gloria'* [FIG. 41] and El Greco in *The Adoration of the Name of Jesus* [CAT. 6].

The depiction of donors, less subject to the requirements of decorum than the independent portrait, in particular the court portrait, also has that need for 'realism' to ensure the effectiveness mentioned earlier with respect to wax figures. In fact, the donors liked to transfer to the pictorial plane those free-standing *ex votos* on tabernacles in front of altars, with all the connotations this involved of 'invasion' of the space previously reserved exclusively for the divinity. Although it is impossible to gauge the degree of faithfulness of the donors, documents repeatedly mention this quality, and for example the Barcelona magistrates in *Our Lady of the Councillors* required Dalmau to show them 'as effigies with the proportions and habits of their bodies, with faces like the living have',[36] while in 1480 Martín Torner (fl. 1480–1495) promised the abbess of the monastery of Santa Clara in Valencia to paint in a Last Supper 'la *similitud* de la senyora abadesa agenollada' (the *likeness* of the abbess kneeling), using a term that is in itself very explicit.[37]

But for a portrait to exist it was not sufficient just to commission it; it was equally or even more necessary to have someone able to produce it. However, not all painters were capable of this. Portraitists, along with muralists, were the specialist painters *par excellence* and both were conspicuous by their absence in Spain until the second half of the sixteenth century. In fact, since the mid-fourteenth century the lack of good painters, whether portraitists or not, became evident. The demand for religious and secular paintings multiplied as a consequence of the popularity of the altarpiece and the need of the increasingly powerful and personalised courts to define and augment their representational elements. This obliged the sovereigns – and the civil authorities too – to compete for the most able artists. The portrait painters benefited from this situation, and this is how we should interpret the interest of Juan I of Aragon in 1388 in the Parisian artist Jacques Coene (fl. 1398–1404) in view of his skill at painting faces and physiognomies, at which, it seems, his Aragonese colleagues were not particularly adept.[38] Over the following century and a half, the situation improved only sporadically. In 1486 King Ferdinand apologised to his sister, Queen Joanna of Naples, for not having been able to reciprocate the portraits she had sent because there was nobody to paint them,[39] and even by 1533 Charles V's ambassador was asking the Venetian authorities for the services of Titian, 'whom their majesties the emperor and empress only require to do portraits'.[40] It was not until the 1560s, after Philip II's return to Spain, that there was a permanent portrait painters' 'workshop' at court, discussed below.

In order to meet these needs, the sovereigns almost always resorted to foreign artists, a fairly common practice if we recall the importance of the Brussels painter Jean Clouet (*ca.* 1486–1540) at the court of Francis I of France, or the chronic dependence on foreign portraitists by the English monarchs, for whom the German painters Hans Holbein and Gerlack Flicke and the Flemish artists William Scrots and Hans Eworth worked in the first half of the sixteenth century. In Spain, all the portrait painters who worked for Ferdinand and Isabella were foreigners. The origins of Antonio Inglés (active in Spain 1489–1490) and Juan de Flandes (1496–1504) are revealed by their surnames, whereas Michel Sittow (1492–1504) was an Estonian who had trained in Bruges. The situation remained the same with Charles V (1517–1558), although the presence of royal portrait painters in Spain became even more sporadic, coinciding with the short visits by the court or making the journey specifically for the purpose of painting the empress and her children at the request of one member of the imperial family or another, usually Margarita of Austria and Maria of Hungary. Among those to visit Spain for diverse reasons were Antonio de Holanda (fl. 1495–1540) in 1528,[41] Jan Cornelisz. Vermeyen (*ca.* 1500–1575/76) probably in 1526 and certainly between 1537 and 1539,[42] the German Jacob Seisenegger (1505–1567) between 1538 and 1539,[43] and the Flemish painter Anthonis Mor) (1519–1576) in 1551 and 1553. Mor was brought to Spain by Philip II when he returned to the country, along with Alonso Sánchez Coello (1531/32–1588) – both foreigners who had trained abroad – and his example was followed by members of the nobility such as the Duke of Villahermosa, who returned from Flanders in 1559 with the Brussels painter Roland de Mois (died *ca.* 1590).[44] All this shows that portrait painters came invariably from northern Europe and mainly from Flanders. Leaving aside Titian, who never visited Spain despite Charles' efforts, during this period Flanders and portrait painting came to be linked

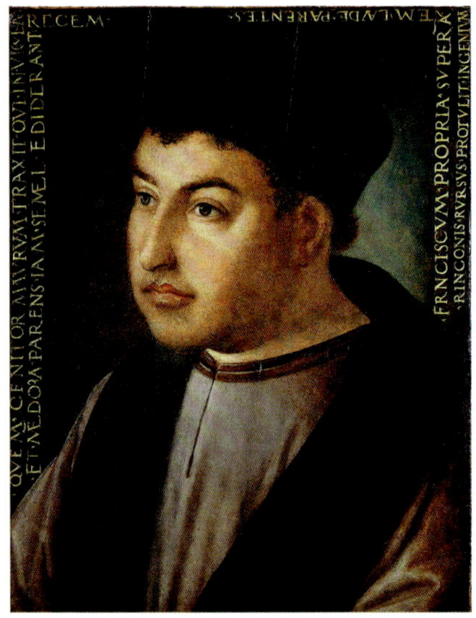

FIG. 34. Hernando del Rincón, *Francisco Fernández de Córdoba y Mendoza*, *ca.* 1520. Madrid, Museo del Prado [P-2518]

together in much the same way as Italy and *fresco* painting. Thus we find that John III of Portugal sent Alonso Sánchez Coello to Flanders to train as a portraitist in 1550, and that Gonzalo Fernández de Oviedo wrote about Alonso de Silva, a nobleman who liked his pages to have some skill, 'and one of the principal ones was to be good at drawing'. When one of them made a very poor drawing of his head in chalk on the wall, following the shadow cast by a candle, 'the gentleman later sent that page to Flanders and spent money on him so that he would learn to paint, and he turned out to be a fine painter'.[45] In addition to its echoing Pliny's well-known passage on the origins of painting, and regardless of its veracity, the interesting thing about the text is that it reflects the widespread association between portraits and Flanders.

And what about the Spaniards or those foreigners who had resided in Spain for a long time? There is no record of any of them producing independent portraits before 1500. Indeed, I have only found reference to a single independent portrait: of Ramón Savall, one of the Barcelona magistrates included in *Our Lady of the Councillors*, which was in the possession of his son Beltrán Ramón Savall in 1488 and was possibly painted by Dalmau.[46] Even after 1500 there were very few. There is a record of a portrait of King Ferdinand by Alejo Fernández in 1508,[47] and we know that Alfonso Berruguete was at least able to copy portraits,[48] while Diego de Arroyo (1498–1551), 'court painter to His Majesty', was admired for his portraits in miniature. Among those that have survived are a signed portrait by Joan de Burgunya from his Italian period,[49] and the portraits of Francisco Fernández de Córdoba y Mendoza [FIG. 34] and Francisco Ruiz (Instituto de Valencia de Don Juan, Madrid), both dated around 1520, which are attributed to Hernando Rincón de Figueroa, the king's painter from 1513–1517;[50] these last two, with their Latin inscriptions (the first includes the painter's name) show the cultivated circles through which portraiture must have spread in the early decades of the sixteenth century. Without any attempt to be exhaustive, let us also mention Juan de Juanes in Valencia and, in Seville, Luis de Vargas (1505–1567) and Pieter Kempeneer from Brussels (1503–*ca.* 1580), whom Pacheco described as 'valiant portrait painters' (*retratadores valientes*).[51] Vargas painted the portrait of the Venerable Fernando de Contreras (Seville Cathedral) in around 1541, while Kempeneer is only known for his images of donors, such as the male and female members of the Caballero family [CATS 4 and 5].

Beyond any facile association between national temperament and artistic skill, the supposed ineptitude of Spanish painters of the late Middle Ages and the Renaissance for portrait painting must be attributed to the way in which painting was taught and practised in the workshops, where priority was given to the repetition of foreign models, to the detriment of the study of nature – a fact denounced by treatise writers such as Felipe de Guevara and Lázaro de Velasco, who echoed the criticism of Spanish painters made by the Italians 'because we have no ability to draw from nature' (*porque no tenemos abilidad para contrazer del natural*).[52] However, this theory is unsatisfactory, for the abundance of donor portraits, some of considerable quality, shows that there were Spanish painters with an aptitude for portraiture. The most plausible explanation obliges us to consider the peculiarities of the court portrait as well. With its established forms of representation, it required artists who were capable when necessary of subordinating likeness (*imitatio*) to decorum (*decorum*), following the principle of *dissimulatio* in classical rhetoric, a task at which Titian excelled.[53]

Of the reasons that led a sovereign to commission a portrait painter the most pressing was of a diplomatic nature, since from the latter part of the fourteenth century portraits played an important role in marriage negotiations, and they were probably used in the search for a wife for Charles VI of France in 1390 and Richard II of England in 1396.[54] This was the purpose of the portrait to which Saint Vincent referred and, as we shall see, the association between portraits and royal marriages was virtually automatic in fifteenth-century Spain. In 1428 Jan van Eyck arrived in Lisbon with an embassy sent by the Duke of Burgundy, Philip the Good, to discuss the possibilities of his marriage to Isabel of Portugal. There he probably met Lluís Dalmau (fl. 1428–1461), who had travelled to the Portuguese capital with another embassy accompanying Isabel of Aragon on her marriage to Peter of Portugal. Dalmau may have studied Van Eyck's portraits both then and again in 1431, when Alfonso V of Aragon sent him to Flanders on a mission whose purpose is unknown, but which probably concerned his training as a portraitist. Whenever it was, between 1443 and 1445 Dalmau demonstrated both his talent for portraiture and his debt to Van Eyck in *Our Lady of the Councillors*. Antonio Inglés, the first portrait painter in the service of Ferdinand and Isabella, arrived in Spain with an embassy sent by Henry VII of England (1485–1509),[55] and Juan de Flandes probably did so too in 1496 with another embassy sent by the Emperor Maximilian.[56] It is precisely Juan de Flandes who is attributed with the authorship of the portrait of Joanna of Castile [CAT. 3], whose marriage to Philip the Fair was arranged during the 1496 embassy. Shortly afterwards, Henry VII of England provided an interesting account of the role of portraits in this context. In 1504 he considered marrying Queen Joanna of Naples, niece of King Ferdinand and widow of Ferdinand II of Naples, who had been living with her mother in Valencia since 1501. With this intention, he sent an embassy to enquire about Joanna's habits, but above all to check on her appearance. One of the instructions that Henry gave his ambassadors was that an artist should paint a faithful portrait of Joanna – an essential matter for a sovereign obsessed with female beauty and aware, probably from experience, of the tendency of painters to 'improve upon' their models. He ordered that if the result was not true to reality the painter should do another portrait, and if he were not able to do so he should be replaced. This was the only one of the instructions that did not receive a written reply, probably because the ambassadors delivered the portrait. Although we do not know whether Henry liked it, the marriage never took place.[57]

In the sixteenth century portraits continued to play an important part in state marriages, and also produced some fascinating anecdotes. One incident occurred after the marriage by proxy in Toro in January 1522 between Joanna of Austria (1535–1573), daughter of Charles V, and her cousin John of Portugal (1537–1554), whom she had never met. On 9 March the Portuguese ambassador, Lourenço Pires de Távora, sent the prince a portrait of Joanna, assuring him that she was even more beautiful in real life, and shortly afterwards she received a picture of her husband. Doña Joanna, wrote Pires de Távora to the court in Lisbon, was delighted when she saw it. She placed it in her chamber and spent a long time gazing at it and talking to it. The young Don Carlos, son of Prince Philip and the late Maria of Portugal, was also enchanted with the portrait, calling its subject 'uncle' and inviting him to meals.[58] Years later, in 1565, Prince Charles himself fell in love with his cousin Anne of Austria through a portrait, although he had not always been so fascinated by them; four years earlier, he had shown nothing but indifference to portraits of several French princesses.[59]

One of the most interesting aspects of portraits was their capacity to produce reactions in the viewer, from Saint Vincent Ferrer's anonymous king kissing the portrait of his betrothed, to the young prince inviting his uncle to dine. Although we find these attitudes in other periods and other countries,[60] it is surprising how early they are documented or mentioned in the Iberian peninsula, both by Saint Vincent Ferrer and by the Majorcan writer Ramon Llull. In the latter's *Llibre de Meravelles* (1288–1289), a father and mother had a portrait of their son drawn on the wall of their house before he went off to battle and were comforted by being able to look at it afterwards.[61] This role of the portrait as substitute can be seen, albeit in a punitive rather than affectionate sense, in a curious passage from the *Dietari del capellà d'Alfons el Magnànim* which describes what happened in 1462, during the war between Barcelona and Juan II, to a certain Agulló, one of the city deputies, who was sent to seek help from Lérida and joined the side of the royalists. The reaction of the Barcelona authorities was swift and a painting of Agulló was hung upside down and tried for treason,[62] a practice which recalls the *pitture infamati* of the enemies of Florence from the fourteenth century, whose artists included Sandro Botticelli.[63]

Although the portrait of the soldier painted on a wall, mentioned by Ramon Llull, would have been always visible to his parents, it was more usual, as in the case quoted by Saint Vincent Ferrer, for such paintings to be in cases most of the time. This was nothing exceptional, and in fact paintings did not form part of domestic decoration in Spain – apart from the occasional devotional image – until the second half of the sixteenth century. As we shall see, when this happened portraits played an essential role.

The dearth of documentation precludes any analysis of the use and viewing of portraits before Queen Isabella. In fact she was the owner of the first set of portraits in Spain, characterised by its large number of pieces (as many as thirty-one) and its mobility. Apparently it accompanied the queen wherever she went as various inventories from 1499 and 1500 show practically the same portraits in Ocaña, Madrid and Granada. Furthermore, in none of these places could they have been on display permanently, for they spent most of the time packed away in cases, like the one 'of wood lined with black leather' (*de madera forrada en cuero negro*) that held the portraits of Emperor Maximilian I and his family. The documentation also shows that these portraits were mainly of relatives or members of royal families connected to Isabella as a result of intermarriage. This explains the proliferation of images of the imperial family and the royal houses of Portugal and England, although one also finds rarities such as the 'ugly woman' listed in an inventory in Granada in 1500. In any case, the variety of supports, types and formats is surprising. Together with portraits on wood, the support for most of those that have survived from the period, there are also numerous ones on canvas – up to fifteen of the thirty-one listed in Granada in 1500. Sizes and formats also varied, and the inventories specify whether they were large or small or, in some cases, round ('round box of a foreign woman with red clothing' – *caxa redonda de una mujer forastera con ropa colorada*). But most interesting of all was the variety of types. There were not only individual but also double portraits, such as a small canvas of the King of the Romans and his wife, and even family portraits, like that of Ferdinand and Isabella with Prince John and the 'princess queen' (*reyna princesa*), kept in a box with the royal arms, which was a kind of 'compression' of other multiple royal portraits designed to be shown together, such as the four canvases referred to earlier with Maximilian, his wife and children in a single case. Other examples were even more unusual, such as the diptych with a portrait of the Duchess of Brittany and opposite her, instead of the usual religious image, a view or map of Brittany.[64]

Many features of Isabella's collection continued into the first half of the sixteenth century, such as the variety of supports, the tendency towards family portraits, and the habit of not having them permanently displayed, even in the case of those who, very much in advance of the times for Spain, used to hang paintings in their homes.[65] Around 1540, however, there were indications of changes, by figures such as the imperial secretary Francisco de los Cobos (1477–1547) and Mencía de Mendoza (1508–1554), Marchioness of Zenete. The fact that Cobos had a painting gallery, probably in his mansion in Valladolid, can be deduced from a letter sent to him by Diego Hurtado de Mendoza from Venice on 8 April 1540 commenting humorously on the way the servants treated portraits.[66] In 1540 this gallery held what was probably the largest number of portraits by Titian in Europe, including those of Diego Hurtado de Mendoza, Pedro González de

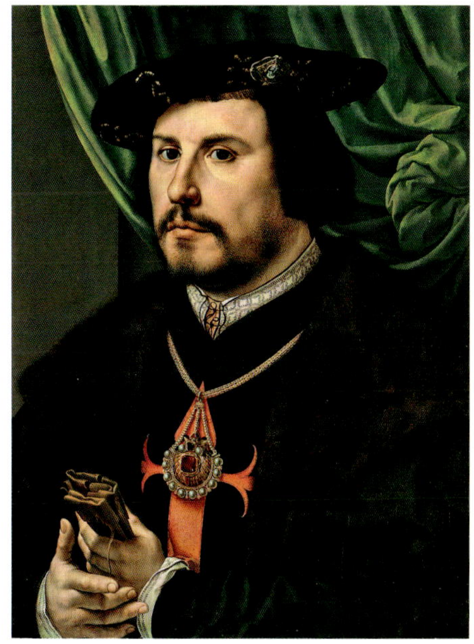

FIG. 35. Jan Gossaert, *Francisco de los Cobos y Medina*, 1530–1532. Los Angeles, The J. Paul Getty Museum [88.PB.43]

Mendoza, the Princess of England, Cornela Malaspina and Alfonso d'Este, as well as Cobos himself and his wife, María de Mendoza.

We have an inventory of Doña Mencía's paintings, which on her death in 1554 numbered a respectable 185 works, of which sixty-three were portraits hanging in different rooms, with their distribution and also the choice of artists following the model of Margarita of Austria.[67] Significantly, Mencía had seen the latter's portrait gallery in Mechelen on her visits to Flanders after her marriage to Henry III of Nassau (in 1530–1532 and 1535–1538).

The fact that this new attitude to portraits was personified by Francisco de los Cobos and Mencía de Mendoza was not fortuitous. A distinctive feature of the Spain of Charles V was the involvement of the ruling classes in imperial politics and the consequent widening of their cultural and artistic horizons.[68] In both Flanders and Italy, Mencía and Cobos moved in circles in which painting enjoyed much greater social, cultural and economic prestige than in Spain, and consequently owning and displaying paintings became a matter of pride and even ostentation. Cobos was able to confirm this personally when Federico Gonzaga and Alfonso d'Este

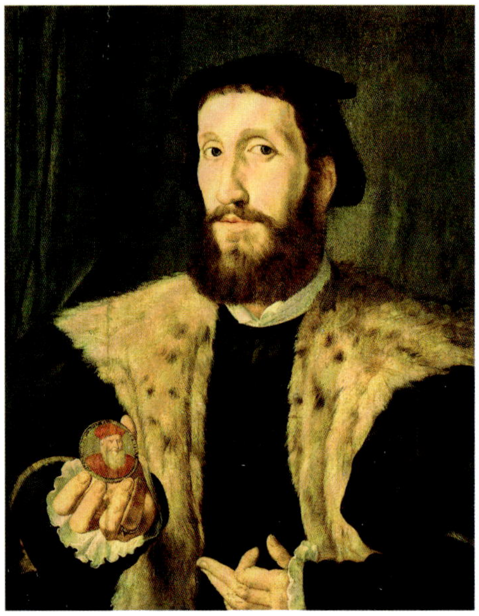

FIG. 36. Style of Jan Cornelisz. Vermeyen, *Juan de Valdés*, *ca.* 1531.
London, The National Gallery [NG 2607]

tried to curry favour with him through paintings, and particularly portraits, the latter being the reason for his exceptional collection of works by Titian.[69] However, nothing illustrates better the consequences of this internationalisation than the extraordinary number of Spaniards whose portraits were painted in Flanders and Italy by the leading artists of the first half of the sixteenth century. Titian painted, among others and in addition to members of the royal family, the Duke of Alba, Antonio de Leiva, Francisco de los Cobos and his wife, Diego Hurtado de Mendoza, Hernando de Alarcón, Pedro González de Mendoza, Gonzalo Pérez and Honorato Juan; Jan Gossaert (*ca.* 1478–*ca.* 1536) portrayed Juan de Zúñiga, Francisco de los Cobos [FIG. 35],[70] Diego de Guevara and Mencía de Mendoza; Jan Cornelisz. Vermeyen painted Alfonso de Valdés and Felipe de Guevara; and Anthonis Mor painted the Duke of Alba.

Portraits also became very popular among humanists, particularly those closest to Erasmus, the European intellectual who best exploited his image in other media (engravings and medallions) as well as painting. Their letters, like those of Erasmus himself, refer constantly to portraits in paintings or on medallions, considering them as an extension and complement to the letters, and both as a testimony of friendship that transcended time, in which the image spoke when the written word was silent, and vice versa.[71] An example of this is provided by Alfonso de Valdés (*ca.* 1500–1532), Latin secretary to Charles V, in a portrait from the studio of Jan Cornelisz. Vermeyen in which he is holding a medallion of his protector, the chancellor Mercurino Gattinara [FIG. 36].[72] This portrait is perhaps the one referred to by Valdés in a letter sent to the Polish humanist Juan Dantisco (Jan Dantyszek) from Ratisbon in October 1531 stating that if Granvela liked it he would have it copied.[73] Dantisco, who lived in Spain for a long time, was the author of a voluminous correspondence containing references to portraits, such as the one he sent in 1529 to Isabel Delgada, a woman from Valladolid by whom he had a daughter in 1527 named Juana Dantisco, or the portrait of Juana painted in Valladolid in 1539 on the instructions of Johan de Weze, Bishop of Lund, by 'a German painter and royal guard' (*un pintor alemán y Guardia de Corps de S.M.*), who must be identified as Jacob Seisenegger.[74]

Separate mention should be made of the sonnets on portraits in the style of Petrarch, which had well-known exponents among what is known as the 'first generation of Spanish Petrarchists' (*primera generación de petrarquistas españoles*), many of whose members participated in the process of internationalisation referred to earlier.[75] I shall mention here just two of these sonnets. The first was dedicated by Diego Hurtado de Mendoza (1503/4–1575) to the portrait of his lady love painted by Titian in Venice in 1542, which also inspired a sonnet by Aretino:

Tu gracia, tu valor, tu hermosura
muestra de todo el cielo retirada
como cosa que está sobre natura
ni pudiera ser vista ni pintada

Pero yo en alma tu figura
tengo en humana forma abreviada
tal hice retratarte de pintura
cual amor te dejó en ella estampada

No por soberbia vana o por memoria
de ti, ni para publicar mis males
ni por verte más veces que te veo

mas por solo gozar con tanta gloria
señora, con los ojos corporales
como con los ojos del alma y del deseo.[76]

[HURTADO DE MENDOZA]

Furtivamente Tiziano e Amore
presi a gara i pennelli e le quadrella,
duo essempi han fatto d'una donna bella
e sacrati al Mendozza, aureo signore

Ond'egli, altier di si divin favore,
per seguir cotal dea come sua stella
con ceremonie apartenenti a quella
l'uno in camera tien, l'altro nel cuore

E, mentre quella effigie e questa imago
dentro a sé scopre e fuor cela ad altrui
e in ciò che piú desia meno appar vago,

vanta il secreto che s'asconde in lui;
ché, s'ognun è del foco suo presago,
ardendo, poi non sa verun di cui.[77]

[ARETINO]

The two sonnets, neither of which describes the portrait, are conceptually similar in that they draw a parallel between the spiritual beauty in Mendoza's heart and the beauty visible to the eye in Titian's portrait, a coincidence that is explained by the sonnets' common roots in Petrarch. We also know from Aretino that Titian painted the portrait without seeing the lady (and Aretino had not seen the portrait either) and that Mendoza covered it with a piece of silk. All this suggests that the lady portrayed was not one of Mendoza's Venetian lovers, all of whom were courtesans. She probably never even set foot in Venice, and was perhaps Marina de Aragón, to whom he dedicated numerous poems but with whom he was never on intimate terms. Mendoza's lover, jealously guarded, responds to the Petrarchist ideal of the sublime woman unsullied by sensuality. In fact, the portrait is more the visual embodiment of Mendoza's ideal of love than the physical representation of his 'loved one', which explains why Titian did not need to see her in order to paint her portrait and why Aretino did not need to see the portrait in order to laud it.

Although Hurtado de Mendoza's sonnet illustrates an accidental but definite relationship between poetry and the painted portrait, most compositions lacked any specific points of reference. Writing sonnets about portraits became a separate genre with rules of its own,[78] and this is reflected in one by Gutierre de Cetina (1514/17–1554/57). Here he transfers the emphasis from the person portrayed to the painter, who is asked by the poet in the tercets whether he did not fall in love with the lady when painting her:

Artífice ingenioso, ¿qué sentiste
cuando tan cuerdamente contemplabas
el sujeto que muestran tus colores?

Dime, si como yo la vi, la viste,
el pincel y la tabla en que pintabas,
Y tú, ¿cómo no ardéis, cual yo, de amores?[79]

This process of internationalisation of the Spanish elite even had an effect on vocabulary, with the word *retrato* being incorporated into Spanish from the Italian. This happened initially in translations such as the one by Boscán of *El Cortesano* by Baltasar de Castiglione, published in Barcelona in 1534, and through writers who had spent time in Italy, such as Gonzalo Fernández de Oviedo (1478–1557). In his *Batallas y Quinquágenas* Oviedo recounts the story of Hugo de Moncada's passion for a Neapolitan lady and how he asked numerous painters 'to draw and paint her from life, and none did it as perfectly as he would have liked, and so he kept all those portraits [*retractos*] and knowing another or other painters he had her drawn. And in this way he had in his chamber with great veneration all those figures for their devotion: some happy, others angry, some in a headdress and nicely dressed, others with loose hair and in different poses.'[80] Once the word had been adopted, it spread rapidly thanks to such popular works as *Silva de varia lección* (1540), in which Pedro Mexía recalled how the ancient Romans used to carry seals with their *retractos*.

Whatever the term used, the fact was that, by the mid-sixteenth century, portraits had extended beyond the confines of palaces and humanist circles and were included in ephemeral events such as the reception given to Prince Philip by the Count of Benavente in 1554,[81] and in literary works where they were the cause of strange adventures, such as *El Cortesano* by Luis de Milán (Valencia, 1561).[82] Printed books were in fact a special vehicle for popularising the portrait, as they included engravings that were often made from paintings. Particular importance was attached to portraits of the authors of works, which became customary from the middle of the sixteenth century, whether the publications were printed abroad, as in the case of Andrés Laguna and his *De Virtutibus* (Cologne, 1543), or in Spain, like the notable portrait of Juan de Iciar in his *Arte Subtilissima* (Zaragoza, 1550).[83]

Did portrait painters benefit from this situation? On analysing the situation we see a gap between artistic theory, which undervalued the portrait and considered it a mechanical reproduction of reality – *ritrarre* as opposed to *imitare* (the representation of reality based on an idea or on its essence) – and artistic practice, which afforded good portrait painters a social standing that was often unattainable otherwise. The association between portraiture and the court was a determining factor in this process and I have already mentioned the benefits to artists – mainly portrait painters – provided by the rivalry between princes and cities in obtaining the services of the most skilled exponents of the genre. This attitude, which could be considered in terms of supply and demand, explains the exceptionally high salary paid to Michel Sittow (*ca.* 1469–1525) by Ferdinand and Isabella as a result of the dearth of portraitists: 50,000 *maravedíes* a year, proportionally more than any other previous or subsequent court painter. It also explains the fact that two of the first three painters to be ennobled by Spanish sovereigns specialised in portraiture (Titian and Mor) and the third (though chronologically earlier) was a distinguished muralist (Dello Delli, *ca.* 1404–?) – these being the two pictorial genres with a chronic scarcity of practitioners in Spain.[84]

Social success was, however, not enough to silence the critics and consequently a theory was formulated that valued the merits of a portrait according to its social implications: its prestige lay in the status of the person portrayed, and therefore only those possessing outstanding moral, intellectual or personal qualities should be painted. In the Iberian peninsula, this idea was expressed by the Portuguese artist Francisco de Holanda (1517–1584) in *Do tirar polo natural* (1548), the first European treatise on portraiture, translated into Spanish by Manuel Denís in 1563. There he criticised those who produced portraits indiscriminately and advised the 'excellent painter, if you like to call him a painter, to paint very few people, who have been specially selected'.[85] The court portrait painters were the ones who most clearly understood that their social and financial success, as well as their recognition as artists, was closely associated with the standing of their patrons, which they proclaimed explicitly by depicting themselves alongside them. Titian did so in a self-portrait (now lost) with the image of Philip II, while Anthonis Mor, in a self-portrait in the Uffizi [FIG. 37], includes an inscription announcing his ties to the Spanish sovereign.[86]

Around 1560, Felipe de Guevara, in his *Comentarios de la pintura*, advised Philip II to hang his paintings, since 'covered and concealed they lose their value, which consists of an outsider's eyes and opinions of men of good understanding and good imagination';[87] and immediately afterwards the Palace of El Pardo became the first royal residence in which painting played a prominent role in the decoration. Philip II brought to El Pardo the Flemish idea of the gallery as an architectural space for housing images of relatives and ancestors in what was named the Sala de Reyes. There he arranged in the form of a frieze forty-five portraits, 'full length or at least to the knee' (*cuerpo entero, poco menos que hasta la rodilla*), by Titian, Mor and Sánchez Coello, including the self-portraits of the first two.[88]

It would, however, be misleading to mention only the novel aspects of the Sala de Reyes. Throughout this essay I have tried to refute the idea of a radical divide between the Late Middle Ages and the Renaissance as far as portraiture is concerned, and hence my insistence on demonstrating, for example, that its capacity to arouse emotions and its leading role in marriage arrangements were present from the very beginning. Also, in the Sala

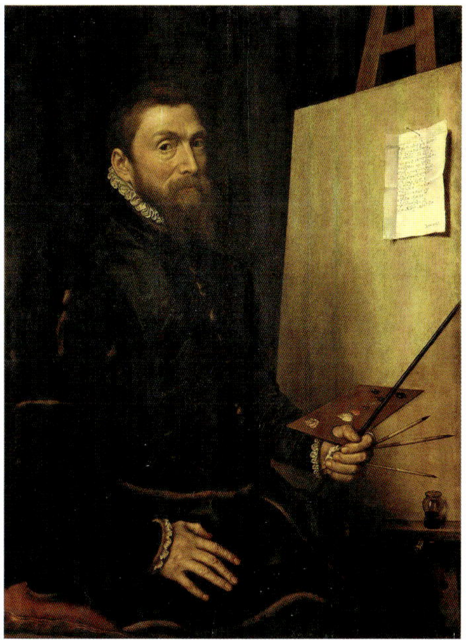

FIG. 37. Anthonis Mor, *Self Portrait*, 1558. Florence, Galleria degli Uffizi

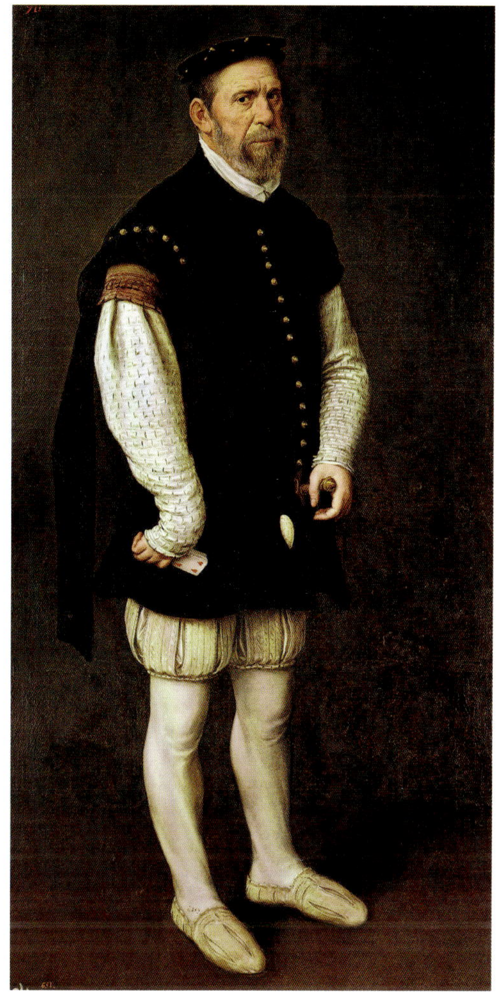

FIG. 38. Anthonis Mor, *The Buffoon Pejerón*, 1559–1560. Madrid, Museo del Prado [P-2107]

de Reyes there are strong underlying elements of continuity with the previous period. For instance, its name, the 'Hall of Kings', recalls the palace rooms that housed the royal series of the Late Middle Ages. Similarly, the dynastic and instructive function of the portraits, and the fact that they were the work of foreigners or of Spaniards who had trained abroad, have earlier precedents. Even the inclusion of the self-portraits of Titian and Mor should be viewed as the culmination of a long process of social recognition of the court painter, prior to and separate from the formulation of the humanist theory of the arts, although it was to benefit from the latter as well.

Why, therefore, terminate this essay at around 1560? The date is only of importance from a Spanish perspective. Philip II's return to Spain and the choice of a permanent capital were decisive factors in the development of court art and consequently of portraiture also. And although the king did not stop employing foreign artists, a palace 'workshop' began to develop around Sánchez Coello that was to satisfy the needs of the monarchy for over a century, until the arrival of French portrait painters with the first Bourbon sovereign, Philip V. But as far as the theme of this exhibition is concerned, the decisive factor was the development, in the mid-sixteenth century, of a type of portrait that was to serve as a reference point not only for other reigning houses but, more importantly, for future generations of Spanish painters, who thereafter could turn to a national tradition in search of inspiration and solutions – and not only for royal portraits; looking at Anthonis Mor's *The Buffoon Pejerón* [FIG. 38], any observant viewer will immediately recognise in it a forerunner for the dignity and the bold spatial composition of Velázquez's buffoons [see CAT. 51].

NOTES

1 Ferrer 1934, I, pp. 197–98. Aspects of this essay were the subject of an initial approach in Falomir 1996a.

2 For some writers, donor portraits are not pure portraits but forms of representation of individuals: Levey 1976, pp. 20–29. The same can be said of sets of portraits I will be discussing below.

3 A list of these images appears in Sánchez Cantón 1948.

4 *(El) Espéculo*, book II, title XIII, law VI: 'Cómmo deven sseer onrradas e guardadas las ymágenes que ffueron pintadas o entalladas del rrey e qué pena deve aver qui las quebrantasse' (How the images that were painted or carved of the king must be honoured and safeguarded and what shame anyone who breaks them must feel), in Alfonso X ed. 1985, p. 167.

5 Some writers describe these portraits as 'typical', to distinguish them from the 'authentic' ones: Castelnuovo 1973, pp. 1036–37.

6 Tormo 1916.

7 Martindale 1988, pp. 8–9.

8 Tormo 1916, pp. 17–29. For this series, continued by Enrique IV and Philip II, which was burnt in 1862, see Collar de Cáceres 1995.

9 This Aragonese series in Tormo 1916, pp. 51–56; its French predecessors in Bracons i Clapés 1989, pp. 212–13; and for Navarra, see Leroy 1986, p. 309.

10 This is suggested in the *Castigos e documentos del rey don Sancho* (1292), 1952, p. 112, which includes advice by Sancho IV of Castile (1285–1295) to his heir: Falomir 1996a, pp. 179–82. Formally and materially different from the series, though similar in concept, are the genealogical rolls and trees that were very popular in the fifteenth century: Serra Desfilis 2002–2003, pp. 57–74.

11 Mena ed. 1989, p. 255; Martorell ed. 1983, p. 225. The passage from *Tirant* was first linked to specific examples in D'Olwer 1933, p. 125.

12 For the vitality of the series in the sixteenth and seventeenth centuries, see Falomir 1998, pp. 203–27 and Falomir 2000, pp. 61–77.

13 *La Catedral de Toledo*, 1999, p. 220. Borgoña and his work in Toledo in Angulo 1954, pp. 20–21.

14 Joan de Joanes 2000, pp. 136–47.

15 Martindale 1988, pp. 31–35. The literature on the portrait of Laura is vast; among more recent publications see Quondam 1989, pp. 9–44; Mann 1998, pp. 15–21 and 191–92; Trapp 2001, pp. 55–192.

16 Martindale 1988, pp. 21–22; Panofsky 1951, pp. 12–19. See also Duby 1991, pp. 206–10.

17 Yarza 1994, pp. 79–83.

18 '[...] fom nats complits los set mesos que fom engenrats, e nasquem tam feble e tan axoquiós, que no·s pensaven les madrines [...] que poguéssem viure' (we were born seven months after conception, and we were so weak and sickly that the midwives did not expect us to live); *Chronique catalane de Pierre IV d'Aragon, III de Catalogne*, Ed. Amédée Pagès, Toulouse 1941, p. 52.

19 Castelnuovo 2002, pp. 39–40.

20 Rubio y Lluch, 1908–1921, vol. I, pp. 156–157 and 185, vol. II, p. 282.

21 Rubió i Lluch 1921, p. 171.

22 Cennini ed. 1988, pp. 226–30.

23 The first person to associate wax figures with the origins of portraiture in Spain was Gudiol i Cunill 1922, p. 11. For its presence in Italian art and particularly Florentine art of the Quattrocento, mentioned by Vasari, see Van der Velden 1998, pp. 126–36 and Wright 2000, pp. 103–04.

24 Representations of *ex votos* in late mediaeval painting in Llompart 1973, pp. 397–403.

25 Freedberg 1992, pp. 192–94, 252 and ff.

26 Gudiol i Cunill 1927, p. 74. The first wax image documented in Florence, of Pope Alexander IV, dates from 1260: Van der Velden 1998, p. 129.

27 Rubió i Lluch 1908–1921, vol. II, p. 125.

28 For the origin and significance of these images and the 'theory of the king's two bodies', see Kantorowicz 1957, pp. 420–36; and Giesey 1960.

29 Caliena Corbero and Iranzo Munio 1991, p. 58. There is no record of this practice in Castile or Navarra: Menjot 1988, pp. 127–38; and Leroy 1988, p. 238.

30 Falomir 1996b, pp. 376–77.

31 Warnke 1993, pp. 212–14.

32 Wright 2000, pp. 86–87.

33 The altarpiece, painted by Sancho de Zamora and Juan de Segovia, was commissioned by María de Luna, daughter of the Condestable Álvaro de Luna and Juana Pimentel. Their images appear on the predella, long after the death in disgrace of the Condestable in 1453. See Berg Sobré 1989, pp. 318–31.

34 Molina 1999, pp. 136–46.

35 For the degrees of Augustinian vision and their relationship with the *imago pietatis*, see González García 2004, pp. 101–04.

36 Falomir 1996b, p. 373.

37 Falomir 1996b, p. 373.

38 Madurell Marimon 1952, p. 89.

39 De la Torre 1961, pp. 167–72.

40 Ferrarino 1975, p. 11. Despite Titian's attempts to diversify, Charles V was to use him mainly as a portraitist. See Hope 1988, pp. 53–54.

41 Bury 1989, p. 87.

42 Horn 1989, pp. 8 and 25–31.

43 Matthews 2001, p. 81.

44 Morte 1999, pp. 445–68.

45 Fernández de Oviedo 2000, vol. III, pp. 64–65.

46 Molina 1999, p. 194.

47 Gestoso y Pérez 1899, vol. II, p. 33.

48 In 1546 Mencía de Mendoza commissioned Berruguete to copy a portrait of Juan de Zúñiga owned by Cobos, which was not produced because of disagreement over the price: see José Mª March 1948, pp. 299–300.

49 Condorelli 1965, pp. 77–84.

50 Ramos Gómez 1996, pp. 80–83.

51 Pacheco (1638) 1990, p. 524.

52 Sánchez Cantón 1923, vol. I, p. 212.

53 Warnke 1993, pp. 212–17; Falomir 2001, pp. 71–86.

54 Warnke 1993, p. 220.

55 Inglés stayed at court for a year. In 1497, the painter Luis de París also arrived with an embassy, sent by the Archduke

Philip the Fair. See Domínguez Casas 1993, pp. 131–32.

56 Silva Maroto 2004, p. 125.

57 *Dos opúsculos isabelinos* 1979, p. 97. The ambassadors' visit to Joanna took place on 22 June 1505.

58 Jordan 1994, pp. 179–82.

59 Gachard 1984, pp. 144–45 and 157.

60 Freedberg 1992, pp. 375–80.

61 Molina 1999, p. 194.

62 '[...] pintat, lo penjaren cap avall, fent-li procés de traïdor' (painted, they hung it upside down, condemning him as a traitor). Miralles 1988, p. 163.

63 Edgerton 1985, pp. 59–125.

64 Azcárate 1982, vol. II pp. 61–74.

65 Such was the case of the ambassador to Rome and vice-chancellor of Aragon, Miquel May, who continued to keep the three portraits in his house in Barcelona encased, where nonetheless other paintings were hung on the walls. See Duran i Sanpere 1960, p. 112.

66 'I expect Titian, who is in Mantua, to paint the portrait of Señor Pedro, which will go with mine, and I do not want to lose the right to a place in Your Lordship's house, where you should place one in bronze that I will have made here, but it will not be on the staircase, as you said, so that the pages will not throw dirt in my eyes'. Ferrarino 1975, p. 17.

67 Hidalgo Ogáyar 1997, pp. 83–102; concerning Margarita, see Eichberger 1995, pp. 225–47. Mencía had as many portraits as Margarita and more than María, whose inventory after her death indicates twenty-nine.

68 Falomir 2000, pp. 375–405.

69 Bodart 1998, pp. 51–149.

70 The portrait of Cobos at the J. Paul Getty Museum. Only a photograph survives of the portrait of Zúñiga, which belonged to the Palau (San Cugat del Vallés, Barcelona) up until the Civil War and formed a diptych with *Our Lady of the Pear*, also lost. In 1576 inventory of possessions of Zúñiga's son, Luis de Requesens, the diptych was described as follows: 'On one part is a painted image of Our Lady with her Son on her arm, and Our Lady has a pear in her hand, and on the other part is a portrait of Don Joan Çunyga with his hands folded'. (March 1941, vol. I, p. 88 and reproductions of the diptych in vol. II, plates XIX and XX.) Given the fact that Zúñiga bears no resemblance at all to the portrait in the Getty Museum, which is certainly similar to the medallion of Cobos produced by Christopher Weiditz in 1531, the recent identification of the Getty portrait as Zúñiga does not seem viable: Álvarez 2003, pp. 488–89.

71 Bodar 1990, pp. 17–68.

72 Horn 1989, p. 12.

73 'S. Dominus Granvella libenter videret meum simulacrum ut, si placeret ei, per eundem pictorem suum quoque depingi faceret; si extrema manus imposta est fac obsecro ut habeamus': Valdés 1996, p. 98.

74 Fontán and Axer 1994, pp. 74 and 108–09. There is documentary evidence of Seisenegger's presence in Spain in 1539.

75 Concerning sonnets on portraits and Petrarch's influence in the early sixteenth century, for example on Pietro Bembo, see Pommier 1998, pp. 65–74.

76 Hurtado de Mendoza 1990, p. 269. This is a literal translation:

Your charm, your valour, your beauty
a sample from the entire heaven taken
as something above nature
that could not be seen or painted.
But in my soul I have your image
in condensed human form
as I had you portrayed in paint
so love left you imprinted on it.
Not in vain pride or in memory
of you, nor for publishing my ills
nor for seeing you more often than I do
but simply to enjoy such glory,
lady, with the eyes of the body
as with the eyes of the soul and of desire.

77 Aretino 1916, II, p. 245. For Aretino's Petrarchism, see Freedman 1995, pp. 16–20. This is a literal translation of the sonnet:

Secretly Titian and Love
took up paint brush and canvas;
they've made two images of a lovely woman,
both sacred to the golden Mendoza.
He, proud of such divine favour
in order to follow this goddess as his star,
with due ceremonies unto her
keeps one image in his room, t'other in his heart.
And whilst he gazes upon the one within
and hides the second from others' view
so as to appear, as is his wish, less rapt
he boasts of the secret hidden in his breast;
so that, though all can see the flames therein,
he, though burning, for whom he burns conceals.

78 Lecercle 1987, pp. 79–143.

79 Cetina 1990, p. 128. The artist in love with the woman he is painting refers to the passage about Apelles and Campaspe, well known through Pliny.

Ingenious artist, what did you feel
when you so knowledgeably contemplated
the subject your colours disclose?
Tell me if you saw her as I did,
the brush and the panel on which you painted,
And you, how is it you do not burn, like me, with love?

80 Fernández de Oviedo Ms. 359, fol. 936. Oviedo lived in Naples between 1500 and 1502.

81 Muñoz 1554, fol. 17.

82 Falomir 1994, p. 75.

83 In the absence of a similar work on Spain to that by Zappella 1988, see Checa 1987, pp. 179–82. The Laguna portrait is discussed in Carolus 2000, no. 183.

84 Most of the Spaniards mentioned as authors of independent portraits prior to 1550 worked for the court: Llorens Saragossa, Dalmau, Hernando Rincón, Alonso Berruguete, Diego de Arroyo. In none of the documents naming them court painters, however, is portrait painting mentioned among their attributions, and in fact many others must not have had the skill to work in this genre.

85 Holanda 1921, p. 254.

86 Woodall 1990, pp. 69–89.

87 Felipe de Guevara, *Comentarios de la pintura*, Madrid, Guevara ed. 1788, pp. 4–5.

88 To these were added, at a lower level, two of the dwarf Stanislao, four views of cities and eight triumphs of Charles V by Vermeyen. For the Sala de Reyes, see Woodall 1995, pp. 53–103.

CAT. I. Bartolomé Bermejo. *Saint Dominic of Silos*, 1474–1477. Madrid, Museo del Prado [P-1323]

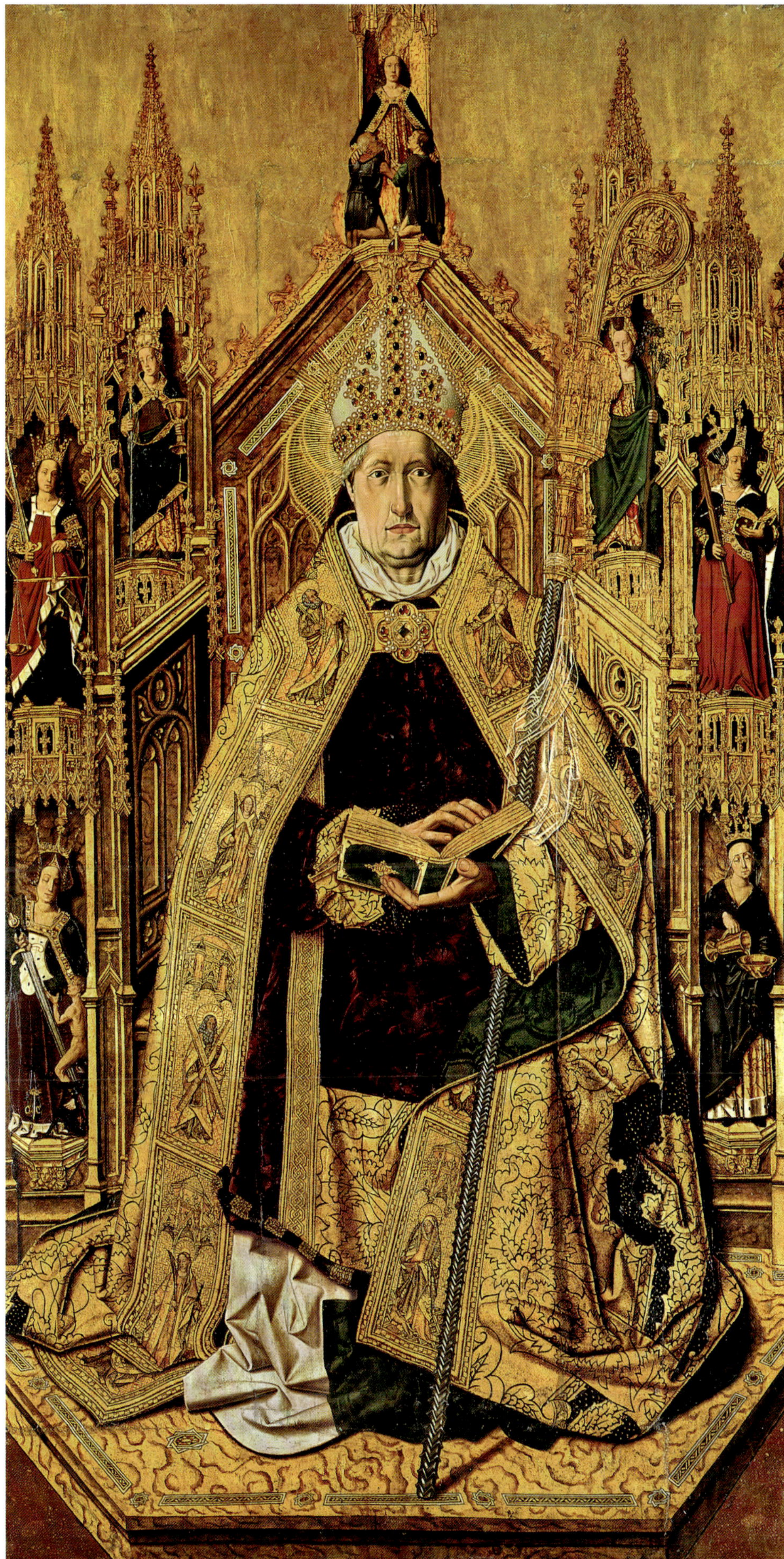

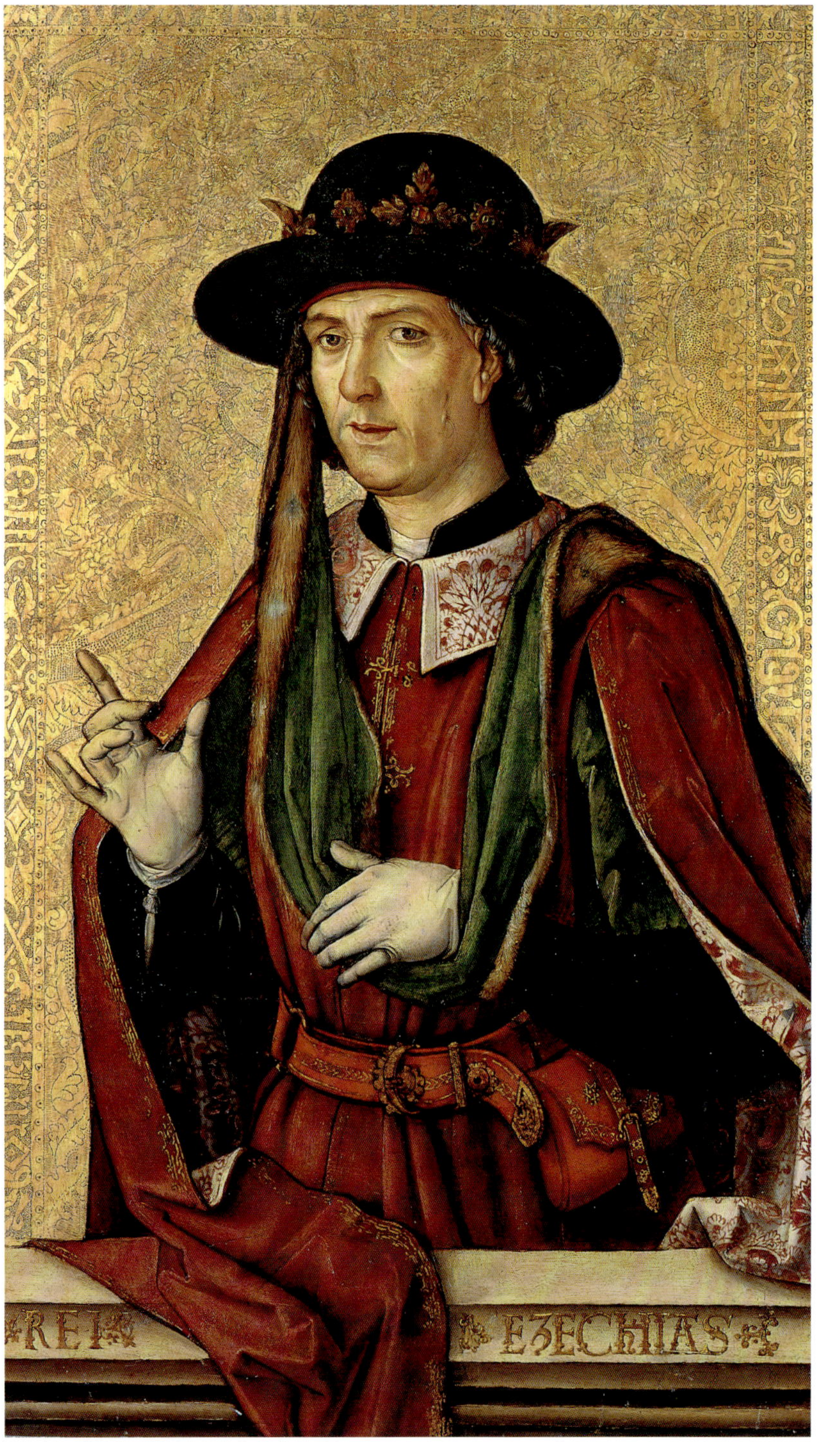

CAT. 2. Pedro Berruguete. *Hezekiah, ca.* 1490. Paredes de Nava, Museo Parroquial de Santa Eulalia

CAT. 3. Juan de Flandes. *Portrait of an Infanta, ca.* 1496. Madrid, Museo Thyssen-Bornemisza [141 (1930 36)]

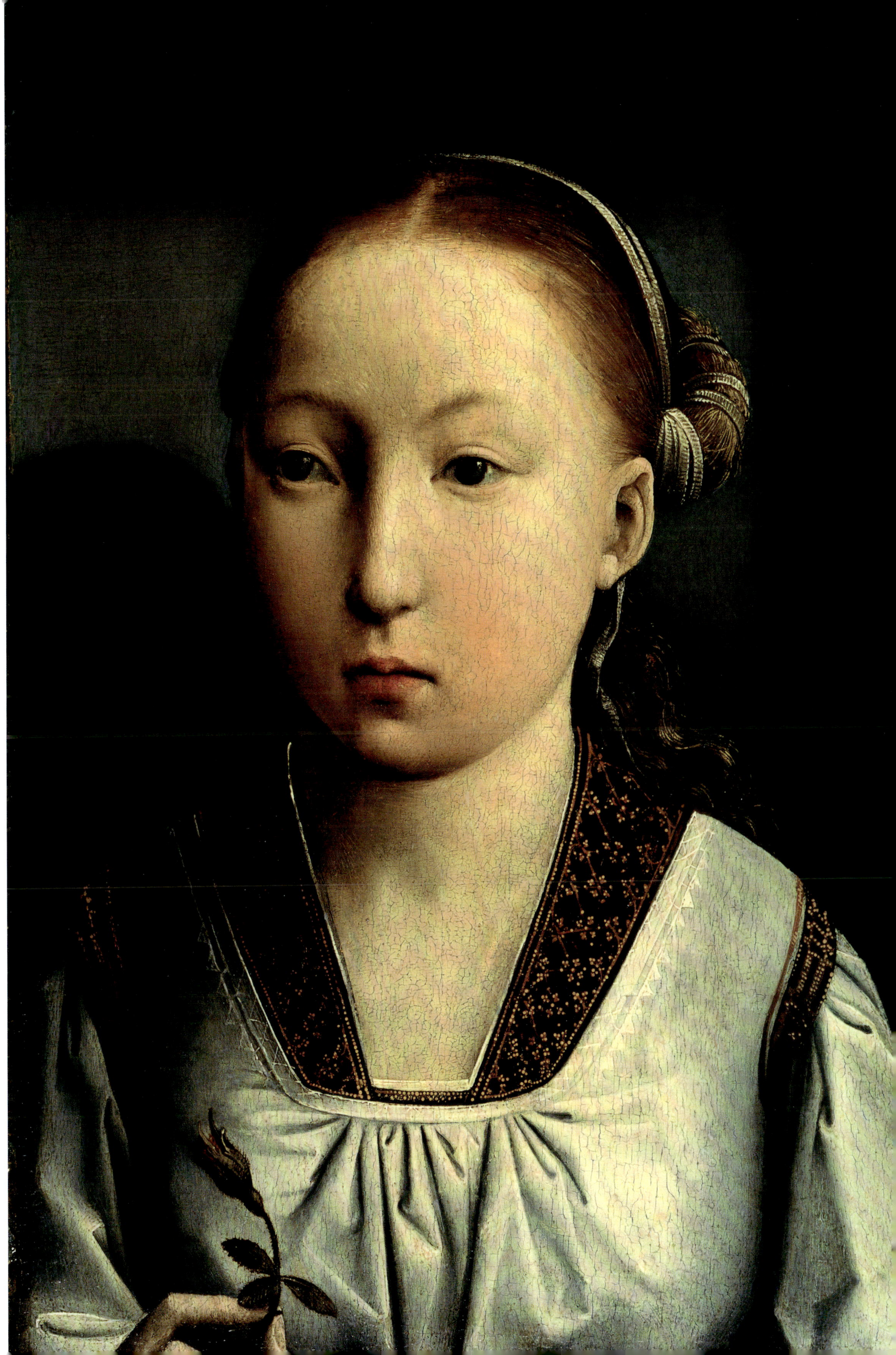

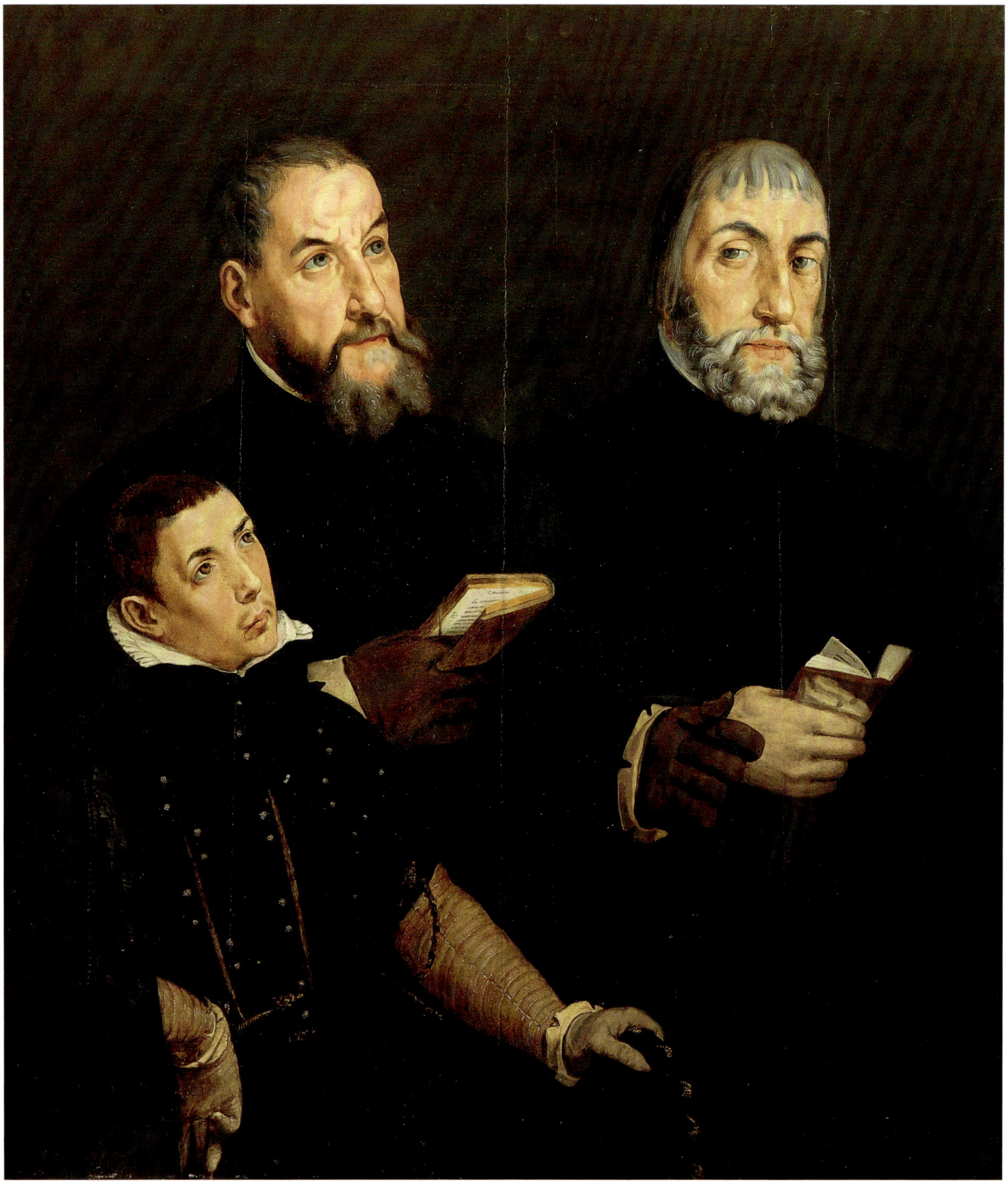

CAT. 4. Pedro de Campaña. *Don Diego with Don Alonso Caballero and his Son*, 1555–1556. Seville, Cathedral

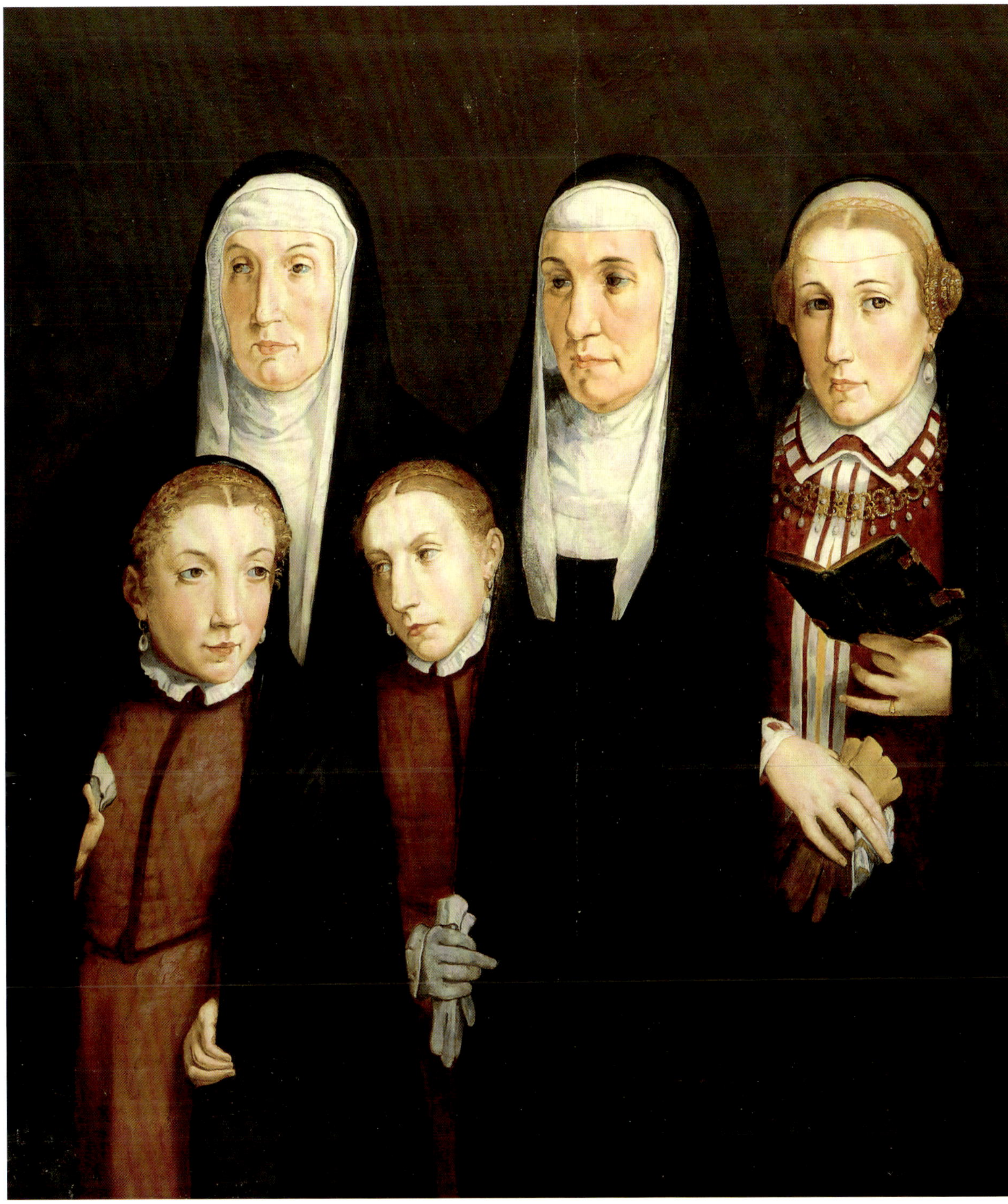

CAT. 5. Pedro de Campaña. *Doña Leonor with Doña Mencía de Cabrera and her Daughters*, 1555–1556. Seville, Cathedral

CAT. 6. El Greco. *The Adoration of the Name of Jesus*, 1577–1580.
Patrimonio Nacional. Real Monasterio de San Lorenzo de El Escorial [10014683]

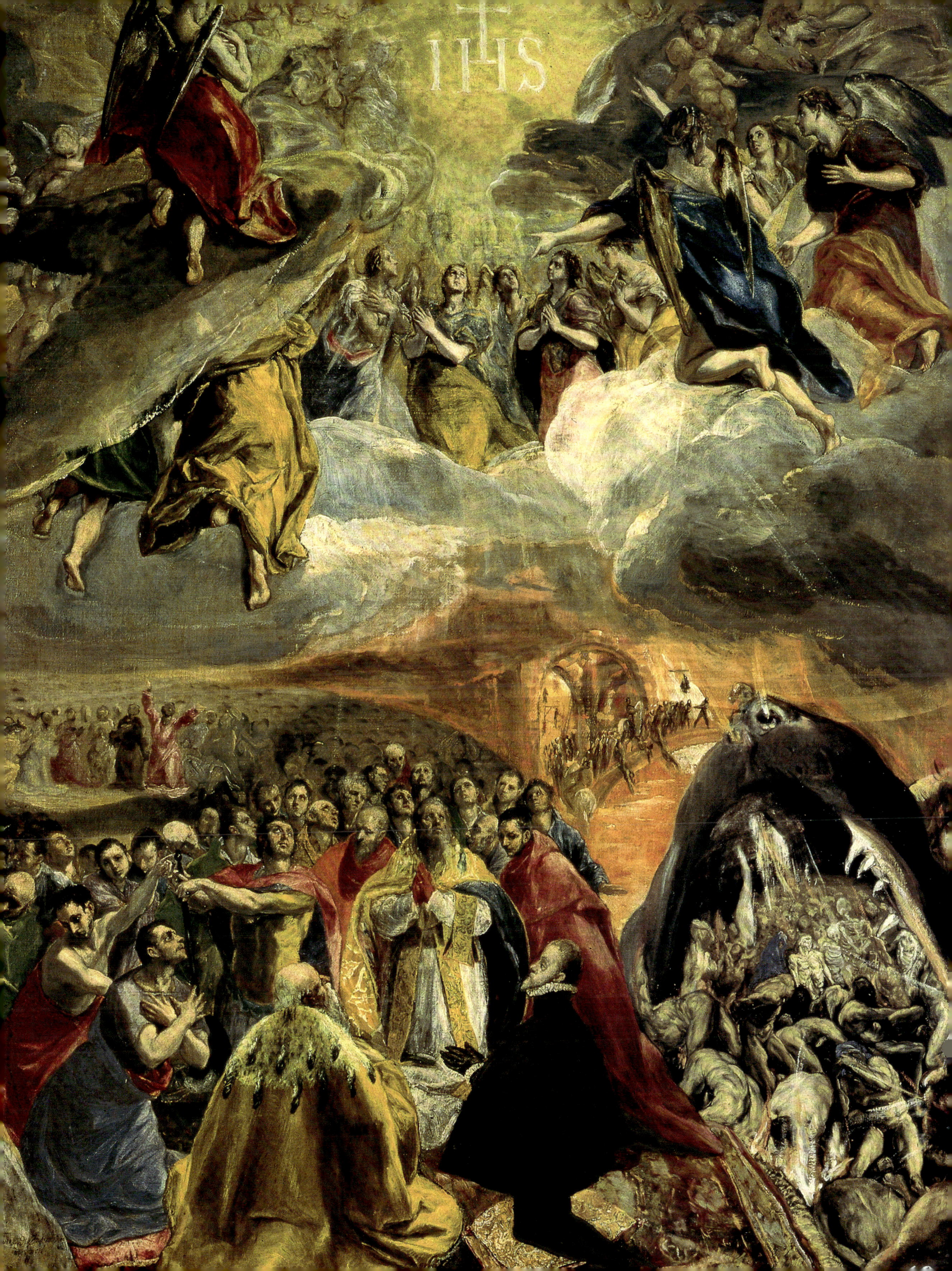
IHS

2 Court Portraits in the Spanish Monarchy (1530–1660)

Leticia Ruiz Gómez

When Charles V and Titian met in the city of Bologna in 1530, both enjoyed European reputations. Charles V had been crowned Holy Roman Emperor by Pope Clement VII, thereby becoming the foremost ruler of his time. For his part, Titian had been acclaimed as one of the most illustrious painters of the century, with a particular facility for portraiture.[1] As a portraitist he excelled in idealising his sitters without forfeiting veracity. Charles V had been portrayed many times; the family of his grandfather Maximilian I had engaged since the end of the fifteenth century in a complex strategy of dynastic exaltation and propaganda, through the use of medals, prints and numerous portraits. Several iconographic traditions converged in the portraits of Charles V, crafted by artists of origins as varied as the territorial possessions of the Empire.[2]

In that first encounter with Charles V, we know that Titian painted an effigy that showed him 'half-length, armed with a bare sword in his hand and with his helmet on a table'.[3] In this portrait, known through copies and engravings, the Emperor had the air of a victorious warrior *all'antica*. In 1533 Titian was called again to Bologna, but

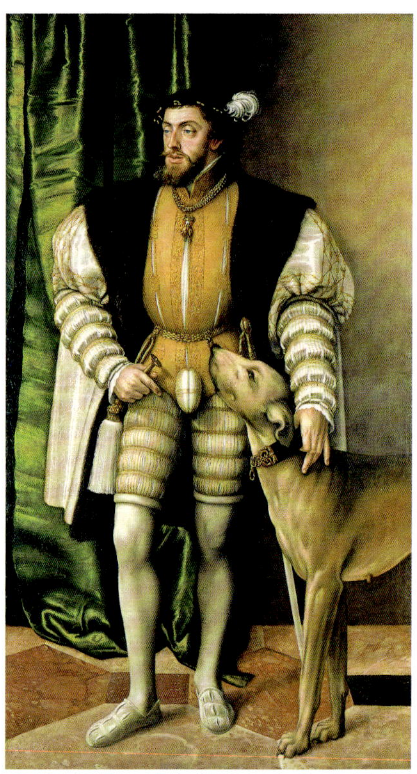

FIG. 39. Jakob Seisenegger, *Charles V with a Dog*, 1532. Vienna, Kunsthistorisches Museum [GG 114]

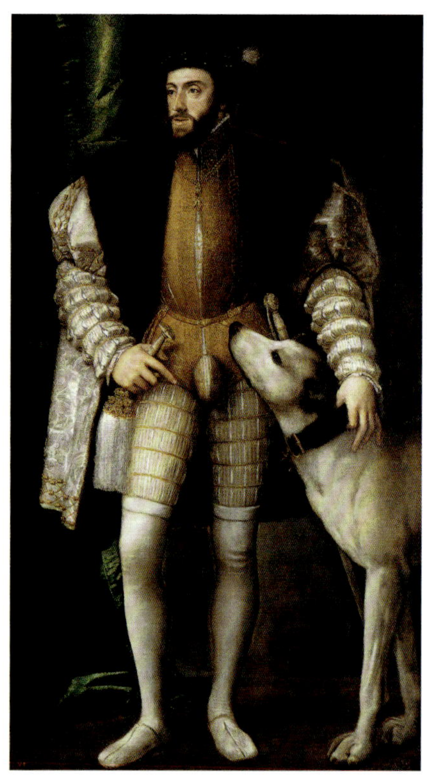

FIG. 40. Titian, *The Emperor Charles V*, 1533. Madrid, Museo del Prado [P-409]

this time he was asked to make a copy from an original that had been painted a year earlier by the German Jakob Seisenegger (1505–1567). Seisenegger was the court painter to Charles's brother, Ferdinand II, and had returned to the old Germanic tradition of the state portrait, showing the sitter full-length and standing in a rather simple setting.[4] The work by Seisenegger depicted Charles V with a dog [FIG. 39] and commemorated his visit to Bassano in November 1532. In a setting defined by a green drape, the imposing figure of the Emperor stands out in the foreground, magnificently attired and accompanied by a hound. The copy by Titian is almost identical, but he recreated the image with certain alterations in spatial terms, subtly elongating the sitter and softening his conspicuous facial features. Thus Titian achieved an intelligent readaptation of the northern European model that the German artist had re-established, giving the Emperor a distinctive appearance.[5] The Emperor would certainly have recognised himself in the portrait, but Titian did not permit his drooping eyelids, nor his pronounced lower lip giving the impression of someone who was insecure in his position. Instead, he painted these features in such a way that they conformed with the general image of the sitter as an elegant and Apollonian man, at ease and yet ready for action. The image conveyed a majestic splendour, the main quality of the ruler in the Early Modern Period. This was a hitherto vague concept, but later it was to feature much in the laudatory writings that appeared on Titian's portraits.[6] For his version, *The Emperor Charles V* [FIG. 40], Titian was paid the considerable sum of 500 *scudi*, and his standing as the foremost portrait artist of the time was confirmed. This was the result of his ability to bring together within a single portrait the northern European tradition, a decorous resolution of the problem posed by the Emperor's prognathism by transforming it into a point of reference and pride, and the most avant-garde pictorial form of the time.[7]

The association between Titian and Charles V would reach its highest point in 1549, when the artist travelled to Augsburg, having been commissioned to paint a complete gallery of portraits of the Emperor and his family

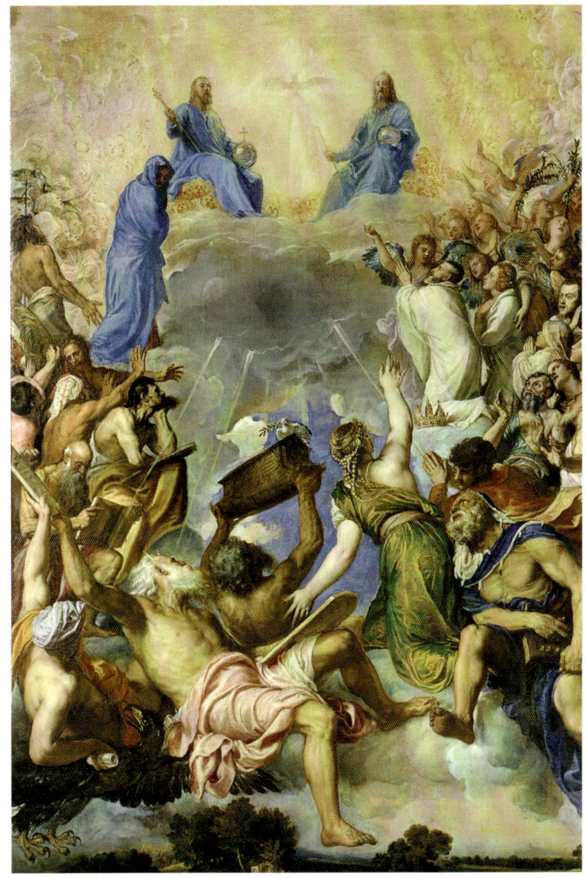

FIG. 41. Titian, *'La Gloria'*, 1553–1554. Madrid, Museo del Prado [P-432]

during the crucial moment of the Diet of Augsburg. It was around this same time that Titian painted the imposing equestrian portrait of *Charles V at Mühlberg* [FIG. 52] as well as several seated portraits, such as *Charles V Seated*, which is in Munich (Alte Pinakothek), and a double portrait with the Empress Isabel, known from the copy by Rubens (Madrid, Casa de Alba Foundation).[8] The Empress had died in 1539, but Titian had already painted her in 1543, taking the likeness from a minor portrait of her, but with changes directed by the Emperor.[9] Both Isabel and Charles were painted again by Titian in the early 1550s in *'La Gloria'* [FIG. 41], a very large canvas painted as an altarpiece for the Monastery of Yuste and subsequently taken to El Escorial in 1574. He portrayed the imperial couple together with other family members, draped in shrouds and praying to the Holy Trinity as part of the Celestial Court. With *'La Gloria'* we find

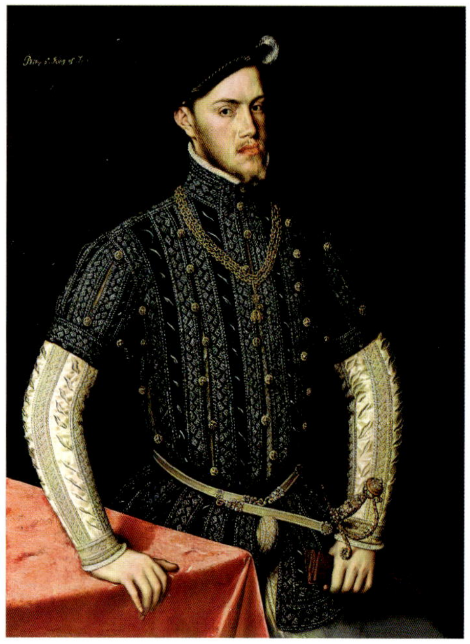

FIG. 42. Anthonis Mor, *Philip II*, *ca.* 1549–1550. Bilbao, Museo de Bellas Artes [92/253]

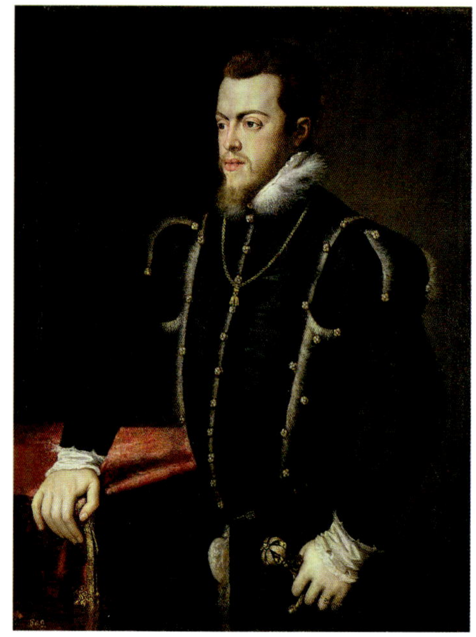

FIG. 43. Workshop of Titian, *Philip II in Black*, *ca.* 1551–1553, Madrid, Museo del Prado [P-452]

ourselves in front of an intriguing collective portrait, shaped by the spirit of the Counter-Reformation.[10] This work would later influence sepulchral portraiture, especially the sculptures of the Leoni, but also other portraits in which family members were shown in scenes from the stories of the saints, often lending their features to the sacred figures of the Scriptures and Christian hagiography.[11] It was a trend which, although far from being new,[12] Titian reinforced in this impressive canvas. The painting was to become a major reference point for the imagery of the Hapsburg dynasty.

Titian's association with the Hapsburg dynasty extended into the reign of Philip II. He painted a portrait of Philip around 1550 during the latter's visit through the heartlands of the imperial territories. We have a detailed chronicle of this journey which helps us to understand the importance of the period between 1549 and 1551 in the dynastic, political and artistic tutoring of the future King of Spain.[13] At the same time, another portraitist was making his mark on the Hapsburg dynasty. Anthonis Mor (1519–1576, known in Spain and Italy as Antonio Moro) was an artist who had been trained in the Netherlandish precision of his master, Jan van Scorel, but also had great admiration for Titian. In 1549 Mor became the painter of Cardinal Antoine Granvelle, a great art collector and a figure of considerable influence in the Spanish Court. Granvelle introduced Mor to the Emperor's sister, Mary of Hungary, ruler of the Netherlands, who – following in the footsteps of their aunt, Margaret – had a great interest in developing a dynastic record. Among her large collection of paintings she therefore held a gallery of portraits of the family, some of which were the very ones painted by Titian during the family gathering in Augsburg. Mary placed these in a special hall in her palace at Turnhout, together with other portraits of her relatives, many of them painted by Mor after 1549, when she had commissioned from him portraits of both herself and her sister Leonor.[14] Everything points to Mor having carried out these works under the influence of Titian's elegant models, though without losing his own identity as very much a Netherlandish painter. In his three-quarter-length portraits of Granvelle (Vienna, Kunsthistorisches Museum) and the Duke of Alba (New York, The Hispanic Society of America), the imposing physical presence of these sitters contrasts with a neutral background, and he endows them with a quiet dignity far removed from the rhetoric of the Netherlandish portraits of the previous generation.[15]

As can be seen in Mor's panel in the Museo de Bellas Artes in Bilbao [FIG. 42],[16] his portraits of Philip II dating from this time present a courtly image of the Prince, in the same way as does the *Philip II in Black* from Titian's workshop [FIG. 43].[17] In each of these portraits the sitter dresses sumptuously and wears the insignia of the Order of the Golden Fleece, the main identifying symbol of the family. Both Titian and Mor resolve the always problematic positioning of the hands by placing one on a nearby table and the other on or by the sword hilt. This compositional solution could not be more expressive, since it explicitly portrays the future ruler as ready to take charge of his military duties and the administrative tasks of his office. In both paintings, which are of very similar size,[18] the Prince is depicted in the manner recommended by Francisco de Holanda (1517–1584) in 1549 in the first treatise on portraiture in the Renaissance, *Do tirar polo natural*.[19] Holanda put forward a large number of recommendations which tied in neatly with the practice of court portraiture as it was developing at that time, beginning with the aristocractic and restrained nature of the genre. His observations in this respect were to be echoed in *Tesoro de la Lengua Castellana* (Madrid, 1611) by Covarrubias, who defined the portrait as 'the contrived likeness of any prominent person of high standing whose image should rightly be preserved for centuries to come'. Francisco de Holanda also recommended that the sitter should be shown in a three-quarter view, neither looking straight ahead nor appearing in profile. Furthermore, he held that illumination should be from the front, to prevent any shadows from interfering with proper contemplation of the sitter's features. The mouth should remain closed in order to avoid showing any teeth, and the hands should be low as a sign of the calmness of the subject. Though it is true that Titian, like Mor, seems to have been guided by Holanda's precepts (or rather, we should say that Holanda reflected current practice), the portrait by Mor proves to be a more incisive image of the young prince, with no concession towards 'idealising' the distinctive Hapsburg features by softening mouth and chin, the result being a likeness as magnificent as it is distant, as convention required.

It is interesting to see how both artists achieve the same facial typology of Philip II, possibly through the use of some *modellino* or *ricordo* that had particularly pleased him and would therefore have been used, with only slight variations, as the basis for a great many of the portraits of that decade. This practice standardised not only images of the Prince but also methods of working in the portraitists' workshops, allowing reproduction of the Sovereign's image without his having to pose on a regular basis. At the same time, in every portrait the sitter's approval of his facial features – the fundamental aspect of the work – was assured. The use of models also facilitated the production of later replicas and copies by both the master and his workshop.[20] Once the head, painted from life during a normally brief sitting,[21] was finished, completion of the portrait by the addition of the dress and the necessary paraphernalia was a simple exercise – and one that was repeated again and again by court painters over the years, as can be seen from the works of Sánchez Coello, Pantoja de la Cruz, Bartolomé González and Velázquez.

From 1550 Anthonis Mor travelled between several courts in Europe: Madrid, Valladolid, Lisbon, London and Brussels. This was an indication of the favourable reception his paintings received, and of his availability to serve the particular needs of the various courts. Mor is an early example of a portrait specialist or *retratador* (the term used at the time). Although the treatise writers considered the portrait to be an inferior genre, the portraitist actually played a very important role among the sovereign's painters. Sometimes, to be a portraitist was the essential requirement for entering the court, as was the case with the arrival from Seville of the young Velázquez. His skills as a painter of portraits allowed him to establish his position within the complex structure of competing interests among the court painters.

Through his travels Mor achieved further international recognition of the 'Hapsburg' type of portrait. In 1550, in Spain, he painted a portrait of Maximilian, husband of Mary of Austria, the daughter of Charles V. In the absence of the Emperor and his son Philip, Maximilian (who would become Emperor Maximilian II) and Mary were regents of Spain at this time. Mor painted full-length portraits of both of them, which would have an important influence on later works, for they came to be considered the model for the depiction of a Hapsburg ruler. The portrait of Maximilian [FIG. 44] is usually compared to that of Philip II by Titian [CAT. 7], painted during his second encounter with the Emperor in Augsburg in 1551. The similarities between these two portraits give an indication of the decisive influence that Titian had over the production of Mor – although in this particular instance Mor's portrait of Maximilian was painted a year earlier than Titian's of Philip II. They are both full-length life-size portraits, in which a similar pose is struck: the body turns slightly, with the weight on one leg while the other leg appears relaxed, slightly flexed, a *contrapposto* that elegantly enhances the manifest verticality of the subject. In Titian's portrait one hand holds the sword tightly, and the other rests on a helmet that sits on a table covered with a crimson cloth; from then onwards, this arrangement would be regarded as a codified expression of majesty and military power. The head is bathed in bright light and the eyes stand out impressively, lending the monarch a powerful presence.[22] The size of these paintings and the fact that the figures are in the foreground combine to give the illusion of the real presence of Philip II and Maximilian II. The portraits convey an image of containment and remoteness, as well as regalness.

The portrait of Philip II in a suit of armour marked an explicit return to the paternal model, recalling a full-length portrait of Charles V with half armour that was destroyed in a fire in the Palace of El Pardo in 1604; we know about this painting from copies by Juan Pantoja de la Cruz (1553–1608) [FIG. 45].[23] In fact, the radiograph of Titian's canvas [FIG. 46] shows that beneath the portrait of Philip II there is an image of the Emperor corresponding to the lost portrait, probably painted shortly before. It was common practice for the master to repeat his compositions, as Miguel Falomir has brilliantly shown in connection with Titian's replicas.[24] The image of the Crown Prince would be associated with the military semblance of his father, depicted in the classical tradition, even though such an image did not fit his hardly bellicose disposition. Only the table, larger in both breadth and height, gives us a clue as to the natural inclinations of the Prince: his interest in state papers.

When Philip II received Titian's portrait he appears not to have been pleased and is reported to have said laconically: 'It can be seen that he did it in a hurry, and were there more time I would make him do it again'.[25] This has been interpreted as an indication that he was as yet little aware of Titian's artistry, but the comments may have been influenced by recommendations from his aunt, Mary of Hungary, about the way to hang the portrait *Philip II in Black*. In her view, this work required appropriate lighting and had to be seen from afar, 'because the works by Titian were not always legible from close up'.[26]

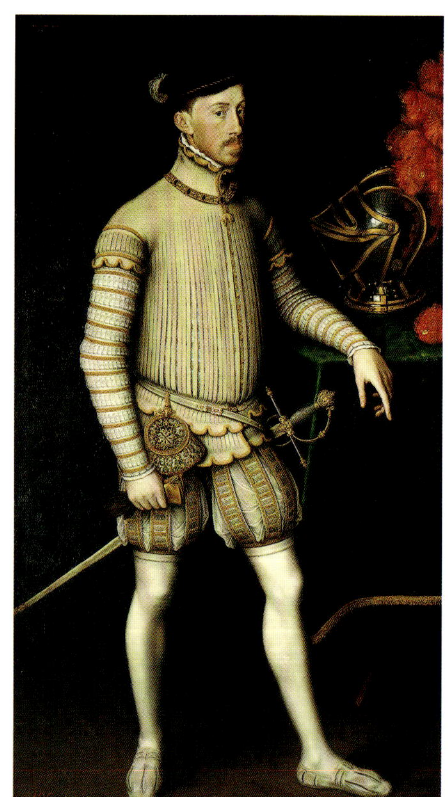

FIG. 44. Anthonis Mor, *Maximilian II*, 1550. Madrid, Museo del Prado [P-2111]

Mary agreed with her nephew's opinion of the artist as a painter of patches or blotches, and saw this style as not entirely adequate for works such as portraits, which she felt needed to be seen from close up. Their shared conception of Titian's painting was anchored in a vision that would prevail in Spanish writings of the seventeenth century, in which it was stated that 'with blotches he did admirable things, and the whole Venetian School followed this bizarre and daring manner with such licence that some paintings are barely recognisable from close up, although at a convenient distance one discovers with contentment the art of those who painted them'.[27]

Philip II soon came to understand the character of the great Venetian master's art, at the same time recognising that the subjects best suited to his warm, sumptuous and vibrant brushstrokes, brimming with intensity, were mythologies, sensuous nudes and landscapes, and the intensely felt religious themes that he painted at the end of his life.

In his portraits of the Hapsburgs, Titian had learnt from and revitalised the central European chivalrous model, and gave the features of Charles V such transcendence that they became the standard reference. This was an exercise that reconciled the faithfulness required of the genre with the majestic tone that was understood to be intrinsic to the sovereign and his family. Titian invested common elements such as chairs, drapes, columns, balustrades, tables or clocks, with dynastic associations and a timeless quality. Mor, however, responded more effectively to the tastes and needs of the future King, and made himself available to travel. Philip II preferred to leave the portraits to Mor, while to Titian he assigned the responsibility of history paintings, the foremost genre in the artistic hierarchy of the Renaissance. Thus, Anthonis Mor established the most convincing

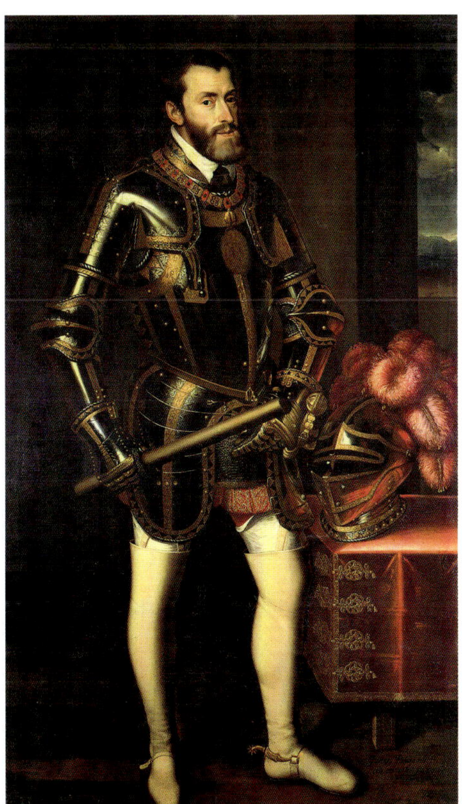

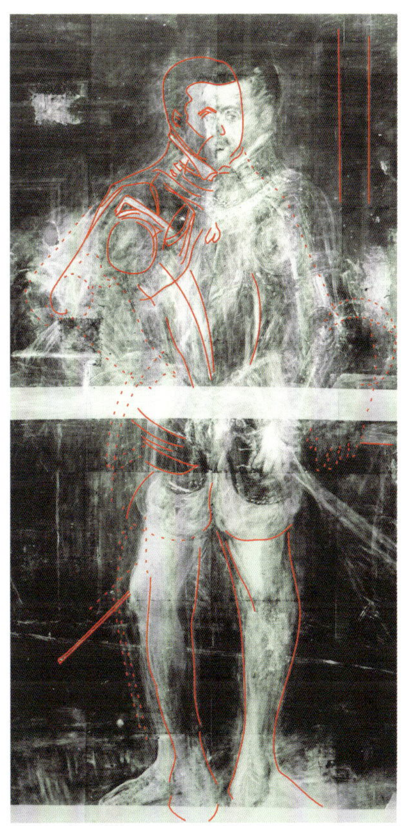

FIGS 45 and 46. Juan Pantoja de la Cruz after Titian, *Charles V in Armour*, 1605, Madrid, Museo del Prado [P-1033]; and radiograph of Titian's *Philip II* [CAT. 7]

pictorial models for the purposes of the Spanish monarchy, linked especially to the 'matrimonial imperialism' of the dynasty.[28] More distinct and descriptive brushstrokes and a greater interest in detailing facial features, as well as a distinctive chromatic restraint, allowed for a more intense illusion in representing the King; thus could the King be substituted by his own image. The notion of the King's presence was strongly linked to palace practices and the idea of the sacredness of the monarchy during the reign of Philip II. One historian has contrasted Philip II's 'counter-reformatory withdrawal' with the 'triumphant and *all'antica* world of the princes and generals of his father the Emperor'.[29]

The old principle *Regis imago Rex est* (The King's image is the King), of such importance for an 'absent King' such as Charles V, becomes even more relevant for a 'hidden King', as was the case with Philip II.[30] In the latter's images the heroic overtones of his father's portraits were replaced by the image of a more restrained and distant persona, although they were nevertheless still the expression of the dual nature of the King. Any image of the King had to show his appearance, by portraying his physical features and suggesting certain facets of character and psychology against a relevant regal backdrop, but the person of the King also represented a concept of the state, the dynasty and society itself – with all its hierarchy – and this too had to be conveyed in the portrait. This formula symbolised the idea of the two bodies of the King: 'Every Prince is made up of two Persons. One is Nature's work, with which he communicates with all other men. The other is, by grace of Fortune and favour of Heaven, made for government and for the protection of the public interest, and we will call it his public persona.' These are the words of Fadrique Furió Querol in 1559, establishing the theory of the two natures of the King, which was to be endorsed by later writers.[31] Thus the features of the King and his family should reflect the virtues which were considered typical of the dynasty, and which had been granted by divine design so that they would govern successfully: severity, gravity, remoteness and impassivity.

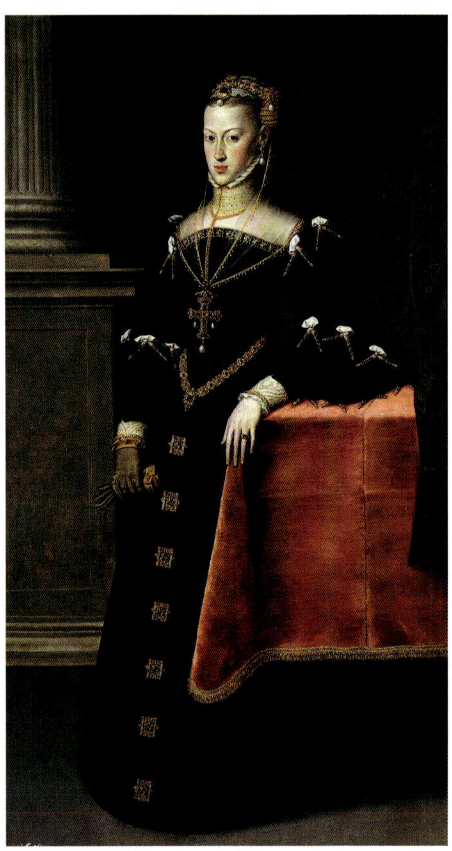

FIG. 47. Anthonis Mor, *The Empress Mary of Austria, Wife of Maximilian II*, 1551. Madrid, Museo del Prado [P-2110]

This concept of royalty, which conferred moral values upon the features of the monarch, also affected the women of the royal family, who were responsible for the continuation of the lineage and the strength of dynastic unions, and who from time to time acted as regents. In 1551 Anthonis Mor painted a portrait in Spain of the future Empress Mary of Austria [FIG. 47]. The canvas is signed and dated a year after the portrait of her husband. Despite the two portraits being of a different size,[32] it is thought that Mary's was considered a *pendant* of Maximilian's portrait, in what became a formula for marriage portraits for some time to come. The portraits are separate and yet complementary, so that they can be exhibited opposite each other. It is interesting to note that we have here one of the first examples of a full-length portrait of the women of the Hapsburg dynasty.[33] At the beginning of the 1550s the elements used to fashion the royal portrait – cold detachment and elegant restraint – are also present in the portraits of female sitters. The magnificence of the sitter is manifest in her attire: a black dress with *décolletage*, with rich jewels standing out on the fabric, testifying to her high rank. The table might be a reference to her position as ruler of Spain during those years, and was a novel element in a female portrait, which cannot be said of the column, already used by Titian in other family portraits.[34] The proximity and height of the table allows the left forearm to rest on it, a formula that again points to the role of the table as a symbol of the duties of state, as well as resolving the matter of where to place the hands. Mary holds an amber glove, an object of aristocratic distinction, which replaces the traditional items appearing in male portraits (swords, daggers, helmets, sallets, sceptres or batons).

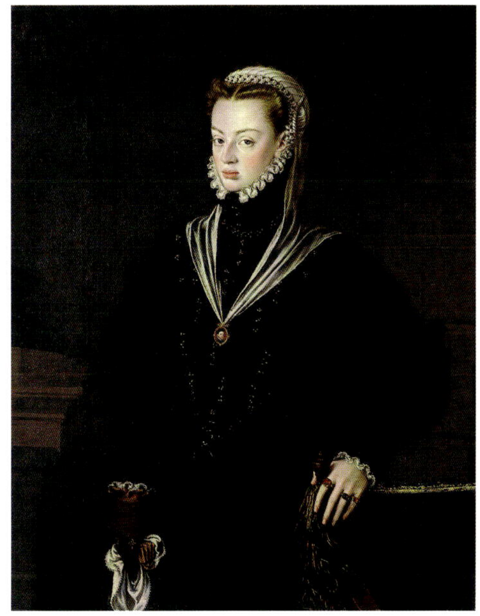

FIG. 48. Alonso Sánchez Coello, *Joanna of Portugal with a Cameo*, *ca.* 1557. Bilbao, Museo de Bellas Artes [90/15]

The female portrait of the dynasty would culminate with Anthonis Mor's 1559 portrait of Joanna of Portugal, sister of Mary and the King, and one of the most representative figures of the period. The influence of some of the most powerful images of the Hapsburg women was crystallised in this portrait. Joanna had been painted on several occasions throughout the 1550s by other portraitists, such as Cristóbal de Morales[35] from Portugal and Alonso Sánchez Coello from Valencia. The former had followed the Portuguese tradition in portraying the Princess accompanied by a small black page on whom she leans (Brussels, Musées Royaux des Beaux-Arts de Belgique), a compositional ploy charged with significance. The page would be replaced by a large dog in the portrait painted by Sánchez Coello (Vienna, Kunsthistorisches Museum), in a manner similar to the portraits of Charles V with a dog by Seisenegger and Titian. In another portrait of Joanna, Sánchez Coello represents her holding a miniature of Philip II, a sign of dependence, dynastic filiation and subordination to the King (Bilbao, Museo de Bellas Artes) [FIG. 48][36] which is seen in many female portraits. As in other works, Mor paints Joanna dressed in black as a widow, with her hair tied back and her head held high, emphasised by the large collar that was then the fashion in Spain. She holds a handkerchief and her right hand rests on a chair, a symbol of her high rank.[37] But beyond the conventions that all these portraits reflect, the work by Mor [CAT. 8] allows us to visualise Fray Juan de Carrillo's 1616 description of her as a woman in whom 'solemnity, maturity, severity and good sense' clearly demonstrated that she was 'the daughter of whom she was'.[38] Simple in composition, Mor's portrait summarises all the devices of the court portrait. The notion of majesty is conveyed by the very presence of the princess, a woman of a compellingly haughty expression with an inquisitorial gaze that seems to recognise, as if holding an audience, the demands of the viewer. This image is successful in conveying the same impression as the King's sister herself, who inspired 'respect and fear', just as her brother Philip II did.[39]

It is not surprising then that a monarchy which credited itself with sacred values and made a complex ritual of its appearance wanted to perpetuate its public image in its portraits, so that such paintings would inspire the same respect. The anthropologist Carmelo Lisón recently summarised the qualities that images of the King should embody: 'sacredness, a hieratic remoteness and the same splendour as their public appearances; that they required a response of reverence and veneration'.[40] On the value of the portraits as *substitutes*,[41] it is important to remember Pacheco's assertion that Philip II 'greatly honoured his ancestors, and he would remove his hat before their portraits'.[42] A century later, during the reign of Philip IV, in Juan Bautista Maíno's monumental canvas of 1635, *The Recapture of Bahía*, the soldiers who have been defeated by Spain kneel in front of a portrait of the monarch as if in the presence of the King himself [FIG. 49]. According to the play by Lope de Vega on which the work by Maíno is based, a conversation took place between Fadrique de Toledo, captain of the victorious Portuguese-Spanish army that had recaptured the stronghold, the defeated Dutch troops and the King, who was known throughout the extensive Spanish territories only by means of his portraits.[43]

Perhaps because of the devotion he felt towards his ancestors, and his conviction that he had to preserve their memory by exhibiting their portraits, Philip II followed the example of his aunt, Mary of Hungary, and planned to have in the Palace of El Pardo a gallery of portraits where images by Titian and Mor would hang side by side, reflecting the two portrait traditions of the reign.[44] Mor worked in the gallery after travelling to Spain in 1557 with the King, at a time when he seemed to have attached himself definitively to the Spanish Court. However, what supposedly could have been a brilliant career was cut short in 1560 when Mor had to return temporarily to Flanders because of problems, it seems, with the Inquisition.[45] Mor's departure favoured the gradual advancement of one of his pupils, the Spaniard Sánchez Coello.

Coello (*ca.* 1532–1588) was a painter who had been with Mor since the time of his association with Granvelle and Mary of Hungary in the Netherlands;[46] we have already considered his portrait of Joanna of Portugal in 1557. With both Joanna and Prince Carlos (1545–1568) Sánchez Coello established himself towards the middle of the 1550s, completing works of considerable artistic worth in complete harmony with the requirements of the rituals and etiquette of the Spanish Court. In the portraits of Don Carlos[47] he convincingly resolved the problem posed by the depiction of a person of high rank who was also mentally disturbed and deformed. His manner of dignifying the sitter followed the Renaissance conventions concerning the image that a ruler should convey.[48] In the example in the Prado [FIG. 50] there was also an allegorical reference in the sky, visible through the open window to the right of the sitter, in the form of Jupiter and an eagle bearing a column. This was appropriate iconography for the crown prince of Spain, but curiously it was later covered up for no obvious reason.[49] Generally, such allegorical references were not used in painted portraits, although they were found in books, medals, engravings or ephemeral architectural representations. The rare exceptions, such as the Allegory of *the Education of Philip II* by Justus Tiel (Madrid, Museo del Prado, P-1846) or the *Allegory: Birth of the Infante don Fernando, Son of Philip II* by Michele Parrasio (Madrid, Museo del Prado, P-479), only confirm the rule.

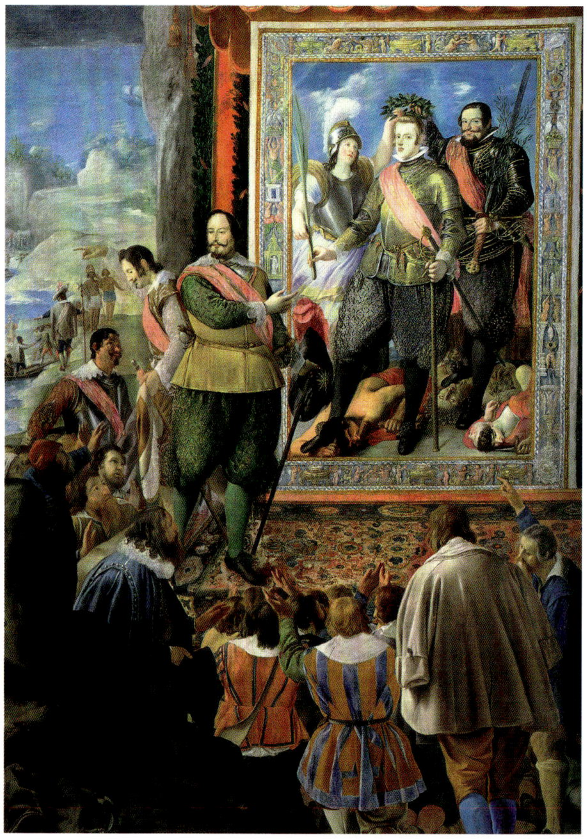

FIG. 49. Juan Bautista Maíno, *The Recapture of Bahía* (detail of the right-hand side of the painting), 1635. Madrid, Museo del Prado [P-885]

From what we know, Sánchez Coello adapted to the needs of Philip's court, establishing terms similar to those the sovereign maintained with other Spanish artists, such as Juan Fernández Navarrete, '*el Mudo*'. He gained Philip II's confidence by showing a docile versatility, with no aspirations other than to render his services to satisfy the King's requirements.

In the 1560s Sánchez Coello completed the Gallery of Portraits in El Pardo. This work included painting copies, restoring works and adapting paintings of diverse origin to formats that were more or less harmonised.[50] He also painted many portraits and replicas of portraits, some miniatures, and copies of works by other painters such as Mor[51] and Sofonisba Anguissola (1535–1625), a remarkable portraitist from Cremona who had joined the Spanish Court as lady-in-waiting to Queen Isabel de Valois.[52] We owe to her the delicate portraits of Isabel, dated 1561, in which the painter's portrayal of the Queen follows the traditions of the Spanish female portrait. However, these are less austere images, imbued with the sophistication and love of luxury of the French Queen.[53] During her reign other portraitists entered the scene. Some were directly commissioned by the court, for example Manuel Dionis, the Flemish painter Jorge de la Rúa or the Frenchman Esteban de Humotre.[54] Others became associated with a particular member of the court, as in the case of Cristóbal de Morales from Portugal, who painted portraits of Princess Joanna.[55] The Fleming Rolán de Moys (doc. 1571–1592), was a mediocre painter in the service of the Duke and Duchess of Villahermosa, in Aragón.[56]

After the death of Queen Isabel, Sánchez Coello played an even more prominent role. He was responsible for nearly all the portraits of the last Queen, Anne of Austria (1549–1580), who arrived in Spain in 1570 hoping to provide male heirs for the Spanish dynasty. His portraits of children stand out in his works from this date onwards. There were many such portraits, compared to the very few we have of Philip II, and only some of the latter can be attributed to Sánchez Coello with total certainty: the portrait of the King in armour that was paired with the portrait of Anne of Austria, both half-length, dating from around 1570–1571 (Glasgow, Pollok House), and *Philip II in Black* in the Palazzo Pitti [FIG. 51] in Florence, signed 1587.[57] If in the first case Sánchez Coello readapted the portrait that Anthonis Mor had painted in 1557 (Monastery of El Escorial), a work he knew well since he had to copy it in 1566 (Vienna, Kunsthistorisches Museum), the painting in Florence is one of the most significant court portraits of the late sixteenth century. The attire, the pose, the solemnity, the lack of attributes other than the Golden Fleece, and above all the spatial arrangement, anticipate the portraits of Philip IV that Velázquez would paint nearly three decades later.

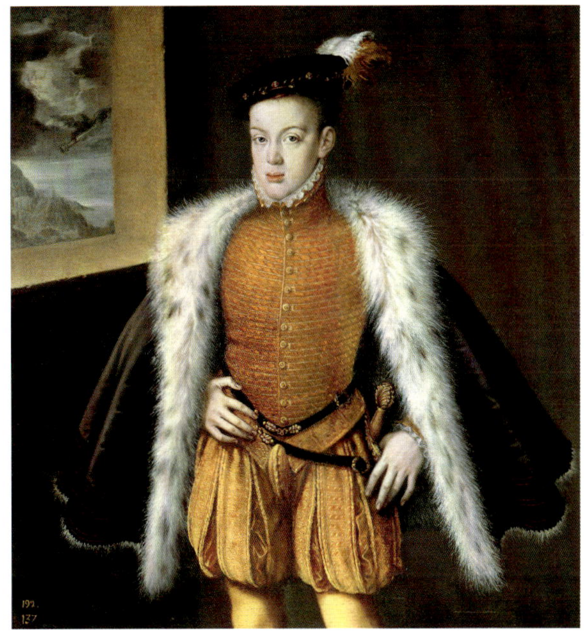

FIG. 50. Alonso Sánchez Coello, *Prince Don Carlos*, *ca.* 1557. Madrid, Museo del Prado [P-1136]

The portraits of royal children were meant to record the development of the younger members of the family, and were commissioned as much out of parental love and the affection of close relatives as because of the need to formalise future marriages. But whatever their purpose, such images went beyond the private sphere, not least because until recent years little or no privacy existed for sovereigns and their families. An interesting case is that of Isabel Clara Eugenia (1566–1633) and Catalina Micaela (1567–1597), daughters of Philip and Isabel de

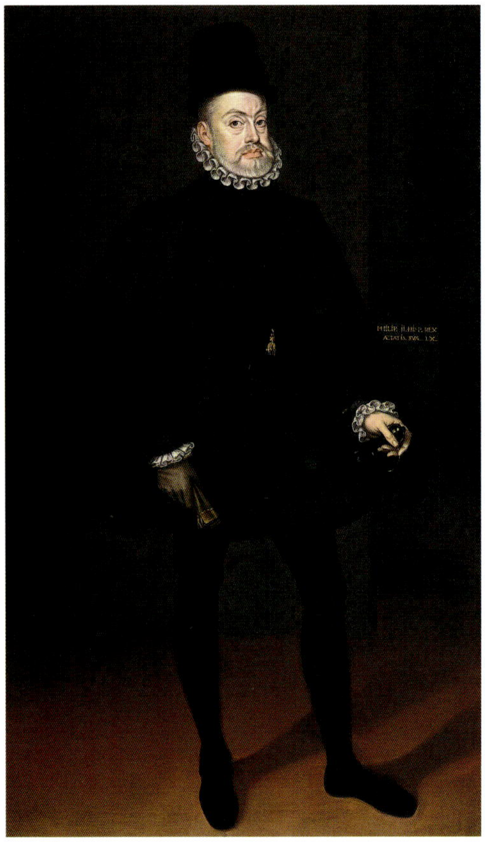

FIG. 51. Alonso Sánchez Coello, *Philip II in Black*, 1587. Florence, Palazzo Pitti [276]

Valois. Alonso Sánchez Coello painted several portraits of them [see CAT. 9].[58] In the three paintings of the two girls together, beyond the sitters' physical changes the image that is conveyed is very similar. They are both dressed as adults, their little bodies encased within the tight geometric shapes that were worn at the time. Not only the clothing of the two princesses but also their attitude conveys the severity, calmness and remoteness of their elders.

By the time of Sánchez Coello's death in 1588, the Spanish court portrait had reached its zenith. The conventions that were required to depict the King and his family were firmly established. The painters who succeeded Sánchez Coello watched over their legacy by honouring the past, but their interpretations were as unexceptional as the artistic skill of most of them. They repeated the existing models assiduously, completely assimilating them so that their individual personalities became blurred. The most outstanding among them was Juan Pantoja de la Cruz (*ca.* 1553–1608), who collaborated with Sánchez Coello in his final years and had had previous training in other European courts, where the example of Mor had exerted a profound influence. He followed closely in the footsteps of Sánchez Coello, but in his best works Pantoja introduced an impressive combination of sophistication and geometric abstraction, achieved by means of powerful contrasts of light and shadow.[59] Pantoja began to paint for the Court in the mid-1580s, but it was not until 1596 that he was appointed Court Painter. Just before 1594 he must have painted the portrait of Philip II 'wearing a cape, a hat and black boots of leather, with a golden fleece around his neck' [CAT. 10],[60] a work that includes the essential elements of Philip's portraits: the austere chair, the column and the drapes, against which the figure of the monarch stands out, more grave and solemn than ever. It was painted towards the end of the reign for the library of the Royal Monastery of El Escorial as part of a small family series, with the portraits of the Emperor, Philip III and Philip IV as a child. This portrait has been considered one of those which best express the idea of Spanish majesty, based on the remoteness of the monarch.[61] When Pantoja died in 1608, he left behind him a workshop full of his pupils, which, with its commissions from the Hapsburg dynasty, must have been a prosperous concern. Not only had its works been popular in court collections at the end of the sixteenth century but they remained so during the whole of the seventeenth, and many were exported.[62]

Another of the King's painters was Bartolomé González (*ca.* 1583–1627), who trained by making copies of earlier portraits, including replicas on panel of heads by Mor.[63] He worked in Pantoja's workshop, and in 1617 was appointed Painter to the King, after several years of making portraits of Philip III and Queen Margarita, and especially of her numerous relatives. Like Sánchez Coello and Pantoja, he established a small 'industry' of portrait-making thanks to his court position.[64] Other artists, such as Santiago Morán (d. 1626), Francisco López and Rodrigo de Villandrando (*ca.* 1588–1622), also became the makers of royal images. In such a lacklustre environment one can understand the success of Diego Velázquez (1599–1660).

In 1623 Velázquez established himself in Court after a failed first attempt the previous year. Philip IV had ascended to the throne two years earlier and, as a young man of intelligence and artistic sensitivity, he immediately recognised Velázquez's merits. In fact, after seeing a bust portrait of himself that Velázquez had sketched from life, he granted him the exclusive right to depict his image, an honour that would endure for nearly four decades, until the painter's death.[65] Philip IV would enable Velázquez to become the painter *par excellence* in the Kingdom and allow him to develop an artistic career that was to be very different from that of other Spanish painters. Velázquez used this advantageous position to climb gradually in the Spanish court. As a result he was to have long and extensive access to the royal art collections. This, together with his two trips to Italy, were determining factors in his development as an artist.

When he first entered the Court, Velázquez adopted the portrait tradition that had been consolidated under Philip II. He followed the established convention in portraying the King, although he introduced, without breaking the rules, new possibilities for their interpretation. In the first portraits he painted of Philip IV [CAT. 11], the image is similar to the portrait of Philip II by Sánchez Coello from half a century earlier.[66] The King, diffident and remote, dressed in black like his grandfather, comes across as an immature and inexpressive young man Having mythologised the reign of Philip II, he aspired to emulate him personally and in the way he governed. The *Philip IV* in the Prado was later modified and repainted by Velázquez, as was to be the case with many of his canvases. But in this case he trimmed the span of the cloak enveloping the King, changed the position of the legs and softened the jawline. The reasons for these changes are not clear and have provoked some debate as to the most likely date of the work or the relationship between this painting and other existing versions. However, in these various portraits of Philip IV, as in the portrait of his brother, *The Infante Don Carlos* (Madrid, Museo del Prado, P-1188), Velázquez introduced subtle spatial differences compared with the work by Sánchez Coello, establishing a new balance between the sitter and the surrounding space. The sitter appears to rest more lightly on the floor, the background shifts towards a pearly grey tonality, and he paints with progressively richer and more pictorial brushstrokes. This process became more marked after his return to Spain in 1631, when Velázquez broadened his palette, moving away from the blacks, greys and browns of the 1620s to achieve surprising artistic results. This can be seen in *Philip IV of Spain in Brown and Silver* (London, The National Gallery) [FIG. 74], a portrait in which he admirably maintains all the compositional formalities of the Spanish court portrait, yet invigorates it by means of a very effective and vivid pictorial technique.[67]

In the 1630s, Velázquez together with Rubens, the European painter and courtier *par excellence* and a personal model for the Spaniard after their encounter in Madrid in 1628, would be the protagonists of the most outstanding artistic projects of the reign: the Salón de Reinos and the Torre de la Parada.[68] The Salón (Hall of Realms) in the Buen Retiro Palace was decorated with twelve large canvases of battles depicting the triumphs of the Spanish monarchy. The continuation of the dynasty was affirmed in a series of equestrian portraits of Philip IV and his wife Queen Isabel of Bourbon, the parents of the monarch, Philip III and Margarita of Austria, and the Crown Prince Baltasar Carlos. The vision of the sovereign on horseback was a prestigious image that followed a long tradition and was highly effective in conveying the idea of power and royalty.[69] The Spanish collections included one of the foremost and influential examples of the genre: *Charles V at Mühlberg* by Titian [FIG. 52], a work that was full of historical resonance for the Hapsburgs. In 1626 Velázquez had had the chance to paint an equestrian portrait of the King. This lost work was paired with Titian's canvas but did not arouse much enthusiasm, and it was replaced two years later by another equestrian portrait by Rubens, known from a copy since the original was destroyed in the Alcázar fire of 1734.[70] For the Salón de Reinos,

Velázquez had a new opportunity to paint an equestrian portrait of the monarch. In his *Philip IV on Horseback* [CAT. 47] he preferred to distance himself from the grand allegorical tone of Rubens and return fundamentally to Titian's model, both in the image of serene and melancholy majesty that the portrait projects as well as in the role played by the 'plein air' landscape, which becomes much more than a mere backdrop. In this painting the landscape is an enveloping element,[71] which goes well beyond the classicist landscapes the painter would have seen during his first visit to Rome, several examples of which were sent from Italy for the decoration of the Buen Retiro Palace.[72] The view of the mountains outside Madrid, which the painter could admire from the old Alcázar, reappears in *The Prince Baltasar Carlos* (Madrid, Museo del Prado, P-1180), a delightful portrait bathed in light, providing a fully convincing rendition of the outdoors and perfectly combining the required formality and the youthful freshness. He does the same again in the portraits he paints of the King, the Cardinal *Infante* and Prince Baltasar Carlos as hunters,[73] which were meant for the Torre de la Parada, a hunting lodge that no longer exists. Hunting was, of course, considered a fitting activity for the nobility. In these canvases the Sevillian painter takes into the open air the kind of courtly image that Seisenegger had created of Charles V in 1532. But he emphasises the natural elegance of Titian's version and provides novel images of the King and his family that are full of life. The dogs accompanying each figure are not there simply to provide balance to the composition; they are portraits in themselves, a mastiff and a hound in the first two paintings, and setter and a greyhound in the portrait of Baltasar Carlos.[74]

In 1640 problems arose both for Spain and for Philip IV. After Portugal regained its independence from Spain, there were revolts in Catalonia and Naples; Olivares ceased to be the King's *valido*, and both Queen Isabel of Bourbon and Prince Baltasar Carlos died. In 1649 the King remarried; this time his bride was his niece, Mariana of Austria. This gave rise to a wave of portraits of the new Queen and the children of the royal marriage. The first portrait of the Queen by Velázquez was made when the painter returned from his second journey to Italy, which lasted from the end of 1648 until June 1651. In that canvas, which is today in the Prado [CAT. 13], the then adolescent Mariana (1634–1696) was convalescing after the birth of Margarita. At first glance we are confronted with a portrait of the Queen along the lines of the Philippine tradition, displaying the statue-like impassivity that court protocol demanded.[75] However, the serious, circumspect and not very graceful face of the young Queen is offset by the pictorial breadth of the elements surrounding it, especially the dress and the hairstyle. Formally and chromatically the portrait is both showy and harmonious. Velázquez, the painter of admirable heads, prefers this time to 'dignify' the Queen by investing her features with the splendid beauty of his art. As Professor Julián Gállego states: 'While retaining the traditional format of the Hapsburg portrait, Velázquez, with his customary discretion, is demolishing its basic principles'.[76]

As with Alonso Sánchez Coello a century earlier, Velázquez's portraits of the Infantes were an expression of parental love. At the same time, they were useful instruments in the arrangement of marriage unions. Velázquez gave this particular variant of the court portrait a remarkable treatment. In the many portraits of Baltasar Carlos in the 1630s, which was an optimistic period in the life of the King and, naturally, the court itself, the artist maintained the fiction of the 'child adult' that had been established by Sánchez Coello, giving the boy the attire, pose and gravity that majesty demanded. We can always find Velázquez, however, subtly subverting established convention, as in the curious portrait of *Baltasar Carlos with a Dwarf* (Boston, Museum of Fine Arts), where the dwarf acquires an unusual prominence, anticipating the personal vision that Velázquez would convey to his later portraits of dwarfs and buffoons. Twenty years after these portraits of Baltasar Carlos, the feeling in the Alcázar was very different. The painting of *Prince*

FIG. 52. Titian, *Charles V at Mühlberg*, 1548.
Madrid, Museo del Prado [P-410]

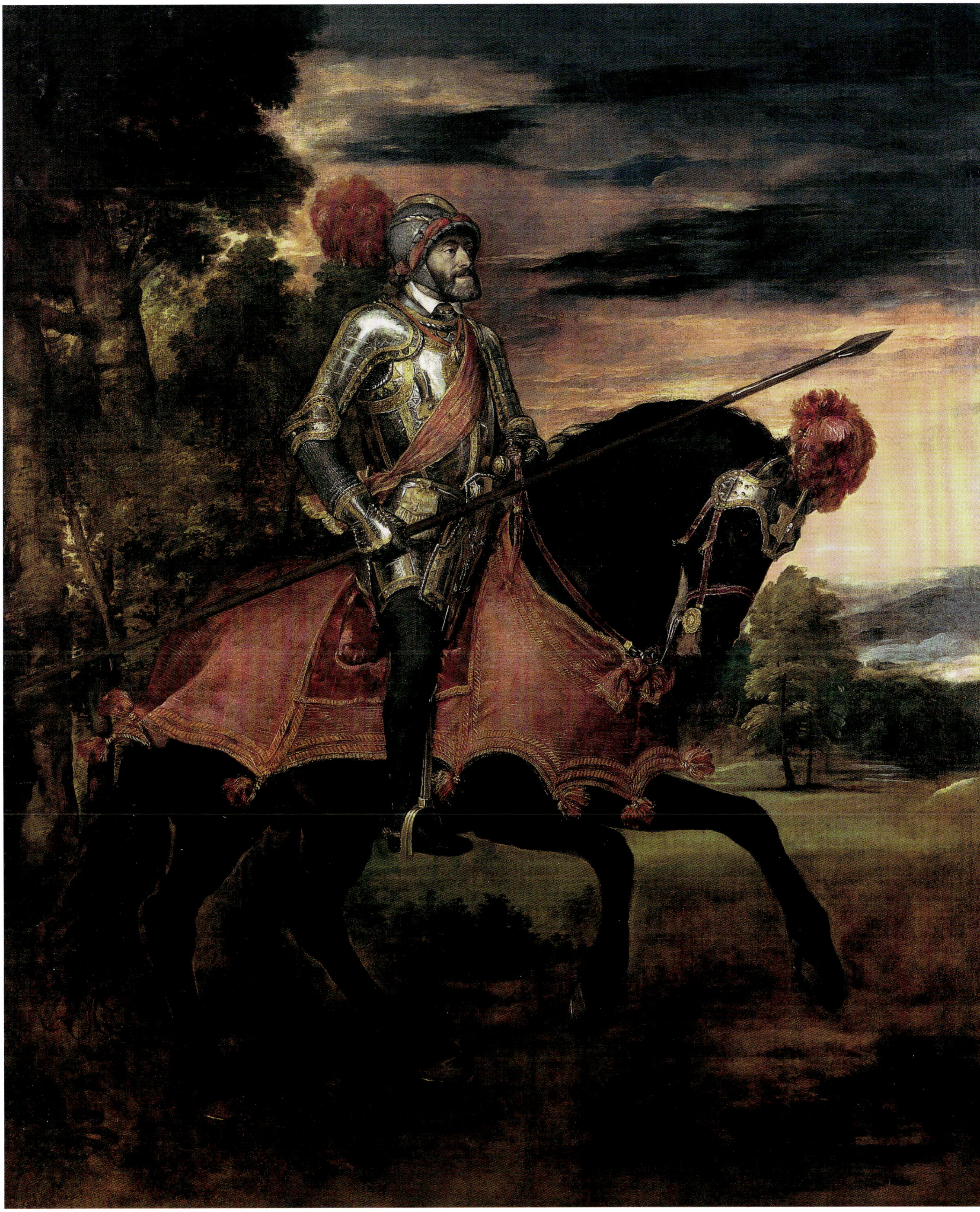

Felipe Próspero (1657–1661) in Vienna (Kunsthistorisches Museum) [CAT. 54] is that of a two-year-old child who is full of dignity despite his frail health. Perhaps that is the reason why the painter portrays him without a sword, or armour, or a nearby table that might anticipate his future as a ruler. The portrait of Felipe Próspero is very similar to the sweet and delicate image of his sister Margarita, even in the manner of leaning on the nearby armchair, and in the childish attire covered with charms and amulets to dispel evil, which are far removed from the portraits of the time and recall the images of the children of Philip III and Margarita of Austria [CAT. 14].[77] The hunting dog that slept confidently beside Baltasar Carlos as a hunter has been replaced by a lapdog sitting on a nearby chair and looking mournfully at the spectator. Among his portraits of children, Velázquez paid most attention to the Infanta Margarita, since her grandfather, Emperor Ferdinand III, requested images of the child. Between 1654 and 1659 Philip IV sent three portraits so that the Austrian Hapsburgs could have a record of her development. The purpose of these images went beyond merely satisfying family interest, since she was promised in marriage to the future Emperor Leopold. In these paintings one can see the increasing freedom with which Velázquez approached the traditional portrait, apparent not only in the artistic qualities of each portrait but also in his special appreciation of the sitter's character. Velázquez combined a sense of dynastic dignity with the particular personality of the Princess, and this combination can be seen in the late bust portraits of Philip IV, painted at a time charged with uncertainty. The painting in the Prado [CAT. 12] belongs to the typology of the bust portrait that developed in Spain from the second half of the sixteenth century. These are simple images, without any context beyond the black attire and the white collar; not even the Golden Fleece, the quintessential identifying mark of the Spanish noble that appears in the painting in London (The National Gallery, NG 745). It may be that what we have here is one of those *modelli* used both by the artist and by his assistants for the purposes of painting official portraits. These images, heavy with pictorial wisdom and emotional depth, are clearly related to the portraits of noblemen that El Greco had painted some decades earlier [CATS 15 and 18]. Velázquez did, of course, own portraits painted by the Cretan artist, and he kept them in the rooms he occupied in the Cuarto del Príncipe in the Royal Palace.[78] The King's countenance, devoid of anything that could betray his status, had become the symbol itself of Royal Majesty, the perfect synthesis to which the Spanish court portrait had aspired ever since Titian subtly transformed the features of Emperor Charles V. In his bust portrait of Philip IV, Velázquez shares those same Titianesque aspirations, but at the same time shows a stooping, mortal man – the King as presented to us by the anthropologist Lisón:

> The King (that very specific person, barely perceptible under his all-encompassing symbolic mantle) replicates the King himself; he is a mimesis of the King. The King is king in his own image.[79]

NOTES

1 Wethey 1971, pp. 18–22; Eisler 1981, Checa 1987a, pp. 40–45; Mancini 2000, pp. 221–34.

2 For the creation of the image of Charles V, see Checa 1987a. As well as other depictions in engravings, medals, etc., there is an analysis of those painters who, within the Netherlandish context, painted the King from his childhood, from the *Diptych of the Children of Joanna the Mad of Castile and Philip the Handsome of Austria*, by an anonymous artist dating from 1507 (formerly in Museo de Santa Cruz, Toledo), to the group portrait of Bernard Strigel (Vienna, Kunsthistorisches Museum), and the bust portraits of Bernard Van Orley (Edinburgh, National Gallery of Scotland, and Budapest, Szépmüvészeti Múzeum).

3 Inventory of El Pardo, 1614–1617, in Wethey 1971, p. 192.

4 Concerning the tradition of the Germanic portrait painting and the full-length portrait of the Emperor by Seisenegger, see Kusche 2003, pp. 29–38.

5 Matthews 2001, pp. 86–90; Falomir 2003, cat. 18.

6 Carlo Ridolfi referred to the 'maestà leggiadra' emanating from the Emperor in the portraits by Titian, see Manzini 2000, p. 221. For his part, Aretino said that in Titian's portrait, Philip II appeared 'in gesto bel di maestà reale'. Aretino, *Lettere*, 1957 edn, II, p. 277, quoted by Wethey 1971, p. 42.

7 Checa 1987a, pp. 44–45. Concerning the state portraits, see Jenkins 1977.

8 Titian and his workshop painted two further seated portraits of Philip II in 1551 (Cincinnati Art Museum and private collection, Geneva). This iconocraphic model of the ruler, showing the King as the wise dispenser of justice was hardly employed at the Spanish Court. One of the few exceptions is the *Philip III* by Bartolomé González, which the Prado has in the Spanish Embassy in London (P-2918).

9 On the portraits of Isabel of Portugal, see Falomir 1998, pp. 203 and 204.

10 Checa 1992, quoting Harbison 1976, pp. 244–46.

11 García Sanz and Ruiz Gómez 2000, with bibliography on the subject.

12 Possibly the most common antecedent is *The Virgin of the Reyes Católicos*, anon. fifteenth-century Spanish panel (Madrid, Museo del Prado, P-1260), in which the maternal grandparents of Charles V also appear kneeling in front of the Virgin Mary, though it is still an image in which the King and Queen are represented as donors in a religious tableau. A portrait 'a lo divino' of Charles V as Saint Sebastian, in a painting in a private collection in Madrid, was included in the exh. cat. of *The Emperor's Lineage* (no. 3.2), and reflects more adequately a formula that would have considerable influence during the reign of Philip III.

13 See the Chronicle of J. C. Calvete de Estrella 1552, quoted in the edition of the Sociedad de Bibliófilos Españoles, Santander 1930. On the importance of that journey for his artistic training, see Checa 1992.

14 The two portraits are lost; we know the portrait of Leonor from a copy that is kept in the Monastery of Las Descalzas Reales in Madrid. After those portraits, around 1554 Maria commissioned from Mor the portrait of her niece, Cristina of Denmark. See Kusche 2002, pp. 77 and 78.

15 On Mor, see Hymans 1910; Marlier 1934; Frerichs 1947 and Woodall 1990b.

16 Woodall (1992) thinks that the work was carried out between April 1549 and May 1550.

17 This canvas was received by don Felipe in 1553, and was considered to be an original by Titian. Also from the workshop, but of a somewhat later date (towards 1554) are the full-length canvases of Philip II, with a version in Naples (Capodimonte, Gallerie Nazionali) and another in Florence (Palazzo Pitti).

18 The painting by Mor is 107.5 x 83.5 cm, and that by Titian is 103 x 82 cm.

19 Edition of José da Felicidade Alves 1984. Translated into Castilian by Manuel Denis (in 1563), Madrid, 1921. On Holanda, see J. B. Bury 1989, pp. 87–103.

20 This facial typology was repeated, with very few variations, by Titian and his workshop. Concerning Mor, the existence of some paintings of the monarch's head, without any background, on a panel and of similar dimensions, suggests that they were used to produce series of images: Madrid, Museo del Prado, P-2118 (41 x 31 cm) and Muzeul National de Arta al Romanei of Bucharest (41.5 x 33 cm). These examples could be either preparatory works or simple models to be repeated at a later stage. A similar case is the splendid panel, attributed to Lucas de Heere (Gante, 1534–1584), also in the Prado, although of a later date judging by the age of the model (*ca.* 1553).

21 Pacheco mentions that the time required for Sánchez Coello to make a sketch of a head did not exceed three hours, and it was advisable to do this work during the morning, with the light from the north (quoted by Serrera 1990, p. 61). Pacheco also tells us that Velázquez needed a day for the first portrait of Philip IV, probably the head. Van der Hamen took about 'half an hour or little more' to paint the head of Cardinal Barberini (quoted by Harris 1970, p. 364; Brown 1986, p. 47).

22 Campbell 1990, p. 238.

23 The full-length portrait of Charles V with half armour, baton and helmet had the lower half cut off when it became part of the Gallery of Portraits in the Palace of El Pardo. The remaining upper section was kept and inventoried at the death of Philip II in the 'Pieça tercera de la Casa del Tesoro'. Sánchez Cantón (ed.) 1959, p. 248. See also Falomir 1998, p. 222.

24 Falomir 2003, pp. 77–91.

25 Cloulas, 'Documents concernant Titien. Les premiers portraits

d'apparat', *Mélanges de la Casa de Velázquez*, III, 1967, p. 213. Quoted by Wethey 1971, no. 78.

26 Fletcher 2003, p. 63. The portrait was sent from Brussels to London so that Mary Tudor would see what her future husband looked like. A workshop version of this work is in the Museo del Prado (P-452). The text of the letter is quoted in French by Campbell 1990, no. 129.

27 Carducho 1633, p. 35.

28 The expression is found in Parker 1999, pp. 26 and 27. Concerning the use and functions of the court portrait during the reign of Philip II, see Falomir 1999 and 1998.

29 Checa 1998, p. 36.

30 On the concealment of Philip II and the manner in which he showed himself publicly, see Bouza 1994b.

31 Furió Querol Henry Méchoulan (ed.) 1993, p. 5. See also Kantorowicz 1985 and Lisón 1992, especially pp. 182–86.

32 Maximilian II's is 148 x 100 cm, and Mary's, 181 x 90 cm.

33 Campbell states that the full-length standing female portrait derives from a lost original by Titian which is known from a mediocre copy in Innsbruck (Ambras Castle). It would appear to have been a full-length portrait of the seated Empress, with roses, also lost but known from an engraving by Pieter de Jode (Madrid, Real Academia Española) (Campbell 1990, p. 219, no. 242). However, the portrait at Innsbruck could be a reworking of the bronze sculpture by Leoni, finished in 1564 (Madrid, Museo del Prado, E-274), inspired by Titian's portrait but also by the sepulchral sculptures of Maximilian I in Innsbruck.

34 As in the half-length portrait of Mary of Hungary (*ca.* 1548), when she ruled as regent, and in the portrait of Philip II in armour. The portrait of Mary of Hungary is known from workshop copies. The original was lost but the copy in the Musée des Arts Décoratifs in Paris is considered the closest to it. Earlier, Titian had included a column in the *Portrait of Giacomo Doria*, *ca.* 1533–1535 (Oxford, Ashmolean Museum). The column was a recurrent symbolic element, a reference to Hercules, with whom the Hapsburg dynasty were identified. For the symbolism of this element, see Rosenthal 1971 and Mancini 2000.

35 Jordan 1994, pp. 31–47.

36 According to Maria Kusche, the paintings of Joanna are the work of the Flemish painter established in Aragón under the patronage of the Duke of Villahermosa, Rolan de Moys. See especially Kusche 2003.

37 On this element of representation which Mor introduced to Hapsburg portraiture, see Gállego 1984, pp. 226 and 227.

38 Carrillo 1616, folios 4 and 13.

39 On Philip II's appearance and the emotions this aroused, see Bouza 1994b, pp. 48 and 49.

40 Lisón 1992, p. 183.

41 The substitutive character of portraits is frequently referred to in the plays of the period; see examples in Portús 2000, p. 29.

42 Pacheco 1599, p. 302, quoted by Serrera 1990, p. 44.

43 The play by Lope de Vega was *El Brasil restituido*. See Brown and Elliott 1981, pp. 195–98. Gállego points out other examples in which a portrait replaces the subject being portrayed: 'We know that for the celebration of the capture of Lérida by this Monarch, the portrait made of him by Velázquez (the so-called 'Fraga' portrait) was placed in the church of San Martín, in Madrid, during the Te Deum', Gállego 1984, p. 218.

44 Kusche 1991, pp. 1–22 and Kusche 2003, pp. 161–78. See also Woodall 1995, pp. 53–103.

45 In 1563 he was still receiving a salary, and Granvelle wrote to the King to ask about his return to Spain but the King considered that this was inappropriate. Kusche, Archivo General de Simancas (CM, 1ª época, leg. 1353, primer tercio; leg. CM, 1ª época, leg. 1388). Quoted by Kusche 2003, p. 163, note 374.

46 On Sánchez Coello, see the exh. cat. on the painter, 1990, Museo del Prado, and the work by Maria Kusche 2003, which includes the most recent bibliography.

47 Versions in Madrid (Museo del Prado, *ca.* 1559) and Vienna (Kunsthistorisches Museum, 1564).

48 *Dissimulatio*, combining *imitatio* and *decorum*, is discussed by Falomir 1998, pp. 210 and 211. Among quotes from classical times on the subject are Pliny the Elder, *Historia Naturalis*, lib. XXXV, 36.90, and Quintilian, *Institutio Oratoria*, book II, chapter XIV. On the XVI, Leon B. Alberti, De pictura II, 40.

49 This part of the painting was uncovered when the canvas was restored for an exhibition on Alonso Sánchez Coello, in 1990. In the inventories of the Alcázar (1666) there is no reference to the window, probably because by then it had already been covered. Serrera 1990 relates this iconography of the painting of Don Carlos to the decorative elements of the sepulchral monument of Philip II that was erected in 1598 in the Cathedral of Seville, pp. 42 and 43.

50 At this time, Titian's portrait of Charles V in armour was reduced to three-quarter length.

51 In 1566 he copied Mor's the portrait of Philip II in armour (Vienna, Kunsthistorisches Museum), the original of which had been painted in 1557 to commemorate the battle of Saint Quentin (Monastery of San Lorenzo de El Escorial), the only battle in which the King was directly involved.

52 The post allowed her to be close to the royal family, and perhaps because of this she was able to introduce certain variations to the formalities imposed on Spanish portraiture, such as a greater vivacity in the sitter and more intimate spaces, enveloped by a golden light and soft outlines. On the painter, see Ferino-Pagden and Kusche 1995 and Kusche 2003.

53 The originals and replicas by the painter herself have been lost; we have later copies. There is a copy attributed to Rubens of the portrait of Isabel with a sable in her hand (Toledo, private collection) and a three-quarter version by Juan Pantoja de la Cruz (Madrid, Museo del Prado, P-1030). Of the portrait of the Queen leaning on a column and holding a miniature of Philip II, the Prado keeps another copy attributed to Pantoja (P-1031).

54 Amezúa 1949, I, p. 265. There is documentary information on the three painters: Dionis painted a portrait of the King; payments for several Jorge de la Rúa portraits are recorded, although the only one that can be surely said to be his is the portrait of Isabel of France (Madrid, Monastery of Las Descalzas Reales), which was painted in France in 1573 following the models by Clouet, as can be seen by comparing it with the *Charles IX* (of France) of 1566 (Vienna, Kunsthistorisches Museum). As for Humotre, the French portraitist, he was 'granted the grace of 200 escudos so that he would return to France', on 23 April 1565.

55 On Cristóbal de Morales, see Jordan 1994.

56 Morte 1999, pp. 445–68, and Kusche 2003, pp. 99–124; the latter attributes many portraits of Joanna of Portugal to him.

57 Mulcahy 1996, pp. 517–21.

58 Madrid, Monastery of Las Descalzas Reales, in 1568; London, Buckingham Palace, a portrait of 1571; Madrid, Museo del Prado, canvas of 1575 [CAT. 9].

59 The pair of portraits of Philip III and Margarita of Austria, in the Museo del Prado (P-2562 and P-2563, respectively), were indicative of the painter's style. Pantoja's production concentrated mainly on the King and Queen, their children and devotional portraits with the inclusion of members of Queen Margarita's family. See Marías 1997b, with a bibliography on the painter, which includes the contributions of Maria Kusche.

60 Asiento de la Entrega 1597, fol. 46c.

61 See García-Frías 2001, pp. 407 and 408, which provides a bibliography on this, including the views of Maria Kusche, who considers that the painter of this work must have been Alonso Sánchez Coello. She also maintains this view in her most recent work, Kusche 2003, pp. 473–82.

62 On the distribution of these portraits outside the palace and on the 'other' painters whose production generated this, see Varela 2000.

63 The panel *Caballero de la Orden de Santiago* in the Museo del Prado (P-1143) is attributed to González and is a copy from an original by Mor which is in Budapest, in the Szépmüvészeti Múzeum (P-2532). The sketches of heads of Philip II, copying those by Mor, which are in the museum in Budapest and the Museo del Prado (P-2118), seem to be by the same painter.

64 Cherry 1993, p. 4.

65 On the introduction of Velázquez to the court and the role played by the Count-Duke of Olivares and other courtiers such as Juan de Fonseca or Gaspar de Bracamonte, see López Rey 1999, p. 48.

66 Versions in the Palazzo Pitti in Florence, and in the Museo del Prado (P-6181) (probably a workshop production), deposited in the Spanish Embassy in Paris.

67 Brown 1986, pp. 85–88.

68 On the Salón de Reinos, see Brown and Elliot 1981, pp. 149–202. On the Torre de la Parada, see Mena 2000 and Cruz Valdovinos 1999, pp. 141–67.

69 On the subject of equestrian portraits in the Early Modern Period, see Liedtke 1984.

70 The copy is in the Galleria degli Uffizi, Florence.

71 Gállego 1990, no. 38.

72 There is a good analysis of the painting in Brown 1999, no. 7.

73 They are all in the Museo del Prado (P-1184, P-1186 and P-1189).

74 Gállego, 1990, nos. 43–45.

75 On the statuesque poses of Philip IV and Mariana of Austria, see Gállego 1987, p. 231.

76 Gállego 1990, no. 71.

77 Other examples are portraits of *Ana Mauricia* by Juan Pantoja de la Cruz (Madrid, Monastery of the Descalzas Reales, and Vienna, Kunsthistorisches Museum) and of the *Infanta Margarita Francisca* by Santiago Morán (Madrid, Museo del Prado, P-1282, deposited in the Pontevedra Museum). See Marías 1997, pp. 106 and 112–16, and García Sanz and Ruiz Gómez 2000, p. 146.

78 On this subject, see Álvarez Lopera 2003, pp. 175–215; and the same author's contribution to this catalogue.

79 Lisón 1992, p. 184.

CAT. 7. Titian. *Philip II*, 1551. Madrid, Museo del Prado [P-411]

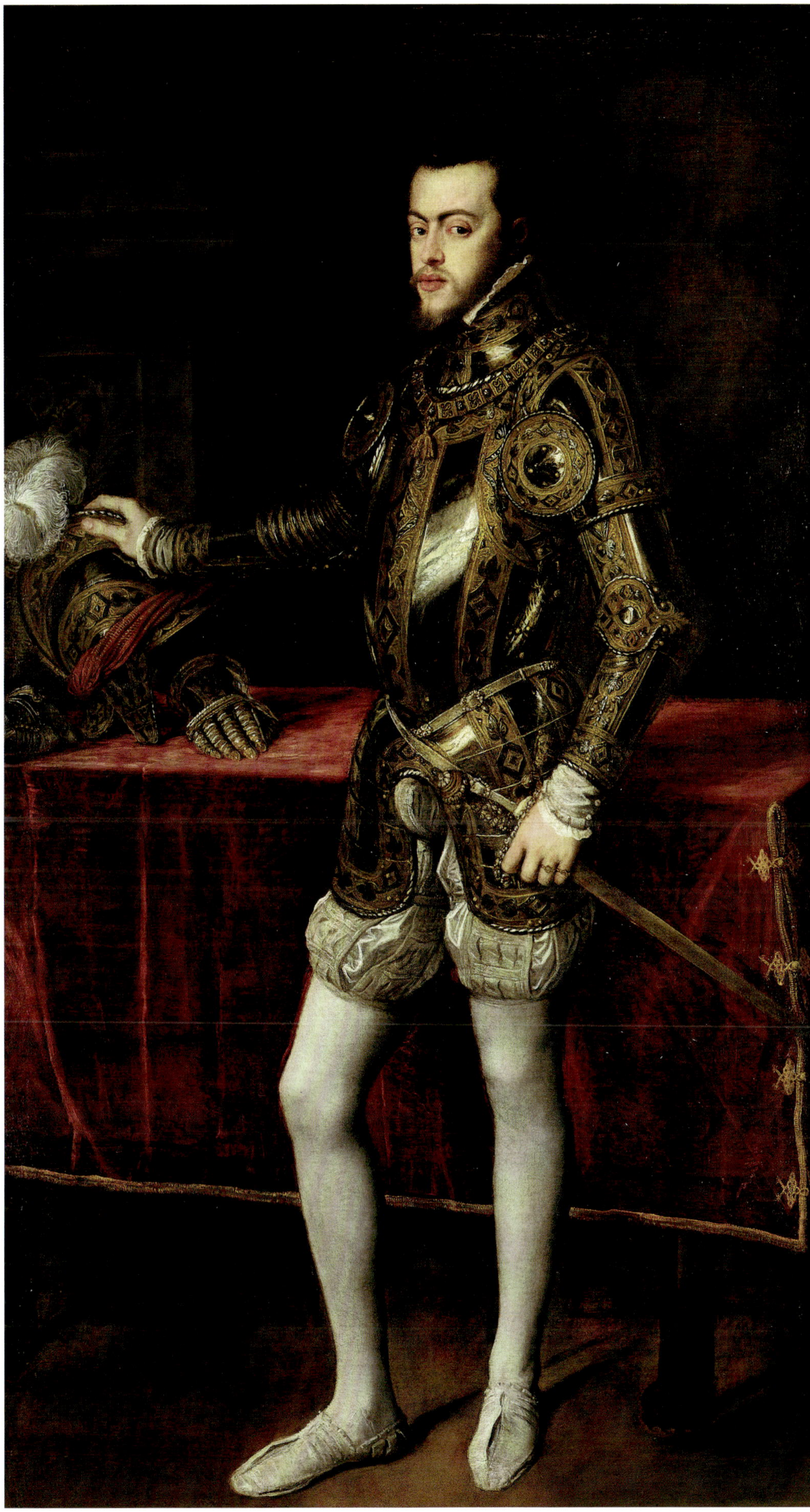

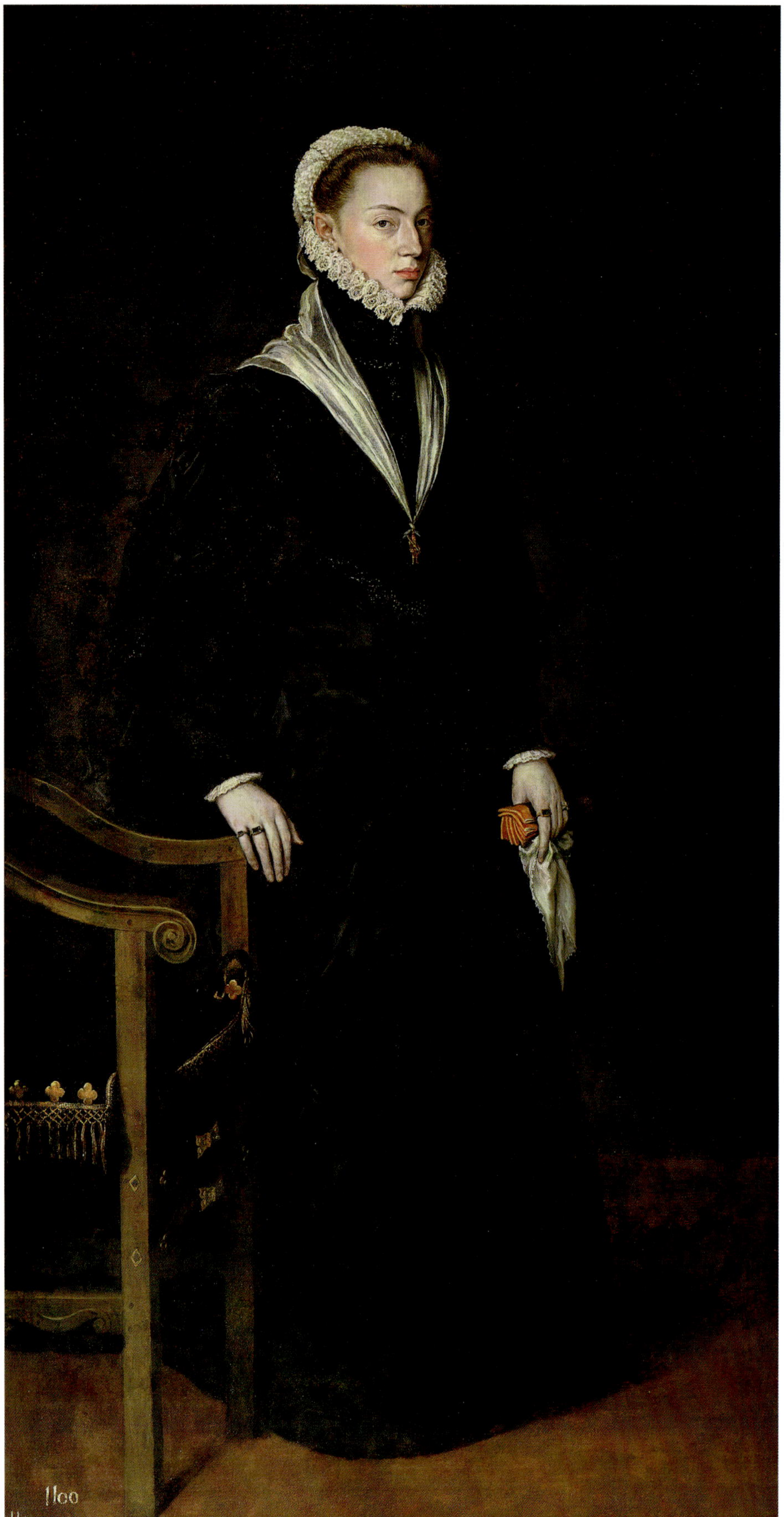

CAT. 8. Anthonis Mor. *Joanna of Austria*, *ca.* 1549. Madrid, Museo del Prado [P-2112]

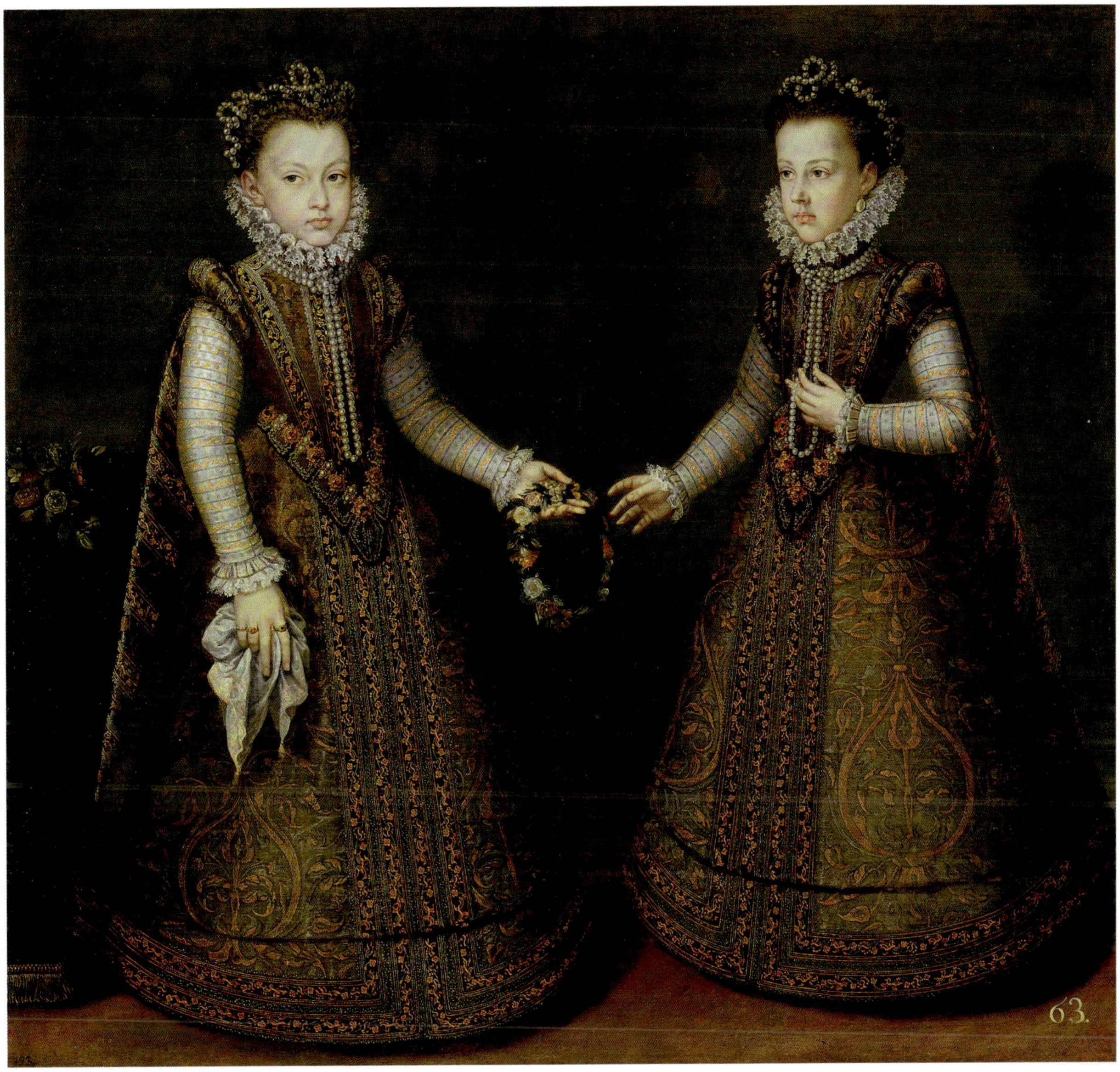

CAT. 9. Alonso Sánchez Coello. *The Infantas Isabel Clara Eugenia and Catalina Micaela*, 1575. Madrid, Museo del Prado [P-1138]

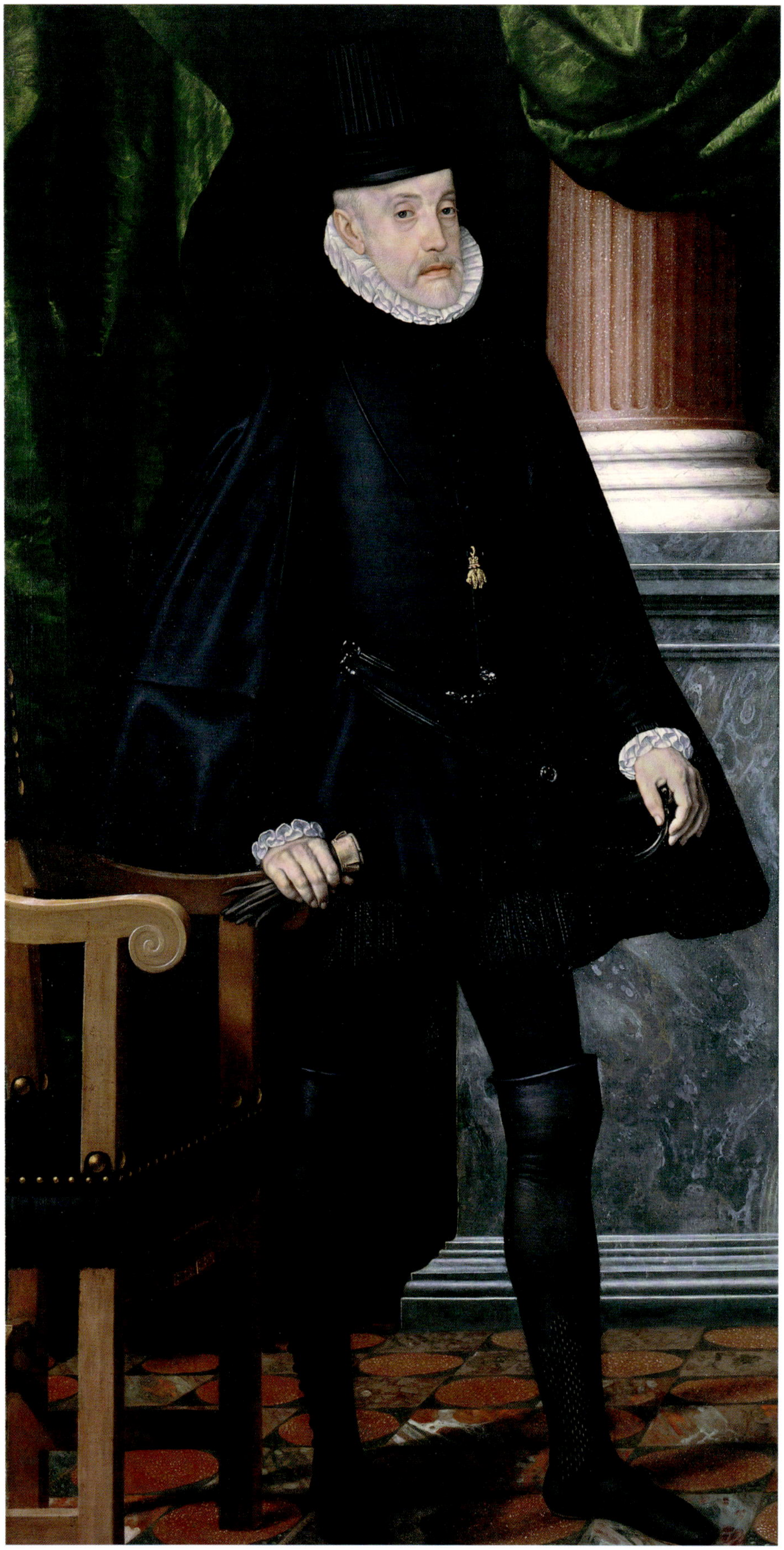

CAT. 10. Juan Pantoja de la Cruz. *Philip II*, *ca.* 1590.
Patrimonio Nacional. Real Monasterio de San Lorenzo de El Escorial [10034484]

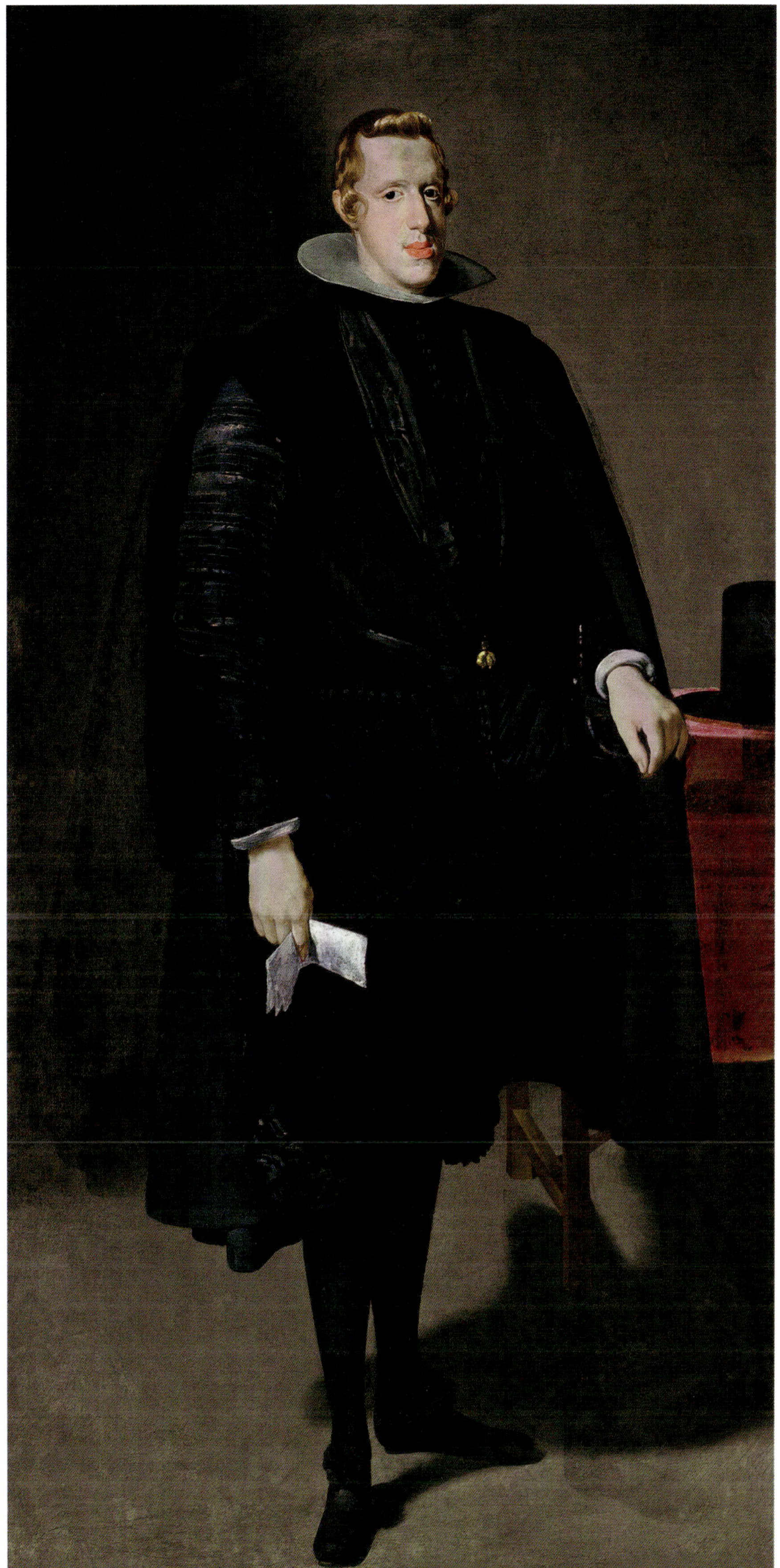

CAT. 11. Diego Velázquez. *Philip IV*, 1623–1627. Madrid, Museo del Prado [P-1182]

CAT. 12. Diego Velázquez. *Philip IV*, *ca.* 1653. Madrid, Museo del Prado [P-1185]

121

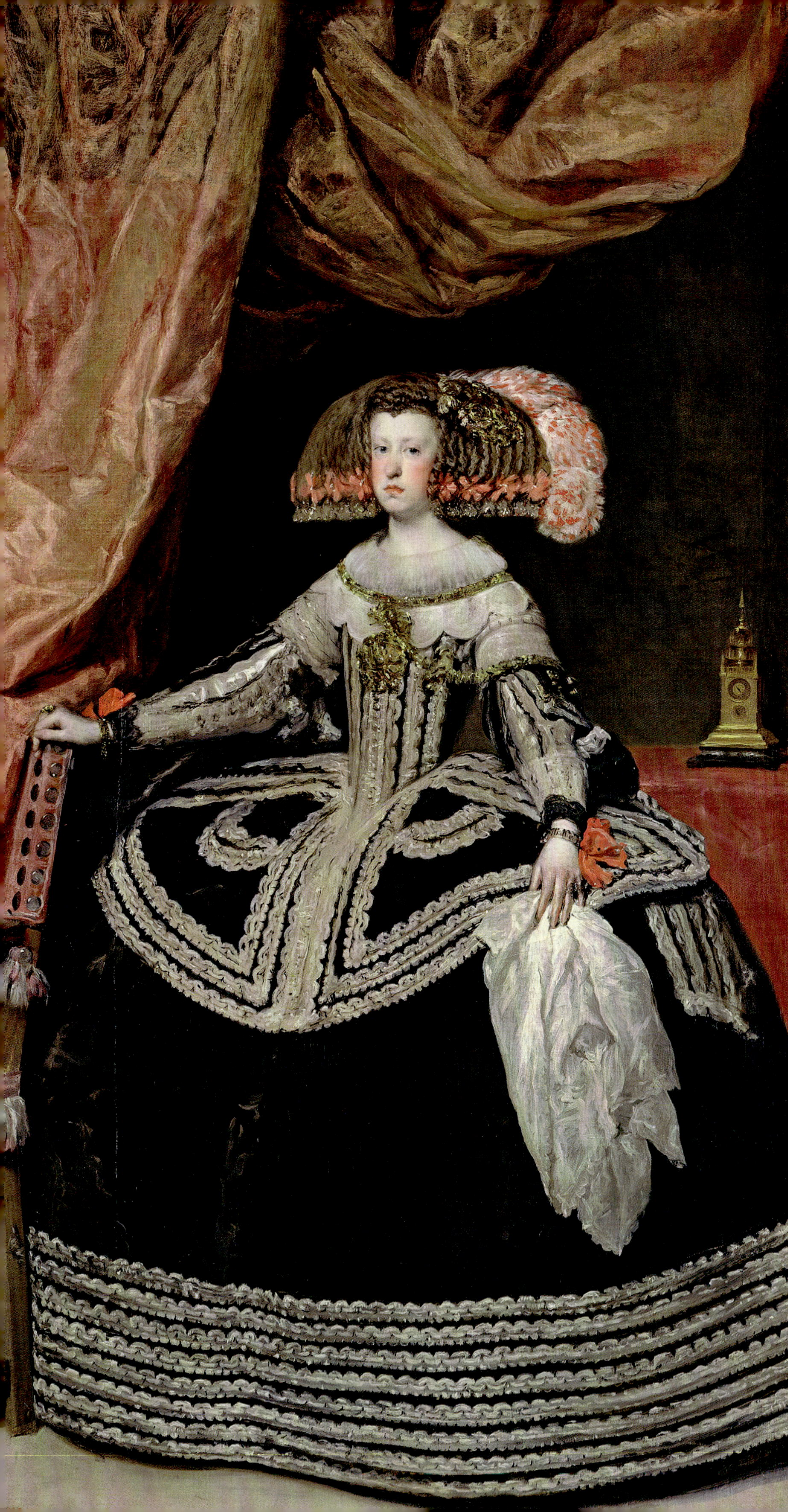

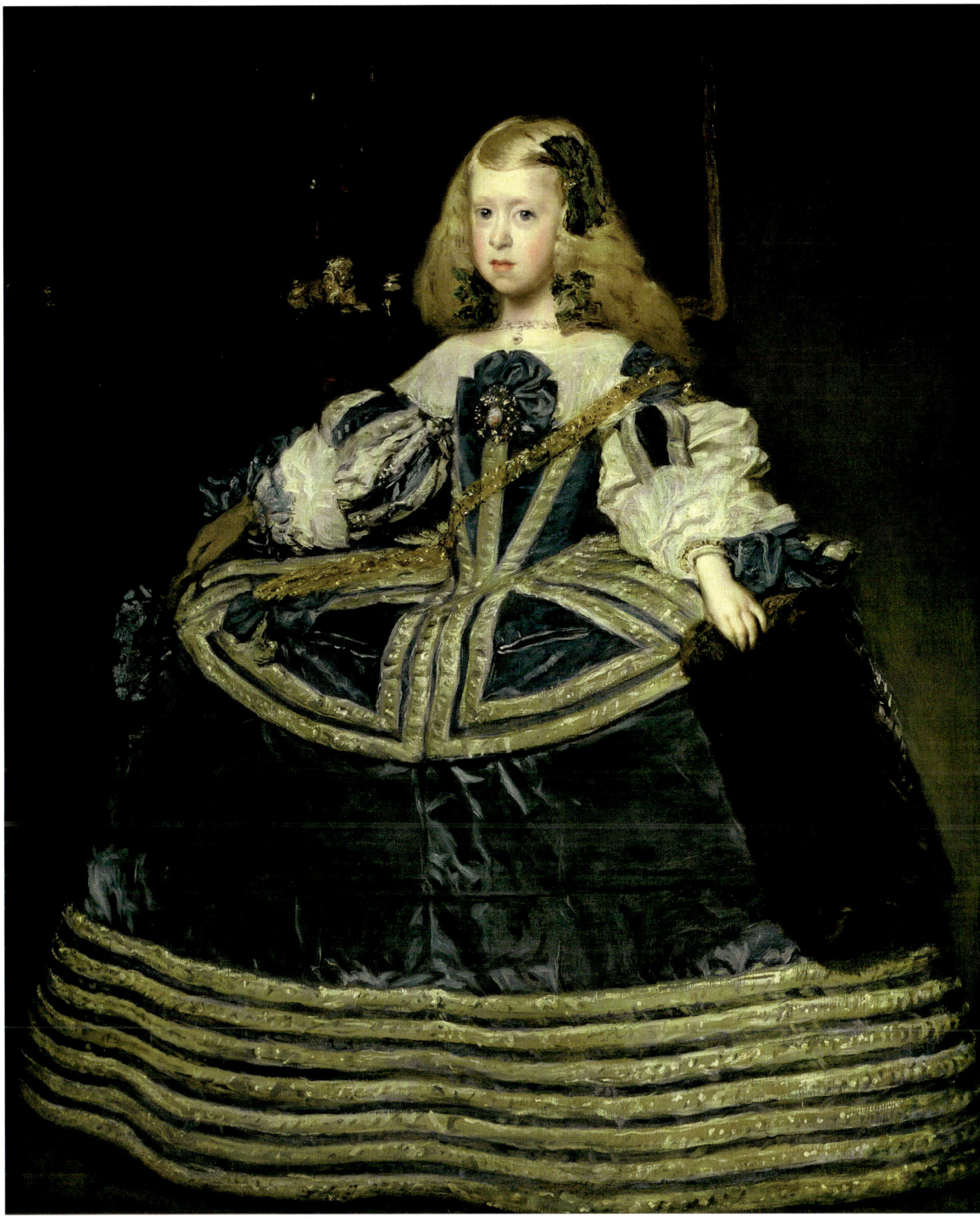

CAT. 13. Diego Velázquez.
Queen Mariana of Austria, ca. 1652–1653.
Madrid, Museo del Prado [P-1191]

CAT. 14. Diego Velázquez.
The Infanta Margarita in Blue, ca. 1659.
Vienna, Kunsthistorisches Museum, Gemäldegalerie [2130]

3 The Portraits of El Greco

José Álvarez Lopera

ITALIAN PORTRAITS

When, in November 1570, El Greco arrived in Rome from Venice, Giulio Clovio introduced him to Cardinal Alessandro Farnese as a 'young man from Candia, a disciple of Titian who, in my view, is among those excelling in painting', and stated that 'among other things he has painted a self-portrait that has caused amazement among all artists in Rome'.[1] Regrettably neither that self-portrait (probably conceived as a 'letter of introduction' to Roman society) nor the five small portraits by El Greco that Fulvio Orsini, the Cardinal's librarian, had at the time of his death in 1600 (one of a 'young man with a red cap' and four small tondos on copper with the effigies of Cardinals Alessandro and Ranuccio Farnese, and also Cardinal Bessarion and Pope Marcello Cervini)[2] have survived. Be that as it may, it seems that El Greco was unable to make his way as a portraitist in Rome. In his *Considerazioni sulla Pittura* written in about 1620, Giulio Mancini said that 'in some particular commissions he did provide great satisfaction',[3] but it is unlikely that he was referring to El Greco's portraits. Today only three portraits from this period are known and accepted as his, which seems to show that El Greco's ability as a portraitist was not entirely appreciated in Rome, where the dominant styles, especially from the point of view of technique and finish, were very different from what El Greco had assimilated in Venice.

The three known portraits of El Greco's Italian period (there is a fourth portrait, of *Charles de Guise, Cardinal of Lorraine*, which is probably also his, although it cannot be attributed conclusively to him) make up a compact and coherent group, set apart by its Venetian roots both in style and technique, and are united by their emphasis on physical reality and by the aim to strike a balance between the representation of the sitter's status and the individual personality.

The earliest of these portraits, the *Portrait of Giulio Clovio* [FIG. 53], adheres to a specific formula: a half-length portrait with the subject set close-up against a dark and neutral wall. A window opens on one side to show a distant landscape. There are many similar approaches to portraiture in works by Titian, Tintoretto, Sebastiano del Piombo and other Venetian painters. However, El Greco distanced himself from these painters when he adopted the uncommon horizontal format. This could suggest that he was acquainted with the works of Passerotti,[4] and perhaps with double portraits by Titian himself, such as *Charles V and Empress Isabel*, which is now lost, or the one of *Georges d'Armagnac and his Secretary Guillaume Philandrier* (Alnwick Castle, Duke of Northumberland). In my opinion, although until now it has not been noticed, it is clear that, aside from the spatial mood, the way of depicting Giulio Clovio (a half-length portrait with the sitter gazing at the spectator, his head strongly lit in front of a dark background and holding his work in one hand while pointing towards it with the forefinger of his other hand) has been influenced by the *Portrait of Giulio Romano* by Titian (Mantua, Palazzo Te). Particularly interesting is the identical gesture of the hand with which both sitters point to their work. El Greco's approach, during a period that was still one of assimilation (in which he frequently adopted motifs taken from engravings by others, using them as the pieces of a puzzle that fitted his own compositional ideas), was to resort to the fusion of two formats which, whilst revealing his origins perhaps with some pride (we must not forget that he introduced himself in Rome as the 'discepolo di Titiano'), proved his desire for originality and his capacity for invention.

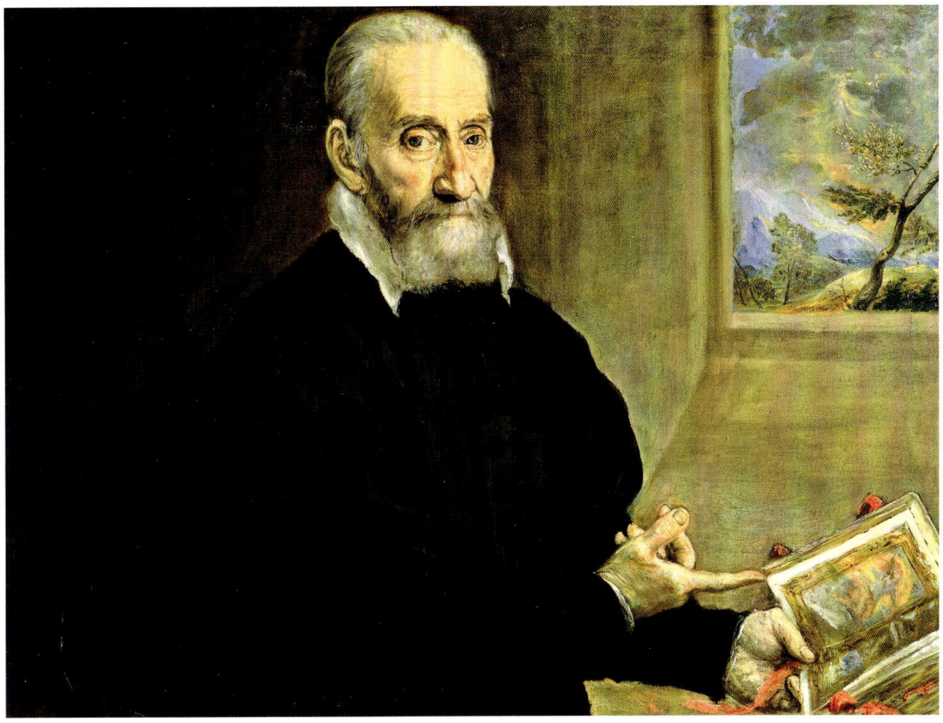

FIG. 53. El Greco, *Portrait of Giulio Clovio, ca.* 1570–1572. Naples, Galleria Nazionale di Capodimonte [Q191]

The *Portrait of an Architect* [FIG. 54], whose identity and profession remain the subject of debate,[5] is intimately related to Venetian painting of the time, which features an abundance of similar pyramidal three-quarter-length figures facing the spectator against a neutral background, sometimes with a hand on a table and usually with the same illustrative gesture as that of the sitter in this portrait. Examples are the *Portrait of a Scholar with a Black Beard* (Copenhagen, Statens Museum for Kunst) and the portrait of *Cardinal Bembo* (Washington, National Gallery of Art) by Titian, as well as *A Nobleman with a Fur Coat* (formerly in Florence, Collection Contini-Bonacossi) and *The Procurator Antonio Cappello* (Venice, Gallerie dell'Accademia) by Tintoretto. However, except in that rhetorical gesture, as befits a man who is displaying his knowledge or conveying his ideas (a gesture frequently used by Tintoretto in his portraits of renowned men[6]), El Greco did not faithfully follow any of his models, but adapted the format to his own ends.

The same can be said of the *Portrait of Vincenzo Anastagi* [FIG. 55], probably painted in 1575 on the occasion of his appointment as *sergente maggiore* of the Castel Sant'Angelo in Rome.[7] It is almost certainly the last of the known portraits that El Greco painted in Italy. As Waterhouse has observed, this portrait is 'the direct successor to Titian's portraits of Philip II and to Veronese's *Pasio Guarienti*,[8] while it leads us to a picture such as Caravaggio's *Alof de Wignacourt*'.[9] On the other hand, certain details of the portrait might be based on other recent paintings: the placing of the helmet on the floor and the position of the protagonist, who stands firmly and with a seemingly defiant attitude in front of a window (although this particular one does not afford a view of the outside), remind us of the *Portrait of a Soldier* by Tintoretto, which is in a private collection in Venice.[10] Also, the curtain that frames the sitter recalls the portraits of monarchs and nobles of the time (Wethey pointed to the portrait of *Philip II Seated, with a Crown*, in the Cincinnati Art Museum[11]), and the posture with the arms akimbo is practically identical to that of the *Unknown Gentleman* by Titian in the Louvre.[12]

However, it is much less tied to its models than the two previous portraits. In fact, the emptiness of the setting (possibly the guards' room in a guardhouse) is rather unusual, as is the especially discrete display of weapons. One should compare, by contrast, the portraits of *Francesco Maria I della Rovere, Duke of Urbino* (Florence, Uffizi) and *Giovanni Battista Castaldo* (Dortmund, Becker Collection) by Titian. It is evident that El Greco wished to convey the determination, strength and authority that were inherent in the sitter's military status by means only of his pose, his spatial location and the relationship with the spectator. What actually makes this portrait unique among those of its genre – and heralds the future El Greco – is the treatment of space and the sophisticated play of rhythms on the surface, full of contrasts and interactions. This is apparent in the contrast between the curvilinear rhythms of the wide pantaloons and drapes on the one hand and the diagonals and acute rhythms of the arms and half-armour on the other, in the subtle continuity on the right side of the painting from the contour of the drape to Anastagi's arm, and in the way in which the dividing line between floor and wall coincides exactly with that between pantaloons and hose. All this allows a play of chromatic and luminous masses that will not reappear in the history of painting until Manet and his *Victorine Meurent in the Costume of an Espada*. (One could also say that the continuation of the linear rhythms on the surface, the play of formal simplification and the sub-

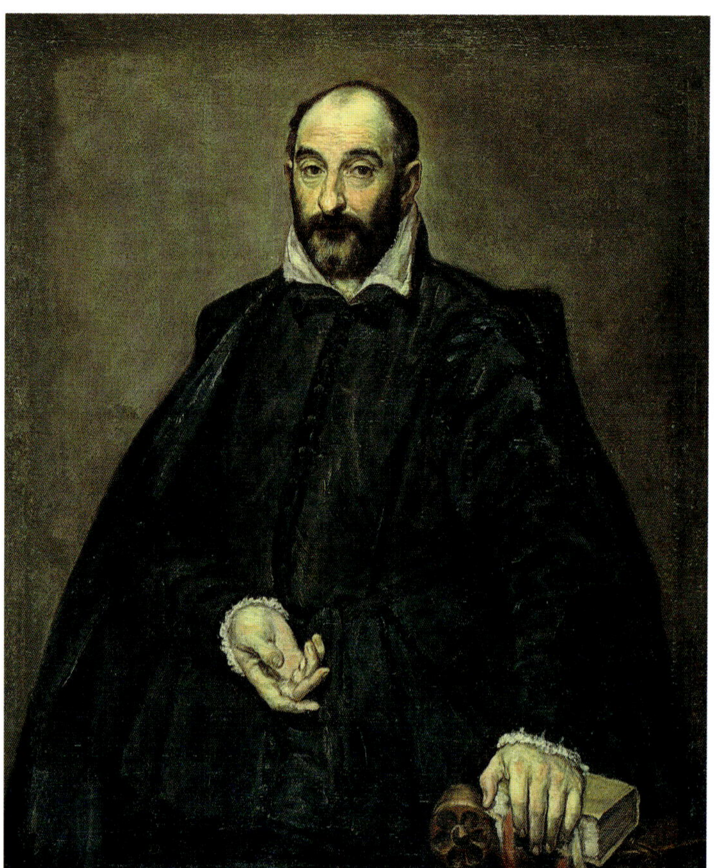

FIG. 54. El Greco, *Portrait of an Architect*, *ca.* 1575–1576. Copenhagen, Statens Museum for Kunst [KMSSP 146]

ordination of the parts to an abstract whole bring to mind both Cézanne and his *Les Grandes Baigneuses* and Matisse and *Le Luxe II*). Pope-Hennessy was probably referring to those abstract qualities when, in a somewhat unappreciative way, he wrote that what El Greco had created in this portrait was 'an acceptable pictorial setting for the figure, and not a space illusion in the conventional sense'.[13] What must be stressed is that the artist was able to combine those abstract qualities in the creation of the image with the powerful expression of physical reality. The result, as Wethey pointed out, is 'a peculiarly earthy interpretation of the man'.[14]

From Mayer (who wrote that the portrait of Anastagi 'gives no indication of the development manifest in the works of Greco's later period'[15]) onwards, most critics have pointed to the 'dissonance' between the portraits of the Italian period and those of the Spanish period. This is obvious in El Greco's technique and in his expression of physical reality, but it is the result of his artistic development and not, as has been written on many occasions, of changes in his approach to the psychological characterisation of the subject.

In the Italian portraits, El Greco appears strongly indebted to the technique of the great Venetian artists (and – as has been frequently pointed out – more to Tintoretto and Bassano than to Titian). The faces are carefully painted (almost 'painfully', as Waterhouse puts it[16]) using short brushstrokes and strong impastos, while the hands are more softly modelled. The garments, though full of tactile qualities, seem to be rendered in a more simplistic fashion (this artifice, together with the use of light, forces our attention on the facial features, which are endowed with a strong naturalism).

Later on, once he was in Spain, El Greco would become inclined towards a more delicate impasto and a certain 'dematerialisation' of the image. One can understand how disoriented Méndez Casal felt when he was confronted, halfway through the 1930s, with the *Portrait of an Architect* in Copenhagen.[17] But although, with time, the methods changed, and even agreeing with Pope-Hennessy's opinion that 'the longer he explored the portrait, the more strenuously did Greco concentrate on the portrayal of the mind and personality, to the detriment of the physique',[18] there is no doubt that the El Greco of the Italian period anticipates the painter of the Spanish period.

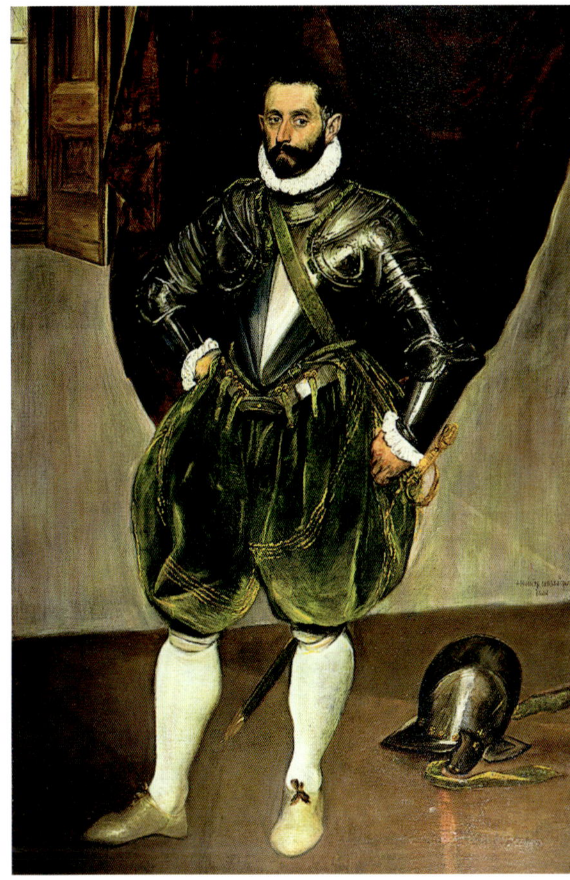

FIG. 55. El Greco, *Portrait of Vincenzo Anastagi, ca.* 1575. New York, The Frick Collection [13.1.68]

The *Portrait of Giulio Clovio* is, just like the *Portrait of an Old Man (presumed Self Portrait)* [FIG. 60], an image of the deterioration of old age; the *Portrait of an Architect* is a precursor of the composition used in the *Portrait of a Doctor (Rodrigo de la Fuente)* [FIG. 59], and its expression of melancholy spirit anticipates the *Elderly Gentleman* in the Prado [CAT. 18]; the *Portrait of Vincenzo Anastagi* [FIG. 55] (often, and understandably, viewed as evidence of El Greco being a 'forerunner' to Velázquez[19]) anticipates, from its energetic charge and the way the subject imposes himself on the spectator, the *Portrait of Cardinal Fernando Niño de Guevara* [FIG. 63].

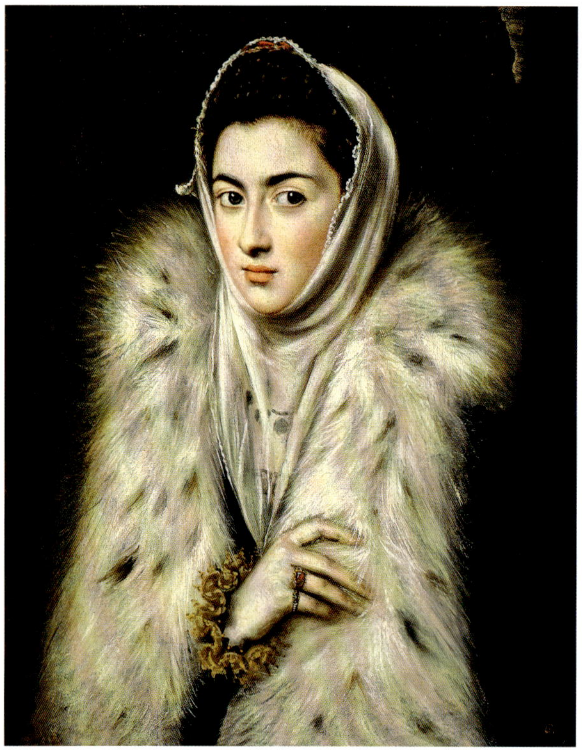

FIG. 56. El Greco, *A Lady in a Fur Wrap*, *ca.* 1577–1579. Glasgow, Pollok House, Stirling-Maxwell Collection [PG 18]

FIRST PORTRAITS IN SPAIN – ADAPTING TO THE NEW ENVIRONMENT

El Greco's development as a portrait painter in Spain can only be explained with reference to his adapting to his new environment. The *Portrait of Pompeo Leoni* (private collection), probably painted shortly after his arrival in Madrid, in 1576 or at the beginning of 1577, is still, from a technical point of view, totally Venetian (so much so that Adolfo Venturi attributed the portrait to Jacopo Bassano[20]). It shows clear stylistic links with the *Portrait of an Architect* in Copenhagen. If not the first, it is one of the earliest portraits of a sculptor portrayed in the act of sculpting, and undoubtedly it is the clearest precedent of *Portrait of a Sculptor* by Velázquez in the Prado (P-1194). Adapting an approach which is typical of self-portraits, El Greco shows us Leoni standing in a three-quarter view, with a neutral and light background, engaged in giving the final touches to a marble bust of Philip II and looking at the spectator (in theory towards the king), with whom a frank and immediate relationship is established. The contrast between the cold and livid gaze of the statue and the eyes of the sculptor brimming with life, already drawn attention to by Venturi,[21] has been interpreted by Davies as a possible indication, albeit very subtle, of the superiority of painting over sculpture. Whether that is the case or not, what is certain is that, as Davies himself points out, 'ironically the bust portrait of the king is more typical of the ideals embodied in his person and society than the more naturalistic or life-like representation of the sculptor'.[22] In the years that followed, El Greco would have to adapt his ideas and his style to the court portrait of the time in order to satisfy his clients.

I believe it is from this point of view that one must approach *A Lady in a Fur Wrap* [FIG. 56], a highly controversial portrait in terms of its authorship and the identity of the sitter.[23] However, I consider that it should not be excluded from El Greco's oeuvre. In fact, the soft modelling of the face is the most striking aspect in the portrait, and it has been linked by Wethey, Baticle and others to some of the earlier works of El Greco in Spain.[24] From Cossío[25] onwards attention has been drawn to the prodigious technique, so similar to that of the master himself, apparent in the fur lining, the transparent veil of the head-dress or the frilly edge of the sleeve. And aside from the appealing and gentle asymmetries already pointed out in 1914 by the painter José Garnelo,[26] other elements have to be emphasised: namely, the expressive aspects (the elegant gesture of the hand or the air of distinguished reserve, and at the same time the psychological closeness of the subject) that link the portrait to El Greco. It is in fact a *unicum* in the work of the artist. But it should be stated that it would not be the first time that the painter, trying to prove that he could surpass his rivals on their own territory, changed his style unexpectedly and produced a work that does not seem to fit in with his stylistic evolution. Suffice it to recall *The Martyrdom of Saint Maurice* for the Monastery of El Escorial.

The first effigies of noblemen, painted in Madrid or Toledo between 1577 and 1580, must also be interpreted as an adaptation to the new environment: *A Nobleman with his Hand on his Chest* [CAT. 15], *The Gentleman of the House of Leiva* (Montreal, Museum of Fine Arts) and the *Portrait of a Gentleman (the supposed Duke of Benavente)* [FIG. 57].

A Nobleman with his Hand on his Chest is probably the portrait by El Greco that has attracted most literary commentary. Here El Greco established the type of portrait that he would paint in later years: the half-length or bust portrait with the sitter emerging from a neutral background, and with the light and expressivity concentrated on the face and hands. This is a dense and austere portrait of obvious psychological refinement; the sobriety in the dress of the sitter contrasts with the air of affectation and aloofness. When the painting was restored towards the end of 1996 not only was it cleaned of surface dirt and varnishes but also of the heavy repaints making the figure of the sitter in black stand out against the grey background, typical of other portraits by El Greco. This also allows us to see the slight forward projection of the left shoulder, which partly nullifies the effect of frontality and dramatism that were mentioned earlier and generated so much commentary. It also emphasised the affected elegance of the sitter, very similar to other portraits of those same years, such as *The Gentleman of the House of Leiva* in Montreal. The technique is of clear Venetian influence and the handling smooth and unified, as is typical of the works of those years, but El Greco achieves exceptional expression through his use of texture. And so despite the frontality of the face, we witness him making a subtle and restrained use of asymmetry and linear deformation (for example, in the different height of the eyes, the nearly imperceptible lateral displacement of the lower lip or the asymmetry of the cheeks). On the other hand, as pointed out by Beruete in 1914, El Greco, 'though he does not forget what he learnt in Venice', here 'shakes off the rich colours, the reds and golds that characterize Venetian art, in search of tones which are colder, greyer', and from those dark tones he proceeds to make the lighter ones stand out, ending with the whites.[27]

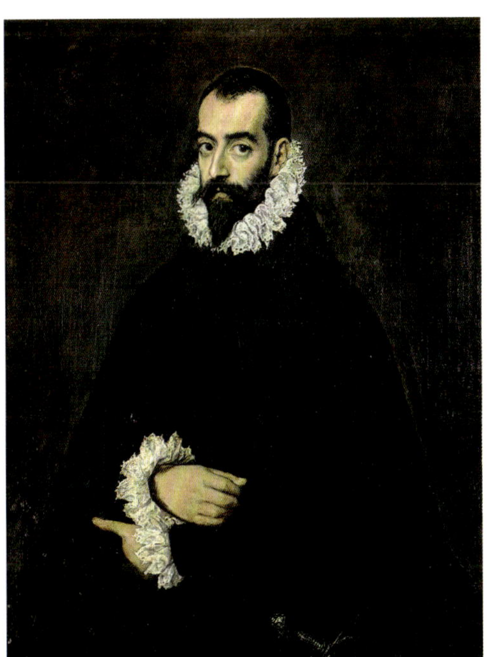

FIG. 57. El Greco, *Portrait of a Gentleman (the supposed Duke of Benavente)*, *ca.* 1580–1586. Bayonne, Musée Bonnat

In any case, what has to be noted here is that *A Nobleman with his Hand on his Chest* represents an approach to portraiture that El Greco seems to have used only during his first years in Spain. This should perhaps be interpreted as an attempt to adapt to his environment by assimilating some of the characteristics of the court portrait in the style of Anthonis Mor or Sánchez Coello (the sobriety, reserve and remoteness of the sitter, a certain meticulousness of detail and preciousness in the depiction of garments and accessories), which was in fashion at that time. In a lecture delivered at the Warburg Institute some years ago, Nicos Hadjinicolaou referred to the 'rigidity' that he seemed to perceive in portraits such as this one, or the *Portrait of Rodrigo Vázquez* or the supposed Duke of Benavente in the Musée Bonnat in Bayonne. Hadjinicolaou compared *A Nobleman with his Hand on his Chest* with the *Portrait of an Architect* in Copenhagen in order to illustrate the conviction that, when El Greco arrived in Spain, 'his presence in a society in which he felt a total stranger and the traditionalist values of his new clients had as a result an incredible decline in the quality and inventiveness of his work *in portraiture*'. For Hadjinicolaou, those portraits are 'conventional' and 'exterior representations of a physiognomy and a social status rather than of the individual'.[28] However, it should be noted that what Hadjinicolaou interprets as rigidity is actually remoteness and reserve, two of the basic features of the Spanish court portrait at the time (neither *A Nobleman with his Hand on his Chest* nor *The Gentleman of the House of Leiva*, with their subtle forward movements, their vivacity and elegance, can be qualified as being rigid). In addition, these are portraits of nobles and they needed to convey the qualities associated with high social class, apart from the individual personality of the subject. On this matter, I think Fernando Checa was right in saying, with regard to *A Nobleman with his Hand on his Chest*, that these portraits by El Greco respond to a 'Renaissance mentality, a specific idea and image of the aristocratic and stratified society in which he lived'.[29] This type of portrait (sitters from the nobility, in half or three-quarter length, with their affected elegance and the display of symbols such as the sword) dates from his early years in Spain and does not reappear later. This may be an indication of the kind of patronage that El Greco enjoyed in Madrid and Toledo during this period – a patronage which, except for his ecclesiastical commissions, remains little known.

CLIENTS, RELATIVES AND FRIENDS

In Spain El Greco did not secure the 'favour of princes' that he believed was indispensable to becoming fully successful as a painter, so in order to succeed, he probably relied on his ability as a portraitist. He did paint Philip II in *The Adoration of the Name of Jesus* [CAT. 6] and in the glory of *The Burial of the Count of Orgaz* [FIG. 17], but as far as we know, he did not paint any portraits of members of the King's family, nor any members of the high aristocracy or (with the exception of Cardinal Quiroga[30] and Cardinal Niño de Guevara) any of the great ecclesiastical dignitaries of the time. Excluding the portraits that appear in *The Burial of the Count of Orgaz* (which cannot be treated here and which is almost an expression of a collective state of mind) and the portraits of donors included in several religious paintings, of which El Greco painted more than is usually assumed,[31] today we know of about thirty portraits from the Spanish period. It is significant that only a dozen of these portray people who have been certainly or reliably identified; the rest, especially the group of noblemen attired with a ruff, remain anonymous.

There are, however, elements that can shed light on the various groups from which El Greco drew his sitters. One such element is the relationship between the identifiable sitters. First, there is a group of family portraits, which includes the *Portrait of an Old Man (presumed Self Portrait)* [FIG. 60], which may show his brother Manusos, the *Portrait of a Lady with a Flower in her Hair* [FIG. 61], probably his daughter-in-law Alfonsa de los Morales, and the *Portrait of a Painter (Jorge Manuel Theotocopouli)* [CAT. 17], certainly his son, Jorge Manuel. The subjects in the second group were intellectuals and scholars who were friends of El Greco (Dr Rodrigo de la Fuente, Covarrubias). Then there was another, much larger group, with portraits of clergymen who were, in some instances, close to him (Cardinal Niño de Guevara, Paravicino, probably Francisco de Pisa). Finally there were the portraits of lawyers and politicians who were involved in the government of the Kingdom (though in this case, only one painting, Don Rodrigo Vázquez de Arce, President of the Councils of the Treasury and of Castile) or local government (the *licenciado* Jerónimo de Cevallos, Councillor of Toledo from 1605).

One should also bear in mind the evidence provided by the list of portraits unquestionably painted by El Greco, which were in his son Jorge Manuel's possession in 1621 but which today we cannot identify, even supposing they have survived. This is the case of the portraits of Luis Fernández de Córdoba (*Corregidor* of Toledo in 1592), Soria de Herrera (*Corregidor* during 1592–1593, after the death of Fernández de Córdoba),[32] Jerónimo Pacheco (not identified), a monk of the Jeronomite Order

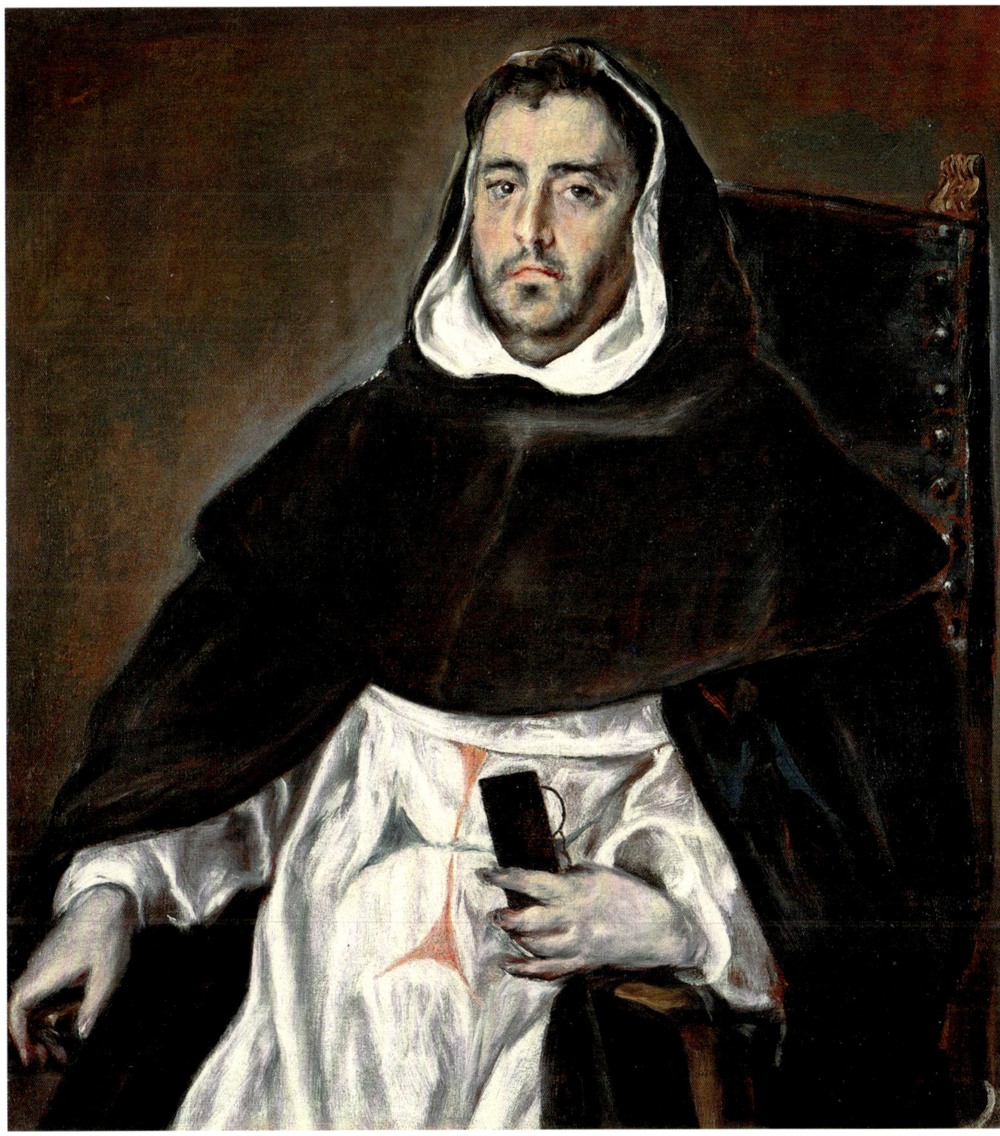

FIG. 58. El Greco, *Portrait of a Trinitarian Friar, ca.* 1608–1614. Kansas City, The Nelson-Atkins Museum of Art [Nelson Trust 52–53]

(not identified)[33] and Ávila de Vera (probably the *licenciado* of the same name, cleric and canon lawyer, who was a member of the Council of Government in the archbishopric of Toledo in 1610).[34]

Thanks to this series and to what we can gather from the documentary references (which in only a few cases identify the sitters: a self-portrait and two portraits of Rodrigo Vázquez which were the property of the Counsellor of Castile, Don Agustín del Hierro, in 1660,[35] another of Covarrubias in the collection of the Marquis of Leganés in 1655,[36] and another of Alonso de Villegas in the collection of Andrés González de Bricianos, 'senior official in the Accounting Offices of the Royal Secret Expenses of His Majesty', in 1708[37]), we can gain a very precise idea about who El Greco's sitters were. They included his relatives and friends, people belonging to the intellectual and literary circles in Toledo,[38] clerics of varying status[39] and members of the local nobility and government institutions in the city. It is telling that El Greco seems to have painted few portraits of women,[40] while those of men are practically all bust or half-length portraits set against a neutral background. In fact, only that of Cardinal Niño de Guevara is a full-length portrait with a clearly defined interior setting, and there are barely five or six in which the intellectual personality or profession of the subject is explicitly depicted by means of the pose or the accessories. In view of this, we can be sure that most of El Greco's portraits would have had a private purpose and, given their characteristics, would not have brought him considerable financial gain.[41] But the environment in which El Greco lived and the specific nature of his clientele allowed him to establish, as Portús writes in his introduction to this catalogue, one of the cornerstones of the 'civil' portrait in Spain. Such clients also gave him the freedom to combine what was distinctive and what was typical, and allowed him, at least from the beginning of the new century, a technical and expressive autonomy that was unthinkable at court.

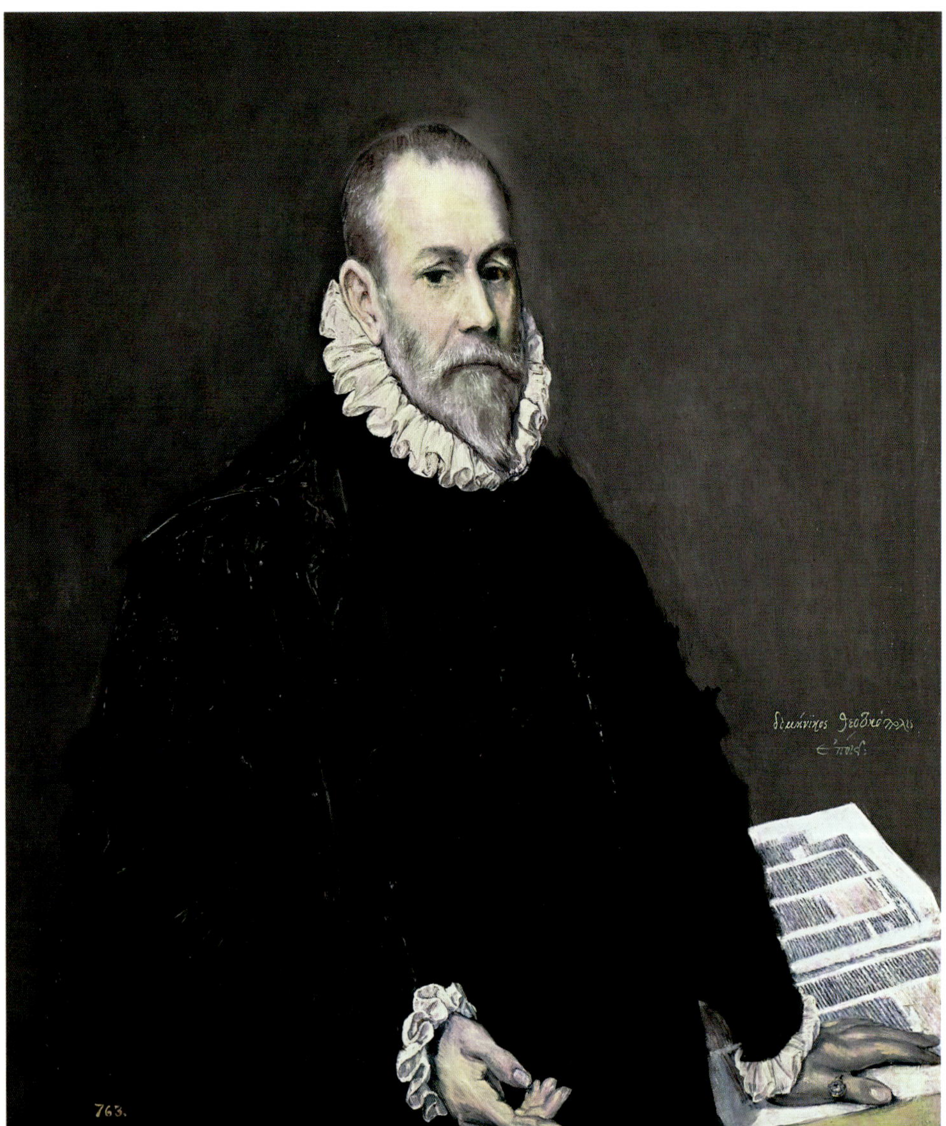

FIG. 59. El Greco, *Portrait of a Doctor (Rodrigo de la Fuente), ca.* 1585–1589. Madrid, Museo del Prado [P-807]

PORTRAITS OF GENTLEMEN – BUST AND THREE-QUARTER VIEWS

With the exception of the *Portrait of a Doctor (Rodrigo de la Fuente)* [FIG. 59] – an image of a learned man in which El Greco returned to the format, and the rhetorical gesture of the right hand, seen in the *Portrait of an Architect* in Copenhagen [FIG. 54] and also used in some paintings of saints[42] – and the portrait *A Student* (perhaps Saint Aloysius Gonzaga), today in a private American collection, practically all the other portraits painted by El Greco between 1580 and 1600 are images of gentlemen that conform to the same pattern: bust portraits against a neutral background, the face in three-quarter view and the gaze turned towards the viewer. There are considerable differences in quality between these portraits, and, since they were painted over a very long period, the technical aspects also vary substantially. However, the formula, which was established at a very early stage, remained unchanged throughout El Greco's years in Spain. This, together with the air of reserve conveyed by the sitters, indicates that here we have images that aim to define their social status as much as or even more than their individuality. The sobriety and the similarity of their dress and the lack of accessories or symbols make it difficult to identify them.

The earliest of these portraits is, undoubtedly, the *Unknown Gentleman* (Museo del Prado, P-813) painted most likely towards the middle of the 1580s, around the time of *The Burial of the Count of Orgaz*. One can see the evolution of the artist's style when comparing this portrait to two other unknown gentlemen in the Prado (P-810 and P-811), dating from after 1600 and both highly typical of El Greco's oeuvre. Through them we can appreciate how, as pointed out by Cossío, with the passing of time the painter's technique became lighter and he became the 'owner […], with an increasingly determined grasp, of the difficult secrets of his art'.[43]

Although the two portraits are similar both technically and conceptually, and are usually dated to much the same time (1600–1605), the first one, which according to many historians recalls Velázquez, seems to be more developed and subtle. It is similar to *An Elderly Gentleman* [CAT. 18] in the way in which the bone structure of the face is rendered and the subtle qualities that differentiate the hair on the head, the moustache and the goatee beard. However, the modelling is already of an 'impressionistic lightness', as described by Camón Aznar.[44] Light seems to move across the face making it pulsate with life, and the touches of carmine enliven the surface with tremendous effect. The handling is remarkably thin and the painter allows the reddish preparation to show through in order to create shape and volume. Prefiguring what he would paint in his final years, a thick dark contour surrounds the face. As a further illusionistic detail, the face makes a shadow fall on the ruff, giving a sense of volume and depth.

'HEADS'

The *Unknown Gentleman* (Museo del Prado, P-810) represents one of the pinnacles of illusionistic realism in the portraiture of El Greco. For this reason and because of its chromatic range, the portrait is often considered a precursor of the portraits of Velázquez, who, according to Palomino, 'in his portraits imitated Dominico Greco, because his heads were such that they could never be sufficiently praised'.[45] We know that Velázquez, at the time of his death, had in his apartments in the Cuarto del Príncipe in the Alcázar three portraits by El Greco: 'a portrait by the Greek, of the head of a cleric', 'A portrait by the Greek, half-length of a woman' and 'Another by the same [painter] of an elderly man'. None of these portraits has survived,[46] but it is not difficult to see what Velázquez must have learnt from El Greco if one considers paintings such as the *Nobleman of the Order of Santiago* in the Gemäldegalerie in Dresden or the bust portrait of *Philip IV* in the Prado [CAT. 12].

It is virtually certain that Velázquez must have studied *An Elderly Gentleman* [CAT. 18], the formula for which El Greco used again, interestingly, in another portrait of an old man: the supposed self-portrait [FIG. 60] which,

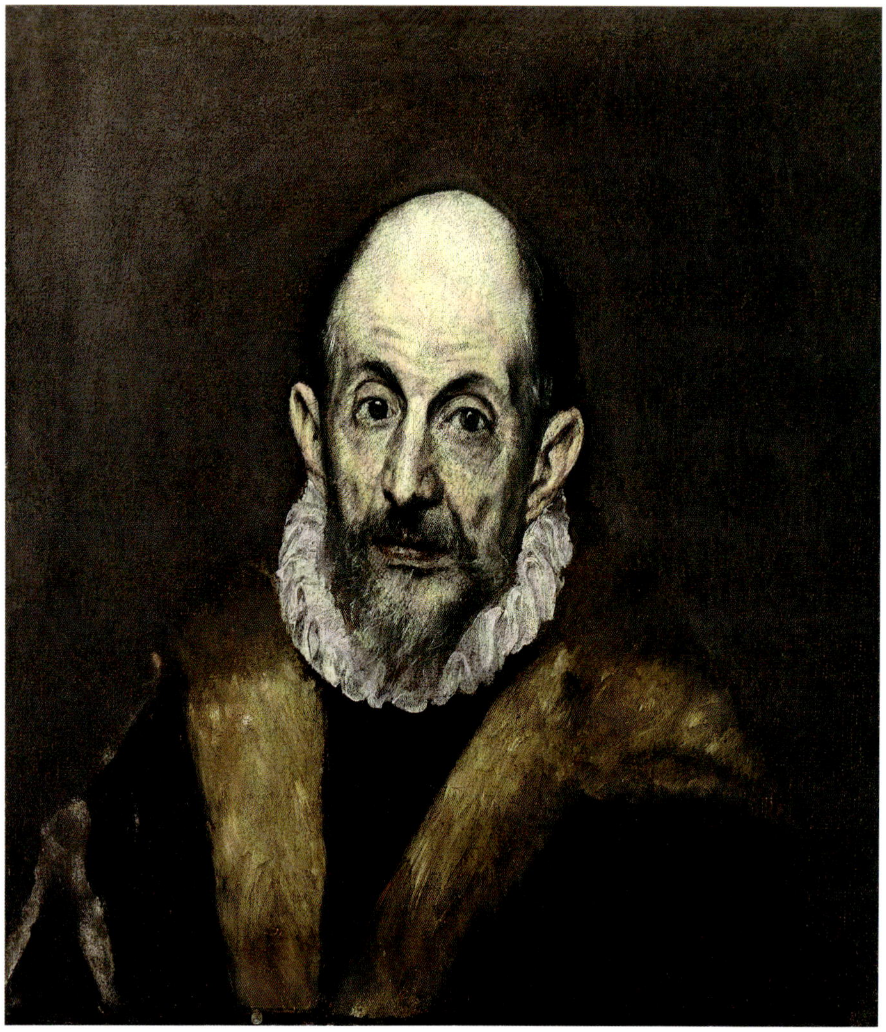

FIG. 60. El Greco, *Portrait of an Old Man (presumed Self Portrait), ca.* 1597–1603. New York, The Metropolitan Museum of Art [Joseph Pulitzer Bequest, 1924, inv. 24.197.1]

as mentioned earlier, may in fact show his brother Manusos. The composition is extremely simple; rather than a bust, it is a forward-facing head which stands out against the whiteness of the collar before a neutral background. This simplicity, the immediacy of the presentation and the acuity of his vision – the depth of the psychological insight – indicate that, although in neither case can we be sure of the identity of the sitter, these are intimate portraits whose purpose is exclusively private, for the family. The sitter in the Prado portrait is immersed in deep thought, looking towards the viewer without any communication but, rather, allowing himself to be scrutinised. The air of sadness and melancholy that he exudes has caused much ink to be spilt. Baroja named the painting 'An old hidalgo',[47] and Cossío thought he saw in it the prototype of the Castilian *hidalgo*, the personification of the 'people, yet elegant and well-groomed'.[48]

But beyond these types of characterisation – which are ultimately the product of their time – what has to

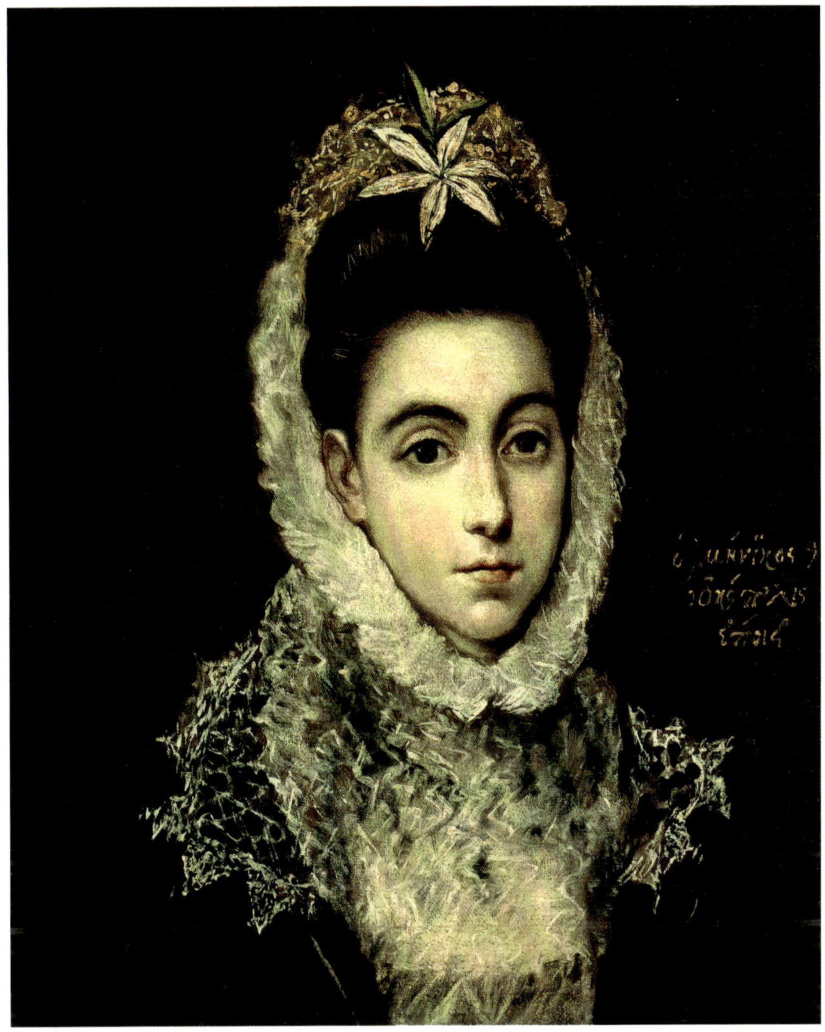

FIG. 61. El Greco, *Portrait of a Lady with a Flower in her Hair*, *ca.* 1603. New York, private collection

be borne in mind is that it is precisely in portraits such as this one and the one in the Metropolitan, totally lacking in affectation, that El Greco's extraordinary capacity for individual characterisation is expressed; in other words, his capacity to delve deep within his subjects. Gómez-Moreno wrote that 'El Greco, and after him Velázquez and Goya, undressed their sitters in their portraits, whereas other painters dress them and mask them'.[49] This may not always be true, but it is so at least in this instance. When Trapier wrote, concerning this portrait, that compared to the El Greco of this period Tintoretto and Bassano seem 'dull and conventional' portraitists,[50] she was referring not only to the sharpness of vision of the artist, but also to the prodigious technique of the painting, full of subtleties and complexities that bring to mind the awareness the Cretan artist had of his own qualities and the disapproval he expressed of Michelangelo the painter: 'He did not know how to paint portraits, nor paint hair, nor anything that could resemble flesh and [...] in what concerns oil

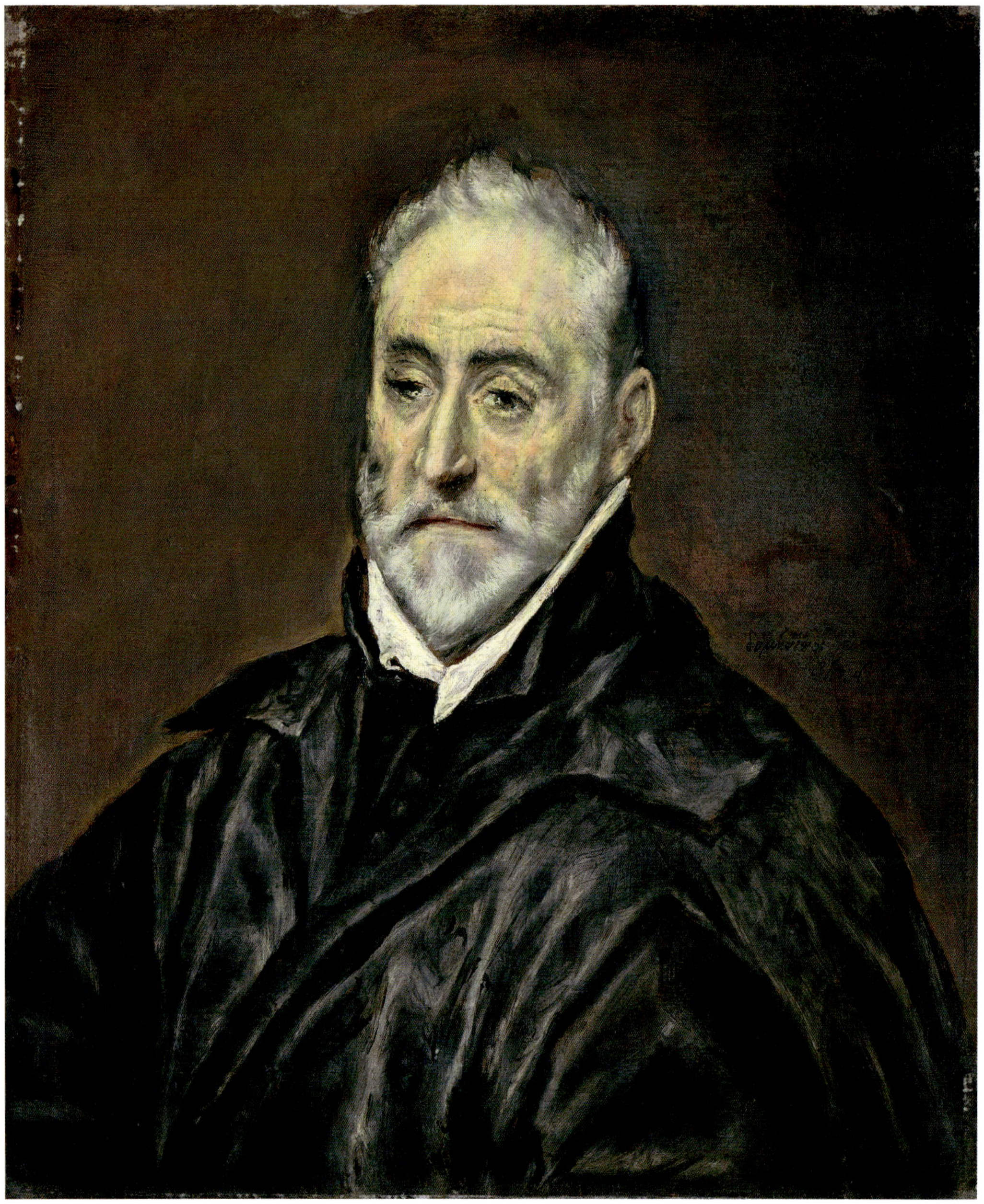

FIG. 62. El Greco, *Portrait of Antonio de Covarrubias*, *ca.* 1600–1602.
París, Musée du Louvre [R.F. 1941–32]

painting it cannot be denied that he was lacking in such delicate skills'.[51] El Greco's evolution as a painter and portraitist is apparent in the increasingly accentuated asymmetries and the distortion of the facial features, as well as the extraordinary way in which the painter submits the various elements of the painting to a specific rhythm that governs the composition. Note, for example, the sinuous line that descends from the central section of hair to the tip of the chin, passing through the nose.

Although they are not straightforward 'heads', we must also include in this category of 'intimate' portraits the *Portrait of a Lady with a Flower in her Hair* [FIG. 61] and the *Portrait of Antonio de Covarrubias* [FIG. 62]. The identity of the sitter in the first portrait has not been firmly established, although it is quite likely that, as suggested for the first time by Sánchez Cantón,[52] it may be Alfonsa de los Morales, the first wife of El Greco's son Jorge Manuel. The identity of the second is beyond doubt. Covarrubias was intellectually very close to El Greco, who had already painted him in *The Burial of the Count of Orgaz* and paid him an obsequious homage of admiration in his annotations in Barbaro's edition of Vitruvius.[53]

In any case, we must note how in these two portraits of people who are close to the artist, presented in a similar way and painted around the same time (the portrait of the lady, supposing she is Alfonsa de los Morales, must have been done in 1603 when she married Jorge Manuel, and the one of Covarrubias shortly before his death in 1602), El Greco was able to differentiate clearly between the two representations. Typically, in both portraits he concentrated on the facial features and approached the dress in a more summary manner (especially in the case of the lady, whose shawl, as Gudiol stated,[54] was a simple notation of zigzags painted at speed). But in the painting of the lady, as befitted a portrait which was in a way celebratory, he introduced a symbolic element (the white lily, which denotes virtue and innocence) and renounced a certain licence (the modelling of the face is relatively smooth and, except for the eyebrows, there are no marked distortions or asymmetries). El Greco painted an unquestionably idealised rendition of the young woman but also an appropriate image of her social person. This is the portrait of a discreet and prudent girl who looks towards the viewer but remains remote, barely allowing her individuality to show through.

The portrait of Covarrubias, on the other hand, is a *tour de force* of psychological penetration and individual characterisation. In this case, the very composition of the portrait tells us of the painter's intentions. El Greco could not have found in Toledo a better candidate than Covarrubias for a three-quarter-length portrait of a scholarly man, complete with books and other accessories – an arrangement he had used on other occasions. But instead, he concentrated on the face of his friend, since he was interested in the man and not what he symbolised, providing us with an image which is moving, even painful. It is significant that this is the only portrait by El Greco in which the subject does not look at the viewer. The feeling of isolation that is conveyed is further emphasised as a result of the pupils not being focused and the asymmetry of the mouth. As has been written so many times, one can feel his deafness. But at the same time, the nearly imperceptible movement of the body moving forward and the vivid modelling of the face, executed with small and careful brushstrokes that reach remarkable levels of virtuosity when it comes to the beard and the bristly hair, imbue the image with remarkable energy and reveal the rich inner life of the sitter.

A STATE PORTRAIT

Between December 1599 and March 1602 (or perhaps January 1604, when the Cardinal visited Toledo), El Greco painted his only state portrait: the *Portrait of Cardinal Fernando Niño de Guevara* [FIG. 63]. As has often been stated, the representation is ultimately based on Raphael's *Julius II* (London, The National Gallery), the prototype for a whole line of Papal portraits: the Pope sits on a throne placed diagonally in relation to the picture plane, with one hand holding on to the armrest, the other hand open, and the head and the gaze slightly turned. Titian had used the same formula in his two portraits of *Paul III* and *Paul III with his Grandsons Alessandro and Ottavio Farnese*, in the Museo Nazionale di Capodimonte in Naples; these were portraits which El Greco knew well, since they were in the Palazzo Farnese during his stay in Rome. The latter of the two portraits, in which Titian portrayed the Pontiff with an expression of shrewdness that was at odds with the conventions of the State portrait, has been considered a precursor of the freedoms that El Greco enjoyed in his stark psychological characterisation of the Cardinal.[55] However, this is only one of the elements of the portrait. In conceiving it the artist seems to have worked with similar principles to the ones he applied in Italy in the portraits of Giulio Clovio [FIG. 53] and Vincenzo Anastagi [FIG. 55]. These images are based on models sanctioned by tradition, which El Greco used merely as a starting point for a new approach. In fact, he steered away from convention when he depicted the Cardinal in a full-length portrait (earlier official portraits of Popes had all been three-quarter portraits, that of Paul III with his grandchildren being an exception because it is a 'family group'). As first Baetjer[56] and later Brown and Carr showed in relation to the *Portrait of Charles V Seated* by Titian (Munich, Alte Pinakothek), and especially in the depiction of the sitter in front of a tapestry of honour,[57] it seems clear that in this painting El Greco blended two different yet complementary modes (as he had done in the *Portrait of Giulio Clovio*) of depicting those in a position of power, in order to highlight the authority of the sitter. Furthermore, he broke away from traditional practice by merging the official *persona* of the sitter and the characterisation of his individual personality. The way in which the sitter imposes himself and the feeling of self-assuredness, strength and authority that the portrait conveys are dependent partly on the faithful transcription of the facial features, but also on details such as the rapid turn of the gaze in a face which is still and impervious, the connection between that gaze and the twitch of the left hand, or the contrast between that hand and the right one, which hangs gently and elegantly. They are dependent also, as in the *Portrait of Vincenzo Anastagi*, on other details, such as the relationship between the sitter and the frame – with the sitter appearing magnified in the foreground and filling most of the surface of the canvas – or the sophisticated play of rhythms on the surface and the bold use of perspective and spatial associations. The design of the flooring, which seems to lift as we advance into the depth of the painting, introduces an element of instability and apprehension that makes the figure of the Cardinal even more imposing. The Cardinal is solidly set and his decisiveness is highlighted by the powerful play of the vertical and horizontal lines of the background. From what we know about the painting it is unlikely that Velázquez was aware of it, but it is certainly difficult to disassociate it from his portrait of *Pope Innocent X* [FIG. 9]. Both portraits were indeed conceived in the same spirit and with the same freedom.

PORTRAITS OF THE FINAL PERIOD

During his final years El Greco reached the peak of his talent for psychological characterisation and for communicating the inner life of his sitters. During this time he combined the individual and the representational in the most extraordinary way, showing a versatility in his modes of expression and presentation that one does not find in the portraits painted during his two first decades in Spain. The *Portrait of a Painter (Jorge Manuel Theotocopouli)* [CAT. 17] is an image like the *Portrait of Cardinal Fernando Niño de Guevara*, in which the individual and the generic merge, although the artist's intention is, of course, to ennoble his sitter. If we isolate the top half of the painting we revealingly find yet again one of his bust portraits of gentlemen (it is interesting to point out that the *Unknown Gentleman* (Museo del Prado P-811) has also been considered to depict Jorge Manuel[58]). And yet it seems obvious that the elegance of the pose, the absence of physical effort, the air of mental concentration by Jorge Manuel, staring at us and with his brush suspended in the air, refer to the intellectual nature – one could say the nobility – of the art of painting. It was not by any coincidence that Velázquez depicted himself in a practically identical manner in *Las Meninas*. If in the portrait of his son El Greco seems to have departed from his bust images of gentlemen, in other portraits of ecclesiastical figures painted during these years, like the

FIG. 63. El Greco, *Portrait of Cardinal Fernando Niño de Guevara, ca.* 1600. New York, The Metropolitan Museum of Art [H.O. Havemeyer Collection, inv. 29.100.5]

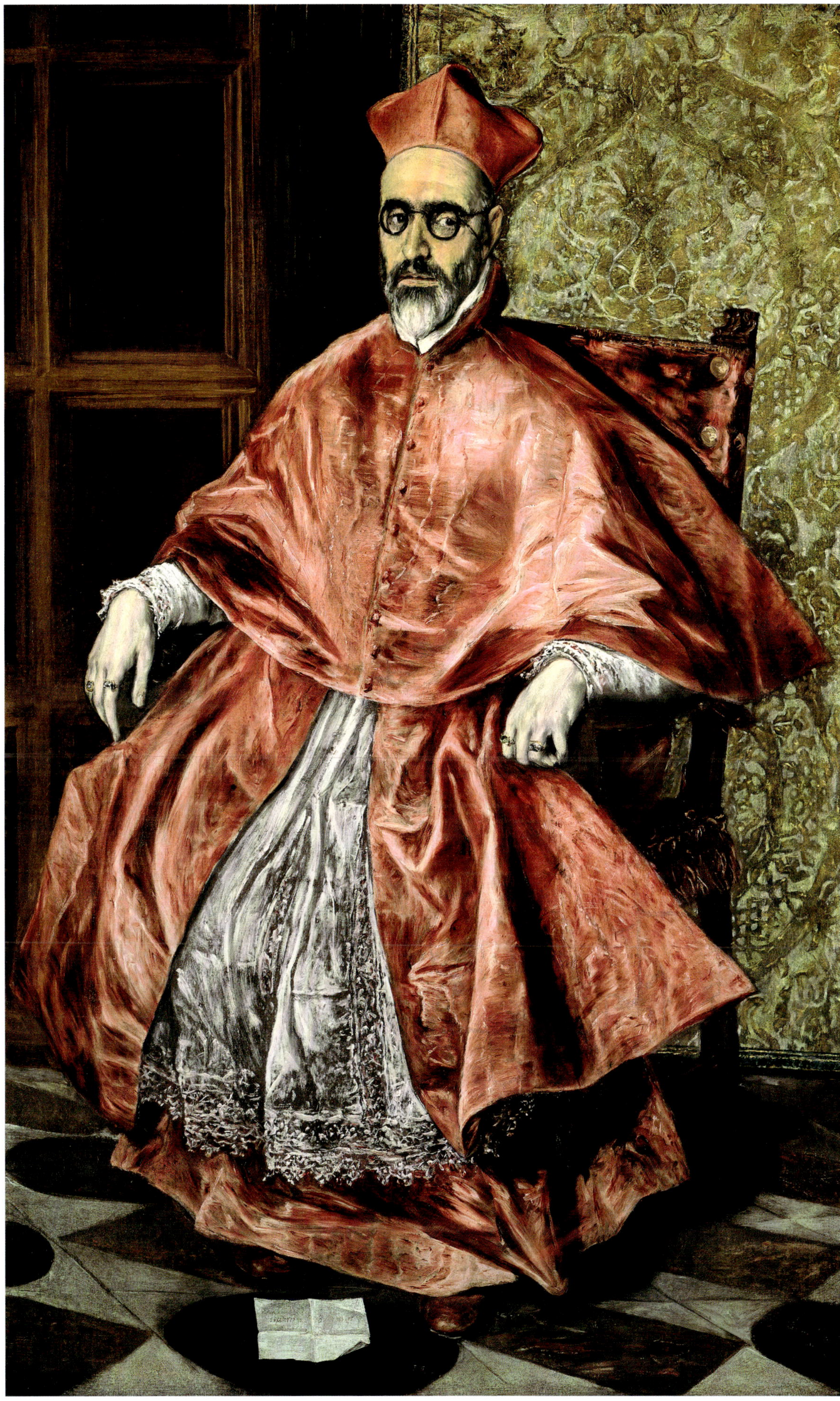

one of *Cardinal Tavera* (Toledo, Tavera Hospital) or the *Portrait of a Canon Lawyer (Francisco de Pisa?)* [FIG. 65], it seems clear that he used the composition from an earlier religious painting (*Saint Jerome as Cardinal* [FIG. 64]), in that exchange between portraits and depictions of saints that we have pointed out earlier in relation to *A Nobleman with his Hand on his Chest* and the *Portrait of a Doctor (Rodrigo de la Fuente)*. A portrait such as *Jerónimo de Cevallos* [CAT. 16], represents the culmination of the bust portraits of gentlemen, while that of *Fray Hortensio Félix Paravicino* [CAT. 19] is fashioned in a totally novel way. It is precisely in the two latter portraits, and in the *Portrait of a Canon Lawyer (Francisco de Pisa?)*, all of them painted after 1608, that the extraordinary degree of technical and expressive freedom that the artist achieved in his final years is most clearly apparent. In his *Spanische Reise*, Meier-Graefe singled out the portrait of Cevallos from all those in the Prado, stating that it was 'the pearl' amongst them. Meier-Graefe analysed its qualities in specifically modern terms: 'If one stops to consider the anatomy of the face,' he wrote, 'one receives the impression of a fantastic structure. The right eye is far lower than the left; were it not for the beard the mouth would be a shapeless piece of flesh; the left ear, almost separated from the head, would seem monstrous. The fact is that one can separate nothing, that the coloured flow of dark pink and yellow binds the separate parts more organically than any draughtsmanship could do. Where the hair begins (always the mark of a good portrait) is as difficult to see as it is in nature. The eyes swim in their hollows, they are not fixed, but move; they see. The red of the ear grows out of the red of the flesh; it is substance before it becomes form and similarly the whole face grows out of the reddish-brown background, and it is marvellous how, somehow, it fits into the grey-white collar without separating itself from the background'.[59]

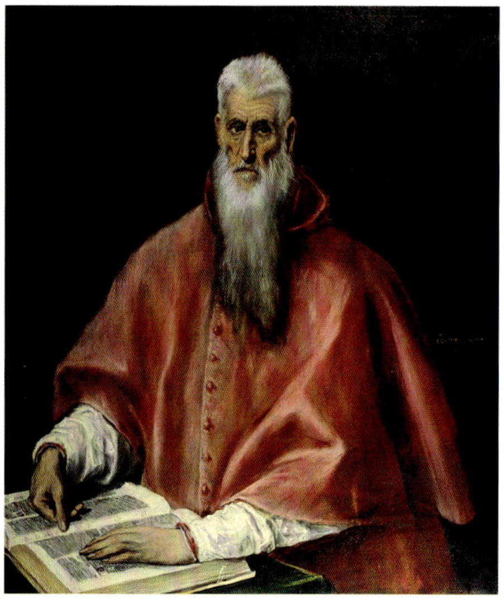

FIG. 64. El Greco, *Saint Jerome as Cardinal*, *ca.* 1590–1600. New York, The Frick Collection [05.1.67]

We find the same degree of technical freedom and vivaciousness, and ability at capturing the transient, in the portrait of *Fray Hortensio Félix Paravicino* in Boston, a painting which is much more complex than the one of Cevallos, but which shares with it an artifice that seems to have been exclusive to some of the portraits of the final years: although facing the spectator, the sitter looks away, thus creating a barely perceptible, but at the same time highly effective, sensation of instantaneous movement. In this case, the impression of life is extraordinarily reinforced by the frontal pose of the friar, and by the freedom that El Greco allowed himself in representing space, creating the feeling of depth while the sitter and the back of the chair seem to have been brought towards the picture plane. The instability, the general design and the licence in the use of perspective bring to mind certain portraits by Cézanne which adopt a similar format, with the sitter on a chair, viewed from the front and depicted only down to the knees. This is the case in the portrait *Mme Cézanne in a Yellow Armchair*, in the Metropolitan Museum of Art, New York. In this work, as in the portrait by El Greco, we have the feeling that the sitter is about to stand up. In such portraits, however, Cézanne did not generally aim to fathom the interior life of his sitter or transmit a feeling of life and transience (although he does achieve this in the *Portrait of Joachim Gasquet*, in the Národni Galerie, Prague), but limited himself to using

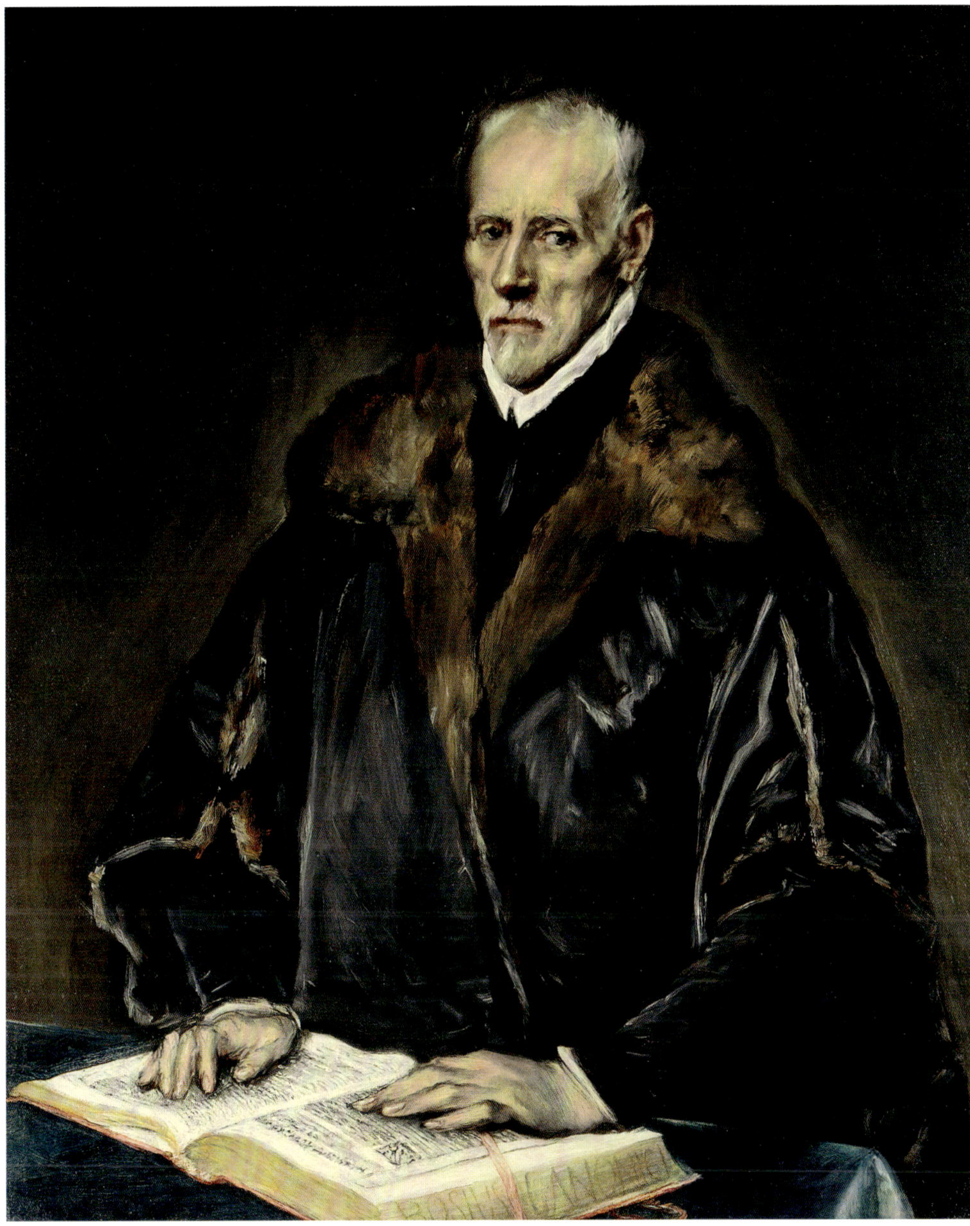

FIG. 65. El Greco, *Portrait of a Canon Lawyer (Francisco de Pisa?), ca.* 1608–1614. Fort Worth, Kimbell Art Museum [AP 1977.05]

the human figure as one more element in an abstract compositional design. El Greco, in contrast, used such liberties to fill his interpretation with life. We sense, and this has been pointed out more than once, that the friar, whose reading has been interrupted, has become aware of our presence and is ready to welcome us. On the other hand, although this is practically a 'state' portrait since both the format and the presentation are more typical of the portraits of high ecclesiastical dignitaries than of those of a simple friar, it is at the same time alive with informality and apparent casualness. While the portrait undoubtedly conveys the closeness between artist and sitter, there is no doubt that El Greco faithfully depicted not only the friar's brilliant and lively personality but also – and this in spite of his ecclesiastical condition – his haughty character and worldliness.

NOTES

1 This letter is dated 16 November 1570 and asks the Cardinal to give El Greco apartments in his Palace. Published by Ronchini 1865.

2 Inventory of the assets of Fulvio Orsini. Published by Nolhac 1884.

3 Published by Longhi 1914.

4 Pallucchini 1966, pp. 366–67.

5 As is known, the names that have most insistently been put forward are Giambattista Porta and Andrea Palladio. For a summary of the various views until then, see the entry by Hadjinicolaou in *El Greco in Italy*, 1995, no. 48, pp. 538–40. See also Marías 1997a, p. 112, who titles the portrait *Man with Writing Implements*. Recently, Bray has proposed, in a purely speculative way, another set of names: Orsini, Arias Montano or the lawyer Lancilotti mentioned by Mancini in his *Considerazioni sulla Pittura* (entry in *El Greco*, New York 2003, no. 71, p. 264).

6 For example, in the portrait of *The Procurator Antonio Cappello*, already mentioned, in the portrait of *A Venetian Senator of 46 Years of Age* (Los Angeles County Museum of Art) or in the portrait of *The Doge Pietro Loredan* (Melbourne, National Gallery of Victoria).

7 See Wethey 1984, pp. 175–76.

8 On the problems relating to the attribution of this portrait, see *The Genius of Venice*, 1983, no. 24.

9 Waterhouse 1930, p. 83.

10 Rossi 1974, cat. no. 133, ill. no. 33.

11 Wethey 1967, I, pp. 45–46 and 110, no. 107.

12 *Ibid.*

13 Pope-Hennessy 1966, p. 153.

14 Wethey 1967, I, p. 46.

15 Mayer 1916, p. 248.

16 Waterhouse 1930 p. 78, concerning the *Portrait of Giulio Clovio*.

17 '... It is an excellent painting,' he wrote, 'but despite our best will we cannot see any link with the production of El Greco. The colouring, the tone, the modelling, the way of resolving the intense shadows – so distinctive in El Greco – everything is different': Méndez Casal 1936, p. 9.

18 Pope-Hennessy 1966, p. 153.

19 See for example, Mayer 1916, p. 248, and Camón Aznar 1950, p. 129.

20 Venturi 1929, pp. 1.171–1.173.

21 *Ibid.*

22 Davies 2003b, p. 253.

23 See the recent summaries of the various hypotheses on the identity of the lady and the authorship of the painting, the entries by Davies in *Felipe II. Un monarca*, 1998 no. 234, pp. 607–10; the one by Lopera in *El Greco, Identidad* 1999 no. 27, pp. 364–65, and the one by Finaldi in *El Greco*, New York 2003, no. 73, p. 268.

24 See Wethey 1962 and 1967, no. 148, and Baticle 1984, p. 17.

25 Cossío 1908, pp. 395–98.

26 'Returning to El Greco, and choosing one of his portraits, the most regular, beautiful and perfect that we know among his paintings, *A Lady in a Fur Wrap*, one can point out as an exquisite example of the subtlety of the irregular, how the right eyebrow, when linking to the bridge of the nose, descends more than the left, how the axis of the mouth ascends in the opposite direction, and how the plane of the forehead is perfectly parallel to the plane of the chin': Garnelo 1914, pp. 222–23.

27 Beruete 1914, p. 17.

28 Hadjinicolaou 1993, pp. 175–212.

29 Entry in *El Greco y su revalorización*, 1996, pp. 110–11.

30 Concerning the existence of a portrait of the Cardinal by El Greco, as stated by Jerónimo Román de la Higuera in his *Historia eclesiástica de la Imperial Ciudad de Toledo* (*Ecclesiastical History of the Imperial City of Toledo*), see Vegué and Goldoni 1928. Today it is impossible to be certain of the identity of the artist who painted the profile bust from the Convent of Santa Úrsula in Toledo (Wethey 1967, no. X-192), which for decades has not been located. Cossío, Mayer and Camón Aznar considered it a work by El Greco, but Wethey, who did not actually see the portrait, assigned it to the school of the painter.

31 Today we only know of those that appear at the feet of *Christ Crucified* in the Louvre and the portrait of the *Christ on the Cross* made for Martín Muñoz de las Posadas (perhaps Andrés Núñez, the parish priest of Santo Tomé) and of course, the portrait of his son in the *Virgin of Charity* in Illescas. Nevertheless, there are documentary references to others. In the inventory of Jorge Manuel in 1621 there is a 'painting of the Angel Saint Gabriel giving the solemn message to Zachariah, with a portrait of a monk from the Jeronomite Order below': San Román 1927, doc. XXXV, no. 2; and in 1701 a canvas of 'Saint Ildefonso writing in front of an image of Our Lady with a portrait in the same canvas by the Greek', was registered in the Royal Collections: Álvarez Lopera 2003, pp. 184–85.

32 This has been sometimes identified as *Unknown Gentleman*, in the Musée de Picardie, in Amiens. However, this seems to portray a teacher or lawyer, not a politician. See Wethey 1962, pp. 278–80.

33 San Román 1927, doc. XXXV, no. 119. It could be the one registered in the inventory of assets of Dr Pedro Pacheco, Counsellor of Castile, in Madrid, 1662. 'Another portrait of a Jeronomite friar, by the same hand [of Dominico Greco] and same size, with its black frame, valued at 300 *Reales*.': Burke and Cherry, I, 1997, no. 57, p. 566.

34 See Gómez-Menor 1967.

35 Marías 1993, p. 62.

36 'A portrait of President Cobarrubias, *by the hand of the Greek*, a quarter [of a *vara*] in height and a quarter in width': López

Navío 1962, p. 318. From the size one could think that it would be different to the two known portraits.

37 'Another portrait of the *licenciado* Alonso de Villegas, original by the hand of the Greek, with its black frame, the size of the previous one [a *vara* and a half high, and a *vara* and a quarter wide]': inventory and valuation of assets published by Barrio Moya 1995, p. 53. Villegas praised *The Burial of the Count of Orgaz* in his *Flos Sanctorum*, but there is no other record that El Greco painted his portrait, and therefore, the identification in the inventory cannot be guaranteed.

38 Undoubtedly among the known portraits belonging to this group are the ones of Dr Rodrigo de la Fuente and Antonio Covarrubias, the one of a canon lawyer (possibly Francisco de Pisa) and the *Unknown Gentleman* from the Museum of Amiens. However, the idea that some portraits of gentlemen in the Prado portray writers who belong to the Academy of the Count of Mora does not seem acceptable (nos P-810 and P-811). See Álvarez Lopera 2003, pp. 200–03.

39 Apart from the posthumous portraits of Diego de Covarrubias and Cardinal Tavera, probably painted for the Gallery of Portraits belonging to Pedro Salazar de Mendoza, we now have around half a dozen: *A Student* (possibly Saint Aloysius Gonzaga), the *Trinitarian Friar or Dominican* in the Prado, *Paravicino*, the *Seated Trinitarian* in The Nelson-Atkins Museum of Art of Kansas City, and *Portrait of a Canon Lawyer (Francisco de Pisa?)* in the Kimbell Art Museum in Fort Worth (Texas). But there must have been more. In the inventory of assets of 1621 the following are registered, as has been mentioned: the portrait of a Jeronomite friar, the one of the canon lawyer and a member of the Governing Council of the Archbishopric of Avila de Vera. We have to include the lost portrait of Cardinal Quiroga, and various others included in inventories of the seventeenth century: the 'head of a cleric' that Velázquez, at his death, had in his rooms in the Cuarto del Príncipe in the Alcázar (see Álvarez Lopera 2003, pp. 175–76), the 'portrait of a priest' and the 'portrait of a Jeronomite friar' (possibly the same picture cited in the inventory of 1621) which appear in the inventory of assets of Dr Pedro Pacheco, Counsellor of Castile, in 1662 (Burke and Cherry 1997, I, p. 566), the 'half-length portrait of a Dominican friar' registered in 1669 in Madrid, in the inventory of assets of Catalina de Alvarado (*ibid.*, p. 625), and even the already mentioned 'portrait of the licenciado Alonso de Villegas' from the inventory of assets of Don Andrés González de Bricianos – whether or not it portrayed Villegas, it must have been the portrait of a clergyman.

40 Apart from the controversial *A Lady in a Fur Wrap*, only one female portrait is known – *Portrait of a Lady with a Flower in her Hair* – nowadays belonging to a private collection in New York. The existence of another two is also known from documentary references: the 'sketch of a portrait of a woman', from the inventory of 1621 (San Román 1927, doc. XXXV, no. 91) and the 'half-length portrait of a woman' that Velázquez had in his rooms in 1660 (probably the 'portrait of a lady with a large ruff', included in the inventories of the Alcázar of Madrid in 1666, 1686 and 1701, which must have been destroyed in the fire of the Alcázar in 1734).

41 Based on the fees paid to other contemporary painters for similar portraits, Marías 1997a (p. 207) suggests that the painter would not have received more than 50 ducats for the paintings. With a few exceptions, like the 'portrait of a man with a collar', a *vara* and a quarter high, which belonged to the painter Antonio Puga (valued at Puga's death in 1648 at 100 *reales*, acquired at auction by the painter Domingo Guerra Coronel for 67 *reales*, and valued again in 1651 at 150 *reales*: see Caturla 1982, pp. 76 and 82, and Saltillo 1944, p. 46), the valuations of portraits by El Greco that are included in seventeenth century collections were between 200 and 400 *reales*. Only the collection of Don Gaspar de Haro and Guzmán, Marquis of Carpio, where in 1689 three portraits were listed at a value of 1,000 *reales* and another at a value of 800 *reales*, were valued at considerably higher figures (Burke and Cherry, I, 1997, pp. 834, 835 and 873).

42 See, for example, the *Saint Benedict* in the Prado, from an altarpiece in the Monastery of Santo Domingo el Antiguo, or the *Saint Paul* in the collection of the Marquesa de Narros.

43 Cossío 1908, pp. 429–30.

44 Camón Aznar 1950, p. 1.122.

45 Palomino 1724/1986, p. 157.

46 See Álvarez Lopera 2003, pp. 175–76.

47 Baroja 1900, p. 1; reproduced in Álvarez Lopera 1987, pp. 454–57.

48 Cossío 1908, p. 404.

49 Gómez-Moreno 1943, p. 16.

50 Trapier 1958, p. 32.

51 Annotations in his copy of Vasari's *Lives*; see Salas 1967, p. 38.

52 Sánchez Cantón 1942, p. 20.

53 'That Antonio de Covarrubias (I would say he is a miracle of Nature) in which not only live…the eloquence and elegance of Cicero and the perfect knowledge of the Greek language, but also infinite kindness and prudence, which shine so brightly that it disturbs the eyes and prevents me from going on': Marías and Bustamante 1981, p. 168.

54 Gudiol 1971, p. 251.

55 Christiansen in *El Greco*, New York 2003, no. 80, pp. 282–85.

56 Baetjer 1981, pp. 41–44.

57 Brown and Carr 1984, pp. 69–73.

58 See the entry by T. de Antonio in *El Greco y su revalorización*, 1996, no. 4, pp. 112–13.

59 Meier-Graefe 1910/1926, pp. 104–05.

CAT. 15. El Greco. *A Nobleman with his Hand on his Chest, ca.* 1577–1580. Museo del Prado [P-809]

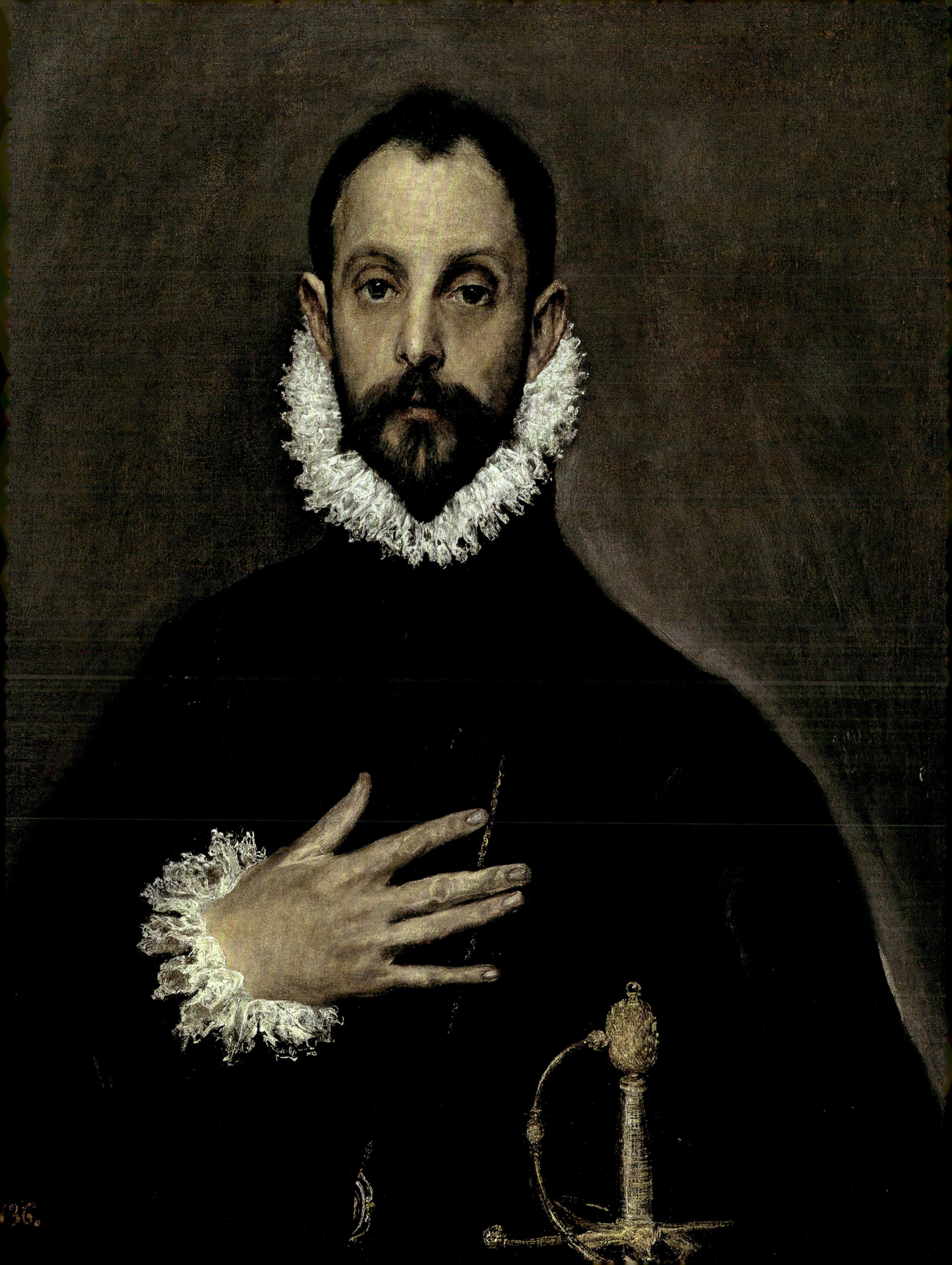

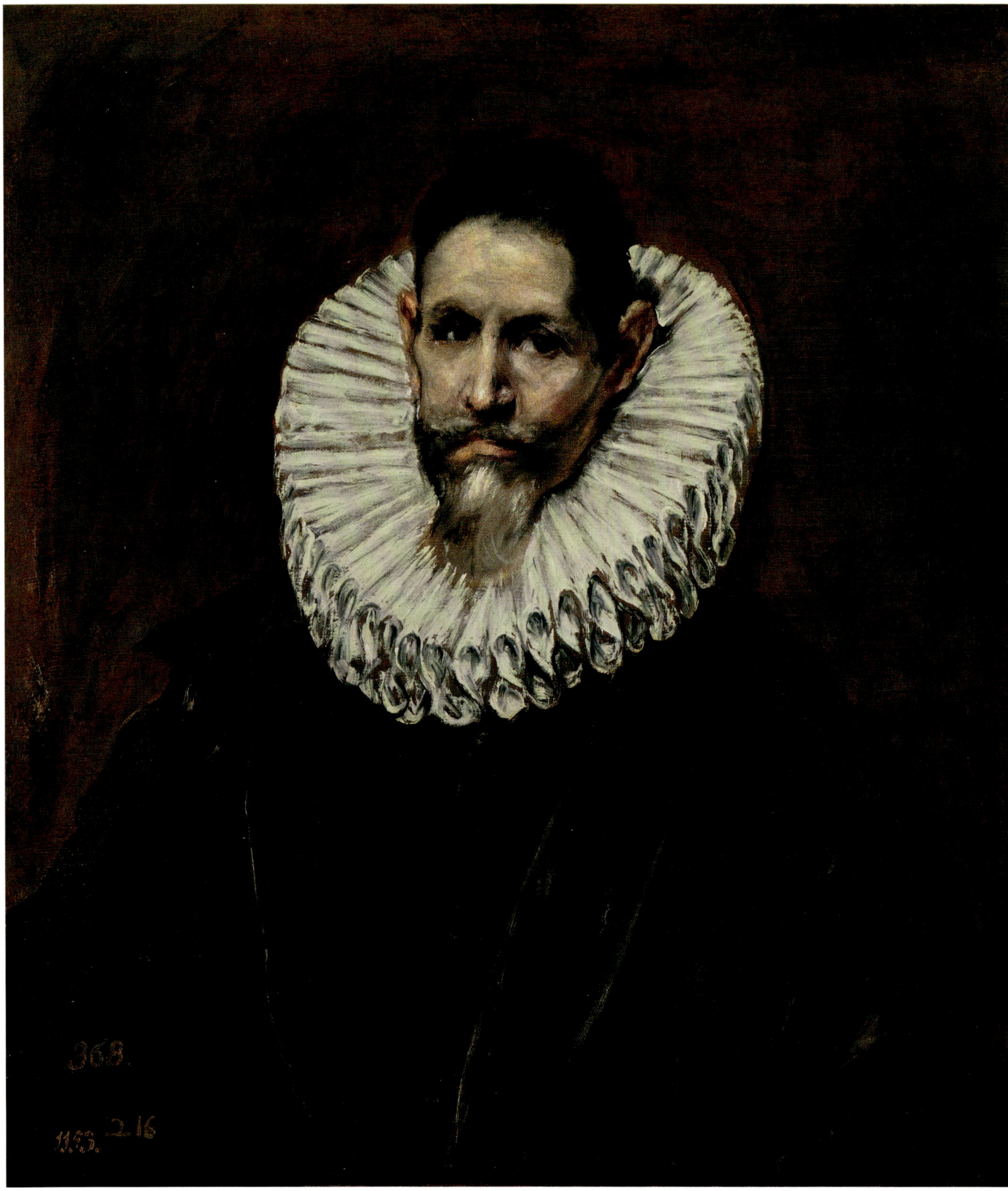

CAT. 16. El Greco. *Jerónimo de Cevallos*, 1613. Museo del Prado [P-812]

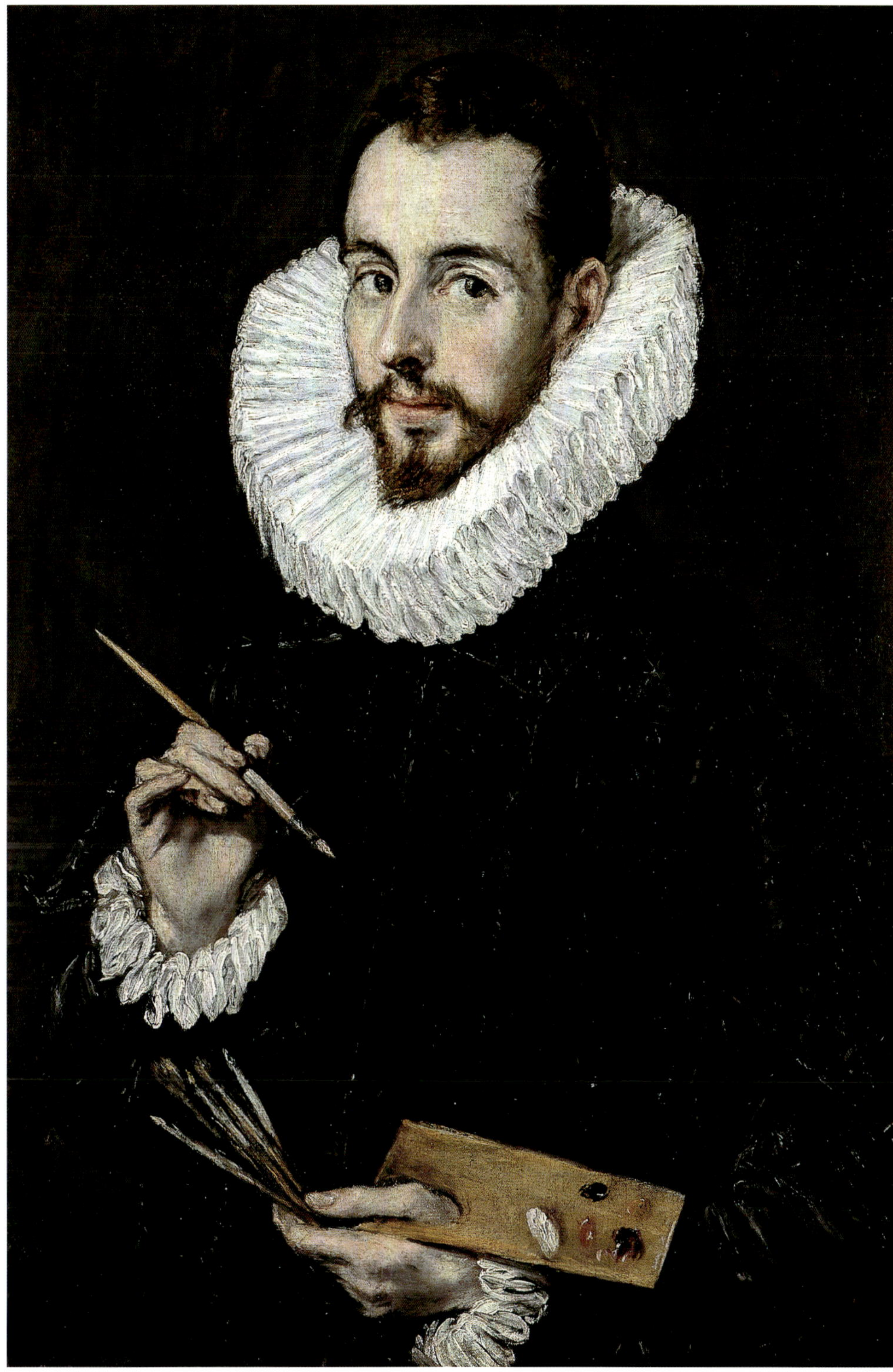

CAT. 17. El Greco. *Portrait of a Painter (Jorge Manuel Theotocopouli), ca.* 1603.
Seville, Museo de Bellas Artes [E.97.P]

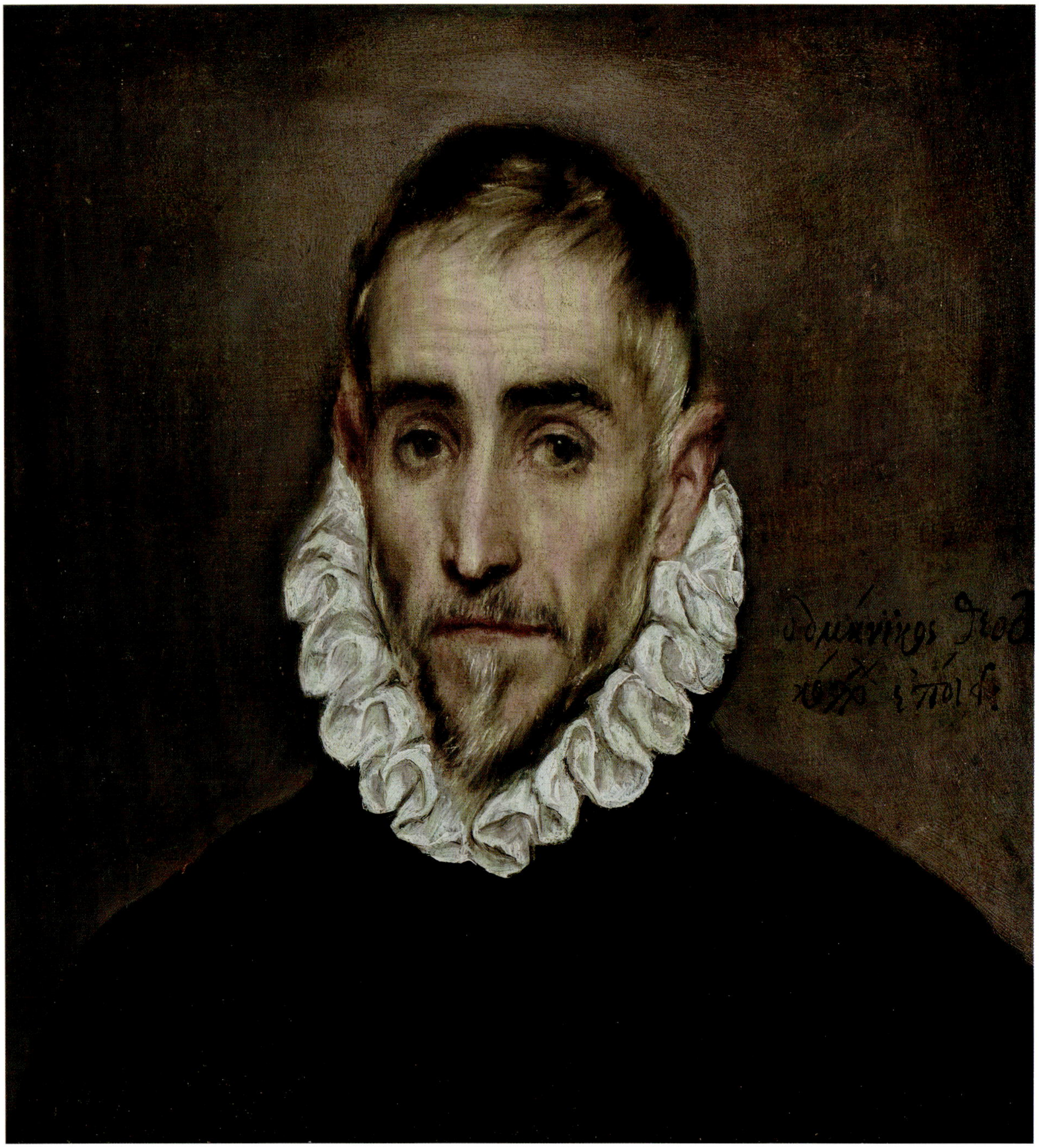

CAT. 18. El Greco. *An Elderly Gentleman, ca.* 1587–1596.
Museo del Prado [P-806]

CAT. 19. El Greco. *Fray Hortensio Félix Paravicino, ca.* 1609–1613.
Boston, Museum of Fine Arts (Isaac Sweetser Fund [04.234])

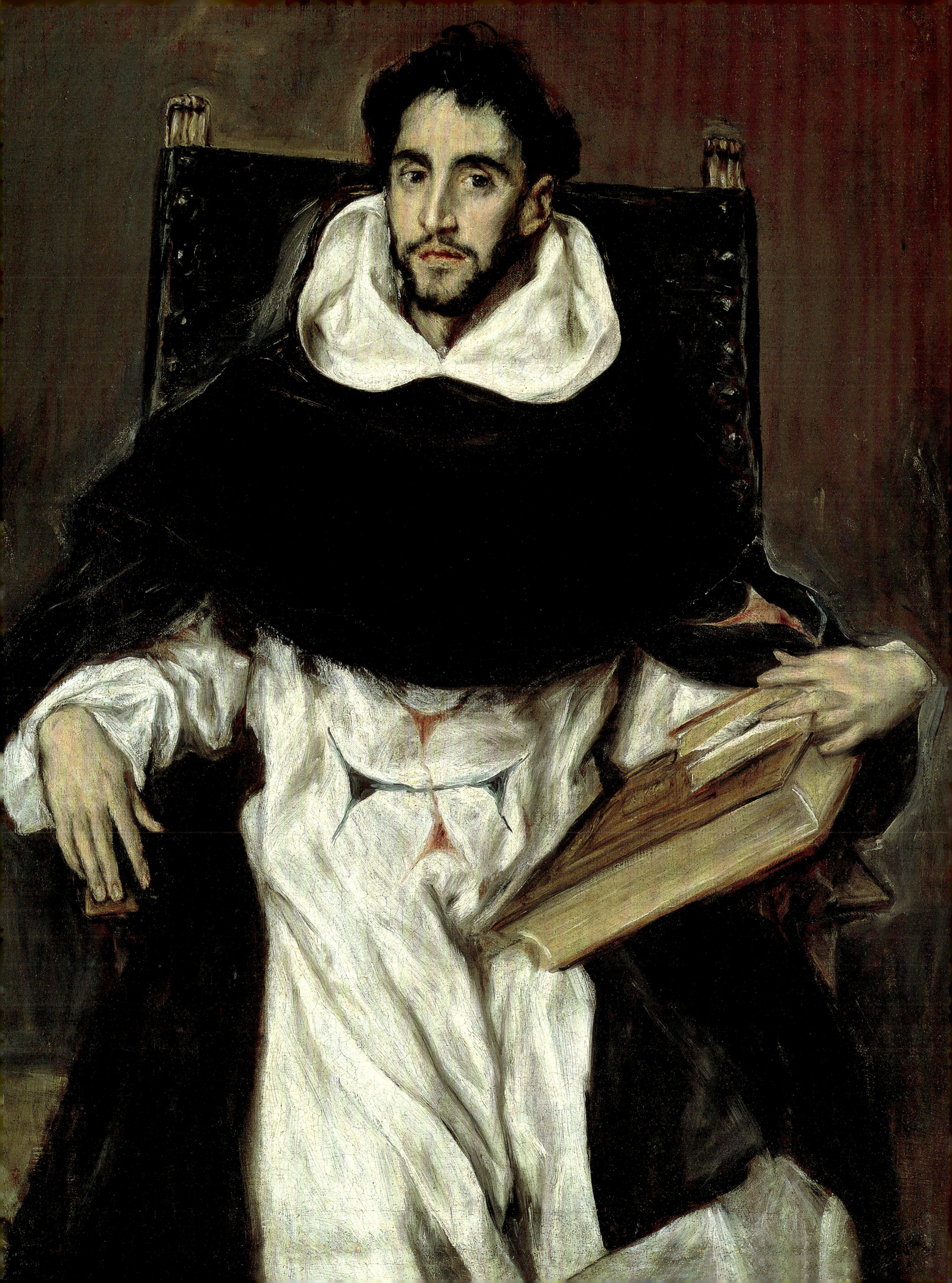

4 Portrait and Reality: Ribalta, Zurbarán, Ribera

Gabriele Finaldi

In the summer of 1612, Francisco Ribalta (1565–1628), the foremost painter in Valencia, executed a portrait of a recently deceased parish priest, Father Francisco Gerónimo Simón, with Christ carrying the cross [FIG. 66]. In spite of the fact that he had not been a celebrated preacher, nor had he published anything, Father Simón (1578–1612) acquired a reputation for sanctity, which after his early death spread rapidly throughout Spain and Catholic Europe. Among his distinguished devotees were the King of Spain, Philip III, the Duke of Lerma, Archduke Albert, Governor of the Netherlands, and most probably Ribalta himself, who effectively became the venerable priest's official image maker.

At first sight the portrait appears to correspond to the typology of the donor portrait in a devotional painting, but in fact what it shows is Father Simón witnessing a vision that he experienced along the Calle de los Caballeros in Valencia, when he heard trumpets and saw Christ bearing the cross followed by the Virgin Mary and Roman soldiers; as Christ approached the kneeling priest, he drew back the locks of hair that covered his face and gazed lovingly at him.[1] Ribalta may have based his posthumous likeness of Simón on an earlier portrait made from life or from his memory of the priest's appearance, but it is noteworthy that in this painting he made no distinction between the styles he employed to paint priest and vision: Christ and Father Simón are treated with the same level of reality and share the same physical presence, the same space and identical lighting. No doubt the aesthetically homogenous treatment was intended to bolster the claims of the truth of Father Simón's visionary experience – viciously challenged by his detractors – but it also reflects a shift in the stylistic vocabulary of Valencian painting in the early part of the seventeenth century towards a more naturalistic manner. A similar shift is apparent in the other artistic centres of Spain, Toledo, Madrid and Seville, and it is of course especially evident in portraiture, where the express purpose of the genre (as defined by Covarrubias in 1611, and by Francisco Pacheco in 1649) was the accurate recording of a sitter's appearance for posterity.

As has been already observed several times in this catalogue, it is not always easy to separate portraiture

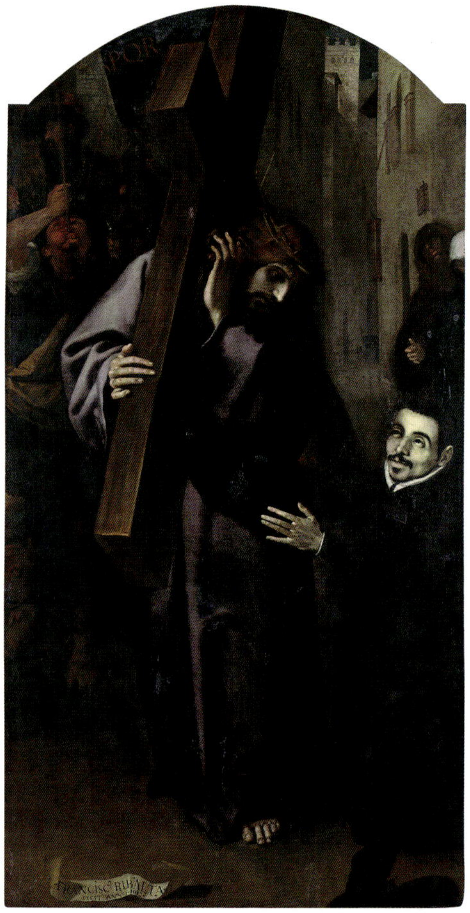

FIG. 66. Francisco Ribalta, *The Vision of Father Simón*, 1612. London, The National Gallery [NG 2930]

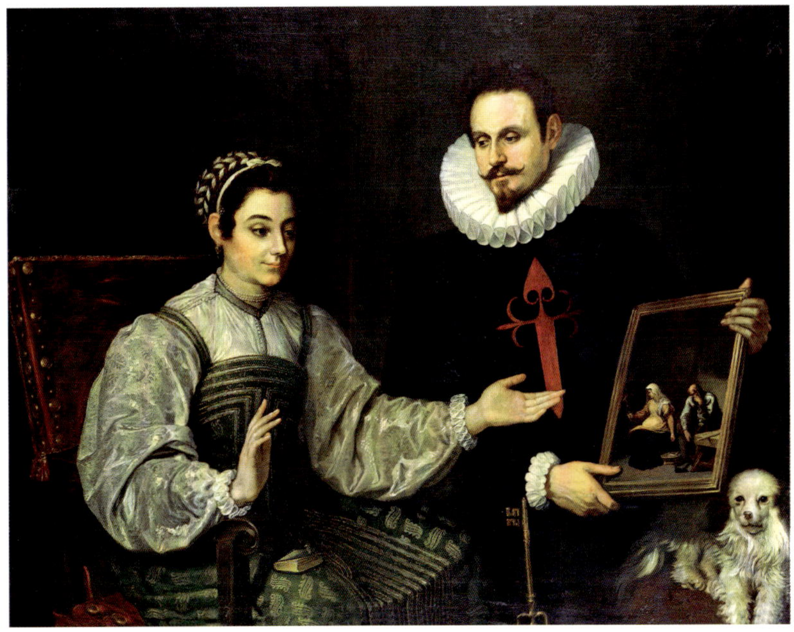

FIG. 67. Anonymous Spanish painter, *A Knight of Santiago and his Lady*, 1610s. Lexington, University of Kentucky Art Museum [Gaines Challenge Fund 1984.18]

and portrait-like images (sometimes inelegantly referred to as 'pseudo-portraits'), and there are particular subjects which take advantage of the ambiguity. Saint Luke was, according to pious legend, a painter and made portraits of the Virgin. When El Greco painted his *Apostolados*, it was natural that he should feel a special empathy with Saint Luke, and the artist's features have often been recognised in those of the evangelist in the Toledo Cathedral apostle series.[2] Ribalta's rendition of Saint Luke in the set of *Evangelists* for the high altarpiece of the charterhouse of Porta Coeli near Valencia [CAT. 20] shows a very distinctive individual, halo-less, determined and brooding, markedly different in character from the traditional and idealised morpohology of the other three evangelists. He is represented in the act of portrait painting – only rarely shown in Spanish art [see CATS 43 and 44 (Velázquez's *Las Meninas* and Mazo's *The Family of the Painter*)] – and his sacred sitter is positioned immediately behind the easel at which he works to enable him to paint her approximately life size. He has turned his piercing gaze momentarily away from the Virgin in order to look at the viewer and show off what is in all probability his own likeness. Jusepe de Ribera (1591–1652) and Luca Giordano (1634–1704) also painted what are presumably self-portraits in the guise of Saint Luke,[3] but the most remarkable image of this kind is surely the picture by Francisco de Zurbarán (1598–1664) in which a painter devoutly contemplates the crucified Christ [CAT. 21]. Often, but mistakenly, assumed to be Saint Luke – who did not paint Christ on the cross – this figure is frequently, and again probably mistakenly, identified as a self-portrait of Zurbarán. In fact, the artist skilfully juggles with a variety of visual ambiguities concerning what is real and what is represented, the differing scale of the figures and the nature of their relationship to one another. Rather than a straightforward self-portrait, the painter in the picture should perhaps be understood as a conceptual portrait of the devout artist, a type with which Zurbarán would have identified.

A fascinating portrait in which a religious painting is the object of contemplation of the sitters is the intriguing double portrait of *A Knight of Santiago and his Lady* in the University of Kentucky Art Museum [FIG. 67].[4] The painting used to be attributed to Francisco Ribalta but is probably by an artist working in Madrid and dates from the second decade of the seventeenth century before

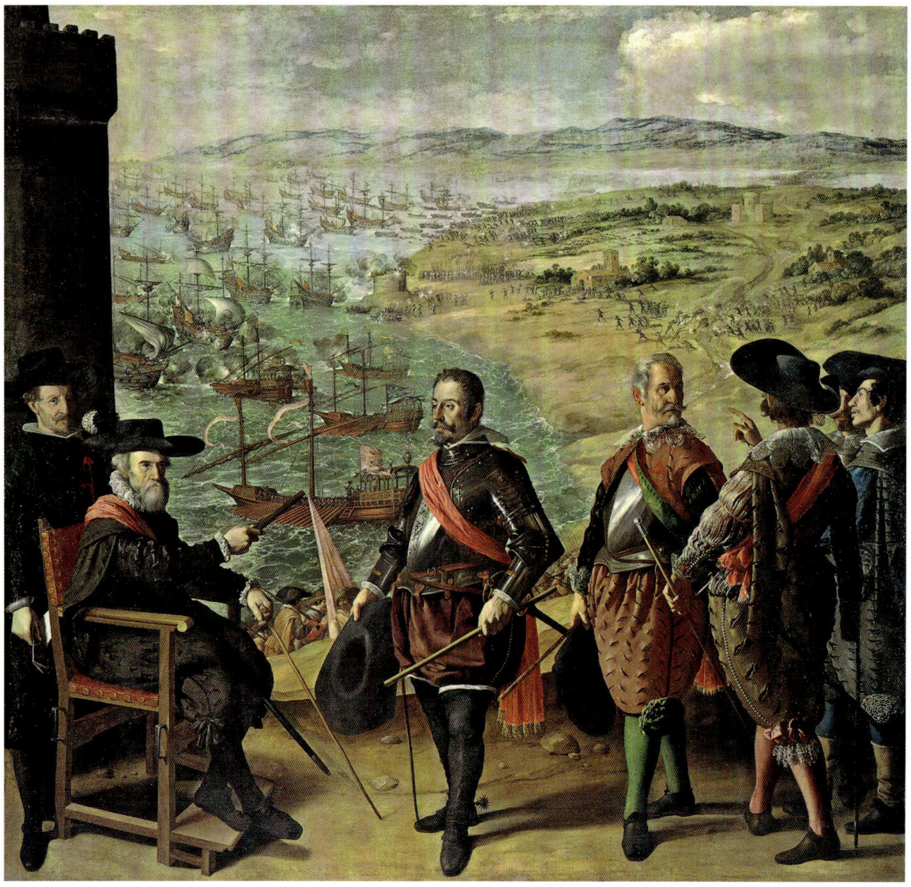

FIG. 68. Francisco de Zurbarán, *The Defence of Cadiz*, 1634. Madrid, Museo del Prado [P-656]

the use of the starched ruff was banned by Philip IV. The knight, who bears the key of a Gentleman of the Bedchamber, a high-ranking court position with frequent access to the king, is showing his wife, who has just laid aside her prayer book, a small devotional painting of the Virgin and Saint Joseph in the carpenter's workshop. The Virgin is heavily pregnant and the solicitous gestures of the woman probably express the couple's hope for a child. One is naturally wary of identifying such a specific narrative in a portrait painting, but given that it is extremely rare for a married couple to be represented together in a Spanish portrait at this time, it may be assumed that the portrait expresses a shared concern of the sitters. The domestic character of the painting is underlined by the presence of the pet dog, also a symbol of marital fidelity, which appears with increasing frequency in Spanish portraits of this period.

Neither Ribalta nor Zurbarán painted many portraits. Fewer than half a dozen by Zurbarán, who worked principally for the monastic foundations of Seville, have survived and these testify that he brought to bear the same searing observation on his sitters as he did to the objects in his still lifes.[5] The portrait of *Don Alonso Verdugo de Albornoz* [CAT. 22] was painted in 1635, probably in Seville, and shows the twelve-year-old knight and military captain regaled with sash, sword and baton. He is sharply lit from the upper left and emerges with a forceful physical presence from the opaque, almost unmodulated dark background, his breastplate flashing and the slashes on his pantaloons casting deep shadows. The artist conveys the sitter's haughty aristocratic bearing but is clearly sensitive to his childlike vulnerability. The work was painted very soon after the large *Defence of Cadiz* [FIG. 68] made for the Hall of Realms (Salón de

Reinos) of the newly-built Buen Retiro Palace in Madrid, which includes a group of life-size portraits (grown-up versions of Don Alonso) set against a landscape background in which Spanish troops fight off the English naval attack of 1625. The military governor of the city, Fernando Girón y Ponce de León, immobilised by gout, gives orders to his stern and elegant captains from the chair on which he was carried. The admirable execution of the heads and the skill apparent in the rendition of textures in dress and armour demonstrates what Zurbarán was capable of in the field of portraiture, but the painting also shows up his limitations as a painter of history subjects, in which the handling of narrative and the interaction of the figures are the elements fundamental to the success of the compositions.

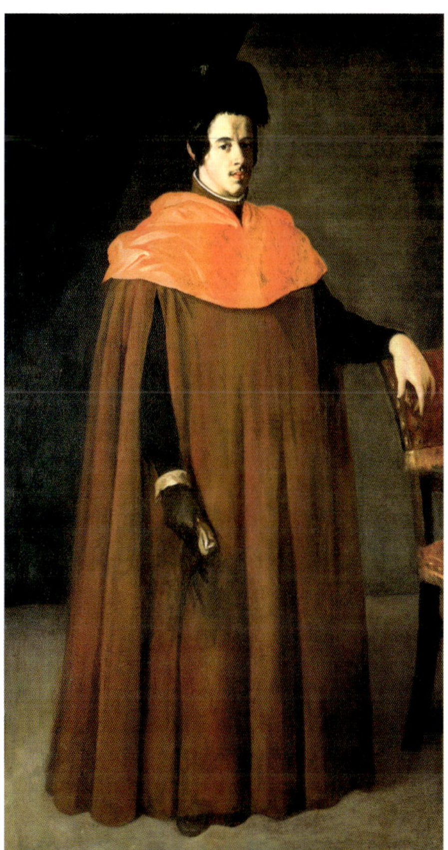

FIG. 69. Francisco de Zurbarán, *A Doctor of Law at the University of Salamanca, ca.* 1635. Boston, Isabella Stewart Gardner Museum

Zurbarán's natural inclination towards the representation of the individual full-length figure, best seen in his series of virgin-martyrs [see FIG. 7], saints and patriarchs, resulted in portraits which are striking for their equilibrium, *gravitas* and concentration, like the *Doctor of Law at the University of Salamanca* in Boston [FIG. 69], or the less well known *Portrait of Doctor Juan Martínez Serrano* (1578–1653), a theologian who taught in Sigüenza, which is in a private collection in the United States.[6] In these works the sitters are shown life-size, close to the picture plane, with plain backgrounds and few attributes or objects, and they gaze directly at the viewer. In spite of his years of activity in the capital (1634 and 1658–1664), he never portrayed any member of the royal family and his sitters appear to have been professionals and minor nobles from outside Madrid.

It remains surprising that he painted so few portraits and the reason may simply be that he had sufficient other activity not to need to cultivate this genre. It is also possible that already in the mid-1630s his portraits looked static and slightly *passé* in style in comparison with those painted at court by Velázquez and Rubens (in Madrid in 1628–1629) which were defining what was fashionable in the genre.

But in a sense, all Zurbarán's figure paintings are portraits. His saints and visionaries, monks and martyrs, are distinctive individuals based on the study of the physiognomies of particular models. When he came to paint the series of 'portraits' of celebrated Mercedarian theologians for the library of the Merced Calzada of Seville, all of whom (with one exception) were dead before he began, he appears to have used a selection of living Mercedarian models who played the part of their forebears. Fray Francisco Zúmel [CAT. 23], a celebrated philosopher and teacher and General of the Order, had died in 1604, but rather than painting a posthumous portrait based on an earlier image or a death mask, Zurbarán decided to employ the traditional imagery of a church doctor, solemn, reflective and divinely inspired in his writings, combine it with the close observation of a living model, and then simply inscribe the canvas with Zúmel's name. The same model in fact appears as another deceased theologian, Fray Pedro Machado (Madrid, Museo de la Real Academia de San Fernando).

Zurbarán's attitude to his models, characterised by a reluctance to stray from the visual datum – indeed bound to it with an almost fervent dogmatism – and resistant to any form of flattering idealisation, is paralleled in the work of his older contemporary, Jusepe de Ribera. Ribera was born in Valencia but his entire career was spent in Italy, where he achieved success and renown as painter to the Spanish viceroys of Naples, the city where he settled in 1616. While his painting developed in proximity to such artists as Guido Reni (1575–1642), Domenichino (1581–1641), Giovanni Lanfranco (1582–1647) and Massimo Stanzione (*ca.* 1585–1656), who were his colleagues and rivals, he worked for a largely Spanish clientele. He was no doubt familiar with developments in painting in Spain, from the reports he received from the viceroys, often themselves cultivated collectors and patrons, from the civil servants who were posted to the viceregal court in Naples, and from the artists who visited him there, the Aragonese painter Jusepe Martínez (1600–1682) who was in Naples in 1625, and Velázquez himself, who visited in 1630 and possibly twice during his second Italian sojourn (1649–51). Most importantly, his pictures were imported into Spain in large numbers, many of them finding their way into the collection of King Philip IV, who had a great admiration for his work. Although Ribera never returned to Spain, the country he described as a 'cruel stepmother to her own native children' (*cruelísima madrastra de los propios naturales*),[7] his paintings were well known and exerted a powerful influence on several generations of Spanish painters including Velázquez himself, Zurbarán, Alonso Cano (1601–1667), Murillo (1617–1682) and Juan Carreño de Miranda (1614–1685).[8]

Jusepe Martínez described Ribera as a *pintor imitador del natural*, and Ribera's astonishing gifts at capturing natural appearances were deployed within a tenebrist idiom, deeply informed by the late paintings of Caravaggio. It is probably no coincidence that, like Caravaggio, Ribera painted few portraits. Generally speaking, Caravaggesque painters in Italy were not given many opportunities to paint portraits, and in Naples such commissions appear to have gone to Stanzione and to artists of Flemish extraction more inclined to produce attractive renditions of their sitters.[9] The portrait for which Ribera is best known is one that he was commissioned to paint precisely because the patron wanted a faithful and unidealised rendition of the sitter's extraordinary appearance, for she was nothing less than, as the inscription on the painting states, EN MAGNV[M] NATVRA MIRACVLVM, 'A great wonder of nature' [CAT. 25]. Maddalena Ventura, the bearded woman of the Abruzzi, was painted at the behest of the Viceroy Duke of Alcalá, who had invited her to the royal palace in Naples, fascinated by her embodiment of an aberrant hermaphroditic nature, a woman who had been a female until the age of thirty-seven and had then begun effectively to transmogrify into a man. Her face is completely masculine, bearing no trace of soft skin texture or feminine lineaments, but the artist has painted the suckling child and the skein of wool as attributes of her eclipsed femininity. Maddalena appears serious and resigned; her husband, Felice De Amici, who hovers in the background, accustomed to his wife being the protagonist in every situation and no doubt profiting from it, looks world-weary and acquiescent. Ribera is sensitive to the complex psychology of their matrimonial situation but also to the artistic possibilities the subject offered for a special display of painterly virtuosity.

By 1637 the portrait hung in the Duke of Alcalá's dining room in his palace in Seville, the Casa de Pilatos.[10] Portraits of the fantastical and the deformed, of dwarves and giants, are frequently listed in the inventories of Spanish noble collections and in the royal palaces.[11] Juan Sánchez Cotán's *Portrait of Brígida del Río*, the bearded woman of Peñaranda, painted in 1590 (Madrid, Museo del Prado), was given by the artist to the royal architect Juan Gómez de Mora and subsequently passed into the royal collections, and Velázquez's portraits of the dwarves who were members of the royal household were painted for King Philip IV [CATS 33 and 34 and FIG. 19]. Alonso Sánchez Coello (1531/32–1588), Diego de Romulo Cincinnato (*ca.* 1580–1625), Juan van der Hamen (1596–

1631) and Ribera also painted portraits of dwarves, and Vicente Carducho (1576–1638) made enormous paintings of heads, probably portraits of giants.[12] Ribera made several drawings and prints of grotesque heads, including figures deformed by large goitres, which reflect a personal fascination for subjects of this kind. For the Duke of Alcalá's successor, the Count of Monterrey (viceroy from 1631 to 1637), he painted the naked portrait of a monstrous child, Andrea Mangone, who at the age of sixteen months was already nearly a metre tall and equally wide.[13] His appearance was so impressive that Monterrey had him brought, like Maddalena Ventura, to the palace where Ribera painted him. The portrait eventually passed from Monterrey's collection to that of the king and was hung in the Buen Retiro palace. Regrettably it is lost, but an echo of it is surely to be found in Carreño's naked portrait of Eugenia Martínez Vallejo, known as 'La monstrua', a child of gigantic proportions who was born in Bárcena near Burgos and was brought to the court in Madrid to be shown off in 1680, when she was six years old [FIGS 87 and 88].[14]

The *Portrait of a Knight of Santiago* [FIG. 70] has been identified tentatively as a portrait of the Count of Monterrey, although there is little evidence to back this up.[15] It is an un-rhetorical representation of a captain-general and projects a strong sense of personal dignity combined with a certain aristocratic *hauteur*. The military paraphernalia is kept to a minimum and instead of a breastplate he wears only a gorget over a leather doublet. His elegant sleeves are unbuttoned in the middle to give his arms greater freedom of movement and he rests his left hand on the hilt of his sword. The draped table and the swathe of crimson curtain signify high status, as does the cockle pendant on his chain bearing the cross of Santiago, but for the moment his identity remains unknown to us. Given the strength of this portrait, it remains something of a surprise that in spite of having served eleven viceroys, Ribera only certainly made images of one of them, Don Juan José of Austria [FIG. 71]. The large equestrian portrait in the collection of Patrimonio Nacional showing the nineteen-year-old Infante on a rearing dappled grey stallion, overlooking the Bay of

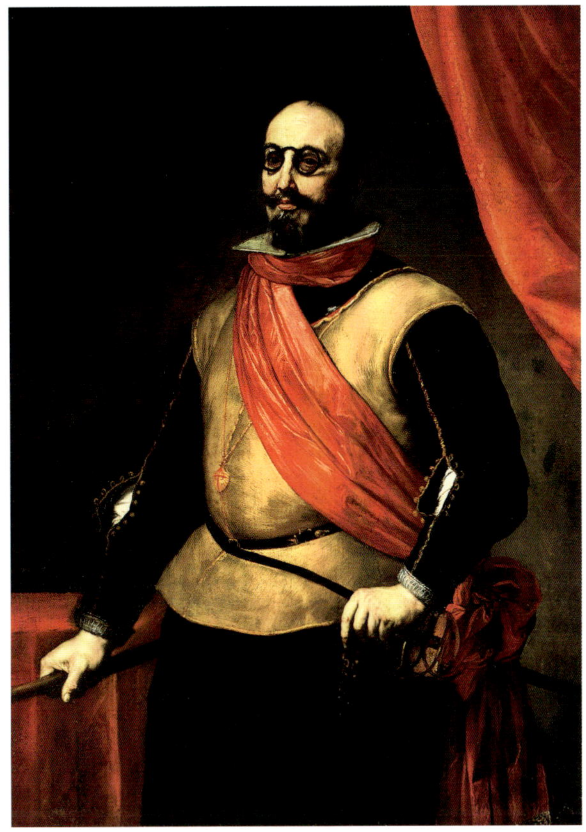

FIG. 70. Jusepe de Ribera, *Portrait of a Knight of Santiago*, mid-1630s. Dallas, Meadows Museum, Southern Methodist University [Algur H. Meadows Collection, 77.02]

Naples, impressively conveys the brilliant and flamboyant character of the sitter, but one senses that the artist was ill-at-ease with the grandiloquent rhetoric of this kind of state portrait.[16] In the etching he made based on this picture (dated 1648), he resolved the spatial infelicities, improved the contour of the horse and completely reworked the view of Naples, creating an image that was considerably more effective as political propaganda.[17] For a painter whose principal concern was faithfulness to nature, political imagery in portraiture was never going to be a primary interest.

In Naples, as in Spain, a significant sub-genre in portraiture was that of images of ecclesiastics and other religious figures. Many of El Greco's sitters and several of Velázquez's were churchmen and women [CATS 19 and 29], admired for their learning or zeal, and their portraits were intended for friends and admirers, or to grace the walls of the orders to which they belonged. Ribera's sober *Portrait of a Jesuit* [CAT. 24] belongs to this category of the religious portrait, but the scale and format of the painting indicate that the sitter had considerable social standing. The black Jesuit cassock provided a particular pictorial challenge (like the white habits of the Carthusians and Mercedarians that Zurbarán painted) and Ribera uses the great swathe of black that dominates the picture to emphasise the seriousness and gravity that is conveyed in the sitter's face. His left hand, situated in the centre of this stretch of black, marks the rhythm of the pictorial composition, defining the diagonal axis that runs across the picture from right to left, where the sitter's right hand rests on a lion, a significant symbolic attribute (like those employed in the portrait of Maddalena Ventura), whose significance remains hidden to us at present. It may refer to the Jesuit's name or to some virtue with which he was richly endowed, or, as has traditionally been thought, it may allude to his missionary activities.

These paintings and a few others constitute Ribera's entire portrait oeuvre,[18] but, as has been observed above in relation to Zurbarán, the artist's close reliance on highly distinctive models for his religious and genre paintings makes the relationship between his portrait and his non-portrait oeuvre a fluid and very interesting one. A comparison between the head of the ragged philosopher *Democritus (?)* [CAT. 26] and that of Maddalena Ventura not only reveals intriguing similarities in handling and characterisation but suggests that the process of elaboration, which involves detailed observation of the sitter-model, is very similar in the two pictures.

In his celebrated letter to Teodoro (Dirck) Ameyden, *Discorso sopra la Pittura*, on the different modes of modern painting, written in Rome in 1617–18, the writer and collector Vincenzo Giustiniani described Ribera's method as 'painting with the natural objects before the eyes' (*dipingere con avere gli oggetti naturali davanti*). He added that this was not simply a question of making a *portrait* of them (*non basta farne il semplice ritratto*), for the artist must know how to handle the contours, design and *chiaroscuro*.[19] In the present context it is noteworthy that Giustiniani uses the word 'ritratto' not in relation to painting a sitter but to describe an attitude in painting any subject from nature. The same kind of scrutiny and observation that is focused on the sitter when making a portrait is likewise applied to all other natural subjects. The accuracy of the statement in relation to Ribera's work is apparent in his series of the *Five Senses* painted in Rome just before Giustiniani was writing, in which the artist brilliantly conflates painting of everyday life, rooted in profound natural observation, with allegorical intent, and also in his masterpiece of genre painting of 1642, the *Clubfooted Boy* in the Louvre [FIG. 72].[20]

Set against a scrubby landscape with a low horizon line which confers an unexpected monumentality on the sitter, this young Neapolitan beggar stands like a child pikeman with his crutch resting on his shoulder like a weapon, engaging the viewer with a resplendent smile, the very personification of triumph in adversity. The piece of paper he bears says, 'Give me alms, for the love of God' (*DA MIHI ELEMOSINAM PROPTER AMOREM DEI*), and invites the spectator to Christian charity. This boy is of course a type, a representation of a member of the Neapolitan underclass, the army of rogues, beggars, *lazzaroni* and ne'er-do-wells that populated the streets of the capital, but in Ribera's hands he is an individual with a real existence beyond the moment of the picture. The artist has given this genre painting a portrait-like treatment, investing his model with individual character and psychology; he has given him a soul. This is a quality that is apparent in his pictures of philosophers in the 1630s and in his personification of the five senses. *The Clubfooted Boy*, perhaps commissioned by the immensely wealthy Flemish merchant resident in Naples, Ferdinand Vandeneynden (d. 1674), never went to Spain, but when it was seen in Paris by Ignacio Zuloaga (1870–1945) it inspired him to produce one of his finest portraits, that of the *Dwarf Gregorio Botero in Sepúlveda* (1907, Moscow, Pushkin Museum of Fine Art).

Murillo's urchins are evidently relatives of Ribera's boy, but theirs is a more idealised, lyrical poverty [CAT. 28].[21] Although his entire career was spent in Seville, Murillo was certainly familiar with the works of Ribera and the early paintings of Velázquez, and in his pictures of poor children he effected an original and personal synthesis influenced by the scenes of everyday life of northern European painters, particularly those of the *Bamboccianti* who worked in Rome in the middle decades of the seventeenth century painting small-scale pictures of beggars, tavern scenes and lowly traders. Murillo's portraits proper are treated elsewhere in this book, but in paintings like *Four Figures on a Step* in the Kimbell Art Museum [CAT. 27] he shows a profound empathy with the reality of contemporary life and a concern to transmit a believable family situation with its attendant psychological relationships. Whether this is a straightforward and uncomplicated 'portrait' of a Sevillian family, which seems unlikely, or a scene of solicitation and prostitution, the artist employs certain conventions which are directly associated with the genre of portraiture: the individual characterisations, the use of contemporary dress, the life-size scale and the gazes directed at the viewer.

Murillo's portraiture, one of the most attractive and brilliant aspects of his oeuvre, reveals his ready absorption of the techniques, poses and formats of Rubens and Anthony Van Dyck (1599–1641), as well as those of Guido Reni, as demonstrated in the portrait of *Don Justino de Neve* in the National Gallery, London [CAT. 41]. His greatest debt though, is of course to Velázquez, whose titanic contribution to the genre is the subject of the next chapter.

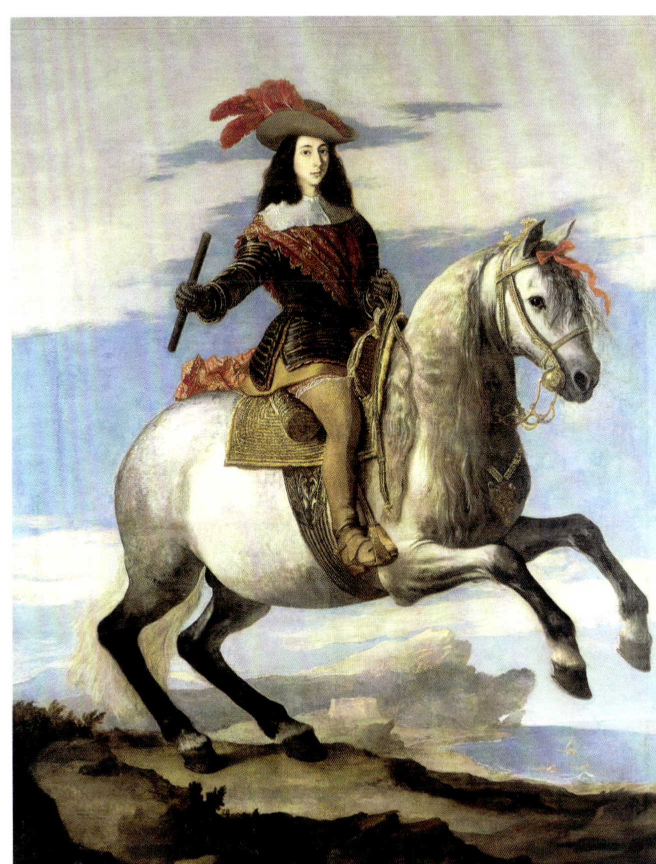

FIG. 71. Jusepe de Ribera, *Equestrian Portrait of Don Juan José of Austria*, 1648. Madrid, Palacio Real, Patrimonio Nacional

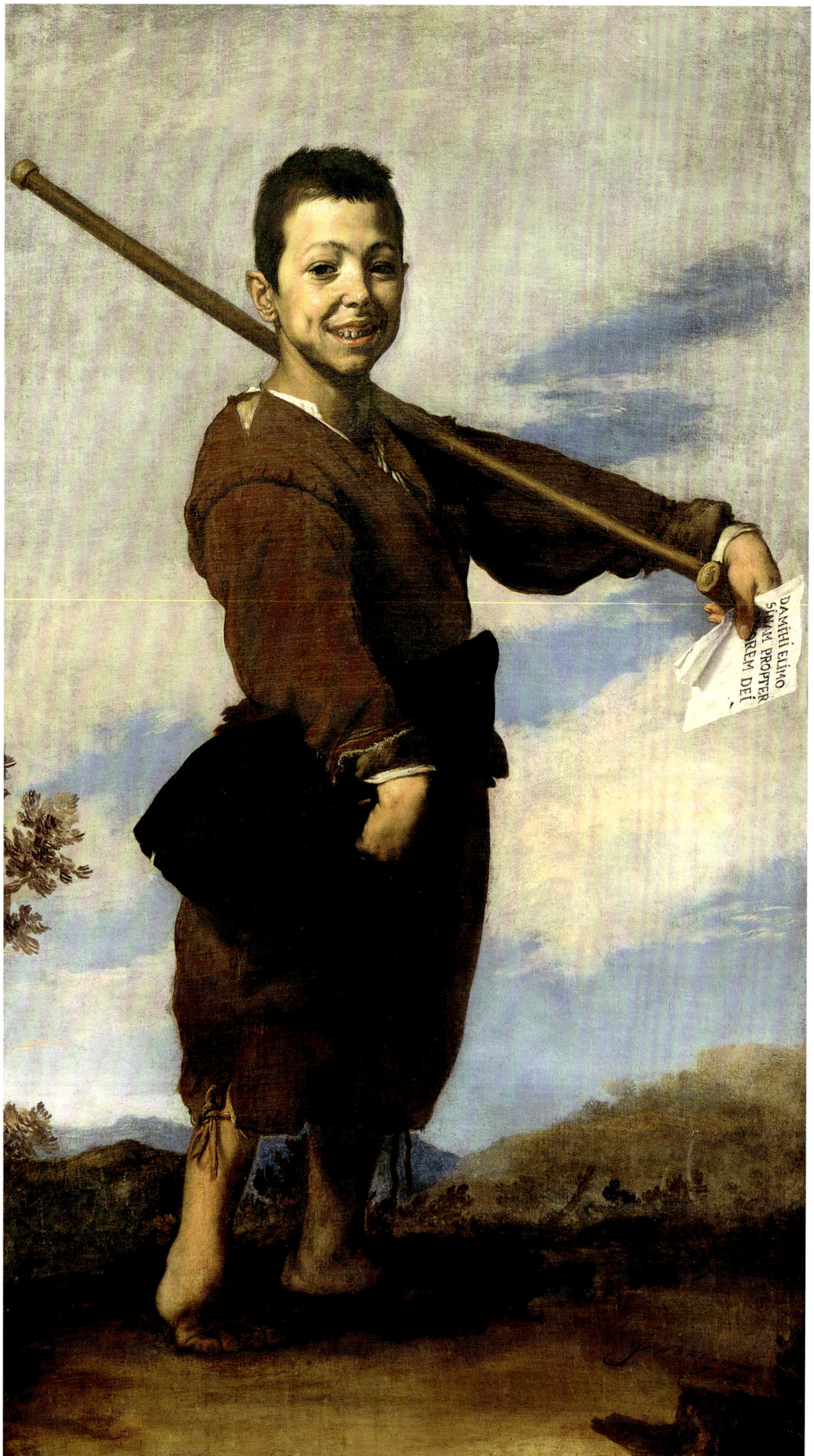

FIG. 72. Jusepe de Ribera, *The Clubfooted Boy*, 1642. Paris, Musée du Louvre [MI 893]

NOTES

1 See MacLaren/Braham, 1970, pp. 87–91 and more recently, on the controversies surrounding Father Simón and the use of his images, Falomir 1998–1999.

2 On El Greco's *Apostolados*, see the exh. cat., *El Greco: Apostolados, Museo de Bellas Artes de La Coruña*, 2002; on the *Saint Luke*, see Wethey 1962, II, no. 166.

3 For Ribera's painting, see Pérez Sánchez 1981, and the comments in *Ribera, 1591–1652 (Madrid)*, pp. 487, 489 (note 46) and 504. For Giordano's, see Ferrari and Scavizzi 1992, cat. nos A13 and A14, figs 72 and 73.

4 The painting has also been attributed to Pedro Orrente and to Luis Tristán, see Kowal 1985, cat. S-13, p. 309 (with bibliography); Haraszti-Takács 1983, cat. 168, pp. 207–08; Benito 1994, p. 191.

5 On Zurbarán's portraits, see specifically López Rey 1971, and the references in Caturla/Delenda 1994.

6 The latter is reproduced in colour in Caturla/Delenda 1994, p. 212.

7 Reported by Jusepe Martínez in his *Discursos praticables del nobilísimo arte de la pintura*, compiled in 1675, quoted in *Ribera, 1591–1652 (Madrid)*, 1992, p. 495.

8 See the essay 'Ribera y España' by A. E. Pérez Sánchez in the exh. cat. *Ribera, 1591–1652 (Madrid)*, 1992, pp. 79–105.

9 Portrait painting in Naples in this period remains little studied. See some general observations drawn from the evidence of inventories of picture collections in Labrot 1992, pp. 32–35.

10 'Un lienço sin g^on^ de una muger Barbuda con su marido de mano de Joseph de rrivera [...]', Brown and Kagan 1987, p. 251 (item V.19).

11 On this subject, see Moreno Villa 1939; Bouza 1991; *Monstruos, enanos y bufones* 1986.

12 Madrid, Museo del Prado, P-638 (246 x 205 cm), see Angulo Iñiguez and Pérez Sánchez 1969, no. 472, p. 181, fig. 142; another is in a private collection in Spain (information from Leticia Ruiz).

13 See Finaldi 2003a, p. 385.

14 *Carreño, Rizi, Herrera* 1986, cat. nos 49 and 50, pp. 228–29; Bouza 1991, pp. 49–50; *Monstruos, enanos y bufones* 1986, cat. nos 31–32, pp. 108–11.

15 See the lengthy entry on the painting by C. Felton in *Jusepe de Ribera, lo Spagnoletto, 1591–1652 (Fort Worth)*, 1982, cat. no. 24. The problems with the identification rest on the differences between the appearance of Ribera's sitter and the documented portraits of Monterrey (several prints and Giuliano Finelli's portrait sculpture in the church of the Agustinas Recoletas in Salamanca) in which he is never shown with glasses, he has more hair and has a differently shaped beard. He is, however, always shown with the cross of Santiago. The 1835 inventory of the collection of the Infante Don Sebastián Gabriel de Borbón, who owned the picture in the nineteenth century, describes it as '29. Otro cuadro en lienzo de 5 pies y 2 pulgadas de alto por 3 pies y 10 pulgadas de ancho. Retrato de don Fernando de Moncada, vulgo el del coleto. Está restaurado por Bueno, y tiene marco tallado y dorado', see Agueda 1982, p. 106, item 29, and p. 115, note 34. This identification remains to be explored.

16 See *Ribera, 1591–1652 (Madrid)*, 1992, cat. no. 121.

17 For the print, see *Jusepe de Ribera. Prints and Drawings* 1973, cat. no. 16, pp. 77–78 and 110–11.

18 The others are: *Saint Augustine with a Page* (1637, Poznan, National Museum) in which the page is the portrait of a child wearing contemporary military dress, *golilla* collar and a sash; the *Portrait of a Musician* (1638, Toledo (Ohio), Museum of Art); *Portrait of a Dwarf with a Dog* (1643, formerly Vienna Lederer Collection, present whereabouts unknown). See Spinosa 2003, nos A183, A205 and A256, respectively.

19 Quoted in Spinosa 2003, p. 367. For the dating of the *Discorso*, see M. G. Aurigemma, 'Vincenzo Giustiniani: manoscritti ed edizioni', in *Caravaggio e i Giustiniani*, exh. cat., S. Danesi Squarzina, Rome, 2001, pp. 167–72.

20 Most recently on this painting, see the entry in Gerard Powell and Ressort 2002, pp. 228–31.

21 On Murillo's genre paintings, see the exh. cat., *Murillo. Scenes of Childhood*, 2001.

CAT. 20. Francisco Ribalta. *Saint Luke*, 1625–1627. Valencia, Museo de Bellas Artes [471]

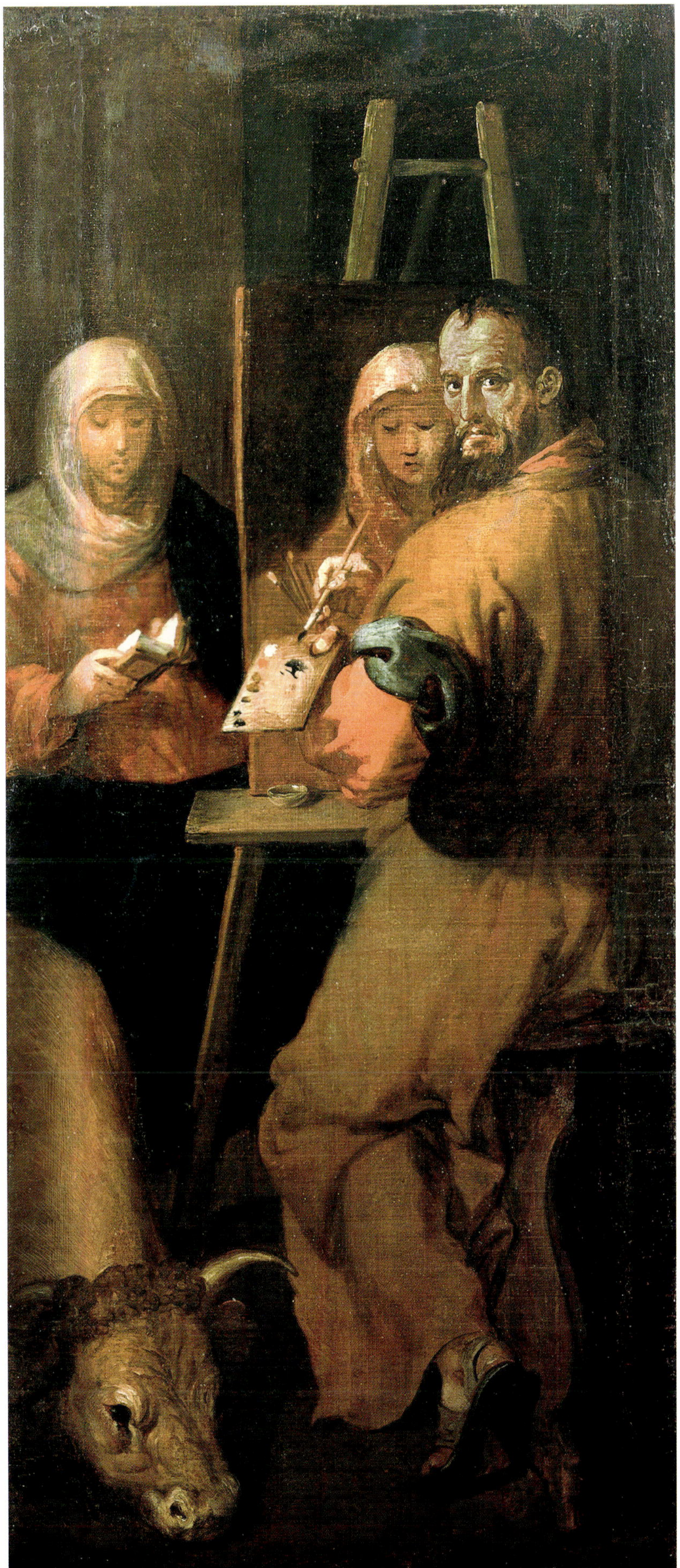

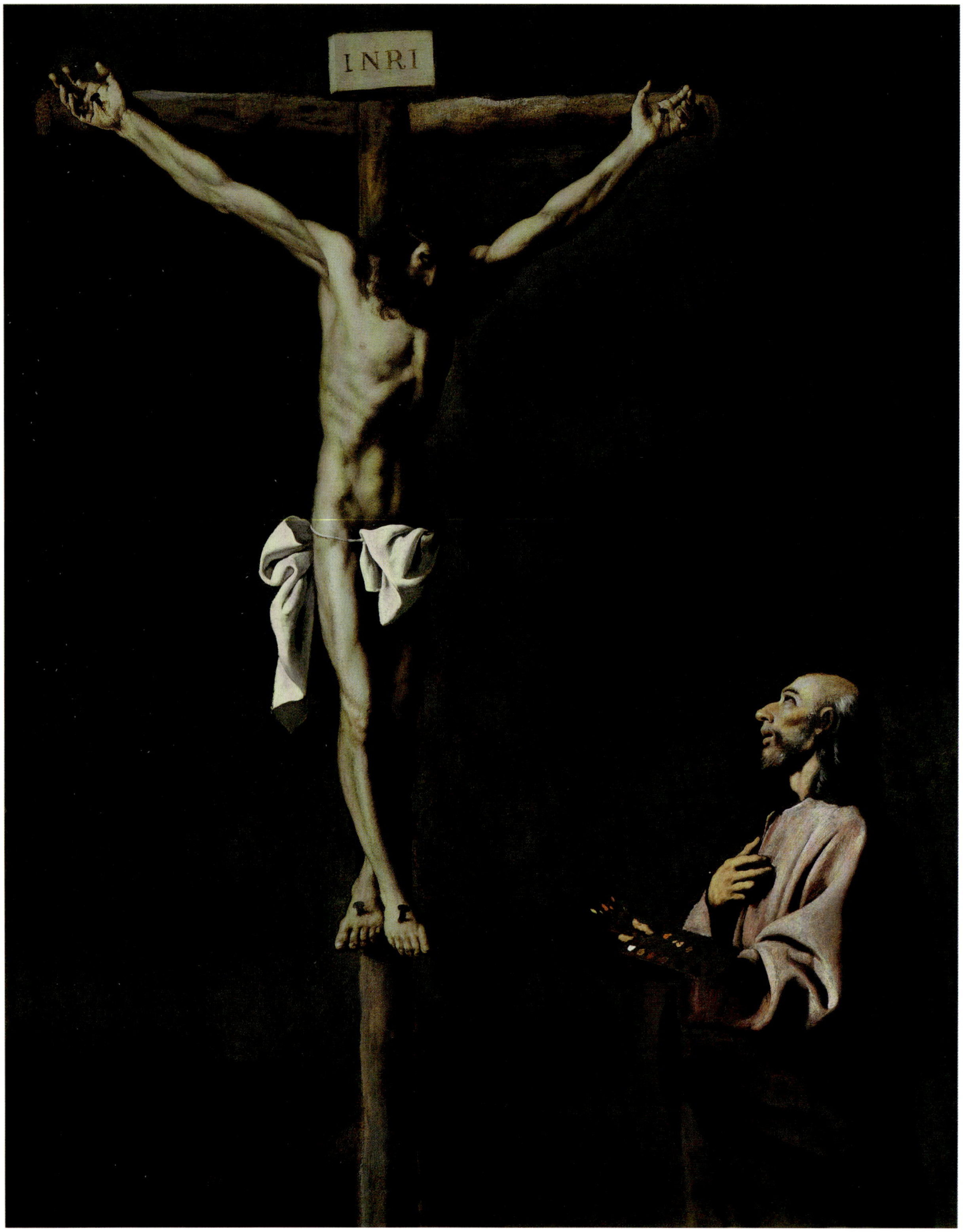

CAT. 21. Francisco de Zurbarán. *The Crucified Christ contemplated by a Painter, ca.* 1630–1639. Museo del Prado [P-2594]

CAT. 22. Francisco de Zurbarán. *Don Alonso Verdugo de Albornoz*, 1635. Berlin, Staatliche Museen zu Berlin, Gemäldegalerie [404C]

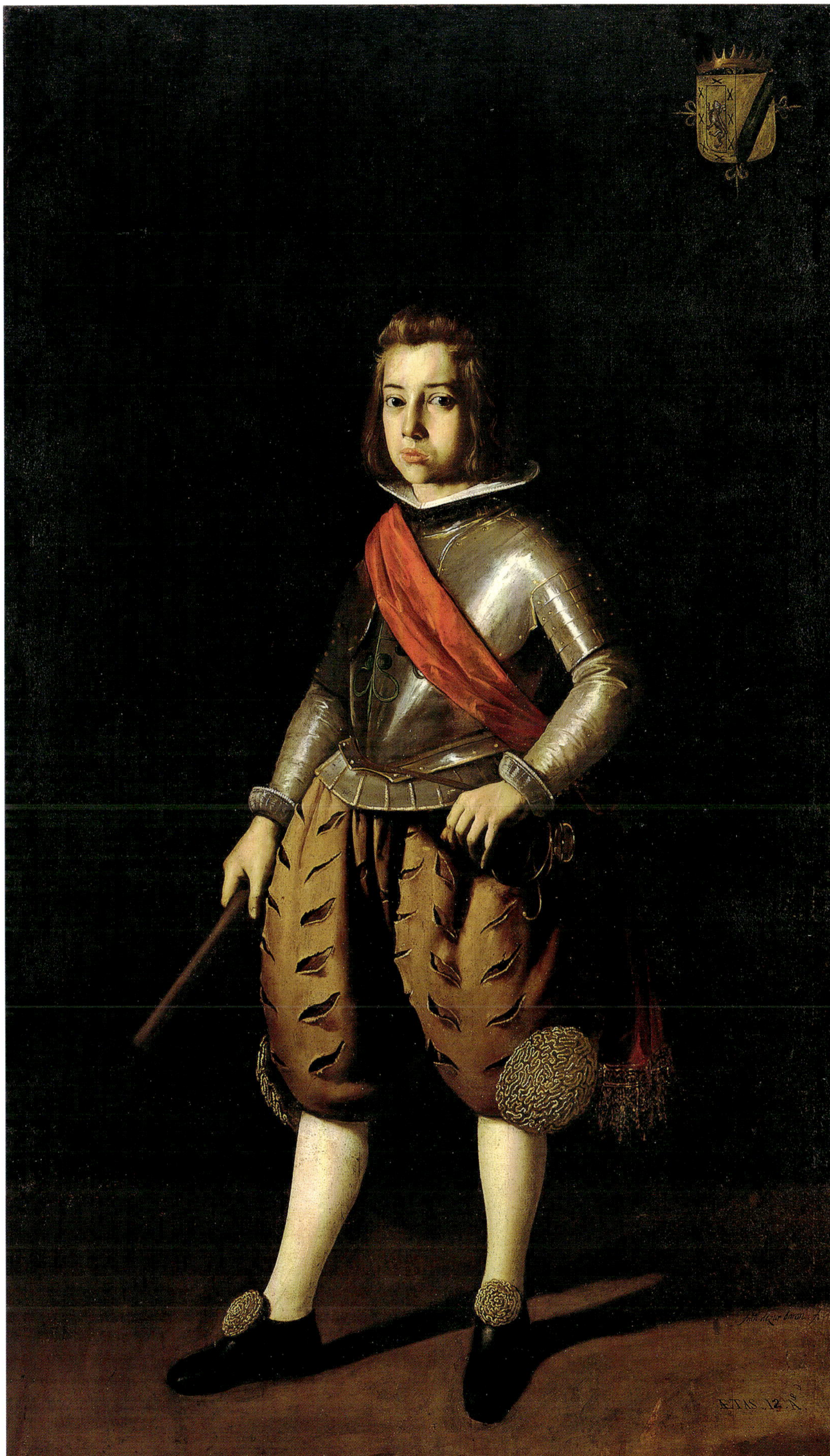
ÆTAS. 12. A.

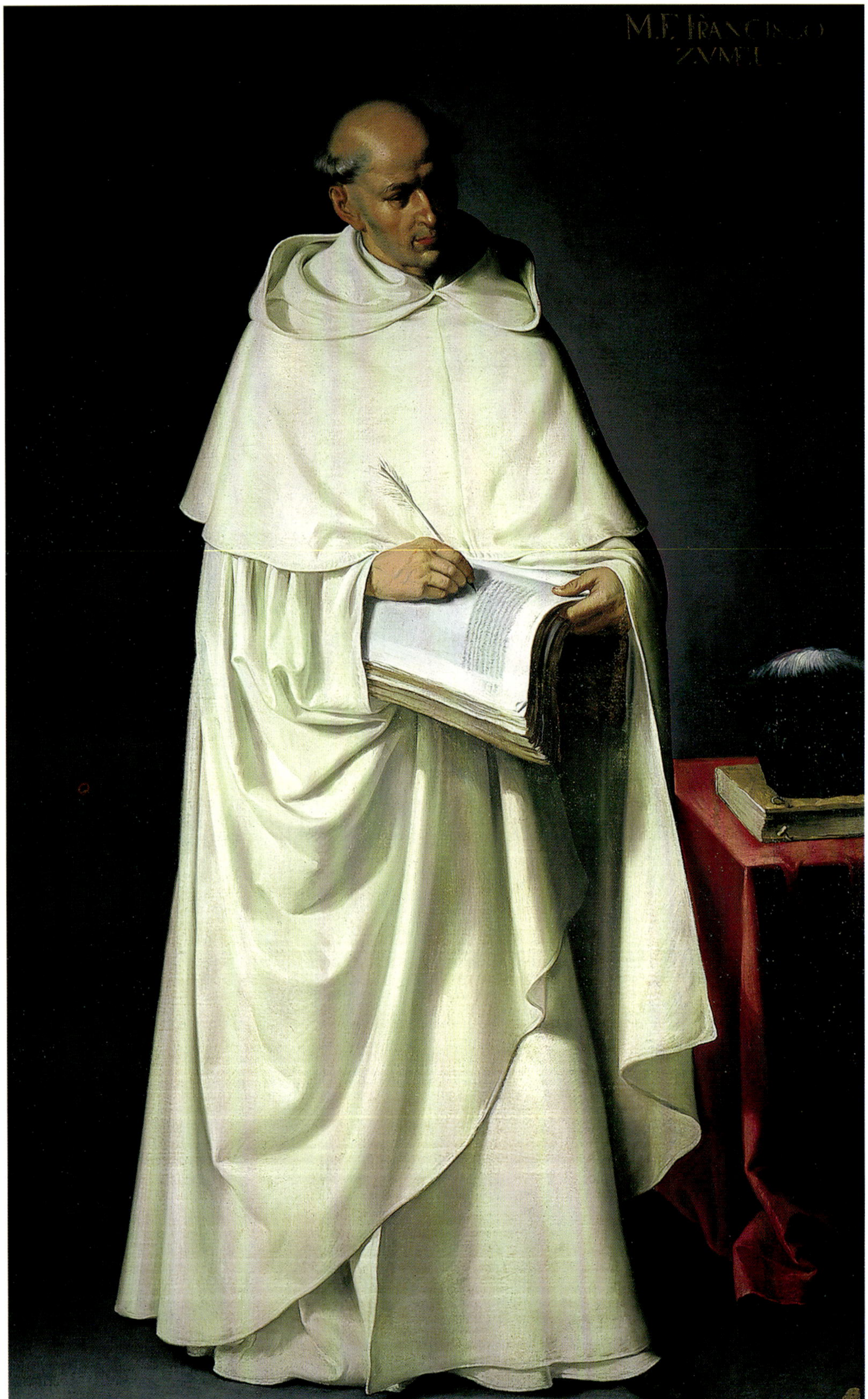

CAT. 23. Francisco de Zurbarán. *Fray Francisco Zúmel*, *ca.* 1630.
Madrid, Museo de la Real Academia de Bellas Artes de San Fernando [664]

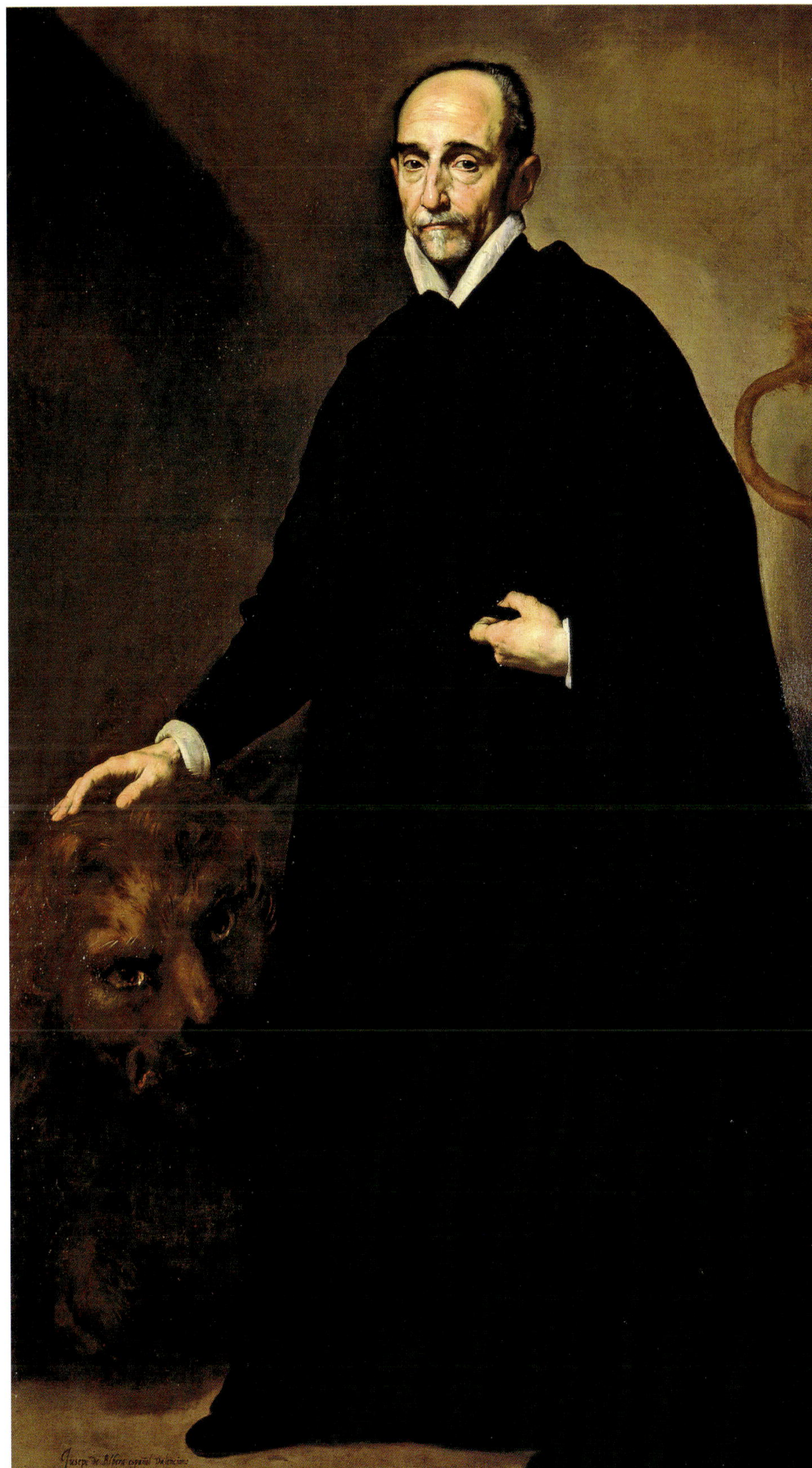

CAT. 24. Jusepe de Ribera. *Portrait of a Jesuit*, 1638. Milan, Museo Poldi Pezzoli [332-95]

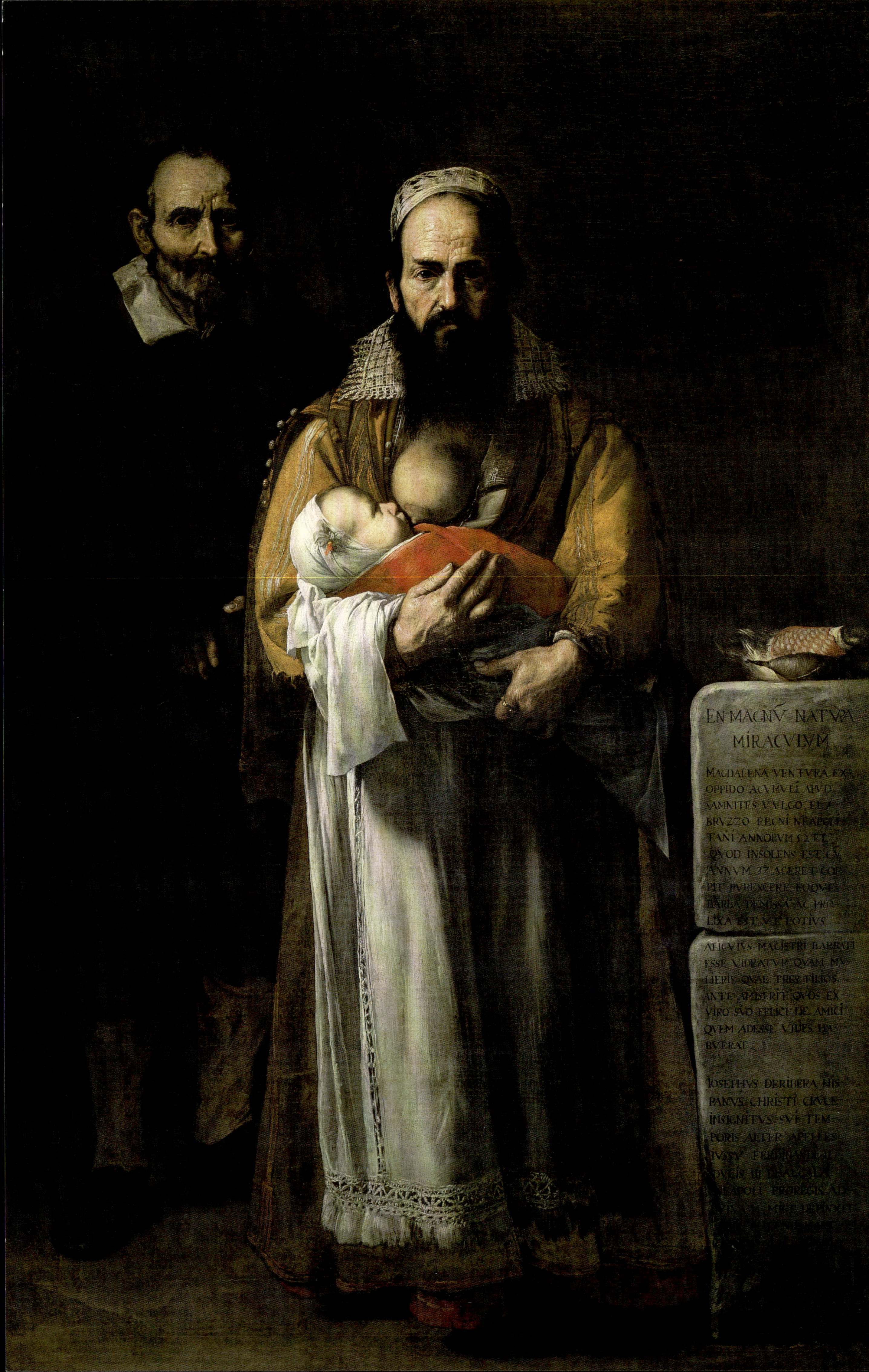
EN MAGNV NATVRA
MIRACVLVM
MAGDALENA VENTVRA EX
OPPIDO ACVMVLI APVD
SAMNITES VVLGO EL A
BRVZZO REGNI NEAPOLI
TANI ANNORVM 52 ET
QVOD INSOLENS EST CV
ANNVM 37 AGERET COE
PIT PVBESCERE EOQVE
BARBA DEMISSA AC PRO
LIXA EST VT POTIVS
ALICVIVS MAGISTRI BARBATI
ESSE VIDEATVR QVAM MV
LIERIS QVAE TRES FILIOS
ANTE AMISERIT QVOS EX
VIRO SVO FELICI DE AMICI
QVEM ADESSE VIDES HA
BVERAT
IOSEPHVS DE RIBERA HIS
PANVS CHRISTI CRVCE
INSIGNITVS SVI TEM
PORIS ALTER APELLES

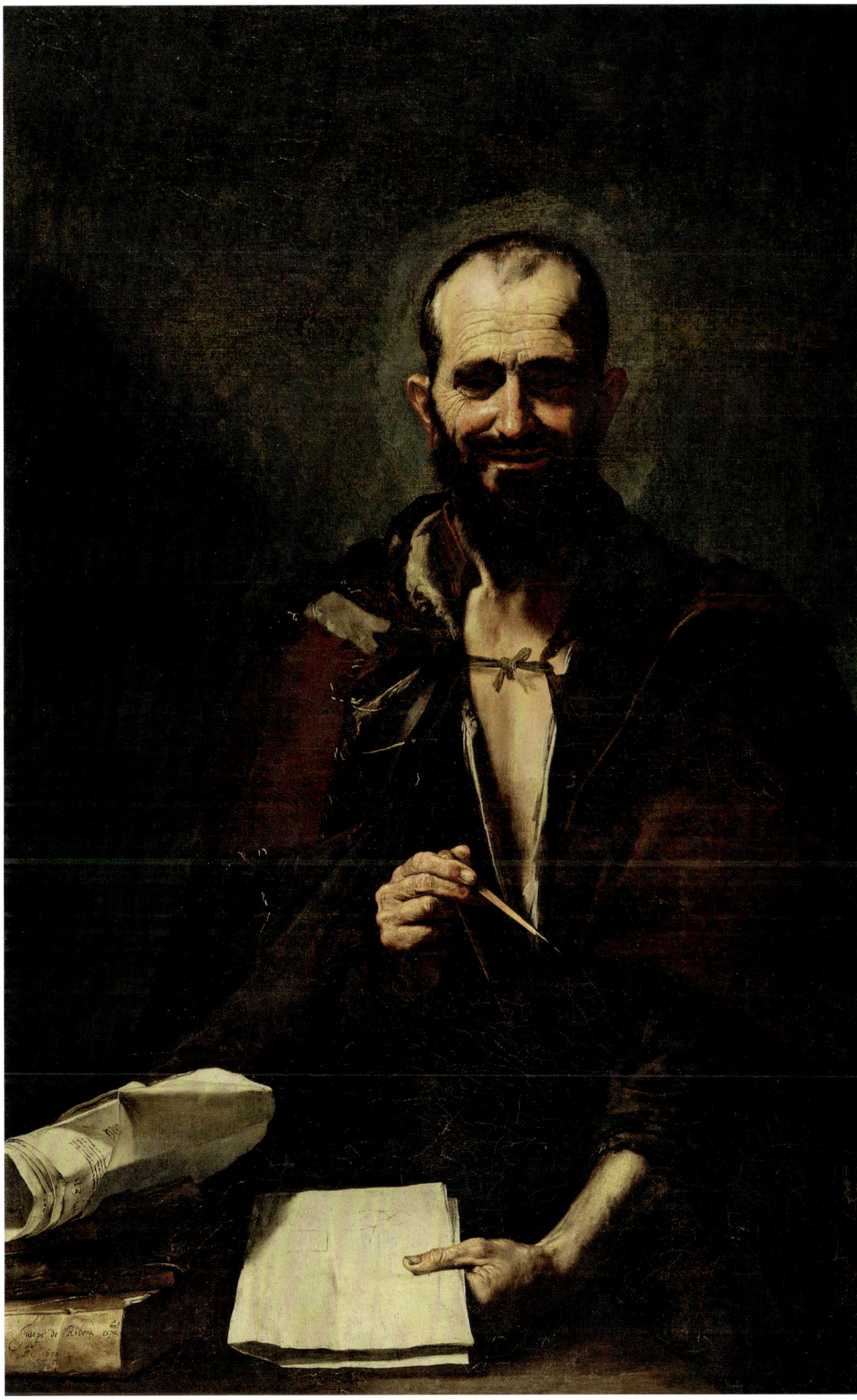

CAT. 25. Jusepe de Ribera. *Maddalena Ventura with her Husband ('The Bearded Woman')*, 1631. The Lerma Bequest. Toledo, Palacio Tavera, Fundación Casa Ducal de Medinaceli

CAT. 26. Jusepe de Ribera. *Democritus (?)*, 1630. Museo del Prado [P-1121]

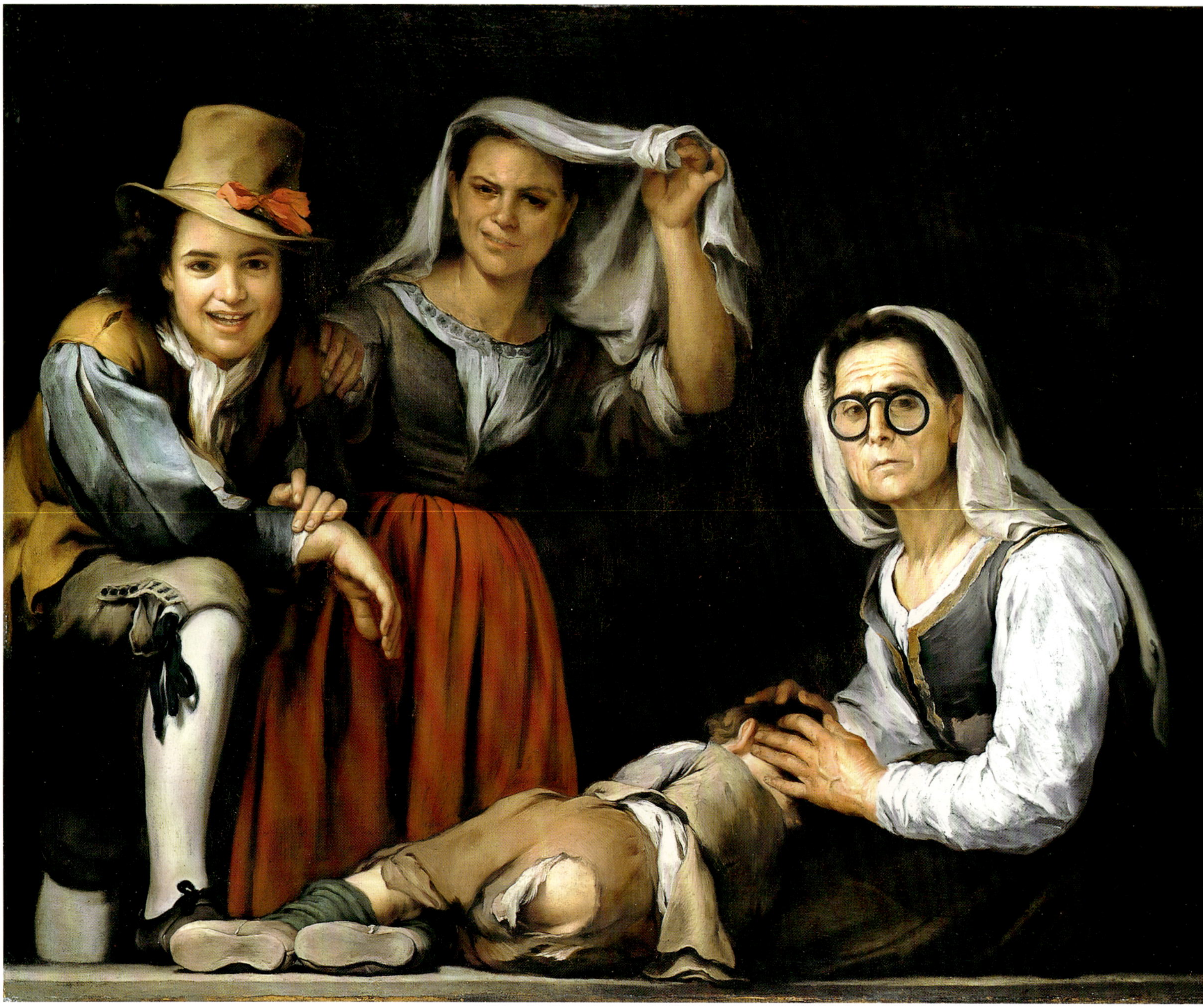

CAT. 27. Bartolomé E. Murillo. *Four Figures on a Step*, *ca.* 1655–1660. Fort Worth, Texas, Kimbell Art Museum [AP 1984.18]

CAT. 28. Bartolomé E. Murillo. *Boy Leaning on a Sill*, *ca.* 1660–1669. London, The National Gallery [NG 74]

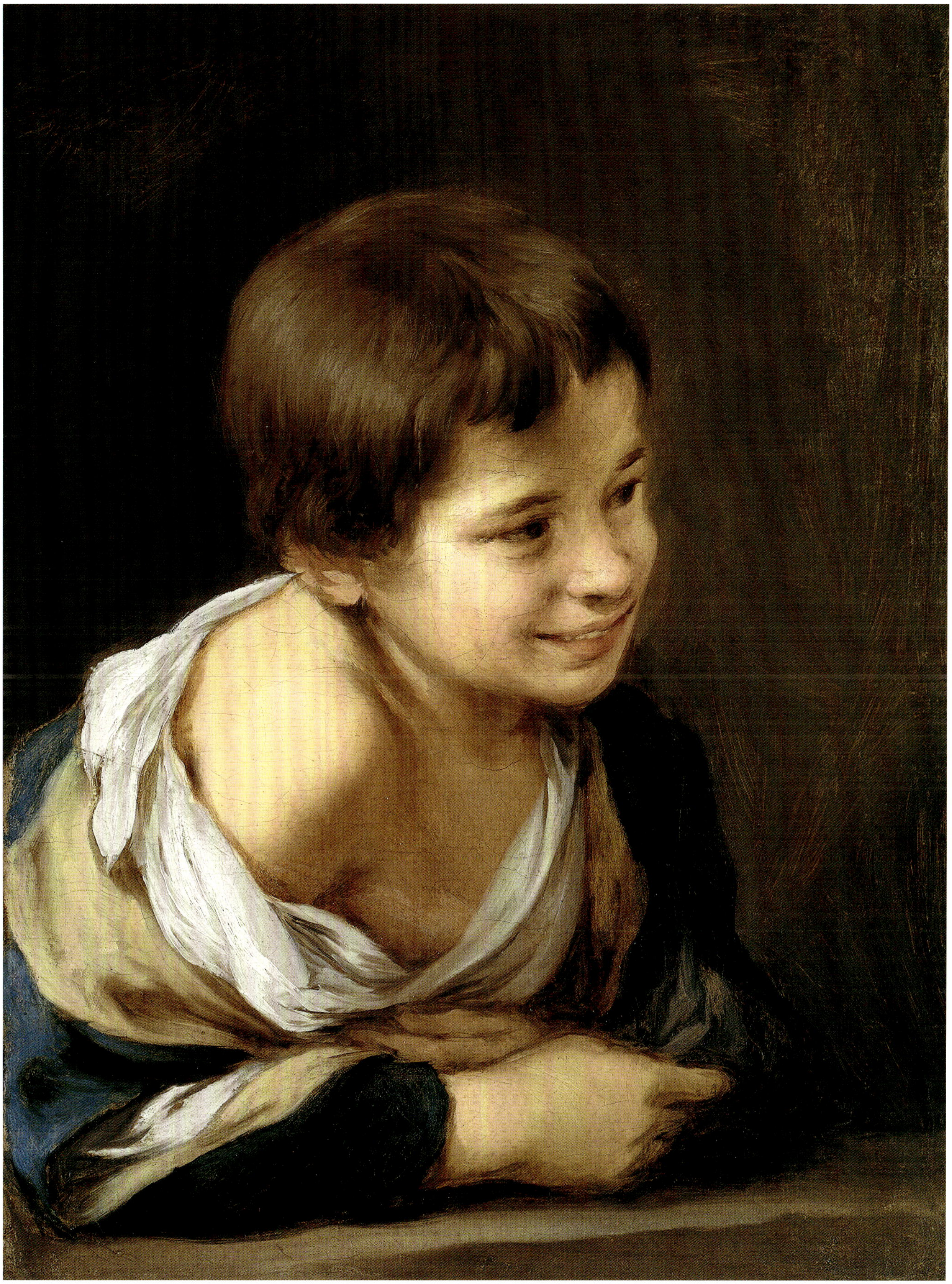

5 Velázquez and the Baroque Portrait

Alfonso E. Pérez Sánchez

The arrival of Velázquez in Madrid and his appointment as court painter in 1624 marked a noticeable change in the whole concept of court portraiture.

During the reign of Philip III the tradition that had begun under Philip II still survived, with an attention to detail inherited from Flanders and a certain Venetian influence in the treatment of expression and colour. Although Juan Pantoja de la Cruz, court painter to Philip II, died in 1608, his pupils, who remained active during Velázquez's early years in Madrid, continued the traditions of portraiture first established by Sánchez Coello and Sofonisba Anguissola.

The painters who lived at court, some of whom had been there for many years, remained faithful to the ideals of the previous generation. Their subjects appeared standing erect, almost rigid, a hand resting lightly on a table or desk, in a gloomy interior in which the only impression of depth was created by the device of a curtain, drawn aside, which was also a symbol of authority and nobility. The sitters' elegant attire was always painted in minute detail, reproducing every embroidered motif, every jewel, every scrap of lace.

The subjects always had an intense gaze which did little to create any feeling of vitality as they stood imprisoned in their stiff-looking garments, especially the ladies, whose silhouettes resembled traditional Spanish cruets. Even in some devotional images the figures were presented dressed in this style.

Rodrigo de Villandrando (*ca.* 1580–1623), Bartolomé González (1564–1627), the Italian Antonio Ricci (d. 1631) and several other less important and less famous painters were happy with these principles, whose obvious purpose was to ensure greater distance between subject and spectator. As Carducho said, 'this gravity of attire and posture…is the due of royalty and nobility'. He went on to bemoan the fact that 'very common men and women' were also painted in this fashion.

During his early days at court Velázquez kept to the rules, but it was not long before he was able to transcend them as he discovered his own language – one that not only dictated the formal aspects of his paintings but also enabled him to draw on his deepest spiritual reserves and his talent for subtly analysing the individuals who came to him to be painted.

Apart from the 'official' portraits of the sovereign, his wife and children and leading figures at court, in which he had to temper his objectivity with a degree of respectful distance, Velázquez very soon proved to be an exceptional interpreter of the human soul. His portrait of *The Venerable Mother Jerónima de la Fuente* [CAT. 29] shows her brandishing a crucifix as if it were a weapon, revealing the unbending and fanatical vigour that drove her, at a very advanced age, to found convents in the Philippines. The more intimate portrait of *Luis de Góngora* [CAT. 30] exposes the poet's underlying resentment and bitterness, once again showing the Sevillian artist as a pitiless observer of the depths of the human heart in all its grandeur and weakness, who presents his subjects to the viewer as genuine human beings. At the same time, as he became better acquainted with the treasures of the royal art collections, he refined his technique, learning from the Venetians, abandoning the darkness of tenebrism and substituting direct light with a diffuse light that gently enveloped his subjects, softening their contours and imbuing them with a magical veracity, a quality of momentariness and a spiritual presence that Ortega y Gasset described as 'phantom-like'. By taking his subject and transforming it impressionistically into a mass of insubstantial brushstrokes, which Quevedo termed 'distant blobs' which from a distance became truth, 'not appearance', Velázquez achieved a configuration within the portrait where all that really mattered was the immediate reality of the person portrayed. The art historian Enrique Lafuente Ferrari speaks of the 'salvation of the individual'. Whether jester, prince or king, the subject is presented to us with little attention to the trappings that would tell us something of his social status. Of course the artist had to submit to a certain 'discipline' dictated by his position as painter to the King. The Velázquez scholar, José López Rey, has observed that this type of 'impressionism' occurs less in the faces of royalty, since the artist was constrained by the need for decorum. It was not enough to produce vague strokes to be put together in the eye of the viewer, for the portrait had to convey with clarity the features that reflected the near-divine status of the sovereign.

But in other portraits the individuality of the person portrayed, whatever his or her social condition, is achieved with prodigious freedom. The painter merely suggests, but nonetheless succeeds in creating, a marvellous presence whose proximity and real humanity we immediately feel.

Throughout his career, Velázquez always analysed in depth the person in front of him, resorting to ever more subtle techniques. He employed, in the elegant words of Rafael Alberti, 'the fleeting touch of a transparent wing', but he did not incorporate the dynamic formal elements used by Rubens, whom he must surely have met during the Flemish artist's stay in Madrid from 1628 to 1629.

Nevertheless, slowly but surely, with that 'phlegmatic' nature that even the king acknowledged, he began to break through the conventions of portrait painting. The tenebrist backdrops he used as a young man in Seville and even in his first Madrid canvases were gradually changed to let in more light and generate a less oppressive mood. Instead of isolating his subjects in a pool of light he created an almost transparent atmosphere around them.

The royal portraits that were his main occupation at the palace became progressively more naturalistic. He even attempted to avoid the traditional rigidity of masculine portraits by having the subjects stand with their legs together, rather than apart as was the custom,

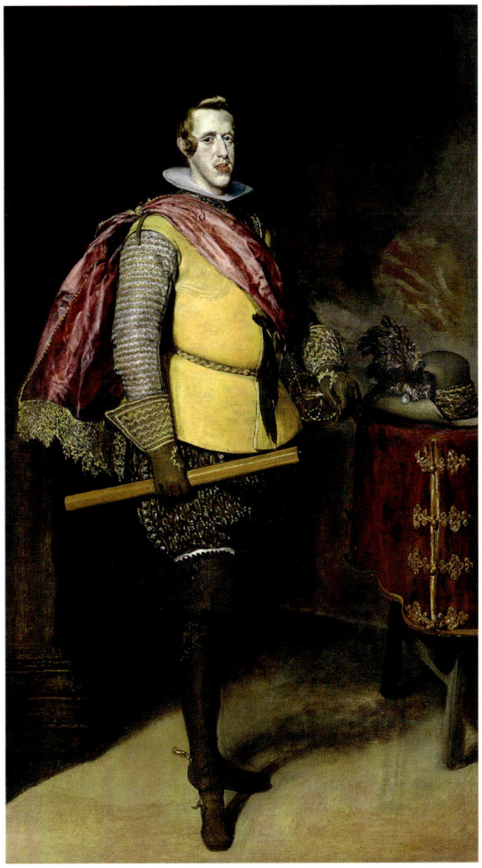

FIG. 73. Diego Velázquez, *Philip IV*, 1625–1628. Sarasota, Ringling Art Museum [SN 336]

so producing a more slender silhouette. From radiographs and even to the naked eye, it is clear that the portrait of the young Philip IV now in the Prado was initially painted in line with tradition but was later repainted with the subject in a more 'modern' stance, although the artist respected the convention of showing the monarch wearing black.

The portrait of the king in military dress in the Ringling Museum of Art in Sarasota (Florida) [FIG. 73] represents a step forward. As in the modified portrait, the legs are placed almost at right angles to each other, with the right foot forward and the left drawn back. The figure in three-quarter view facing right is exceedingly slender and majestic. His opulent garments include a yellow buckskin doublet with silk sleeves shot with gold and silver thread, chamois gloves with wide gauntlets, gold-embroidered baggy silk breeches and high riding boots with silver spurs. In his right hand he carries a

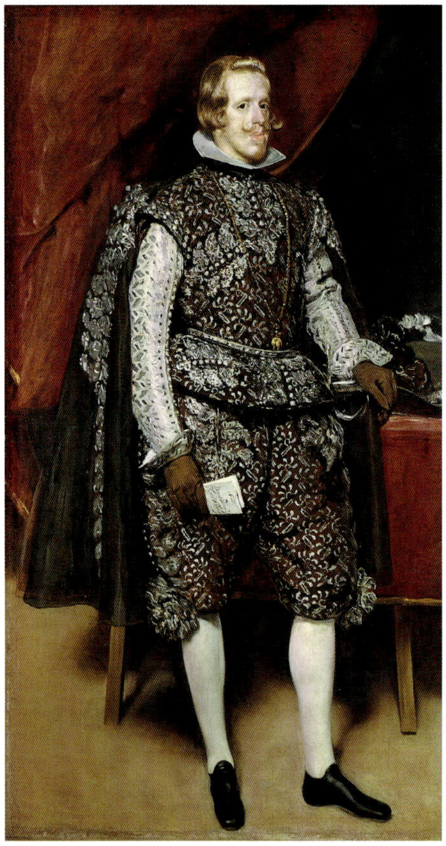

FIG. 74. Diego Velázquez, *Philip IV of Spain in Brown and Silver*, 1631–1632. London, The National Gallery [NG 1129]

general's baton while his left rests on the hilt of his sword. On a table covered with red velvet trimmed with gold braid we see a broad-brimmed hat adorned with plumes secured with a pearl brooch.

The whole composition creates a feeling of richness and colour and the vigorous brushwork leads us to surmise that Velázquez had watched Rubens at work – this admirable portrait appears to date from the time when the Flemish artist was in Madrid – and some of Rubens's exuberant style had rubbed off on him.

After his trip to Italy, Velázquez made further advances towards a style that we could call baroque, were his art not so restrained, in comparison with the extremes that some of his contemporaries went to.

The portrait of *Philip IV of Spain in Brown and Silver* in London's National Gallery [FIG. 74], also known as the '*Silver Philip*', painted immediately after his return from Italy, offers a dazzling and innovative display of dabs of silver against the monarch's brown suit. Even so, the king is shown in the 'old' stance, with feet apart.

However, in the portraits of royalty in hunting garb, painted for the Torre de la Parada, the royal hunting lodge deep in the countryside outside Madrid, Velázquez manages to envelop his subjects in an atmosphere so vibrant that even the leaves on the trees appear to tremble. They are also accompanied by dogs, seen at rest but truly life-like (see, for example, CAT. 50). The portraits for the Buen Retiro, especially those executed entirely by Velázquez, *Philip IV on Horseback* [CAT. 47] and *Prince Baltasar Carlos on Horseback* (Madrid, Museo del Prado, P-1180), suggest a further move in the direction of the baroque, but without the freedom and dynamism of Rubens and the Flemish school. Even the superbly atmospheric portrait of the prince, a tender image of a very serious-looking little boy, is ultimately based on the composition of a mannerist engraving. *Philip IV*, with the horse in profile parallel to the plane of the canvas, is marvellous, but connects more readily with the works of Renaissance painters than with Rubens.

The equestrian portrait is the preserve of royalty, since the horse is a metaphor for the throne and the reins represent instruments of good government capable of both encouragement and restraint.

Only on one occasion did Velázquez – as always using an earlier etching as a model – embark on a powerful equestrian portrait infused with energy that was truly baroque. The subject was Don Gaspar de Guzmán, Count-Duke of Olivares [FIG. 75]; his horse gallops away from the viewer but he turns his head and casts a haughty glance. The choice of this form of representation may have been a mark of the artist's gratitude for the protection he received from Olivares, but also a recognition of the latter's well-known vanity. However, it leaves us with an unforgettable image of the Count-Duke, perhaps telling us more about his character than hundreds of pages written by his contemporaries.

As for court paintings of female subjects, here the artist seems to have been rather more conservative in his presentation. The portraits of Isabel of Bourbon, first wife of Philip IV, are arranged in the same way as those of the

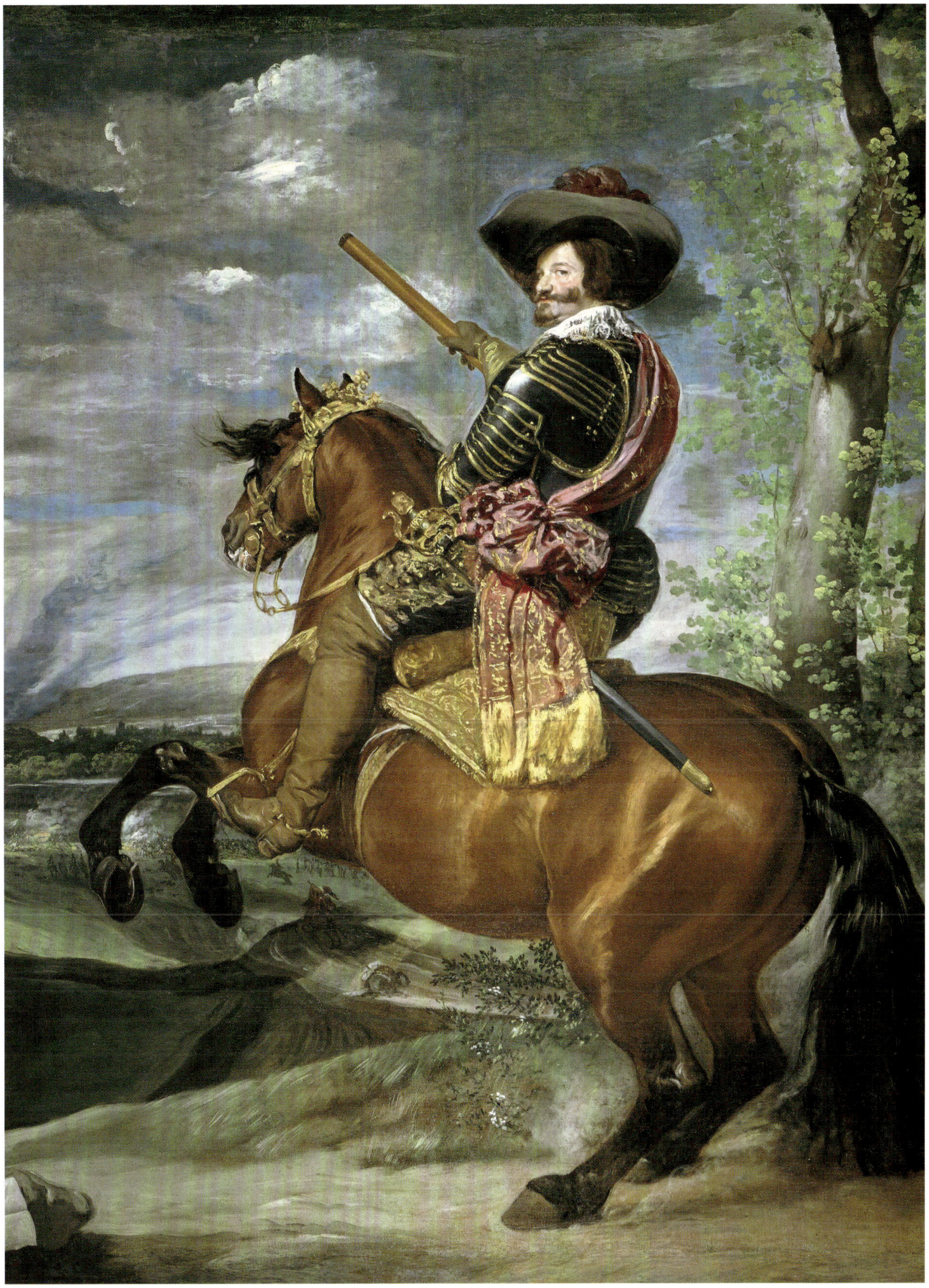

FIG. 75. Diego Velázquez, *Don Gaspar de Guzmán, the Count-Duke of Olivares, on Horseback*, *ca.* 1631. Madrid, Museo del Prado [P-1181]

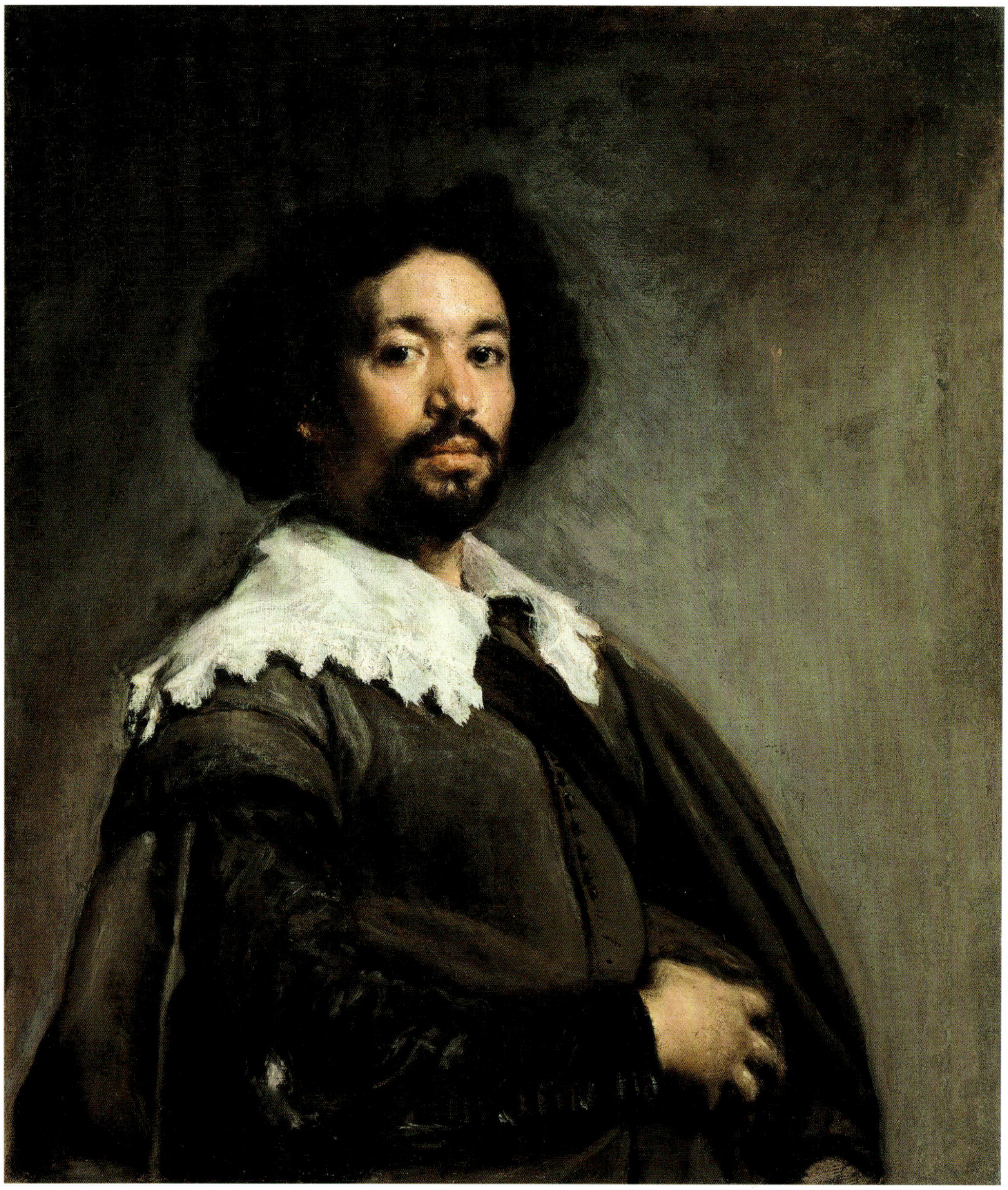

FIG. 76. Diego Velázquez, *Juan de Pareja*, 1649–1650. New York, The Metropolitan Museum of Arts [1971.86]

previous generation, although the brushstrokes are more vibrant and the curtain is given greater prominence.

Those of Queen Mariana of Austria, the king's second wife who arrived in Madrid while Velázquez was on his second trip to Italy, already respond to a change in fashion [CAT. 13]. The queen's huge hooped skirt and spectacular head-dress with its ribbons and feathers, the magnificent curtain and the table with the clock, the handkerchief against the rich black silk of the skirt, all indicate the degree of subtlety achieved by the artist, creating a luminous and colourful vibrancy that distinguishes this serene and relaxed royal image from his earlier works.

As court painter Velázquez also produced some significant portraits of the young princes and princesses, full of tenderness and subtle delicacy. The first of these, *Prince Baltasar Carlos with a Dwarf*, now in the Boston Museum of Fine Arts, was painted when Velázquez returned from his first visit to Italy, full of technical innovations and inspired by new moral considerations. The royal child, barely sixteen months old, wears richly embroidered adult ceremonial dress with a scarlet sash and carries his baton of command like a miniature general. The female dwarf, placed on a lower level, holding a rattle and an apple, turns her face sideways to where the little boy's plumed hat rests on a cushion trimmed with gold braid. The composition, with its varying planes and rich, warm colours predominated by shades of red, strikes a new note in court painting, albeit with prudence and restraint.

Other, much later, portraits of royal children include *Prince Felipe Próspero*, now in Vienna [CAT. 54], with a charming little dog in the armchair on which the prince rests his tiny hand. On a number of occasions Velázquez painted the Infanta Doña Margarita – who features in *Las Meninas* – each time in different attire [CAT. 14]. Each portrait was filled with technical inventiveness and a deep human understanding that seemed to be leading towards a kind of baroque freedom, although this was never fully developed in his portraiture.

And so we come to the culmination of Velázquez's art and the most revolutionary painting of this period on the brink of the full-blown baroque style, which, as we have seen, was slow to take hold in the Spanish portrait. The work in question is *Las Meninas*, or, as it was known at the time, *The Family* [CAT. 43]. An enigmatic picture, which has also engendered vast numbers of critical interpretations, it is essentially a group portrait showing a number of people in a space that extends away into the distance, characterised by an extraordinarily atmospheric sensation. The protagonists, especially the Infanta Margarita and the ladies-in-waiting around whom the scene revolves, are vividly and intensely brought to life, creating a feeling of intimacy with the viewer. The boy captured in movement as he teases the dog, and the painter – Velázquez himself – peering out from behind his canvas for a better view of his models who are outside the picture, engender an interchange of gazes and movements that is totally baroque, despite the almost ritual solemnity of the composition as a whole. The significance of the canvas, the subject of so many contradictory theories, adds a touch of mystery and controversy. The portrait is transformed into a conceptual game, perhaps interweaving ideas about Spanish political life at the time, the painter's own aspiration to nobility, the dignity of the painter's art and its value as a means of recording the real and the imaginary.

At the same time, the portrait of *Pope Innocent X* [FIG. 9] painted in 1650 during the artist's second stay in Rome, can – and should – be considered a court portrait. Seated in a red throne and wearing a white alb, a cape of intense, brilliant crimson and a biretta of the same hue, the pontiff is portrayed in a manner traditional in Italy for members of the religious hierarchy, especially popes. But Velázquez exploits the traditional pose to picture an astute, dynamic and sceptical Pope whose penetrating gaze looks right through the viewer. In a display of his technical skill the painter employs an astonishing economy of means to create a pontiff who will live for ever in the eye of the beholder, as if the two had met in real life.

But even outside the environs of the court, Velázquez proved himself as a painter of portraits that were not about ostentation and status but about friendship, pleasure and appreciation.

From the outset, although imbued with the tenebrist tradition as in the portrait of Góngora mentioned above, the series of bust and half-length portraits painted throughout his career testify to his insightfulness and depth of vision. At the same time they are priceless documents that tell us much about us the real lives of his contemporaries, providing us with keys to the character of the Spaniard, severe and sober in his attire and with an air of grandeur and majesty which, in the words of Maréchal de Gramont, who visited Spain in 1659, 'had not been seen anywhere'.

Among the principal milestones along his career path are the melancholy *Portrait of a Young Man* in the Alte Pinakothek, Munich, the imposing *Portrait of a Man* in Detroit, *Portrait of a Gentleman, probably Juan Mateos* in Dresden, or *Portrait of a Man* in Apsley House, London [CAT. 36], identified, probably correctly, by Enriqueta Harris as José Nieto, aposentador, or Palace Marshall, to the Queen, who appears in the background of *Las Meninas*. The impressive *Juan de Pareja* [FIG. 76],

Velázquez's studio assistant and pupil, painted in Rome, displays the slightly brutish vitality of a man of humble origins but conscious of his own worth. According to Palomino the likeness was painted 'to practice' before embarking on the portrait of the Pope.

The few representations of female subjects also fit into this category of what we might call 'intimate' portraits, especially the wonderful *Lady with a Fan* in the Wallace Collection in London [FIG. 77], believed by some to have been the painter's wife, so great is the feeling of spontaneity and warm intimacy she conveys.

The *Portrait of a Woman* from the Duke of Devonshire's collection, seen in a similar pose, may be a less complex representation but it displays identical emotion. The Hispanic Society's *Portrait of a Girl* [CAT. 38], may simply be a spontaneously executed record of someone very close to the artist, whose delicate features are reproduced with subtlety and gentleness. More spontaneous still is the portrait, called 'La Gallega' (*The Galician Girl*) (private collection), a brilliantly executed work that is not a conventional portrait but something painted for sheer pleasure. Born out of the artist's delight in discovering an unexpected image of dreamy melancholy, it allows the viewer to share his powerful emotional response.

While in Rome from 1649 to 1650, Velázquez painted a series of portraits of dignitaries of the papal court, probably in an attempt to win their support for his pretensions to ennoblement. *Camillo Massimi*, *Camillo Astalli* and *Portrait of a Man, 'The Pope's Barber'*, which has recently become part of the Prado collection [CAT. 35], blend objectivity with a degree of intimacy, but are tempered by the sensation of distance and a certain haughtiness, characteristic of 'official' portraits. An extreme example of this is the *Knight of the Order of Santiago* in Dresden, who looks at the viewer with deep disdain.

Another, very different, face of Velázquez's art is revealed in the portraits of buffoons and dwarves kept for the court's amusement – which constitute one of the best known and best loved parts of his oeuvre. A definite distinction has to be made between the various types of likeness. There are full-length, standing figures like *Pablo de Valladolid* [CAT. 51], in which the subject, who strikes a theatrical pose of the kind that earned him the nickname 'the Actor', is positioned in space without any geometric reference whatsoever. A baroque tendency is apparent in the mock seriousness of the *Buffoon 'Barbarroja'* and the elaborate setting and attributes of *Don Juan de Austria*.

Confronted with such mad and consequently free-spirited characters, Velázquez himself is free of any obligation and so uses a lighter technique to create a more truly human image.

The four 'dwarf' portraits in the Museo del Prado, identified as *El Niño de Vallecas* [CAT. 34], *The Buffoon Calabacillas* [CAT. 33], *Diego de Acedo 'El Primo'* and *The Dwarf Sebastián de Morra*, are a different proposition. They are obviously portraits whose deep humanity has caused much to be written in praise of their 'truthfulness' and the approach of the artist, who avoids insensitivity in his depiction of physical defects, painting with deep human understanding and even affection. But the identity of the sitters is not totally clear and, as Manuela Mena has pointed out, it is possible that these canvases hide some allegorical or symbolic meaning responding to the painter's own intellectual frames of reference. But as portraits, whoever the models were, they are works of incomparable vitality and represent an advance in the treatment of the figure in relation to surrounding space.

The singular personality of Velázquez – virtually the only Spanish representative of seventeenth-century classicism – and his special sensibility, baroque in spirit but somewhat restrained in form, meant that he had few followers except among court painters, in whose work his influence can be traced. This is particularly true of his son-in-law Juan Martínez del Mazo (1605–1667), to whom are attributed those so-called 'Velazquian' works which lacked the qualities of those genuinely painted by the master. However, we also know the names of several artists sometimes mentioned as pupils or collaborators of Velázquez who were no doubt responsible for portraits that were, and continue to be, claimed as his.

FIG. 77. Diego Velázquez, *Lady with a Fan*, *ca.* 1635. London, The Wallace Collection [P. 88]

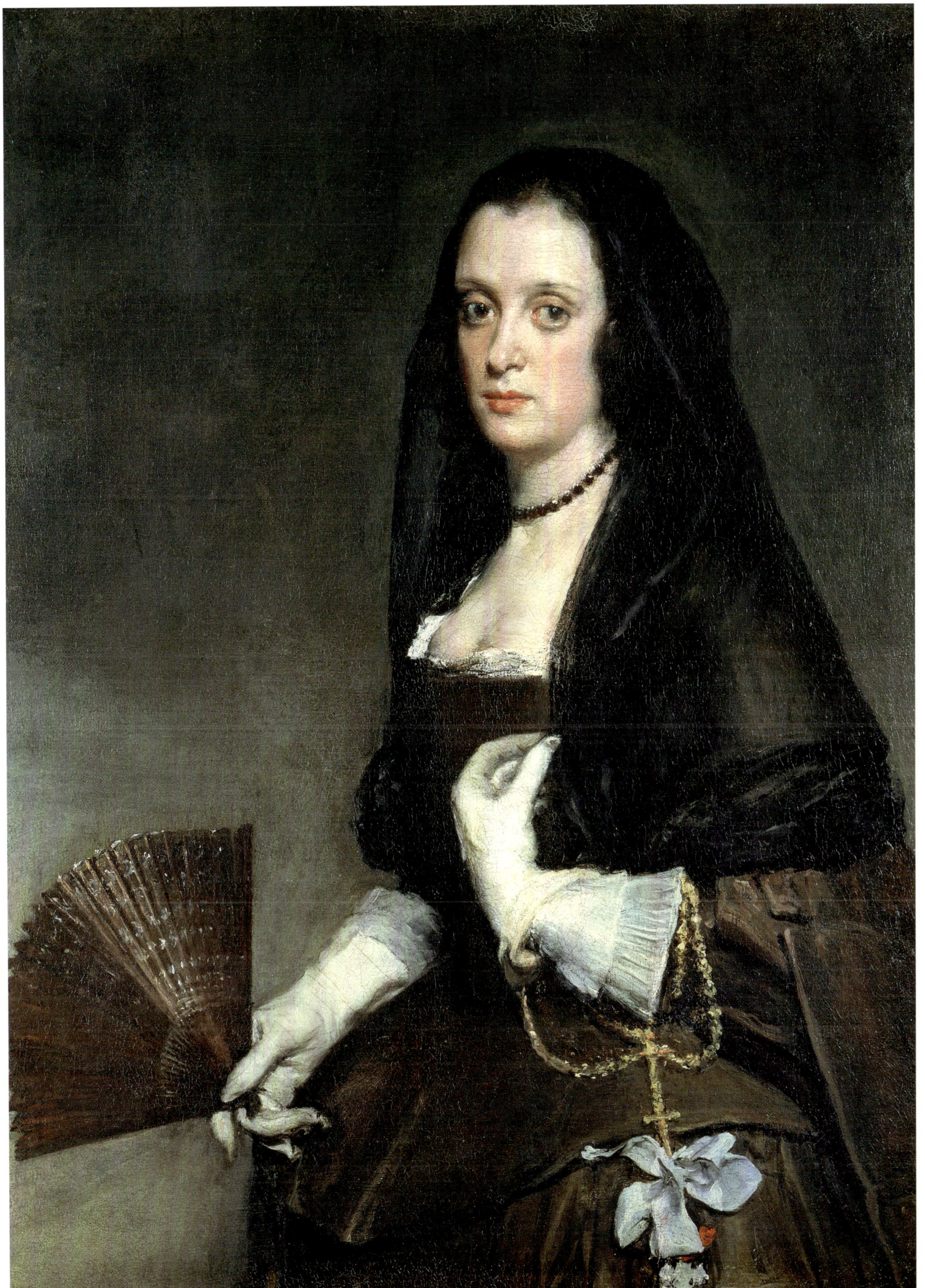

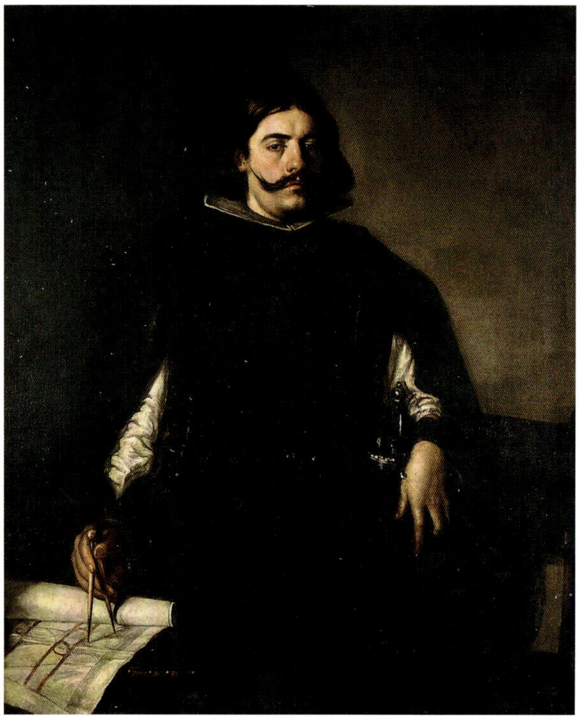

FIG. 78. Juan de Pareja, *Portrait of the Architect José de Ratés Dalmau*, *ca.* 1660–1670. Valencia, Museo de Bellas Artes [2/91]

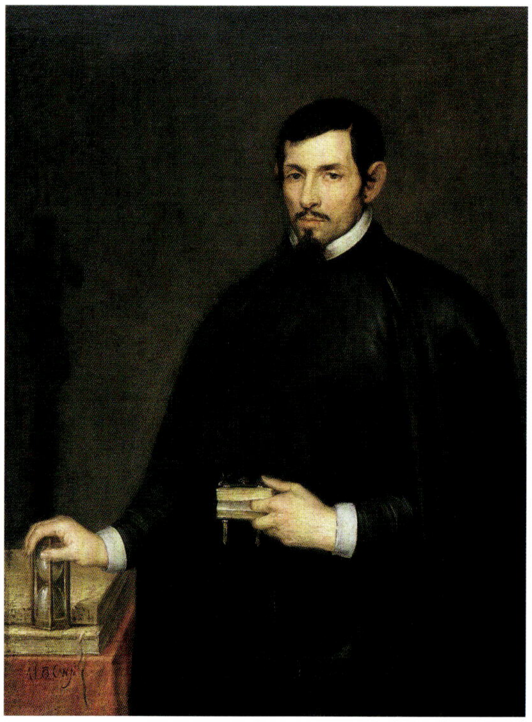

FIG. 79. Alonso Cano, *Portrait of an Ecclesiastic*, *ca.* 1625–1630. New York, The Hispanic Society of America

Velázquez's taste for restraint and austerity, the sobriety of his settings and his subjects' seriousness of expression and pose contrast with the exuberant energy and theatricality of the baroque in its heyday, which occurred towards the end of the life of this inspired painter. His most immediate successors, especially Mazo, structured their paintings in a similar way but made their settings more complex.

Mazo carried to extremes the free, exuberant brushwork of his master and father-in-law but did not achieve the same precision or *gravitas*. His figures seem to float in their surroundings, lacking the solid support that Velázquez accomplishes with his mastery of space.

Portraits such as *A Child in Ecclesiastical Dress* in the Toledo Museum of Art (Ohio), or *The Infanta Margarita of Austria* in the Prado (P-888), pay tribute to the master but introduce new elements that accentuate, not always convincingly, depth of space and introduce baroque-type elements in the middle distance which perhaps stem from his mentor, but which seem superficial in comparison with the total truthfulness of *Las Meninas*. The group portrait of *The Family of the Painter* in Vienna [CAT. 44], to which we shall return later, derives from Velázquez's masterpiece, but the diagonal alignment of the figures, betraying distinctly baroque tendencies, is completely alien to Velázquez.

Another artist with a personal connection to Velázquez was his slave – later freed – Juan de Pareja (*ca.* 1606–1670), the sitter in the superb portrait discussed above. A few of his canvases survive, in which, following in his master's footsteps, he paints with extraordinary energy and vitality.

The *Portrait of the Architect José de Ratés Dalmau* in the Museo de Bellas Artes in Valencia [FIG. 78] is a notable example. In a totally Velazquian atmosphere with a sombre palette of blacks and greys, the subject, very conscious of his own status and importance, holds in his right hand a compass, which he rests on a plan while placing his left hand on the hilt of his sword. This is the portrait of a proud man, sure of himself and confident in his calling, completely characteristic of the ostentation of the baroque.

Sadly, no portraits by Francisco Burgos Mantilla (1610–1672) or Francisco de Palacios (*ca.* 1622–1652) have come to light. According to Palomino, both were highly skilled portrait painters in the 'manner' of Velázquez, with whose works their own were sometimes confused. The delicate range of greys and pinks in their still lifes leads us to assume that they might have used the same colour ranges in their portraits, created with the same air of *gravitas* and serenity as those of Velázquez. But this is purely hypothetical.

Radiating that same Velazquian serenity are the few known portraits by Alonso Cano (1601–1667). These emphasise the two artists' common training in Seville, painting in the tenebrist manner and then studying the Venetian painters in the Royal Collection. A delicate, meditative tone makes the Hispanic Society's *Portrait of an Ecclesiastic* [FIG. 79] extraordinarily enigmatic, while the presence of the hourglass anticipates the moralistic messages of later portraits painted at the height of the baroque era. Cano's few portraits also share aspects of Velázquez's technique; his treatment is less audacious, but equally subtle.

Some portraits also survive by an artist who, as a very young man, knew Velázquez: the Cordovan Juan de Alfaro (1643–1680). His portraits of the ladies of the Morales family mentioned by Palomino (Madrid and Bilbao, private collection), long attributed to Carreño, show his devotion to Velázquez as well as some of Van Dyck's ingenious elegance. These same characteristics mark the work of Madrid's most significant baroque portrait painter, Juan Carreño de Miranda (1614–1685).

But after Velázquez and Mazo the artist who took the definitive step towards the creation of the royal image in the baroque style was Sebastián Herrera Barnuevo (1619–1671), who held the post of Court Painter for several years after Mazo's death. It was he who painted portraits of Charles II as a child, opulently dressed and surrounded by angels and cherubs holding attributes of kingship, with the crowned eagle of the Hapsburgs much in evidence, in a palace setting opening onto a view of the Casa de Campo. This painting has a direct connection with another, anonymous, work in the Museo Lázaro Galdiano [FIG. 14], which shows the boy king surrounded by portraits of his forebears in various poses, with a huge flower vase in the foreground. Whether or not the vase symbolises future matrimony, as has been suggested, it is obvious that this canvas is very different from the severe elegance of those of Velázquez, and is a very Spanish example of a ceremonial portrait.

The triumph of the baroque, witnessed in Italy around 1630 (a famous article by Giuliano Briganti was entitled '1630, or the Baroque'), and in Flanders much earlier when Rubens returned from Italy in 1609, was late in reaching Spain. It was not until the second half of the seventeenth century, and especially during the reign of Charles II, that it manifested itself in all its glory.

In the portrait the baroque shows up in greater ostentation in dress and trappings, in more expansive gestures and more lavish settings, and sometimes through the introduction of pages and servants in the role of 'extras'. There were also some, albeit rarer, examples of the group portraits so common in the Low Countries.

The Spanish baroque portrait retained the seriousness, composure and haughtiness that distinguished it from works from the rest of Europe. But it could not ignore for long the new forms, formulae and models imported from abroad, and particularly the canvases brought home by military men, politicians and churchmen who had their portraits painted in Italy or Flanders. Another important influence came from the thriving trade in prints, which provided a repertoire of poses and gestures that soon made an impression on Spanish artists.

Above all it was original works by Rubens and Van Dyck, and prints based on them, that most strongly influenced Spanish portraiture in the second half of the century and well into the next. Beyond the confines of the court, it took a while to assimilate the new French style of portrait painting, which would completely transform the way of 'seeing' the subject.

The baroque portrait par excellence that would inspire lavish displays of allegorical elements and symbols of power was the royal portrait, and, as we have seen, Velázquez's ways of defining power and authority had a certain sobriety. Carreño, who fulfilled the same role at the court of Charles II as Velázquez had during the reign of Philip IV, used the master's methods as a starting point for his own efforts to add baroque flavour to his depiction of the sovereign.

His portraits of Charles II, starting with what appears to be the first of the series (now in the Museo de Bellas Artes de Asturias in Oviedo), signed and dated 1671, show the monarch in the spacious 'Salón de los Espejos' (Hall of Mirrors) in the Alcázar standing beside a splendid table supported by bronze lions, with gold-tasselled curtains and mirrors with gilded frames shaped like eagles in which are reflected the paintings hanging around the room. The boy king, dressed in sombre black, may look as impassive as his father, Philip IV, but the composition as a whole is much more complex and attaches special significance to the splendour of the palace decor, something to which Velázquez barely alludes.

Other representations of the king, such as those showing him in military attire (Toledo, Museo del Greco and Monastery of Guadalupe), with shining armour and a view onto a terrace beyond which we glimpse violent scenes of battle, or standing proud in the regalia of Master of the Order of the Golden Fleece (Harrach Collection) [FIG. 11] – in which, making an almost unique appearance, the royal crown resting on the table reinforces the opulence of the velvet robe and cap – are perhaps the ultimate expression of the baroque principle of devoting so much attention to luxurious adornment. In this case the baroque splendour presents a terrible contrast with the sickly, fragile figure of the king called 'el hechizado' – the bewitched.

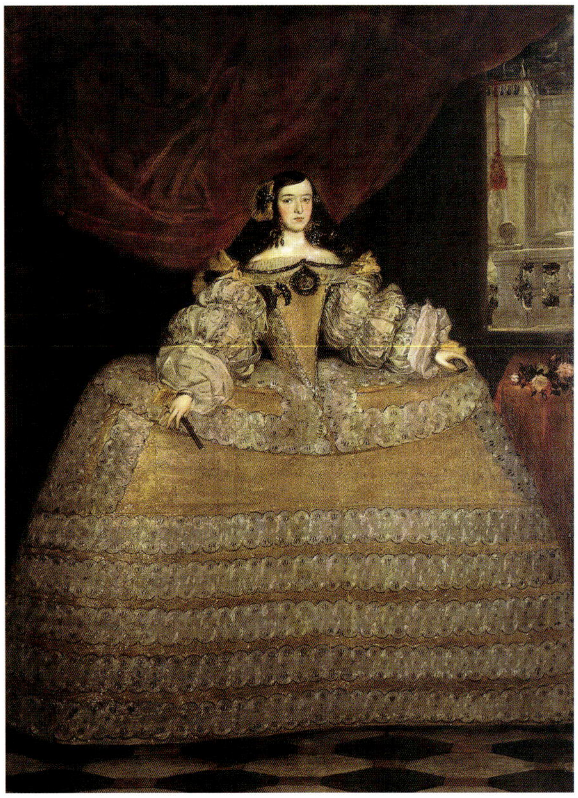

FIG. 80. Juan Carreño de Miranda, *The Marquesa de Santa Cruz*, *ca.* 1665–1670. Madrid, private collection

After portraits of royal personages, with all their affectation and flamboyant displays of power, came those of the aristocrats, proud of their noble blood and lineage. These too became more extravagant, influenced considerably by changes in fashion and the French finery that did much to brighten up late seventeenth-century life. Settings opened up to catch luminous perspectives and sweeping landscapes. Interiors were adorned with ever more opulent drapes, and sitters were often accompanied by animals, most frequently dogs, the traditional embodiment of fidelity. Often, however, these were depicted as playful creatures adorned with ribbons and bows to emphasise their decorative value.

Beyond the confines of the royal palace, with its rituals and etiquette that imposed conventions and a certain continuity with the past, Carreño could more freely resort to some of the innovations arriving from Flanders. His famous portrait of *The Duke of Pastrana* in the Prado [CAT. 40] combines the Velazquian *gravitas* of the main figure with a vibrant sense of movement in the attendants and in the horse, which connect it to the most elegant and elaborate works of Van Dyck.

The two portraits of the nuncio Cardinal Sabas Millini in the Gil Collection and the Guadalupe Monastery offer an extravagant display of dazzling purples that links them closely with some of the most magnificent examples of Flemish and Roman ecclesiastical portraits executed at the very height of the baroque era.

It is equally obvious that, taking as his starting point Velázquez's last portraits of female subjects, especially

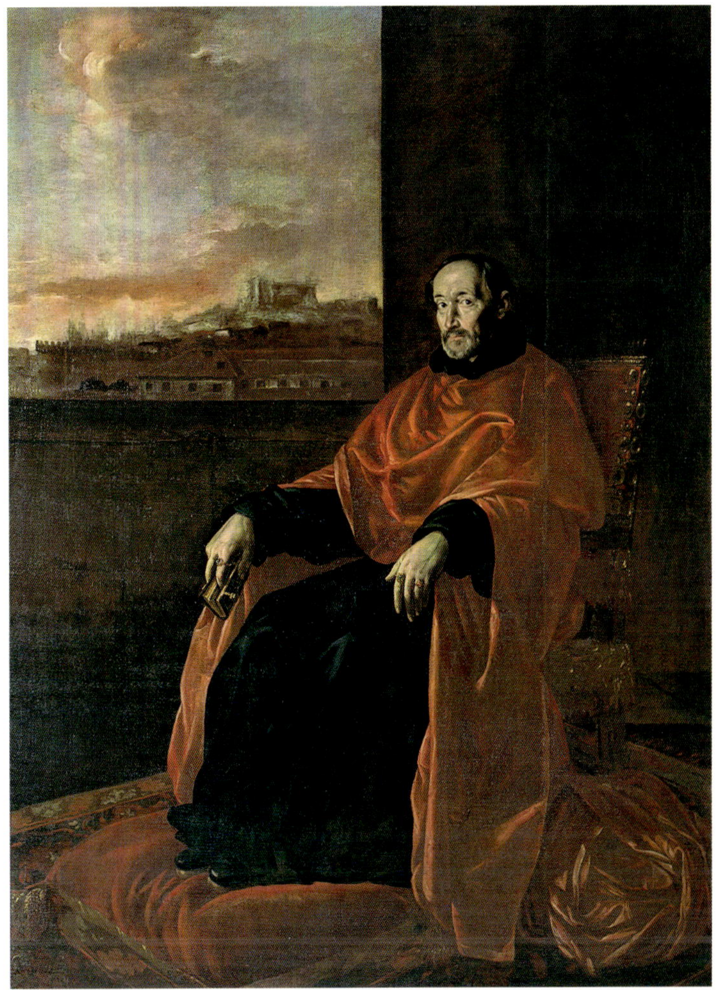

FIG. 81. Fray Juan Andrés Rizzi, *Fray Alonso de San Vitores*, 1651. Burgos, Museo de Burgos [201]

The Infanta Margarita de Austria, now usually attributed to Mazo [CAT. 37], Carreño embellishes the huge hooped skirts, makes the curtains even more splendid, and opens up vistas of gardens, terraces and balustrades as in the portrait of the *Marquesa de Santa Cruz* [FIG. 80].

And where there are no glimpses of external landscapes, the beautiful clothes, the sumptuous hangings, the jewels and trappings move even further away from the manner in which Velázquez or Mazo would have painted them, while retaining these painters' impressionistic technique. One example is the portrait of *Marie Louise of Orleans*, in the Monastery of Guadalupe, wearing a fabulously embroidered dress and posed in front of a lustrous curtain.

Sometimes painters use the device of presenting their subjects sitting down to underline their dignity and prestige. This is especially true of portraits of churchmen, of which the most glorious and significant example is *Don Justino de Neve* by Murillo (1617–1682) [CAT. 41]. Clad in austere black, the cleric sits at an angle to the surface of the canvas, facing the viewer, beside a table on which there is a clock, a bell and a book. Behind him we see the balustrade of a terrace overlooking a landscape, and in front is a playful dog gazing up at its master. Each element of the portrait carries some special meaning but all fit quite naturally into the overall composition.

Juan de Valdés Leal (1622–1690), in his portrait of *Don Miguel de Mañara* in Seville's Hospital de la Caridad [CAT. 42], presents his subject in a spacious study with paintings on the walls, reading the Rules of the Brotherhood of Charity or his *Discurso de la Verdad* ('Discourse on Truth'). Don Miguel is seated at a velvet-covered desk with a book rest and a crucifix, looking towards the viewer. A small boy wearing the habit of the brotherhood sits in a corner, his finger to his lips in a gesture demanding silence, inviting the viewer's complicity and lending the painting the very baroque characteristics of interior dynamism and extension of the action beyond the limits of the canvas.

Another superb example of a portrait of a seated ecclesiastic was painted in about 1656 by the Benedictine monk Fray Juan Andrés Rizzi. *Fray Alonso de San Vitores* [FIG. 81] is one of the most beautiful and vibrant portraits in the whole of Spanish painting, unmistakably drawing on Velázquez but interpreted using a technique that is at the same time vigorous and austere. The subject, wearing the magnificent robes of a cardinal over his black cassock, appears seated in front of a large window overlooking a landscape with the castle of Burgos and providing a source of bright light in a conception that is entirely baroque.

While it was unusual to present the sovereign seated, Carreño did so during the regency of Queen Mariana, doubtless as a tribute to the Queen Mother's punctilious attention to affairs of state. The various portraits of the queen in the Prado, the Museo de Bellas Artes, Bilbao, the Academia de San Fernando and elsewhere show her at a desk, official documents in hand, austerely dressed in widow's weeds in a spacious room with sumptuous mirrors and paintings that reinforce the portrait's allegorical meaning. One of the paintings shown is Tintoretto's *Judith and Holofernes* (now in the Museo del Prado), an exemplar of a strong woman fighting for her people.

However, seated portraits were actually quite rare. It was more usual for portrait subjects to be standing, in all their finery, next to a table on which were arranged objects loaded with meaning that would have been evident to a contemporary viewer. The clock, which as we have seen appears frequently, is a measure of time and symbol of the virtue of restraint and precision, a desirable attribute of the powerful.

Less frequent, but more obviously baroque in that they clearly echo the Flemish models of Rubens and Van Dyck, are portraits in which the subject appears attended by servants. Carreño's *Duke of Pastrana* and Murillo's magnificent *Don Antonio Hurtado de Salcedo*, familiarly known as *The Hunter* because he appears with his dogs and a servant against the backdrop of a fine landscape [FIG. 82], are excellent examples of this type of portrait, in which the artist draws on his familiarity with Van Dyck's dynamic and luminous portraits.

All the remarks made by Carducho (1633) about the dignity of the subject and the inadvisability of painting 'common persons' with 'highly unsuitable manners, apparel and insignia standing next to a table or beneath a hanging with the gravity of attire and posture associated with kings and the nobility' apply more readily to the baroque than to the period when Carducho was writing.

Conspicuous flaunting of wealth, ostentatious dress and the insistence on being seen as an extraordinary and significant individual were all intensified by the new, freer and more colourful style of painting incorporating Flemish and French influences. The severe black garments still worn by the king appeared less formal and more lavish when trimmed with silk and lace. Backdrops opened up to show landscapes, and female portraits, in which colour could be used more liberally, displayed an enormous wealth of tones and textures influenced by the marvellous freedom employed by Velázquez, which became the norm among his followers.

To the despair of those such as Carducho who believed that portraiture should be confined to those who had accomplished 'great things' worthy of imitation, artists depicted men 'of mechanical trades' (though wealthy) with all the arrogance of 'the great'. One such was *Don Luis García de Cerecedo* (Madrid, private collection), who made his money trading in horses and devoted himself to good works in his native village of Aldeavieja in the province of Ávila. He was shown soberly dressed, standing beside a table, in a splendid portrait of uncertain attribution, possibly the work of Francisco Camilo (1615–1673) or Herrera the Younger (*ca.* 1627–1685), painted some time between 1676 and 1678. In the case of many portraits of unnamed subjects, characterised by austerity of composition and freedom of technique and dating to the last quarter of the seventeenth century, we shall never know whether they represent genuine 'nobles' or bourgeois who had made a fortune and, proud of their achievements, wished to be painted for all the world to see.

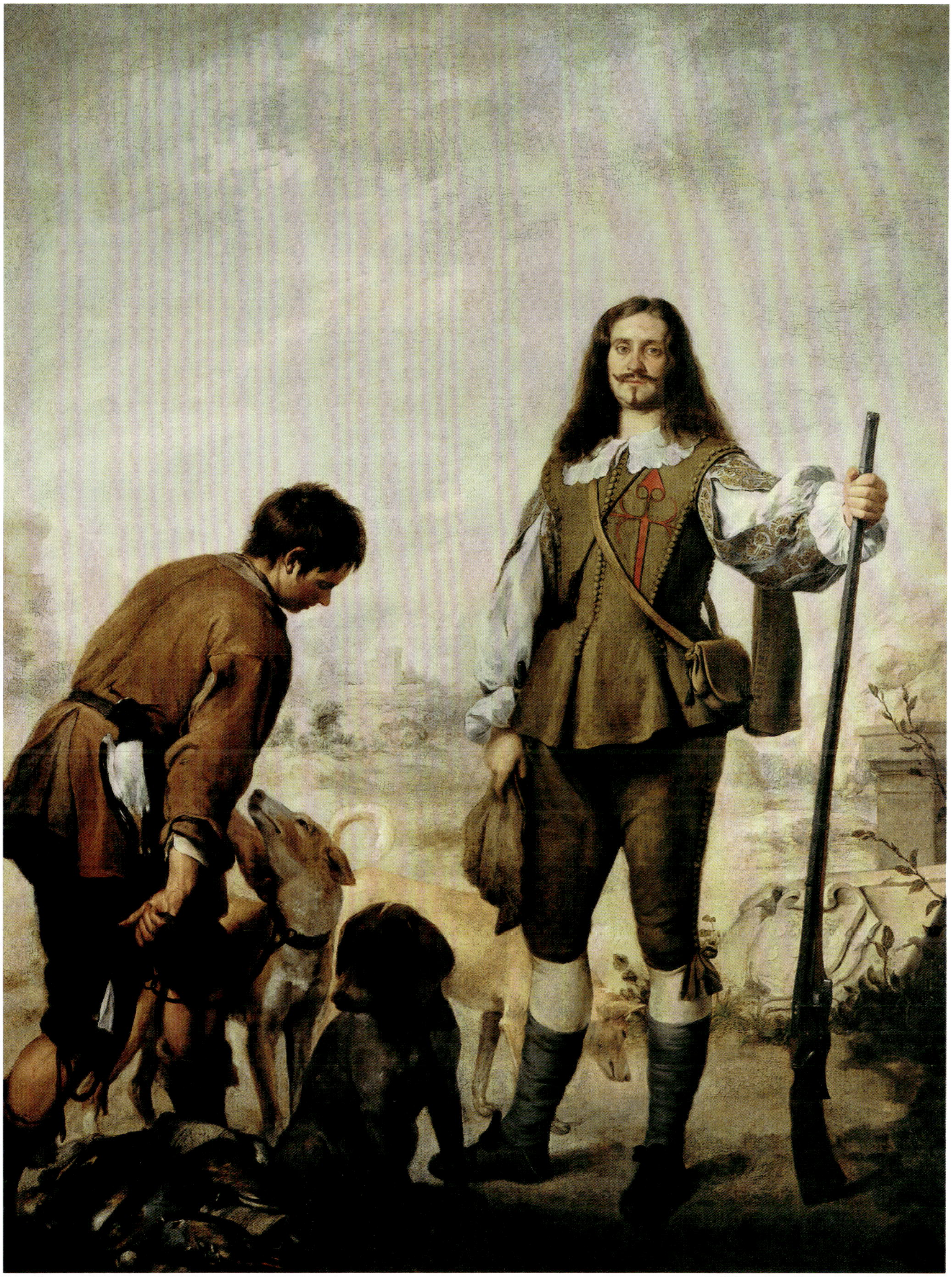

FIG. 82. Bartolomé Esteban Murillo, *Portrait of Don Antonio Hurtado de Salcedo, Marqués de Legarda, as a Huntsman*, *ca.* 1664. Private collection

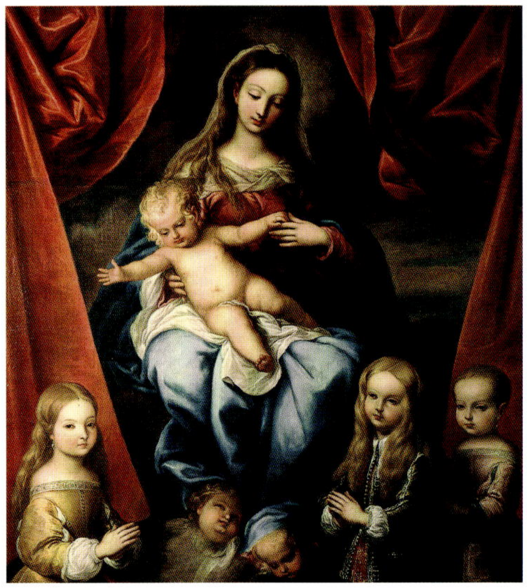

FIG. 83. Pedro Atanasio Bocanegra, *The Virgin and Child with Portraits*, *ca.* 1680. Bilbao, Museo de Bellas Artes [02/151]

One type of baroque representation so far reserved for kings was the equestrian portrait. There were illustrious prototypes of this ultimate accolade and manifestation of power, executed by such great artists as Titian, Rubens and Velázquez, but there were very few examples, at least in Spain, of aristocrats seeking to claim this privilege for themselves. However, towards the end of the seventeenth century we find examples of the equestrian portrait being used to represent generals, victorious or otherwise, and allowing them to parade their vanity and arrogance.

It was in Flanders that this form of representation was most familiar. From Rubens's *Duke of Lerma*, dated 1603 (Madrid, Museo del Prado, P-3137), or Van Dyck's *Don Francisco de Moncada*, *ca.* 1635 (Paris, Musée du Louvre), there is no shortage of examples of horses presented frontally, breaking through the surface of the canvas, and reinterpretations of Titian's magnificent version of the genre are echoed in Rubens and Gaspar de Crayer.

Apart from the flamboyant image of the Count-Duke of Olivares, where Velázquez forsook his usual objectivity and gave way to adulation, equestrian portraits were rare in Spain until the latter part of the century. Examples include *Don Baltasar Juliá y Montpalau* by Miguel March (1633–1670) (Valencia, private collection) and *Don Carlos San Gil y Lajusticia* by Senén Vila (1640–1707) (Madrid, private collection), although the latter already belongs to the eighteenth century since it is dated 1705 and was modified in 1708, perhaps in an unfortunate attempt at restoration.

But in the baroque world of the second half of the seventeenth century there were also other noteworthy types of portraiture, not without antecedents in earlier periods. An earlier convention that still survived was the inclusion of donor portraits in religious paintings. From the Middle Ages onwards praying figures were frequently shown at the foot of a devotional image and these were closely bound up with origins of the portrait as a genre.

This tradition continued but was manifested in a variety of ways. Traditional donors – including those in the first half of the century, like the two boys at the feet of the Virgin, their hands joined in prayer, in Zurbarán's *Immaculate Conception* in the Museo Nacional de Arte de Cataluña – are shown looking upwards at the image.

Then, however, at the zenith of the baroque, donors looked out towards the spectator, conscious of their own importance. Valdés Leal's superb *Immaculate Conception* in the National Gallery in London has a gentleman and an old woman at the feet of the Virgin. The woman is represented in the traditional way, but the man directs his gaze towards the viewer, pointing to the Virgin with an elegant movement of the hand, betraying the influence of Van Dyck.

One of the finest works of Pedro Atanasio Bocanegra (1638–1689), a native of Granada, shows a Virgin and Child, with three children praying at her feet, looking out shyly at the viewer [FIG. 83]. Clearly, the donor, almost certainly the children's father, as well as expressing his devotion to Mary took advantage of the occasion to capture the tender images of his offspring.

Sebastián de Llanos Valdés (1605–1677), in his 1667 *Virgin of the Rosary*, originally in the Dominican College of Santo Tomás in Seville and now in the National Gallery of Ireland in Dublin, also places a choir of schoolboys in the lower part of the painting. They are not actually donors but represent the college to which the donor is connected. But the individual attention devoted to each face makes it clear that these are portraits. Some

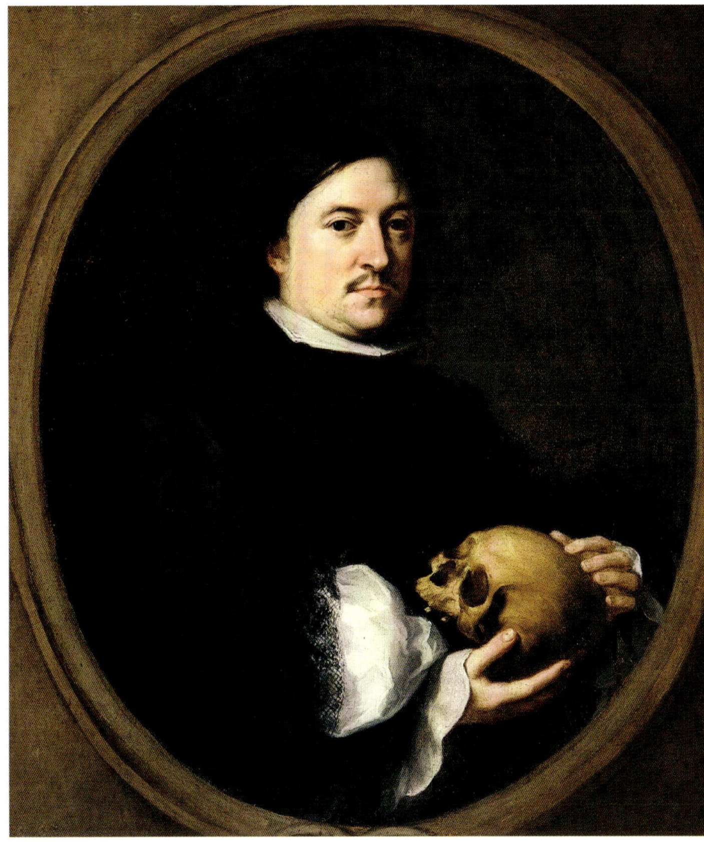

FIG. 84. Bartolomé Esteban Murillo, *Nicolás Omazur*, 1672. Madrid, Museo del Prado [P-3060]

are gazing up at the divine image while others stare out at the viewer, obviously interested in what is happening outside the painting, thereby pointing to a new and different mentality, where the affirmation of personality counts as much as, or even more than, religious devotion.

In a charming anonymous painting formerly in the collection of the dealer Rafael García Palencia, which, from the cut of the protagonists' clothes, appears to date from around 1680, very close to the era of Claudio Coello, we see a family kneeling before an altar dedicated to the Virgin. The parents on either side are looking at the holy image while the children in the foreground turn towards the viewer, pointing to the altar with playful gestures.

Another more intimate and more direct type of representation is the bust or half-length portrait, in which there is no space for decorative paraphernalia. The intensity of the sitter's gaze brings us much closer to his or her personality. We feel as though we know the person, and that their expression of trust or haughtiness, their smile or scorn, is directed specifically at us.

The tradition of bust portraits had been a very long-standing one, but in the final quarter of the seventeenth century an innovation arrived from the Low Countries, more especially from Holland, which soon became fashionable. It was the half-length or extended bust portrait enclosed in a feigned oval frame, which allowed artists to indulge in visual trickery. For example, the subject's hand might extend beyond the frame, clutching some significant item that reflected his or her character. Perhaps this new, very baroque, device was first adopted in Seville, the most frequent port of arrival for Flemish and Dutch works of art from 1648 onwards. The leading Spanish exponent of this form of portraiture was indisputably Murillo, who used it to splendid effect in his *Self Portrait* in the National Gallery in London [FIG. 1], a picture within a picture, in which the oval frame rests on a table on which compasses, a palette, brushes and sheets with drawings are set out. The artist convincingly creates the illusion that his hand is resting on the frame as if it were a windowsill. In another youthful *Self Portrait* (USA, private collection) this time without the illusionism, Murillo is seen in an oval frame that appears to rest on a marble-like stone. The portrait of his friend, the Dutch merchant *Nicolás Omazur*, in the Prado [FIG. 84], and the matching portrait of his wife, *Isabel Malcampo*, now lost, add symbolic and moralistic meaning to the oval format. In his hands the husband clutches a skull, while his wife holds a rose, allusions to the fragility of life and the transience of beauty which baroque art frequently used as a counterbalance to the tawdriness of worldly glory.

Valdés Leal also resorts to this format. A similarly bleak message is carried by a somewhat battered portrait of *Miguel de Mañara*, also holding a death's head in his hands, in the Hospital de la Caridad in Seville, of which Don Miguel was the founder.

Valdés Leal's son, Lucas Valdés (1661–1725), who inherited his father's talent and commissions, painted an oval portrait of *Admiral Pedro Corbet*, now in the Hospital de Venerables Sacerdotes in Seville. The subject's hand rests on the frame and, as in Murillo's self-portrait, attributes of his profession are laid out on a ledge outside the frame: a plumed helmet, an armillary sphere, some military treatises, a plan of a fortress and a coat of arms, showing his profession and his high status.

Although most examples of this kind of portrait are found in Seville, there are also similar ones in Madrid. An engraving in the Biblioteca Nacional, undoubtedly based on a painting that has not survived, shows Carreño de Miranda in an oval frame on which is inscribed his name, his title of Court Painter and the year of his death, confirming that the engraving was posthumous. Another instance is the portrait of the elderly *Duchess of Aveiro*, signed by Francisco Ignacio Ruiz de la Iglesia (1649–1704), in the Museo del Prado (P-3029), which also displays the painter's name and signature inside a feigned frame.

There are also many anonymous portraits in this format dating from the final decades of the seventeenth century. In the eighteenth century, obviously influenced by French court painting, the use of the feigned oval format combined and contrasted the tradition of restraint in the depiction of important personages, and of showing them with solemn expressions, with the newer and more complex configuration of the portrait.

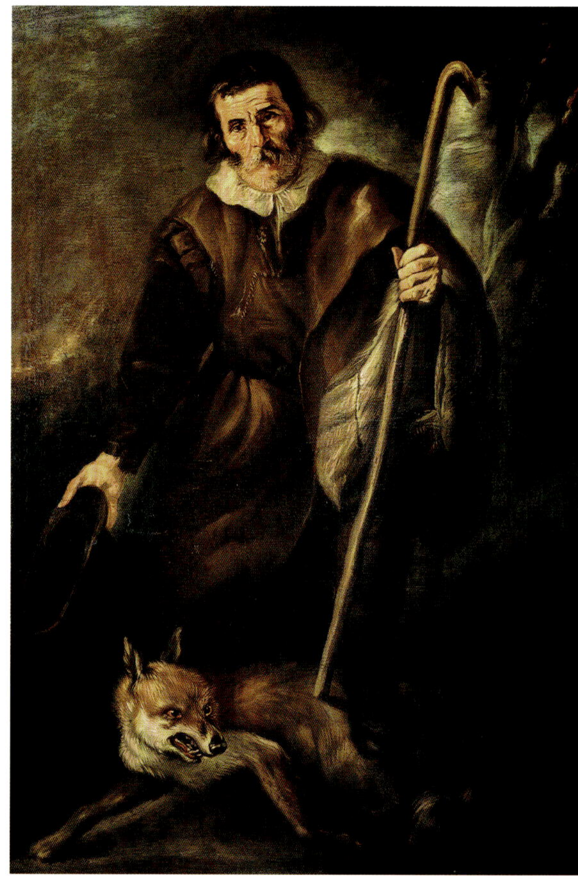

FIG. 85. Francisco Rizi, *The King's Foxhunter*, before 1661. Madrid, Fundación Casa de Alba

There still remains one type of portrait that might be termed the representation of professional people exercising their activity. Theologians and professors were shown seated at a table or desk, artists appear standing at their easels, brush and palette in hand, and there are some rare examples of people practising unusual occupations. One example is the so-called *King's Foxhunter* by Francisco Rizi (1619–1685) [FIG. 85], which is a superb example of the baroque portrait with all the characteristic ingredients: expansive gestures, a sweeping setting and the presence of an animal, in this case the vixen, nervous and alert as she is controlled by the man. The strong personality of the subject leaves us in no doubt that we are looking at the likeness of a real person.

Carducho, writing in 1633, pointed out that those who engaged in the unseemly activity of painting ordinary 'working' men as if they were nobles should at least show them 'with some tool of their trade, so that the notary might appear with a pen behind his ear, the merchant with something indicative of his activity and the painter with brushes and paints'. Painters at least followed his suggestion to the letter, including Carducho himself, whose self-portrait (Glasgow, Pollok House) shows him as both man of letters and painter, seated at a desk writing but with a palette and bundle of brushes next to the inkwell.

Juan de Pareja's *José de Ratés* [FIG. 78], discussed earlier, is a good example of this type of portrait, with plan and compass identifying the sitter as an architect, but at the same time showing him as a self-confident individual content with his lot in life.

Dating from a little earlier is a curious portrait in the Museo de Bellas Artes in Oviedo, showing a painter whom some have identified as Carreño or Rizzi. He appears soberly dressed, looking outwards as he stands in front of a large easel, painting a canvas of the Immaculate Conception.

An even more significant illustration of how a portrait is transformed into the depiction of a subject 'caught in the act' is the presumed self-portrait of the Granada-born artist Pedro de Moya (d. 1674) [FIG. 86]. Sitting in front of his easel, he turns to face the viewer in a rapid

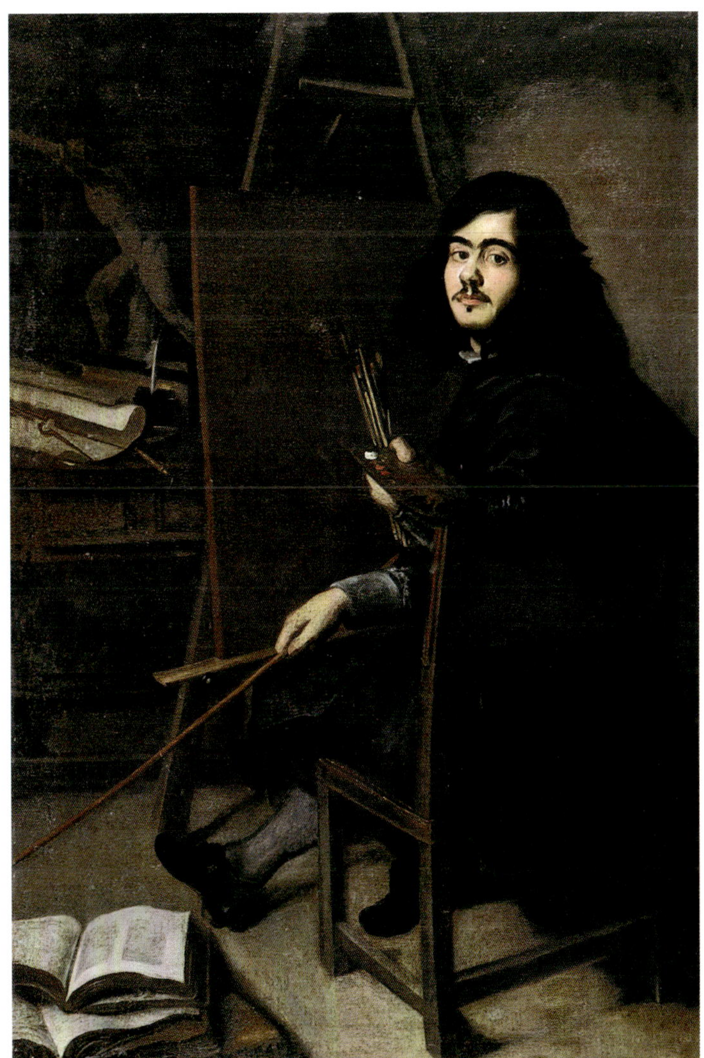

FIG. 86. Pedro de Moya (?), *Self Portrait*. Bordeaux, Musée des Beaux-Arts

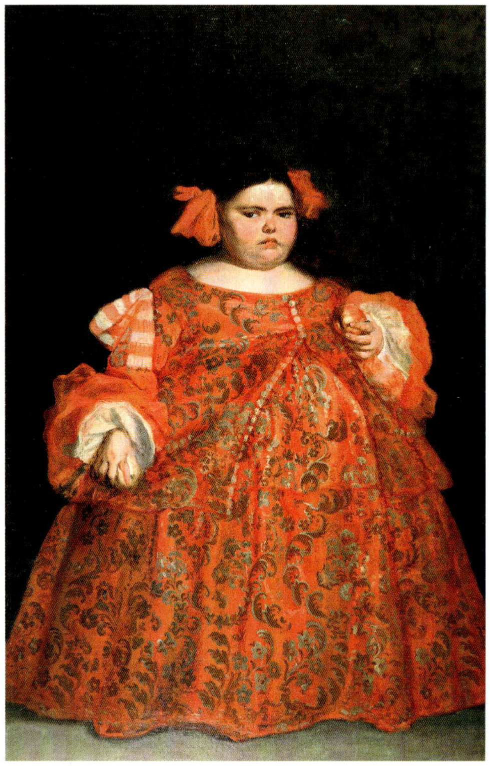

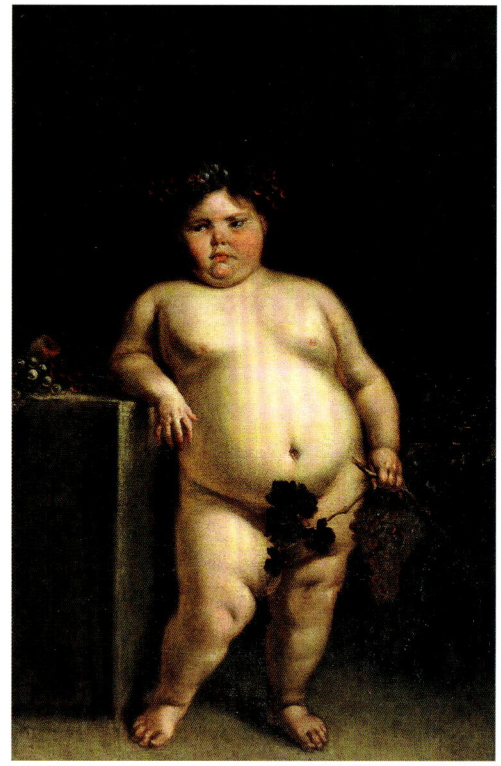

FIGS 87 and 88. Juan Carreño de Miranda, *Eugenia Martínez Vallejo, known as 'La monstrua', dressed* and *'La monstrua', naked*, 1680. Madrid, Museo del Prado [P-646 and P-2800]

movement, supporting the maulstick in his right hand and the palette and brushes in his left. He is surrounded by plaster casts, papers, books and inkwells in a very realistic representation of an artist's studio.

Another example of this type of portrait of people at work that almost borders on genre painting is José Antolinez's *Picture Vendor* (Munich, Alte Pinakothek), perhaps a dealer of devotional paintings. The image conveys the appearance of the modest workshop of a Madrid artist, in which the treatment of space derives directly from Velázquez.

A distinctive form of the baroque portrait is that which brings together subjects made 'different' from others by some quirk of nature: dwarves, lunatics and grotesque individuals, presented to the curious viewer as they might be today if subjects of a science documentary. Compared with the cold, impassive observation of the subject and the loving attention to detail that characterised sixteenth-century portraiture (think of Sánchez Cotán's *Brígida del Río, The Bearded Woman of Peñaranda* in the Museo del Prado and even the naturalism of Ribera's work in the first three decades of the seventeenth century [CAT. 25]), interpretation was freer and not without a certain charm. *Michol the Dwarf* (USA, private collection) poses for Carreño in his palace finery surrounded by exotic creatures: white cockatoos, brilliantly coloured birds and small dogs. When Carreño was commissioned to paint the hugely fat, so-called 'monster' *Eugenia Martínez Vallejo*, clothed and naked, he showed the child dressed in a gorgeous red gown, a gift from the king, and then as the god Bacchus, with vine tendrils and bunches of grapes [FIGS 87 and 88]. His *Buffoon Francisco Bazán* is caught standing unsteadily, as if about to move, in an attitude of gentle pleading and deep respect. All three works are in the Prado.

Of course, these extraordinary individuals have much in common with the wonderful characters painted by Velázquez, but perhaps differ because they lack the complex web of meaning woven around them by the great Sevillian painter's rich imagination.

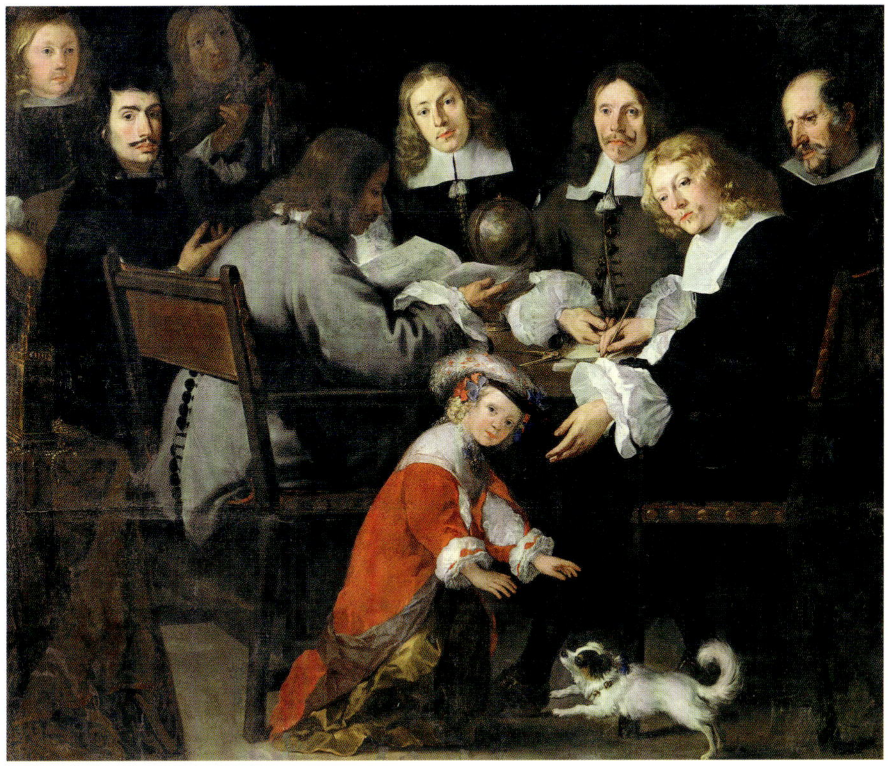

FIG. 89. José Antolínez, *The Ambassador Lerche and his Friends*, 1662. Copenhagen, Statens Museum for Kunst [1646]

Finally, we should mention the category of group portraits, rare in Spanish art and no doubt influenced by northern European traditions. As a rule Spaniards, proud of their individuality and conscious of their importance, did not cultivate the group portrait, which always raised complicated issues of precedence. It is significant that the best known and most outstanding examples are either painted by foreign artists who had settled in Spain or feature groups of foreigners painted by a Spanish artist.

The most 'Spanish' of such portraits is *The Family of the Painter* by Mazo, mentioned above [CAT. 44], a homage to Velázquez and *Las Meninas* with a spatial configuration in some ways similar to that of the prototype but lacking its magical and enigmatic atmosphere. The painting sets out to portray a family – the painter's own – very much aware of its own importance and of its rise up the social scale made possible by the art of painting, alluded to in the room in the background. The portrait of *Ambassador Lerche and his Friends* by the Madrid artist José Antolínez (1635–1675) in the Statens Museum in Copenhagen [FIG. 89] is an exceptionally well-executed work along the lines of Dutch and English conversation pieces. It shows a group of gentlemen engaged in animated literary debate, interrupted by a child and his dog, which add movement and introduce a touch of tender humour.

The Flemish artist Jan Van Kessel the Younger (1654–1708) painted at least two family portraits, lively scenes fully of vivacity and movement set in a garden where the subjects, including two children, dogs and birds, are less constrained by protocol. These portraits – one signed in 1679 (National Museum of Warsaw) and the other in 1680 (Prado, P-2525) – were probably painted as a tribute to the Flemish family who brought the artist to Madrid. Of course, attire and setting in such portraits document the social life of the Spanish court at the height of the reign of Charles II before French fashions became dominant, at least in the most cultured circles, in the eighteenth century.

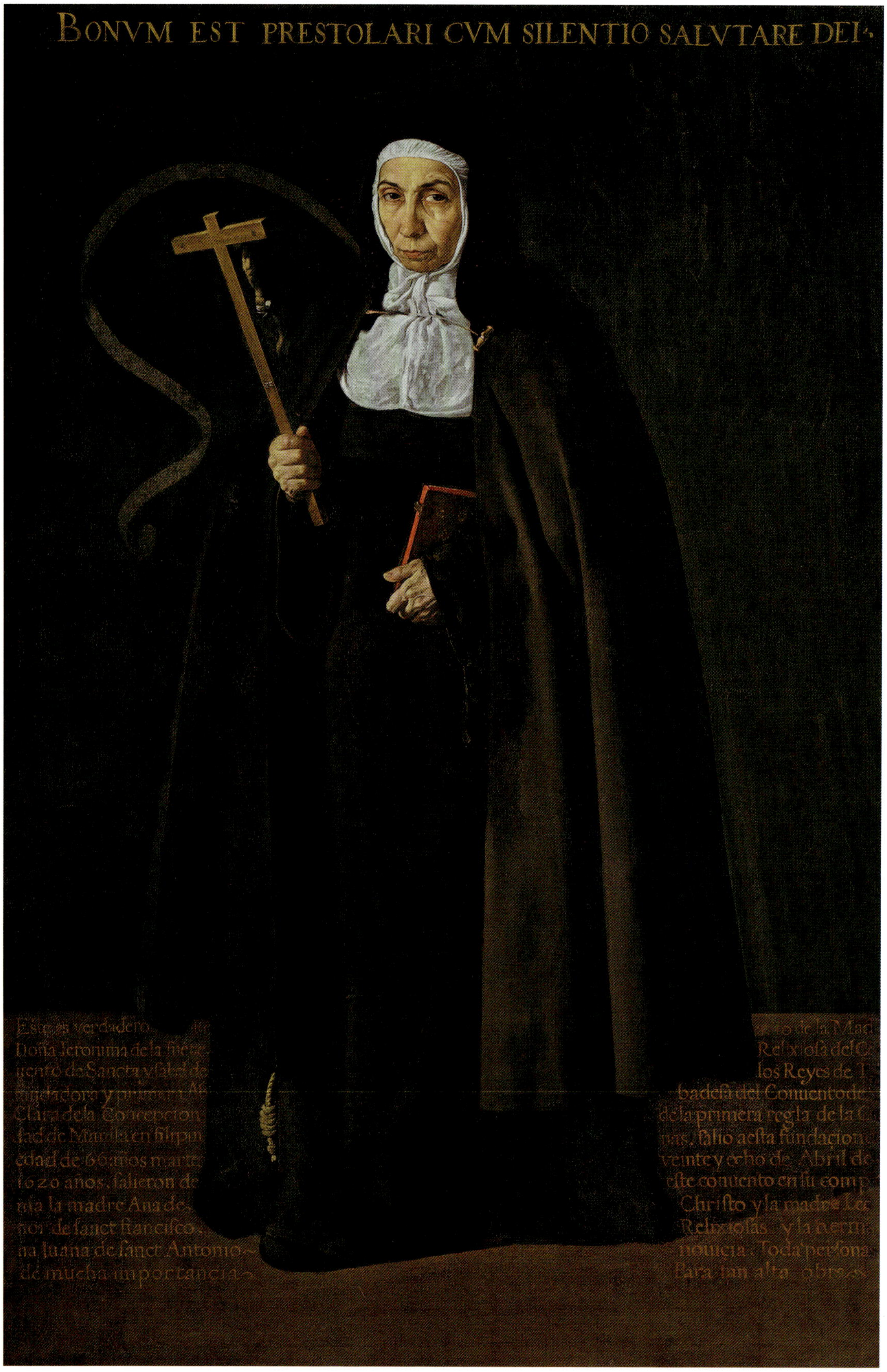

CAT. 29. Diego Velázquez. *The Venerable Mother Jerónima de la Fuente*, 1620. Museo del Prado [P-2873]

CAT. 30. Diego Velázquez. *Luis de Góngora*, 1622. Boston, Museum of Fine Arts (Maria Antoinette Evans Fund [32.79])

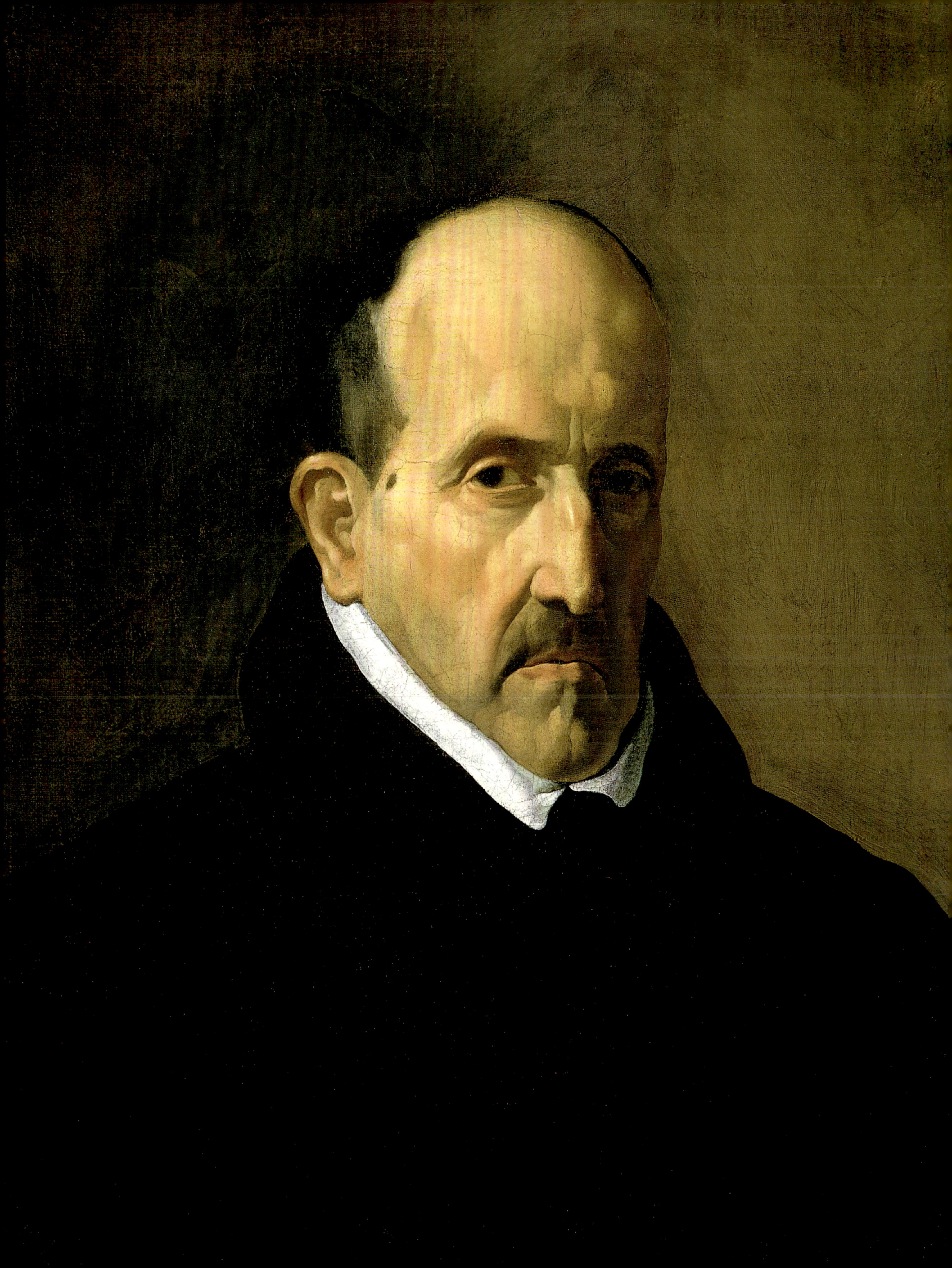

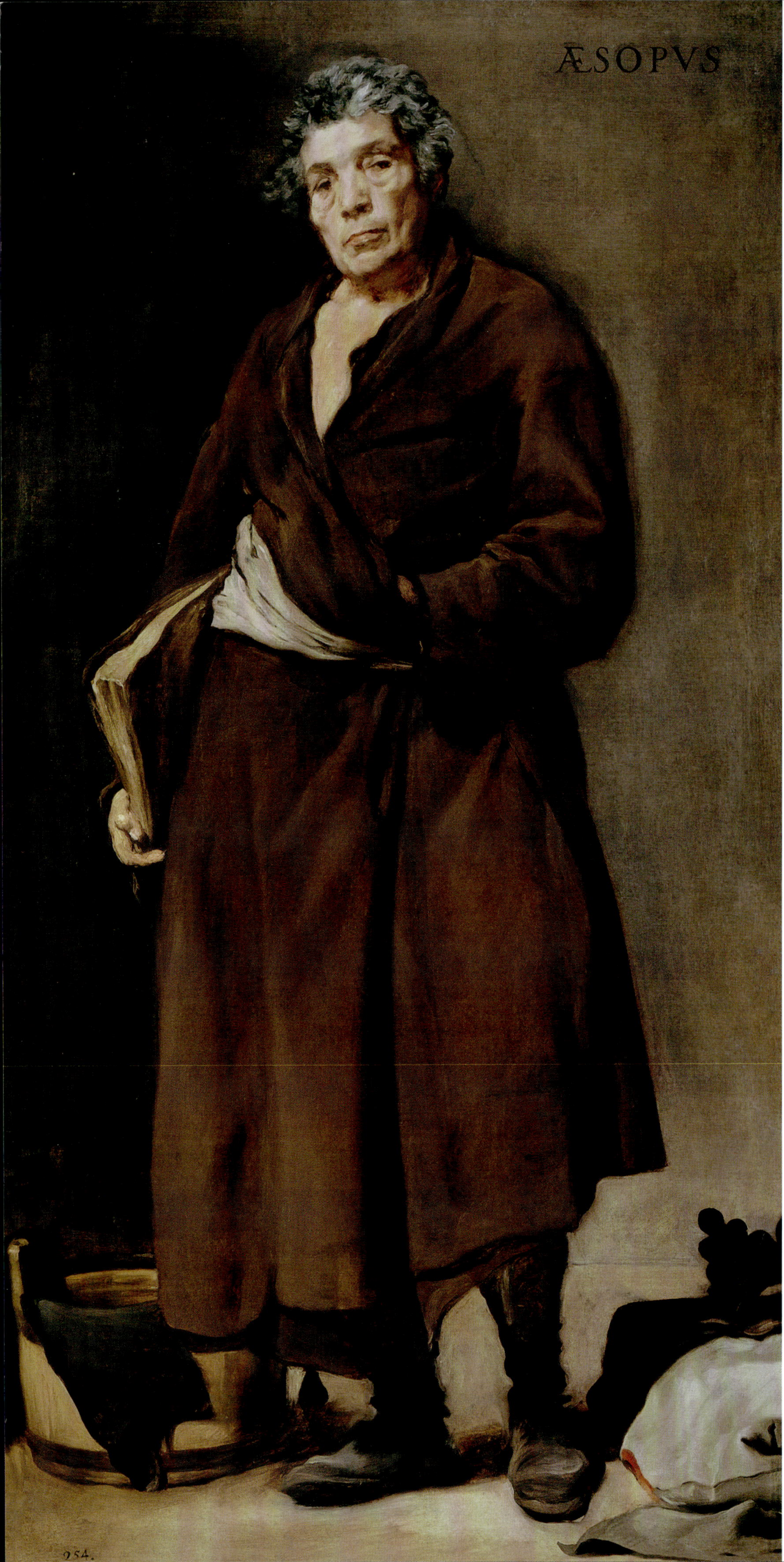
ÆSOPVS
254.

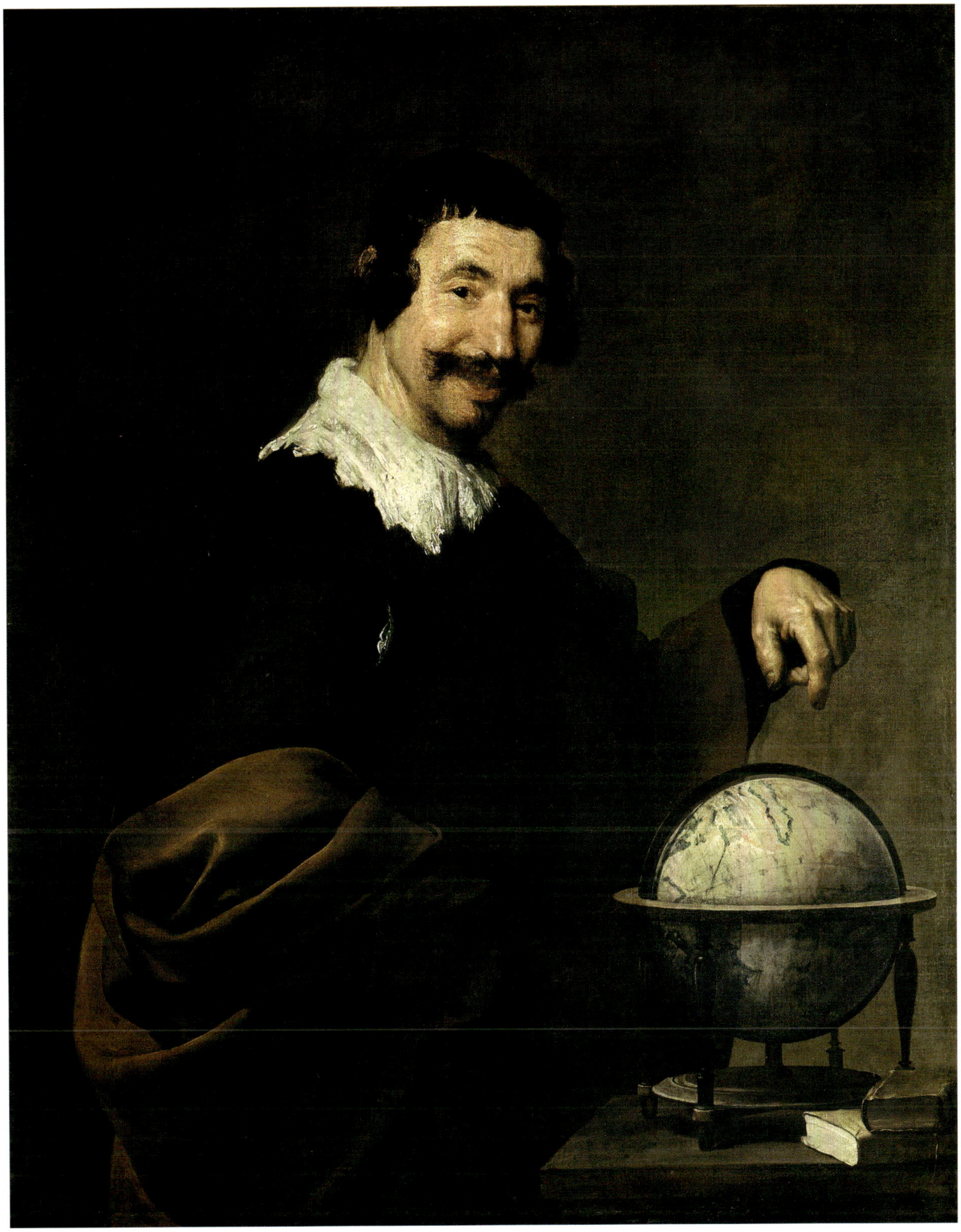

CAT. 31. Diego Velázquez. *Aesop*, *ca.* 1638. Museo del Prado [P-1206]

CAT. 32. Diego Velázquez. *Democritus*, 1625–1627 and 1639–1640. Rouen, Musée des Beaux-Arts. [Collection Gabriel Lemonnier, 822.1.16]

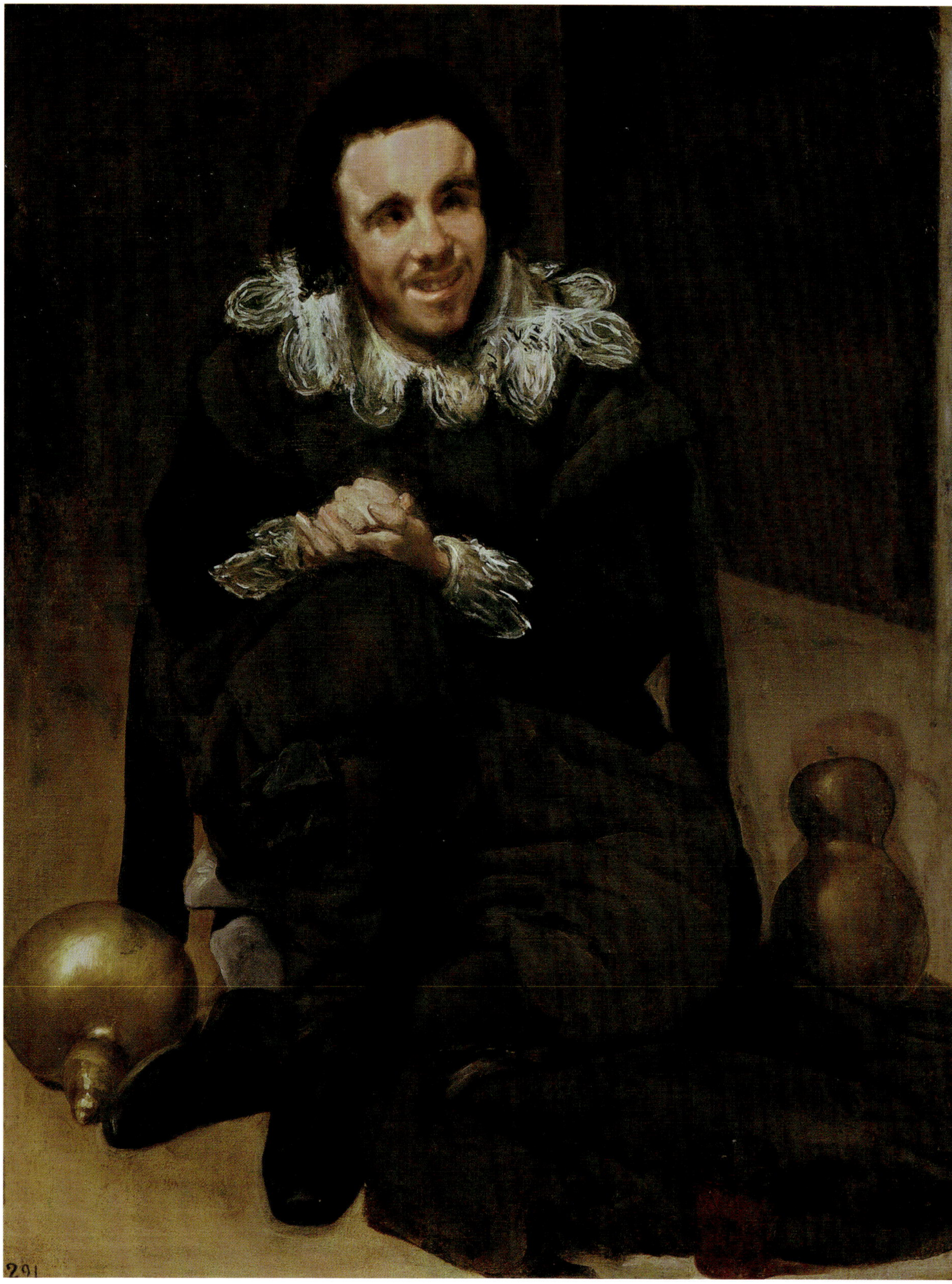

CAT. 33. Diego Velázquez. *The Buffoon Calabacillas, ca.* 1635–1640. Museo del Prado [P-1205]

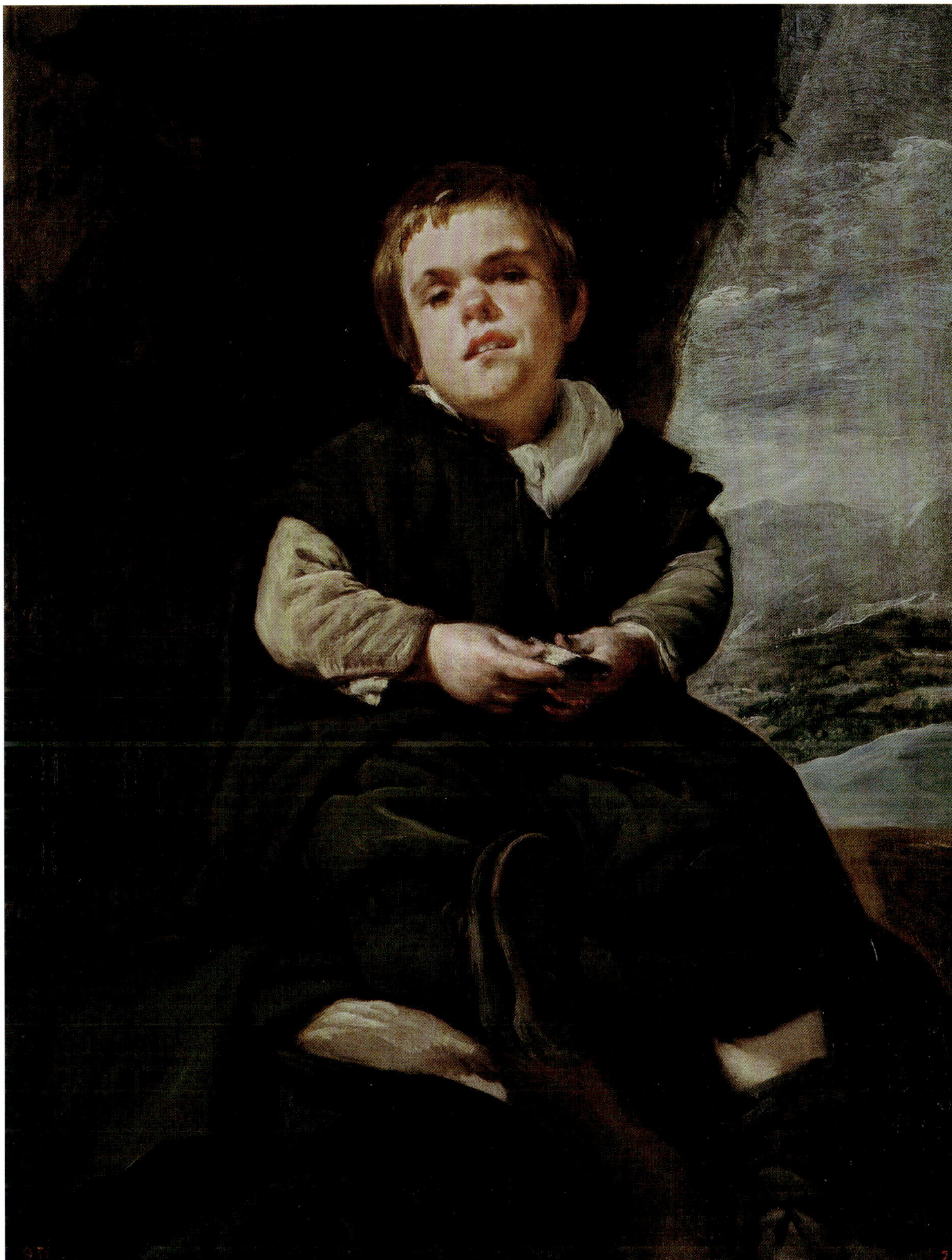

CAT. 34. Diego Velázquez. *El Niño de Vallecas, ca.* 1635–1645. Museo del Prado [P-1204]

CAT. 35. Diego Velázquez. *Portrait of a Man, 'The Pope's Barber', ca.* 1650. Museo del Prado [P-7858]

CAT. 36. Diego Velázquez. *Portrait of a Man, ca.* 1640–1650. London, English Heritage (Apsley House)

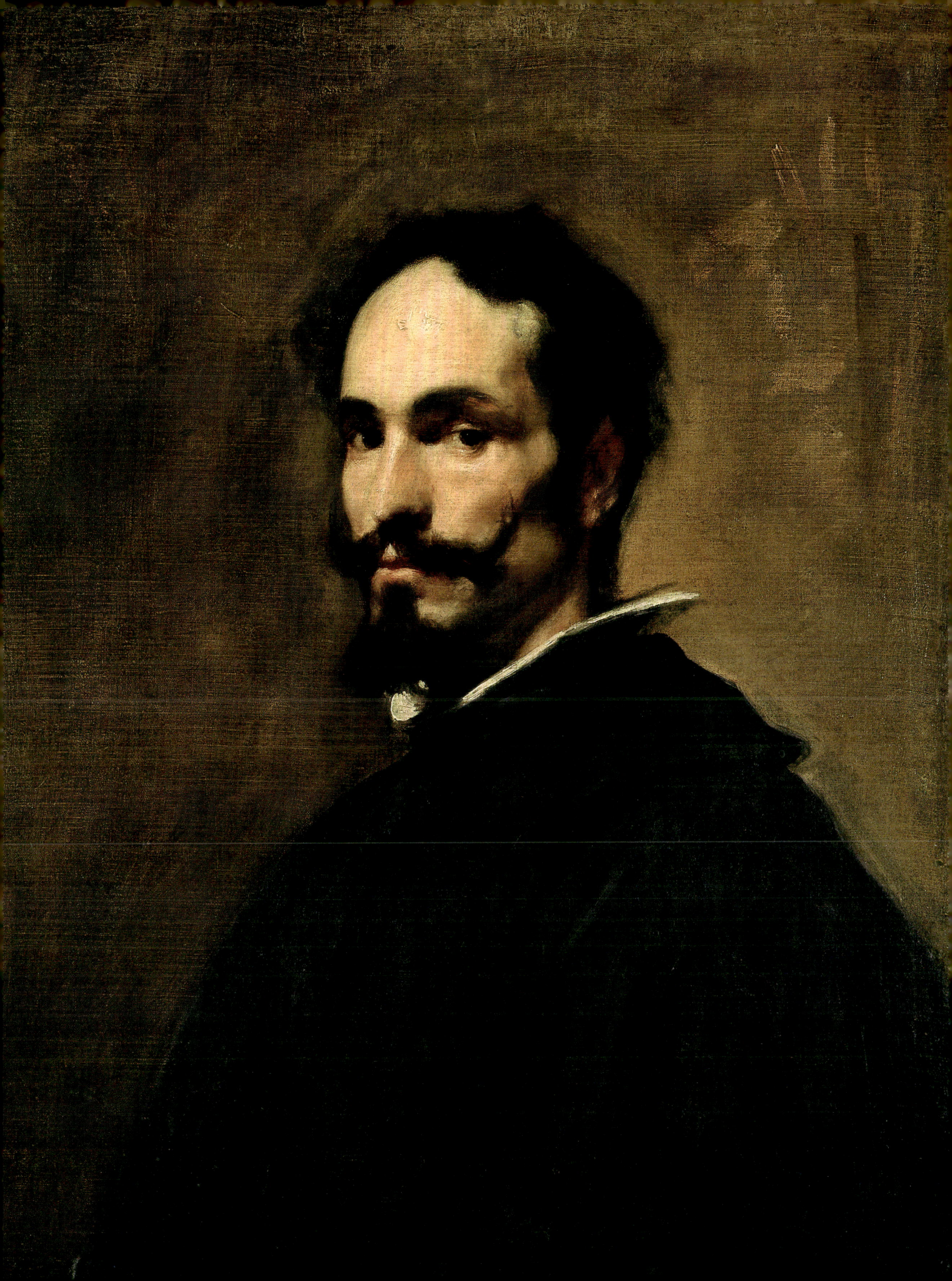

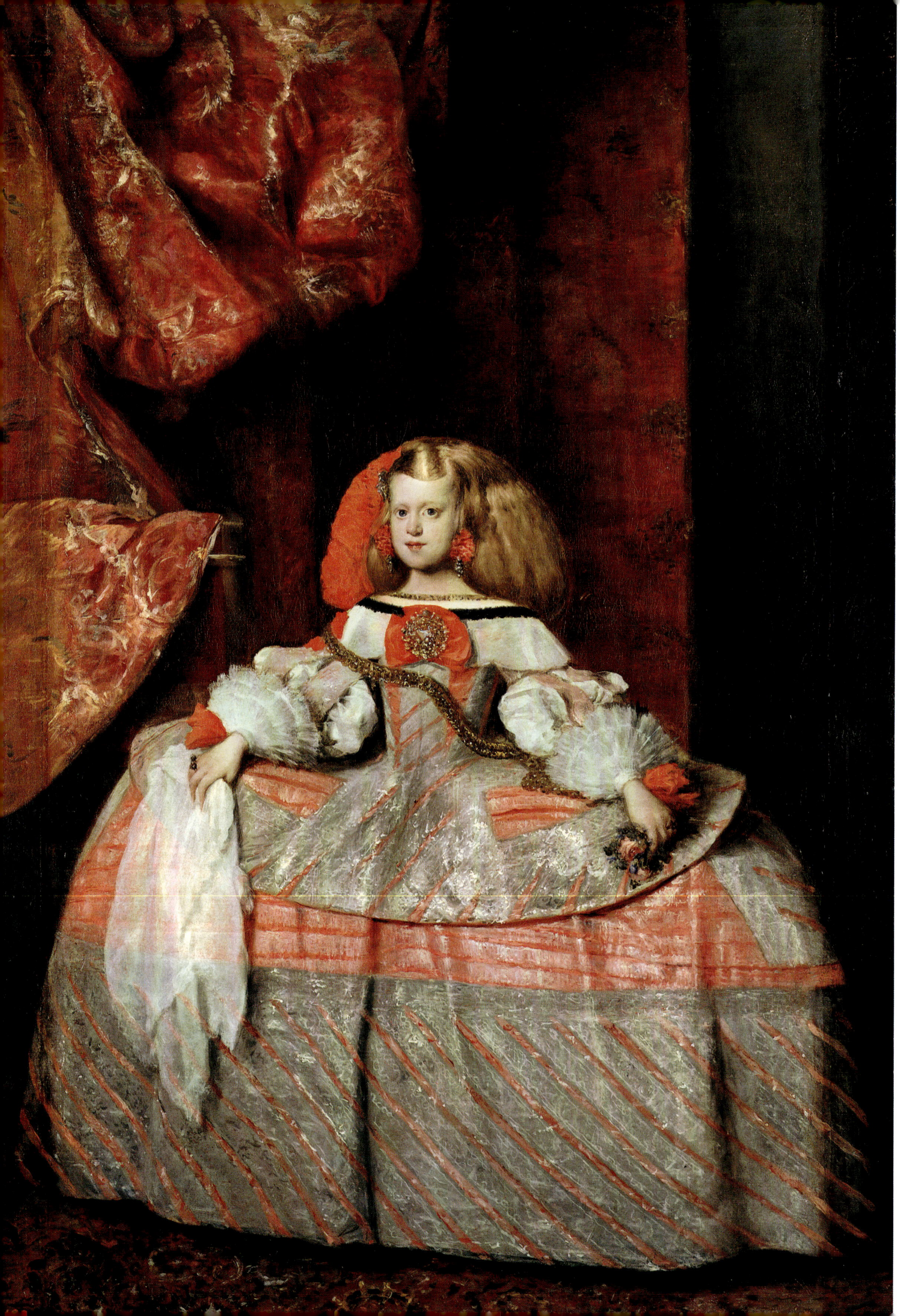

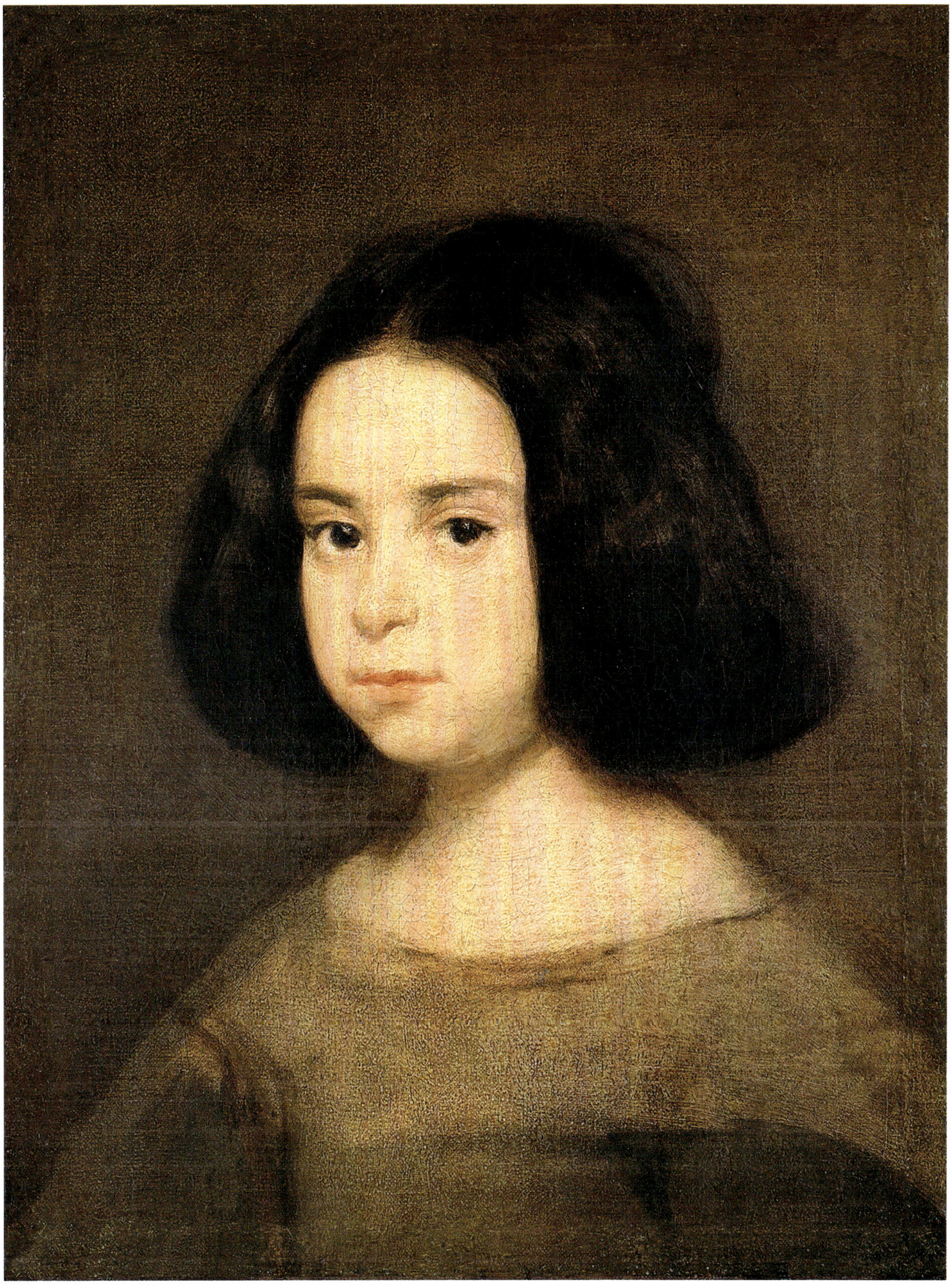

CAT. 37. Juan Bautista Martínez del Mazo. *The Infanta Margarita de Austria*, *ca.* 1665. Museo del Prado [P-1192]

CAT. 38. Diego Velázquez. *Portrait of a Girl*, *ca.* 1640–1642. New York, The Hispanic Society of America [A108]

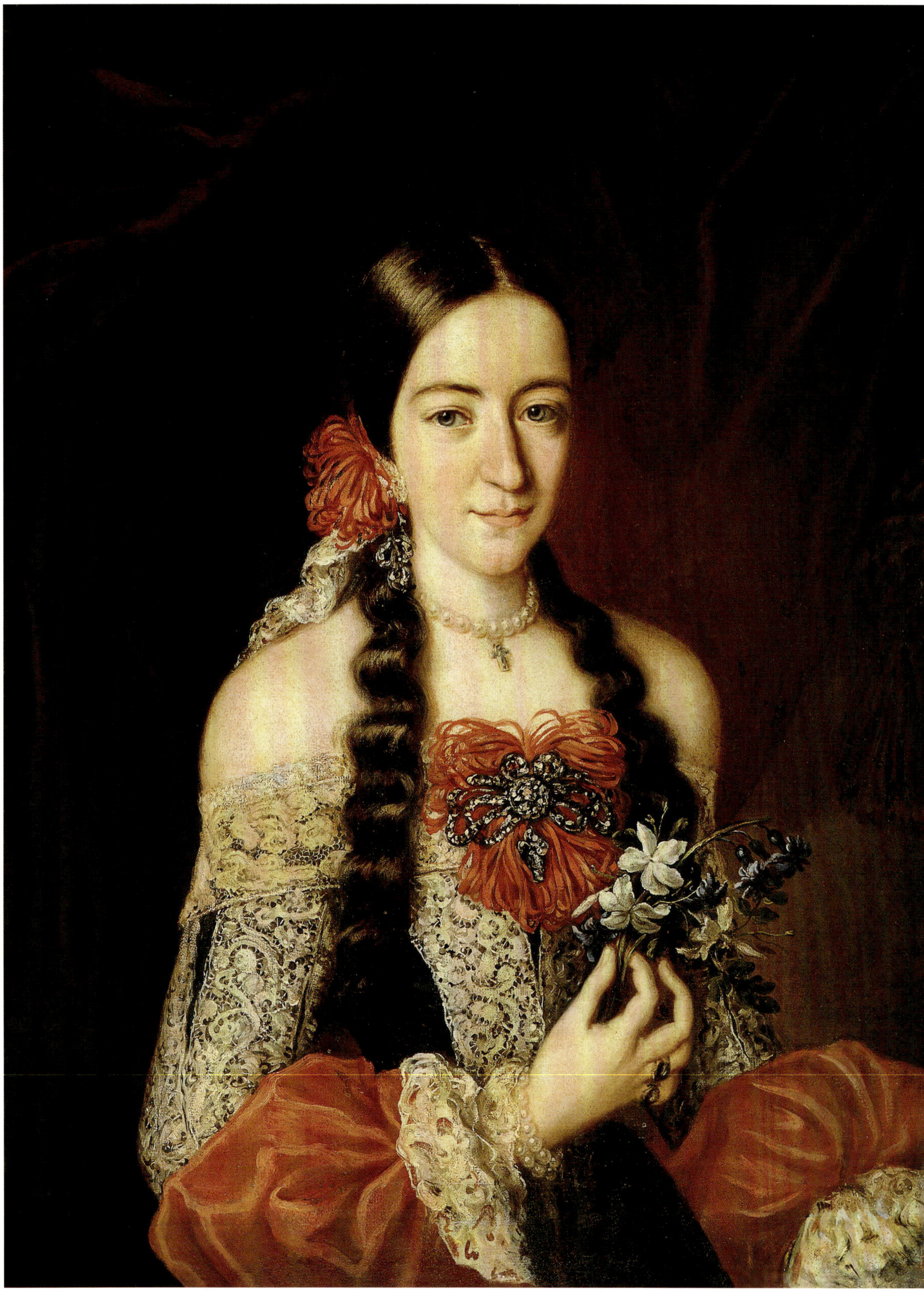

CAT. 39. Claudio Coello. *Doña Nicolasa Manrique, ca.* 1690–1692. Madrid, Instituto Valencia de Don Juan

CAT. 40. Juan Carreño de Miranda. *The Duke of Pastrana*, 1666. Museo del Prado [P-650]

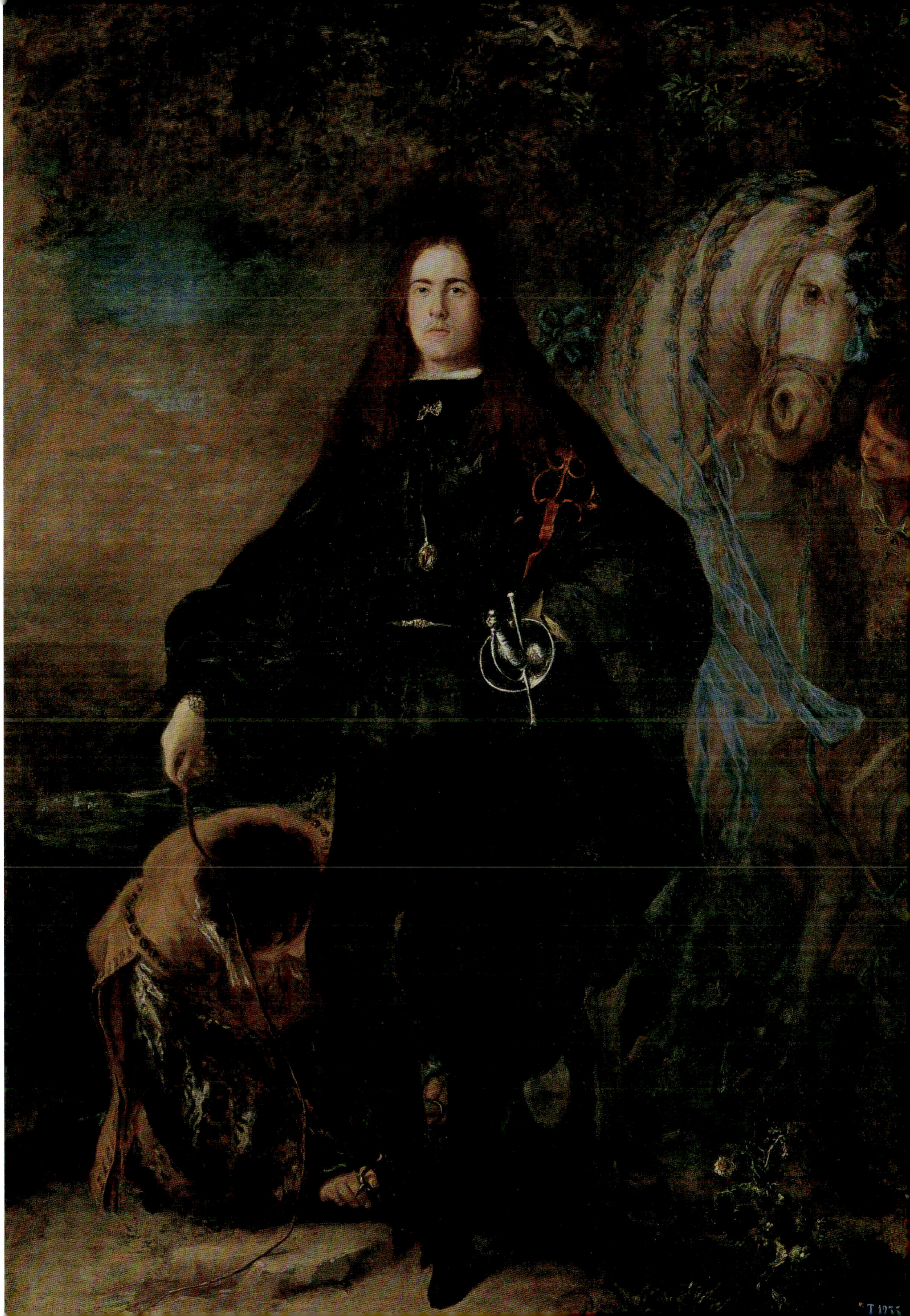

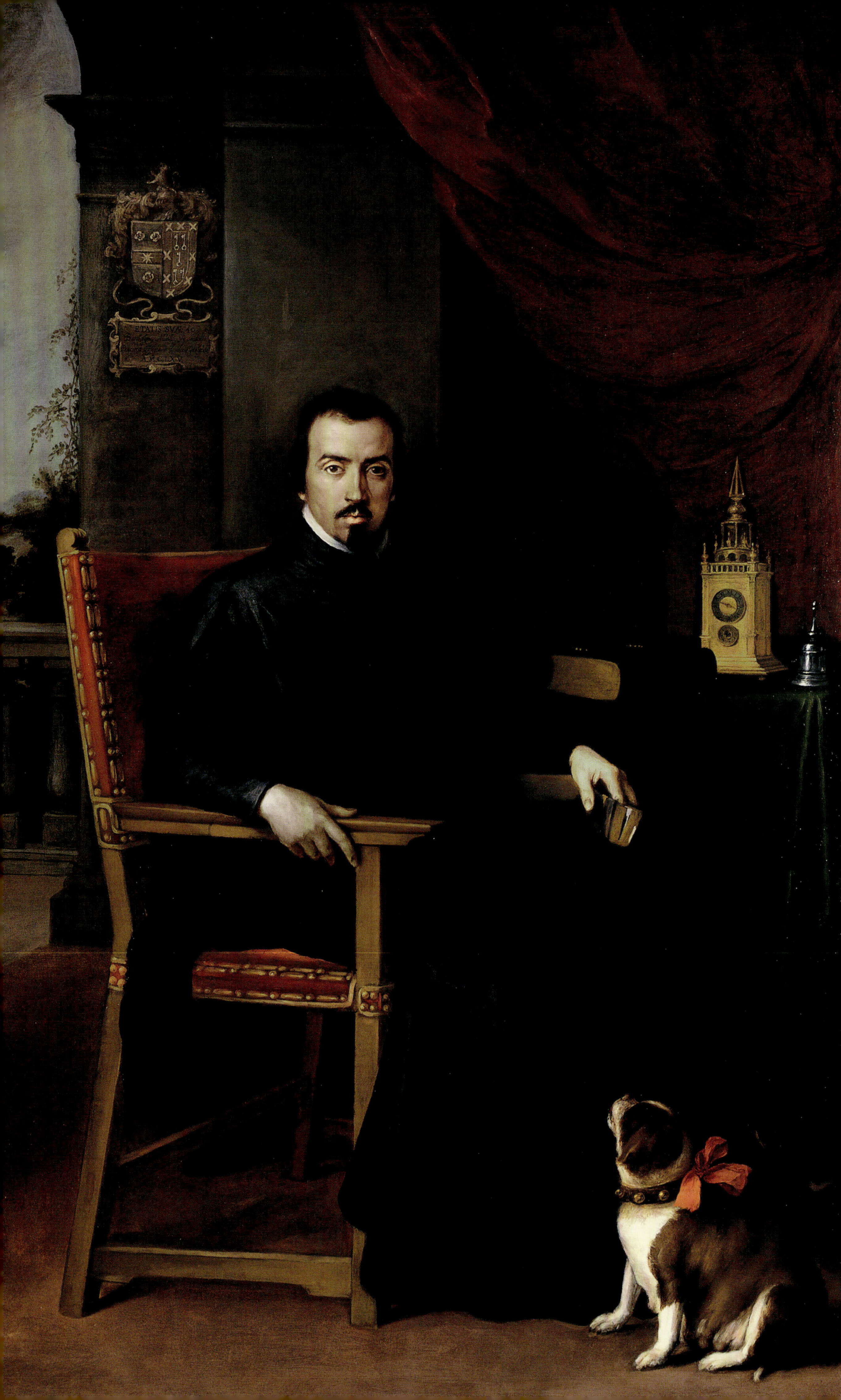

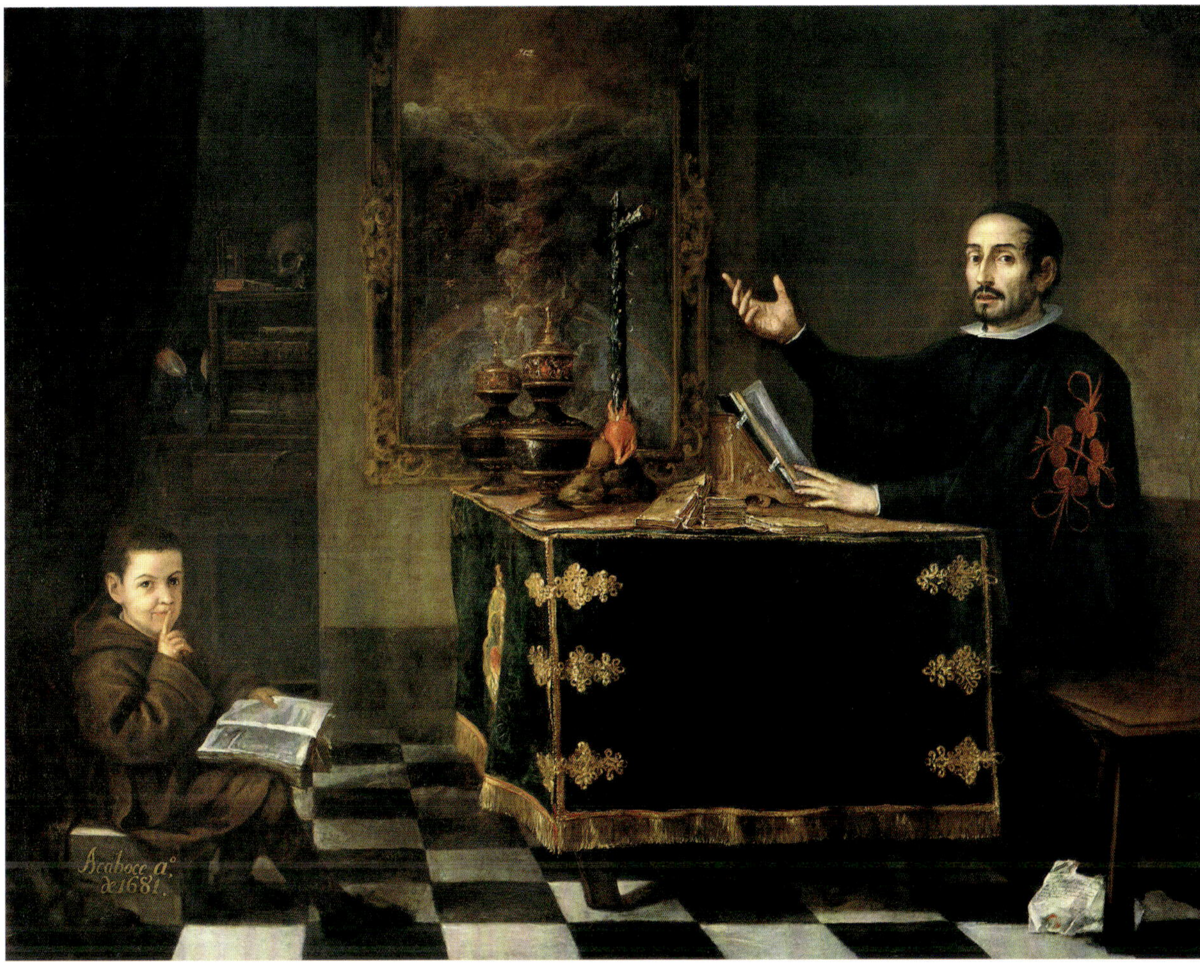

CAT. 41. Bartolomé E. Murillo.
Don Justino de Neve, 1665. London,
The National Gallery [NG 6448]

CAT. 42. Juan Valdés Leal.
Don Miguel de Mañara, 1681. Seville,
Hermandad de la Santa Caridad

6 Goya, a Free 'Disciple' of Velázquez

Manuela B. Mena Marqués

By Goya's time, Velázquez had become something of a legend, at least in the cultured circles of the Spanish court. In the eyes of the German artist and critic Anton Raphael Mengs, the painter and scholar Antonio Ponz and the politician and intellectual Gaspar Melchor de Jovellanos, Velázquez had been the master of masters and thus would never be equalled: 'when he died, the glory of Painting in Spain died with him'.[1] He had not always been so widely revered, even though two Spanish art theorists, his father-in-law Francisco Pacheco and later Antonio Palomino, considered him unrivalled as a painter. Certainly neither his most direct disciple, Juan Bautista Martínez del Mazo, nor his successor as court painter, Juan Carreño – both excellent painters – ever attained the greatness of Velázquez, despite their close contact with him. Nor did Luca Giordano, who, according to Palomino, coined for *Las Meninas* the apt description 'Theology of painting' and whose *Homage to Velázquez*, now correctly identified as a portrait of the Count of Santisteban and his family (London, The National Gallery, NG 1434),[2] was the first tribute by a foreign artist to Velázquez's best-known work. Other highly regarded artists in Spain, the only country where Velázquez was well known in the seventeenth and early eighteenth centuries (his European fame came later) equally failed to see his value as a modernising factor in their own work.[3] It was exactly this that distinguished them from Goya. For just as Velázquez and Rubens had studied Titian as the starting point for a more modern approach, Goya studied Velázquez not as a servile copyist but rather as an intelligent student, in order to refine his own ideas on the representation of nature, his own technique and pictorial resources. If Velázquez's works served as an example and inspiration for his own compositions, these were more a modern tribute than a mere copy.

Goya left too few writings on art to form any clear idea of his views on, or admiration for, Velázquez; such views, therefore, are only to be deduced from an analysis of his work. Indeed, to judge from his private correspondence with Martín Zapater, a childhood friend from Zaragoza, he wrote little on painting in general, and even less on art theory. The Real Academia de Bellas Artes de San Fernando required its members to submit an essay on the teaching of art; significantly, Goya's essay – presented in October 1792 – made no explicit reference to Velázquez. His interest in Velázquez was first brought to public notice by his son Javier, in a biography written in 1831 for the Academia de San Fernando: 'Though a reverent observer of Velázquez and Rembrandt, he neither studied nor observed anything but Nature, which he called his master.'[4] Goya himself, in a brief autobiography for the Museo del Prado catalogue of 1828, the year of his death, makes no direct reference to Velázquez but simply observes, with his usual candour, that he has had 'no master but my observation of painters' things, and famous paintings in Rome and Spain, which is where I learnt most'.[5] In thus stressing his own training as a painter, Goya offered an illustration of his views on the teaching of art, as submitted to the Academy in 1792: 'I shall prove, demonstrating with facts, that there are no rules in Painting, and that oppression and the servile obligation for all to study and follow the same path, are a great impediment to the Young who aspire to such a difficult art.'[6]

The impact of Velázquez's work on Goya became evident at an early stage, when he chose a large group of Velázquez's works as subjects of his prints. Numerous authors have drawn attention to the role of Antonio Ponz in this undertaking. In the fifth volume of his vast *Viage de España* (Travels in Spain), devoted to Madrid – which mentions Goya as one of the young artists working on cartoons of tapestries for the King – Ponz canvasses the idea that the treasures held in the Royal Collections should be made more widely known: 'Europe is vaguely aware that in Madrid, and especially in the Royal Palaces and in El Escorial, there are some outstanding works; but few people know what they are, for they have seen scarcely more than the odd poor print […]. This would have been less surprising in the past, for there were fewer engravers here, but now that we have a fair number of such artists able to undertake this enterprise, it is a shame that they are not put to it.'[7] This enlightened notion was effected the following year, with the rise to power of the Count of Floridablanca. As reported several years later by the engraver Juan Antonio Carmona,[8] one of the Count's first projects on becoming Chief Minister was to commission prints of pictures in the Royal Collection. This fledgling project, if such it was, involved Goya, Ramón Bayeu, Fernando Selma, José del Castillo and perhaps Carmona himself. It is unclear whether Goya came across Ponz's idea in *Viage de España*, or whether he was directly approached – at Floridablanca's behest – by the great scholar himself, then Secretary of the Real Academia de San Fernando and a friend of the art historian Agustín Ceán Bermúdez. Either way, a first set of etchings of Velázquez's work was published in July 1778; a second set followed in December of that year.[9]

Although it is still not wholly clear what led him to play such a leading role in this project, some analysis of Goya's contribution to it is essential in order to understand his interest in Velázquez. Unlike his colleagues, Goya displayed an independent and enthusiastic approach to the task, and – more importantly – his prints did not observe the conventions usual in this type of copying. Goya's etchings were not literal reproductions of Velázquez's paintings; rather, the surviving proofs and drawings after several paintings suggest that he used this medium as a way of studying and understanding the older artist. Occasionally he even modified Velázquez's compositions to reflect his own ideas. In copying Velázquez in 1778, Goya was going back to his early days as an apprentice, when he studied the best prints his master's studio could provide. Now, as a fully-fledged painter, he was able to thoroughly master Velázquez's simplicity, the single full-length figures occupying a whole canvas, the majesty of the equestrian portraits and the range and naturalness of their attitudes and expressions. Goya, by making these prints, was also following the advice of Mengs, who, in a letter to Ponz in 1776, had urged that all students of painting should copy Velázquez's works, for he was a master of 'the Natural style': 'And what better study for any Artist than to contemplate the works of the Author hanging in that room, painted at three different times, and see how they reveal the path he followed to achieve such excellence in imitating Nature. […] and if Titian surpasses him in the use of colour, he in turn surpasses Titian in his awareness of light and shade, and in aerial perspective, which are the most necessary parts of this Style, since through them we are given an idea of the truth […]. Whoever seeks in this genre more than is to be found in the major works of Velázquez, must search for it in Nature itself, for what is most necessary is always to be found in this Author.'

Goya's selection was indeed based on the three periods of Velázquez's career, and included *The Waterseller of Seville*, *The Feast of Bacchus* ('*The Drinkers*'), *Philip IV on Horseback*, and the portrait of the Count, as well as *Las Meninas*. In his etchings, a technique with which he had experimented before,[10] he also displayed a modern approach; like many later artists from the nineteenth century onwards, he showed a remarkable ability to experiment, the flexibility of the technique allowing him to make infinite changes, to consciously shape someone else's ideas until they became his own: 'Many young painters should be urged to study diligently […] for not everyone who copies a work becomes, by doing so, better able to produce something similar, if he does not explore the reasoning of the original author, this being the only value in studying the works of others.'[11]

In December 1778, Goya wrote to Zapater that he was sending him: 'a Set of works after Velázquez that I have engraved, which as you know are in the King's possession; I could not send them before because I have had a thousand problems with them; well, my boy, appreciate them and I shall send them as they come out.'[12] The 'thousand problems' that prevented him from sending them until December, some months after their sale was advertised in the *Gaceta de Madrid* (28 July 1778),[13] are apparently confirmed in a letter to Zapater from a common friend, Goya's brother-in-law Fray Manuel Bayeu: 'My friend, both sets of prints [he was referring only to those by Goya and Ramón Bayeu] have caused a stir at Court. My brother tells me that Goya's are good, if somewhat light. Of my brother's he says nothing; I suppose they must be good, too.'[14] In saying that they caused 'a stir' Fray Manuel may have been referring to their success; but there may have been problems of a different nature, perhaps jealousy among fellow painters or professional engravers, who saw Goya's work as an intrusion into their specialist craft. In June 1778, one month before they were advertised in the *Gaceta de Madrid*, the prints were

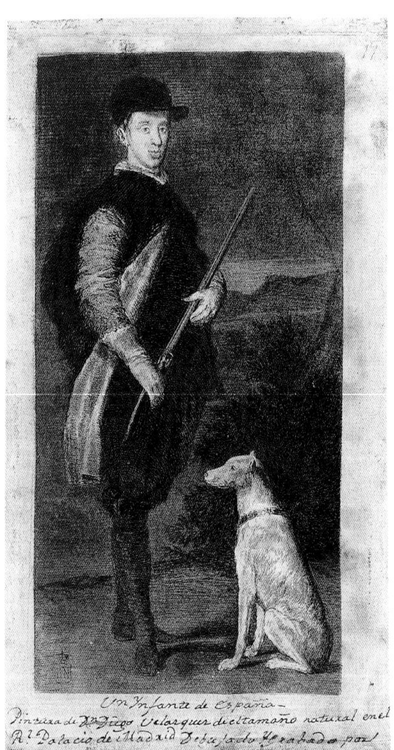

FIG. 90. Francisco de Goya after Velázquez, *The Cardinal Infante Ferdinand of Austria as a Hunter*, 1778–1785, etching, artist's proof. Madrid, Biblioteca Nacional [inv. 45.571]

mentioned by Lord Grantham, the British ambassador to Spain (1771–1779). In August, just after the advertisement, he sent five copies of the set to England, one of them to the painter Sir Joshua Reynolds; on 29 August he also saw the prints hanging in the office of the Chief Minister, the Count of Floridablanca.[15] On 21 October they are mentioned in a letter from Pietro Paolo Giusti, the envoy of Empress Maria Theresa of Austria in Madrid, to her Chancellor, Prince Wenzel Anton Kaunitz. Giusti reported to Kaunitz on various matters at the Spanish court between 1773 and 1778, and supplied news of the major happenings in Madrid's artistic circles. In one letter he referred to Goya, though not by name, and to the first nine Velázquez prints, as though Goya had been the only artist involved in the project, and even its instigator: 'One event of considerable interest for the fine arts in this country is the undertaking, by a Spanish artist, of a project much desired by all, to make engravings of the best pictures in the King's collection. The first test was the etching of some pictures by Velázquez; I am pleased to send your Excellency the nine pieces that have been presented at the Academy. Though their author is not an engraver but a painter, he has been the first to venture here upon this form of engraving, is improving constantly and is keen to continue the work; this will be a great achievement for the arts and for the instruction of those who aspire to them, for the treasures housed in the Palace of Madrid, El Retiro, El Escorial and San Ildefonso are as priceless as they are unknown.'[16]

With the instinct of a true connoisseur, Giusti recognised Goya's importance, and enthusiastically praised his work as a 'painter and engraver'; this combination, most unusual in the contemporary Spanish arts scene, was highlighted by Goya himself in the handwritten title of each print. Giusti also mentioned in passing that the work had received a public showing at the Real Academia de San Fernando.[17] Ponz, who also makes no mention of any problems regarding the prints, refers to them in the prologue to the eighth volume of his *Viage de España*, probably published in late 1778, warmly praising Goya but making no reference to Bayeu or any other artist. Like Giusti, he credits Goya with the instigation of the project: 'Mention should be made of another laudable undertaking, on the part of Don Francisco Goya, Professor of painting: he has set out to make etchings of the famous works of Don Diego Velázquez, which are to be found in the collection of the Royal Palace; in doing so, he has clearly shown his ability, his intelligence and his zeal in serving the nation, for which those who love Velázquez and Painting should be grateful.'[18] Jovellanos also praised Goya for these works; like Giusti, he remarked especially on their originality: 'In drawing and engraving the works of Velázquez, [Goya] has been able to drink in his spirit and has become the most distinguished imitator of his style.'[19] Also of interest is the opinion of the English painter Sir Joshua Reynolds, President of the Royal Academy of Arts, mentioned in a letter to Lord Grantham from his brother Frederick, a fellow art-lover: 'Sir Joshua apparently discerned "a great degree of excellence in the general conception", but could not judge "the extraordinary union of truth & freedom peculiar to the works of Velasquez from these imperfect copies".'[20] It is not known how many copies Goya put on sale, nor whether he sold many,[21] but they had an immediate impact in the most learned and respected circles of the day, and among Spanish and foreign connoisseurs; they also earned him the strong backing of Ponz, Jovellanos and even Ceán Bermúdez, three outstanding figures in the Spanish art world, who were later to provide decisive support in Goya's glittering career both at Court and at the Royal Academy of San Fernando.

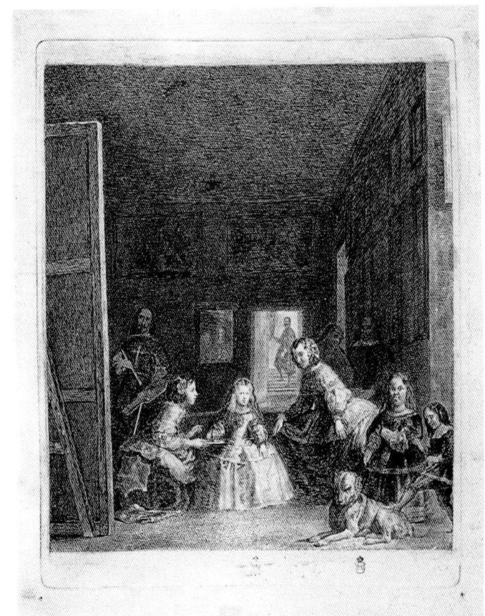

FIG. 91. Francisco de Goya after Velázquez, *Las Meninas*, 1778–1785, etching, artist's proof. Madrid, Biblioteca Nacional [inv. 45.537]

Goya spent several months on the etchings after Velázquez, but was working at the same time on a major set of cartoons for tapestries to be hung in the dining room of the Prince of Asturias at El Escorial (1776–1778), among which were large-scale compositions of great naturalness: *The Parasol*, *The Kite* and *The Brawl at the New Inn* (all now in the Museo del Prado, P-773, P-774 and P-770, respectively). He worked hard and with great enthusiasm on the prints; according to the contemporary reports by Giusti and Ponz quoted earlier, he intended to reproduce all Velázquez's works in the Royal Palace, of which there were then around fifty. The first set comprised equestrian portraits of Philip III and Philip IV, of their respective wives Margarita of Austria and Isabel of Bourbon, and of the Count-Duke of Olivares, *Menippus* and *Aesop*, as well as 'two seated dwarfs', known since the late nineteenth century by the names of Philip IV's court dwarfs, *Sebastián de Morra* [FIG. 94] and *'El Primo'*. The second set contained only two prints, *Prince Baltasar Carlos on Horseback* and *The Drinkers*, the latter described as a 'man playing Bacchus, crowning some drunkards'.[22] The remaining etchings, known only by some surviving proofs, were never put on sale: *The Cardinal Infante Ferdinand of Austria as a Hunter* [FIG. 90], *Las Meninas* [FIG. 91] and *The Buffoon called 'Don Juan de Austria'*. According to Agustín Ceán Bermúdez, Goya made several further copies, known to us by drawings and proofs that remained in his possession; these include *El Niño de Vallecas* – of which there is a drawing and a photograph of what may have been the only etching, now lost,[23] and the etchings *'Barbarossa'*, *Ronquillo* (*Ochoa, the Palace Porter*), *The Waterseller of Seville* and *The Buffoon Don Francisco de Bazán*. Three original drawings with new compositions give us some idea of

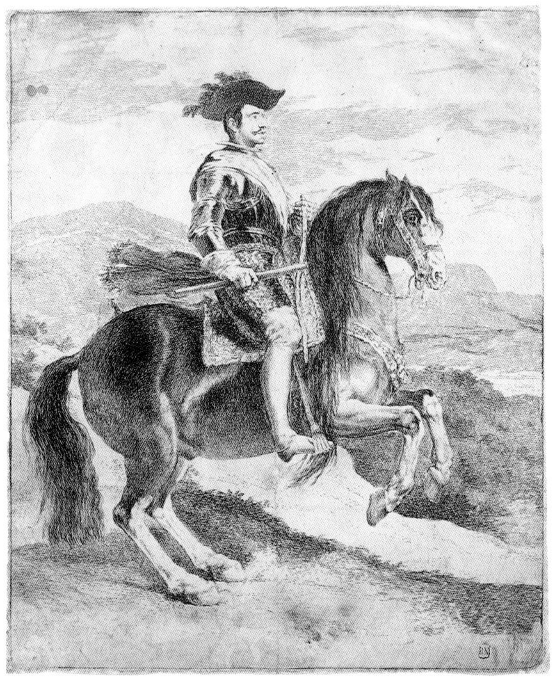

FIG. 92. Francisco de Goya after Velázquez, *Philip IV on Horseback*, *ca.* 1778, etching, artist's proof. Madrid, Biblioteca Nacional [inv. 45.546]

the scale of the project undertaken by Goya: *Philip IV as a Hunter*, *Prince Baltasar Carlos as a Hunter* and *The Infante Don Carlos*.[24]

From the drawings and prints known today, Goya may be assumed to have copied around twenty of Velázquez's paintings in the Royal Collection. This exercise, crucial in transforming his own art, was also the most outstanding individual project undertaken by an artist of Goya's standing, involving pictures from the Spanish Royal Collection or, indeed, any other collection.[25] Comparison of Goya's early works with those painted after 1778 reveals the extent to which this project helped him understand the challenges faced by Velázquez and the resources with which he addressed them. Goya became skilled enough to handle the composition of single figures, set alone in difficult, ambiguous or empty spaces, a technique of which he was later to show complete mastery in his own work. At the same time, he learnt to recognise the nobility and dignity with which Velázquez had endowed his male and female figures, and to fully grasp the complexity of scenes containing numerous figures arranged naturally and harmoniously. The support he derived from Velázquez's work is evident in the way he adapted the stiff poses characteristic of seventeenth-century monarchs and courtiers to the more natural, more 'homely' requirements of his modern patrons: the new kings of the House of Bourbon and the enlightened aristocracy, who in this radical shift towards the modern lost neither their majesty nor their distinction. At the same time, Goya discovered another facet of Velázquez's work that he was soon to make his own, a facet that Jeannine Baticle considers to be of incalculable importance: 'An acceptance of the subhuman, the presence in the master's work of a world of ugliness, peopled by deformed, sometimes even monstrous beings, dwarfs and Palace fools; this can be seen as the first step towards a formal break with tradition, adumbrating the boldness and the freedom in choosing subjects that came to characterise Goya's modern approach.'[26]

Although the full extent of Goya's debt to Velázquez remains far from clear, that early set of etchings and drawings, made in 1778 when Goya had just turned thirty, was undoubtedly decisive. Paintings such as *The Forge of Vulcan*, *The Surrender of Breda* [see FIG. 5] and *The Spinners* (Madrid, Museo del Prado, P-1171, P-1172 and P-1173 respectively) hung close to those etched or drawn by Goya, but there is no evidence of his having copied them. It may be that the challenge posed by these large compositions, full of figures in evidently complex spaces, was such that Goya decided to leave them to the end, starting with the easier ones; it is also possible, however, that he concentrated on those that were likely to prove most useful to him in his own work, such as the royal portraits and the highly expressive single figures – almost portraits – of philosophers and dwarfs. The first set of prints put on sale comprised the four royal equestrian portraits and that of the Count-Duke of Olivares, while the second contained a portrait of the young Prince Baltasar Carlos, also on horseback. But Goya showed an unexpected and almost revolutionary freedom in unashamedly adapting the Velázquez originals to reflect his own views and style. The most significant change was a simplification of the background landscape, which took on a starkness similar to that of *Philip III on Horseback* (Madrid, Museo del Prado, P-1176); Goya removed the distant groves and forests of the original, reducing the presence of Nature to some small, low-lying bushes and scrubland that would not detract from the greatness of the figures in the foreground. This approach is particularly evident in his copies of the portraits of Isabel of Bourbon and Philip IV [FIG. 92]; the King now rides alone, no longer protected by the enormous tree of the Velázquez original; the figures of both King and Queen stand out against a bright white background, which in both portraits takes on a marked abstract quality. Since Goya took some trouble to draw, in marvellously precise detail, the monarchs' clothing and armour, this abstraction of the background landscape should not be seen as an attempt to make his work easier, but rather as a new, personal, modern handling of backgrounds, for which he used the dazzling white light already employed in the etchings of a contemporary artist whom Goya much admired, Giovanni Battista Tiepolo. Goya was also to apply this new use of light in his portraits of Charles IV [CAT. 48] and Maria Luisa on horseback, as well as in the planned portraits of Godoy and Palafox. The portrait of the young Prince Baltasar Carlos on horseback, undoubtedly the most spectacular and harmonious of the etchings [FIG. 93], reveals the most radical change in dimensions with respect to Velázquez's portrait; Goya increased the overall space to almost twice that of the original, notably enlarging the upper portion of the sky to create new sunlit skyscapes over the child's head. At the same time, he 'corrected' the proportions of the horse's somewhat bulky body, which Velázquez had intended to be seen with the compulsory upward perspective of the Salón de Reinos at the Buen Retiro. Through all these changes, Goya achieved a splendid, spectacular representation of the Crown Prince's power, but at the same time the portrait is more airy, and succeeds better than Velázquez's original in capturing a certain majesty as well as a childish charm.

Goya's equestrian portraits reveal a clear 'humanising' of their royal subjects; though hardly modifying their facial expressions, he achieved that sense of vitality and approachability that informs his best posed portraits. Slight, almost imperceptible variations in the clothing, which more closely reflects eighteenth-century fashions, turn Velázquez's solemn effigies into something more realistic, more familiar; this perhaps marked the influence of an age in which 'enlightened' Spaniards felt that the royal family should be closer to the common people. Goya was soon to take full advantage of these pictures; first they served as the basis for the equestrian portrait of Maria Teresa de Vallabriga (1783),[27] for whose preparatory sketches he recreated the portrait of *Queen Isabel of Bourbon on Horseback*, and even the equestrian portrait of *Prince Baltasar Carlos*. Surviving sketches for the equestrian portrait of Godoy of 1792, who had by now become 'Prince of the Peace', clearly reveal that he was inspired by the horseback portrait of Philip IV. At the time, Goya told Zapater that the equestrian portrait was 'among the most difficult things a Painter can be given

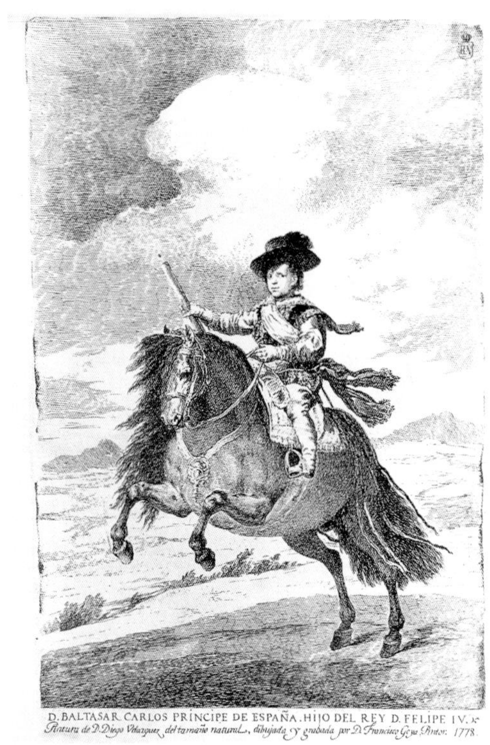

FIG. 93. Francisco de Goya after Velázquez, *Baltasar Carlos on Horseback*, 1778, etching, first edition. Madrid, Biblioteca Nacional [inv. 45.557]

to do. Bayeu should have done it, but he couldn't deal with the body, though not for want of trying.'[28] Goya was again to make use of his familiarity with Velázquez's equestrian portraits in 1800, in his own portraits of Charles IV [CAT. 48] and Maria Luisa; here the posture of riders and animals alike recalls Velázquez's canvases, with which Goya's works would inevitably be compared since they all hung in the rooms of the Palace.[29] In the portrait *Queen Maria Luisa on Horseback* (Madrid, Museo del Prado, P-720), the Queen is shown in profile, her horse 'Marcial' at the trot; here, Goya sought to convey the Queen's serenity. In contrast, in his portrait of Charles IV the King fearlessly reins in a huge, powerful horse, against a dark, stormy, almost nocturnal landscape. The majestic figures of man and horse were drawn from the portrait of *Queen Margarita of Austria*,[30] advancing out of the canvas towards the spectator.[31] Goya used his knowledge of Velázquez in still other equestrian portraits. The most interesting, because again it was a portrait of the reigning monarch, was that of King Ferdinand VII (Madrid, Real Academia de San Fernando), commissioned by the Academy and painted in 1808; the horse is placed exactly as in Velázquez's equestrian portrait of Philip III. Subsequently, Goya was to paint two further equestrian portraits: the *Duke of Wellington* (London, Apsley House) in 1812 and *General Palafox* (Madrid, Museo del Prado, P-725) in 1814. In both, however, he abandoned the traditional pose of the royal equestrian portrait, which he had employed in earlier works for the Court, in favour of a more dynamic, expressive and clearly modern approach, which he was to reserve for that class of aristocratic officers to which the two subjects, in their varying degrees, belonged. He modified the excessive and somewhat dangerous movement of the horse in Velázquez's portrait of the Count-Duke of Olivares, which in other respects remained highly classical; even so, the horse's hindquarters are displayed in the foreground, in a forced view of the animal galloping out of control, which seems to shed doubt on the rider's ability and his mastery of the situation.

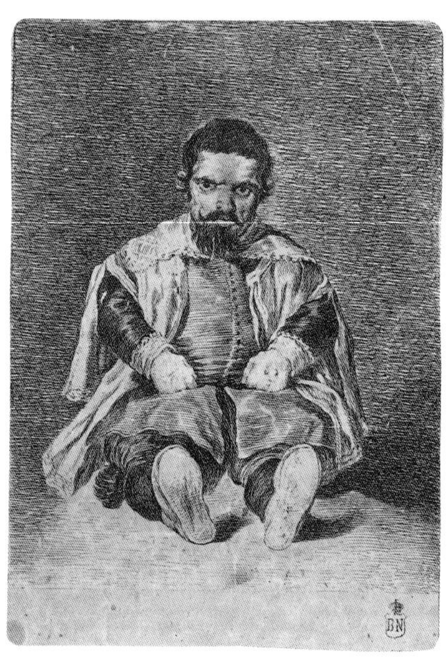

FIG. 94. Francisco de Goya after Velázquez, *Sebastián de Morra*, *ca.* 1778, etching, artist's proof. Madrid, Biblioteca Nacional [inv. 45.588]

Perhaps of greater significance for his own paintings were his copies of other Velázquez compositions: the large, solitary figures like *Aesop* and *Menippus*, *The Buffoon called 'Don Juan de Austria'*, *'Barbarossa'*, *Ochoa*, *El Primo*, *Sebastián de Morra*; one might also add the portraits of Philip IV and the Infante Don Fernando in hunting dress, and other drawings mentioned earlier, especially *The Infante Don Carlos* and *Prince Baltasar Carlos as a Hunter*. A number of compositions – the dwarfs, even then assumed to be portraits, or *Aesop* [CAT. 31] and *Menippus*, or the central group in *The Drinkers* – suggest that Goya was deeply attracted by the singular nature of these figures; in the seventeenth century, and clearly even more in the late eighteenth century, these compositions revealed a high degree of sophistication, both intellectual and human, and straddled the dividing line between 'invention' and portrait [CATS 31 and 32]. Though he had freely modified the royal portraits, here he made no change to expressions or facial features, rigorously respecting the Velázquez originals. A possible exception might be the shrewd gaze of *Sebastián de Morra* [FIG. 94]: in Goya's drawing, the expression becomes aggressive, angry, while in the original it conveys resigned acceptance. In this group of pictures 'invented' by Velázquez, Goya clearly took pains to achieve the exact proportions of expressiveness and dignity that give the original figures their balance and harmony. Goya was to use these 'portraits'[32] as the basis for many of the figures in his own paintings. Even the dogs were to appear in his own works, captured with all the fresh, direct naturalness achieved by Velázquez, but now more suited to an age in which allegory played only a small part. Velázquez's paintings were outstanding for their characterisation of the sitter, their naturalness, their psychological insight, as well as for their essential vibrant technique. Yet other key qualities – the simplicity of the figures, the elegance befitting their social status, and their overall austerity – were of little interest to Goya. The society he sought to capture in his paintings had changed since the seventeenth century, even in Spain. The austerity of Velázquez's portraits, surprisingly modern in their simplicity, was due in no small measure to contemporary Spanish fashions. Clothes were plain and sober: blacks and whites for the gentlemen, elegant tones for the velvets and dark silks of the court ladies. By the eighteenth century, men and women had started to wear light, bright colours; smart materials for dresses and jackets, and multicoloured embroidery, had become the last word in fashion, testifying to the distinction and social status of the wearer. Yet beneath the bright colours, we can still discern in Goya the expressiveness and sometimes the composition of Velázquez's portraits [FIGS 77 and 95].

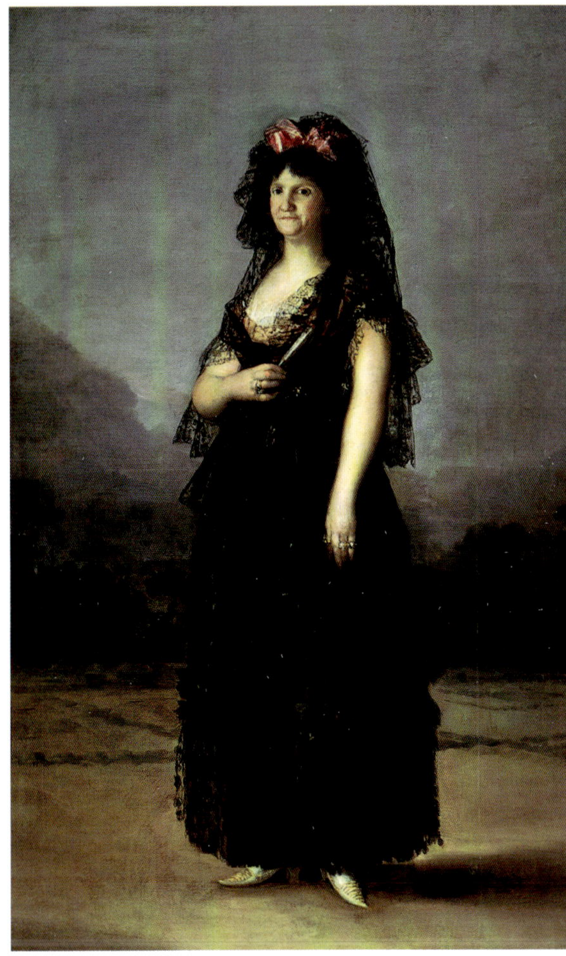

FIG. 95. Francisco de Goya, *Queen María Luisa with a Mantilla*, 1799, Patrimonio Nacional, Madrid, Palacio Real [10002935]

Goya came to portraiture relatively late. In the 1770s he had received a number of important commissions for religious paintings, as well as two or three cartoons for the King's tapestries; yet, other than himself in an early *Self Portrait* (Zaragoza, Ibercaja), nobody had yet trusted him enough to commission a likeness. Soon, however, portraits were to become the most sought-after branch of his art. Among the first people to sit for Goya, in the early 1780s, were two 'modernists', Jovellanos and the Count of Floridablanca. The portraits, very much ahead of their time, have yet to receive the acclaim they deserve: *Jovellanos by the River at Gijón* (Oviedo, Museo de Bellas Artes de Asturias) and *Don José Moñino, Count of Floridablanca* [FIG. 96], which portrays the Chief Minister presenting the King the handwritten paper marking the founding of the Banco de San Carlos; certain details in both portraits recall Goya's recent copies of Velázquez. However, he also took techniques and solutions from other contemporary artists: Mengs' great subtlety in capturing the changing expression of his sitters, Pompeo Batoni's studied elegance, and the intimate, domestic naturalness of the British portrait painters, wholly alien to traditional Spanish tastes. In starting out as a portrait painter with two full-length portraits of well-known public figures, one set against his native landscape and the other in a subtly lit interior, Goya clearly showed his

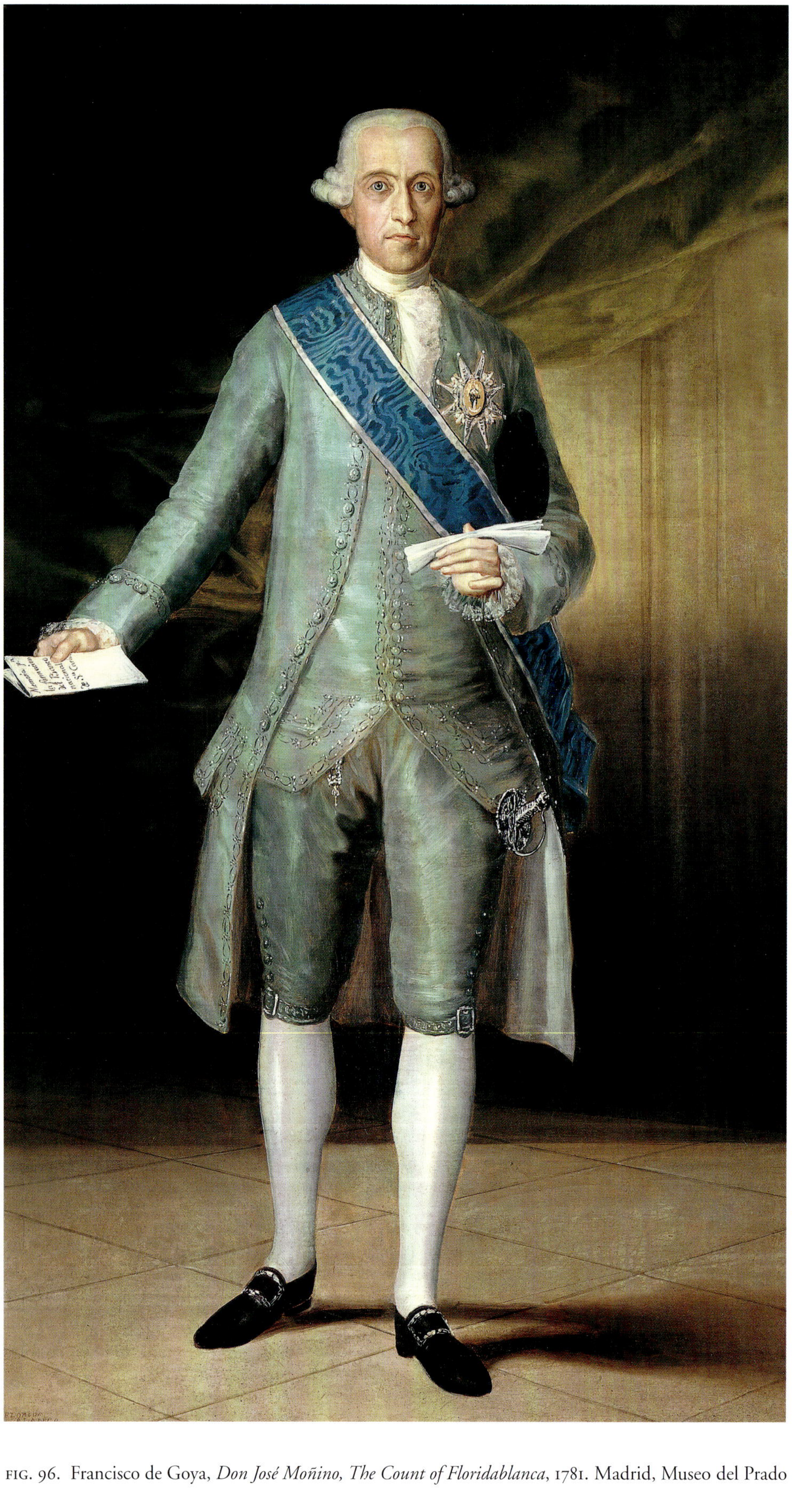

FIG. 96. Francisco de Goya, *Don José Moñino, The Count of Floridablanca*, 1781. Madrid, Museo del Prado [P-3255]

confidence and his ability to execute highly ambitious, large-format portraits of courtiers, in itself a difficult genre. The aristocratic presence of the elegant young Jovellanos, for example, owes much to the distinction and detachment achieved by Velázquez in his portraits of Philip IV and his brother the Infante Don Ferdinand. The delicate *Marchioness of Pontejos* (Washington, National Gallery of Art), painted in 1786, blends aspects of Velázquez's male portraits with the childish grace of little Margarita in *Las Meninas* – a grace tempered by her awareness of her power. Floridablanca steps forward, holding the paper in his right hand, in a movement strongly reminiscent of *Pablo de Valladolid* [CAT. 51] in its active, dynamic effect, though not in its colours. This same portrait, not included in Goya's etchings, was used again for a somewhat later portrait, that of Francisco Cabarrús, painted in 1788 (Madrid, Banco de España) [CAT. 52]. The portrait, which bears a much closer resemblance to Velázquez's *Pablo de Valladolid*, suggests that Goya had by now attained a clear psychological understanding of his sitters. Moreover, in both *Floridablanca* and *Cabarrús*, despite the modern, shockingly bright colours, the background suggests the dimly-lit shadows and lack of spatial definition characteristic of Velázquez's actor, a strikingly modern touch which Goya grasped and used long before Manet.[33] The movement of a single figure in an ambiguous space, against a shadowy, unevenly lit background, is also a key feature of Velázquez's *The Infante Don Carlos*. Goya, too, was to make this ambiguous space a hallmark of his portraits: it recurs in some of his best single-figure ones, including *The Marchioness of La Solana* (Paris, Musée du Louvre), *Queen Maria Luisa in Court Dress* (Madrid, Palacio Real), the portrait of his own daughter-in-law, Gumersinda Goicoechea (Paris, private collection), and, above all, *The Condesa de Chinchón*, painted in 1800 [CAT. 64]. Despite the enormous complexities of group portraits, this deliberately undefined space can also be discerned in the families of the Duques de Osuna [FIG. 21] and of Charles IV [CAT. 46]. In both portraits, light merges into shade with no definition of angles or distances, a technique used by Velázquez and Goya to suggest the personality or the profession of the sitters: the actor Pablo de Valladolid acts in the unreal, invented space of the stage; the Condesa de Chinchón, or the King and his family, move across the difficult scenery of the court.

It is not easy to chart Velázquez's influence, or to say exactly where it begins and ends, since Goya considerably transformed the originals, skilfully erasing his sources and relying on his visual genius to capture the essence of Velázquez's images and thus create his own pictures, as though they were his alone.[34] A simple example of this process of transformation is the portrait of *Queen Maria Luisa wearing a Farthingale*, painted in 1789 (Madrid, Museo del Prado, P-2862); here, Goya gave an eighteenth-century air to Velázquez's portrait of *Queen Mariana of Austria*, in the Museo del Prado [CAT. 13]. Another example is the portrait of *Charles III as a Hunter* (Madrid, collection of the Duke and Duchess of Fernán Núñez; there is another version in the Museo del Prado), which was clearly inspired, at least superficially, by the portraits of members of the Hapsburg dynasty in hunting dress, painted for the Torre de la Parada and copied by Goya, which also served as a basis for a later portrait of *Charles IV as a Hunter* (Madrid, Palacio Real). The portrait of Charles III, however, bears a stronger resemblance to Goya's splendid etching of Velázquez's *The Buffoon called 'Don Juan de Austria'* in the positioning of the legs and the turn of the head, which give both portraits their peculiar and slightly caricatured expressiveness. In the late eighteenth century, royal inventories classified this Velázquez portrait not as the fool known as 'Don Juan de Austria', but as an 'artilleryman' in the 1772 inventory, and as a 'Spanish general' in the 1792 version, compiled among others by Goya himself;[35] this would suggest that he had no intention of caricaturing the King in this surprising portrait. It is even more difficult to chart Goya's debt to Velázquez in group works, such as the portrait of *The Family of the Infante Don Luis* [CAT. 45] or *The Duques de Osuna and their Children* [FIG. 21], which also differ from each other in terms of formal composition and expression. These innovative works were painted when Goya had finally gained access both to the ruling class and to the power struggles involving the royal family and the great aristocratic families. For the first time, he used *Las Meninas* as a basis. Having made prints from this portrait, he was well aware that it achieved a unique blend of figures and planes of light, of social classes and of adults and children, making it an essentially human, timeless symbol, that has an added subliminal, subconscious attraction. In the portrait of the Duke of Osuna and his family, parents and children are clearly arranged with a view to conveying a sense of hierarchy; the power of the family is held by the Duke, and flows from him to his children, heirs to the family titles, who are shown playing with a lapdog, a charming eighteenth-century substitute for Velázquez's hound. Goya was clearly fascinated by the bold foregrounding of the Infanta Margarita in *Las Meninas*, a key element of the scene, which Goya was to use more than once for the same expressive purpose as Velázquez. He employed this device for the Duchess and her elder daughter in the Osuna family portrait, and in his portraits of the Marchioness of Pontejos (Washington, National Gallery of Art) and the Duchess of Alba in white [CAT. 61], repeating it again in the posture and position of Queen Maria Luisa in his group portrait *The Family of Charles IV* [CAT. 46]. All these noble female figures share the same distinction, the same arrogant awareness of lineage and supremacy, that is shown, even in childhood, by the young Infanta Margarita; but, like her, they lack the stiffness of similar iconic figures in the works of other contemporary artists who sought to convey that effect.[36] Goya captured the same childish blend of naivety and arrogance in *Manuel Osorio Manrique de Zúñiga* [CAT. 53], a portrait of a boy similar in age to the Infanta Margarita. Here, however, despite certain similarities of form (the child looks straight out at the spectator), Goya has rejected Velázquez's elaborate approach to children as seen, for example, in *Prince Baltasar Carlos with a Dwarf* (Boston, Museum of Fine Arts) or the portrait of Prince Felipe Próspero with his dog [CAT. 54]. He has eliminated the rich hangings, cushions and silk armchairs in favour of the stark, bare space and shadowy lighting typical of Velázquez's more sombre works, thus enhancing the intensity of the child's red suit.

Goya made similar use of the visual ideas in *Las Meninas* in his portrait *The Family of the Infante Don Luis* [CAT. 45]. Don Luis lived with his family in exile, at Arenas de San Pedro, having lost his claim to the throne following his morganatic marriage. Yet the portraits commissioned from Goya in 1783 and 1784 seemed to meet the requirements of a ruling family enjoying real power, rather than those of a prince whose way to the throne was barred, and whose children could not bear his name. Goya painted portraits of the Infante and his family, a large-format equestrian portrait of his wife to match a similar portrait of him, and the imposing family portrait, of clearly exaggerated, truly palatial proportions. The Infante lamented his loss of position, and was aware that he had surrendered for ever his claim to the throne. He used art as his father Philip V and his brother Charles III had done before him: as propaganda for his views, to further his dynastic power, and perhaps also as a private compensation for the indignities his situation probably entailed. His children, stripped of the Bourbon name, might yet attain through paintings the status denied them by the King. Goya was able to capture all this on canvas to the entire satisfaction of the Infante 'with unexpected acclaim, for other painters had been there and not managed it'.[37]

The portrait of *The Family of the Infante Don Luis*, dated 1784, was the first in which Goya used specific ideas drawn from *Las Meninas*, but subjected to a radical modernisation in terms of their visual appearance. His aim was to achieve a natural, private portrayal of a family that remained 'royal' even despite Charles III's decree. To achieve this, he used the same simple strategy that Velázquez had adopted to portray the Hapsburgs, the dynasty and their power. Velázquez had captured a trivial moment in the family's daily life: the little princess is offered water by her maids of honour while the King and Queen, reflected in a mirror, look on; to the left, Velázquez himself stands with his brushes before a huge canvas. In Goya's portrait, the couple are playing cards, a game of chance with all its symbolic significance; the wife, placed at the centre of the scene and brightly lit, gazes out at the spectator, while the valet approaches to brush her hair and her maidservants hold out a tray containing a silk hairnet and a silver jewellery box. To the right, other household servants look on, while to the left – again – the painter sits on a low stool, before an almost empty canvas on which he has already sketched in the outline of the figures. The arrangement of the scene echoes that of *Las Meninas* in that all the figures are spread out to both sides of the brightly-lit central axis of Maria Teresa de Vallabriga, who looks straight out; the positions of the other figures, in profile or face-on, also looking out at the spectator, closely resemble those in Velázquez's painting. Goya produces a modern transformation of *Las Meninas*: he tones down the sense of family power and elaborate protocol of the Hapsburg dynasty and modifies the portrayal of the servants, who in Velázquez were less handsome than their masters, like the dwarf Maribárbola. The glorious past is thus turned into a British-style domestic 'conversation piece', a popular contemporary genre with which Goya was probably familiar. Here, however, the grandiose dimensions of the painting suggest a greater interest in dynastic intentions than in the trivial details of everyday life at the Palace of Arenas de San Pedro. In *Las Meninas*, the presence of Philip IV, reflected in the mirror in the background, seems to guarantee the inheritance to be received by his daughter Margarita; similarly, in Goya's portrait, the father is shown in the profile characteristically used for medals and coins, a pose echoed, or shadowed, by the profile of his eldest son, placed immediately behind him and further into the background.

Goya's debt to *Las Meninas*, a painting greatly admired by Mengs, is also apparent in his portrait of *The Family of Charles IV*. Here he was to contrast his own idea of the Bourbons with Velázquez's dynastic concept of the Hapsburg dynasty, using some elements of Velázquez's composition but achieving an altogether more modern effect. The differences between the two compositions are evident: Goya was required to portray the entire family, which – for reasons of dynastic weight – included those who had died, like the Infanta Maria Amalia, and those who were yet to be part of the family, like the future wife of the heir to the throne, not yet selected from among the princesses of Europe.[38] Although Goya again portrays himself in *The Family of Charles IV*, there are no ladies-in-waiting and no servants; the composition aims at the hidden symmetry of figures and groups that marked *Las Meninas*. The Queen is placed, like Maria Teresa de Vallabriga, and, indeed, like the little Infanta Margarita, at the centre of the portrait, serving as the axis for the whole group, towards which the other figures converge from right and left, with a perfect balance of number and pose. The space here is greatly reduced, the figures arranged in a strict frieze, as on the Roman sarcophagi so fondly admired in this Neoclassical period. But Goya has also made use of the stark austerity of Velázquez's setting, the Palace belonging to the previous ruling dynasty, thereby creating a visual link of considerable allegorical significance between the old castle – destroyed by fire in 1734 – and the New Palace of the recently enthroned Bourbon family (whose interiors and decoration were in fact quite different from those depicted here). Other essential formal elements that help establish the influence of *Las Meninas* on *The Family of Charles IV* are the two paintings shown in the background in both works, and the presence of the painter before an easel and a large canvas – in both cases placed at the left of the scene, although Goya positions himself further back.

However, the last echo of *Las Meninas* is to be found in the vast *Meeting of the Royal Philippines Company*, painted by Goya in 1815 (Castres, Musée Goya). Here, King Ferdinand VII chairs the board meeting of a leading trading company, in a large, dimly-lit room. Although the scene is wholly different from that depicted by Velázquez, the use of space and light is directly inspired by *Las Meninas*; in both pictures, the windows on the right throw light into a central space, in which distances are marked by planes of light and shadow, in an extreme illustration of the concept of aerial perspective established by Mengs years earlier.

A key issue in understanding the interest of later artists in Velázquez's work, as remarked on by Mengs and other eighteenth-century theorists, was his wholly natural style, a style which, according to his admirers, derived from an essential confident lightness of touch. These are also the outstanding features of Goya's style. Jovellanos described Velázquez's technique with a succinctness that must have served as a spur to other painters: 'He stands out for his swift touch, his concise self-expression; with a single bold stroke [...] he captures what other painters, for all their painstakingly studious methods, are unable to represent.'[39] Mengs also referred to Velázquez's highly personal style, in terms which verge on the metaphysical; he remarked that *The Spinners* had been painted 'in such a way that it appears the hand had no part in its execution, but rather that he painted it by sheer force of will'.[40] Goya's only written reference to Velázquez, dating from the final Bordeaux years, also concerned matters of technique. In a letter to his friend Joaquín Maria Ferrer in 1825, speaking of his latest work, Goya remarked: 'Indeed, last winter I painted on ivory, and I have a collection of about 40 experiments, but it is a new kind of miniature that I have never seen before, for everything is made up of dots and things, that look more like the brushwork of Velázquez than of Mengs.'[41] Goya here underlines the contrast between Mengs' smooth, decorative style and the 'dots and things' that characterise the looser, freer style of Velázquez, in which forms take on clarity and a real meaning only with distance. This indeed is what made Velázquez modern.[42] At the time of Goya's letter, in 1825, this technique – which was to change the future course of painting – had few followers; Mengs' polished style was still the yardstick for the last of the Neoclassicals, like Ingres and the academicians, and Goya himself was probably not familiar with the works of Delacroix, who was to serve as the link with the modern innovators of the late nineteenth century. In the light of Goya's remarks, his own use of Velázquez's technique may be best exemplified in his Bordeaux miniatures, painted on ivory and undoubtedly made up of 'dots and things'. The subjects are extraordinary burlesques, expressive but deformed beings; although Goya himself prized these works above his *Caprichos*, which he considered dated now that he had 'better ideas', these last works clearly met with little understanding. Some last vestiges of Velázquez's technique might therefore be sought in Goya's last portraits of his friends in France, *Leandro Fernández de Moratín* (Bilbao, Museo de Bellas Artes), *Juan de Muguiro* [CAT. 67] and *Jacques Galos* (Philadelphia, Barnes Foundation). Though the style no longer bears any real resemblance to that of Velázquez, these portraits to an extent represent its final consequences, and at the same time pave the way to modern painting.

As in other aspects of his use of Velázquez, Goya was by no means a slavish imitator of his technique. He had his own way of painting, his own personal technique, built on countless experiences and on his knowledge of many leading artists: he readily recognised his debt to what he had seen in Italy, to Correggio and the sixteenth-century Venetian masters, to Titian and, in particular, to Tintoretto, as well as to Rubens and Luca Giordano, and to more modern painters such as Corrado Giaquinto, Mengs and above all Tiepolo. Goya's own unmistakable technique was shaped by other factors, other approaches to painting, the result of an eclectic process in which Velázquez was only one of his masters. The use of chiaroscuro and aerial perspective, which Mengs attributed to Velázquez but much more to Correggio, and the brilliant lightness of touch and brushstroke are all to be found in Goya's work. Although a certain reliance on Velázquez may be charted, it is only to be found in specific paintings and it always serves a particular purpose; Goya would turn to Velázquez when he needed to achieve a special effect, for example to produce a strongly modelled, almost sculptural head without sacrificing naturalness [FIGS 97 and 98].

The debt to Velázquez is undoubtedly clearest in those deft light touches whose meaning only becomes evident with distance [FIG. 100]. Goya studied those 'dots and things' for his own painting, although his thick, energetic brushstrokes are quite different from Velázquez's light, vibrant touch. Goya made use of this technique to reflect the effect of light on objects, to enhance brightness and contrast, to convey the sense of reality that underlies the beauty and realism of his portraits [FIG. 99]. Although, like Velázquez, Goya was economical and self-assured in his technique, his method of applying brush to canvas was highly personal; he made much greater use than

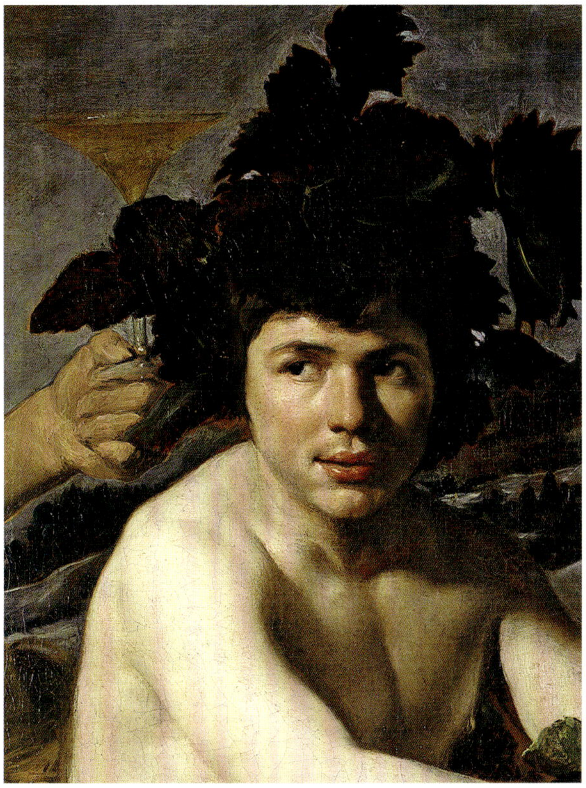

FIG. 97. Diego Velázquez, *The Drinkers* (detail of the head of Bacchus), *ca.* 1628–1629. Madrid, Museo del Prado [P-1170]

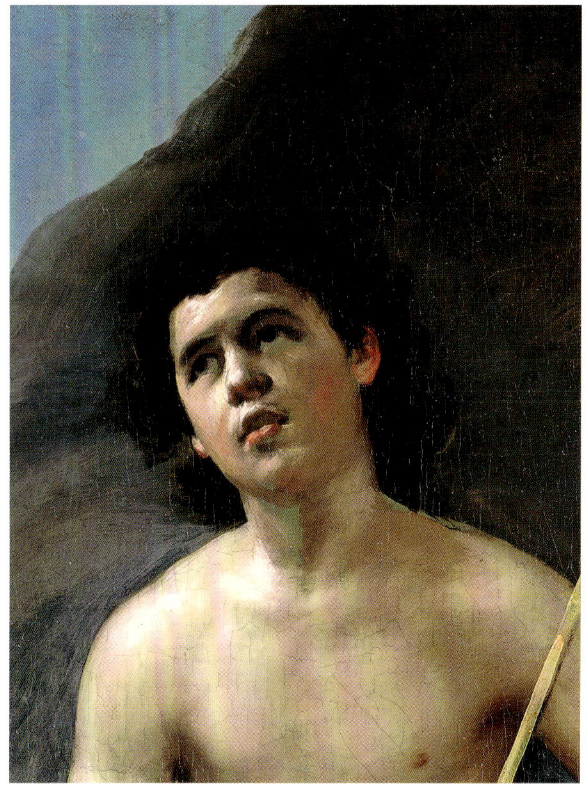

FIG. 98. Francisco de Goya, *Saint John the Baptist as a Child* (detail of the head), *ca.* 1805–1812. Madrid, Museo del Prado [P-7853]

Velázquez of vibrant preparatory sketches, defining his outlines with long, precise strokes of the sort used in drawing, which Velázquez rarely employed. Velázquez created a sense of light by making use of large spaces to give volume to forms and models, and to direct the spectator's gaze towards the essential central point of the composition. In contrast, Goya conveys light through overlapping strokes and vibrations, enclosed by clearly defined, perfectly calculated black outlines, thus heralding the 'impression' of light that was to be favoured by the French Impressionists.

As models of expressiveness and technique, Velázquez's works clearly had a profound effect on Goya's approach to painting. Despite the distance in time, Goya was a 'disciple' in the strictest sense, but he was – as he himself suggests – a *free* disciple. Rather than following the rules, he studied and interpreted them, and in so doing advanced further along the path opened up by Velázquez. In his portraits of royalty and nobility, he made use of Velázquez's models; in other pictures, he approached his subjects with the psychological insight to which his 'master' had introduced him a hundred years earlier.

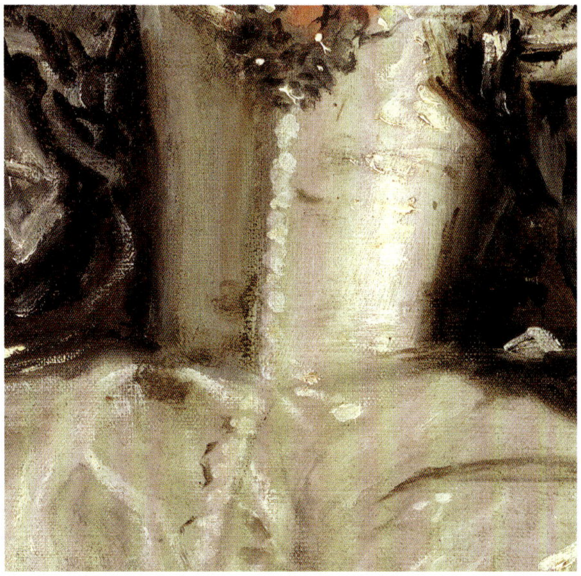

FIG. 99. Francisco de Goya, *The Family of Charles IV* (detail of the Queen's dress) [see CAT. 46]

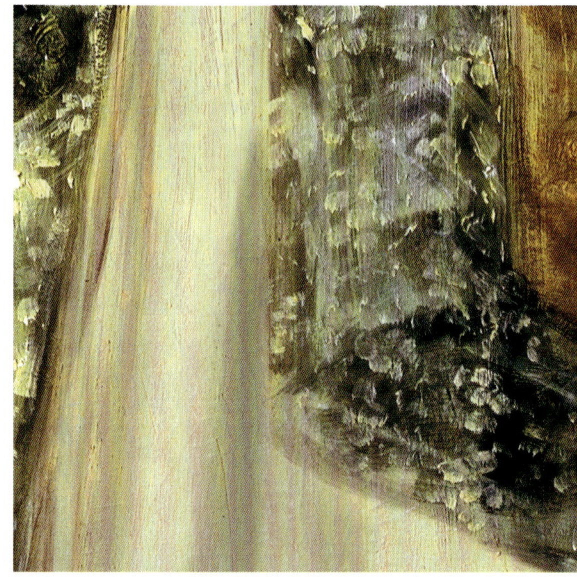

FIG. 100. Diego Velázquez, *Las Meninas* (detail of the dress of the Infanta Margarita) [see CAT. 43]

NOTES

1 Jovellanos 1781, pp. 36–37.

2 Aterido 1994, pp. 369–99 and Finaldi 2002, no. 26, pp. 152–58.

3 On the role of foreign agents and ambassadors in Madrid in spreading Velázquez's fame in Europe in the latter half of the eighteenth century, see Glendinning and Harris 1999, pp. 598–605.

4 This appears in the extended version held by the Museo del Prado, published in Beroqui 1927, pp. 99–100.

5 Published in Eusebi 1828, p. 67.

6 In Canellas (ed.) 1981, no. 184.

7 Ponz (vol. VI, 1776) 1947, p. 555.

8 See Rose 1981, pp. 173–81, and also Vega, Glendinning and Portús 2002.

9 Rose 1981, p. 173. Ramón Bayeu and José del Castillo were also, strictly speaking, painters rather than engravers like Carmona; they were colleagues of Goya at court, and followed Ponz's advice, reproducing paintings by Ribera and Guercino. The Real Calcografía was founded some years later, in 1789, and over the years produced various sets of prints of the works of other artists in the Royal Collections.

10 A small etching of a religious subject (*Flight into Egypt*, *ca.* 1774) was probably made before the set of Velázquez prints. Other early etchings, including *Saint Isidore the Farmer*, *Saint Francis of Paola* and *The Blind Guitarist*, may have been produced at around the same time as the prints.

11 The three quotations from Mengs are drawn from a letter to Antonio Ponz published in Ponz (1772–1794) 1947, pp. 570, 574 and 582.

12 Águeda and Salas (eds) 1982 (2nd edn, 2003), no. 7, pp. 47–48.

13 *Gaceta de Madrid*, 1778, p. 300 (reproduced in many books on the subject): 'Nine prints drawn and etched by Don Francisco Goya, Painter; whose life-size originals, painted by Don Diego Velázquez, are to be found in the collection of the Royal Palace of this Court. They portray the equestrian figures of the Kings *Philip III* and *Philip IV*, and of the Queens *Margarita of Austria* and *Isabel of Bourbon*, and of *Don Gaspar de Guzmán Count-Duke of Olivares*; the standing figures of *Menippus* and *Aesop*, and two seated dwarfs. To be sold at the Bookshops of Don Antonio Sancha, in the Old Customs House, and Don Manuel Barzo Carrera at San Jerónimo. Their prices are: the five equestrian figures at 6 *Reales* and the other four at 3 *Reales*; to be sold together or separately'.

14 Calvo Ruata 1996, letter no. 20, p. 66.

15 Glendinning and Harris 1999, p. 601, and nn 28–35.

16 I am grateful to Gudrun Maurer for drawing my attention to this important historical and bibliographical reference, quoted in part in Wilson-Bareau 2003, p. 142 and notes. The complete quote is to be found in 'Razón del 21 de oct. de 1778' from Pietro Paolo Giusti to Prince Kaunitz, *Rapport sur les progrès littéraires pour ce dernier semestre*, Vienna, Staatskanzlei des

Haus-, Hof- und Staatsarchivs, Fasz. 138, fols 21–26v, published in Juretschke and Kleinmann (eds) 1987, vol. XII, doc. no. 12, pp. 79–81. Giusti mentions the problems faced by the Real Academia de San Fernando after Mengs' departure, which left something of a power vacuum. He also refers to an engraving in the Royal Collection, a portrait of Charles V by Titian, as being the work of Selma; Carmona – mentioned as being currently in Rome – is referred to not as part of the project but as the author of two allegorical engravings of his own invention: 'The pieces on show at the Salon this time, particularly the paintings, serve merely as evidence of an institution still in its infancy, which is due less to any sterility of the Spanish genius than to the lack of a great man capable of firmly guiding young people in this career, it being impossible to find a replacement after the departure of the Gentleman. // Better results have been achieved in engraving, as Your Excellency will be able to judge from the print of a fine Charles V by Titian, engraved by a 22-year-old, which I am pleased to enclose, and which met with general acclaim; I also enclose two pieces by Carmona, allegorical representations of the Order of the Golden Fleece and the Order of Charles III. This artist is now in Rome, where he is to marry one of Mengs' daughters'. The Giusti–Kaunitz correspondence is also published in Velázquez 1963, pp. 176 ff.

17 There is no reference to this presentation in the records of the Real Academia de Bellas Artes, but for 18 September 1778 (i.e. the same year) there is a report of a prize-giving ceremony and an exhibition of the works of the young artists, which were hung for eight days in the rooms of the Academy.

18 Ponz (1772–1794) 1947, p. 666.

19 Jovellanos [1781].

20 Quoted in Glendinning and Harris 1999, p. 601.

21 The plates were acquired by the Real Calcografía, which produced new prints in 1792 and thereafter several times during the nineteenth century: see Wilson-Bareau 2003, p. 142 and n. 17, and Glendinning 1989.

22 This was how Velázquez's picture was interpreted in the eighteenth century, and Goya simply based his title on the description given by Mengs in a letter to Antonio Ponz, published by Ponz in 1776: 'His picture of a man playing Bacchus, crowning some drunkards, shows a looser, freer Style, for he imitated the truth, not as it is but as it appears': Ponz (1772–1794) 1947, p. 574. Ponz had made similar references to the painting, although in different terms: 'In another, one man plays the part of Bacchus, with various figures forming a sort of Bacchanal': *ibid.*, p. 525.

23 From the old photograph, now in the Instituto Jovellanos, Gijón, one cannot judge the quality or technique of this lost work; therefore, it is impossible to know whether it is an original by Goya, or a copy of the drawing now in the Hamburg Kunsthalle: see Pérez Sánchez 2003, no. 383, ill. p. 292.

24 The drawings are in the Hamburg Kunsthalle and are reproduced in *Goya und Velázquez*, 1992, nos 12–14.

25 Amongst other publications, they are listed in *Catálogo de las estampas de Goya*, 1996, pp. 25–26 and nos 5–60.

26 Baticle 1988, p. 9 (translated from the French by Manuela Mena Marqués).

27 The portrait, now lost, is known only by the preparatory sketch, now in the Uffizi Gallery, Florence.

28 Agueda and Salas (eds) 1978, letter no. 135, August 1794, p. 226.

29 See Maurer 2002, pp. 227 ff. and p. 234.

30 For a study of these portraits by Goya, see M. Mena Marqués 2002, pp. 84–111.

31 Maurer 2002, p. 234.

32 Mena 2002, pp. 101–155.

33 Manet's *Tragic Actor* (1865), Washington, National Gallery of Art, and *The Fifer*, Paris, Musée d'Orsay.

34 In [1916], Aureliano de Beruete wrote an essay on Goya which strongly influenced many later studies, and was itself deeply influenced both by the political and cultural ideas then current in Europe and by the rise of nationalism. In his essay he attributed the influence of Velázquez to a natural 'racial' affinity, a view that fails to take into account either the writings of Mengs or the admiration of the foreign critics who had become familiar with Velázquez's work. Beruete's ideas are undoubtedly curious both for their lack of historical rigour and for their evident bias: 'The chain which seemed to have broken in the late seventeenth century was forged anew, and Spain's artistic output continued to express the views of the Spanish race through the artistic language of line and colour…a language that Goya scarcely knew, and that he needed to be able to express himself, a language that he found and learnt in those canvases by Velázquez, the synthesis of pure Spanish production, canvases that were neglected at the time, and that – in order to copy them – Goya had to hunt down in the corridors and dusty back-rooms of the new Palace at Madrid': Beruete 1916, pp. 8–10.

35 Even in the Royal Order of 11 June 1816, transferring the picture to the Academia de San Fernando, it was described as 'The Marquis of Pescara'.

36 For example, Agustín Esteve in his female portraits of the same period.

37 Águeda-Salas 1978, letter no. 49, p. 107. The Infante Don Luis clearly demanded a great deal from his portrait painters, probably less in matters of likeness than because he was anxious that his social standing be clearly conveyed, something that Goya fully understood and captured on canvas.

38 Mena 2002, pp. 174–77.

39 Jovellanos expressed himself in terms similar to those used by Francisco Preciado de la Vega, collected by G. Bottari in his *Raccolta di lettere sulla pittura…*: 'Quella gran bizzaria di pennello, ch'egli ebbe inimitabile e maravigliosa': Bottari (ed.) 1822–1825, vol. VI, p. 229, quoted in Glendinning and Harris 1999, p. 599 and n. 8.

40 Ponz (1772–1794) 1947, p. 574.

41 Canellas (ed.) 1981, doc. 273, p. 390.

42 Baticle 1988, p. 7.

CAT. 43. Diego Velázquez. *Las Meninas, ca.* 1656. Museo del Prado [P-1174]

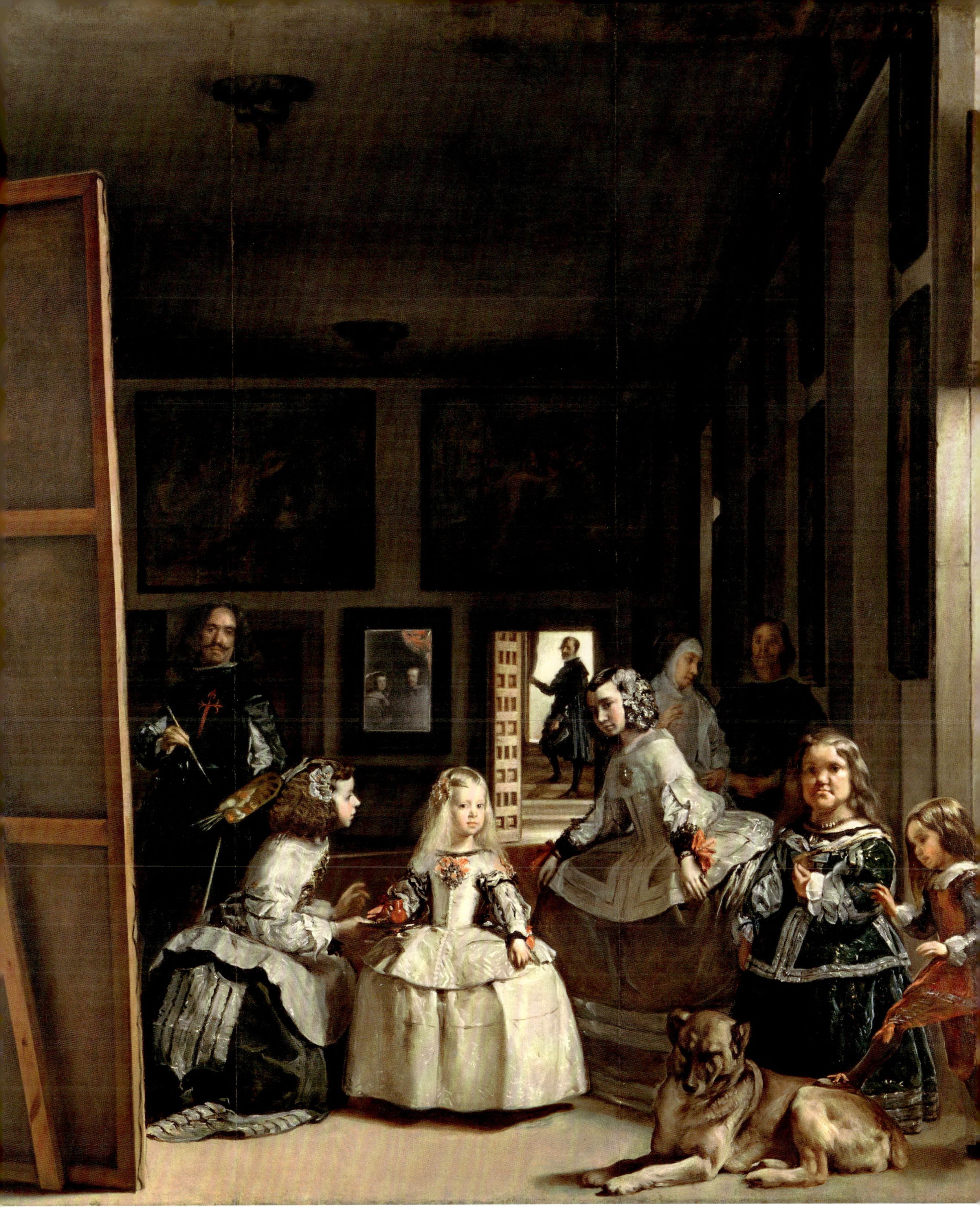

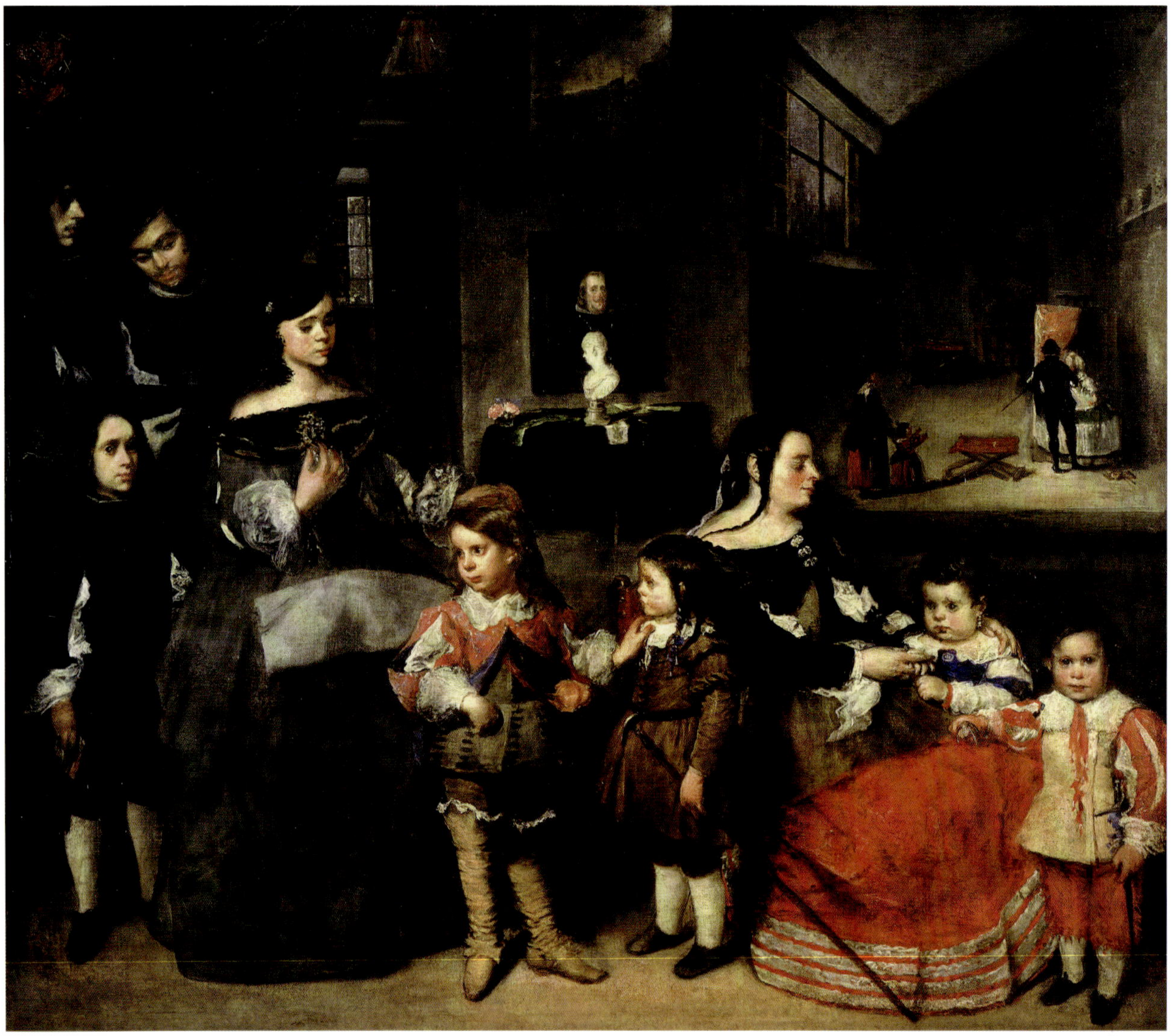

CAT. 44. Juan Bautista Martínez del Mazo. *The Family of the Painter*, 1664–1665.
Vienna, Kunsthistorisches Museum, Gemäldegalerie [320]

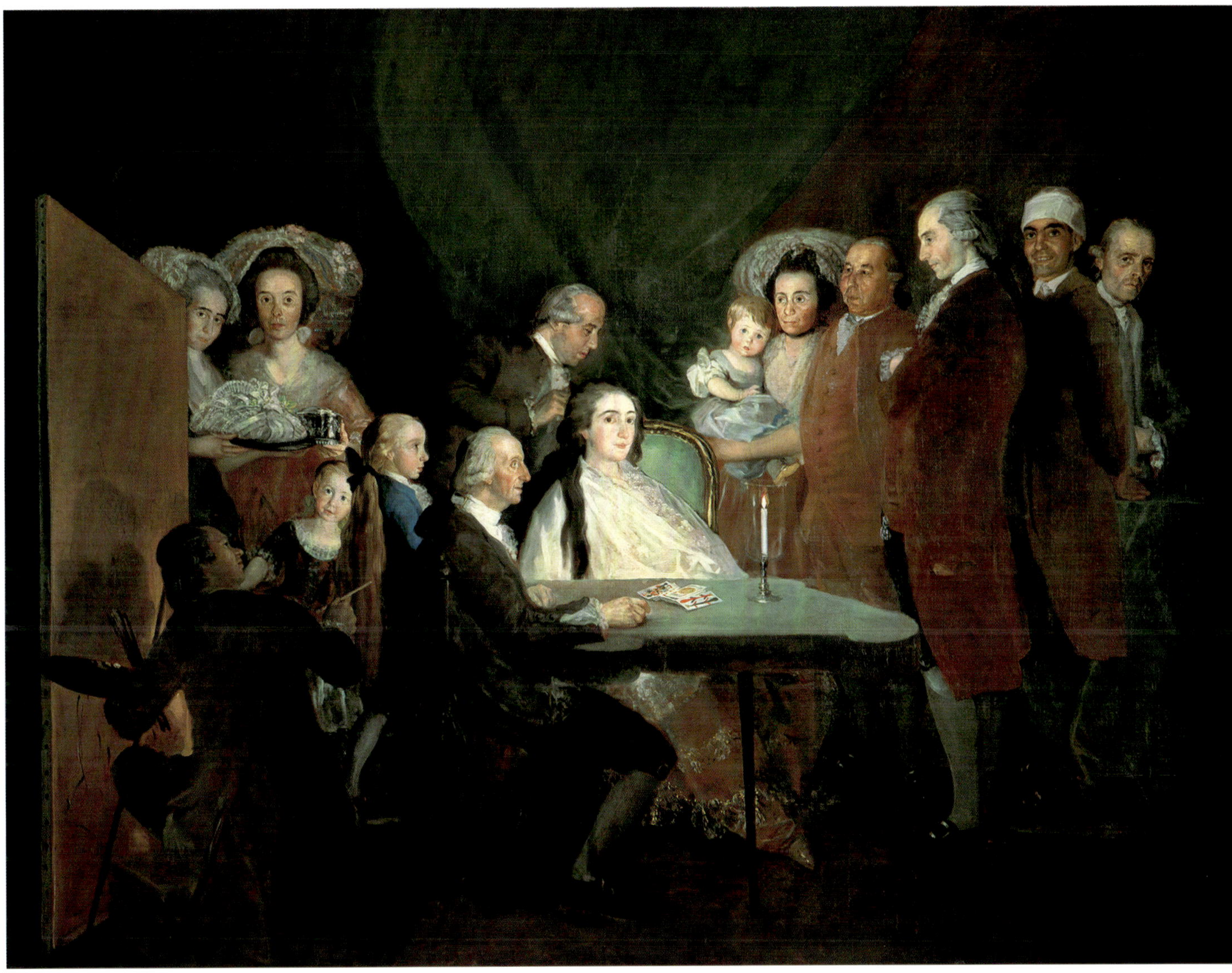

CAT. 45. Francisco de Goya. *The Family of the Infante Don Luis*, 1783.
Parma, Fondazione Magnani-Rocca

CAT. 46. Francisco de Goya. *The Family of Charles IV*, 1800. Museo del Prado [P-726]

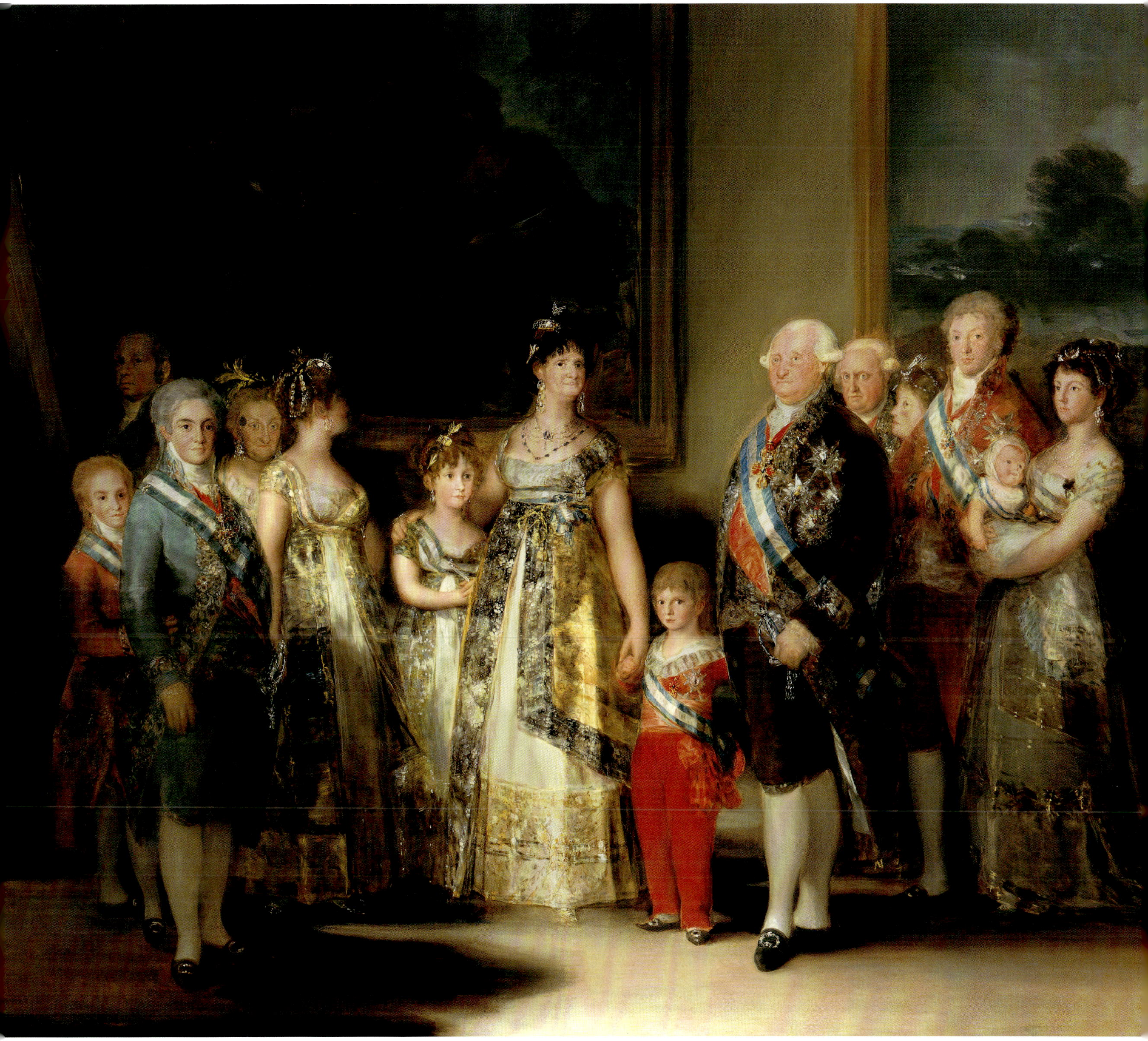

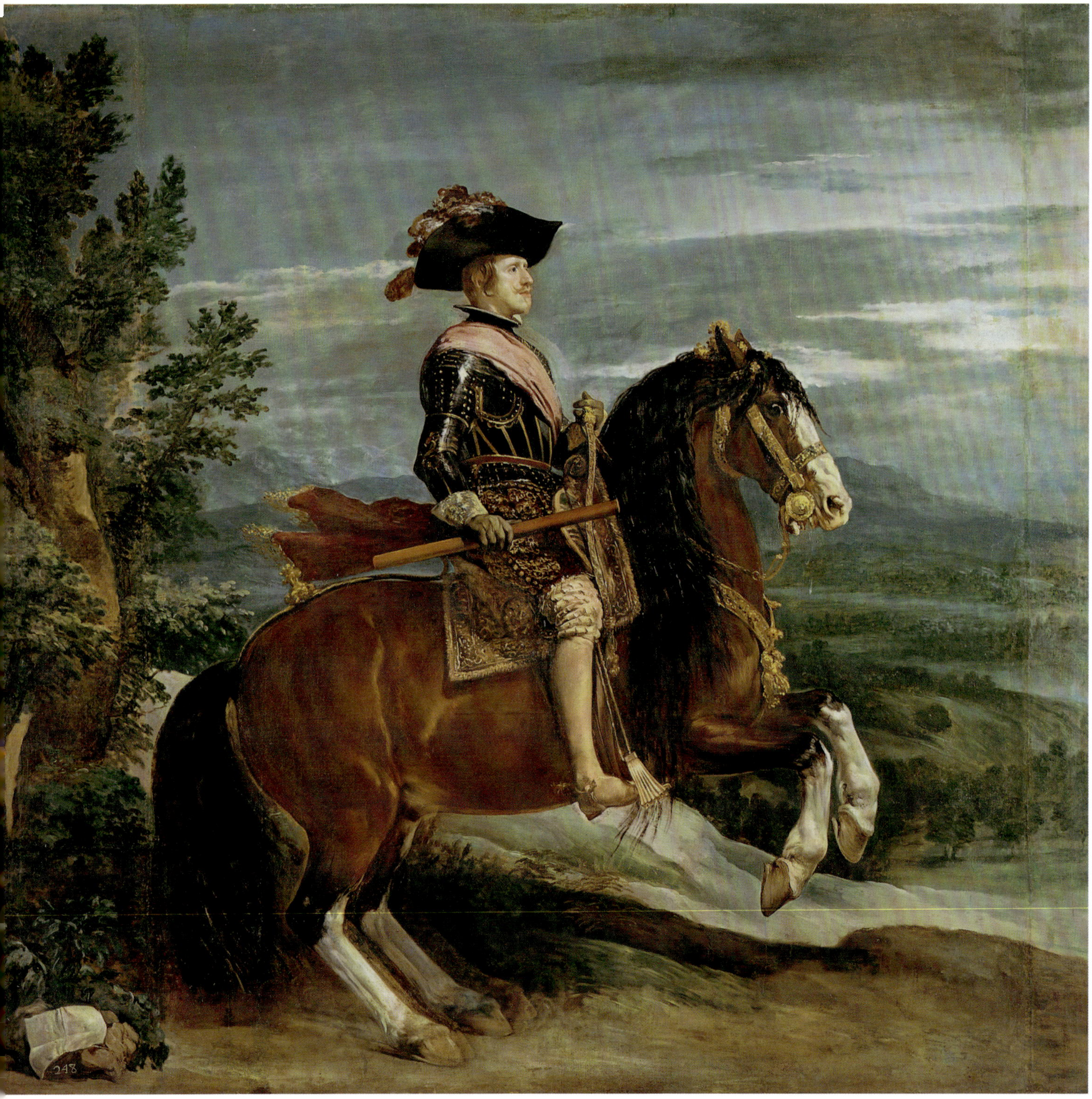

CAT. 47. Diego Velázquez. *Philip IV on Horseback, ca.* 1635–1636. Museo del Prado [P-1178]

CAT. 48. Francisco de Goya. *Charles IV on Horseback* 1800. Museo del Prado [P-719]

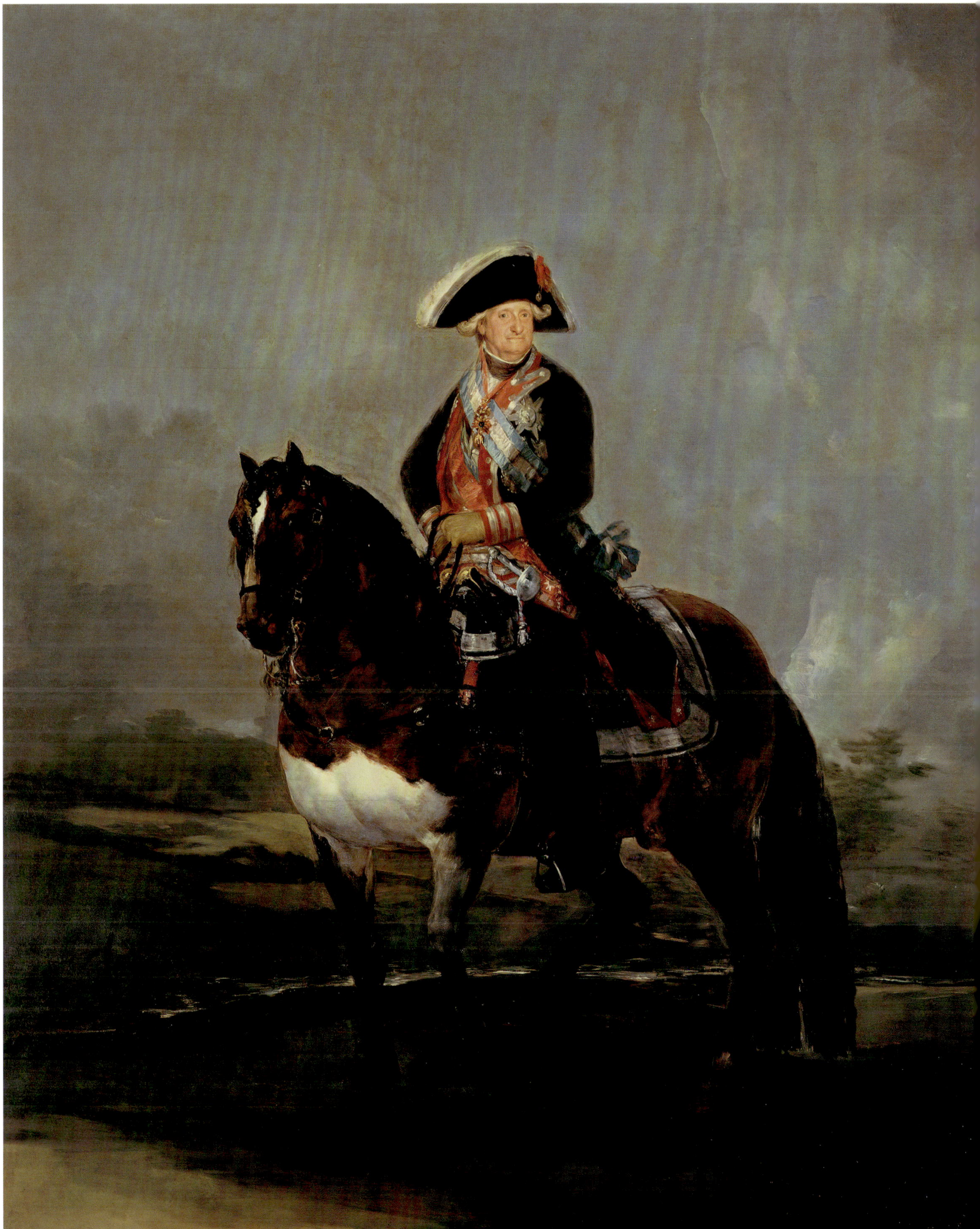

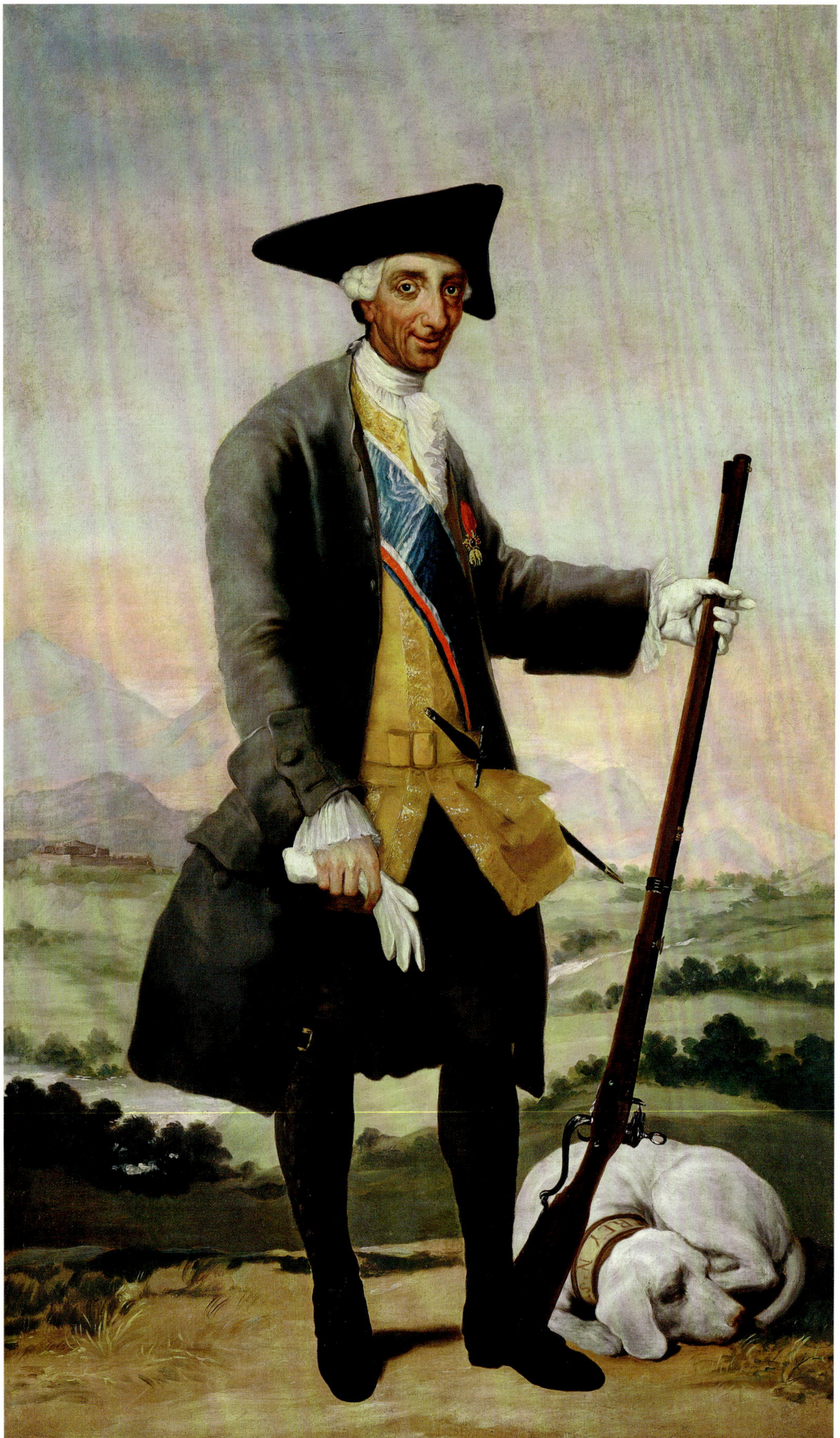

CAT. 49. Francisco de Goya. *Charles III as a Hunter*, *ca.* 1788. Museo del Prado [P-737]

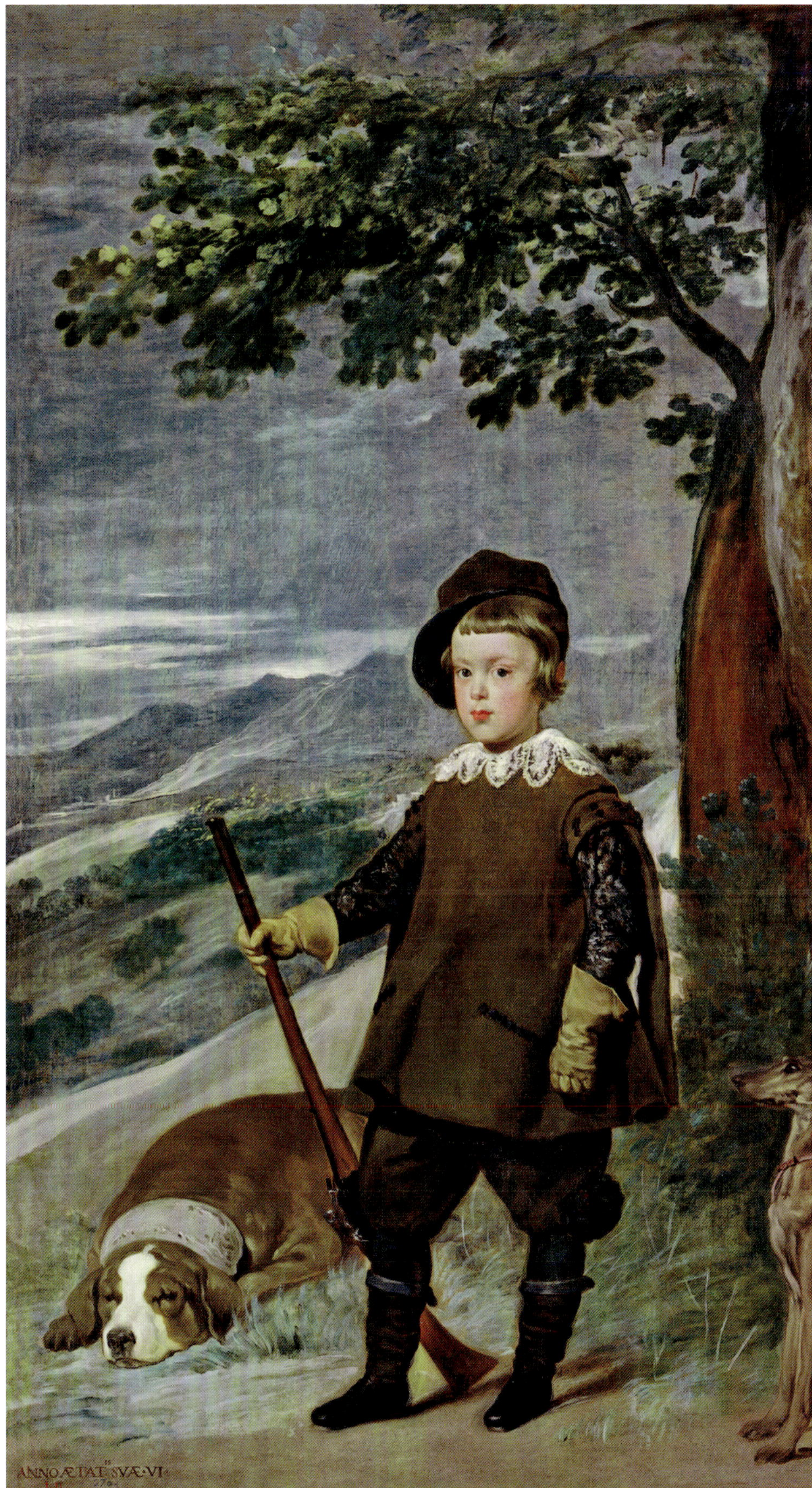

CAT. 50. Diego Velázquez. *Prince Baltasar Carlos as a Hunter*, 1635–1636. Museo del Prado [P-1189]

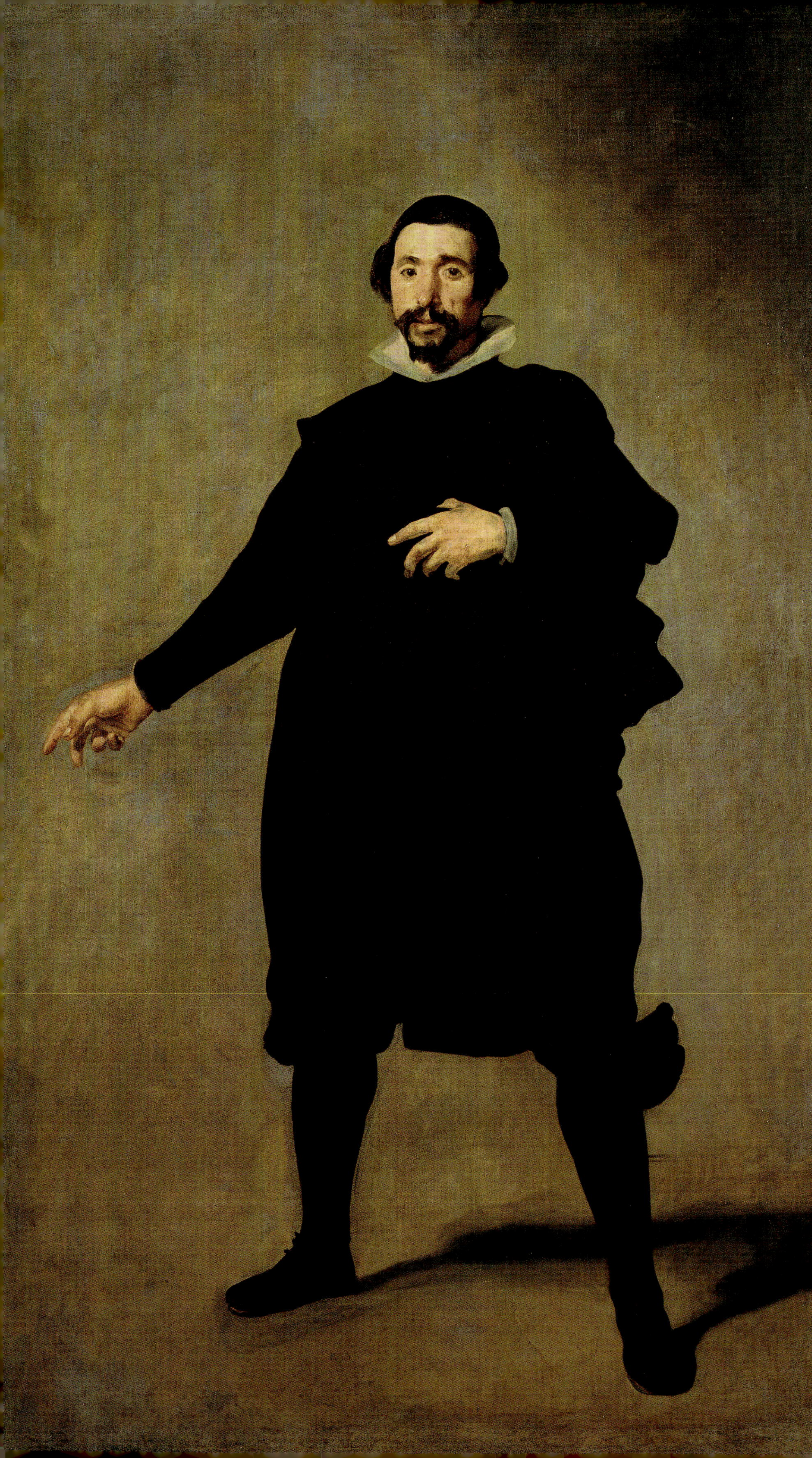

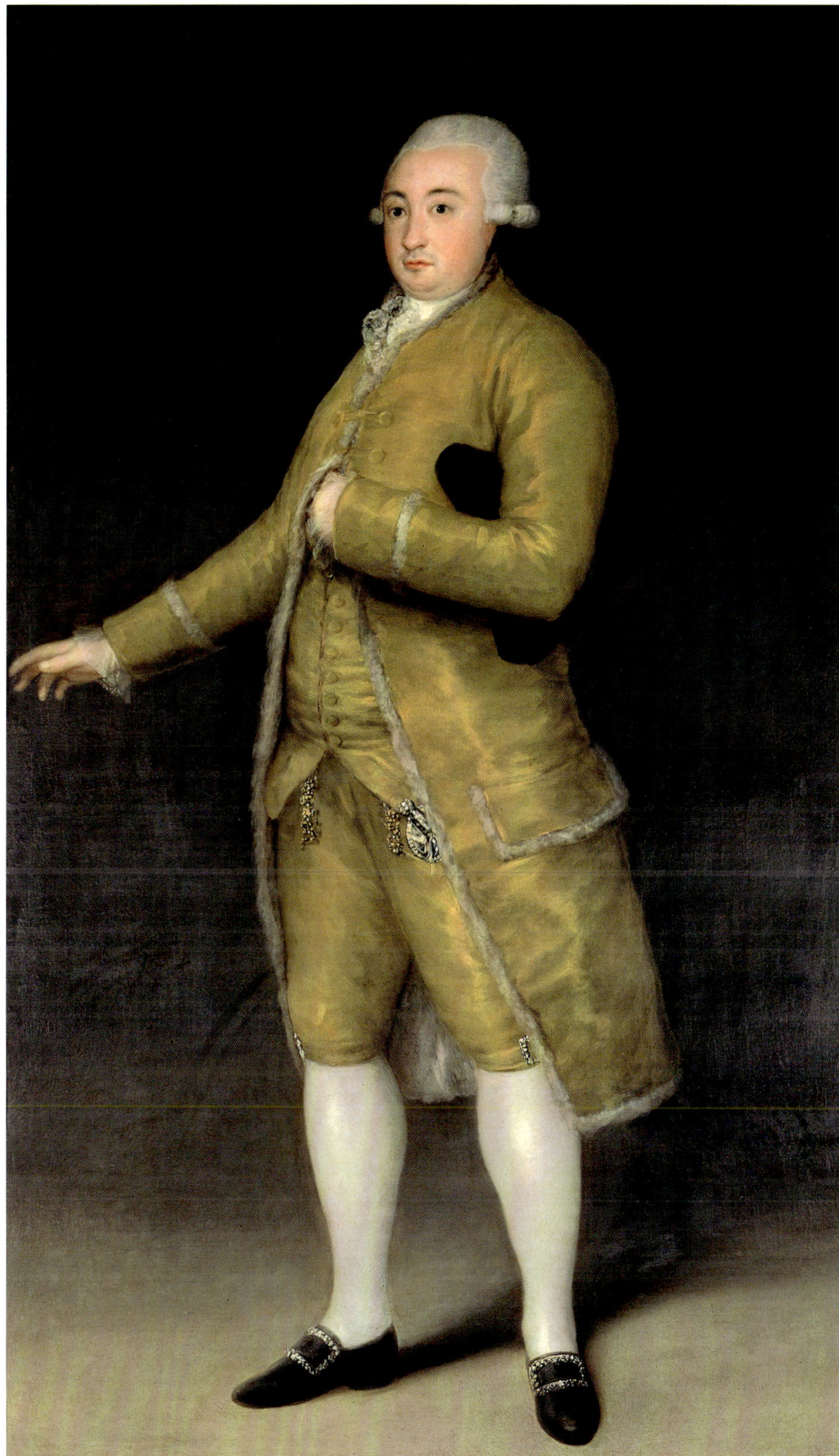

CAT. 51. Diego Velázquez.
Pablo de Valladolid, *ca.* 1635.
Museo del Prado [P-1198]

CAT. 52. Francisco de Goya.
Francisco Cabarrús, 1788.
Madrid, Colección Banco de España

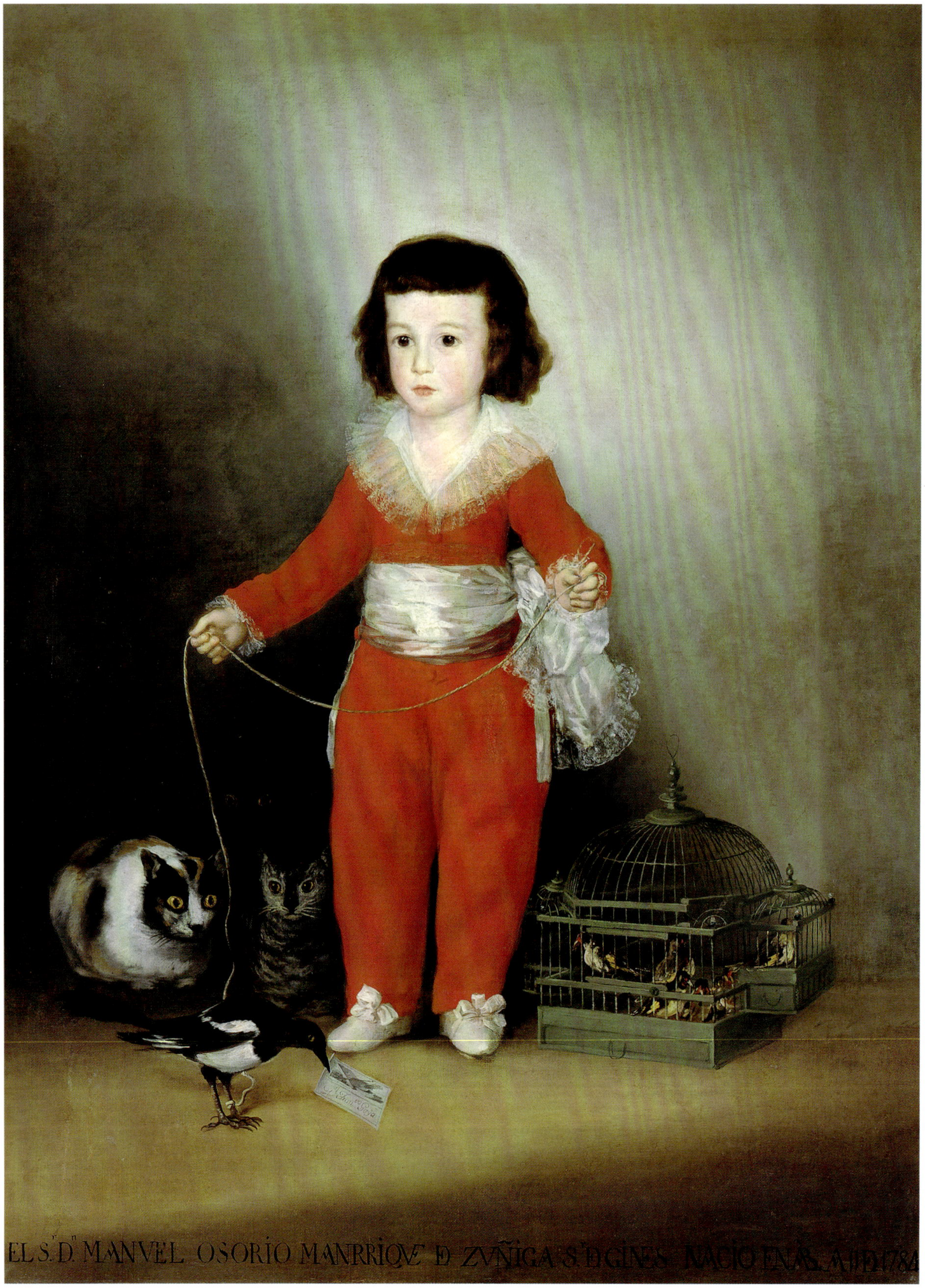

CAT. 53. Francisco de Goya.
Manuel Osorio Manrique de Zúñiga, 1788.
New York, The Metropolitan Museum of Art.
The Jules Blanche Collection, 1949 [49.7.41]

CAT. 54. Diego Velázquez.
Prince Felipe Próspero, ca. 1659.
Vienna, Kunsthistorisches Museum,
Gemäldegalerie [319]

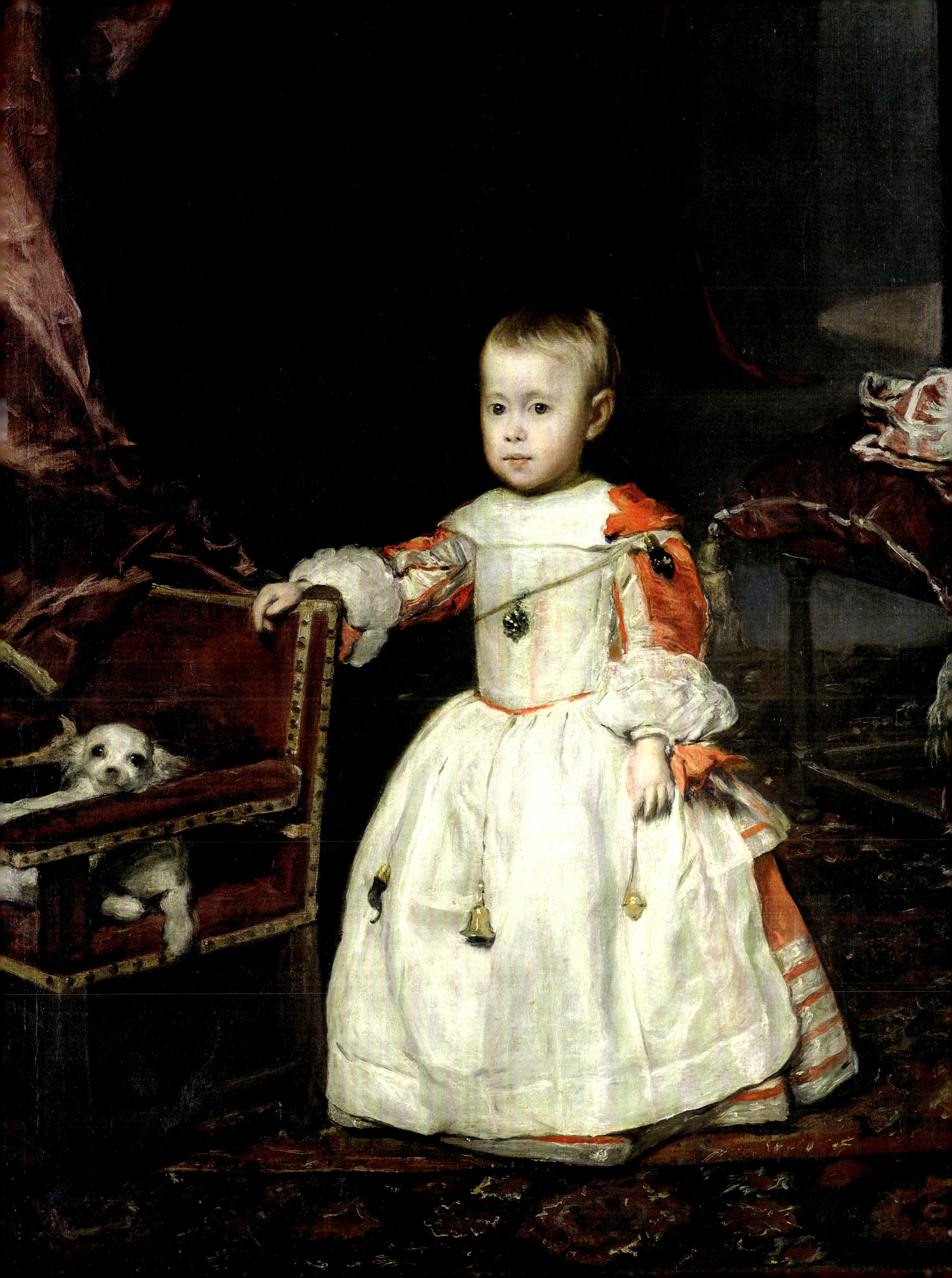

7 The Spanish Portrait in the Eighteenth Century

Nigel Glendinning

There are certain constant factors in portraiture which have to be borne in mind when tracing the historical development of the genre. Some of these change very little over time, and there is a basic pattern of types that seems to be fairly widespread. Analysis of such basics may seem otiose; they are too obvious. But the underlying human motives that determine these constants are ultimately as crucial to the growth of the genre as the involvement of great artists. It goes without saying that variety of size and the materials used in portraits are key factors. They determine the impact of the person portrayed. A large portrait on canvas – life-size, three-quarter or half-length – catches the eye at some distance and is obviously intended for display in a public place, or one that is relatively public even in a private house. Smaller portraits, on the other hand – heads or busts – on any kind of support, are by nature a more intimate or private affair. The smaller the portrait the more intimate it generally becomes, as miniature portraits seem to show; although, of course, maximum impact for an important image – like those of kings, viceroys, ministers of state, bishops and generals – is usually achieved via prints, and scale and materials are less significant in that case. So the nature of the impact varies according to the type of image created. And variations are achieved in a number of different ways: chiefly through the manner in which facial features and the subject's body are depicted, which may be realistic or idealised, for instance, serene or energetic, depending on whether the portraits in question are official or private, designed to impress or enhance, or represent the reality of an individual more literally.

The wishes of the person or persons commissioning a portrait are of major importance. A man will clearly have a specific image of himself in mind when commissioning his portrait. Most people want to highlight their status, their career, their successes and achievements; and they want their physical appearance to reflect this, and to look as good as possible, downplaying their less attractive features. Sometimes the sitter wants his portrait to show his personal pursuits and hobbies as opposed to his social class or profession, and images of this kind become more common in the second half of the eighteenth century, when aesthetic taste and sensitivity were appreciated and deemed worthy of cultivation by a new elite, mainly amongst the untitled nobility and the middle classes. This is not an entirely new kind of image in the eighteenth century, but leisure pursuits depicted in earlier portraits in Spain were mostly confined to hunting. The portraits of Philip IV and members of the royal family in Spain painted in hunting dress by Velázquez, with their dogs and their guns and landscapes in the background, are a memorable example of this kind of portraiture [CAT. 50], and so is Murillo's portrait of a gentleman accompanied by a huntsman in a country setting [FIG. 82]. However, this is clearly a pastime with a rather specific, elitist, social significance: a sport for princes and aristocrats in the sixteenth and seventeenth centuries, and in the Middle Ages before that, since it required good horsemanship and skill in the use of weapons, and a well developed knowledge of tactics into the bargain. Hunting was, in short, an appropriate leisure exercise for warrior princes and military leaders. Velázquez's image of Mars resting was a highly appropriate one for the royal hunting lodge, the Torre de la Parada, as well as the hunting portraits already mentioned.

Clothes and personal adornments also help to define or exalt sitters, and hairstyling and makeup, like dress in the case of women more particularly, increase the impact of the portrait whether they are fashionable or not. For female portraits, especially when not paired with portraits of their husbands, the sex of the person commissioning the portrait is frequently relevant. It seems fairly obvious, for example, that Diego de Corral engaged Velázquez to paint the pair of portraits of himself, his wife and their firstborn child (Museo del Prado, P-1195 and P-1196). Don Diego himself stands beside a table, which is a standard way of indicating the high social status of the sitter, and wears the Cross of the Order of Saint James. His energetic look and the movement of his head make a strong contrast with the more reposeful stance of his wife. It is true that the artist has underlined her high status too. She wears a gold necklace with a jewel hanging from it, and has been placed next to a chair – another sign of upper-class status, according to Carducho.[1] But it is really the young male firstborn child that attracts the spectator's attention. His mother's right hand seems to point at him and his rich clothing stands out against her dark dress, its bright tone heightened by the stripes and gold embroidery of the sleeves and the gold girdle around his waist.

Portraits of women on their own are very different. In female portraits of the seventeenth century, faces, hairstyles and dresses are eye-catching, regardless of who commissioned the portraits in question. A distinction has to be drawn, however, between the portraits of women of very high status and those of the lesser gentry. In his portraits of the Queen and the Infantas, for instance, Velázquez uses all his technical power and symbolic details to underline the standing of his subjects. Mariana of Austria is placed under a curtain, close to a chair, and with a desk or table beside her (Museo del Prado, P-1191). The Infanta Margarita is also beneath a curtain [CAT. 14]. Furthermore, both women wear the huge hooped skirts called *guarda-infantes* (or farthingales), whose span isolates them from other people and hides the lines of their lower limbs, their style of hairdressing creating another defensive *guarda-infante* on their heads. The half-length portrait of the *Lady with a Fan* from the Wallace Collection in London, also by Velázquez [FIG. 77], on the other hand, brings the subject closer to the spectator, and the open fan suggests the lady's discreet availability, good will or desire to be of service. Could the lady's father have asked Velázquez to paint the portrait of his daughter? Could this be the excellent portrait of a lady from Zaragoza painted by the master when in that area, according to Jusepe Martínez,[2] and might her father have asked him to paint her? Martínez reports that she complained because the artist had failed to show the lace collar she was wearing when the portrait was painted – and is indeed wearing in another portrait of the same lady – which would have preserved her better from the male gaze. As it is, it hardly seems a portrait that tries to keep us at a distance, and one wonders if it is not close in spirit to the so-called 'pocket or amorous portraits' mentioned by Palomino with a certain distaste.[3] Such portraits were dangerous for Catholic artists to undertake in Palomino's view, because the image might be put to improper use by the gentlemen who commissioned them. They could also raise problems with the code of honour in Spain, and would be less troubling, so Palomino thought, elsewhere in Europe. In spite of these supposed difficulties, more portraits were painted of women on their own in the eighteenth century than previously, and there were more painted portraits where the woman was as important as the man who accompanied her. Indeed, in Goya's *Marquesa de Villafranca* [FIG. 101] the marquesa's husband is present in his army uniform merely because his wife is painting his portrait, and she appears more important than he does in consequence. There is a very great difference between this portrait and a family group of the Villafrancas by Agustín Esteve (Madrid, Alba Collection), where the husband is standing in his uniform, protectively hovering over his seated wife and their son.

Self-portraits are not normally commissioned works. Frequently the artist simply decides to record his features following one or other of the two major traditions for this type of work: either to show himself with palette and brushes painting a picture; or in ordinary dress, with no indication whatsoever of his profession. There is another type of self-portrait, to be sure, where the artist includes his own face in a painting with a large number of figures in it, and a variant on this – or a mixture of the self-portrait as artist and a group portrait – is Velázquez's *Las Meninas* [CAT. 43], which led Goya to take a similar line in two works: first by including himself with easel and canvas in *The Family of the Infante Don Luis* [CAT. 45], and later in *The Family of Charles IV* [CAT. 46].

Although self-portraits of artists working at their easel continued to be painted, the other type of self-portrait, which makes no overt reference to the artist's working life, became more common in the course of the eighteenth century. Presumably artists were now more conscious of the social status their profession had achieved in the previous centuries, rising above the handicrafts category with which they were originally associated. So they preferred to depict themselves as individuals and not simply artists, or as people of exceptional sensitivity. No doubt, in the matter of status, Spanish artists were influenced by the attitudes of foreigners – more particularly those from France and Italy, who worked for the early Bourbon monarchs. The creation of the Academy of San Fernando (and other Fine Arts Academies) may also have increased their awareness of their upward mobility, since these institutions encouraged the wider use of the term 'professor' for those who taught, and those who worked in the profession, than had previously been the case.[4] An especially interesting example of a self-portrait that reflects this increased awareness of social status amongst French artists in the first half of the eighteenth century is one painted by Nicholas de Largillière. In it the artist depicts himself in hunting costume, out in the country with his well-dressed wife, his dog and his gun. They are listening to their elegantly attired daughter singing a song (Paris, Louvre). There is no Spanish self-portrait of an artist of the period to compare with this, but a small-scale one by Paret is not far short of it. This shows the painter in smart attire – probably that of the *majo* of the period, involving materials like satin and velvet, and a hairnet – in some senses sitting under a curtain in his studio, looking pensive or melancholy, his elbow resting on a map on a table beside him, and stroking a silken handkerchief with the fingers of his right hand [CAT. 58]. This stroking of silk reminds one of the composer Richard Wagner, who also stroked silken materials, which he liked to have around him, for inspiration, doubtless to evoke the comforting memory of stroking his mother's breast when he was a babe in arms. It is true that Paret, in this self-portrait, is sitting beside a large oval picture on which he was working, depicting a contemporary event. He is also surrounded by many other objects: antique busts, books, drawings (some loose, some in a portfolio) and his palette, which he is not using for the time being. His intention is presumably to underline his commitment to study and the idea of the 'painter philosopher', whose circulation had been encouraged by Mengs in Spain, another artist who depicted himself thinking rather than painting at this period, with a large portfolio of prints or drawings by his side, in the early *Self Portrait*, now in the Alba Collection [CAT. 55].

The eighteenth-century tendency of painters to portray themselves as people of exceptional sensitivity and mental powers, rather than just skilful artists, is in part the result of the new importance and value that was being attached at the time to the opinions of individuals, and the contribution they could make to the progress of society. The tendency may also reflect the considerable change in the class structure and the sense of hierarchy in European societies that is a major factor of the second half of the century. In Spain, anti-hierarchical developments are first of all apparent in the criticism of aristocrats who play no useful part in national life or abuse their power: a criticism common in writers during the reign of Charles III. There are also protests at that period against people in power who fail to encourage those whose obvious abilities are unrecognised or who are underemployed in the posts they hold. A character invented by the writer José Cadalso in his *Noches lúgubres* (*Lugubrious Nights*) written in about 1773, for instance, inveighs against the 'arbitrary and useless class divisions' into which people are born by chance, when they are, in reality, all one and the same species.[5] Manuel José Quintana, in the next generation after Cadalso, explains in his famous 'Ode to the Printing Press' how that invention had first of all brought freedom for the nations, and then a sense of universal equality. This egalitarian and anti-hierarchical impulse was given additional force by a fundamental change in the meaning of the expression 'public opinion' at this time. Initially it had referred to the good or bad reputation an individual was believed to have in society, but in the 1790s in Spain it began to be used in the modern sense, and applied to the general views held by the mass of the people.[6] This

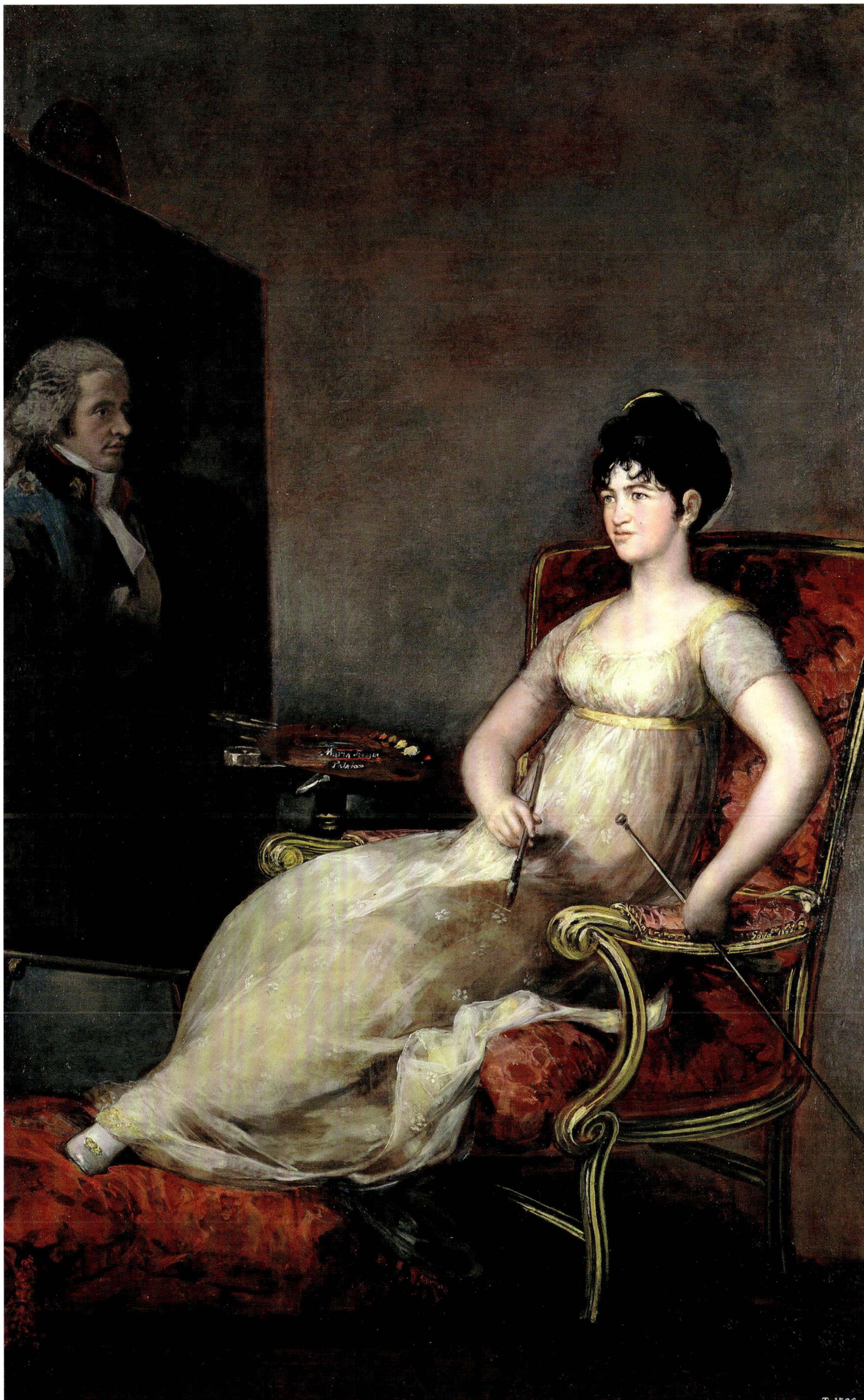

FIG. 101. Francisco de Goya, *María Tomasa Palafox, Marquesa de Villafranca*, 1804. Madrid, Museo del Prado [P-2448]

shift in meaning, which had happened earlier in France, is a clear consequence of the broadening of the 'Public Sphere' in the eighteenth century, to use Jürgen Habermas's term: the participation of an increasing number of people in the discussions of the period, with a growing sense of their right to hold their own opinions and criticise those in power.

Portraiture reflects these changes in a fairly blatant fashion, even if old conventions and new approaches frequently intermingle in this genre. The underlying concept of portraits in the sixteenth and seventeenth centuries, which remained valid for part of the eighteenth also, was that only very exceptional individuals, or those who could be held up as a particular example to others, should have their portraits painted. In the middle of the sixteenth century, Francisco de Holanda stated that 'only the highest Princes and Kings or Emperors are worthy of being portrayed, so that their images and figures may be preserved and properly remembered by posterity [...], and amongst such people may be included those who are famous for feats of arms, or for art and letters, or for outstanding generosity or other virtue, and no other person at all'.[7] Vincencio Carducho (and Palomino too at a later date) are slightly less inflexible and exclusive on the subject of portraiture, although they basically follow the same line, and Carducho, for instance, holds that if an artist paints members of his family or friends, he must make them 'worthy of being imitated for the virtues which adorn them'.[8] It is certainly the case that Murillo makes a moral example of two of his friends when painting their portraits, despite the fact that they were not of the very highest social class or particularly outstanding in their careers, and he may have followed convention in so doing. The two people in question were Nicolás Omazur (Museo del Prado, P-3060 [FIG. 84]), a poet and merchant in Seville of Flemish extraction, who was keen on art and a major collector, and his second wife, Isabel Malcampo. Murillo does not paint them with works of art around them to reflect their particular interests or symbolise their social status, but holding a skull and a rose in their respective hands: emblems of the brevity of life, and the fleeting nature of time and earthly beauty. So it seems that either they or the artist still took seriously in 1672 the convention that portraiture should have some status or moral justification. However, not all artists and patrons appear to have held such views in Spain at that date. And Murillo himself, when painting Josua van Belle, a person of similar social standing and merchant background to Omazur, fails to include any moral element, and seems to have had no qualms about enhancing his subject's status. He portrays him underneath a curtain, wearing a sword at his side. Van Belle was involved in Seville's overseas trade and was Dutch in origin, so it may be that Murillo applied the norms appropriate to portraiture in the Low Countries rather than Spain in this case, translating the implication of the sitter's 'van' before his surname into Spanish conventions of high social status. ('Van', like the German 'von' was an indicator of untitled nobility in the Netherlands.) Alternatively, of course, there may have been a gap between theory and practice in these matters in Spain, as there often was in other countries.

It is not easy to get to the heart of these problems in portraiture. In order to find out exactly what proportions of artists and patrons followed the theoretical norms of the period, we would need to know the complete range of the portraits painted. And that is naturally out of the question. Museums, foundations and a few aristocratic and upper middle-class families have preserved the relatively small number of portraits we know today, and these may well be the work of painters of the highest quality, or in the greatest demand, who generally kept to the conventions. We know, nevertheless, that not everyone was obedient to those laws, nor followed the supposedly approved principles in the seventeenth century, since Carducho himself complained about it. 'I have seen portraits painted,' he said, 'of very ordinary men and women, from a wealthy but artisan background, placed next to a table and beneath a curtain, dressed in the style and posed in the manner that is appropriate for Royalty and the highest members of the nobility (without their even being outstanding in their trade to justify portrayal; some of them carrying arms, or a general's baton, as if they were the Duke of Alba or the Marqués del Vasto.'[9] This kind of prejudice and the limitations on portraiture, however widely applied in the seventeenth century, seem not to have continued far into the eighteenth. There are even portraits of artisans at that period, like that of Andrés del Peral, for example, the court gilder painted by Goya (1797–1798, London, The National Gallery). Furthermore, in the eighteenth century an artisan with a trade no longer forfeited the possibility of proving the good stock and honourable background of his family for the purpose of claiming *hidalgo* status (*hidalguía*), as the Royal Provision of 18 March 1783 guaranteed.[10] In the world of commerce, self-made men, like Sebastián Martínez or Tomás Pérez de Estala, were painted by the leading artists of the period, including Goya (1792, New York, Metropolitan Museum of Art [CAT. 60]; and 1800–1805, Hamburg, Kunsthalle). Goya portrays them as well-dressed individuals, totally sure of themselves, and very different in temperament: Pérez de Estala, a clearly energetic individual and perhaps a little obstinate – typically Aragonese in that respect; and Sebastián Martínez [CAT. 60], a more thoughtful and shrewd person by the look of him, with a sheet of blue paper in his hand that could be either a letter or, perhaps, a drawing, which Goya inscribed with the affirmation that the sitter was his friend. In the seventeenth century, friendship did not warrant the painting of a portrait, but in the more egalitarian and sociable (and even sentimental) environment of the end of the eighteenth century, the artist had no reason to hide the affection he felt for some of his sitters.

These two Goya portraits of merchants make no reference at all to their careers, unless the handsome jacket of don Tomás (or just plain Tomás more accurately, since he was not of *hidalgo* origins), was also intended to advertise the textile mills he ran in Segovia. They capture the personality of the two sitters without needing to refer to their social class, their success or their exemplary nature. The same could be said of many other Goya portraits: those of the businessman and intimate friend of the artist, Martín Zapater, for instance; writers (and friends too) like Juan Meléndez Valdés and Leandro Fernández de Moratín; the print-maker Bartolomé Sureda and his wife; actors and actresses like Máiquez, La Tirana and Antonia de Zárate [FIG. 102]; singers like Lorenza Correa and

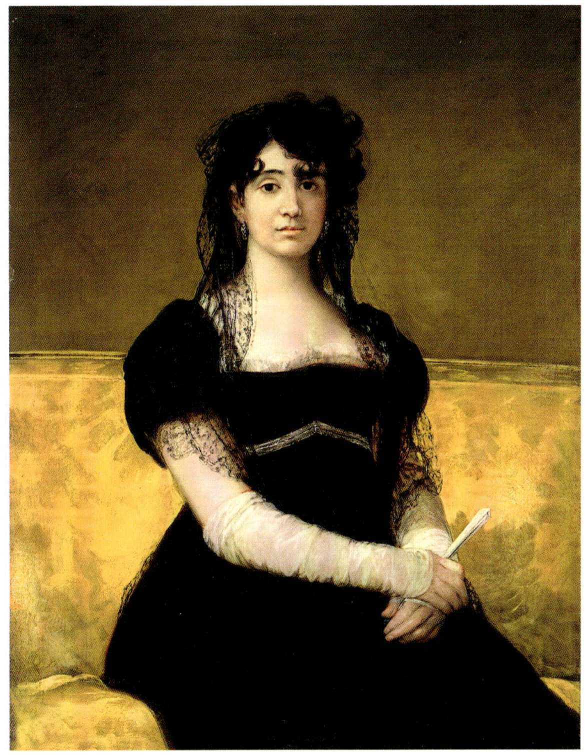

FIG. 102. Francisco de Goya, *Doña Antonia de Zárate*, 1805–1806. Dublin, National Gallery of Ireland [4539]

Manuel García; and the musician and composer Manuel Quijano. Goya painted one of his sitters – Pedro Mocarte, a member of the Toledo cathedral choir – wearing a cape and apparently dressed as a *majo* or bullfighter, underlining his character and temperament while revealing nothing of his career as a church musician, which brought him into conflict with the cathedral authorities from time to time, as the documentation provided years ago by Elizabeth du Gué Trapier shows.[11] It is hardly surprising that this painting – as bold in its brushwork as it is unrestrainedly open and direct in its character portrayal – should have aroused the enthusiasm of a later artist like Fortuny, whose vigorous copy of Goya's portrait can be seen next to the original in the Hispanic Society of America in New York. An interesting contrast to Goya's approach to businessmen is that of Maella, in his depiction of a leading merchant, comparable in standing to Sebastián Martínez and Pérez de Estala: *Don Juan Sixto García de la Prada* (Madrid, San Fernando Academy [FIG. 103]). Juan Sixto was a member of the Guild of Drapers. He had been born in Penilla (in the diocese of Santander) in 1735,

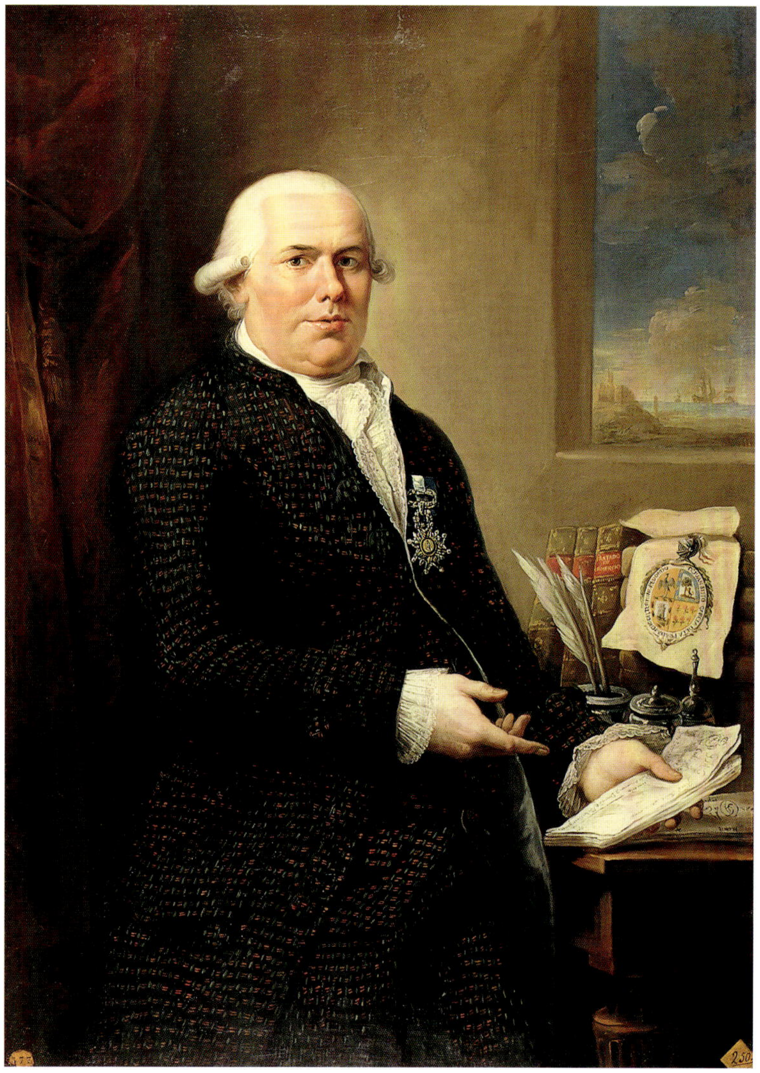

FIG. 103. Mariano Salvador Maella, *Don Juan Sixto García de la Prada*, *ca.* 1798. Madrid, Museo de la Real Academia de Bellas Artes de San Fernando

and had settled in Madrid, in a house on the Calle de Postas, in 1764, at the age of twenty-nine. Over time he became one of the four directors of the Five Major Guilds and a member of the Royal Council, as honorary Minister of the Board of Trade, Commerce, Currency and Mines. He was awarded the Order of Charles III in 1794, and Maella probably painted him at that time, when he was nearly sixty years old, since he wears the insignia of the Order on the lapel of his jacket. He fell ill in 1796 and died four years later. The portrait includes references to a number of different aspects of his life and stresses the importance of his business career. The table, the inkstand and quills and the bundles of letters no doubt stand for his commercial activities; the escutcheon of his family underlines the pride he took in his *hidalgo* background and the honorary posts held by earlier generations of his family and himself in Penilla, the town of his birth. Sea and ships in the background emphasise the centrality of overseas trade in his life.

It is also useful to contrast Goya's portraits of actors, actresses and bullfighters with the engraved portraits of the stars of stage and bullring in Juan Cano y Olmedilla's *Colección de trajes de España tanto antiguos como modernos* ('Anthology of Spanish Dress, both Ancient and Modern') (1777–1788). In these hand-coloured prints, the profession of the people portrayed is underlined: Pedro Romero and Joaquín Costillares, dressed as bullfighters, with sword and cape in hand, and the bull, killed with a single thrust of the sword no doubt, dead at their side; actors and actresses playing the parts for which they were famous, and wearing their stage costumes. Amongst the latter the series includes the celebrated comic actor Miguel Garrido, dressed as a gypsy, and in the last plate, Josef Espejo in a scene from the *Confrontation of Maja Witnesses*, written by Juan Cano's elder brother, best known for his short comedies called *sainetes*, Ramón de la Cruz Cano y Olmedilla.[12] Espejo [FIG. 104] specialised in comic old men's roles, and was the senior *barba* ('beard') in various theatre companies in the 1760s and early 1770s. In 1782, he was one of those responsible for checking accounts intended to support retired actors, on behalf of the Guild of Our Lady of the Novena.[13] The print captures brilliantly the ability of the actor to enter fully into the part of the character he plays, but fails to reveal what he looked like offstage or to give us a sense of his own personality.

Despite the increasing interest in the depiction of real characters in portraits, the possibility of idealising sitters in some respects is not entirely eliminated in the eighteenth century. Probably it never is at any period. Goya certainly mocks the idealising tendency in his *Capricho 41* (1799): 'Just like that'. In this particular etching a monkey – representing the artist as an imitator of nature – is painting a portrait of an ass, and covering up the latter's prominent ears with a wig in the canvas on which he is working. In this way the artist underlines the high social status of the sitter and diminishes the impact of his stupidity. The caption suggests, with heavy irony, that the artist has perfectly captured the likeness of this braying upper-class fool. But the artist is left-handed (cack-handed) and incapable of showing the true nature of the sitter, or unwilling to do so. In the preliminary drawing for this *Capricho*, the material advantage of producing flattering images of sitters is all too plain in the sarcastic caption: 'You won't die of hunger!' The question of idealisation, which Goya seems to ridicule here, will need further examination later.

Whatever the differences of approach, there was certainly a new public interest at the end of the eighteenth century in portraits recording likenesses for private use. Portrait painters begin to make their presence felt in newspaper advertisements at that period, doubtless reflecting a demand for portraits from people with relatively modest incomes, who now thought they had as much right to be depicted as those with more money or status. This created a demand that was not previously evident. In the *Diario de Madrid* for 10 March 1797, for instance, a miniature painter called Manuel de Castro advertised his readiness to paint 'portraits with a good likeness at the Flemish Inn in the Calle del Carmen'. The following year Castro moved house on more than one occasion, and announced his new address in the *Diario* so that clients could continue to knock on his door. By 1799, he no longer confined his work to miniatures, and diversification led him to offer 'large or small portraits, very true to life and reasonably priced'. The same advertisement was repeated in January 1800, adding his willingness to teach drawing. This time his portraits were not merely 'large or small', but also in 'various styles and prices'. This reference to style as well as price – which was normally related to the size of the picture – probably implies that he was able to do full-length, three-quarter, half-length or bust portraits, conceivably in pencil, pastels or paint.[14] In the last year of the century, namely in 1800, don Alejandro Curty, who was 'Roman in origin, professor of miniature painting and a member

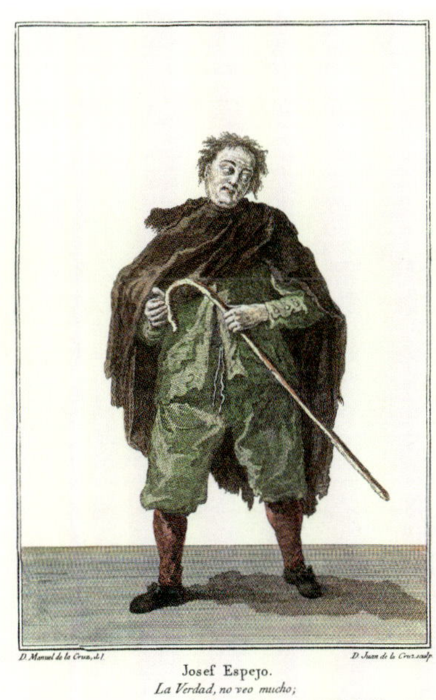

FIG. 104. Manuel de la Cruz (designer) and Juan de la Cruz Cano y Olmedilla (engraver), *Josef Espejo*, in *Colección de trajes de España tanto antiguos como modernos*, no. 85, *ca.* 1777.

of the Barcelona Academy' also advertised his various skills in Madrid. He could paint all kinds of men and women, 'capturing their facial features perfectly', and furthermore, he would take back any portraits that were not a good likeness.[15]

The desire for a good likeness – a desire that is not always genuine – is a constant in portraiture and not confined to any particular period. And at the end of the eighteenth century there were new ways of achieving it, recording the features of people's faces by more or less mechanical means. Artists had used the camera obscura for centuries to increase the accuracy of their paintings, and guarantee their truth to life. But the camera was chiefly used to copy accurately the details and positions of objects in space, more particularly in landscapes, interior and exterior views, rather than portraits. Ceán Bermúdez, for example, who was very knowledgeable about the history of art and well informed about the techniques employed by artists, having had some training as a painter himself, considered that Velázquez had employed the camera to study 'the gradual decrease of light and shade at a distance, and the sharper contrasts in the foreground'. Ceán believed that the camera was useful for fixing colours and tones precisely, and for distinguishing foreground groups of people from the background behind them. But he makes no comment about the possible employment of the camera for portraits.[16] Other techniques existed for making exact copies in Spain in the 1770s, but they seem not to have been used for portraits either. However, then Gilles-Louis Chrétien appeared on the scene, in France if not in Spain, with a new invention he called the *physionotrace*. The apparatus Chrétien created – by profession he was a musician and engraver – traced the full-size profile of the face on paper in a very few minutes. An assistant then reduced this mechanical drawing in size so that Chrétien could engrave the image as a medallion. In the Paris *salon* of 1793, a hundred portraits produced by this method were on show; 600 in Year IV of the Revolutionary Era (that is, between September 1795 and August 1796), with further increases in numbers between 1797 and 1799.[17] A similar apparatus was advertised in Madrid in the *Diario* on 1 December 1798, when subscriptions were invited for 'profile portraits engraved in the style of Chinese Ink' at Barco's bookshop on the Carrera de San Jerónimo. The drawings were rapidly made, according to the advertisement 'using a machine, and naturally a likeness is guaranteed'. Each engraved plate cost 120 *reales*, and the price included two prints of every portrait.[18] Naturally at this price those on very modest incomes could not afford to have their portraits made: day-labourers, who only earned 6 *reales* a day (one-twentieth of the sum required for a portrait of this sort), or house servants earning 25 *reales* a month. But these new methods of making portraits clearly encouraged the democratisation of the genre. So far as Spanish portraits of this new variety were concerned, only one named artist who appears to have used this mechanical device is at present known. This was Francisco de Paula Martí, an etcher, printmaker and expert in shorthand in Madrid. At least, it was he who signed the image of a lady linked in some way to the Marqués de Almenara, whose features were apparently copied by the same process used by Chrétien in Paris for Almenara.[19] The marquess, for his part, was not, in fact, the only Spaniard portrayed by Chrétien himself. There is a whole series of *physionotraces* of the Duke and Duchess of Osuna and their children made in Paris around 1798 [FIG. 105].

There may be something to the claim that these automatic portrait machines were bound to produce a good likeness, but it is as well to remember that profile portraits were often made to conceal defects in the sitter rather than show the face as it really was. The famous half-face portrait of King Antigonus, made because the monarch was blind in one eye, was used in the middle of the seventeenth century as an example from Antiquity to show how valuable it was for an artist to display prudence when painting royal portraits.[20] In the eighteenth century Palomino and Mayans y Siscar took a similar line. Palomino thought it was legitimate to 'diminish the impact of defects unfavourable to the sitter, such as minor furrows, weak points or poor skin colour, always making sure, however, that the main lines of a person's features were preserved'. Palomino believed that the painter, from an elitist point of view, should not take such liberties

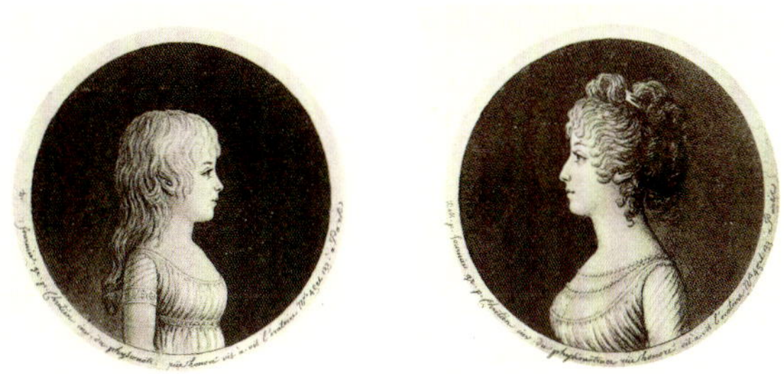

FIG. 105. Gilles-Louis Chrétien, *Doña Joaquina and Doña Manuela Téllez-Girón y Pimentel (daughters of the Duke and Duchess of Osuna)*, physionotrace, *ca.* 1798.

with 'people of every class'. But he went on to encourage artists to favour more illustrious personages, selecting 'times and occasions when the sitter's face is at its best, and he has a pleasant mien and a good colour [...], and this applies more especially to the highest members of the ruling class'.[21] Gregorio Mayans y Siscar, for his part, in his *Arte de pintar* recommends the artist to place the sitter 'at a sensible distance', so that his freckles, patches or pockmarks cannot be seen. Such precautions had more especially to be taken when portraying high-born people, so as to preserve their honour.[22]

When it came to it, some eighteenth-century artists concealed the physical problems of some sitters while others did not. Portraits of Count Aranda, for instance, who was President of the Council of Castile at the end of the 1760s and the early 1770s, provide an interesting variety of approaches. It seems that the count had a squint in one eye, and the amatory expert Casanova refers openly to his misfortune in his *Memoirs*. 'This great Lord was fairly ugly,' he writes, about his first encounter with Aranda in 1768. 'He had a rather unpleasant squint and received me pretty coldly.'[23] A range of portraits of the Tenth Count, by a variety of artists in different media, give us a somewhat vague indication of the extent of the problem. There are portraits in oils by Ramón Bayeu (1769) and Joaquín Inza (1771), for example; a coloured clay relief by Julián López (*ca.* 1760); a print based on a drawing by a Frenchman called Méon, who taught at the Royal Military College in Paris (1767); and a ceramic plaque by an anonymous artist (*ca.* 1780).[24] There is an obvious problem with the right eye, to judge from a print engraved by Mateo González, an artist from Zaragoza, at the centre of the count's seat of power in Aragon; rather less of a defect in Inza's equestrian portrait (Seville, Palacio de Dueñas, Alba Collection), showing Aranda as Captain General – the highest military rank, which he had already reached in 1763 – wearing the insignia of the Order of the Golden Fleece, which had been granted him on 13 April 1756. And hardly a hint of a squint in Ramón Bayeu's portrait, where he is also dressed in Captain General's uniform, though carrying in addition the doctoral regalia of the University of Huesca, since the portrait was painted to commemorate the award of an honorary degree to the count (Huesca, Provincial Museum).

What conclusions can be drawn from these differences? We cannot know precisely how Aranda's looks were; nor do we know whether his eye problem was the result of a battle wound – as seems possible, to judge from the anonymous plaque referred to earlier – or a congenital defect. But the different poses selected by the artists, and no doubt the different requirements of those who commissioned these works, appear to reflect a clear variety of approach in Spain at the period in question, suggesting more than one possible explanation of these images of Aranda. On the one hand, the impact of foreign artists working for the early Bourbon monarchs favoured a certain idealisation; and Mengs's Platonic ideas gave new impetus to that approach. Respect for the social hierarchies also encouraged the concealment of certain truths about the way people looked, if these might prove detrimental to the offices the individuals held, and there was a long tradition of this. From a different point of view, the sense that all men were equal before God, and the growing egalitarianism of Enlightenment thought, favoured honesty in portraiture. In Spain, furthermore, the tradition of Velázquez's portraits upheld the pursuit of realism and truth in portraits, even in court circles, whatever the reality was.

At all events, it is perfectly possible to find instances of idealisation in portraits of Count Floridablanca and the Infante Don Luis, which were painted by Goya in the early 1780s. Goya's portrait of Floridablanca as chief minister of the crown at the age of fifty-five, is a case

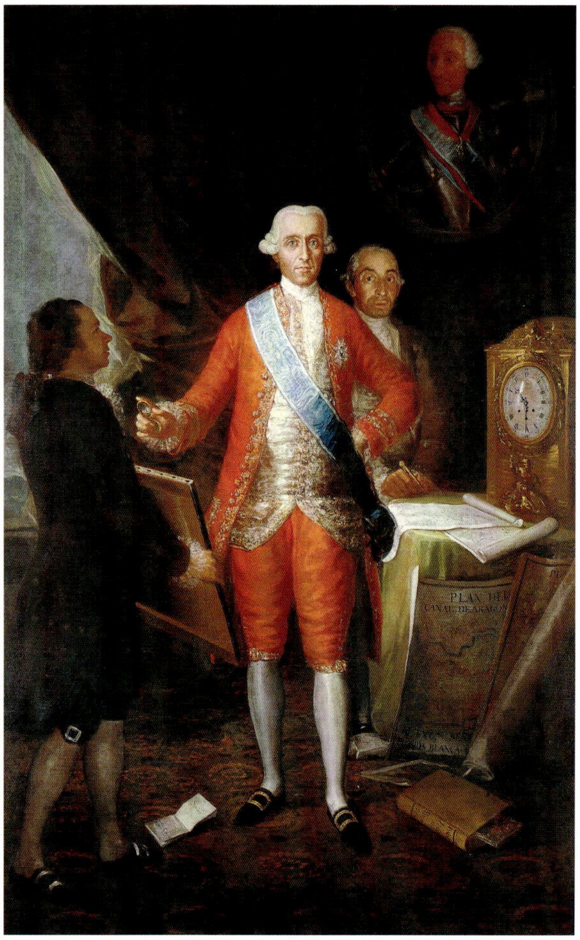

FIG. 106. Francisco de Goya, *The Count of Floridablanca*, 1783. Madrid, Colección del Banco de España

in point [FIG. 106]. It shows him discharging various functions in his office in the presence of the artist and another person. In the first place, the portrait exaggerates Floridablanca's height – contemporary evidence suggests that he was not particularly tall – and also makes him less fat in the cheeks and more refined in his facial lines than depicted by other artists: notably Batoni in a drawing for a print published in Rome a very few years earlier. Furthermore, the composition underlines the relative position of the figures depicted in the social hierarchy, in a somewhat schematic fashion. At the top on the right is the portrait of King Charles III; the count himself is in the centre of the picture, seen in a strong light, and dressed in a red jacket and breeches whose colour appears to have had some link with high status at the period, since Count Aranda mocked Floridablanca for wearing it.[25] Behind Floridablanca is one of his assistants or advisers, half in shadow, while the artist reduces his own size so as not to overshadow the chief minister. Logically, since Goya stands in the foreground at the left, we would expect him to look larger than he in fact appears.

Despite the measure of personal idealisation in this picture, and others like it, there is no exaggerated glorification of great lords. The details within the painting, furthermore, invite us to think of the beneficial effects of the policies put in place by the minister on behalf of the king, rather than simply of Floridablanca himself. He is shown as a protector of the Arts, for instance, thanks to the presence of a copy of Palomino's *Practice of Painting* on the floor at his feet, and because he is about to scrutinise a canvas that Goya has brought to show him: a small sketch for a large-scale, public work in all probability. We are also made aware of the measures being taken to stimulate commerce and agriculture in Spain. A piece of paper, with an estimate of costs and plans for the Canal in Aragon, which can be seen, shows the minister's concern with the economic development of the country. It is also likely that the third person present in the room has some relationship to the canal project. Recently he has been identified with Julián Sánchez Bort, the military engineer in charge of the construction of the canal from 1776.[26] But it is equally possible that the person in the painting is the architect Sabatini, who was Director of Hydraulic Works and Civil Architecture, according to the official publications of the period. A later portrait of Sabatini, wearing a wig, by an anonymous artist, does not seem to overturn this possibility.[27] And the fact that the Italian was sixty-two years old in 1783, makes him perhaps marginally a more likely candidate for the unidentified person in Goya's group portrait than Sánchez Bort, who was fifty-nine. It is certainly the case that Sabatini was not a good-looking man, and the same is true of the person in this picture. Casanova inevitably emphasises his relative ugliness in his *Memoirs*,[28] and the British architect, Sir William Chambers, was of the same opinion. The latter admired Sabatini's qualities as an architect, but stated that he was 'one of the ugliest fellows in Italy', who had done well to join the army instead of pursuing his vocation as a priest, since his head, like that of Medusa, 'may be useful in war', presumably turning the advancing forces of the enemy to stone.[29]

A portrait, which fairly evidently avoids the excessive idealisation sometimes applied to senior members of the nobility, is that of the Count of Altamira, painted by Goya, as Director of the Bank of Saint Charles (1786, Madrid, Banco de España). The count also had the title of Marquess of Astorga (amongst others) and was a descendant of the Count-Duke of Olivares. Goya certainly includes some symbolic elements which enhance the sense of the count's high social status. He wears what appears to be court rather than military uniform, for instance, whose decorative patterns of gold embroidery and braiding changed from one reign to the next, without there being at present any published guide to help us identify the precise rank or post of most of these. Probably he is wearing the uniform of Gentleman of the Royal Bedchamber, since Goya has also portrayed him with the handle of the gold key (associated with that office) protruding from his pocket. The most surprising element in the depiction, however, is the fact that Goya has not concealed or attenuated in any way the count's extraordinarily small stature, having him sit on a fairly low chair, beside what seems an outsize table. Altamira himself must have said that he did not want any dissimulation, since his smallness was too well known. Lord Holland claimed that he was 'the least man [he] ever saw in society and smaller than many dwarfs exhibited for money'.[30] But it looks as if the count was untroubled by the standard court jibes on this subject, and perhaps he preferred to be painted in a dignified way without exaggeration, instead of trying to cover up the truth, as Agustín Esteve attempted to do in a portrait of the count painted for the University of Granada (1792–1795, University of Granada). Esteve has him standing by a small table and beside a far from large chair, with an immense column in the background: the traditional symbol of power.[31] Goya has not eliminated symbolism altogether, as we have seen, but the most striking thing about his portrayal of Altamira is the refined and intelligent quality he has given his facial features, and the handsome proportions of his body and limbs.

A common way in which the meaning of a portrait is extended in the eighteenth century, is through the use of visual metaphors and symbols, as we have already seen. A fine example of the process early in the century occurs in Jean Ranc's portrait of the future Charles III, painted in about 1723 as a young prince, with flowers in his hand and a book open on a desk before him, with a sprig of flowers on top of it (Museo del Prado, P-2334). The flowers used to be taken literally, and it was deduced from these that the prince studied botany in his youth, as if the point of the portrait were to record reality. But recent investigations, concentrating on the Latin verses inscribed in the book open in front of the prince, and the probable emblematic significance of the flowers, have reached a very different conclusion. The painting appears to provide a compendium of the moral and heroic virtues which princes were expected to acquire. The text in Latin – whose words form a classic heroic couplet (a hexameter followed by a pentameter) with an additional hexameter after it – invites the spectator to seek out the metaphorical meaning of other details in the painting.[32]

Naturally, the presence of books in a portrait can signify a variety of things. In some Goya portraits the genuine publications of the sitter are depicted, extending our sense of his or her personality and temperament. The titles of books in the background can often be read, as is the case in Goya's portraits of Admiral Mazarredo (private collection), Munárriz (1815, Madrid, San Fernando Academy) and Félix Colón de Larreátegui (1794, Indianapolis Museum of Art), in which the books remind us of the sitters' careers, scholarly activity and value to the state. Books held by the Archbishop of Zaragoza, Joaquín Company (Zaragoza, Archbishop's Palace), or Cardinal Luis María de Borbón (*ca.* 1800, Museo del Prado, P-738), on the other hand, are likely to be missals or other religious books, related to the vocation rather than the personality of these individuals. The books in the background of Miguel Jacinto Meléndez's portraits of Philip V, Queen Isabel Farnese, and the two princes, with books in their hands or beside them, have a very different import (1727, Madrid, National Library). These pictures were painted to hang in the recently founded Royal Library and the books are shown primarily because they are relevant to the place where these portraits were intended to be seen. The rules of Decorum clearly operate here: the norms which laid down that subjects of paintings should relate to the physical context in which they were placed: landscapes were appropriate for a country house, for instance, and book-related themes (including portraits of famous authors) for a library. Beyond the idea of Decorum, in this particular case, there is a political point: to reaffirm official protection for scholarship in Spain, and assert the value of the pursuit of knowledge for the State.

There is a similar range of different meanings in backgrounds of portraits depicting the sea. We have already seen Maella use the sea and ships to denote international trade and commerce in the portrait of Juan Sixto García de la Prada. In portraits like those of Admiral Mazarredo by Goya and Dubos (private collection; and Madrid, Museo Naval), they normally relate to the navy itself. But in Paret's portrait of a naval officer (1787, Madrid, private collection), who has been identified as Francisco Javier Muñoz y Goosens, the boat and the coastline have a more specific significance. It seems that Muñoz y Goosens, who was a naval captain, was charged with the recovery of seven million *pesos fuertes*, which were on board a ship called *San Pedro de Alcántara*, when it foundered in 1786, and it is thought that the same subject is also exploited by Paret in his *Self Portrait* [CAT. 58] in the Prado Museum.[33] Such details take on a more personal note in the portrait of Muñoz y Goosens, and refer to one of the sitter's specific achievements rather than simply to his relationship to the sea and ships as a naval man, although there is no sense that Paret has sought to draw the real site where the shipwreck took place on the Portuguese coast near Peniche. The ships in the background of Amigoni's portrait of the Marqués de la Ensenada, don Cenón Somodevilla y Bencoechea [FIG. 107], by contrast, are more clearly symbolic. The columns behind the minister are the usual emblems of power, while the harbour scene doubtless refers to the marquess's title ('ensenada' in Spanish means a cove or a natural harbour) and also reflects the politician's contribution to the development of the Spanish navy and overseas trade.

A coastal scene in a portrait, which has a more intimate connection with the sitter, appears in the earlier of two images painted by Goya of his friend and patron Jovellanos (*ca.* 1783, Oviedo, Museo de Bellas Artes de Asturias). The coastal area depicted has recently been identified with San Lorenzo near Gijón, which the artist himself is unlikely to have seen.[34] Since the port of Gijón itself was Jovellanos's birthplace, it is a highly appropriate backdrop for this Asturian author, legal expert and politician. But the San Lorenzo area was the subject of a major project for improvements in the port's harbour facilities launched in 1782, when Jovellanos himself presented the plans to the Municipal Authorities on 30 August that year.[35] Although no harbour wall or mole can be seen, Goya indicates its proximity by showing the boats nearest the shore following different directions. One is inward and the other outward bound. It seems that Goya put the San Lorenzo area (no doubt following the indications of Jovellanos himself, and at his suggestion) in the background of the portrait to commemorate the impulse the statesman had personally given to the commercial development of his native province.

In portraits of ladies, their dress, and the environment or context in which they are depicted, can signify a variety of things. At this period, for instance, artists frequently painted aristocratic ladies in gardens, woods or meadows which sometimes genuinely belonged to them, and at others stood metaphorically for their estates. Often the beauties of Nature and the charms of the sitter counterbalanced one another, enhancing real beauty with the ideal beauty around her. But Goya was not strongly influenced by these traditions. In his two full-length portraits of the Duchess of Alba, the dull coloured landscape element is a perfect foil for the reds and golds of the Duchess's clothes and accessories (1795, Madrid, Alba Collection [CAT. 61]; and 1797, New York, Hispanic Society of America [CAT. 62]). On the other hand, a contrast between feminine beauty and the delights of Nature throws the latter into relief in Goya's portraits of the Countess of Fernán-Núñez (1803, Madrid, Fernán-Núñez collection) and the Marquesa de Santiago (1804, Malibu, J. Paul Getty Museum). The grace and beauty of woods

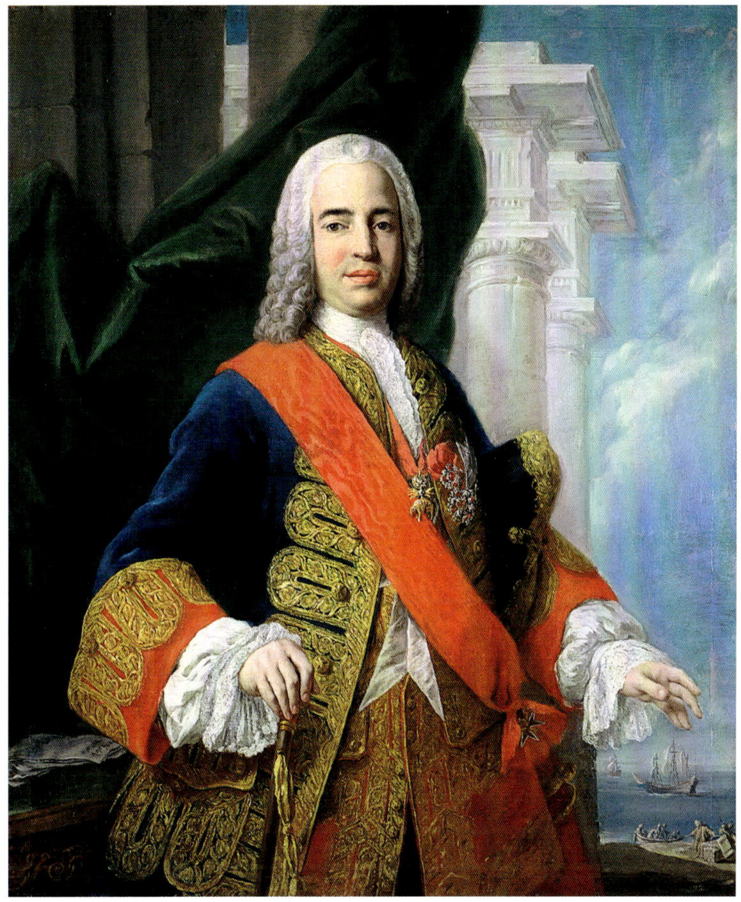

FIG. 107. Jacopo Amigoni, *The Marqués de la Ensenada*, *ca.* 1750. Madrid, Museo del Prado [P-2939]

and fields in these cases is somewhat ironically contrasted with the lesser charms of the ladies in question: the heavily made-up face of the marquesa and the beefy haunches of the countess. The backgrounds in these portraits seem poetic, but the ladies themselves are not poeticised. The landscape background of the Duchess of Alba, on the other hand – the stream, the sandy areas, pine trees and poplars which occur in both these portraits – recalls the real Andalusian landscape near Sanlúcar, and the Duchess's estates which Goya knew.

Although the *maja* dress worn by the Duchess of Alba may have a particularly (Andalusian) overtone in her case, it was widely adopted by high-born Spanish ladies at the end of the eighteenth century, in part, presumably, as a reflection of the taste for national dress. Stimulated no doubt by the early prints in the *Colección de trajes de España* of Juan Cano, issued in 1777, regional dress was soon the rage. Writing to his brother, Lord Grantham, the British ambassador, describes a visit to the Marquesa de Valdecarzana in July 1778, and notes that the lady 'has nearly as large a chignon and ring as the youngest and most foolish Maja there'. The same month, Grantham writes in another letter that the Duchess of Bejar has received a commission for a Majo and Maja dress from Russia.[36] To judge from Paret's painting of *A Masked Ball* (*ca.* 1767, Museo del Prado, P-2875), it would seem that such dresses would not have been out of place in such gatherings in the late 1760s. One of the earliest portraits of an aristocrat in *maja*-type dress is that of the Marquesa de Llano by Mengs [FIG. 108]. The dress is specifically associated with *majas* by the artist's friend Azara, in his catalogue of Mengs's work, where he also mentions that there were two versions of this portrait.[37] It seems that when Mengs began the portrait in Parma in 1771, the sitter's brother-in-law asked the artist for a replica, which was duly made and is now in the Rijksmuseum in Amsterdam. The original portrait, said to be a good likeness, was in fact finished in 1772 in Rome, where it was much

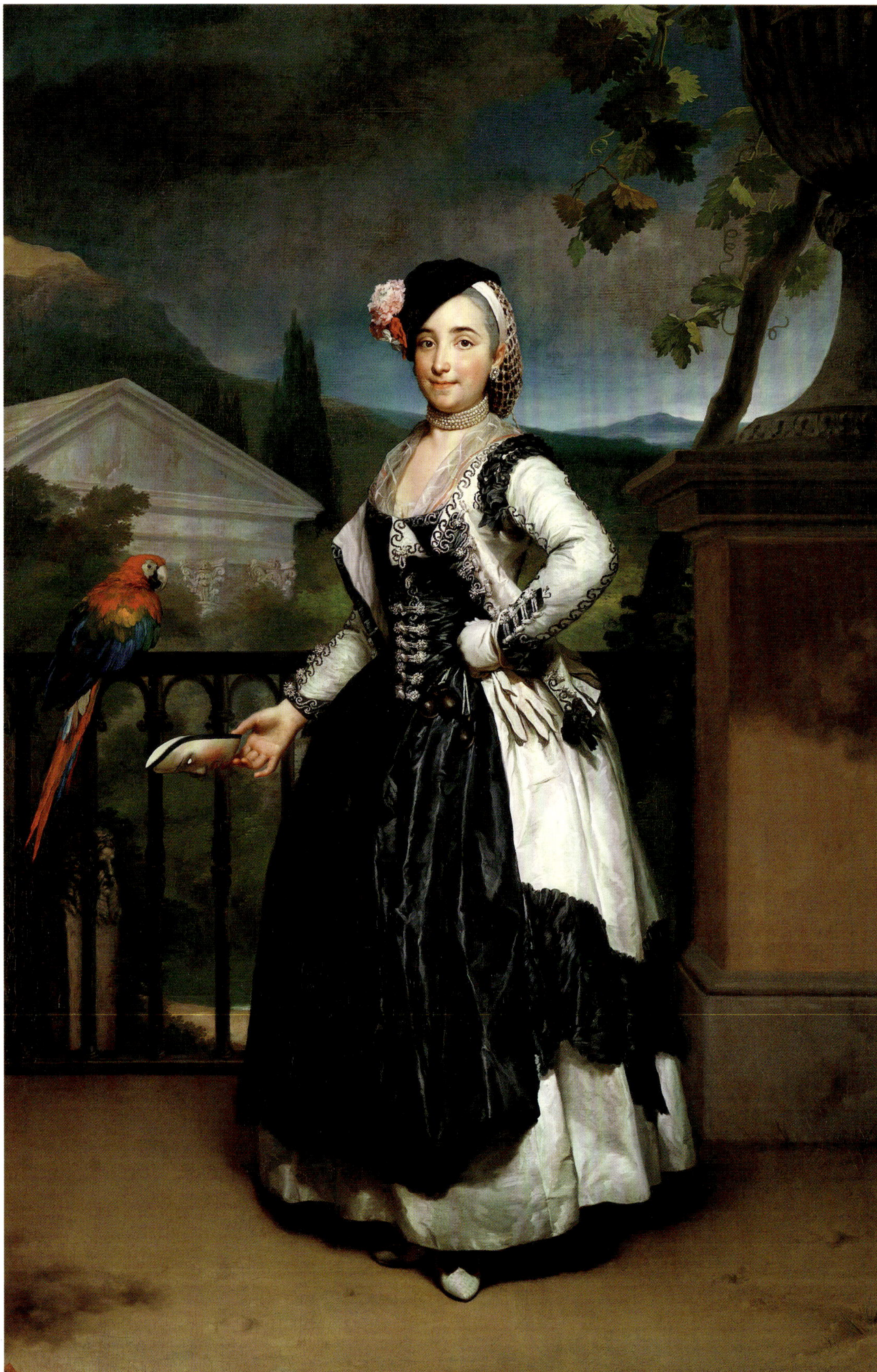

FIG. 108. Antón Rafael Mengs, *The Marquesa de Llano*, 1771–1772. Madrid, Museo de la Real Academia de Bellas Artes de San Fernando

admired by Italian connoisseurs and apparently copied by English aficionados on the Grand Tour. The Marquesa – Doña Isabel Parreño y Arce, who was apparently eighteen years old when the portrait was painted – carries a mask in her hand, as if she were about to attend a ball or party. She wears a dark apron over her dress, tied at the waist, which seems to be characteristic of traditional dress in La Mancha; to judge from Plate 81 of Juan Cano's *Colección de trajes*. Doña Isabel was evidently proud of her regional origins, noting in her will that her parents came from La Puebla de Don Fadrique, then in the mountainous southern part of La Mancha and now in the province of Granada.[38] Her friends even gave her the nickname 'La manchega' (The girl from La Mancha), according to references in Azara's letters and later ones, in the diaries of Jovellanos.[39] Her surroundings in the painting, however, are not in the least Spanish. They look like some Italianate garden, in the late afternoon, whose Classical temple with Corinthian columns, bearded antique head on a pedestal, and decorative urn, invoke an idealised context for a portrait of a female member of the Spanish aristocracy with a taste for Italy and Antiquity. This is, in fact, very reminiscent of the setting in which Mengs had earlier placed Arabella Swimmer in his portrait of her (*ca.* 1753, Scotland, Dalmeny House, Rosebery Collection). Doña Isabel smiles, as people in Mengs's portraits often do, giving signs of vitality and animation rather after the manner of French eighteenth-century portraits.

Apart from the importance of dress and hairstyle in female portraits of the eighteenth century, in which there was nothing very novel apart from fashion itself, we must return to the portrayal of taste and sensibility in some of these pictures. This is a striking aspect of eighteenth-century female portraiture, and we have already drawn attention to Goya's painting of *La marquesa de Villafranca*, in which the lady in question is depicted at work on a portrait of her husband. Goya also included musical instruments and scores in portraits of two of the daughters of the Dukes of Osuna, who were all keen amateur musicians: *The Marquesa de Santa Cruz* (1805, Museo del Prado, P-7070), and *The Duchess of Abrantes* (1816, Museo del Prado, P-7713). The latter holds up a piece of music for our delectation, probably an aria from an opera or a song, whilst her sister, reclining on a sofa, carries a lyre in her hand as a classical emblem of music-making. In one of the miniature portraits collected by the same family there is a painting of the third Osuna sister, Josefa Manuela, done by Jean-Baptiste Augustin in France in 1799, in which she is playing a piano.[40] This type of portrait, inspired no doubt by French precedents from the time of Madame de Pompadour, is common in the second half of the eighteenth century.[41] Inza painted Doña Josefa Tilly y Montaner, future countess of Tilly, and Agustín Esteve the marquesa de Ariza, with their respective pianos and scores that are more or less legible. Amongst male portraits of a similar type, Goya's *Duke of Alba* is particularly admirable (1795, Museo del Prado, P-2449). The Duke is portrayed with a Haydn score in his hands, leaning on his piano and with his preferred instrument, the viola, in full view on the top of it. So that some indication is given of the Duke's less personal activities in this portrait, primarily of an amateur musician and music lover, the sitter has had himself portrayed in his riding boots complete with spurs, which probably refer to his honorary court appointment as Master of the Royal Stables in Córdoba, although they could also allude to his passion for hunting. If the first of these two explanations of equestrian detail were correct, the portrait would have been intended to strike a nice balance between the public and private pursuits of the sitter. Among paintings of middle-class professional musicians and enthusiasts, Vicente López gives us Félix Antonio Máximo López, the organist and composer, with a composition in his right hand, and his left – with nicely caught sensitivity in the performer's fingers – on top of his piano [CAT. 68]. Goya, for his part, captures the enthusiasm of a young amateur musician in the intimate portrait of his grandson *Marianito*, painted on panel, with a roll of paper instead of a conductor's baton in his hand, and an obviously classical score behind him (*ca.* 1815, Madrid, Duke of Alburquerque).

Amid this mixture of, on the one hand, hierarchical, official and professional portraits, and, on the other, personal or intimate studies of individuals, a new phenomenon of Goya's times deserves to be mentioned, which could be called a 'portrait without a portrait'. The subgenre in question provides a meticulously detailed indication of the life, career and interests of an individual without portraying the face or body of the person in question. This novelty is an offshoot of *trompe-l'œil* painting. Not many examples survive or are at present known in Spain, but those we have seen appear to have been created as homages to a friend or acquaintance, and attempt to define them in a witty and enigmatic way. Paret made one such portrait for José Santiago Ruiz de Luzuriaga, a doctor in Bilbao, and there is another by Jorge Juan Guillelmi, who was an amateur artist, as well as a lieutenant colonel in the army and a knight of the Order of Saint James. The only known *trompe-l'œil* portrait of this army officer is one in honour of another distinguished military man, of Irish extraction, Francisco Antonio de Lacy, and it was exhibited in a Madrid art gallery quite recently [FIG. 109].[42] The skilled hand of the artist reproduces in it printed papers and manuscript documents relating to Lacy's career, fragments of nine identifiable prints which Lacy presumably had in his art collection or was known to admire, a page from the *Kalendario Manual*, a religious print of Saint Jude, several leaves torn out of religious publications, a book bound in decorated paper, and a few playing cards, all apparently lying higgledy-piggledy one on top of another. It has been suggested that some of the prints reproduced are intended to allude enigmatically to the life of Lacy rather than to his love of art. A print after a painting by Simon Vouet, for example, may be there to evoke the birthplace of Lacy's mother. The naked wise man who watches the world go round and its changes of fortune in what seems to be a drawing, may be there to hint at the stoicism that a battle-hardened officer is expected to display. The tattered prayer book and a scorched religious print may be other indications of the harsh realities and need for divine support of a military career, the more so since Lacy's patron saint – Saint Jude – is the one we turn to in moments of the most extreme difficulty or anguish, when faced with some terrible disaster or adversity. The picture is very personal and works in part by 'in' jokes, but it certainly gives the flavour of the man Lacy presumably was: a courageous

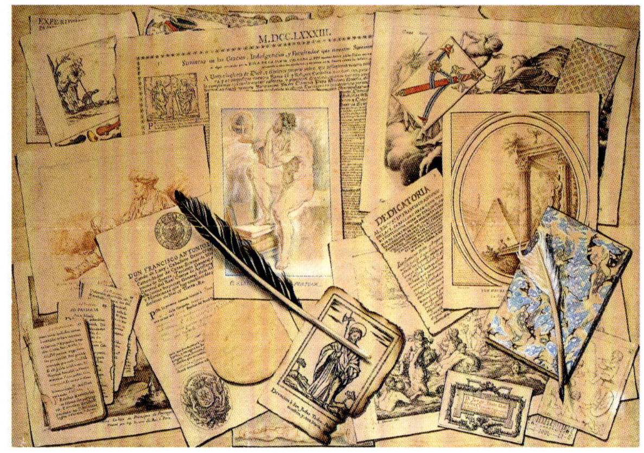

FIG. 109. Jorge Juan Guillelmi, *Trompe l'oeil dedicated to Francisco Antonio de Lacy*, 1783. Madrid, José de la Mano Galería de Arte

individual no doubt, fond of the arts, humour and card games, and religious into the bargain. The portrait is more moral than physical. Yet it includes the same range of references to the 'sitter's' professional career, his social standing and personal tastes, as many of the normal portraits of the period.

There is a great deal of variety, and there are many changes of direction, in Spanish portraiture in the eighteenth century, and we have tried to give some sense of the developments that occurred, and the underlying reasons for them. In passing, we have noted the involvement of foreign artists working for the court in the development of Spanish portraiture, bringing with them their own traditions and conventions, in much the same way that Italian and Flemish artists had done at earlier periods. The exuberance and dash of French portraits, with their flowing swathes of velvet curtains, the shining finish of their materials and clothing, and the slightly theatrical poses and attitudes their sitters adopt, make a major impact. They capture all too well, symbolically, the power and arrogance of the ruling class. Louis-Michel van Loo's portrait of Don Ricardo Wall (1753) is a good example of this flamboyant style [FIG. 110], and the portrait, which is signed and dated in a way that is difficult to read, presumably related to the sitter's appointment as Spanish ambassador to Great Britain in the early 1750s. Van Loo employs some traditional symbolism: making Wall stand by a chair and a richly gilded table, near to a vast column redolent of power, and beneath a swathe of dark velvet curtain. The silvery wig and the face of the sitter stand out against this background and appear more strongly lit in consequence. Wall wears a grey velvet frock coat, embroidered with gold thread, and the red sash and medallion of the Order of Saint James. He also wears a cuirass, which greatly increases the monumentality of the diplomat's body and refers to the rank of Lieutenant General which the sitter held in the army. The folds in the curtain and Wall's cloak give life and movement to the portrait. The position of Wall's feet, the energetic expression in his eyes and the letter (with Latin inscription) he carries in his outstretched hand, also heighten the general effect.

Colour makes an important contribution to the impact of Van Loo's portraits, and sometimes the contrasts are on the garish side. Mengs, in the middle of the century, aims at much gentler effects, creating a sense of elegant refinement in the detailed attention he gives to the embroidered patterns and lacework, and to the gentle and generally satisfied or happy expressions on sitters' faces. His portraits were always favourable to his subjects, and it is not surprising that his time in Spain brought him Spanish pupils, disciples and imitators, such as Maella, Francisco Bayeu and Folch de Cardona. The careful draughtsmanship of the last named of these artists earned him a post as royal portrait painter, and he made a large group portrait of *The Family of Charles IV* (before Goya undertook that subject), which it is unfortunately impossible to assess today because of its seriously deteriorated condition in the vaults of the Museo del Prado. Mengs eschewed most of the mannerisms of French and Italian portrait painters. Although he painted a series of portraits of members of Charles III's family, with the inevitable columns and curtains, he was clever at handling such details with restraint, sometimes placing symbolic elements in areas of shadow in the background so that they were less obtrusive, and softening the impact of relentless detail by clever handling of colour tonalities. He painted many bust or half-length portraits where the dress did not distract attention from the features of the face and the personality of the sitter. He portrayed his friend Azara, for instance, dressed in very simple attire, with no luxurious items at all, and with an unidentifiable book in his hand, which may have been written by him – his edition of Garcilaso's *Poesías* (1765), for example – or conceivably by some other author entirely. The light shines down on his forehead and the upper, more spiritual or intellectual, part of the face; it catches his right hand and one of the fingers which marks the place in the book he is holding.

Goya's portraits, in some sense following this Mengsian path in their preoccupation with the personality and mental activity of the individual depicted, also made new progress by recapturing some of Velázquez's techniques and skills as a portrait painter. The earlier master knew how to tone down the importance of subsidiary material in portraits, and register the essence of details by his impressionistic handling of the brushwork, without forcing the eye to focus on unnecessary minutiae. The

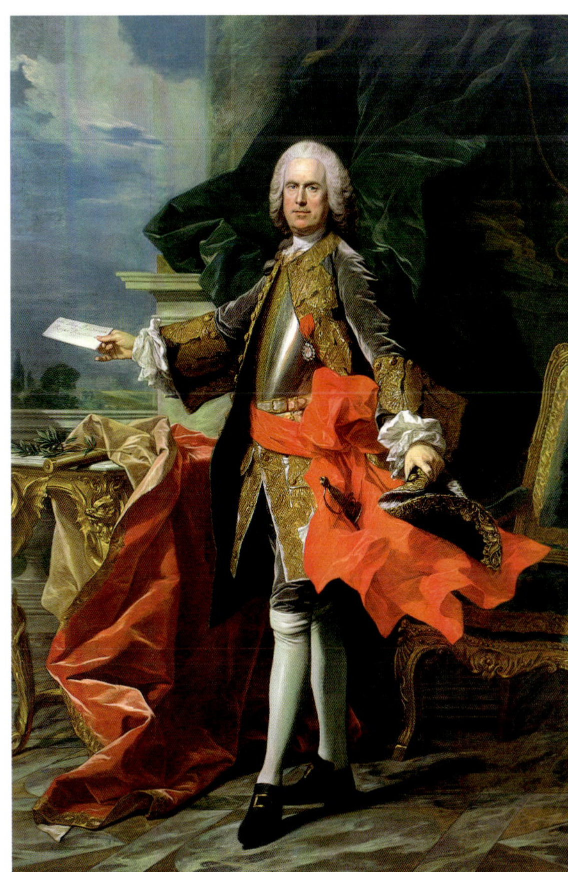

FIG. 110. Louis-Michel van Loo, *Don Ricardo Wall*, *ca.* 1753. Dublin, National Gallery of Ireland [4660]

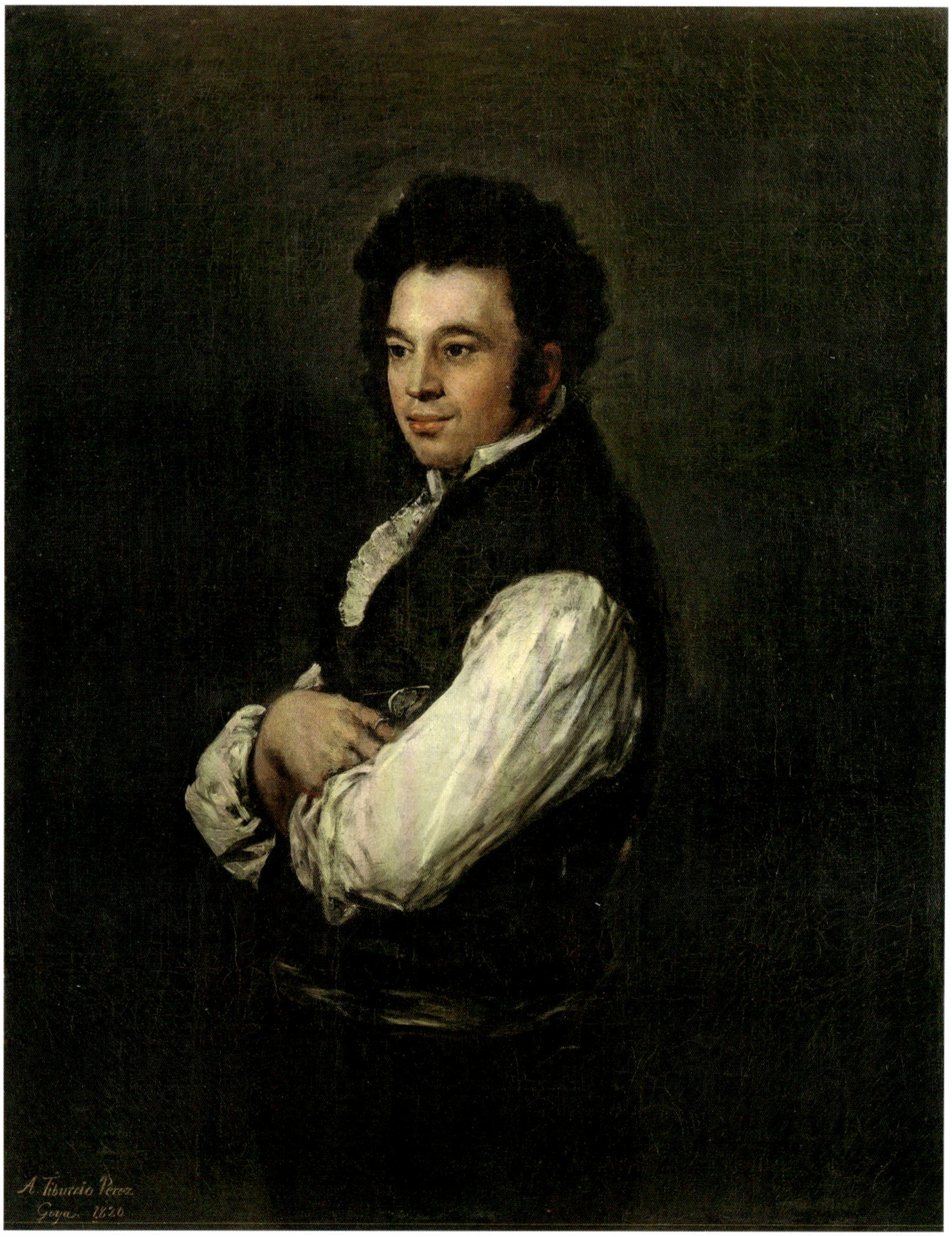

FIG. 111. Francisco de Goya, *Tiburcio Pérez y Cuervo*, 1820. New York, Metropolitan Museum of Art [Theodore M. Davis Collection, Bequest of Theodore M. Davis, 1915 (30.95.242)]

return to Velázquez had initially been impeded by the taste for carefully drawn and sharply defined detail, and the disapproval of naturalism expressed by Mengs and his supporters. But the spread of knowledge of Velázquez's work through prints, above all from the 1770s onwards, led to a reassessment of the virtues of his style, and his pursuit of 'truth', by influential art enthusiasts such as Jovellanos and his friend Ceán Bermúdez, as well as by artists themselves, and this in turn brought Velázquez forward again as a model to follow. Goya was quick to adopt Velázquez's manner in his portraits, often using freer and more audacious brushwork – less accurate too – than his Andalusian predecessor. But the debate about naturalism and idealisation nevertheless persisted, and many adopted a hybrid position. Ceán, for instance, certainly avoided an excessively naturalistic approach that sought to record reality at a specific moment in time, or tended to consider that all details were equally important in the subject in question. He wanted portrait painters to aim for 'an aesthetically pleasing (or beautiful) naturalness as far as possible, while preserving the likeness of the sitter'.[43] His approach is particularly clear in a review he wrote of an exhibition held at the San Fernando Academy, in which he expressed his admiration for the style of Goya's portrait of *Tiburcio Pérez y Cuervo* [FIG. 111]. He does not emphasise the fact that this young architect has been portrayed as an individual rather than as a professional person, but underlines 'the style and freedom with which the painting has been executed'. Ceán was notably less impressed by two portraits painted by Vicente López that were in the same exhibition: *Antonio Aguado* and *Isidro Velázquez*. In his opinion, López had recorded an expression of Aguado's that was not typical or characteristic of the man: 'with a certain air about the way he carried his head and shoulders, that is unusual in the sitter'. The pose of Isidro Velázquez was 'nobler', but 'the braid on his hat, his huge rosette, elegant leather cross-strap, and the stick and gloves in his left hand, are very distracting'. Ceán clearly believes that too much attention to detail is prejudicial to the true image of the sitter and the sense of his personality. He also thinks that the sitters themselves would have preferred verisimilitude – the general air and spirit of the individual – to all these not very revealing if neat and precise minutiae. Verisimilitude, according to Ceán, 'is preferable in works of this kind, as it is in poetry, to servile or run-of-the-mill imitation of nature, which all too often degenerates into mannerism and caricature'.[44] In spite of the neoclassical terminology employed by Ceán, he has an excellent sense of the new direction in which portrait painting was going at the end of the eighteenth century and the beginning of the nineteenth: the concern to focus on the personality of the human being and his or her character, not just the external reality and social status of the person portrayed.

NOTES

1 Carducho (1633) 1979, p. 337.
2 Martínez (*ca.* 1673) 1950, p. 212.
3 Palomino (1715) 1947, p. 574.
4 *Estatutos* 1757, pp. 10, 43, 51, 61 etc.
5 Glendinning 1982, p. 10.
6 Glendinning 1984.
7 Holanda (1548) 1921, p. 255.
8 Carducho (1633) 1979, p. 334; and compare Palomino (1715) 1947, p. 132.
9 Carducho (1633) 1979, pp. 336–37.
10 Aguirre 1793, pp. 11–12.
11 Trapier 1964, p. 29.
12 Cano (1777–1788) 1988, nos 27, 28, 75, 76, 83 and 85.
13 Tobar 2004, p. 633.
14 *Diario de Madrid*, 1797, p. 283; 1798, p. 643; 1799, p. 196; 1800, p. 20.
15 *Diario de Madrid*, 1800, p. 1280.
16 Ceán Bermúdez 1800, IV, p. 175.
17 Pawloswski n.d., p. 256.
18 *Diario de Madrid*, 1798, p. 2151.
19 Tedde de Lorca 1988, unnumbered illustration.
20 Pacheco (1638) 1956, II, p. 152.
21 Palomino (1715) 1947, pp. 529–30.
22 Mayans y Siscar (1776) 1996, p. 124.
23 Casanova 1924–1935, X, p. 274.
24 Albiac Blanco 1998.
25 Olaaechea 1969, p. 113.
26 Pérez Sánchez 1988, pp. 75–76.
27 *Francisco Sabatini*, 1993, p. 24.
28 Casanova 1924–1935, X, p. 278.
29 Bedford County Record Office, L 30/14/71/1.
30 Glendinning 1963–1964, p. 32; and Pérez Sánchez 1988, p. 77.
31 Soria 1957, pp. 99–100, fig. 4.
32 Luxenberg 1997, pp. 136–38; and Luxenberg 2001, pp. 72–88.
33 *Luis Paret y Alcázar, 1746–1799*, exh. cat., Department of Culture of the Basque Autonomous Government at Vitoria-Gasteiz, 1991, pp. 264–65.
34 González Santos 1994a, pp. 82–84.
35 Caso González n.d., I, pp. 134–36.
36 Bedford County Record Office, L 30/15/54/59.
37 Mengs 1780, p. XLIX.
38 Madrid, Archivo Histórico de Protocolos, Po. 21786, f 634.
39 Azara 1846, II, 422–23; and other references on pp, 425 etc.; Jovellanos's diaries have entries referring to her on 3 February 1795, 2 February 1796 and 24 June 1797.
40 Ezquerra del Bayo 1934, pl. XIX, 1.
41 Goodman 2000.
42 Mano 2002, pp. 51–53.
43 Ceán Bermúdez 1821, p. 111.
44 *Ibid.*, pp. 113–14.

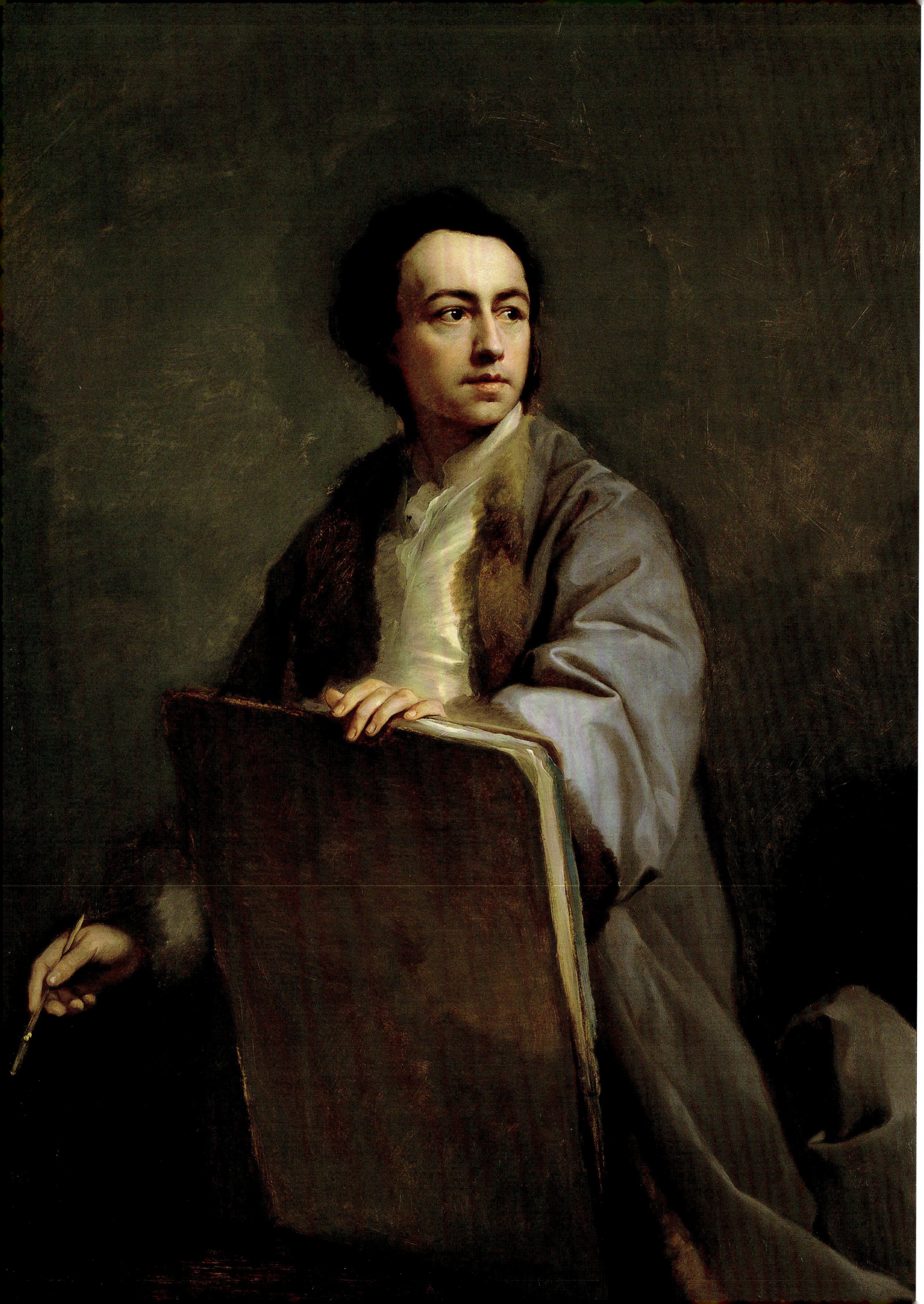

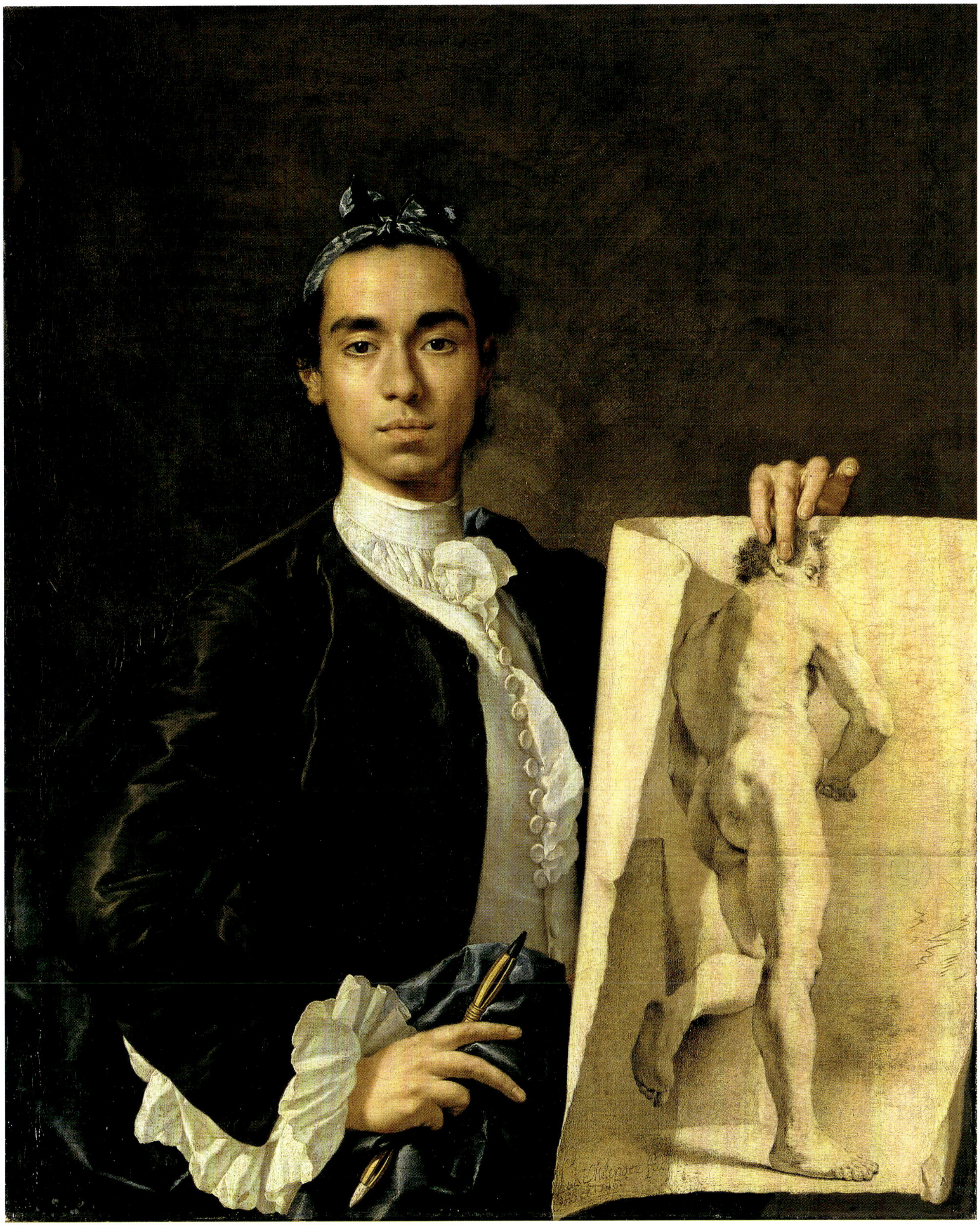

CAT. 55. Antón Rafael Mengs. *Self Portrait*, 1774.
Madrid, Fundación Casa de Alba

CAT. 56. Luis Meléndez. *Self Portrait*, 1746.
Paris, Musée du Louvre. Bequest of Paul Cosson, 1926 [R.F. 2537]

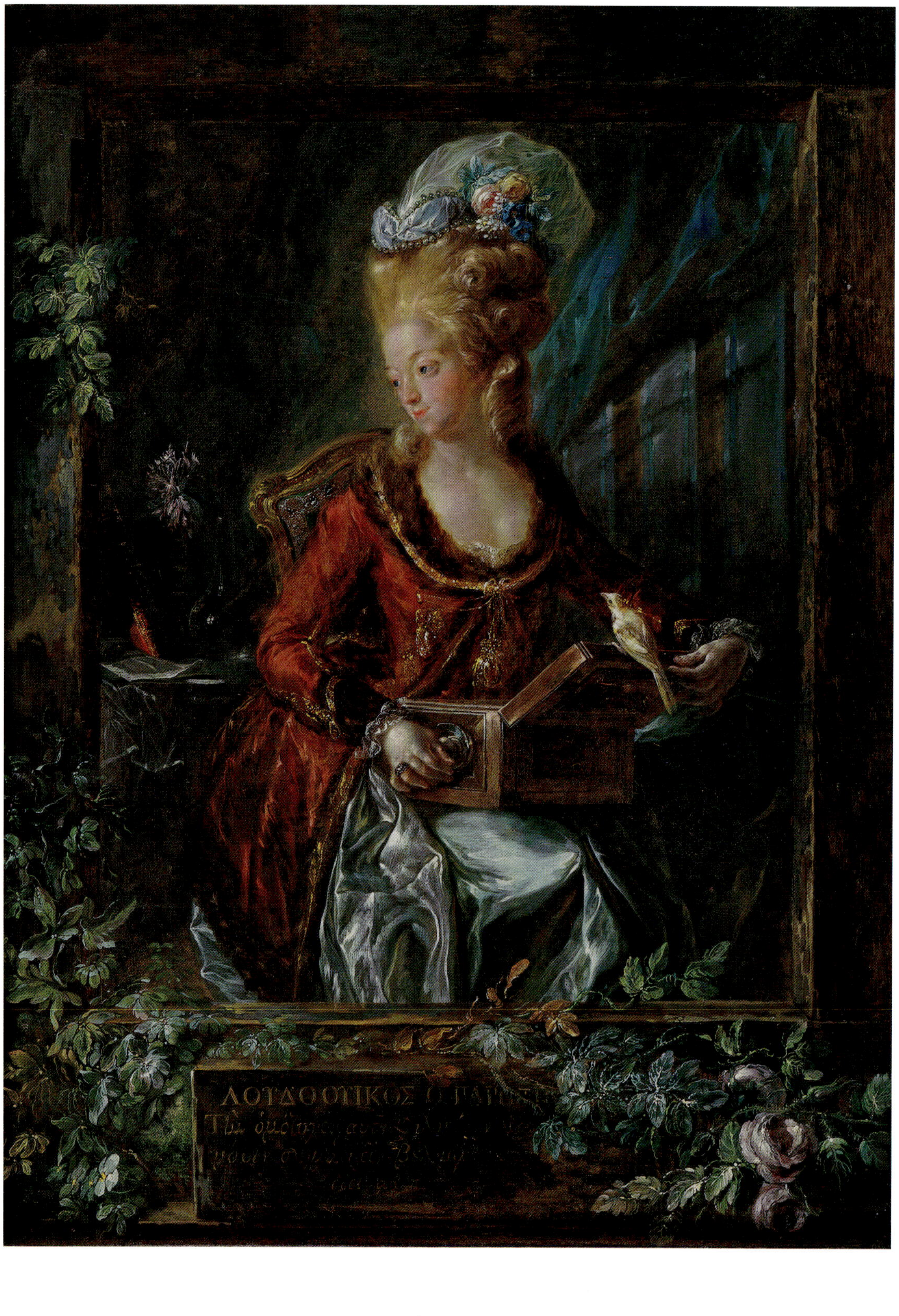

CAT. 57. Luis Paret. *María de las Nieves Micaela Fourdinier, Wife of the Painter, ca.* 1780. Museo del Prado [P-3250]

CAT. 58. Luis Paret. *Self Portrait*, 1786. Museo del Prado [P-7701]

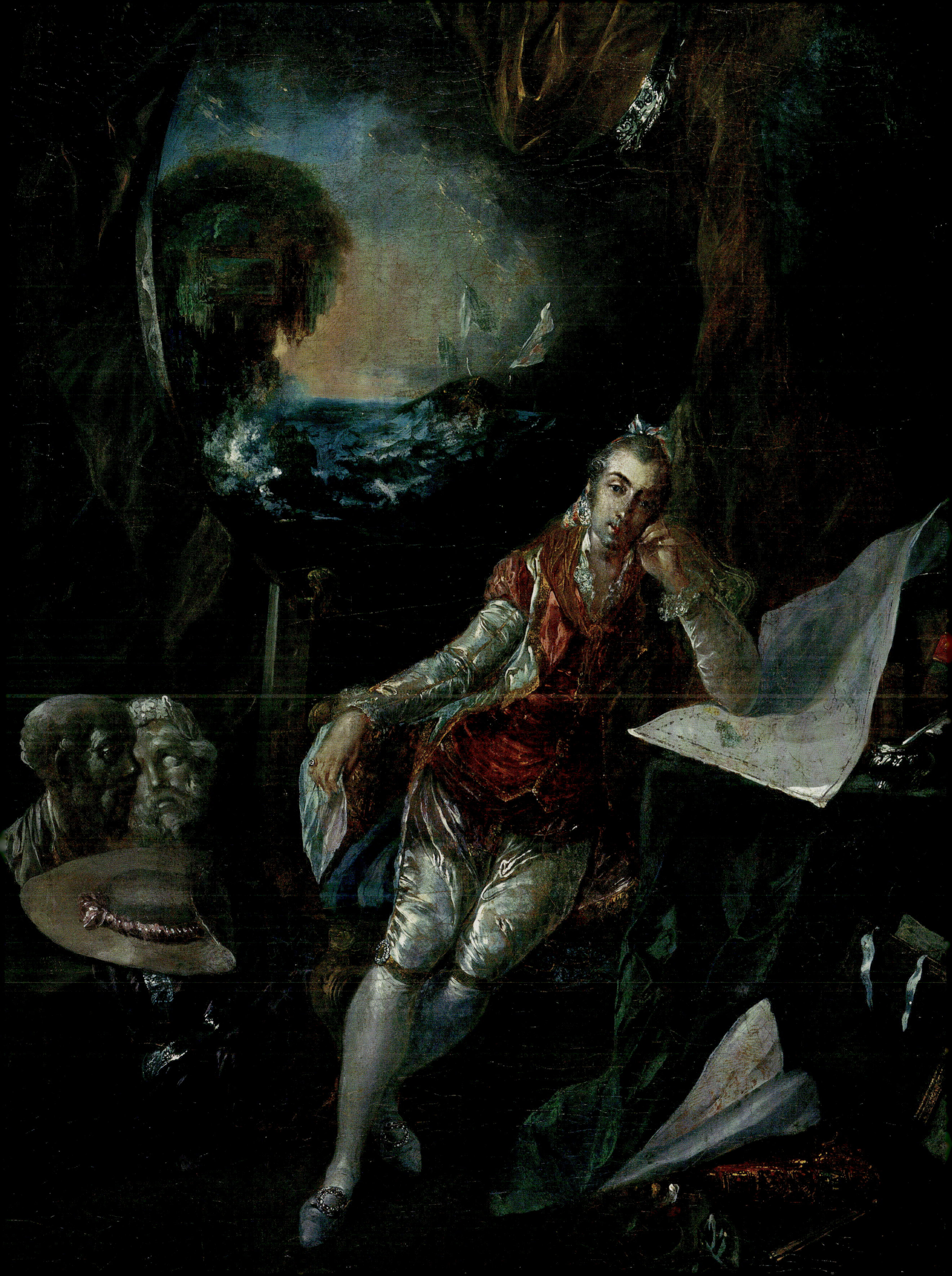

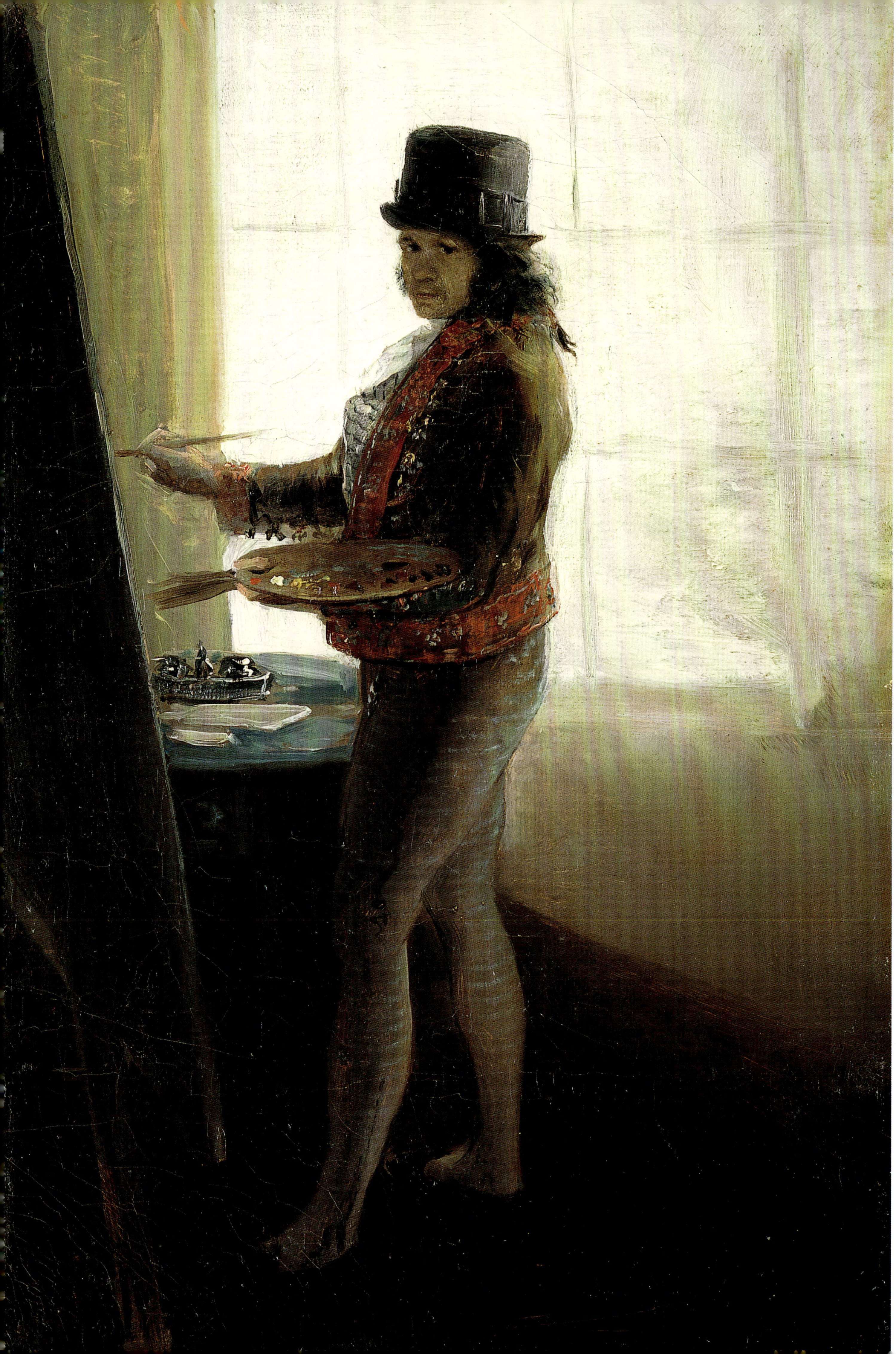

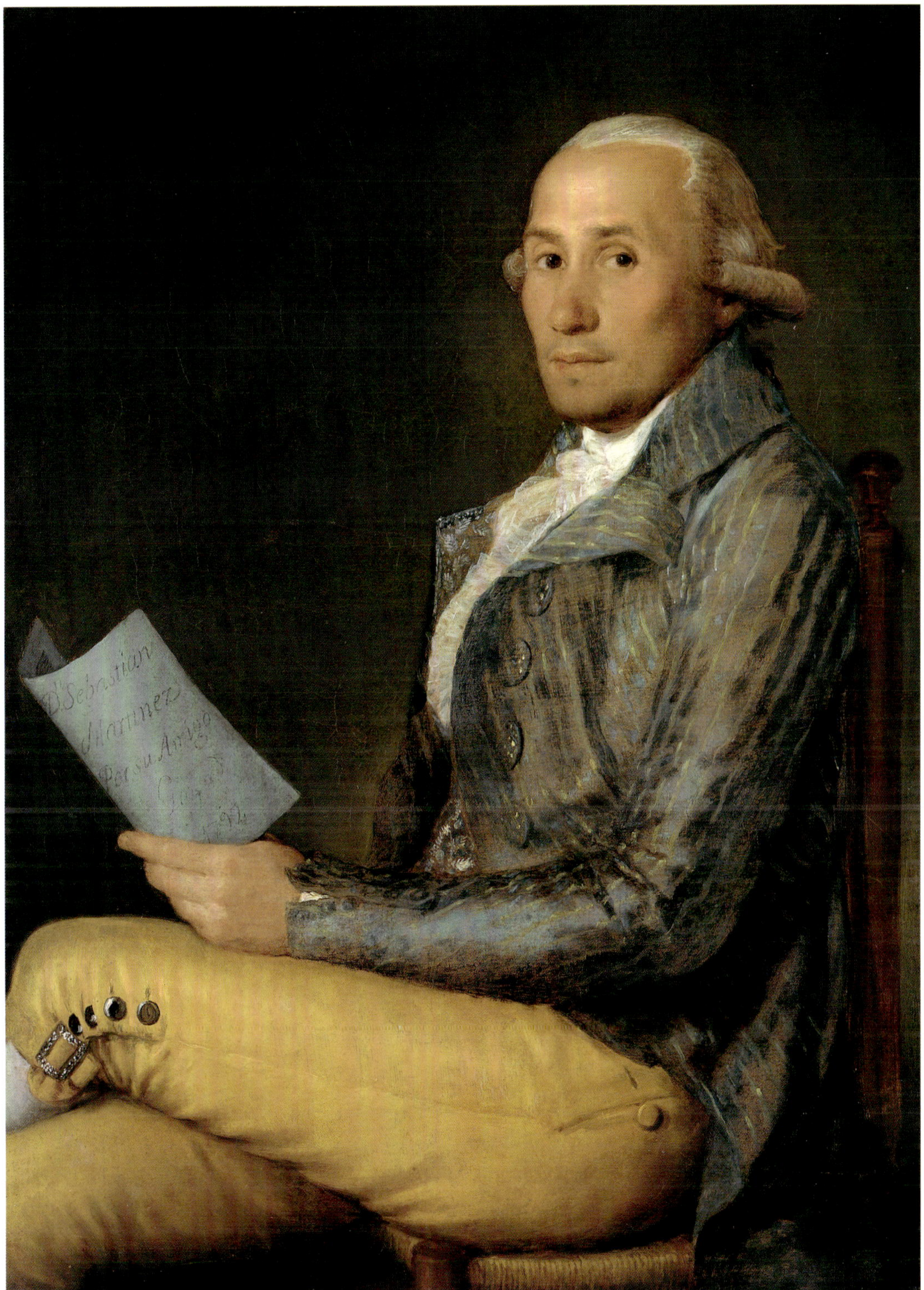

CAT. 59. Francisco de Goya.
Self Portrait while Painting, 1799.
Madrid, Museo de la Real Academia
de Bellas Artes de San Fernando

CAT. 60. Francisco de Goya.
Sebastián Martínez, 1792. New York,
The Metropolitan Museum of Art,
Rogers Fund, 1906 [06.289]

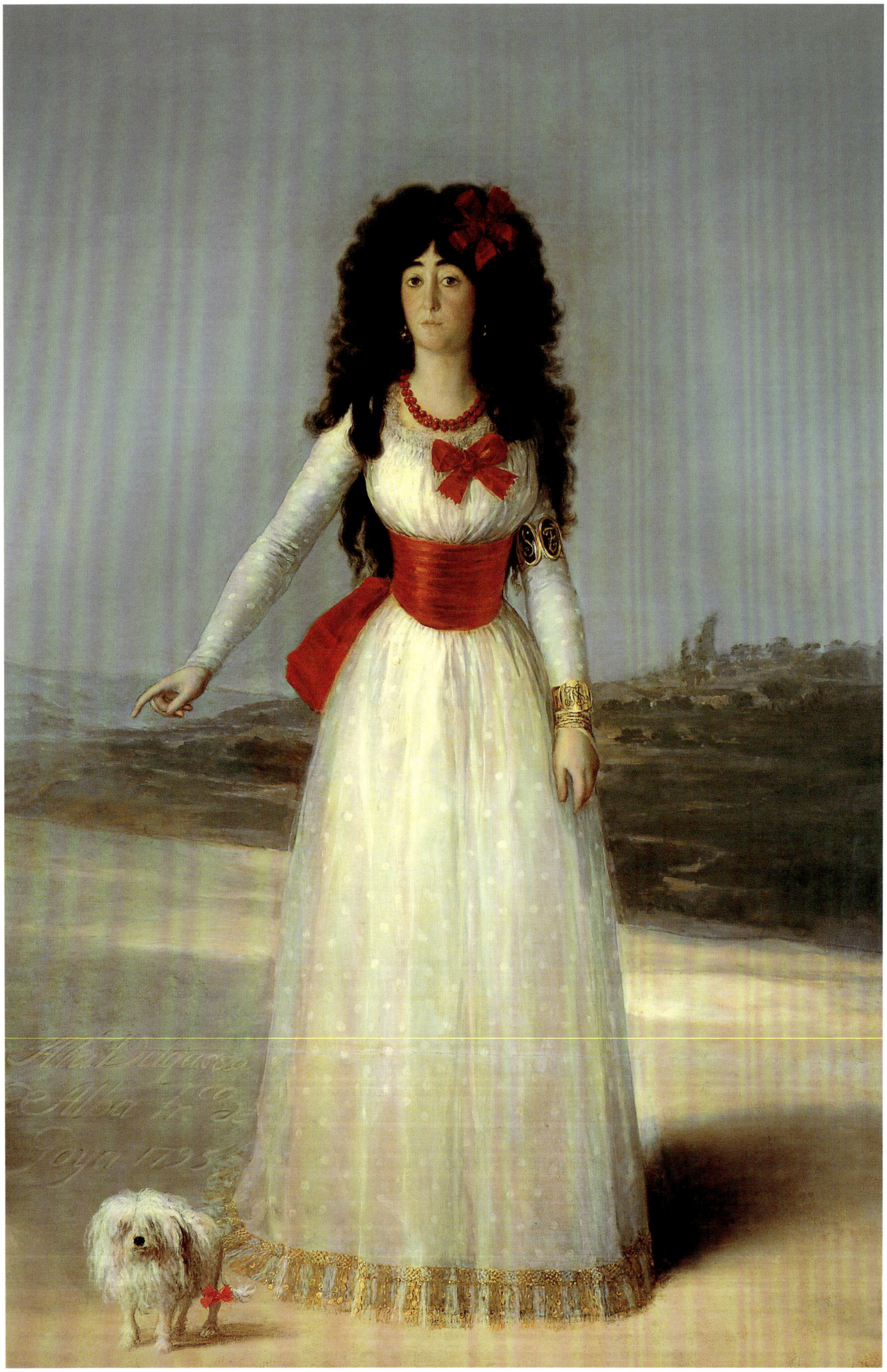

CAT. 61. Francisco de Goya. *The Duchess of Alba*, 1795. Madrid, Fundación Casa de Alba

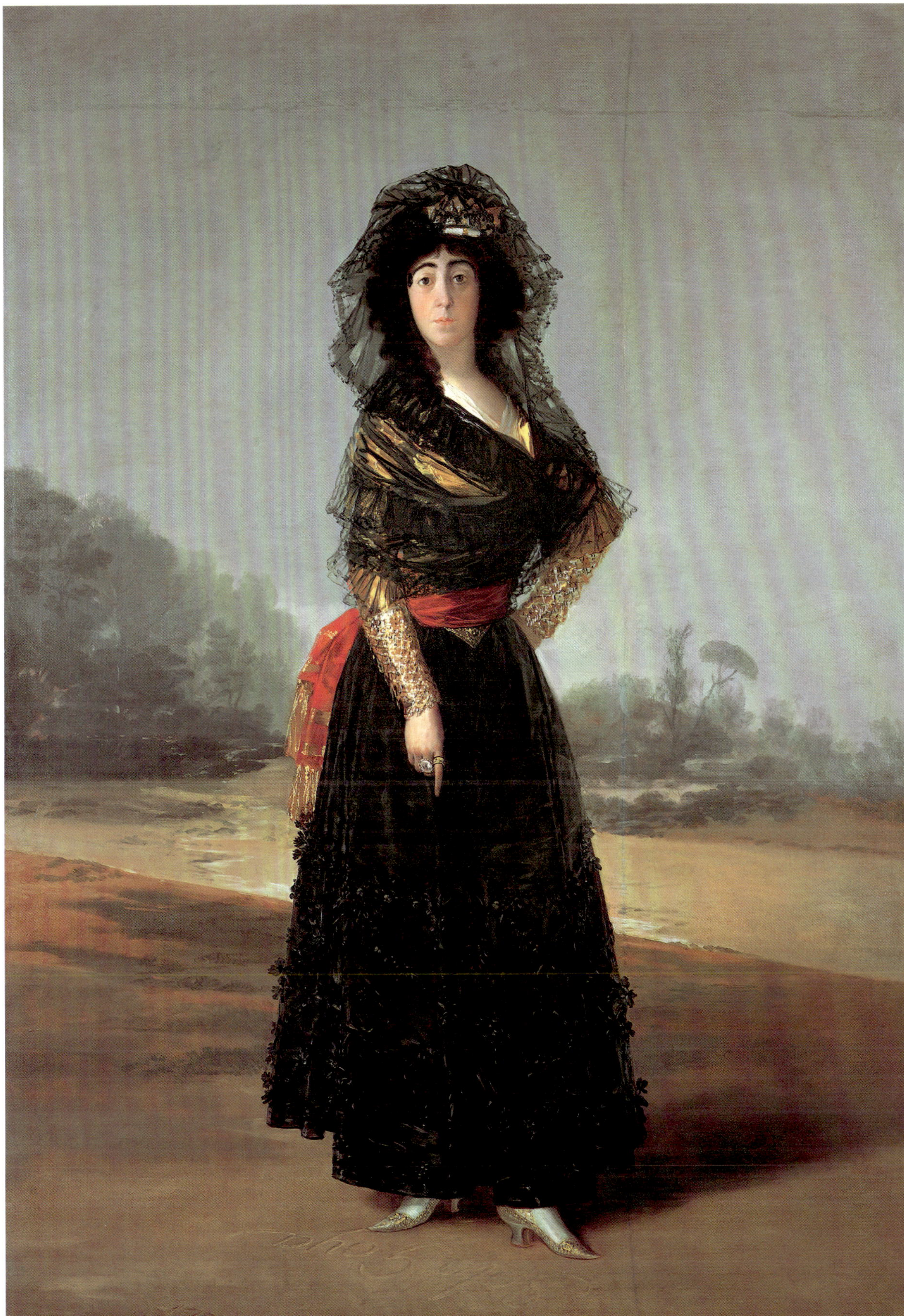

CAT. 62. Francisco de Goya. *The Duchess of Alba*, 1797. New York, The Hispanic Society of America [A 102]

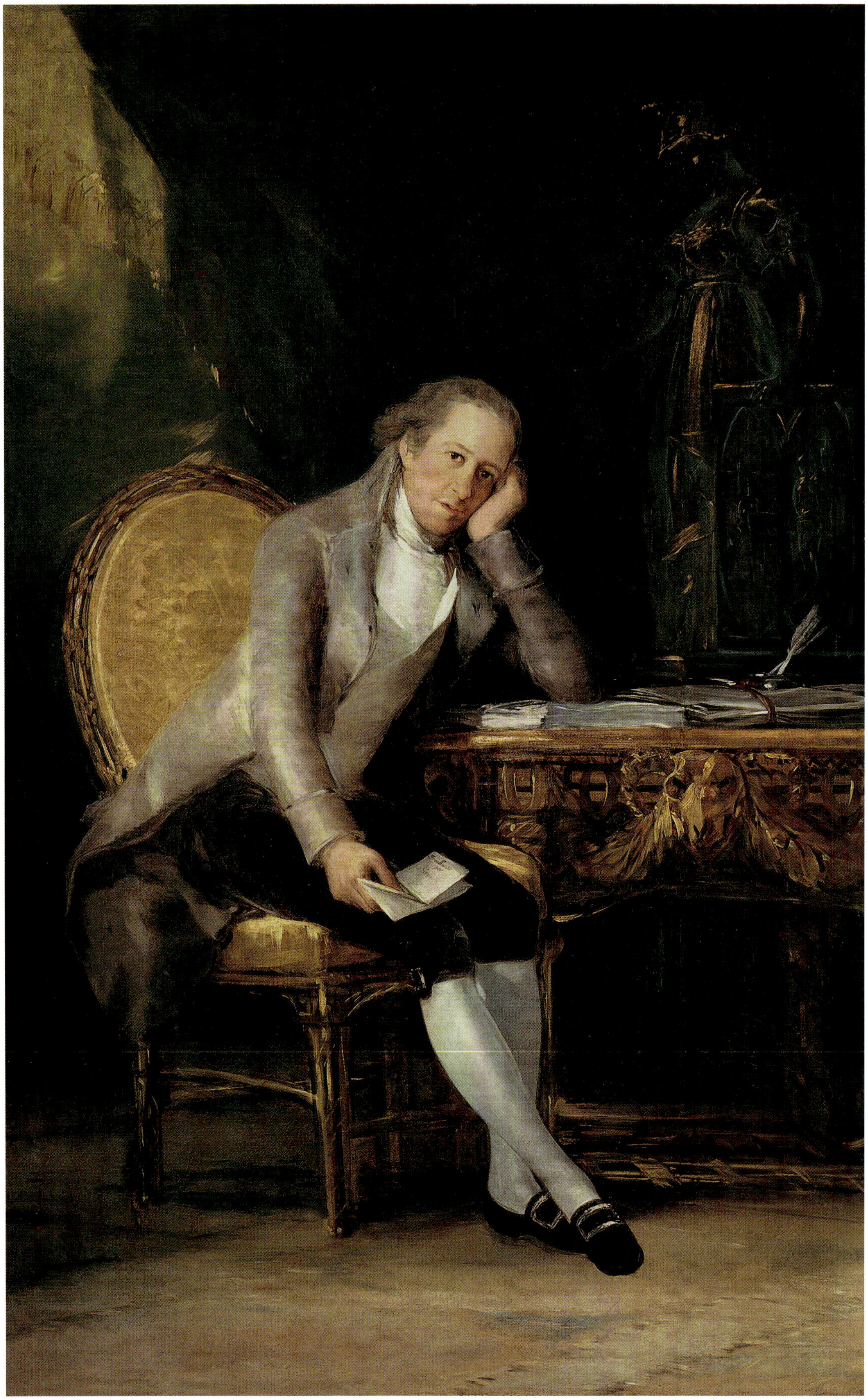

CAT. 63. Francisco de Goya. *Don Gaspar Melchor de Jovellanos*, 1798. Museo del Prado [P-3236]

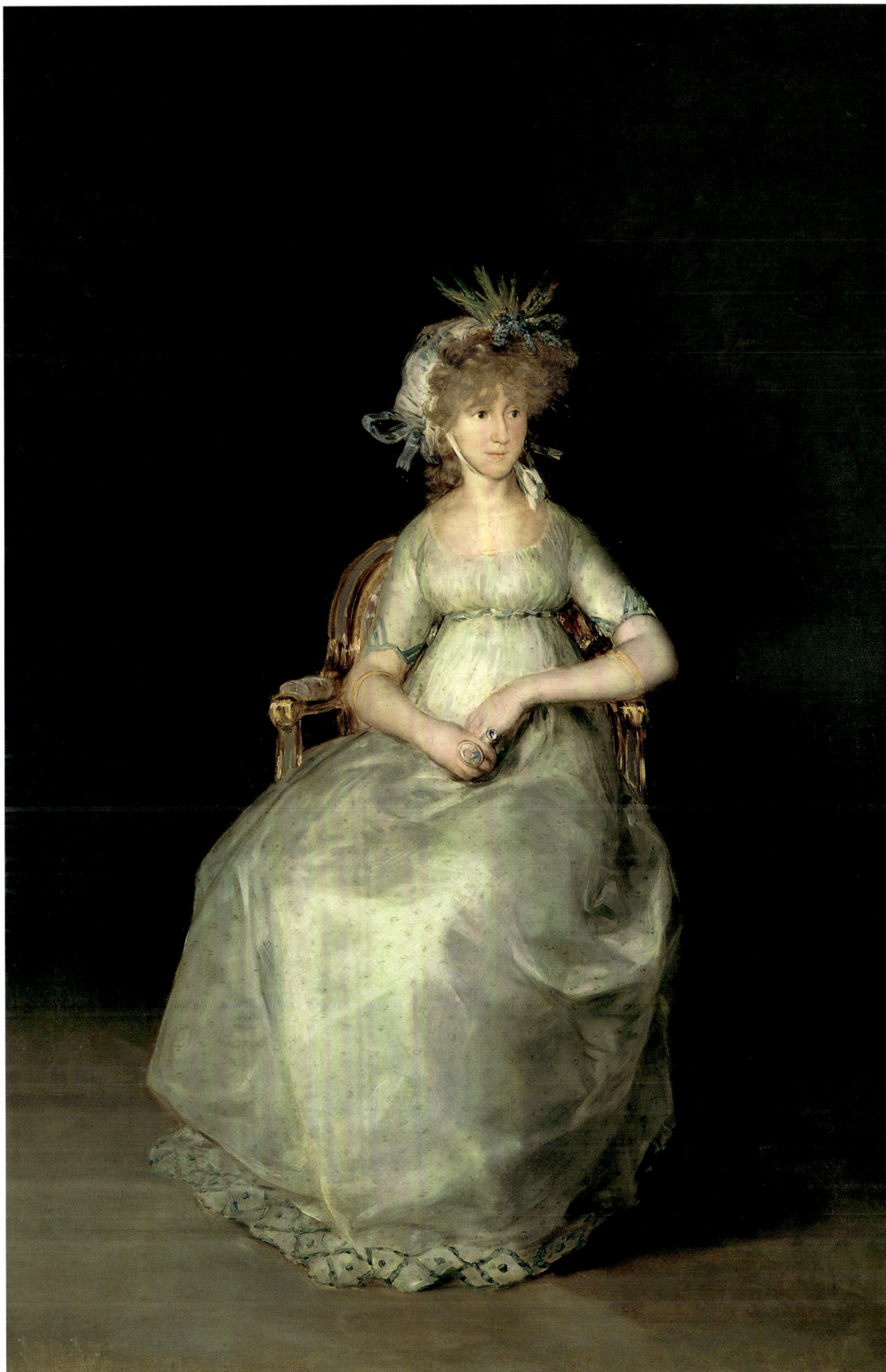

CAT. 64. Francisco de Goya. *The Condesa de Chinchón*, 1800. Museo del Prado [P-7767]

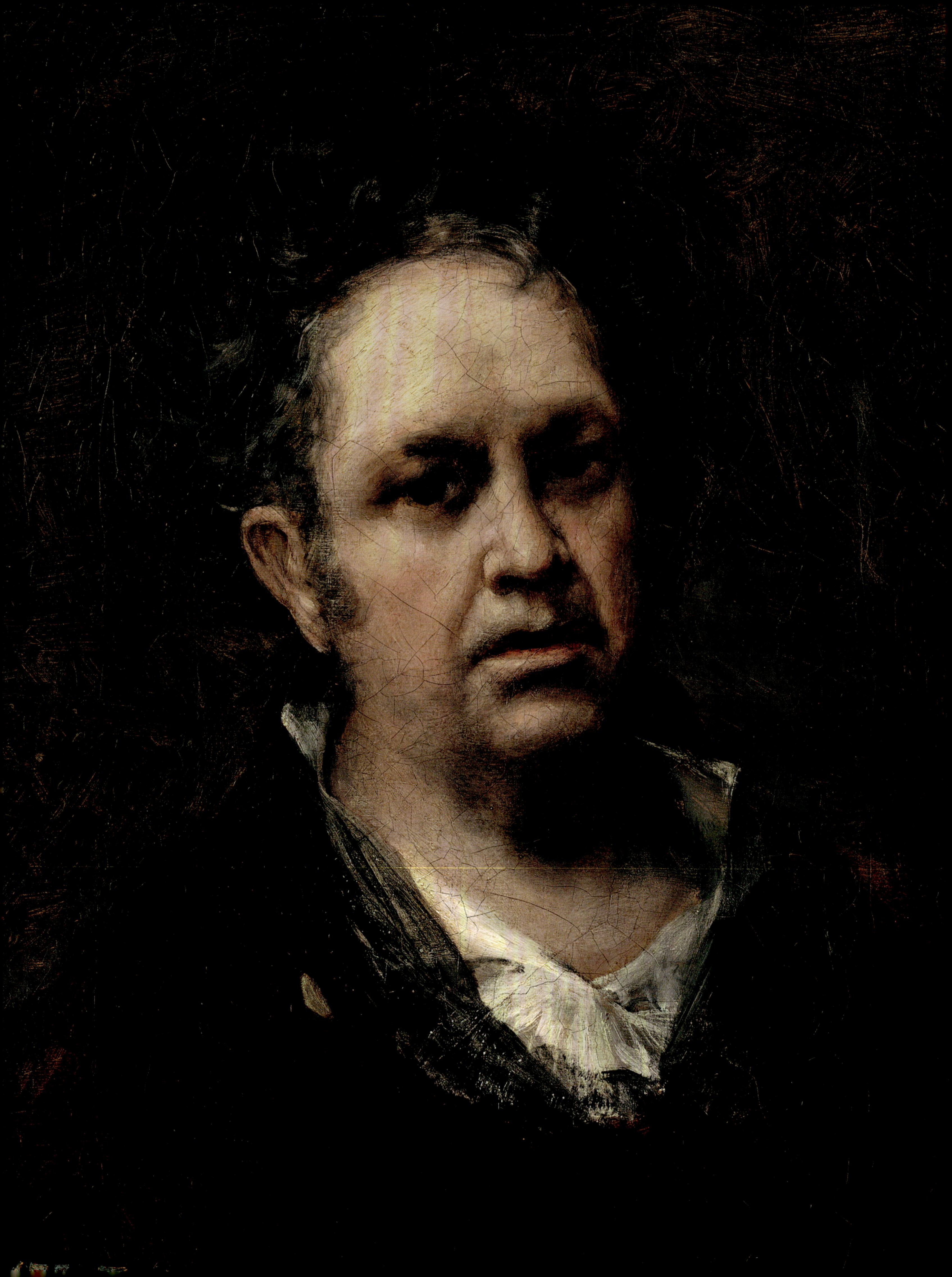

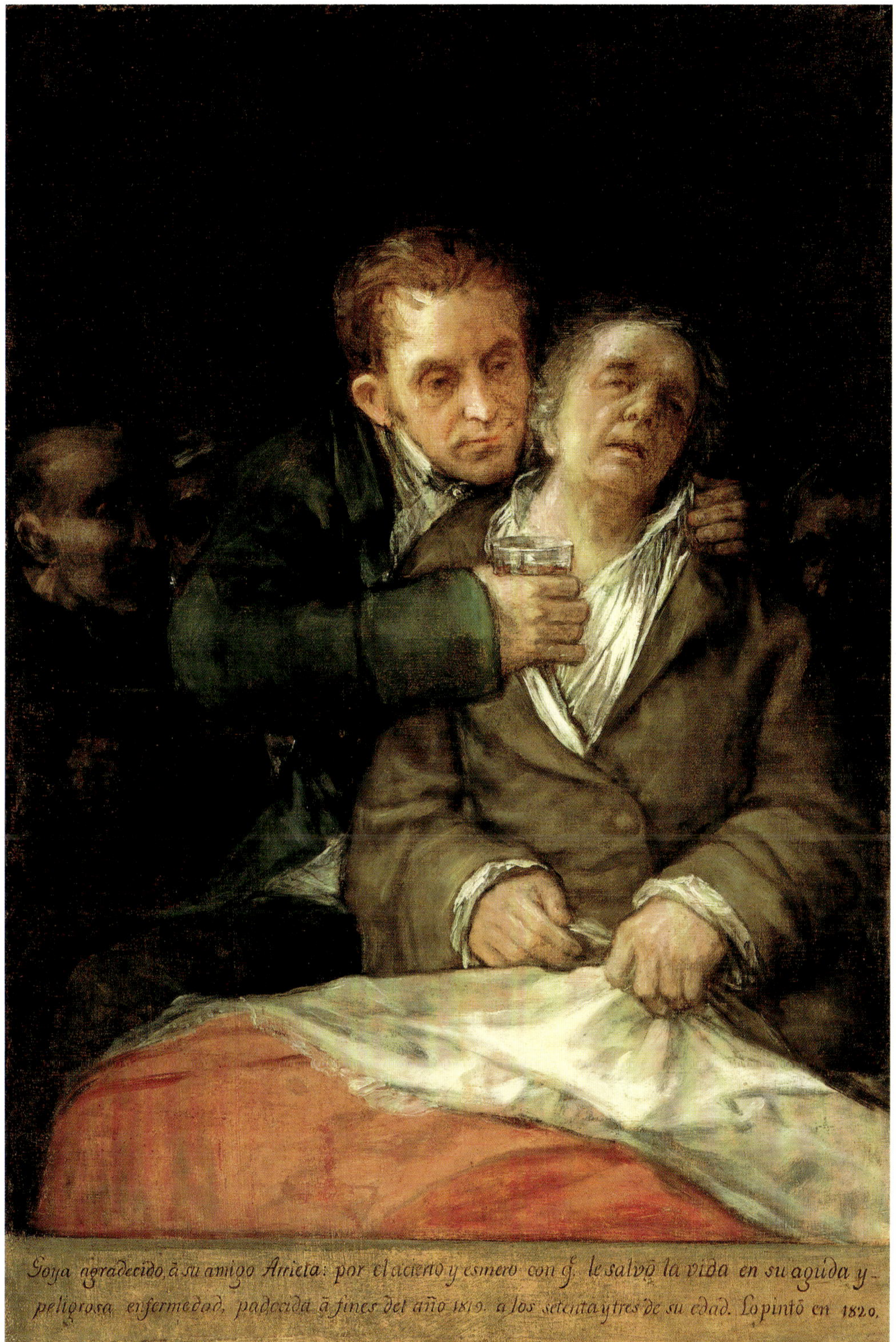

CAT. 65. Francisco de Goya. *Self Portrait, ca.* 1816. Museo del Prado [P-723]

CAT. 66. Francisco de Goya. *Self Portrait with Doctor Arrieta*, 1820. Minneapolis, The Minneapolis Institute of Arts, the Ethel Morrison van Derlip Fund [5214]

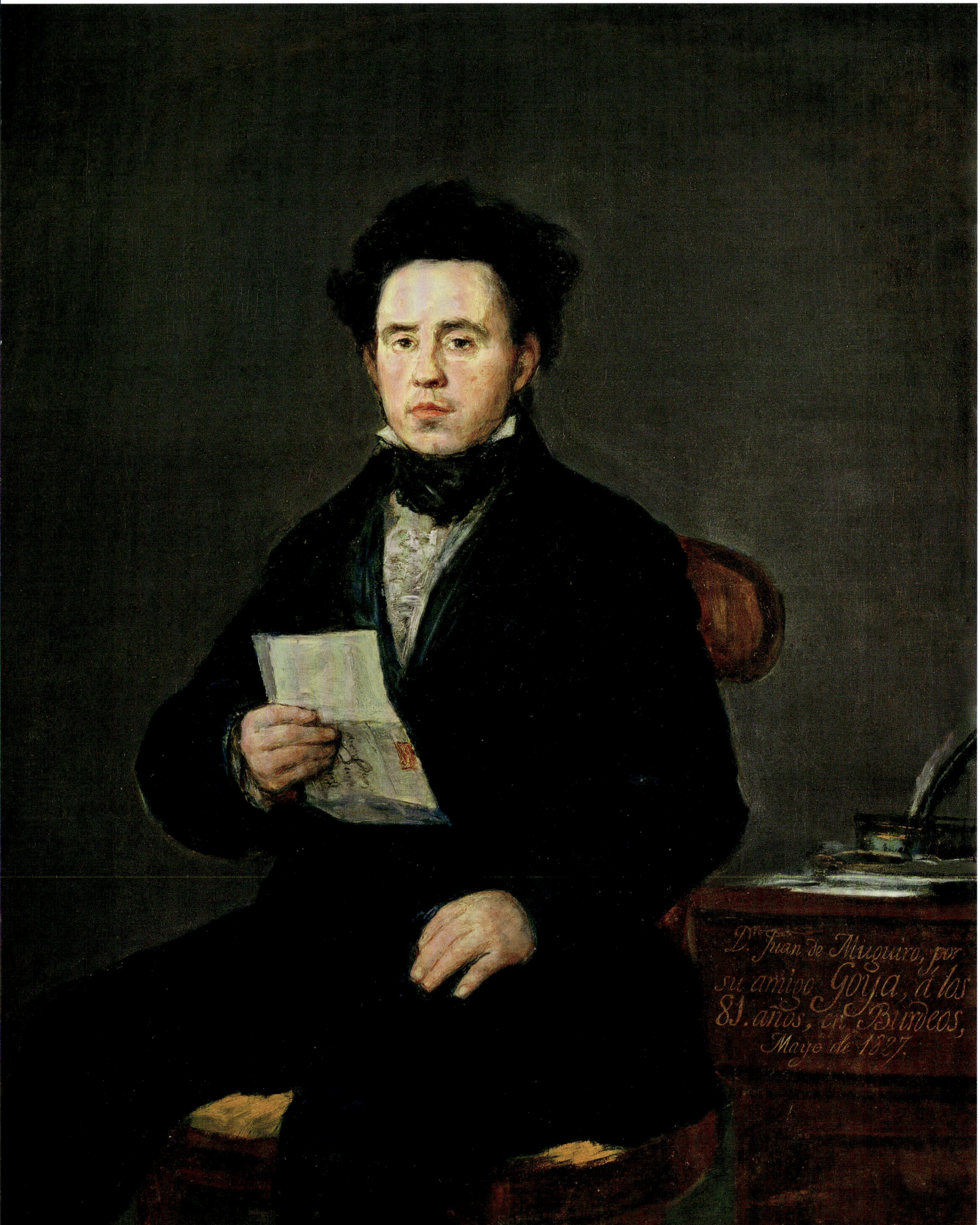
Dn. Juan de Muguiro, por
su amigo Goya, á los
81. años, en Burdeos,
Mayo de 1827.

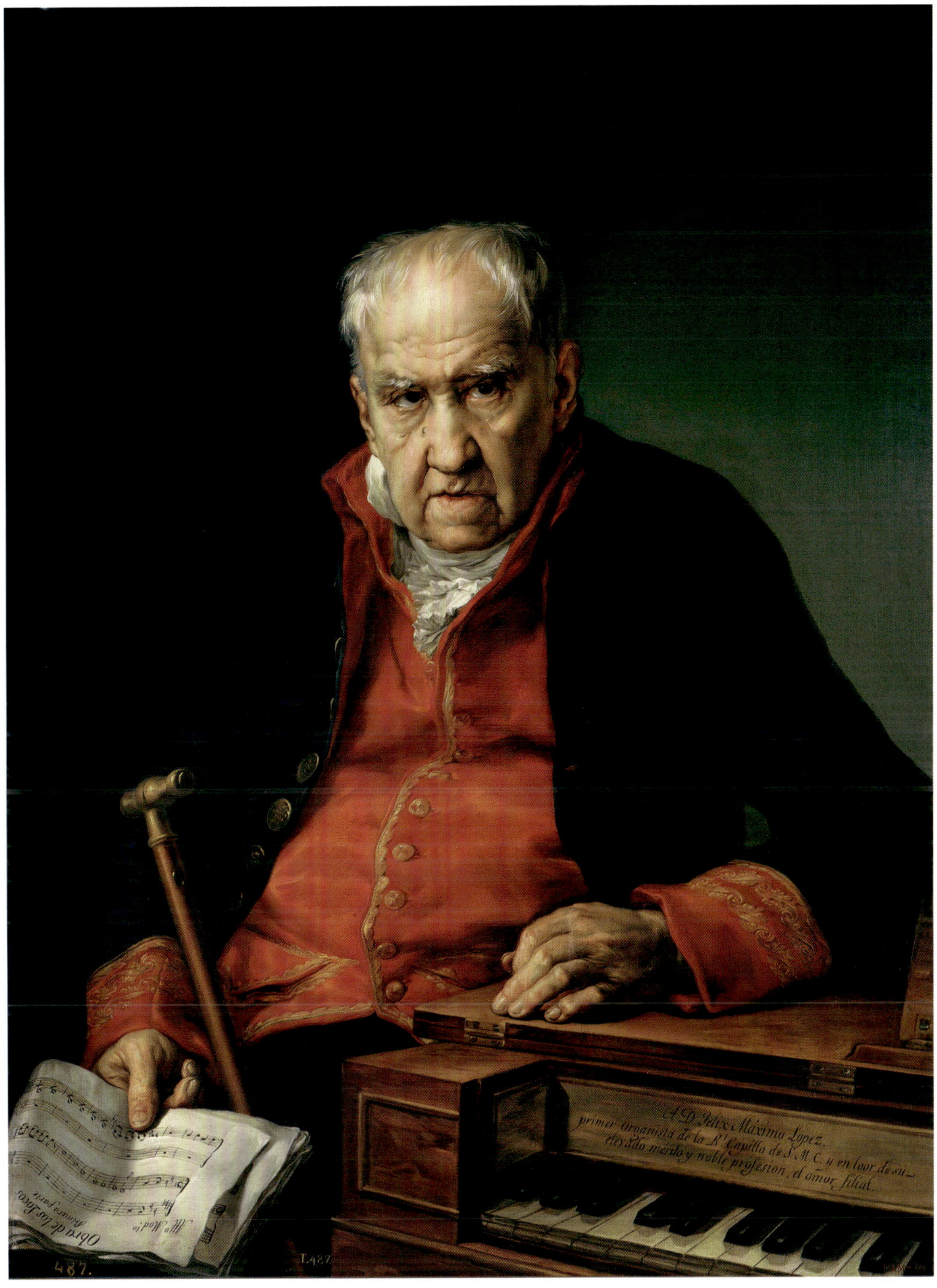

CAT. 67. Francisco de Goya.
Juan de Muguiro, 1827.
Museo del Prado [P-2898]

CAT. 68. Vicente López.
Félix Antonio Máximo López, 1820.
Museo del Prado [P-4405]

8

The Spanish Portrait in the Nineteenth Century

THE TRIUMPH OF A GENRE

José Luis Díez

In the nineteenth century the portrait became the leading genre in Spanish painting, as it did in the rest of Europe. This was a result of changes in the structure of western society. Portraits embodied the changing tastes and perceptions of a new clientele that emerged from the nobility and wealthy upper middle classes and became increasingly powerful in this period, during which the foundations of the modern world were laid.[1]

Official academic circles preferred other artistic genres such as history painting, which was considered more intellectually demanding and was based on solid academic foundations, while collectors favoured genre scenes, still lifes or landscape paintings for the decoration of their homes. But the portrait enjoyed enormous popularity in the private sphere. This reflected the importance of the individual in the new wealthy society of the day and the need for images of its prominent figures which could be enjoyed in the warmth and intimacy of a study or drawing room.

In order to fully understand the precise nature, purpose and value of the various kinds of portraiture that developed in the nineteenth century, several social and artistic considerations should be borne in mind. These help to explain the characteristics of the most common typologies of a period in which portraiture reached its greatest splendour.

Simply to be able to commission a portrait was in itself a sign of social prestige. But this prestige increased in accordance with the artist's repute, since his renown could add a touch of ostentation, and sometimes even influenced the location and size of the signature on the canvas. The portrait demonstrated the sitter's prominent social status and preserved his or her appearance for posterity, just as photography did when it became popular in the final decades of the century.

With a few exceptions, the appearance and nature of a portrait reflected the intentions of the client who commissioned and paid for it, rather than those of the artist who painted it. This led to important commissions of undeniable artistic worth being abandoned in the studios of the century's great portrait painters, merely because the sitter's wishes had not been clearly reflected in the final result. Thus the arrangement and setting, the degree of showiness, the pose of sitters and the accumulation of decorative elements alluding to their identity were all chosen personally by clients who wanted to immortalise themselves precisely as *they* wished to be seen or remembered by others.

Alongside the finest portrait painters of nineteenth-century Spain, who were highly skilled in deploying the complex pictorial resources of the genre, stood a legion of other painters varying considerably in status and ability. Even if more inclined towards other, less profitable genres, they painted portraits because it gave them a guaranteed source of income. Almost always, they carried out their trade in the wake of the successive fashions introduced by the great masters of the genre.

As in any profession with a commercial component, the most highly reputed painters fixed their rates in accordance with the type of portrait the client wanted.[2] Hence female portraits were more expensive than male ones, since they contained more decorative gowns and jewels and more elaborate settings. Full-length portraits were the most costly, followed by half-length pictures. These were even more expensive if the hands were to be shown, because hands were particularly hard to paint. This apparently trivial circumstance led the best portrait painters to flaunt their prowess by making expressive use of the hands, either by projecting them into the foreground to establish a relationship with the spectator, thereby increasing the complexity of the foreshortening, or by investing them with a studied languor to heighten the sitter's elegance. Bust portraits were the least expensive and from these there developed a format known as 'Poussin size', which was one-third life-size and thus partway between a full-size picture and a miniature. This was popular because it was relatively inexpensive and easy to carry.

Nineteenth-century Spanish portraiture was strongly influenced by the social mores of the time, associated with which was an acute sensitivity and a reluctance, bound up with the essence of the Spanish character, to show off in public. This greatly conditioned the way in which sitters decided how others should see them. Modesty of dress and a certain reserve in expressing affection or exposing oneself to public scrutiny left their mark on Spanish etiquette as well as on portrait painting. The concept of 'privacy' profoundly marked the cultural habits of the new society, which allowed spontaneity of gesture and informality of dress only in the most intimate circles. One eloquent testimony to this modesty is the fact that when portraits were shown in public exhibitions, the sitter's identity was usually omitted or specified only by initials.[3]

The defining elements of the nineteenth-century portrait are its overall composition, the choice of setting, the model's bearing and attire, and accompanying objects. A special emphasis was placed on intensity of gaze and facial expression and on the gestural language of the hands. Knowing how to combine all these elements harmoniously, while ensuring that the sitter's likeness was accurately conveyed, was the prime key to success for the great masters of the genre. Such painters gained their clientele through their personal manner of interpreting appearance, responding to clients' desire for honesty while at the same time extolling their social and economic position, or investing them with an air of natural intimacy appropriate to the location for which the portrait was destined.

The new concepts and typologies within the genre reflected the important role of the portrait in the new society, recording the images of prominent figures of the day as they wanted to be seen by posterity. The social reality of nineteenth-century Spain is contained in the genre, and careful historical analysis is required in order to understand it in all its complexity. But even a brief survey of the achievements of the greatest Spanish painters allows a sufficiently broad overview of the portrait's development to understand its significance for the new civil society of the period.

* * *

In Spain, changes in social and artistic habits arrived later than elsewhere. The structures of the *ancien régime* lingered on in the early years of the century during the reign of Ferdinand VII, at which time portrait painting was essentially restricted to the court and the great noble families. He returned to the throne in 1814, after his exile in Valençay during the War of Independence, when he became known as Ferdinand 'El Deseado', the desired. This date marks the real turn of the century in Spain, politically, socially and artistically. The country's economic and cultural reconstruction after the war of liberation was carried out under an absolutist political regime which restored the ideological and social archetypes inherited by the king from his father, Charles IV, and with them the artistic styles rooted in eighteenth-century tradition.

That said, the reign of Ferdinand VII is certainly one of the most interesting artistic periods in nineteenth-century Spain, though it remains little known. It saw the harmonious coexistence of a conflicting and apparently incompatible diversity of styles and aesthetic languages, which mirrored the profound ideological confrontations of Spanish society at this time. An objective historical assessment of the reign, free from inherited prejudice, is long overdue.

The academic Baroque style of the late eighteenth century survived with full recognition under the protection of Ferdinand's court. However, at the same time the Neoclassical avant-garde – imported from France by young artists who had travelled there with pensions from the Crown – was readily absorbed, its tenets incorporated into official teaching and assimilated very quickly even by artists who had never left Spain. The towering figure of Goya, who was a colleague of most of these artists and a friend to some of them, was a respectful witness of the artistic reality of this period, in which his own genius was forged.

Although Goya is dealt with elsewhere in this catalogue, it should be remembered that his work covers no fewer than twenty-eight years of the nineteenth century, in the course of which he far exceeded the innovations of the Romantic portrait, paving the way for its modern manifestation.

A superb example is the portrait of *Juan de Muguiro* [CAT. 67] – a synthesis of blacks, greys and whites painted by the elderly Goya for his friend, 'at the age of 81 years in Bordeaux', just a few months before his death. The powerful presence of the young banker, the black outline of his attire silhouetted against an undefined and undecorated background, the powerful broad-browed face, framed in curls, and the intense, serene and firm gaze anticipate a kind of painting that would not take hold in Spain for another fifty years. Drawing on El Greco's figures in black against a grey background (later reinvented by Velázquez), Goya employed all his accumulated knowledge and experience with an almost feverish insistence to produce the astounding richness of shades we see in this portrait.

Several months after Ferdinand VII returned to Madrid from his exile in Valençay, understandably dissatisfied with the none-too-flattering official portraits painted by the elderly Goya[4] he summoned the painter Vicente López Portaña (1772–1850), whom he had met again in Valencia whilst returning to the capital. López was the absolute antithesis of Goya, of whom he was nevertheless a respectful friend.[5] In 1815 he was appointed first court painter. His exceptional draughtsmanship and observational skills, coupled with a Valencian feeling for intense colour and an instinct for the quality of cloth, jewellery and medals, immediately made him the Court's foremost portraitist.

Vicente López started out as a portrait painter during his first visit to Madrid as a student. On returning to Valencia, he experimented with the stylistic innovations of the acclaimed portrait artists he had met in the capital, in a highly diverse and eclectic expressive language. López had been dazzled by the great court masters such as Maella, and also by Goya, both at the peak of their careers. He attempted to emulate them in his portrait *The Engraver Pedro Pascual Moles*,[6] one of his early attempts in the genre, painted in around 1796. Unable to indulge in Goya's brilliantly incisive displays, López made the most of his exceptional talent for implacable realism. He brought his subjects vibrantly to life, expressing their character traits with absolute sincerity and without the slightest hint of rococo idealisation. While remaining true to his upbringing in the orthodox academic teachings of the late eighteenth century, and particularly influenced by court portraitists such as Mengs and Pompeo Batoni, López skilfully incorporated the Valencian naturalism of Ribera and, more especially, Ribalta, whose works the king commissioned him to copy. This intense realism was the key to his success, and he exploited his unique technical faculties to the full.

His profound empathy for the great masters of the Valencian Baroque underlies his moving portrait of the organist at the royal chapel, Félix Antonio Máximo López [CAT. 68]. The old, worn and shy face, the watery eyes and the hand on the spinet are all strikingly expressive, and the subject appears jaded but alive, like Ribera's saints. Painted in 1820, at the height of López's career, this is a splendid example of the style he cultivated in his professional portraits for Ferdinand VII's most distinguished courtiers.

One of these was a portrait that made him world-famous: *The Painter Francisco de Goya* [FIG. 112].[7] Like the portrait of the organist [CAT. 68], it depicts the elderly and deaf artist with the tools of his trade, and it displays the same sincerity in capturing his face and character. Surprisingly, this much discussed and reproduced painting shows Goya as a perfect gentleman, in a manner diametrically opposed to the customary dishevelled images of him with his shirt unbuttoned. But such formal dress is in keeping with the specific purpose of the portrait, which was painted for the Contemporary Artists' Gallery of the Prado. It was intended to be seen alongside the work of the great masters of the past, immortalising the likeness of a living painter but simultaneously lending him the air of a timeless icon.

Vicente López's style of portraiture remained unchanged throughout his long life, until the new spirit of romanticism became established during the reign of Isabel II. His efforts at working in the new style produced such excellent paintings as *The Condesa Viuda de Calderón* [CAT. 69], but he was barely able to hold his own as the last bastion of the old academic tradition, the sole exponent of an aesthetic language that would die with him.

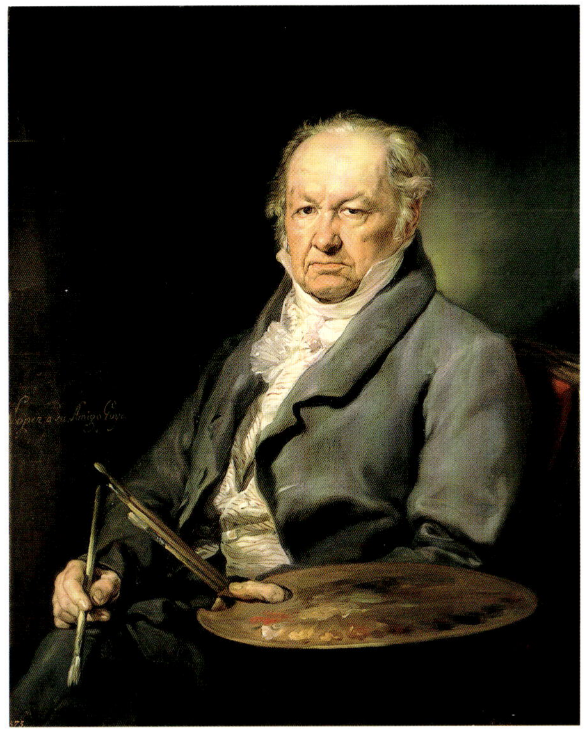

FIG. 112. Vicente López, *The Painter Francisco de Goya*, 1826. Madrid, Museo del Prado [P-864]

* * *

The tradition of academic teachings inherited from Mengs's time substantially influenced the training of Spanish artists in the early nineteenth century. A small number of enterprising young painters who enjoyed the patronage of Charles IV travelled to France to study in the studio of Jacques-Louis David. Here they were able to absorb the new aesthetic ideals of the Neoclassical avant-garde, which was spreading from Paris throughout Europe.[8] They continued to Rome for the second stage in their training, and steeped themselves in the classical antiquity that was being rediscovered in the new artistic order of Napoleonic Europe. Pure Neoclassicism was largely foreign to the considerable number of Spanish painters who displayed middling technical skills and were weighed down by tradition, though many of them adopted its superficial forms.

However, the group studied the literature, monuments and statues of ancient Rome and provided some of the most refined examples of Spanish portraiture of the time. They included Juan Antonio de Ribera (1779–1860),[9] who worked under the patronage of the elderly Charles IV during the latter's exile in Rome. Although very few portraits have been attributed to him with certainty, his depiction of the sculptor José Álvarez Cubero[10] is one of the finest artist's portraits of its time. Ribera portrayed his fellow student and friend in a classical style, wrapped in a Roman patrician's cloak, his bearing powerful and almost arrogant. He gazes at the spectator, the book in his hand a sign of erudition, and points to a clay model of his best-known sculpture, *The Defence of Zaragoza*, made in Rome and now at the Prado.[11] The model's physical solidity and the intensity of his almost heroic presence recall the finest examples of French Neoclassical portraiture.

Ribera's life was to parallel that of his friend, fellow student and, over the years, overt rival José de Madrazo (1781–1859).[12] The latter, fully aware of being a less gifted painter, used his social skills to outdo those of his fellow artists receiving royal patronage, paving the way for the most influential family saga in nineteenth-century Spain. During this period of Roman influence, in 1812 José de Madrazo painted an intriguing picture

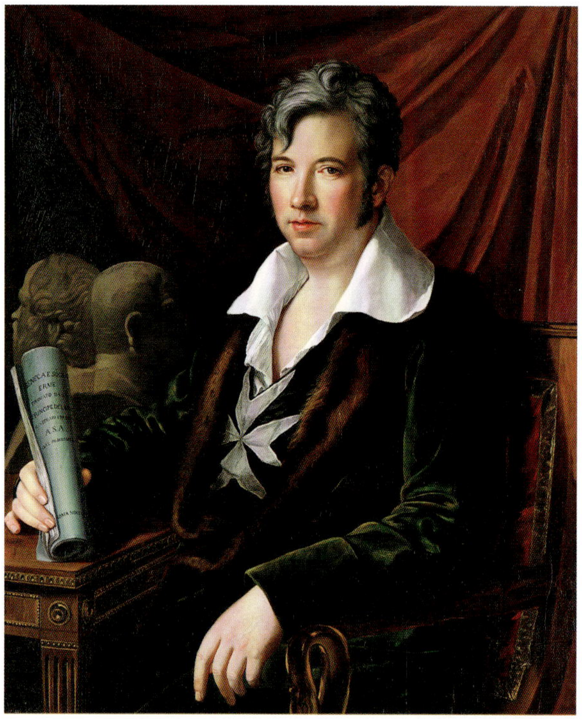

FIG. 113. José de Madrazo, *Manuel Godoy*, 1812. Madrid, private collection

of *Manuel Godoy* [FIG. 113],[13] undoubtedly the most refined portrait of his prolific career, yet unknown until a few years ago. This once all-powerful member of the Spanish court[14] was subsequently exiled to Italy, like the king whom he had served. It was he who inaugurated the portrait of the cultured ruler in nineteenth-century Spanish painting, renouncing the pomp and ceremony of the uniforms and medals used in official portraits and instead reflecting on the subject's enjoyment of intellectual pursuits.

Godoy was also known as 'Prince of the Peace', but his declining role in the history of Spanish politics is eloquently brought out by Madrazo in this canvas. The royal favourite poses in domestic attire, his greying hair dishevelled, in a portrait clearly intended for private contemplation. He holds the brief treatise describing his role in the discovery of the classical herm shown beside him, which had been found in the grounds of his property in Rome; the text reveals a surprising intellectual side to the man, which contrasts with his more established image as a politician. Madrazo's exquisite technique – the texture of the clothes, the flesh tints and hair, the elegant composition and unusual iconography – represents Spanish Neoclassical painting at its finest.

José de Madrazo's immersion in classical antiquity during his years in Rome also gave rise to a curious example of allegorical portraiture, which was highly unusual in Spanish painting at that time. We see it elsewhere in portraits by Goya, such as *The Marquesa de Santa Cruz* and *The Duquesa de Abrantes*.[15] Madrazo never painted such works on commission; they were intended for the intimacy of his own home. His audacious *Allegory of the Five Senses*[16] depicts his wife, Isabel Kuntz, as a great Roman matron, surrounded by her children presented in the form of naked cupids, symbolising the senses.

* * *

Except in the case of the few privileged young artists who had the good fortune to become familiar with French Neoclassical official art at first hand, the academic study of antique models was an essential part of any Spanish artist's training. As a result, the most formal aesthetic aspects of the new Neoclassical portraiture, although not entirely to Spanish tastes, were adopted by some of the most interesting specialists in the genre, even though they had never left Spain.

Zacarías González Velázquez (1763–1834), for instance, had been brought up in the eighteenth-century academic tradition but moved towards a more serene and pure classicism of extraordinary technical precision. The very finest example of this is his exquisite portrait of *Manolita González Velázquez playing the Piano* [FIG. 114],[17] the greatest of all his portraits. The elegant composition, clearly defined draughtsmanship and skill in moulding flesh tints and sculpting folds, highlighted by the glossy surface, is the very essence of academic classicism, emphasised by the little girl's attire and the crown of flowers adorning her hair.

The young sitter's solemn lack of expression, with her big eyes and still, timeless pose, is a distinguishing feature of Spanish child portraiture throughout most of the century. Instead of the naturally restless spontaneity associated with children, they tend to display the distant seriousness of adults grown up before their time. This is often the result of the painter being unable to capture their vitality, but it also reflects the behaviour expected of children at the time, with spontaneous public manifestations of affection being frowned upon. Girls are often shown playing music, as a counterpoint to the hunting scenes and uniforms frequently used in portraits of boys.

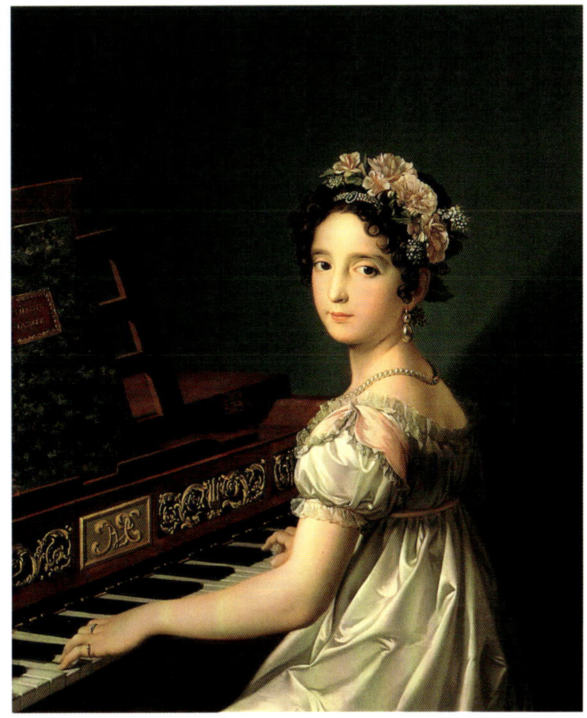

FIG. 114. Zacarías González Velázquez, *Manolita González Velázquez playing the Piano*, *ca.* 1820–1821. Madrid, Museo Fundación Lázaro Galdiano

The early part of the century saw the appearance of another interesting painter, who was working along similar aesthetic lines, though with more measured skills. This was Luis de la Cruz y Ríos (1776–1853), who came from the Canary Islands and was a miniaturist and prolific portrait artist at the court of Ferdinand VII. He was the first to bear witness to the winds of change within Spanish society during the monarch's final years, transforming the king's official iconography of uniforms and regal robes and portraying him as a member of the bourgeoisie, as is the case in the double portrait *King Ferdinand VII and María Cristina de Borbón strolling through the Gardens of Aranjuez.*[18] This eloquent private picture of the sovereign, an extremely rare example of the royal double portrait, reveals the much more accessible and human aspect of the absolute monarch. It reflects the new tastes being imposed at court by his last wife and is a prelude to the profound changes in Spanish society after his death.

But the most outstanding of De la Cruz's many and varied portraits is his great *Full-length Self Portrait* [FIG. 115], painted around 1825. This is perhaps the most eloquent and spectacular picture of an artist painted at any time during Ferdinand's reign.[19] It shows the painter seated and in domestic attire, with the tools of his trade and a folder of sketches and charcoal drawings on his lap. He poses before a portrait of Ferdinand dressed in the robes of the Order of the Golden Fleece, alluding to the position as king's painter that he always sought but never achieved; this is highlighted by the court uniform deliberately folded on the back of the chair. The painting is full of complex artifice: the interplay of internal and external space (suggested by the open window in the background), and of real and virtual space (the room reflected in the mirror and the *trompe l'oeil* of the real and painted portrait, the picture within a picture), all located within a compartmentalised space based on rectangles. The painting's symbolic and conceptual complexity and apparent naturalness display the artist's virtuosity to the full, in one of the most impressive examples of this type of portraiture in the first half of the century.

The long career of the Murcian portraitist Rafael Tejeo (1798–1856) also developed along similar aesthetic lines. His mature work is undoubtedly the most interesting.

imbued as it is with the new Romanticism of the reign of Isabel II. *Portrait of a Girl seated in a Landscape*[20] belongs to this period and is probably one of Tejeo's most sophisticated works in this genre. Here, he deploys his finest skills in reproducing the tactile nature of the little girl's dress – an essential ability in all good portrait painters – and his particular capacity for painting landscapes. These provide the setting for the figure and are customarily used to render child portraits more decorative, often in combination with toys or, as in this case, flowers in the girl's lap.

* * *

The social and political transformation of Spain during the reign of María Cristina and the minority of her young daughter, Isabel II, was also reflected in the country's Romantic portraiture, similar changes having taken place in the rest of Europe several years earlier. The emergence of a new clientele among the fast-expanding moneyed middle classes, the growing warmth and intimacy of private life and the fact that the rigid social codes of the previous regime gave way to a more relaxed climate, which allowed people to give freer rein to their feelings, all introduced a new and much more expressive language into Spanish portraiture.

During the early years of Isabel's reign, Madrid's Romantic portraitists refocused their attention on the work of Goya, giving absolute prominence to the figure of the sitter rather than making concessions to decorative concerns. The presumed self-portrait[21] by Leonardo Alenza (1807–1845) is one of the most intense images of Spanish Romanticism. The figure of the protagonist appears to emerge from a disturbing darkness, enveloped in a dense, intimate atmosphere that underlines the melancholic look on his languid face, a highly impressive example of the Romantic gentleman. He is portrayed bust-length, a format that was to become increasingly popular from this time onwards. Its immediacy, functionality and lack of decoration made it more economical, and thus accessible to a less wealthy clientele.

Eugenio Lucas Velázquez (1817–1870), Spain's finest interpreter of Goya during the Romantic period, was not very keen on portraits and left only a few examples, of varying quality.

However, the highly regarded *Portrait of the Artist's Children*[22] sums up his best qualities in the genre. The two serious and taciturn-looking children are placed in an open, uncluttered landscape, the bold brushstrokes and sense of freedom reflecting the subjects' identity and the fact that the picture was painted for the artist's own home.

* * *

Unlike their colleagues in other regions of Spain, painters in Andalusia remained loyal to the tradition of the great Sevillian masters of the Golden Age – Velázquez and, more especially, Murillo; this was preserved uninterrupted from the eighteenth century all the way through the Romantic period.

Among the most outstanding Andalusian Romantic portrait painters was José Gutiérrez de la Vega (1791–1865). He was strongly influenced by Murillo, whom he imitated over and over again in his pictures of religious themes. However, his best portraits showed the influence of Velázquez, most noticeably in his palette of greys, silvers and reds. This is most exquisitely reflected in the sumptuous portrait of *Queen María Cristina de Borbón dressed in the Fashion of Charles II* [FIG. 116].[23] Her outfit shows her personal love of striking apparel, but the picture is also a splendid example of the fancy-dress portraits that were popular among the aristocracy during the reign of Isabel. This vogue allowed people to combine social distinction with a touch of historical erudition, and lasted until the end of the century, though it was also later popularised by photography.

* * *

Significant numbers of British industrialists and businessmen lived and worked in Seville and elsewhere in Andalusia during the early decades of the nineteenth century. They imported their own style of portraiture to the region, providing local artists with a new source of inspiration and adding further elegance to their portraits of children and families. This can be seen in the work of Antonio María Esquivel (1806–1857), a highly prolific painter of inconsistent quality, who nevertheless produced some of the most beautiful of all Spanish Romantic portraits, such as those of the boy *Manuel Flores Calderón* and his sister *Rafaela Flores Calderón*.[24] These also reveal the artist's special skill in depicting children in the tradition of Murillo.

After he became established at the court, Esquivel introduced his own curious version of the group portrait into Spanish Romantic painting. While firmly established in Dutch painting and in other schools, group portraits were extremely rare in the Spanish

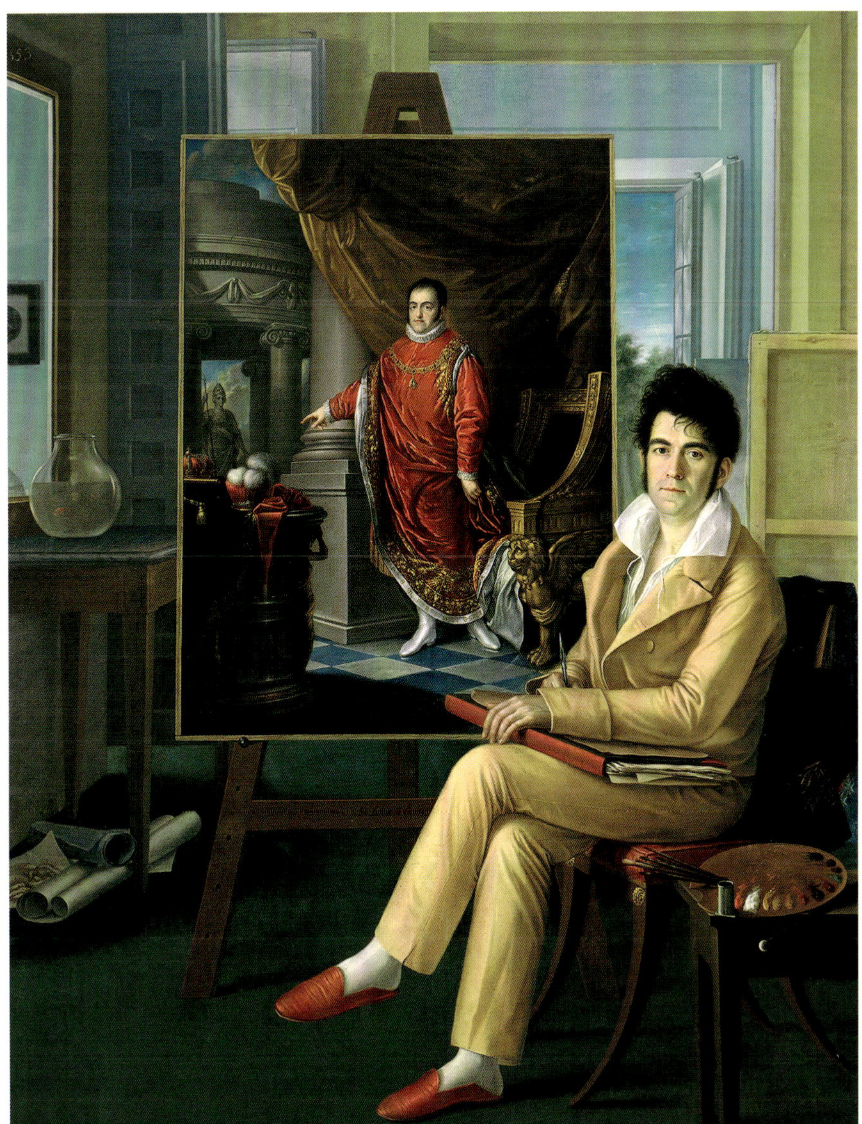

FIG. 115. Luis de la Cruz, *Full-length Self Portrait*, *ca.* 1825. Madrid, private collection

tradition. The finest example is Esquivel's well-known canvas *A Reading of Zorrilla in the Painter's Studio* [FIG. 23],[25] in which he shows himself as part of a large group of contemporary Spanish men of letters. This was the first in a planned series of group portraits of various members of the Madrid intelligentsia during the reign of Isabel II.[26] It uses the spatial conventions of Flemish cabinet painting, and also employs the formula of a picture within a picture by depicting painted portraits alongside real people. This formula was often used as a way of including a person who was absent, either because they had died or because they were too far away.

* * *

The nature of Andalusian society during the Romantic period made it particularly fertile ground for the various types of family portrait. These might depict all the children in a family,[27] occasionally separated by sex or age,[28] or a whole family, and showed a growing trend towards the expression of private warmth, affection and intimacy.[29]

One variant of the family portrait reflected a new and progressive European aristocratic culture, imported first by English families who had settled in Seville and promoted by the enlightened dukes of Montpensier. Such people epitomised a new kind of noble sensibility – very different from the etiquette of the court – which came to be displayed in portraits of unusual domestic immediacy. On the face of it, however, this stood in contradiction to the proud status of these landowners preoccupied with the agricultural and administrative development of their estates.

The best example among works showing this new landed aristocracy is the extremely interesting portrait of the *Marqués de Arco Hermoso and his Family*, which was painted in 1838 by the Sevillian artist Antonio Cabral y Aguado Bejarano (1788–1861). With the obvious influence of English portraiture, the subjects are depicted in the expansive surroundings of their estate at San José de Buenavista, proudly showing off the land from which their title derives. They appear in strict hierarchical order, led by the head of the family dressed as a hunter and observed distractedly by the other family members, who are all holding objects appropriate to their sex and age. They are unaware of the observer's gaze, except for the old servant at the far right, who is holding the smallest child as he plays with the dog – a subtle evocation of *Las Meninas* [CAT. 43].[30]

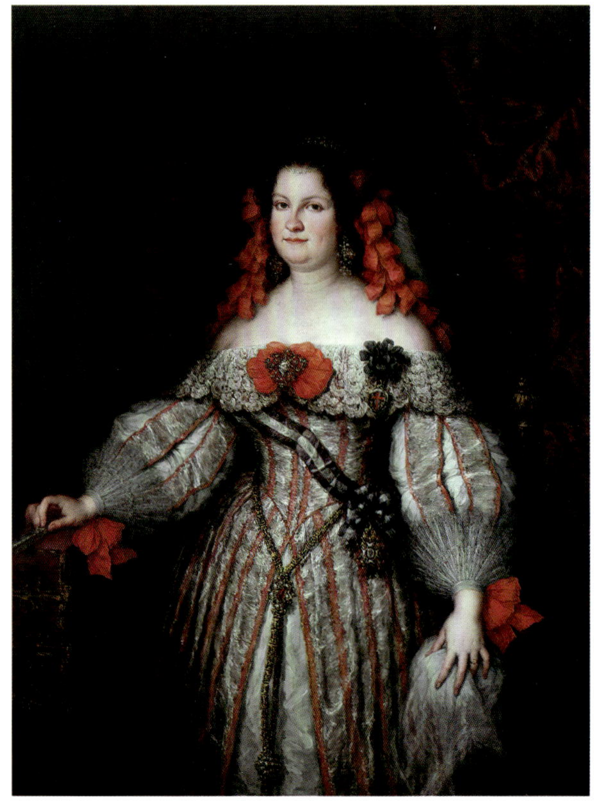

FIG. 116. José Gutiérrez de la Vega, *Queen María Cristina de Borbón dressed in the Fashion of Charles II*, 1838. Madrid, private collection

* * *

The growing political and social openness of Isabel II's reign made Spain much more receptive to foreign cultural influences, mainly from Paris and Rome. The old ways and established tenets of the *ancien regime* within official court portraiture were swept away and replaced by the latest European fashions.

The genre was revitalised by a young artist who, emulating his father, had travelled to France and Italy to complete his education. He rapidly became the most important portraitist at the court of Isabel II and the great master of Spanish portraiture in the middle decades of the century. Federico de Madrazo y Kuntz (1815–1894), the son of José de Madrazo, had an exceptional gift for this type of painting. He adopted the purism of Ingres, who was a friend of his father's, and the academicism of the European Romantic portrait, based on simple forms, elegant poses, technical refinement in reproducing materials and ornaments, and the subtle idealisation of the models' features.

All these aspects, harmoniously combined in serene and balanced compositions, were fundamental to the overwhelming success of Madrazo's portraits among the clientele of the time. He was also fortunate to have easy access to the work of the great masters since his father was a director of the Prado, a post which he himself later assumed.

Compared with the superficial decorativeness of the French or central European court portraitists, each with their own aesthetic parameters, Madrazo's style combined the substance of the Spanish tradition with a mastery of every aspect of the genre, superb technical expertise and the ability to invest his sitters with an elegant poise. This can be seen even in his early works, such as the hitherto unpublished portrait of his friend and fellow student, the painter Carlos Luis de Ribera [CAT. 71]. He painted this in Paris in 1839, in exchange for a portrait of himself by Ribera.[31] Despite his youth, Federico managed to combine both the style of Ingres, whom he greatly admired, and the deep blacks of Velázquez.

A similar restraint can also be seen in his most intimate works, such as the delightful portrait of his children, *Luisa, Rosa and Raimundo de Madrazo, the Painter's Children* [FIG. 117].[32] Here, despite painting the subjects in their own home, he banishes all their natural spontaneity by showing them looking intensely solemn, melancholic and wide-eyed. This reflects both a kind of behaviour and a pride in their social status that marked this family of artists for the remainder of the century.

Behind Federico's best portraits always lie the traces of great Spanish painters of the past. His portrait of *Carolina Coronado*[33] cannot be understood without an in-depth knowledge of the works of Goya, just as it would have been impossible for him to paint the sunflowers on the black satin gown of the Marquesa de Montelo[34] without having studied Velázquez's portraits, from which Madrazo learnt the secrets of simple, restrained and elegant poses.

His brilliant summations of the true Spanish character can be seen, for example, in his portraits of married couples, such as *Segismundo Moret* and *Concepción Remisa*[35] or *Jaime Girona* and *Saturnina Canaleta*,[36] which are fine examples of this master's portraits during his mature period.

However, Federico pulled out all the stops in his most famous and spectacular portrait, *The Condesa de Vilches* [CAT. 70],[37] an outstanding example of Spanish Romantic portraiture and one of the great icons of nineteenth-century Spanish art. In his eagerness to deploy his decorative skills in emulation of Ingres and other French masters, here Federico abandons his usual restricted palette in a portrait of almost brazen sensuality, its sinuous curves accentuated by the rounded corners of the canvas. The audacity of the luxurious dress and the bare arms and shoulders together with the brilliant colours and smooth flesh tints combine with the model's almost provocative pose, apparently seeking to attract our attention. The sitter's irresistibly sweet look borders on frivolity, but she is nevertheless extraordinarily elegant, with elements such as the feather fan and plunging neckline creating an object of desire that can be seen but not touched behind the invisible barrier of the painting.

Madrazo was also a great master of the official court portrait, and particularly of full-length female portraits. The most exquisite examples are delicate ones such as his paintings of *Leocadia Zamora*[38] and the *Marquesa de Espeja*,[39] which have a curiously identical backdrop as well as similarly contrived decorative elements of the kind that would be used in portrait photography later on in the century.

The career of Carlos Luis de Ribera (1815–1891), Juan Antonio Ribera's son, ran parallel to that of his friend Federico. Like his father before him, he lived in the shadow of Madrazo's fame and mastery. A prolific portrait painter, though with a superficiality much more influenced by French styles, his picture *The Family of Gregorio López de Mollinedo*[40] is one of the few examples of a pure Spanish Romantic family portrait. Its academic format is more suited to the drawing rooms of elegant residences during the reign of Isabel. The format was widely taken up in Catalan painting of that time.[41] The skilful composition reveals the artist's special flair for precise, firm drawing and brilliant colour, especially in the fancy dress that was common in child portraits.

Also forged in Madrazo's shadow was his close friend, the learned collector and painter Valentín Carderera (1796–1880). He was a prolific but uneven portraitist, the only one clearly to reflect the direct English influence on court portraits during the reign of Isabel II. In his intriguing portrait *The Duque de Villahermosa and his Brother, the Conde de Sinarca* [FIG. 118],[42] the elegantly dressed teenagers are holding a fencing foil and some papers and a pencil as tokens of their elevated interests. They are posed with their hound in the gardens of the Palacio de Villahermosa, just glimpsed above the treetops, the family residence of the artist's principal patrons throughout his life.

* * *

Although the influence of the great masters of Spanish painting had remained alive to varying degrees within the different schools and movements of the first half of the nineteenth century, it was the Madrid artist Eduardo Rosales (1836–1873) who pointed towards the atmospheric realism of Velázquez's painting as the true path to follow from then onwards. This led to a radical renewal of Spanish painting, with a more open and modern interpretation of the purely pictorial values rediscovered by young artists in the pictures by Velázquez on display at the Prado.

In his great history paintings, Rosales clearly wanted to return to the authentic values of the Spanish tradition as embodied by Velázquez. His *Queen Isabel the Catholic dictating her Testament*[43] marks the beginning of the new realism in nineteenth-century Spanish painting. But his trips to Paris, first in 1865 and then in 1867 to present his great picture at the Universal Exhibition of that year, put him in touch with the modern realism of the French figure painters, including Courbet and Manet. These exerted, perhaps unintentionally, a decisive influence over Rosales' portraits which, although small in number, were of considerable importance.

The solidity and spatial modelling in the painting *The Violinist Héctor Pinelli*[44] are strongly reminiscent of Courbet or Delacroix, while the full-length *Condesa de Santovenia* [CAT. 73] bears traces of Velázquez reflected through the modernity of Manet. The forceful figure beside a tree trunk, in a landscape with a low horizon and silhouetted against a beautiful twilit sky, reminds us of Velázquez's hunting portraits. However, there are also very modern elements: the modelling of the elaborate dress in terms of the reflections on the fabric, the use of black outlines to emphasise the young girl's form, the impasto of the lace and the highlights on the edges of her cloak which are blocks of colour. This is despite the fact that it was a drawing-room portrait, painted to commission.

Such modernity had previously been extremely rare in Spanish painting, but attempts were made to emulate it by younger portrait artists such as Emilio Sala (1850–1910) in his imposing *Ana Colín de Perinat*,[45] a symphony of ochre and black in the purest tradition of Velázquez, and in his portrait *María Guerrero as a Child*,[46] which is very much an echo of Rosales.

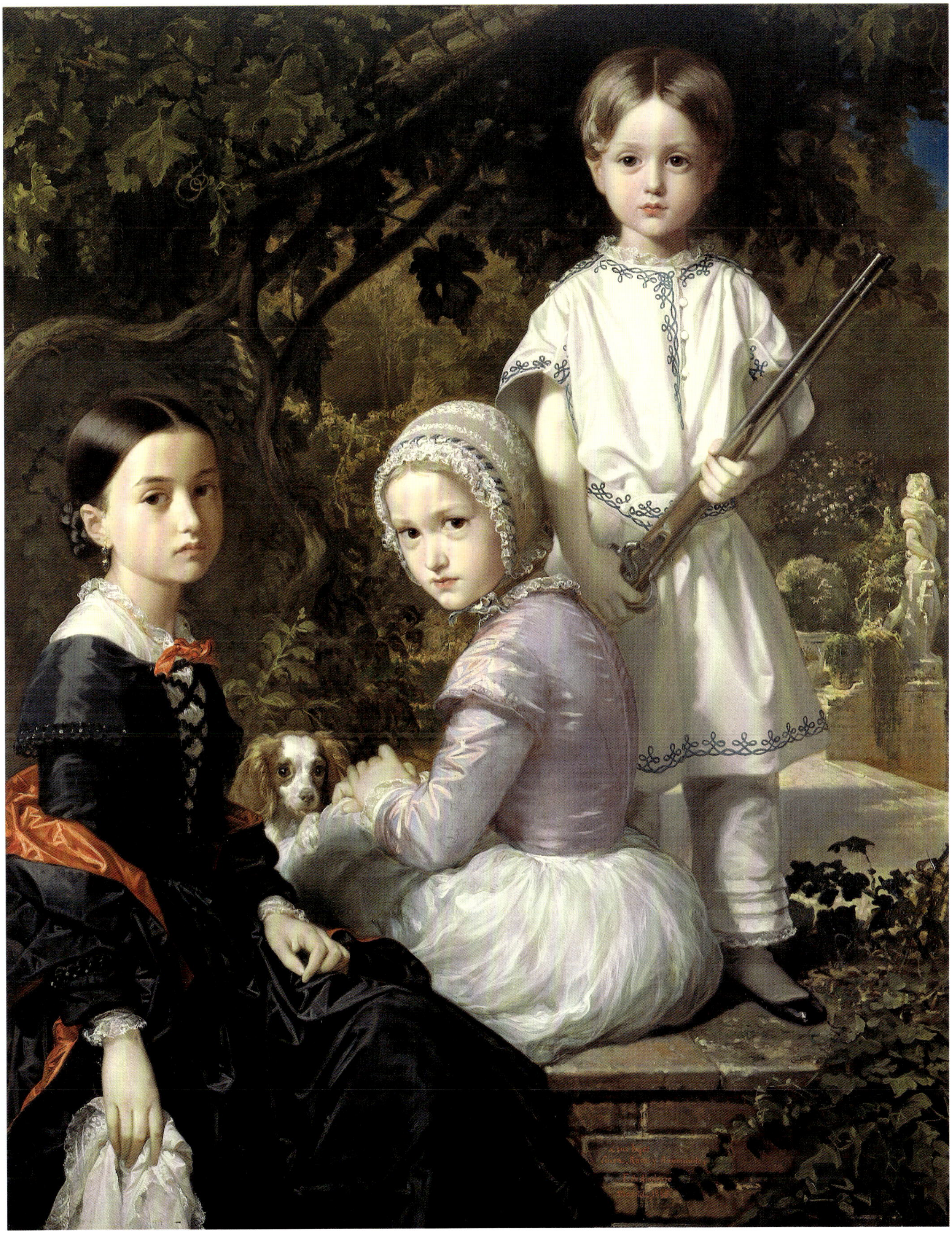

FIG. 117. Federico de Madrazo, *Luisa, Rosa and Raimundo de Madrazo, the Painter's Children*, 1845. Private collection

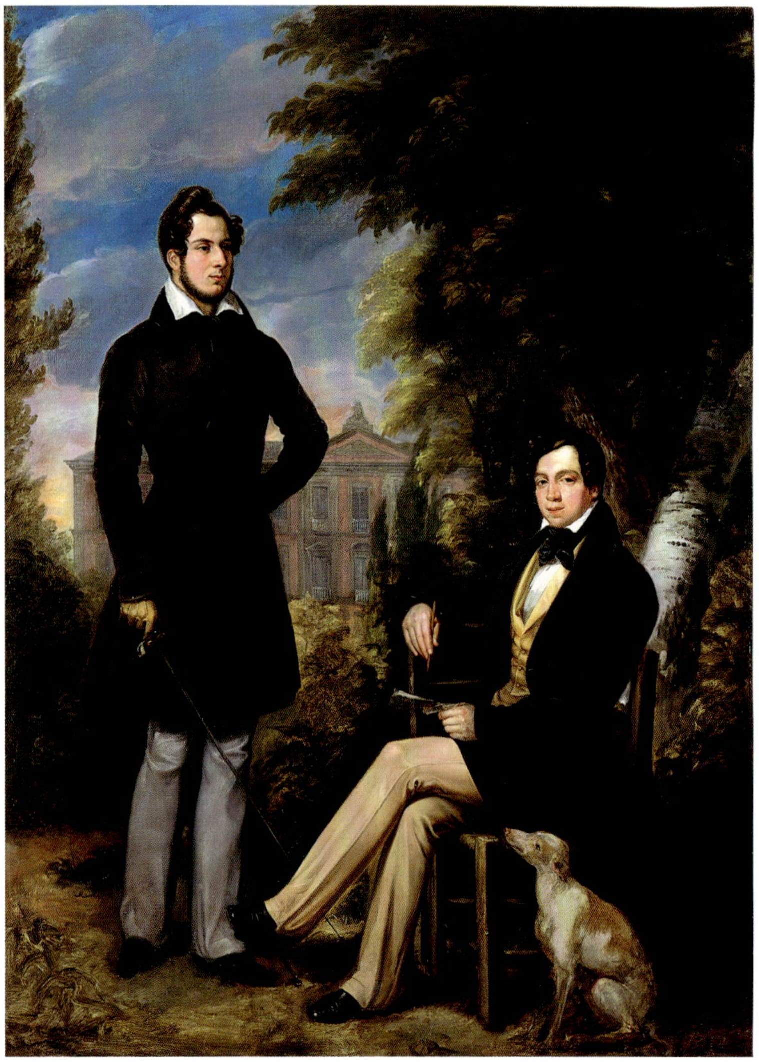

FIG. 118. Valentín de Carderera, *The Duque de Villahermosa and his Brother, the Conde de Sinarca*, 1840. Madrid, private collection

Vicente Palmaroli (1834–1896) was a colleague, benefactor and close friend of Rosales, and also came from Madrid. His technical mastery gave him a rare and almost chameleon-like versatility of style, depending on the nature and purpose of his portraits. In contrast with the immediacy and sincerity of his more private portraits, in keeping with those of Rosales, Palmaroli was one of the first painters to introduce into Spain the large-scale formal portraits that were the height of fashion in the Paris of Napoleon III, continuing the trend started by Madrazo. His spectacular portrayal of *The Infanta Isabel de Borbón in a Ball Gown* [FIG. 119][47] contains all the typical features of this type of painting: luxurious clothing and jewellery, elegant and somewhat affected poses, and magnificent, sometimes overwhelming interiors. These were a response to the ostentation of patrons who commissioned such portraits for their sumptuous residences.

Undoubtedly the great Spanish master of the middle-class portrait in the French tradition during the last few decades of the century was Raimundo de Madrazo (1841–1920), son of Federico and grandson of José. Uniquely among his contemporaries, he combined the brilliantly decorative colours of French portraiture with a sophisticated understanding of the Spanish tradition, acquired alongside his father as a child in the rooms of the Prado. He was also favoured by a truly unique technical ability. Accordingly, in contrast with the deliberate magnificence of portraits such as *The Marquesa de Manzanedo*,[48] emphasised by its impressive carved wood and bronze frame, Raimundo de Madrazo achieved new heights of seductive elegance in such paintings as *Ramón de Errazu* [FIG. 120]. He did this with extraordinary economy, based on greys, whites and blacks and placing the model in an undefined space, in the manner of Velázquez. This highlights the sitter's extremely simple and natural pose, bringing him to life in a truly impressive way.

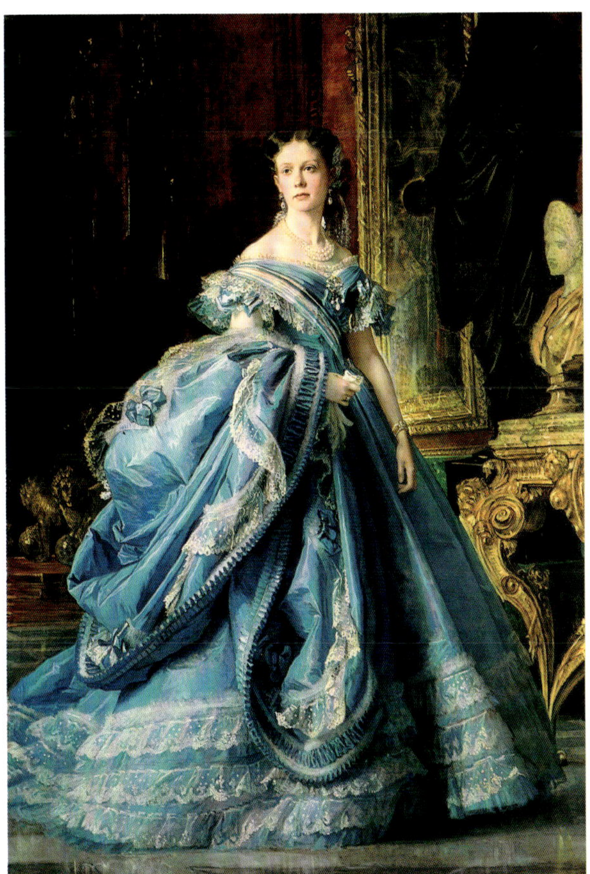

FIG. 119. Vicente Palmaroli, *The Infanta Isabel de Borbón in a Ball Gown*, 1866. Patrimonio Nacional, Madrid, Palacio Real

* * *

At the end of the century, France was also an important source of inspiration for young Catalan painters who were more attracted to the aesthetic innovations taking place on the other side of the Pyrenees than to the academic tradition of Madrid and other Spanish schools. The most avant-garde Catalan masters of the time, among whom the artistic personality of the young Picasso was forged, brought a powerful originality to bear on one specific type of picture: the portrait in an interior in which the sitters are depicted in settings from everyday life, surrounded by furniture and objects that define their personalities. The best portraits by Ramón Casas (1866–1932) contain echoes of Manet or Degas. In the picture of his close friend the painter Santiago Rusiñol [CAT. 75], there are traces of Velázquez in the use of space and in such details as the outfit and boots. There is also a private joke: a fragment of the Infanta Margarita's head copied from *Las Meninas* [CAT. 43] appears behind a landscape painting, alluding to the sitter's specialism.

Santiago Rusiñol (1861–1931) specialised in melancholic portraits of people in shadowy, cheerless interiors, reflecting his sitters' state of mind. An excellent example of this is *Señorita Nantas* [FIG. 121],[49] whose original French title, *Rêverie*, expresses its real intention much better. Painted in 1894 at the Quai Bourbon in Paris, it magnificently sums up this master's portraits. It bears similarities to Fauvist and symbolist painting in its treatment of the female figure, a black silhouette distinguished only by the hands clasped in the lap, and the strictly frontal perspective of the face. The latter is

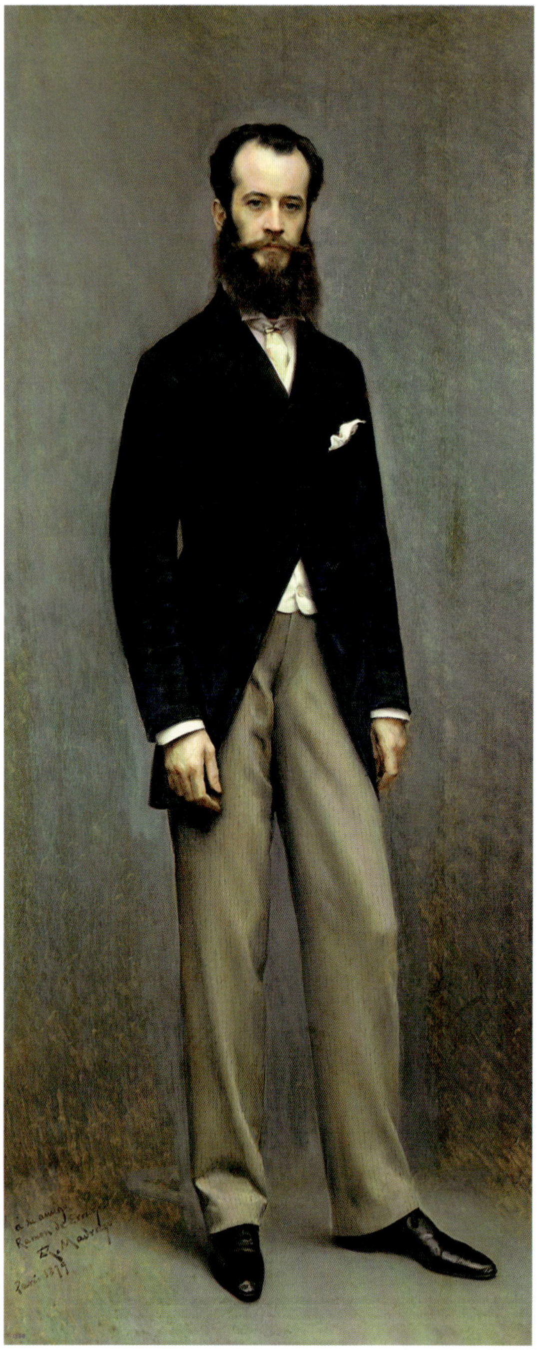

FIG. 120. Raimundo de Madrazo, *Ramón de Errazu*, 1879. Madrid, Museo del Prado [P-2614]

impenetrable and expressionless, the features shaped like the mask of a votive icon. Rusiñol skilfully arranges the subject with her elbow leaning against a cupboard to allow a glimpse of the room. The interior is bathed in a tenuous light that penetrates the net curtains of the balcony and plunges the furniture of this shuttered house into gloom, the white-covered armchairs provoking the same feeling of abandonment and sorrow as the model's face.

* * *

In late nineteenth-century Valencia, progressive portraitists such as Sala achieved complete technical freedom, marked by intense, forceful colour and pure, exultant painting. This was stimulated by the school's profound feeling for Mediterranean light, reflecting the essence of the Valencian character. Great masters such as Ignacio Pinazo (1849–1916) showed a particular inclination for portraits of children, and eventually discovered how to depict their spontaneity and liveliness. This was carried over into more monumental portraits such as the well-known canvas *Learning by Heart* [CAT. 73]. Here, Pinazo's favourite model, his son Ignacio, is shown in scholarly mode with a look of concentration. He is rather formal and elegant for a teenager, and the use of directed light and a predominance of black results in a simple, restrained composition that is profoundly rooted in the Spanish tradition.

The Valencian school also spawned an artist who, on the threshold of the new century, offered a modern reinterpretation of the Golden Age of Spanish painting and the work of Velázquez. Although Joaquín Sorolla (1863–1923) was internationally famous for his beach scenes, portraits were the mainstay of his career. He was responsible for some of the masterpieces of turn-of-the-century European portraiture, thanks to his extraordinary ability to assimilate the essence of Velazquian realism and recreate it in a bold and modern form that paved the way for twentieth-century figure painting. In the superb portrait of his great friend, the painter

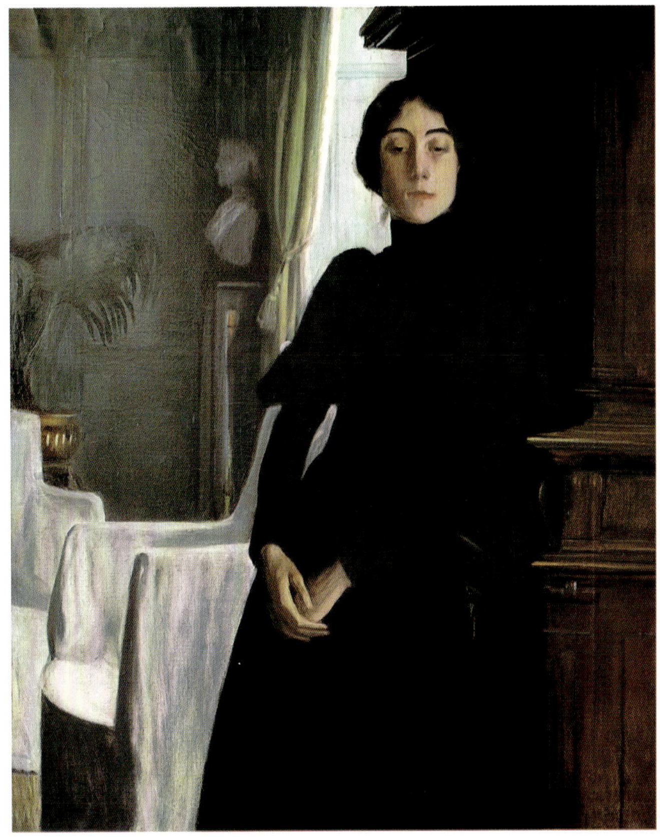

FIG. 121. Santiago Rusiñol, *Señorita Nantas*, *ca.* 1894. Sitges (Barcelona), Museu del Cau Ferrat [32.003]

Aureliano de Beruete [CAT. 74], Sorolla captures the elegant pose of this master of landscape, dressed in walking clothes and sitting in the austere half-light of his studio, using the same greys and browns as Velázquez. The picture concentrates on the artist's face, sun-tanned from his countryside painting forays, communicating his presence with astonishing immediacy. Sorolla's slightly raised viewpoint and confident brushstrokes express the watery intensity of the subject's clear, frank gaze with the same expressiveness as that of Velázquez's late portraits.

On other occasions, the traces of Velázquez in Sorolla's work are more obvious – as in the splendid portrait *The Actress María Guerrero as 'La Dama boba'* (a character from a play by Lope de Vega).[50] She is dressed in the style of Philip IV, in a pink, crimson and silvery white gown, immediately evoking Velázquez's finest court portraits. Sorolla's group portraits also reveal a veritable obsession with the use of space in *Las Meninas*. He was fascinated by the idea of incorporating hidden space into the real space of the looking-glass, thereby envisioning both presence and absence and engaging the participation of the observer standing in front of the canvas.

He used this conceit in some of his most outstanding portraits, such as *My Family*.[51] Here, the artist is reflected in a mirror very similar to the one in Velázquez's picture, as he paints his wife and children in the half-light of the room, enveloping them in an aura of private, intimate tenderness interrupted by the indiscreet eyes of the onlooker. There are direct references to Velázquez in the white dress of Sorolla's daughter María

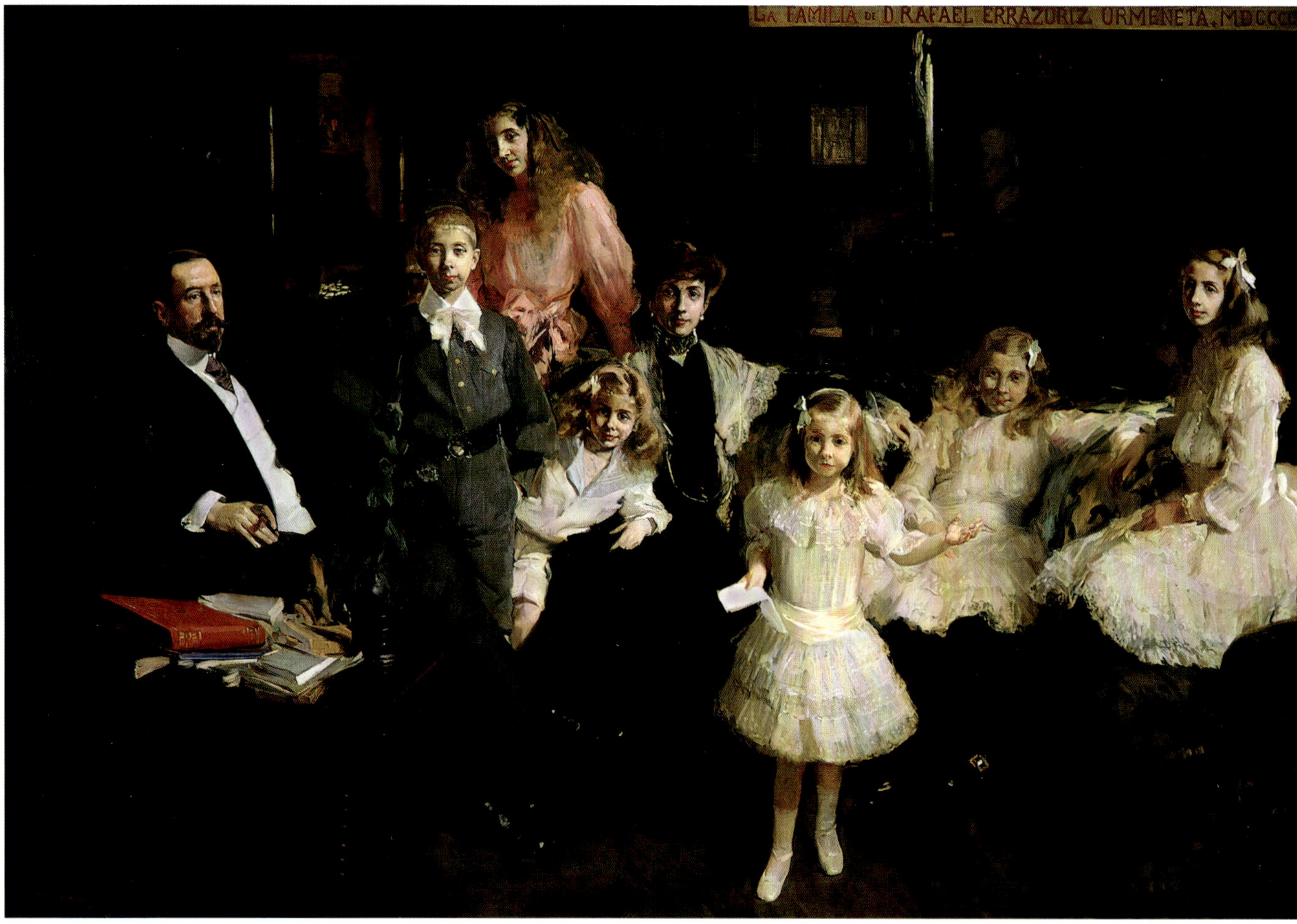

FIG. 122. Joaquín Sorolla, *The Family of Rafael Errázuriz Urmeneta*, 1905. Oviedo, Masaveu Collection [F/M. 218]

Clotilde, which is the main focus of the light, the red of his wife Clotilde's gown, and the distracted attitude of the eldest children, seemingly surprised by their father painting them.

Sorolla uses a similar conceptual interplay in other family portraits such as *Lucrecia Arana with her Son*.[52] Here the subjects appear to be posing not for Sorolla, but for the head of the family, the sculptor Mariano Benlliure, who is reflected sketching in the mirror behind him.

The echoes of Velázquez's deployment of space are at their most dramatic in Sorolla's monumental portrait *The Family of Rafael Errázuriz Urmeneta* [FIG. 122],[53] surely the most sumptuous commissioned portrait of the master's entire career. Here, he seems interested not so much in the subjects themselves as in giving us a painting lesson: the tones of the semi-dark room with its side window allowing a tenuous light to filter through, and the panelled door ajar in the background. This is *Las Meninas* all over again.

The large number of successful young portraitists at the turn of the century included nearly all of the key names in the new Spanish painting. One of these was

Fernando Álvarez de Sotomayor (1875–1960), who pursued Sorolla's luminous realism in such enormously attractive portraits as *The Saridakis in their Motor Car* [FIG. 123],[54] a truly remarkable example of the *retrato elegante*[55] and one of the most delightful statements of the decadent refinement of Spanish high society at the height of the Belle Époque. The couple pose proudly in their brand-new motor car, which has replaced the horse as a symbol of class and becomes an urban emblem of the newly-arrived twentieth century.

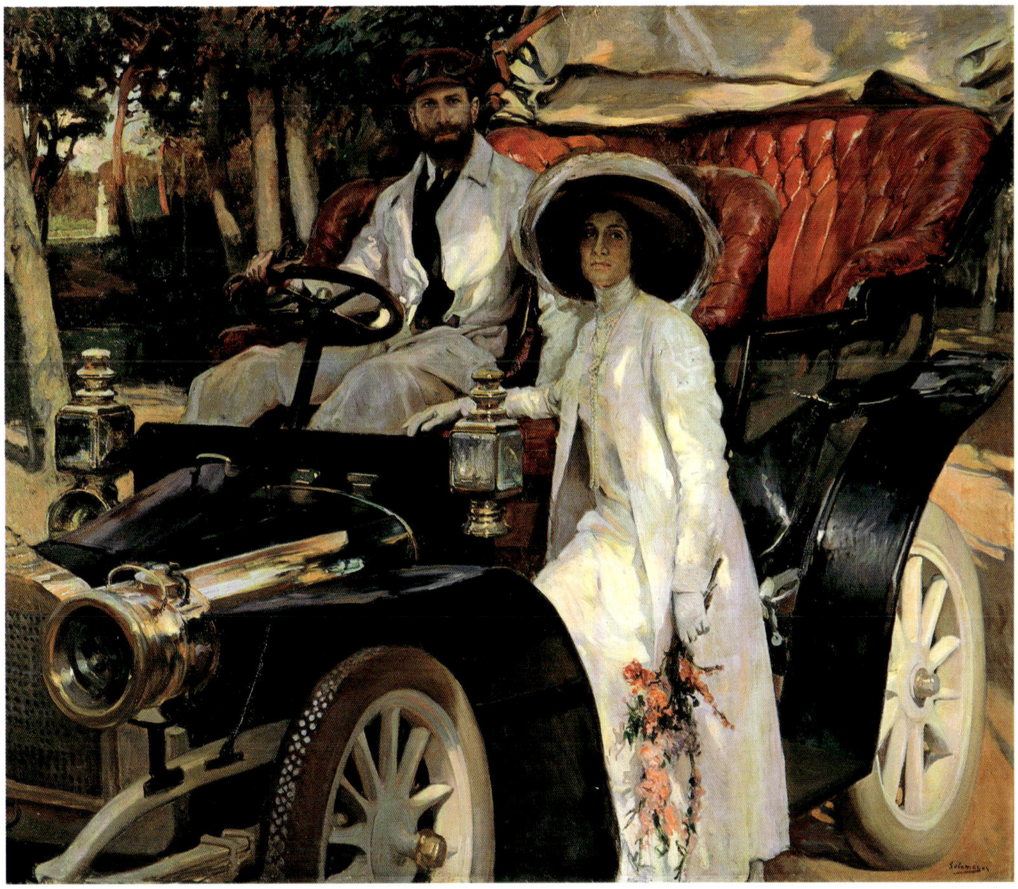

FIG. 123. Fernando Álvarez de Sotomayor, *The Saridakis in their Motor Car*, *ca.* 1905–1910. Masaveu Collection [F/M. 319]

NOTES

1 There is a severe shortage of specific bibliography dedicated to this genre in nineteenth-century Spanish painting. See Díez 1994a, pp. 323–50.

2 The most obvious Spanish case is that of Federico de Madrazo (1815–1894), whose inventory of portraits has been preserved, along with their prices; see Díez 1994b, pp. 435–71.

3 Díez 1991, pp. 45–61.

4 For example, the two portraits of the monarch at the Prado, *Ferdinand VII in his Regalia* [P-735] and *Ferdinand VII before a Military Camp* [P-724], both undertaken as prototypes of official portraits between 1814 and 1815.

5 Hence the dedication on the famous portrait, *The Painter Francisco de Goya* [FIG. 112], painted by López for the Prado in 1826 (see below, note 7).

6 Barcelona, Museu Nacional d'Art de Catalunya [inv. 40.088], painted *ca.* 1794–1796; Díez 1999, vol. II, p. 158, cat. P-640.

7 Madrid, Museo del Prado [P-864], painted in 1826; Díez 1999, vol. I, p. 151 and vol. II, cat. no. P-604, pp. 148–49.

8 See Augé (ed.) 1989.

9 See, in particular, Miguel Egea 1983, pp. 185–212.

10 Formerly in the collection of Manuel Aníbal Álvarez Amoroso; Díez 1997, p. 44.

11 Also entitled *Nestor and Antilochus* (Madrid, Museo del Prado [E-789]).

12 Concerning this artist see, in particular, Díez (ed.) 1998.

13 Díez 1998, pp. 238–41, no. 8.

14 Concerning the changing view of Godoy see, in particular, Rose de Viejo (ed.) 2001.

15 Both Madrid, Museo del Prado [P-7070 and P-7713].

16 Bilbao, private collection, painted *ca.* 1818; Díez 1998, pp. 272–73, cat. no. 17.

17 Madrid, Museo Lázaro Galdiano, painted in 1820–1821; Núñez 2000, pp. 221–22 and 351. Cat. no. 165, plate 59.

18 Oviedo, Museo de Bellas Artes de Asturias; Díez 1991, p. 48.

19 Madrid, private collection; Díez 1997, pp. 38 and 45–76.

20 Madrid, Museo del Prado [P-7619], painted in 1842; *Un mecenas póstumo* 1993, pp. 94–95.

21 Madrid, Museo del Prado [P-4203]; *Artistas pintados* 1997, pp. 78–79, no. 7. This was traditionally considered a self-portrait, but a comparison of the features with engraved portraits of the artist in his youth throws doubts on this identification, which would explain why it was purchased by the Museo de Arte Moderno as *Portrait of a Gentleman.*

22 March collection, painted *ca.* 1862; Arnáiz 1981, p. 502, no. 386.

23 Madrid, private collection, painted in 1838; Arias de Cossío 1978, p. 71, cat. no. 61, fig. 118.

24 Madrid, Museo del Prado [P-4302 and P-4301].

25 Madrid, Museo del Prado [P-4299]; *El mundo literario* 1994, pp. 196–203.

26 A similar purpose is served by the painting *Ventura de la Vega reading a Play to the Actors at the Teatro del Príncipe*, Madrid, Museo del Prado [P-3803], on permanent loan to Madrid, Museo Romántico; *ibid.*, pp. 210–13, no. 41.

27 For example, the *Portrait of the Lara Family Children* by José Roldán (1808–1871), Museo del Prado [P-7722].

28 A combination of both types are the portraits of *Ricardo and Felipe Santaló* and *Enrique, Concepción and Salud Santaló*, Museo del Prado [P-4607 and P-4608].

29 For example, the family portrait entitled *Interior during the Reign of Isabel II*, painted in 1856 by Valeriano Domínguez Bécquer (Cadiz, Museo de Cádiz), or *The Carlist Painter and his Family*, painted in 1869 by the same artist (Madrid, Museo del Prado [P-4235]).

30 Valdivieso 1981, p. 30, plate I, fig. 19.

31 New York, Hispanic Society of America, also painted in Paris in 1839; Miguel Egea 1981, pp. 77–79, no. 2.

32 Private collection, painted in 1845; Díez 1994b, pp. 190–93, no. 20.

33 Madrid, Museo del Prado [P-4451], painted *ca.* 1855; *ibid.*, pp. 260–61, no. 49.

34 Madrid, Museo del Prado [P-4450], painted in 1855; *ibid.*, pp. 264–65, no. 51.

35 Madrid, Museo del Prado [P-4466 and P-4473], deposited in the Jaén, Museum, painted in 1855 and 1886; *ibid.*, pp. 266–69, nos 52 and 53.

36 Madrid, Museo del Prado [P-2813 and P-2814], painted in 1856; *ibid.*, pp. 270–73, nos 54 and 55.

37 Madrid, Museo del Prado [P-2878], painted in 1853; *ibid.*, pp. 240–42, no. 41.

38 Madrid, private collection, painted in 1847; *ibid.*, pp. 196–99, no. 22.

39 Madrid, private collection, painted in 1852; *ibid.*, pp. 234–35, no. 38.

40 Madrid, private collection, painted in 1854; Díez 1992a, pp. 112–13, no. 16.

41 Particularly in the work of Joaquín Espalter (1815–1889), in portraits such as *The Family of the Banker Flaquer*, painted in 1842, Madrid, Museo Romántico.

42 Madrid, private collection, painted in 1840.

43 Madrid, Museo del Prado [P-4625]; Díez 1992b, pp. 212–29, no. 18.

44 Madrid, Museo del Prado [P-4614]; Salas (ed.) 1973, p. 68, cat. no. 24.

45 Valencia, Museo de Bellas Artes, painted in 1874; Espí Valdés 1975, plate 16.

46 Madrid, Museo del Prado [P-4188], deposited in Almagro (Ciudad Real), Museo Nacional del Teatro, painted in 1878; *Maestros valencianos* 1997, pp. 166–67, no. 30.

47 Patrimonio Nacional, Madrid, Palacio Real, painted in 1866; Pérez y Morandeira 1971, plate 13.

48 Madrid, Museo del Prado [P-2603], signed in Paris in 1875.

49 Sitges (Barcelona), Museu del Cau Ferrat, painted in 1894; Coll Mirabent 1986, p. 297.

50 Madrid, Museo del Prado [P-4647], painted in 1897 and reinterpreted in 1906; Díez 1997, pp. 196–97, no. 42.

51 Valencia, town hall, painted in 1901; Pons-Sorolla 2001, p. 187, fig. 93.

52 Private collection, painted in 1906; *ibid.*, pp. 236–37, fig. 130.

53 Masaveu Collection, painted in 1905; *ibid.*, p. 226, fig. 118.

54 Masaveu Collection, painted ca. 1905–1910; Lozoya (ed.) 1975, p. 20, reproduced p. 39, no. 28.

55 Concerning the turn-of-the-century Spanish portrait, see Pérez Rojas 2000 and *Elegantes de 1900*, exh. cat., Granada 2000.

CAT. 69. Vicente López. *The Condesa Viuda de Calderón*, 1846. Madrid, Museo del Prado [P-7041]

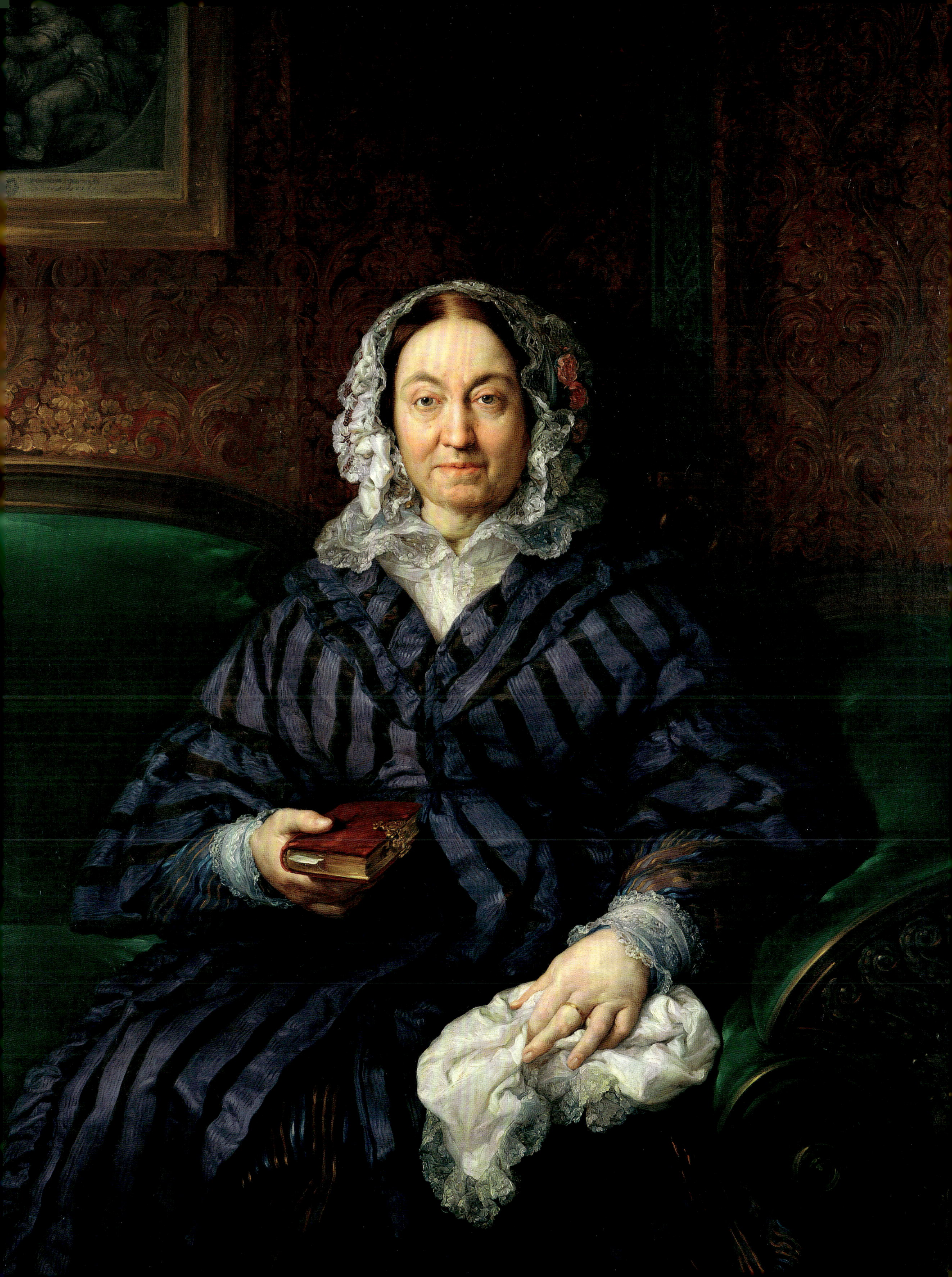

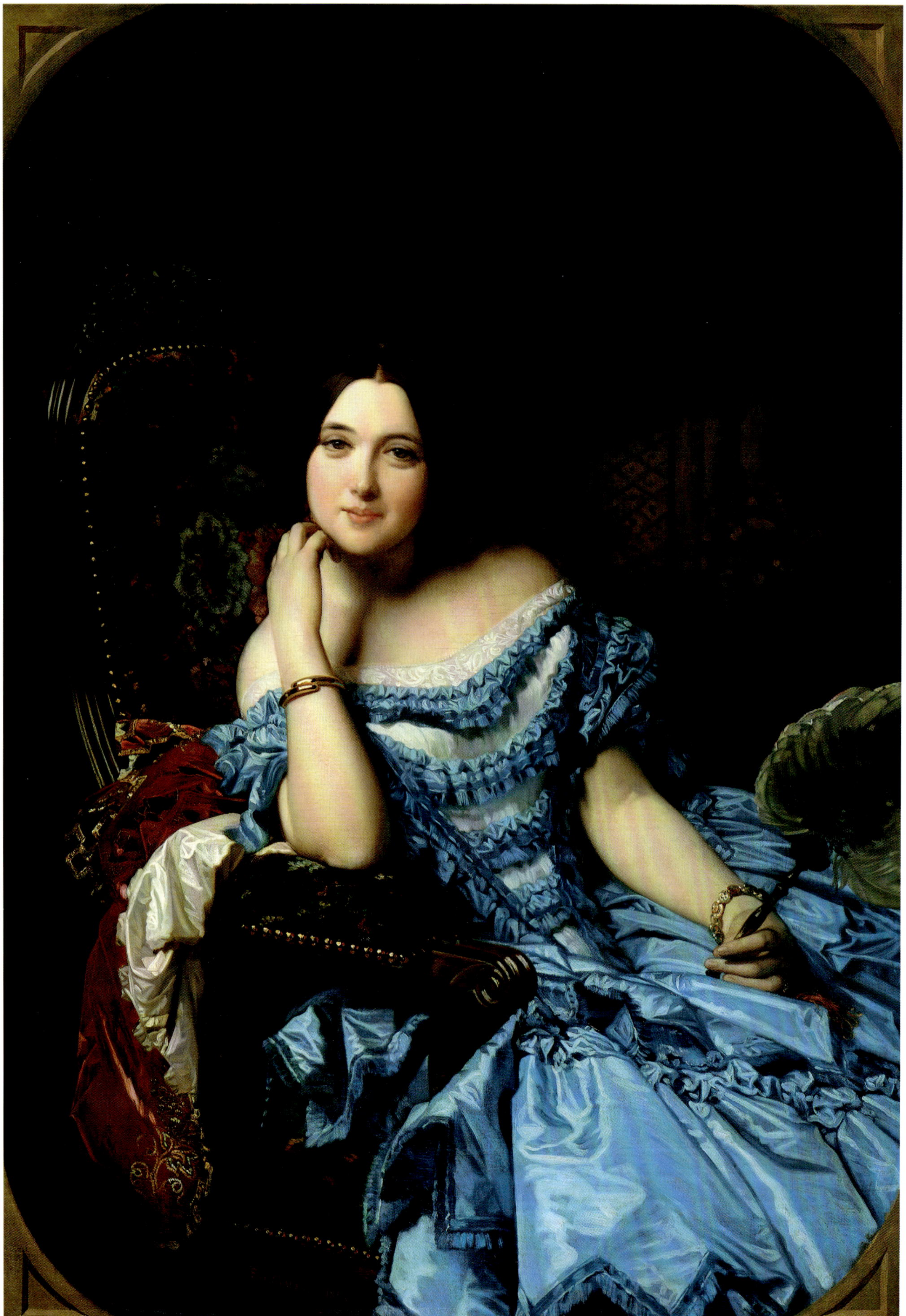

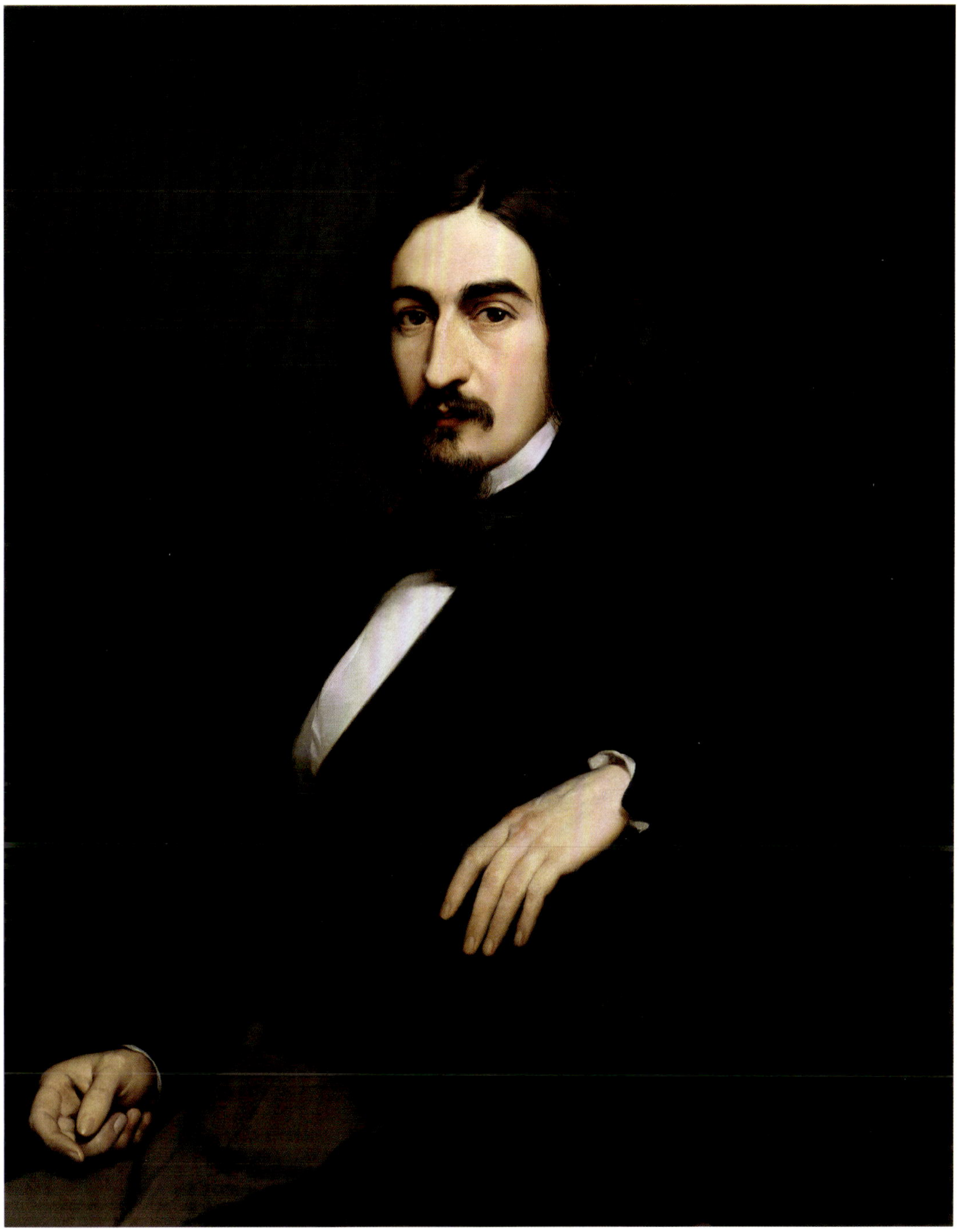

CAT. 70. Federico de Madrazo.
The Condesa de Vilches, 1853.
Madrid, Museo del Prado [P-2878]

CAT. 71. Federico de Madrazo.
Carlos Luis de Ribera, 1839.
Madrid, Museo del Prado [P-7799]

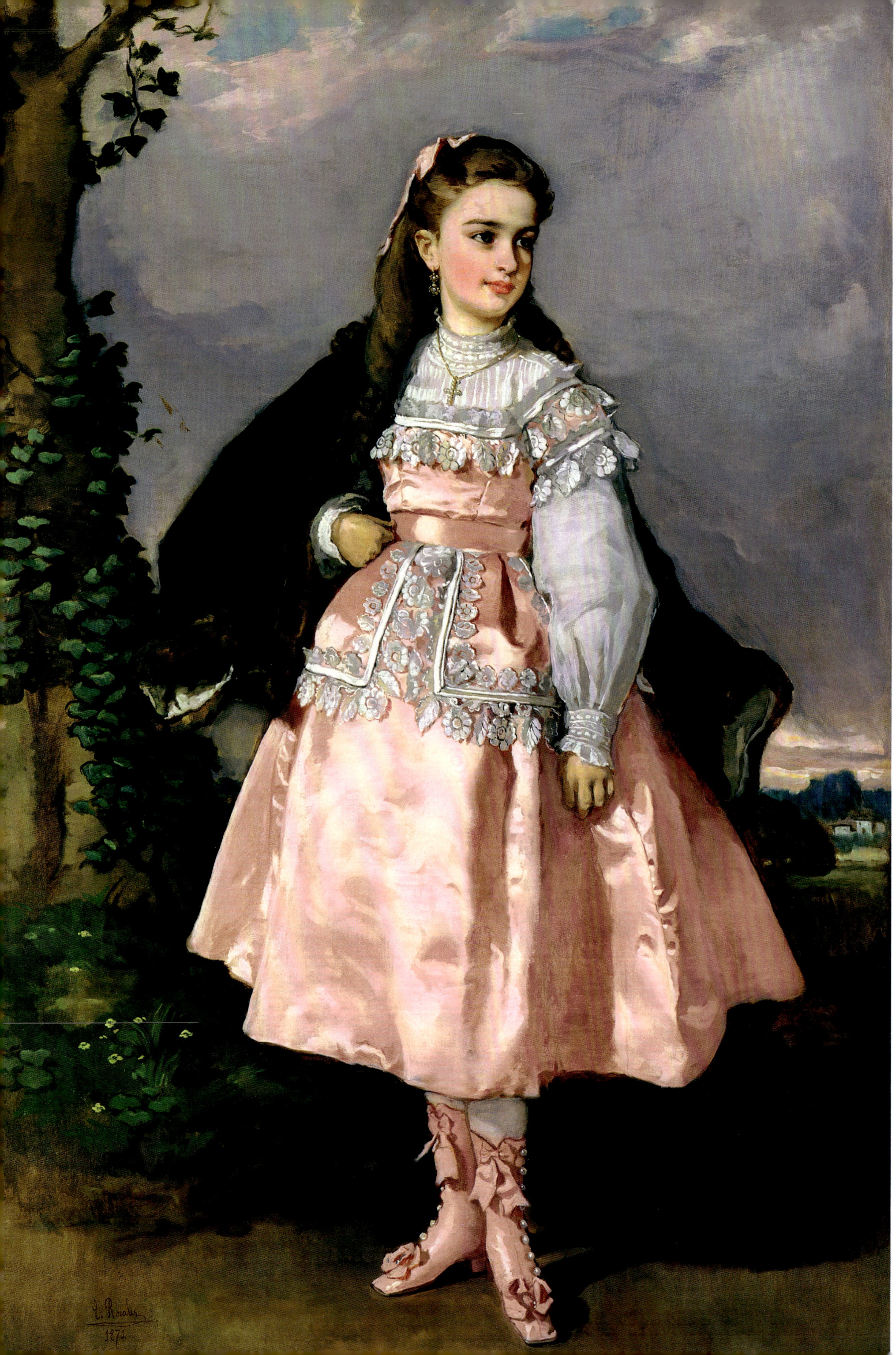

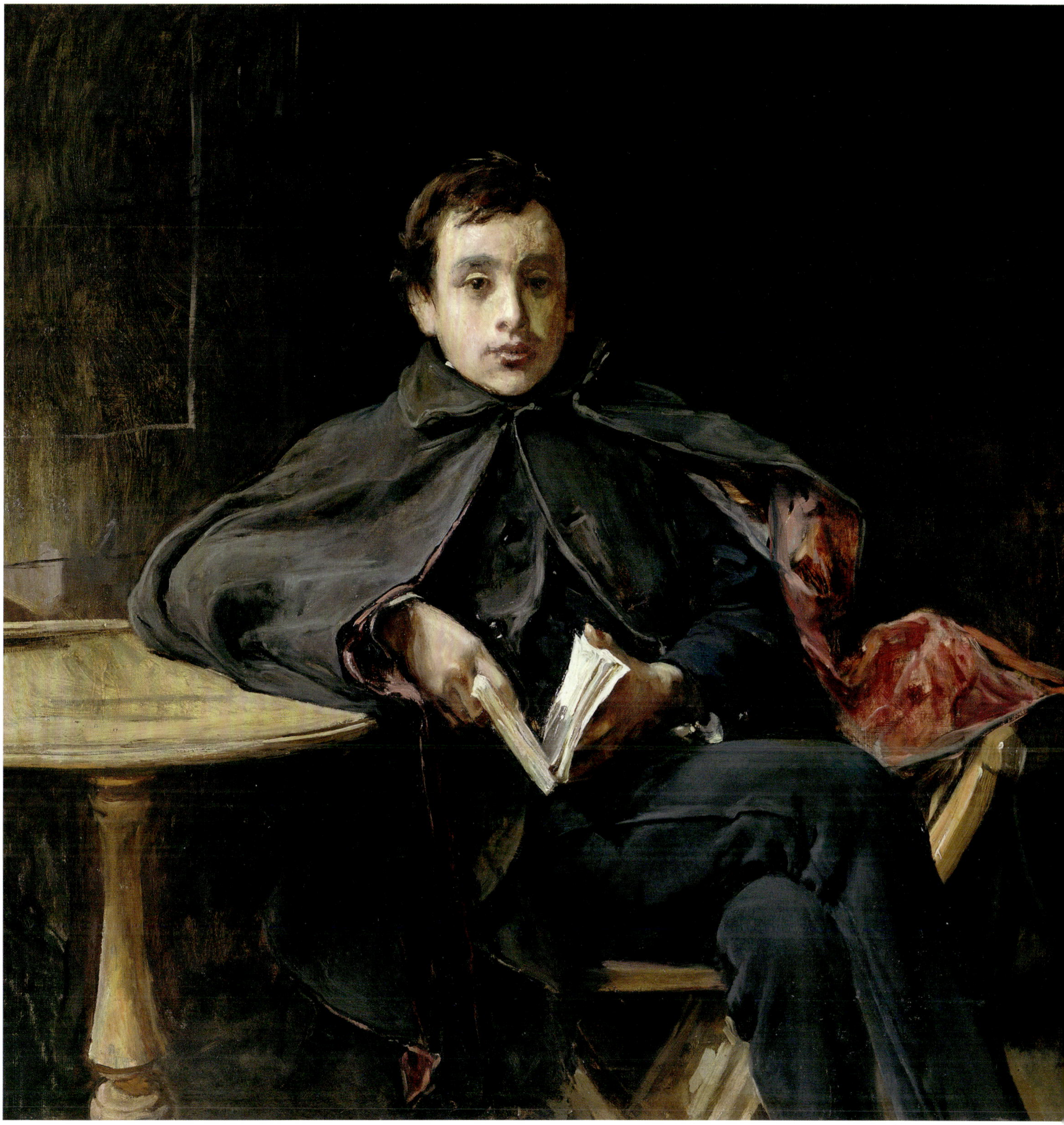

CAT. 72. Eduardo Rosales. *The Condesa de Santovenia*, 1871. Madrid, Museo del Prado [P-6711]

CAT. 73. Ignacio Pinazo. *Learning by Heart*, 1898. Madrid, Museo del Prado [P-4576]

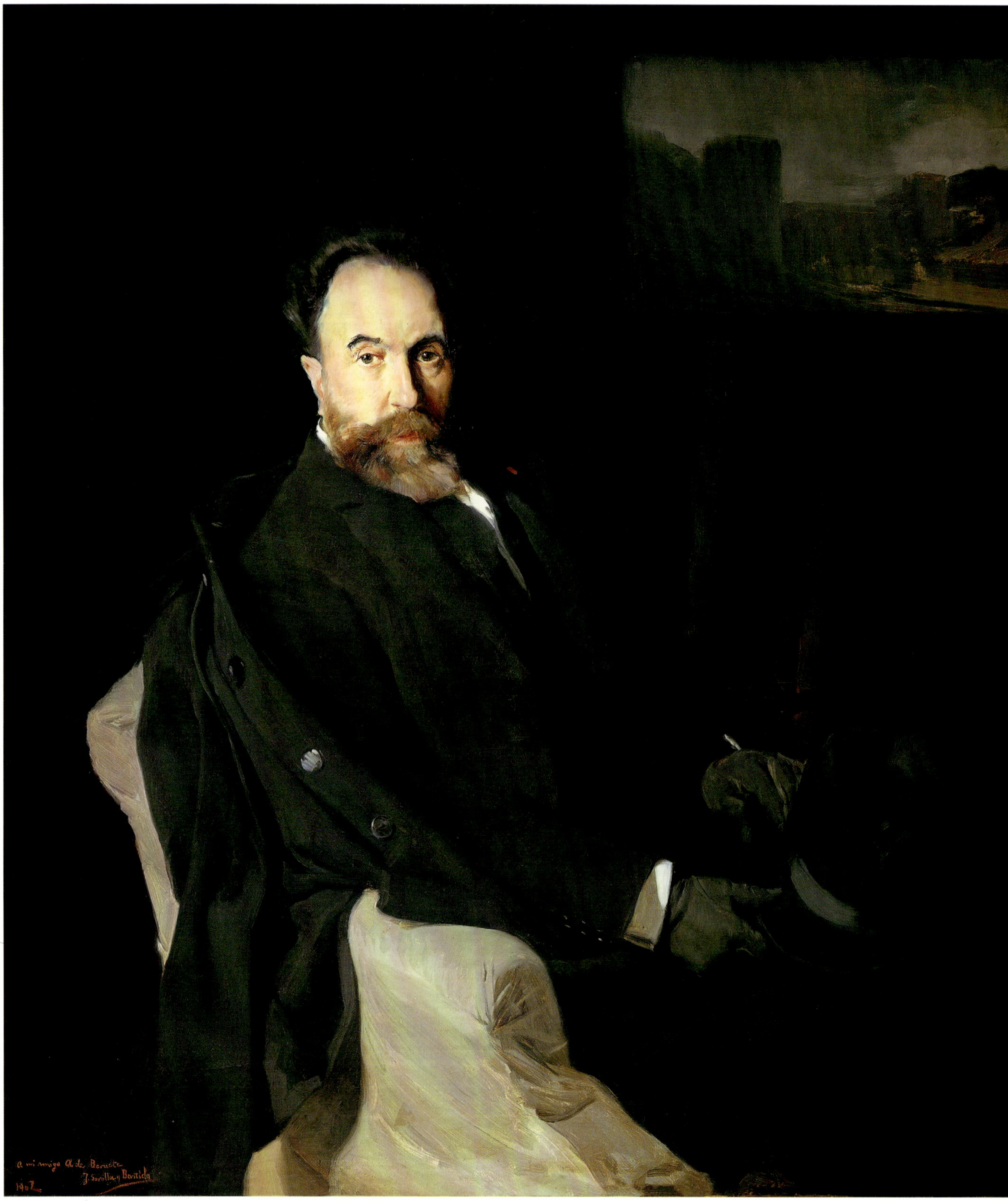

CAT. 74. Joaquín Sorolla. *Aureliano de Beruete, Father*, 1902. Madrid, Museo del Prado [P-4646]

CAT. 75. Ramón Casas. *Santiago Rusiñol*, 1889. Private collection.

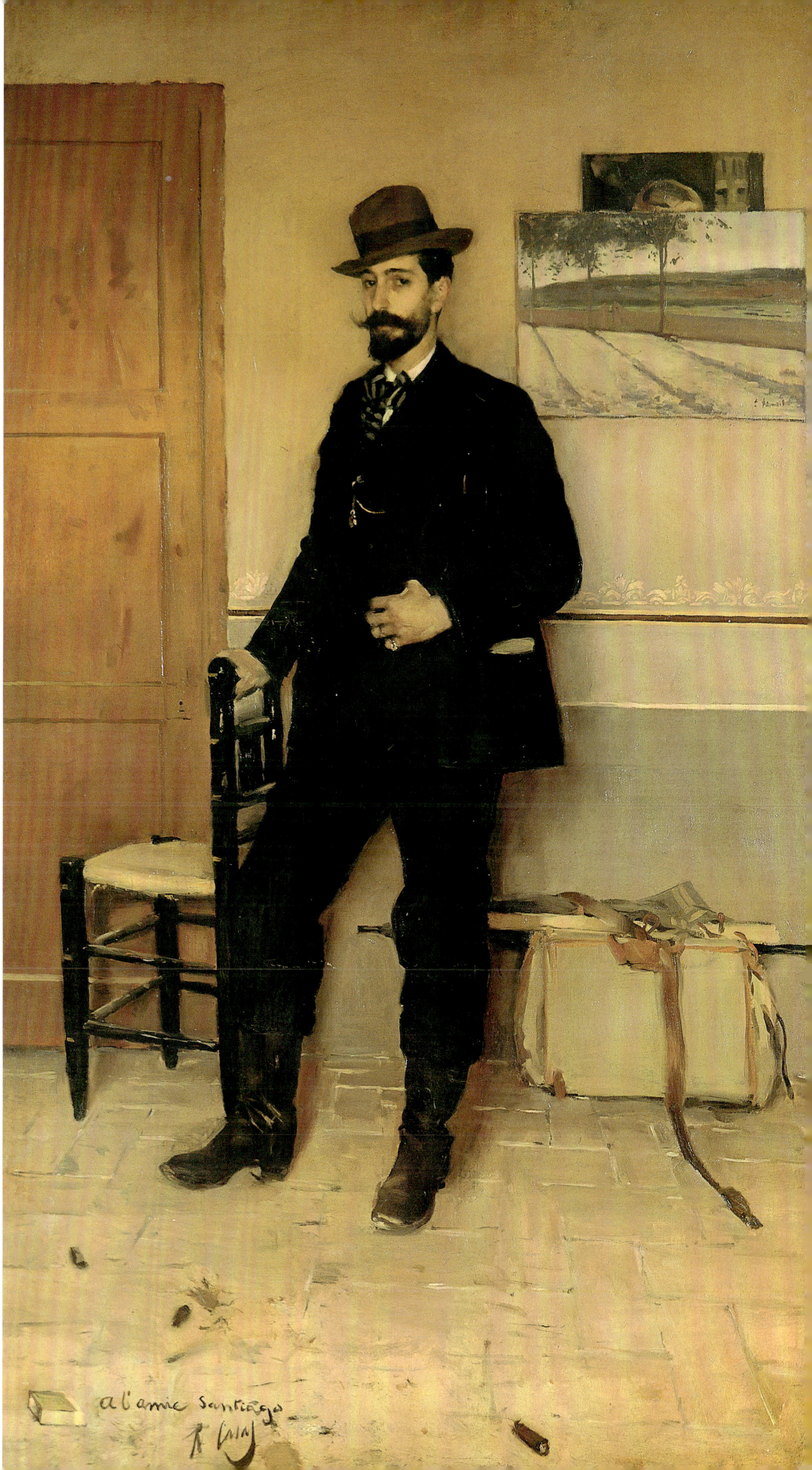
a l'amic Santiago

9 The Spanish Portrait from Zuloaga to Picasso

Javier Barón

Ignacio Zuloaga (1870–1945) and Pablo Picasso (1881–1973) met in Paris during the first few years of the twentieth century. At that time, the portrait was already a major genre in the work of both artists. Unlike Picasso, Zuloaga had won wide recognition in Paris and in Central Europe. There was no experimentation with radical innovations in his painting, although his influence on painters working in Spain was set to increase. However, the real transformation of Spanish painting was to occur in Paris, where the following artists were living, or had been living, in the first decade of the twentieth century: Francisco Iturrino (1864–1924), Ramón Pichot (1871–1925), Isidro Nonell (1872–1911), Evaristo Valle (1873–1951), Joaquín Sunyer (1874–1956), Juan de Echevarría (1875–1931), Ricardo Canals (1876–1931), Julio González (1876–1942), Aurelio Arteta (1879–1940), Cristóbal Ruiz (1881–1962), Daniel Vázquez Díaz (1882–1969) and Juan Gris (1887–1927). For most of them, the portrait formed a major part of their work. Of all of them, only Picasso, Gris and González were to remain in France. The early death of Gris, the fact that González began to concentrate on sculpture and the importance of Picasso's work meant that the latter became a unique and key figure for successive generations of painters who travelled to Paris. This led to a particular development affecting all of Spanish painting in the twentieth century: it became divided between the work carried out in Paris and that performed in Spain by artists affected to differing extents by external innovations.[1]

Among the latter, those who started working at the beginning of the century fought against the painting, then in fashion, of Joaquín Sorolla (1863–1923) and his followers. Portrait painting was a genre much practised in both camps, for instance by Zuloaga himself, by Ricardo Baroja (1871–1953), by the brothers Valentín (1879–1963) and Ramón (1882–1969) de Zubiaurre and, above all as far as portraits of women were concerned, by Julio Romero de Torres (1874–1930), by Miguel Viladrich (1880–1956) and by Anselmo Miguel Nieto (1881–1964). In their work, these artists eliminated both the naturalness of the approach and the appearance of immediacy, which were replaced by the quest to depict the state of mind of the sitter, interpreted as the essential and permanent quality. Thus an awareness developed of the value of the intellectual construction of painting, which was applied to the portrait in the same way as to landscapes. In the latter, despite the infinite variety which previous artists had emphasised, the quest focused on the immutable, on what Unamuno called 'intrahistoria' ('intra-history' or traditional everyday life which served as a background to historical changes). In the same way, a conscious interpretation of history and of the need to make use, as a reference, of the characteristic features of 'the Spanish' began to emerge in the portrait. The form of the naturalistic portrait fluctuated between the extremes of the work of Velázquez on one hand and photography on the other. In the following generation, the influence of photography seems to have lost its force of attraction, but it began to emerge again with great intensity, in the same way as Golden Age painting had in the previous period, but for the opposite reasons. A painting such as *The Dwarf Doña Mercedes* by Zuloaga [CAT. 79] demonstrates this trend very clearly, as does its immediate acceptance in Paris, since it was acquired in 1901 by the Musée du Luxembourg.

This is not odd, since the perception of the Spanish portrait of the time was the same as that of the Golden Age portrait. In the view of Max Nordau, a very well-known writer in the first few decades of the century who was, because of his Lombrosian convictions, greatly

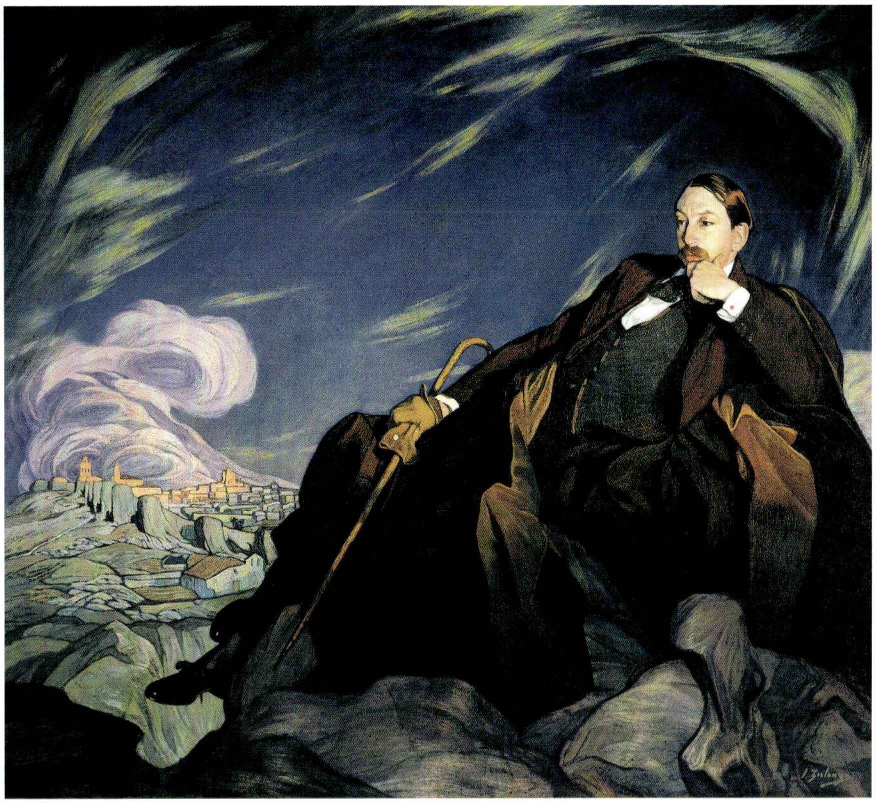

FIG. 124. Ignacio Zuloaga, *Enrique Larreta*, 1912. Buenos Aires, Museo de Arte Español 'Enrique Larreta'

interested in the portrait, Spanish artists 'give the figures in their paintings a firm and gallant attitude thanks to which even a mule driver or a farmhand carting dung looks like a count all dressed up, and they instil in their countenance such contained strength and in their eyes such a dominating gaze which reveal the vigorous courage of the Spanish'. By the same token, the women they depict 'are not in any sense artificial products adulterated by spirituality, morality and social conventions, but rather elemental creatures who embody the vital instincts and physiological norms of the species. The extreme polarity between the male painter and the female model is unmistakably confirmed in the work'.[2] Appreciation of artists like Zuloaga was no doubt based on ideas such as these.

In the Basque painter's wide-ranging trajectory towards the portrait, his work in the first few periods of his career deserves attention. It demonstrates very rich affinities and influences and, together with evidence of the Spanish tradition, reveals a clear proximity to certain modern artists. For instance, in the last decade of the nineteenth century, the portrait *Charles Morice and his Wife* (private collection) is reminiscent of Édouard Manet, while *Valentine Dethomas* (Zumaya, Museo Zuloaga) evokes French Symbolism, and still others contain reminders of James McNeill Whistler and Edgar Degas. Zuloaga was at that time much appreciated by, among others, artists such as Degas himself, Jacques-Émile Blanche and Émile Bernard, to whom he was very close.[3] His method of painting portraits was very intense, according to Fernande Olivier: 'He painted from a distance, with his arm stretched out, and his eyes moving constantly, ceaselessly, from the model to the canvas. He would dab at the canvas, stand back, look intensely at the model and then, ardently and just as intensely, he would rush to the easel, give another dab, stand back again, and engage in the same manoeuvre again, for hours.' Fernande did not much like the way the works were produced, and she wondered whether his 'rich but tedious' execution was a result of this method of working, in which he 'had hardly any time to feel, breathe or think [...], forgetting the model, but without letting himself go'.[4] Despite this immediacy of execution, the painter prepared various types of compositions or sketches beforehand in notebooks, with descriptions such as 'draft for portrait of a mother with two children', or 'draft for portrait of a man: literary person, doctor, etc.',[5] which he used whenever it suited him.

He in fact used this last compositional *parti pris* (or preconceived idea) in the type of portrait which in the end exerted most influence: that of male characters standing against a landscape intimately linked with them – for instance, the portraits of Enrique Larreta [FIG. 124], in 1912, and of Maurice Barrès (Musée de Nancy), in 1913, standing before their main cities, Ávila and Toledo. These may be related to Velázquez's portraits against the backdrop of the Guadarrama. Although the portrait of Larreta has been regarded by critics as being inspired by El Greco (obvious from the depiction of the clouds), the composition is similar to that of the famous portrait painted by Johann Tischbein of Goethe before the ruins in the Roman Campagna (Frankfurt, Städelsches Kunstinstitut). This painting had rejuvenated the portrait of the *Grand Tour* traveller, while those of Zuloaga bore witness to a new kind of tour, to the old cities of Castile. The painter also used this ploy in many other portraits, including those of the most outstanding Spanish writers of his generation. In these paintings, so Unamuno said, 'the men make the setting, rather than the setting making them'.[6] Precisely because of this, and at a time when there were a great many intellectuals (a recently-coined term at that time) in Spanish public life, which they hoped to reform, Zuloaga was the most outstanding portrait painter.

Another type of characteristic portrait by the Basque painter is that of a woman reclining, following the example of Titian and Goya, for instance the *Portrait of Countess Mathieu de Noailles* (Bilbao, Museo de Bellas Artes), in 1913, and the ones he painted in the mid-1920s of Mademoiselle Souty. The influence of Goya, whose first major exhibition had been held in Spain in 1900, was very considerable, not only in this type of portrait but also in other half-length portraits of women, such as *My Cousin Candida* in 1914, and *Portrait of Miss L. S.* in 1915 (both in Madrid, MNCARS).

Zuloaga managed to depict in this way some of the people whose portraits he had painted, using a few of his paintings as a basis for prints (those of Ramón de la Sota and Gregorio Marañón, among others). This was also done by another Spanish artist in France, Fermín Arango (1874–1962), in the 1920s. Engraving was ideal for the type of portrait painted by the Basque artist.

Even before this, Francisco Iturrino (1864–1924) had engraved several of his works, owned by his dealer, Ambroise Vollard. They acquire special expressiveness through this medium, greater than that of his paintings. It is difficult to regard Iturrino as a portrait painter on the basis of his paintings, although he was an outstanding creator of female figures. Much more modern than Zuloaga, with whom he was often compared for his greater frankness and authenticity,[7] Iturrino is situated at a point immediately prior to that of the avant-garde.

Juan de Echevarría (1875–1931), together with Zuloaga, produced the broadest set of portraits of men from the 'Generation of 98'. His obsession with capturing all the complexity of the personality induced him to work assiduously in long sessions. Because of this insistence, the result was often 'tormented'.[8] Therefore, even though he used bright shades due to the influence of French post-Impressionism, his portraits display deep pessimism, in fact in keeping with the thinking of those being depicted. His gypsy figures are interesting, particularly those painted more smoothly and with less concern for volume. Free from the excess purity so lavishly found in Spain, they express freely the influence of Paul Gauguin.

Be that as it may, the great painter of gypsies was to be Isidro Nonell (1872–1911), one of the most original characters in the much-described generation that succeeded Modernism in Catalonia.[9] The 'Popular figures of Barcelona' ('Tipos populares de Barcelona') which he began to publish in *La Vanguardia* in 1894 showed the influence of one of the best draughtsmen in Paris at that time, Théophile Alexandre Steinlen. Two years later, his drawings depicting some of the inhabitants of Caldas de Bohí, a valley in the Pyrenees in which cretinism was endemic, demonstrated his clear preference for a world outside of normality. The works he produced in the following years share some common features with Toulouse-Lautrec and Jean-Louis Forain, and his appreciation of marginal characters in the final years of the century linked him to Picasso, whom he may have influenced at that time. The most obvious precedents for his pronounced expressiveness are Goya and Honoré Daumier.

Having moved to Barcelona in 1900, he devoted himself above all to painting from then on. The intensity with which he painted his gypsy figures led him to a very special style, close to Expressionism, at a time when this movement was beginning to make a name for itself in the centre of Europe. It is true that the artist's attachment to his material in these works, and his famous declaration 'I paint, that is enough' ('yo pinto, y basta'), appear to situate his practice in the Catalan context of emphasis on the picturesque. This is the critical view taken by writers such as Josep Maria Junoy, to whom the gypsies appeared to be a pretext to display, as in a tapestry, his special colourist qualities and the sensuality of his material.[10] Nonetheless, the monumental and intransigent figures in works such as *Consuelo* [FIG. 125] and *Study of a Gypsy* [CAT. 78], wrapped in shawls from which the hands rarely protrude, the deformities of the thick contours of the faces which in some cases, as in *La Juana* (Madrid, MNCARS), are concave, the emphasis on two or three dark colours and the melancholic or anxious expressions of the women make up an ensemble of a depth that cannot be compared with the work of any other Spanish artist, apart from his friend, Picasso.

Although he scarcely painted any portraits at all, Darío de Regoyos (1857–1913), who was thirteen years older than Zuloaga, can be credited with the most innovative examples of Spanish painting in Picasso's formative years. In his *Portrait of Dolores Otaño* (Madrid, MNCARS), of 1892, the frozen, intimate moment of a woman engaged in reading resonates with such intensity that it appears to belong among the best neo-Impressionist works, for instance those of Georges Seurat, a friend of the artist. His Impressionist facet sometimes obscures his Belgian phase, which he called 'neurasthenic' ('*neurasténica*'), and which is closely related to Symbolism. The *Woman Before the Mirror* (Bilbao, Museo de Bellas Artes) clearly shows, in 1885, the influence of Whistler. In addition, the very sharp expressiveness of his figures, not only in the paintings but also in his drawings and prints, is surprising, with his quest for the authentic leading him to the people. This quest was not so much ethnographic, although this aspect did interest him, as a means of coming closer to the original, and, in a broader sense, to the 'primitive' ('*primitivo*'), in which respect he has something in common with Gauguin. His closeness to this artist, whose painting he was familiar with through Paco Durrio, a friend of both, emerges in his painful *Self Portrait* (Oviedo, Museo de Bellas Artes de Asturias), which bears witness to his influence, around 1905, and also to that of Van Gogh.

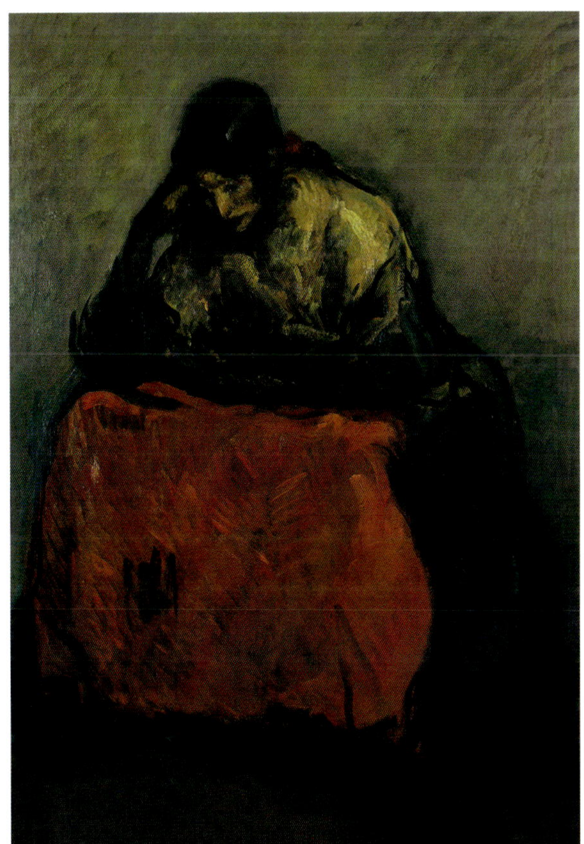

FIG. 125. Isidro Nonell, *Consuelo*, 1905.
Barcelona, Museu Nacional d'Art de Catalunya

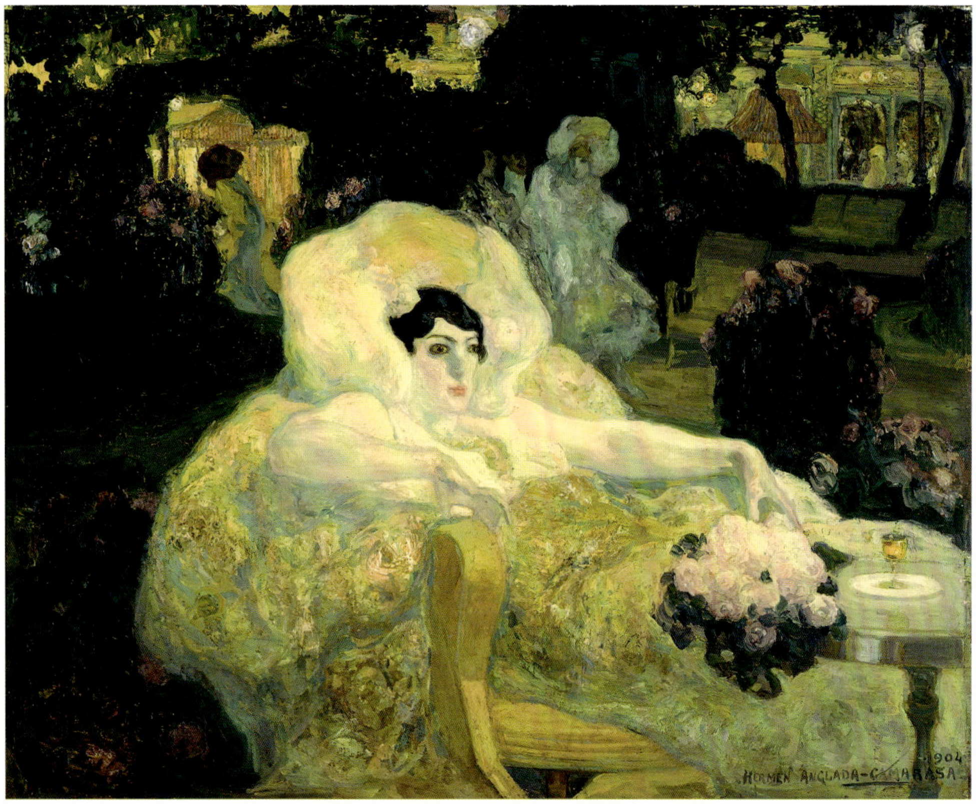

FIG. 126. Hermen Anglada Camarasa, *Le Paon blanc*, 1904. Madrid, Museo Thyssen-Bornemisza [Carmen Thyssen-Bornemisza Collection, 1996.49]

In Spain, Symbolism was not only belated but also eclectic.[11] In 1903, only two artists were regarded as Symbolist (then known as 'neo-idealist'): Rogelio de Egusquiza (1845–1915) and Mariano Fortuny y Madrazo (1871–1949).[12] The former painted veritable archetypal portraits in his series, *Parsifal* (Madrid, Museo del Prado, P-6030). He reworked them in the first decade of the twentieth century, influenced by a divisionist style of brushstroke, which he had come across when attending the Rose + Croix salons, and in the more academic preparation found in the late work of Léon Bonnat, an artist who had been his teacher. Images were defined using drawing and engraving. He used etching to capture an idea of light which, from the upper part, imbues the character with a spiritual feeling, a ploy in keeping with his argument that the stage in Wagnerian operas should be lighted from above, and not from the floor or the footlights as was usual at that time. Although he produced portraits in oil, particularly in his final period, he preferred etching for the portraits of Calderón, Goya, Schopenhauer, Wagner and Ludwig II of Bavaria, as though the severe expressiveness of etching and its lack of colour were more suited to defining a brilliant personality. Fortuny y Madrazo also produced prints, but the most unusual thing was his early devotion to photography, which he used as a basis for his portraits. Despite this, the latter are not naturalistic, since he dressed his models in clothing from another era. He produced a self-portrait in the Venetian style in 1887, and in 1895 he painted his sister in Goya-like attire (Venice, Museo Fortuny), both examples demonstrating his aesthetic taste.

In European painting, Symbolism led to an aura of renewal as regards the depiction of the human figure. From the turn of the century, it was at the root of a number of styles close to Expressionism. Spanish artists rarely took this step, adhering to a very eclectic kind of post-Symbolism, whose most famous international figure was Hermen Anglada-Camarasa (1872–1959). His delightful Parisian figures of *demi-mondaines* at the end of the nineteenth century paved the way for more boldness in gypsy themes at the beginning of the twentieth century, and later for painting with sumptuous material, refined colours and opalescent reflections, which can be seen in exotic female portraits such as *Le Paon blanc* [FIG. 126].

The work of Julio Romero de Torres was linked from 1907 with the painting of a typical female character. Already, in the first decade of the twentieth century, his paintings were much appreciated, which was incomprehensible to masters from the previous generation, such as Aureliano de Beruete and Joaquín Sorolla, who hated them, as did, later, more modern artists. The reason given then, that their immobile nature was precisely what corresponded to their intimate nature, and was what enabled him to depict 'symbolic woman, an archetypal woman of the race',[13] could also be used to justify, from this point of view, the figures in the early Valentín, Zubiaurre and Miguel Viladrich paintings. Be that as it may, the woman painted by Romero de Torres was popular both in educated and working-class circles throughout the painter's life, despite the fact that his most interesting paintings dated from before 1915. Among them, *The Prostitutes* (Fondos de Arte de la Caja Canarias) was rejected by the 1906 Exposición Nacional as being immoral. What must have disturbed the jury was the intense way (usual in his paintings at that time) in which three of the prostitutes gaze at the viewer. This motif was very frequent in the paintings of the time, from the realists to Picasso, whose *Demoiselles d'Avignon* has at times been linked to this work.[14]

Within this nineteenth-century atmosphere, there was a regionalist shift in post-Symbolism, with some artists attempting to capture in their portraits and figures the soul of their regions, in line with what the writers of the time were doing. This occurred among those who were moving furthest away from naturalism, such as Romero de Torres himself in Andalusia, Evaristo Valle in Asturias, the Zubiaurre brothers and Arteta in the Basque Country (and also in Castile), Viladrich in Aragon and Catalonia and Xesús Corredoyra (1889–1939), very much influenced by El Greco after 1910, in Galicia.

One of the differences between the naturalistic portrait and the portrait in the twentieth century is that the former, with the exception of private portraits and self-portraits, was produced on a commission basis. The spread of photographic portraits to all social classes released the painter to a large extent from the need for naturalistic faithfulness to the model and enabled him to regard the genre in a more speculative way. Commissioned pictorial portraits became confined to institutions and high society. In both cases, the genre takes on a specific kind of rhetoric and resorts to emphatic elements which undermine the work because of their insincerity, matching that of both institutional and high society. These clients were quite uninterested in the direction taken by reforming portrait painters. With the exception of Zuloaga, most of the artists who started to paint in the 1890s did not obtain any major commissions for portraits until the second decade of the twentieth century was well under way. Portrait painting continued to be monopolised by the less innovative painters. Thus Azorín lamented the fact that the Congress, Senate and ministries 'commission the painting of such works from whatever dauber is recommended to them by someone powerful', while aristocratic and bourgeois ladies 'order portraits by Moreno Carbonero or Pablo Béjar', who were examples of outmoded painters.[15]

Given the lack of success of the galleries of institutional portraits set up in the nineteenth century with the utmost of dignity, it is not surprising that the most important portrait collection was formed outside Spain – the Iconographic Gallery of Famous Spanish People collected by Archer Milton Huntington for the Hispanic Society of America in New York. Even in this gallery, most of the portraits are by Sorolla, with a few acquired later, which had been produced by Zuloaga, José María López Mezquita, Viladrich and Ramón Zubiaurre.

Moreover, coinciding with the weakness of institutional portraiture, the historical study of the portrait was promoted in specific exhibitions[16] and other exhibitions focusing on the great Spanish masters, for whom this genre formed in effect the core of their work, for instance Velázquez (1899), Goya (1900) and El Greco (1902) at the Museo del Prado. Aureliano de Beruete y Moret (junior), who was later to become Director of the Prado, studied the portraits of these artists the following decade. In addition, in 1901, the National Library (Biblioteca Nacional) published the portraits in its Prints and Fine Arts Section,[17] while the National Iconography Committee (Junta de Iconografía Nacional) collected photographs of the almost four thousand Spanish portraits in existence, an important corpus which it published in 1914.[18] It also published partial studies, including, among others, ones dedicated to royal portraits and to the portraits in the Prado.[19]

The largest number of commissioned portraits came from high society. The carefree life of the bourgeoisie was not interrupted, as it was in the rest of Europe, by the First World War (this was in fact an opportunity to make new fortunes), so there was a continuous demand for portraits by high society up until the 1929 crisis, thus echoing the splendour of the previous period. Unequivocal proof of this boom is the abundant examples of the genre found in the National Fine Arts Exhibitions (Exposiciones Nacionales de Bellas Artes). It was precisely the artists who had been award-winners at these exhibitions from the beginning of the century who were the most assiduous in cultivating portraits which emphasised the favourable features of the person in question and placed him or her in a distinguished setting.[20] These artists included Eduardo Chicharro (1873–1949), José Ramón Zaragoza (1874–1949), Manuel Benedito (1875–1936), Fernando Álvarez de Sotomayor (1875–1960), José María Rodríguez Acosta (1878–1941), José María López Mezquita (1883–1954) and Antonio Ortiz Echagüe (1883–1942). For all of them, Velázquez continued (as did Sorolla) to be the supreme example, although often with the added influence (demonstrating their cosmopolitanism) of the major English and Dutch portrait painters. This dedication to portrait painting, for which there were immediate rewards, fascinated some artists quite a lot: for example Anselmo Miguel Nieto, who, according to Baroja, was lured by the luxury and social position involved.[21] However, the painter who reached the most extreme form of Baroque rhetoric was Julio Moisés (1888–1968). At the opposite extreme, that of elegant sobriety, was María Roesset (1882–1921), whose *Self Portrait* (Madrid, Museo del Prado, P-7642) of 1912, which is of extremely vertical format, is a synthesis of French and English influences with a Velázquez substratum.

A special class within this type of portrait, that of women, focusing on mischievous or fateful seduction intrigues, was a very popular tradition among artists linked to Symbolism and Expressionism. The exotic refinement of the portrait in the work of Hermen Anglada Camarasa, such as the portrait of *Sonia de Klamery* (Madrid, MNCARS), is a very remarkable example.[22] At the other extreme, with more obvious sexuality, there are paintings by a number of artists, including Federico Beltrán Masses (1885–1949) and Gustavo de Maeztu (1887–1947), who (in particular Beltrán) had noticed in Paris the possibility of a kind of pagan erotic painting style, with robust and dominant female figures, following a decadent trend which also interested Néstor Fernández de la Torre (1887–1938) and Chicharro in the 1920s.

For some of these artists, the racial emphasis on the depiction of Spanish women turned into a ploy used for the purpose of frank eroticism. The success which Zuloaga enjoyed among the well-to-do, particularly in North America, can be explained by this. Ladies wanted to be painted not only as attractive women but also as temptresses, therefore they sought out an artist who dressed his models in Spanish clothes and made them look like seductive women, similar to Mérimée's Carmen.[23] Goya's brilliant legacy in fact legitimised this interpretation, as did the courage shown in the execution and the use of contrast between the dark shades of the clothing and the pale shades of the skin, and the intermediary shades of careful greys in the transparent veils. Not all of the models resisted the transformation imposed, and while in some cases the artist managed to enhance the model's own sensuality, in others the result was grotesque, as in 1923 in the *Portrait of the Marquesa de Casati* (Zumaya, Museo Zuloaga), whose open fan displays an image of the *Nude Maja*, which had been interpreted in a very different way by portrait painters such as Giovanni Boldini and Kees van Dongen.

Sitters painted by José Gutiérrez Solana (1886–1945) suffered a different kind of transformation. In his paintings the objects appear to have more life than the people, who are presented frontally, with remarkable archaism for the Spanish painting of his time.[24]

In the self-portrait produced at the end of his life (Santander, Botín Collection), he painted himself in a similar manner, more like a solid object than a human being. Significantly, in this painting the painter is accompanied by two dolls in a close, familial pose. In this fictitious family, the dolls seem more life-like than the painter,[25] who looks helpless, protecting himself with his pallet and brushes.

This is why the type of portrait in which Solana depicts someone in his office, surrounded by the tools of his trade, is particularly fulfilling. The person and the objects complement each other, since they have the same constant character and are equally static. *The Old Shipowner* (1925, Grupo Santander Collection), *The Physicist* (1927, private collection), *The Merchant Navy Captain* [FIG. 127] and *The Book Lover* (*ca.* 1933, Grupo Santander Collection) display a multitude of objects whose abundance recalls the world of Ramón Gómez de la Serna, whose painting was close to that of Solana.

Portraits of groups are rigidly frontal compositions in which the figures are presented in order, without interference, as in the photographs of the time.[26] The intensity of the images is coupled with this immobile quality. It is as if the painter focused more closely and cut down on the framing, with the figures thereby gaining a very characteristic and monumental corporeality. After 1908, paintings such as *The Rejected* (The Detroit Institute of Arts) indicate the early maturity of this type of portrait, which flourished at every stage of the artist's career, and which is particularly evident in *Tertulia in Pombo Café*, 1920, *The Bishop's Visit*, 1926 (both in Madrid, MNCARS), *The Return of the Wealthy Spaniard* (Grupo Santander Collection), *ca.* 1924, *The Young Female Matadors* (Paris, Musée National d'art Moderne), 1931, and *The Family*, *ca.* 1945 (private collection). Sometimes, for instance in the case of chorus girls or prostitutes [CAT. 80], the impoverished colour and ugliness of the figures give the scene

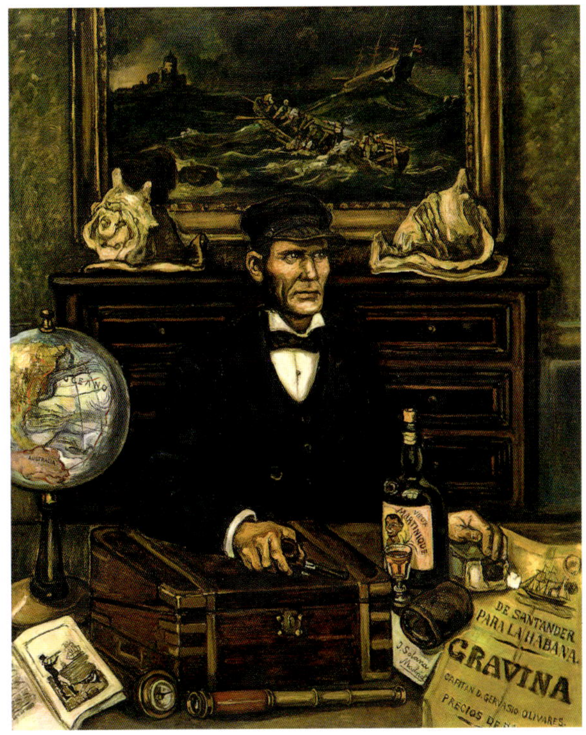

FIG. 127. José Gutiérrez Solana, *The Merchant Navy Captain*, 1930–1934. Santander, Colección Santander Central Hispano

a sense of sad and sombre misery, which cannot be compared with any other Spanish painting of the time.

The considerable body of portrait work by Nicanor Piñole (1878–1978), another artist who sporadically attended the artistic gatherings at the Nuevo Café de Levante, was much influenced, initially, by Velázquez, who inspired Piñole to produce his best work, the *Portrait of Manuel Prendes* (Oviedo, Museo de Bellas Artes de Asturias), 1914. However, the artist's most characteristic feature is his obsession with self-portraits. He produced several hundred, using different techniques. A very expressive vein runs through all of them, reflecting clearly various states of mind which range from melancholy to the most profound anguish. This habitual portrayal of this motif, also in portraits of children, is reminiscent of the personal, expressive Catalan painter, Francisco Gimeno (1858–1927).

Around 1900 it was normal to introduce into painting other techniques, which many artists cultivated simultaneously. These included lithography and illustration drawing. Lithography promoted the development of drawing with deformed outlines, rapidly executed and inclined to simplification and expressive synthesis. The painter Evaristo Valle had in fact trained as a lithographer, and his portraits, above all the figures in his compositions, reflect the influence of this technique. Illustration drawing was cultivated by a large number of the artists of the time, helping to promote the simplification that was later introduced. Photography contributed to an understanding of the conventional nature of the pictorial space. In the case of the portrait, moreover, its influence was very important, given its effectiveness in assisting with the practice of this genre. Zuloaga's scenographic portraits with landscape backgrounds evoke not only Velázquez, as the painter wished, but also photographic studio portraits with painted backcloths. In recent years the influence of photography on Picasso's portraits has been underlined, as well as the importance of his own creative work as a photographer.

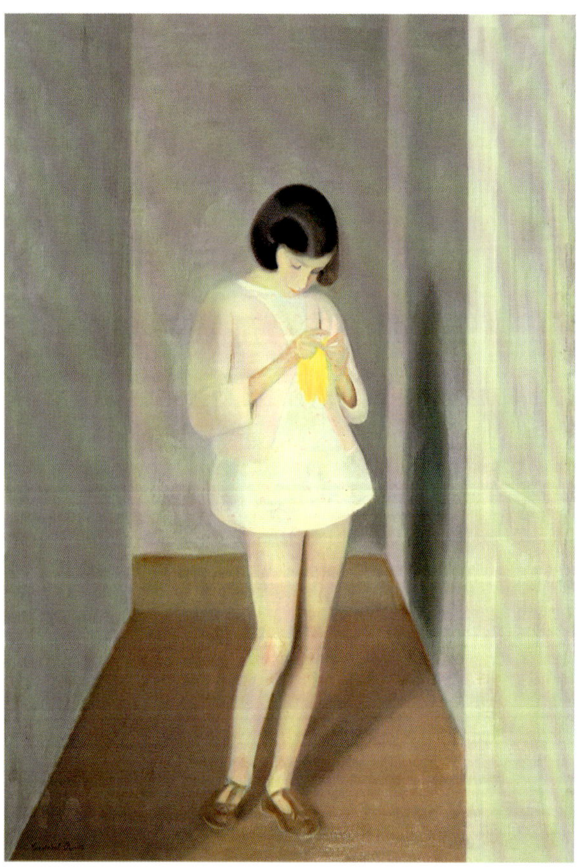

FIG. 128. Cristóbal Ruiz, *Portrait of the Artist's Daughter*, 1923. Madrid, Museo Nacional Centro de Arte Reina Sofía [AS-00319]

Because of their taste for expressive deformation, some painters came close to caricature, which in the nineteenth century already formed part of the artistic avant-garde. This was the reproach which some 'serious' critics made of artists such as Evaristo Valle, as well as of Picasso, whom Félix Fénéon advised, when he saw *Les Demoiselles d'Avignon* [FIG. 129] in his studio, to devote himself to caricature.[27] Throughout the last decade of the nineteenth century and the first few decades of the twentieth, the caricature portrait or *portrait-charge* became very widespread in illustrated magazines, since, unlike in previous periods when the mediation of an engraver was needed, it could by then be reproduced directly.

At the beginning of the twentieth century, caricature became essentially modern. In just a few strokes, it pinned down the features that best defined the person in the portrait. This power of synthesis and functionality became an effective antidote to the obsession in naturalism with detail, as can be seen from the work of artists such as Luis Bagaría (1882–1940), closely linked to José Ortega y Gasset and to his plan to modernise the country. The lucidity of his political criticism, the radical nature of his plans and the originality of his drawings made his work a prime example of the quality which caricature could reach, a veritable axis of artistic renewal. Bagaría himself was at that time aware of the value of caricature and felt, in fact, that 'a caricatural element [...] is the yeast for most works of genius, mainly portraits. [...] Because where this subtle element is not found, academic inanity begins.'[28] His interpretations of writers and artists, the opposite of Zuloaga's portraits of intellectuals, are particularly interesting. The clearest element in the caricatures is the way in which he twists and subverts the style of the painters he is caricaturing, in one case depicting, in fact, an inflated, monumental Zuloaga, from whom a crippled bullfighter is begging for alms, against the backdrop of a bullring and rounded clouds.[29]

Although he also painted, Bagaría was above all a professional illustrator, therefore it is perhaps important when gauging the importance of caricature in painting to turn to Picasso, who formed part of a fertile tradition of great painters attracted by this art, which included Goya. In his drawings, Picasso continually demonstrates his fascination with caricature.[30] Not only does he link up with the tradition of ugliness and deformation in Spanish art, and with the desire for parody that is characteristic of a certain avant-garde, but caricature also forms part of the seeds of the subversive objective present in his work. Even in the portraits from his most objective period, the Cubist period, his skill with caricature and, through it, his ability to extract the most important detail from a face enabled him, unlike Braque, to produce true portraits.[31] It must also be remembered that Juan Gris devoted himself intensely, between 1907 and 1914, to illustration drawing, before, and even after, devoting himself to painting. In all of these cases, the simplification inherent in these works had exemplary value, which was not alien to the avant-garde's objective of purifying art.

The presence in Spain of the Uruguayan painters Joaquín Torres García (1874–1949) and Rafael Barradas (1890–1929) produced a huge shock in terms of the introduction of the avant-garde. The former, despite an initial modernist period, had been a bulwark of Catalan 'Noucentisme'. The insistence on the classicist construction of the human figure owes at least as much to him as it does to Joaquín Sunyer (1874–1956), the other major painter in this area, in which the painting of the sculptor Julio González, a great admirer of Picasso, had its roots.[32] From 1922, Barradas painted portraits which demonstrated a very synthetic definition of the figure based on the predominance of the line and of great areas of uniform and low-range colour planes. His static and simplified design reveals a return to order following the upheaval of Ultraism (a 1920s Spanish poetry movement).

In another aesthetic orientation (although he exhibited with Barradas himself alongside Gabriel García Maroto and Javier de Winthuysen in 1922), a pronounced sense of synthesis can also be felt in the portraits of Cristóbal Ruiz (1881–1962), which, however, reflect quite transparently the remarkably spiritual nature of the model. In paintings such as the *Portrait of the Artist's Daughter* [FIG. 128], the painter is able to capture an atmosphere of privacy involving the character in an emotional yet unsentimental way, within a limpid, empty space.[33]

PICASSO

The basis of the painting of Pablo Picasso (1881–1973) lies in his own individual experience of life, which was deeply felt and originally interpreted. The presence of a powerful and multiform ego spills out into his work, which becomes a kind of continuous and variable register of the artist's subjective responses to the subject matter, even to a person whose portrait he is painting.[34] The numerous series of self-portraits, produced using every technique, including photography, indicate a desire to assert himself which was captured clearly even in his youthful work, such as *I, Picasso* (private collection). It is also a way of facing the events in his life, an example being the portraits of children that he produced around the crises he suffered at the birth of each of his children.[35]

The very physical nature of Picasso's closeness to the objects he painted becomes more intense with people, who stimulated to a greater extent his pictorial response and intensified his desire to show reality. Of his *Woman with a Chemise on a Chair* (New York, Ganz Collection), 1913, Picasso said to Braque that she had to be so real as to give the impression that her armpits smelt.[36] In portraits of women, the profound link between the painter's existence in front of the woman and the painting itself emerges. For this reason, the paintings in which Picasso painted one of his wives or mistresses are revealing. In them, the painting provides a key to his relationship with them, even the sexual aspect.

Painting as an expression of desire was a constant element throughout Picasso's life. The artist confessed that when he was working before models, many times he began to think about other things very different from painting.[37] This was a current topic among artists, but in addition Picasso felt the need to paint his lovers, who appear in his paintings even when the affairs were secret, for instance Marie-Thérèse Walter. Each one of them provoked a different response and the use of a specific pictorial language. In fact *The Painter and his Model* series captures directly the relationship between the artist and the two facets of the woman: sexual being and model. In his recourse to Degas in his late prints, the naked and openly sexual prostitutes are the subject of contemplation by that *alter ego* (here only a *voyeur*) of the painter.

Picasso's art was intended above all to subvert. When applied to the genre of the portrait, this desire to subvert brings out in the paintings elements that are highly ambiguous. Some examples include the use of light in certain self-portraits produced between 1899 and 1901 which in fact leaves half the face in darkness, and the dual view, characteristic of his mature work, of female faces, both frontal and in profile. But perhaps the most eloquent example from this point of view is the use of images like masks which appear to be superimposed on the portraits from 1906 and during the beginning of the Cubist period. They produce a disturbing distortion, in that it is difficult to tell to what extent the features they depict are those of the person in the portrait.

This interest in masks and in the person behind the mask is related to the artist's fascination with the theatre, which began in his childhood. This helps to explain the interplay of multiple, changing personalities appearing in his work, as though on a great stage. Even in his early (*ca.* 1897) painting, for instance *Self Portrait with a Wig* (Barcelona, Museo Picasso), this element of mixing and of humorous transformation of his own image can be perceived. The same thing happens in the portraits of his friend, Jaime Sabartés, whom he introduced as a 'Spanish gentleman', but here with an element of parody that is often cruel or humorous. Even the courtesans who fascinated him in 1901, such as the *Woman in Blue* [CAT. 76] appear through a prism of expressive deformation. In his final period, the many 'musketeers' hark back to the Golden Age in a way that is both ironic and melancholic. In fact, monstrous characters were flourishing in the theatre at that time, the result of a fascination with the deformed which is also reminiscent of seventeenth-century Spain, albeit via Toulouse Lautrec and Van Gogh, in works such as *La Nana* [CAT. 77].

Often, as in the theatre, the comic was combined with the tragic. The need for truth combined with his experience of painting as a kind of diary of his life led Picasso to face up to the tragic suicide of his friend, the painter Carles Casagemas. He painted him recumbent (Paris, Musée Picasso), according to the habitual iconography of the nineteenth century, with post-Impressionist brushstrokes reminiscent of Van Gogh. An absolutely new language emerged from this crisis. When explaining the formation of this language, the influence on the young Picasso of Max Stirner and Nietzsche, via Pompeyo Gener, must be taken into account.[38] The anarchist ideas in vogue in Barcelona may also have had some influence on him. But an idea by Nietzsche, an author who also had a significant influence on Baroja and Azorín, that the disappearance of something released a great energy that could be used in a new creation, is vital in Picasso's work. The concept of history as a burden, as in the *Untimely Considerations*, was very influential at this time. However, despite his desire for novelty, Picasso was inspired, rather than induced to make a veritable *tabula rasa*, by certain artists who were selected by the same sure and absorbing eye that made painters fear his visits to their studios. In a letter to his friend Joaquín Bas concerning his visit to the Museo del Prado in November 1897, Picasso headed the list of what interested him in the museum with the words 'Velázquez, first-rate; El Greco, some magnificent heads'.[39] Both masters, particularly the second, who was not much appreciated at the time, were the focus of his work in the following years. Picasso's fascination with El Greco, which is clear from his Blue Period portraits and, notably, from his *Self Portrait* [CAT. 82] as well as from *La Celestina* [CAT. 81], owed much to his contact at Els Quatre Gats with Santiago Rusiñol (1861–1931) and Miguel Utrillo (1862–1934), who were very enthusiastic about the Cretan painter, as were Regoyos and Zuloaga. He often used a style similar to that of El Greco to depict the marginalised, although they originated from real life, albeit more or less transformed. At the start of the twentieth century, for instance, he painted the prostitutes in the women's hospital of Saint-Lazare in Paris, who appear in his paintings with hoods like that in *La Celestina*. In fact, he painted the latter in accordance with the usual depictions since Goya of an obviously Spanish person.

In the following period, in 1905 Picasso used the image of the harlequin very appropriately to express himself, as indicated by Jung, since Picasso's ability to metamorphose

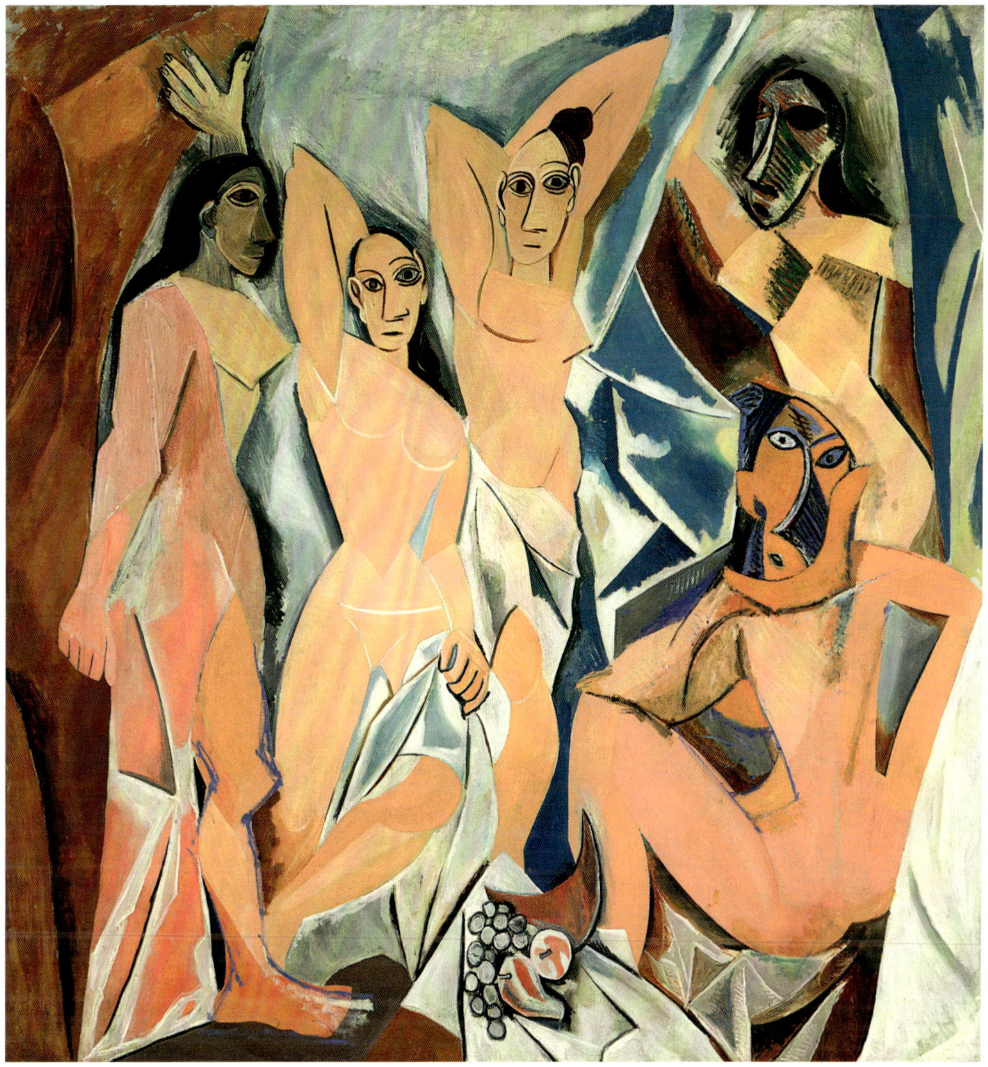

FIG. 129. Pablo Picasso, *Les Demoiselles d'Avignon*, 1907. New York, Museum of Modern Art [Acquired through the Lillie P. Bliss Bequest, 333.1939]

is best defined in iconographic terms by this motif, which also interested Rilke and Apollinaire and relates significantly to the rites of passage to death.[40] This is one of Picasso's many symbolic disguises, like the bull, minotaur, bearded artist and musketeer later on, but the fact that it appears at this time indicates that the painter was now experiencing elusive and changing moods.[41]

We know from Sabartés, whom Picasso had painted twice in 1901, how the artist painted his portraits. He stood, in a rather uncomfortable way which appeared to stimulate him, hunched before the canvas, leaving the pallet on the floor or on some item of furniture, and worked silently with complete concentration.[42] During his initial period, Picasso used models who posed in formal sessions. He also used photography on many occasions. At the time when he painted Benedetta Canals [CAT. 84], he used a camera owned by the painter Ricardo Canals to produce a carefully thought-out self-portrait, with a spacial setting reminiscent of the Baroque style.

In addition, he used the actual printed photographic images for direct inspiration when painting during his Rose Period and at the start of his Cubist period. The images of African figures which appeared in the postcards he used were devoid of the emotion found in photographs of people; this was why they were used in the context of the objective direction which Picasso was taking at that

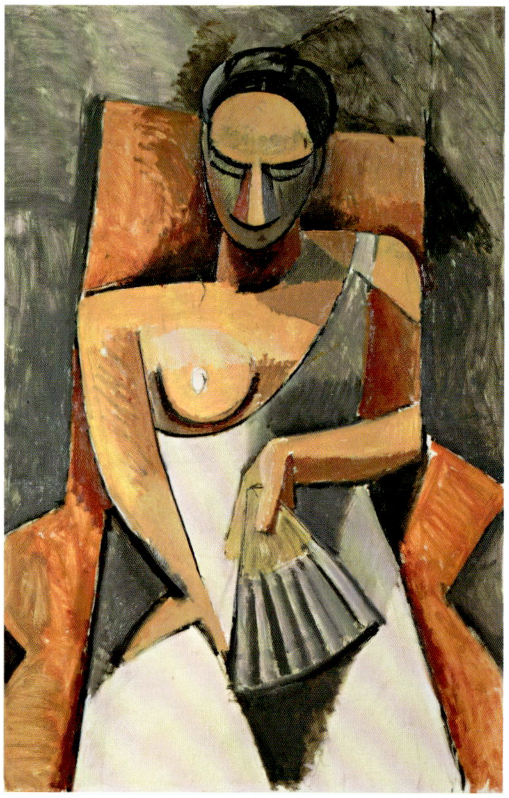

FIG. 130. Pablo Picasso, *Woman with a Fan*, 1908. St Petersburg, The Hermitage

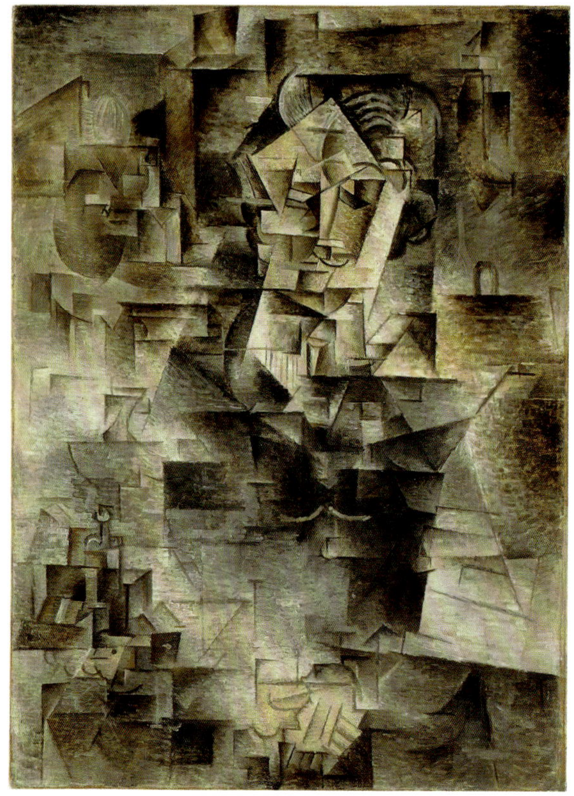

FIG. 131. Pablo Picasso, *Daniel Henry Kahnweiler*, 1910. Chicago, The Art Institute of Chicago

time.[43] They also contributed to his investigation into Cubist reconstruction of the human figure, as did also the powerful images of Egyptian sculpture and the pure Iberian statuettes he could see at the Louvre.

The reflection exercised in the portrait of Gertrude Stein [CAT. 83], produced during over eighty sessions, was another necessary step towards Cubist asceticism. The treatment of the face as a mask and the monumental nature of the figure, which can also be seen in his *Self Portrait with Pallet* (Philadelphia Museum of Art), introduce a completely different character from that of traditional western portraits. Linked to these paintings are the portraits the artist made of Fernande in Gósol in the summer of 1906. There he saw a Romanesque Virgin from the twelfth century,[44] which resulted not only in the extremely monumental nature of the depictions but also in the inscrutability of the facial features. In addition, he was influenced by Ingres since, in 1905, he had seen *The Turkish Bath*.

The origin of Cubism in Picasso's work was in addition related to the presence in his life (a profound experience for him) of his lover, Fernande Olivier, a model whose extremely sculptural features stimulated his painting in Gósol in 1906. Very fertile tension can be felt before the start of Cubism, between the vivid, innovative, formal and original matrices and the intense personality of the figures portrayed in them, whether it was Fernande Olivier, Gertrude Stein or the painter himself in his self-portraits. The artist thus transformed the genre: he approached the portrait with the traditional sessions in front of a model, but turning it into a vehicle headed towards the Cubist revolution.

One question that must be asked is why the portrait, with its individual semantic charge, was of interest to those involved in a movement like Cubism, which was about investigating structure. In fact, the role of the portrait in this search is not alien to the basis of this genre which, for Picasso, acted as a catalyst in transforming his method of painting. His inaugural painting in this genre, *Les Demoiselles d'Avignon* [FIG. 129], can be regarded as a group portrait. A number of influences have been identified in this painting. First, the link with an eminently French tradition of nudes located in interior settings whose antecedents included (apart from Goya) Ingres, Delacroix and Manet. Second, the influence of El Greco and his work *The Opening of the Fifth Seal of the Apocalypse*, which Picasso could have seen since Zuloaga had purchased it. Moreover, other influences adduced include Michelangelo's *Slaves*, the structure used by Raphael, Poussin and Cézanne,[45] and the controversial African masks. However, the artist did not tie himself to any particular national or pictorial tradition. The synthesis between such different elements was surely only possible at that time in a city like Paris, in a district like Montmartre where national differences tended to disappear.[46] In addition, the deformed faces of those suffering from syphilis, whom he saw in Saint-Lazare,[47] have been regarded as potential inspiration; so there is a real starting-point and a direct experience, if we remember the artist's many visits to brothels.

The same occurs with other subsequent paintings such as the *Woman with a Fan* [FIG. 130], in which Fernande's face can be deciphered despite the monumentality and virtual architectural nature of the painting. In these cases, it is clear that the painter was using a *type* in his progress throughout 1909 towards a more refined language.[48] In any case, even during the Analytic Cubist period, the portrait persisted. In the portraits of the art dealers Wilhelm Uhde, Ambroise Vollard and Daniel Henry Kahnweiler in 1910, Picasso had to use his great capacity for characterisation because of the degree of abstraction in the construction of the planes, which was very pronounced in the portrait of the latter [FIG. 131].

In Picasso's subsequent trajectory, the portrait continued to occupy a very important position. His Classical period resulted in a series of painted and drawn portraits in which he recreates a wide gallery of personalities of his time, including his own wife, Olga Koklova. Afterwards, his affairs with Marie Thérèse Walter and Dora Maar marked the years leading up to the Second World War with a profoundly expressionist vision. Extreme pain seems to be expressed in monstrous deformations, with Cubism being used in a way that contradicts completely its original aims, in a typically Picasso subversion, which in this case is performed on the very style he had created himself.

During his last period, an explanation for his previous trajectory emerges. On the one hand, the portraits of women are reworked with great vitality, for instance the images of Jacqueline Roqué. On the other hand, the self-portrait became submerged in interpretations in which Picasso hides behind the often melancholic disguise of a 'musketeer', or appears as an artist, identifying himself with Rembrandt or Degas, or with some other painter. The images are like mirrors in which the subjectivity of the artist is reflected.[49] The meaning of the portrait in terms of specific or extreme individuality is diluted into a set of interpretations that are much more ambiguous and changing within a kind of 'great world stage', with universal value.

If we compare some of the figures which Picasso painted during the Blue Period with his last self-portrait [CAT. 87], we will notice the importance in both cases of the wounded gaze. Picasso was terrified of blindness,[50] and in his Blue Period he linked it to examples of miserable, destitute beings, like the blind beggars he painted, which were like projections of the psychic crisis he was going through. A clear symptom of loneliness was also the 'short-sighted gaze', as described by Sabartés when he saw his own portrait in Paris in 1901.[51] Picasso painted self-portraits at every critical moment in his life, as a kind of exorcism to help him avert a threat. When he produced the last ones a few months before his death, which he confronts in them, a damaged eye appears again, very markedly, anticipating the destruction of the being.

Picasso's painting influenced the work of the many Spanish artists who travelled to Paris in successive waves. The application of Cubist techniques to the human figure and the return to order which occurred at the end of the 1920s and during the 1930s are inspired by his work. One of them, Daniel Vázquez Díaz, produced circa 1918 a synthesis of traditional and post-Cubist painting which was possible because of the years he had spent in Paris.

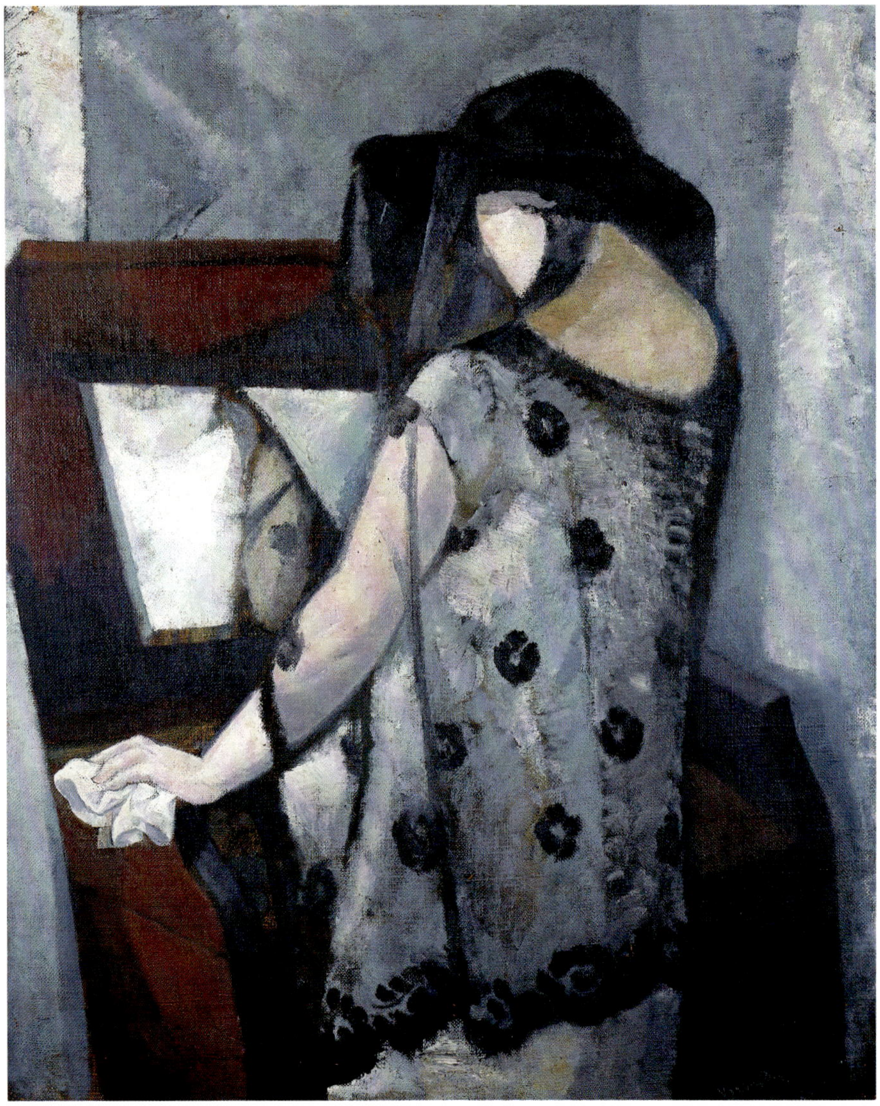

FIG. 132. Daniel Vázquez Díaz, *Woman in Grey*, 1923. Madrid, Laura Vázquez Aggerholm

His pictorial portraits and drawings (the former are grouped together in a large series known as *Men of My Time* produced in the course of over fifty years) are very important in his work. The monumentality and the solidity of the volume of his figures, learnt from Antoine Bourdelle, the careful measuring of his use of colour and the severity of his composition in terms of planes, as can be seen in *Woman in Grey* [FIG. 132], 1923, endow them with an aspect which has been related to typical Spanish austerity (as with Zurbarán), but at the same time they provided a basis for assimilating the avant-garde which exerted considerable influence in Spain.[52]

The artists who really exerted influence in the international arena were the ones who stayed in Paris, including Juan Gris, Joan Miró and Salvador Dalí. Unlike Picasso, Gris, as pointed out by Kahnweiler, disappears in his painting. In his well-known text, *Possibilities of Painting* (*Posibilidades de la pintura*), he describes his work as 'flat, coloured architecture', and this is already clear in his *Homage to Pablo Picasso* [CAT. 85]. In his portraits, he achieves a spiritual objectiveness which enables him to portray the essential permanence in the image of the sitter, as in paintings such as *Josette, the Artist's Wife* [FIG. 133] of 1916. None of his portraits are of types since they all maintain a sufficient amount of specific features.[53] However, the painter ended up abandoning the portrait since his search led him naturally to concentrate on the still life.

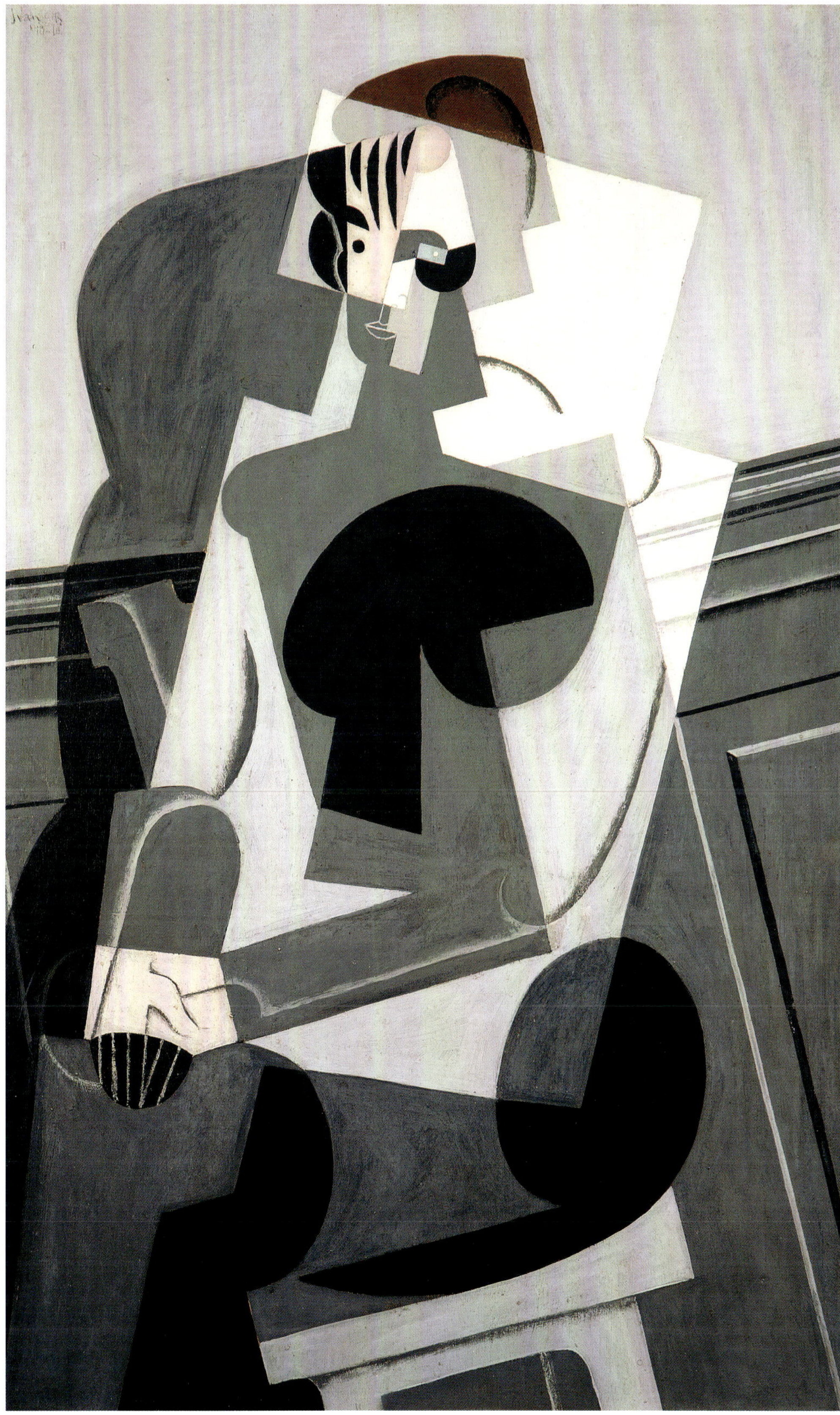

FIG. 133. Juan Gris, *Josette, the Artist's Wife*, 1916. Madrid, Museo Nacional Centro de Arte Reina Sofia [AS-12050]

The 1920s was also the best decade in terms of originality for the painter María Gutiérrez Blanchard (1881–1932), who already in 1914 had demonstrated her special interpretation of the human figure in *The Communicant* (Madrid, MNCARS). This painting comprises, in a surprising way, the almost primitive solidity of the bodies with an imaginative and intense, coloured iridescence. Shortly afterwards she embarked on Cubism with a painting, *Woman with a Fan* (Madrid, MNCARS), which revealed her interest in structure, based on rounded planes of colour. Afterwards, in line with this avant-garde movement, she produced portraits similar to those of Juan Gris. Disillusioned by the almost abstract rigour of these artworks, she created her own special iconography of motherhood and portraits of children and convalescents. Up until 1925, her figures show considerable plasticity, consisting of vivid reflections of cold light, in an atmosphere of strangeness imbued with a spirit that can be linked to the contemporary searches by the Central European New Objectivity movement. Afterwards, the superabundant volumes give way to the spiritualised vision and profound melancholy of invalids and the sick, both in oil and pastels.

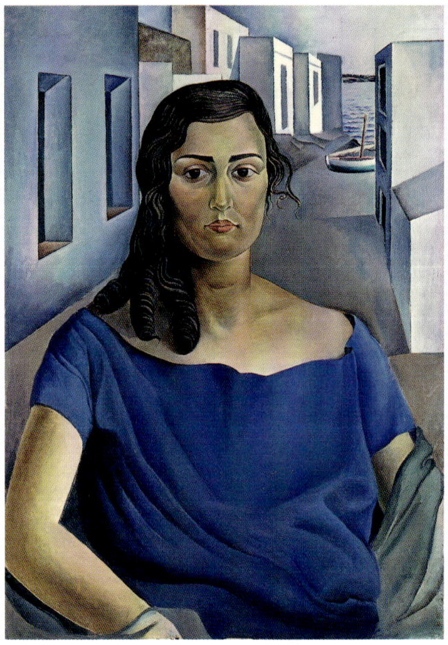

FIG. 134. Salvador Dalí, *Ana María in Cadaqués*, *ca.* 1925. Figueras, Fundación Gala y Salvador Dalí

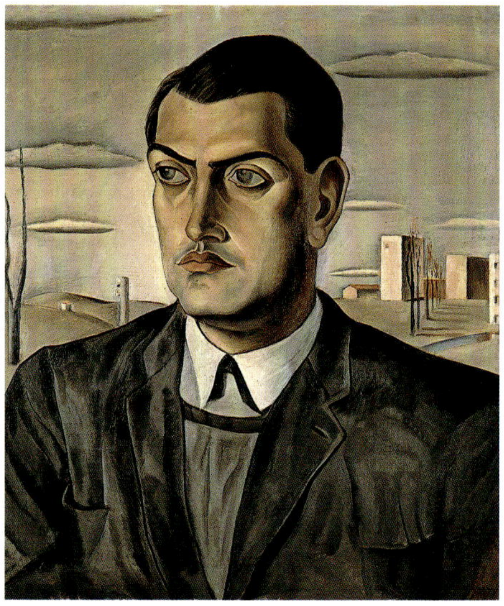

FIG. 135. Salvador Dalí, *Luis Buñuel*, 1924. Madrid, Museo Nacional Centro de Arte Reina Sofia [AS-10530]

Joan Miró (1893–1983) produced his portraits in his period prior to Surrealism, while he was still in Barcelona. They indicate very clearly how the artist looked for a genuine and authentic starting point for his work and, despite his closeness in his first self-portrait to avant-garde movements which had already disappeared, such as Fauvism, or in his second self-portrait [CAT. 86] to ones that were in crisis, such as Cubism, the portraits reveal a Mediterranean sense of a distinct, compact form. His *Portrait of a Spanish Dancer* (Paris, Musée Picasso), 1921, shows the power of drawing in understanding the plastic form with complete objectivity.

This generation consists of a number of artists who were also to make the trip to Paris and turn into defenders of the 'new art'.[54] The main one was José de Togores (1893–1970) who, as an admirer of Torres García, came under the dual influence in Paris of Cubism and of Picasso's Classicist works, which he linked to his *'noucentista'* experience using rounded figures, following the lines of Magic Realism. Lastly, in the initial work of Salvador Dalí (1904–1989), self-portraits occupy an exceptional position. They portray both the characteristic narcissism of the artist and an obvious search for his own identity. After the experimental *Cubist Self Portrait* (Madrid, MNCARS) in 1923, the portrait of his friend

Luis Buñuel [FIG. 135] reveals a return to order inspired by Italian Renaissance masters such as Mantegna. The portraits dedicated to his sister, including *Ana María in Cadaqués* [FIG. 134], depict a limpid Mediterranean vision related to the work of artists such as Valori Plastici. As in Miró, the moment prior to the avant-garde movement is marked, precisely in the portrait, by the abundance and solidity of the form. In the Surrealist period, this was to become *soft*, but the strangeness and desolation of the atmosphere in his future paintings seem to be heralded by the climate of concentrated silence surrounding the figures of this period.

NOTES

1 On this subject and on the question of the avant-garde in Spain, see the many texts written by Juan Manuel Bonet, Valeriano Bozal, Jaime Brihuega, Francisco Calvo Serraller and Eugenio Carmona, among others.
2 Nordau not dated, p. 38.
3 Milhou 1981, vol. 1, p. 107–29.
4 Olivier 1990, p. 142.
5 Lafuente Ferrari 1950a, p. 18, n. 6.
6 Unamuno (1920) not dated, p. 21.
7 Gómez de la Serna (1918) 1986, p. 168.
8 Moreno Villa 1944, p. 165.
9 Fontbona 1975.
10 Junoy 1934, p. 320.
11 Calvo Serraller 1998, p. 34.
12 Beruete y Moret (1903) 1926, p. 147.
13 Nelken 1917, pp. 127 and 128.
14 Pérez Rojas 2003, pp. 123–56.
15 Azorín (1913) 1954, p. 67.
16 The most well-stocked exhibition was the *National Portrait Exhibition* (*Exposición Nacional de Retratos*) in 1902, the catalogue for which was published in Madrid by Casa Editorial Mateu. In Barcelona, the *Exhibition of Ancient and Modern Portraits and Drawings* (*Exposición de retratos y dibujos antiguos y modernos*) was held in 1910, supported by the city council. The 'Society of Friends of Art' ('Sociedad de Amigos del Arte') organised, in addition to its own exhibitions, one on *The Miniature Portrait in Spain* (*La miniatura retrato en España*) (Madrid, 1916), *Portraits of Women by Spanish Artists prior to 1850* (*Retratos de mujeres por artistas españoles anteriores a 1850*) (Madrid, 1918) and *Portraits of Children in Spain* (*Retratos de niño en España*) (Madrid, 1925).
17 Barcia 1901.
18 *Junta de Iconografía Nacional*, 1914.
19 Tormo 1917; Allende-Salazar and Sánchez Cantón 1919. In 1920, the Committee organised a competition to award a prize to the best thesis presented on the theme 'Portraits of Spanish women in the 19th century' ('Retratos de mujeres españolas del siglo XIX'), which was won by Joaquín Ezquerra del Bayo and Luis Pérez Bueno, whose works were published in Madrid in 1924.
20 Pérez Rojas 2000.
21 Baroja 1952, p. 183.
22 López Fernández 2003, p. 26; López de Prado 1999, p. 185.
23 Barón 1999, p. 19 ff.
24 José Moreno Villa (1951, p. 45) wrote that Solana 'sees people like wooden dolls and mummified beings who are in a procession, holding masks or sitting taking coffee a century ago'.
25 Juan Ramón Jiménez (1960, p. 170) described the painter's solitude very well, as if he were 'confined behind thick glass'.
26 Alonso Fernández 1979, p. 99.
27 Parmelin 1968, p. 33.
28 Taken from Encina 1924, p. 169.
29 *La Tribuna*, Madrid, 19 August 1912. See Marcos Villalón 2003, p. 164.
30 See Leal, Ocaña, Cerverau, Bozal *et al.* 2003.
31 Rubin 1991, p. 15.
32 Llorens 1986, p. 20.
33 Abril (1935, p. 96) referred to the person painted by the artist as a 'creature [...] which he leaves alone, isolated, surrounded by a space which is full of soul, nothing else, and in which she, the person, has only the essential corporeal existence'.
34 Rubin 1996, p. 13.
35 Daix 1995, p. 300.
36 Richardson 1988, p. 41.
37 Daix 1988, p. 37.
38 Cirici 1946, p. 134.
39 Salas 1960, p. 483.
40 Starobinski 1970, p. 126. His Rose Period is, in this respect, the most intense, but that of the *Commedia dell'arte*, from 1915, has a playful nature. In 1923 he appears in figures of extreme plasticity, in melancholic reflection. See Leymarie 1985, p. 23; and Clair 2004, pp. 21–33.
41 Penrose 1958, p. 108.
42 Sabartés 1946, pp. 88 and 89.
43 Baldassari 1997, p. 81.
44 Palau i Fabre 1980, p. 477; Richardson 1991, p. 452.
45 Rosenblum 1976, p. 15.
46 Lubar 1999, p. 54.
47 Rubin 1988, p. 423.
48 Weiss 2004, p. 40.
49 Gallwitz 1971, p. 186.
50 Berger 1973, p. 51.
51 Sabartés 1946, p. 72.
52 Brihuega 1981, p. 229.
53 Kahnweiler 1971, p. 220.
54 Carmona 1991, p. 54 ff.

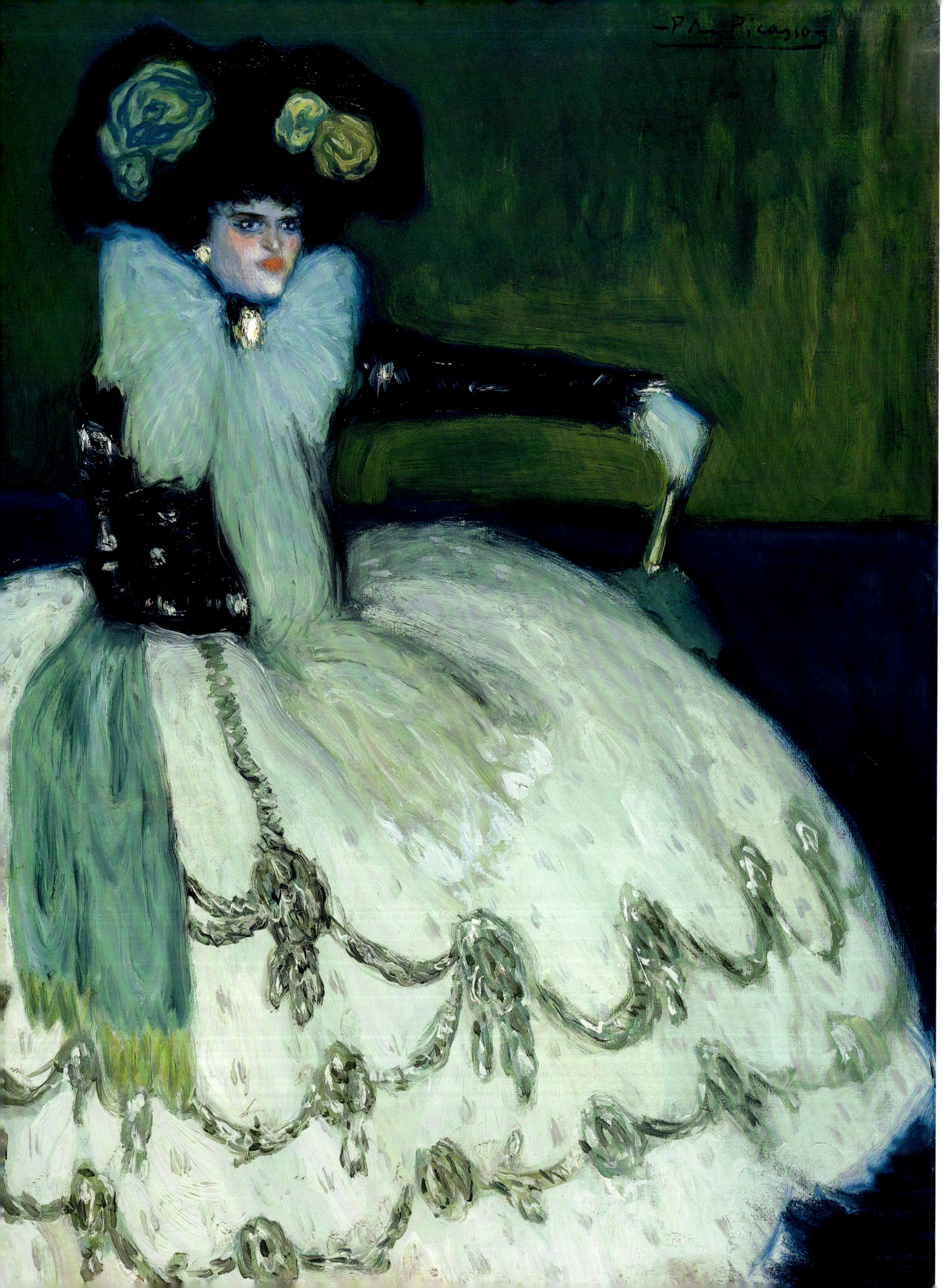

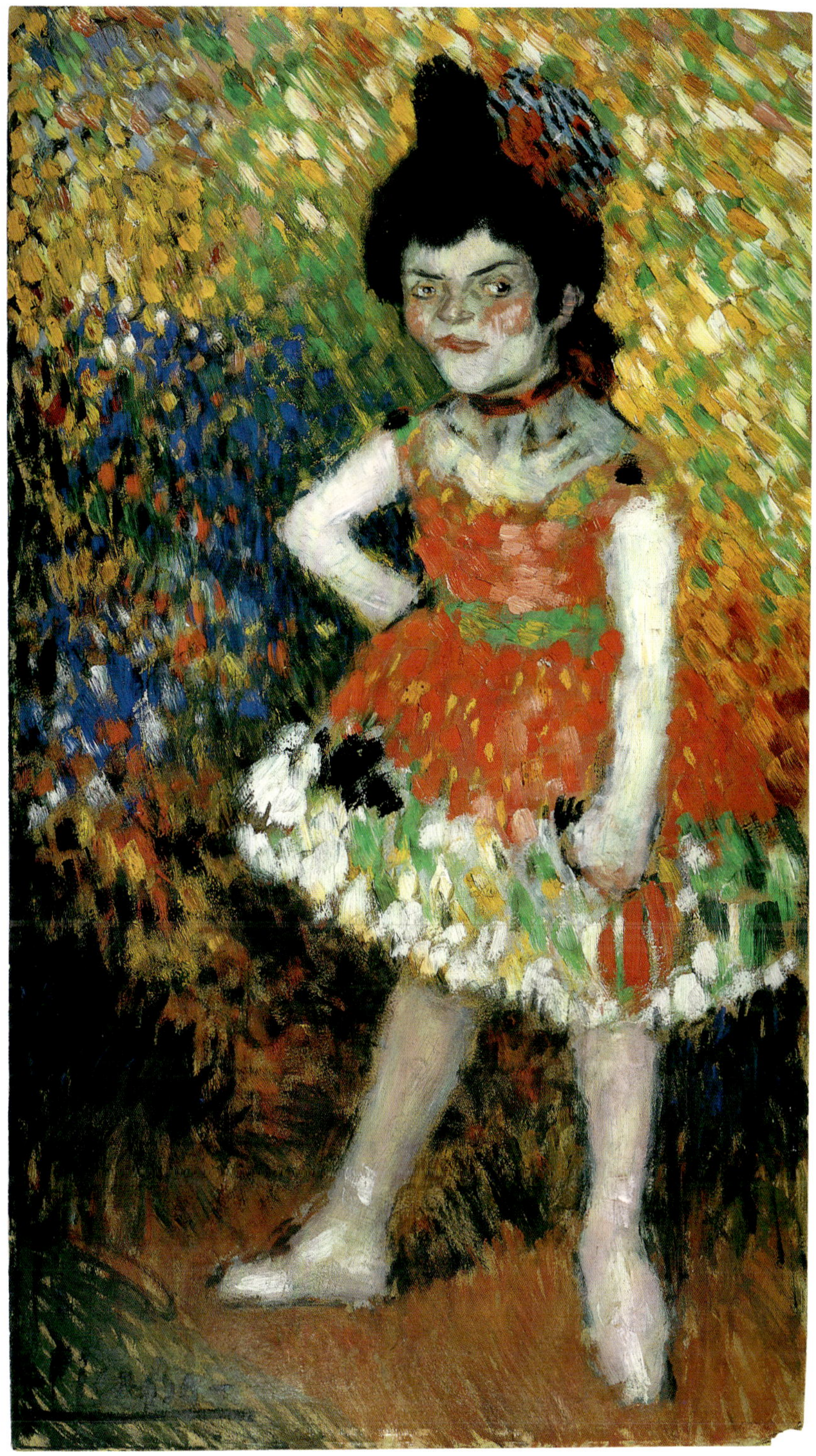

CAT. 76. Pablo Picasso. *Woman in Blue*, 1901. Madrid, Museo Nacional Centro de Arte Reina Sofía [AS-1618]

CAT. 77. Pablo Picasso. *La Nana*, 1901. Barcelona, Museu Picasso [4274]

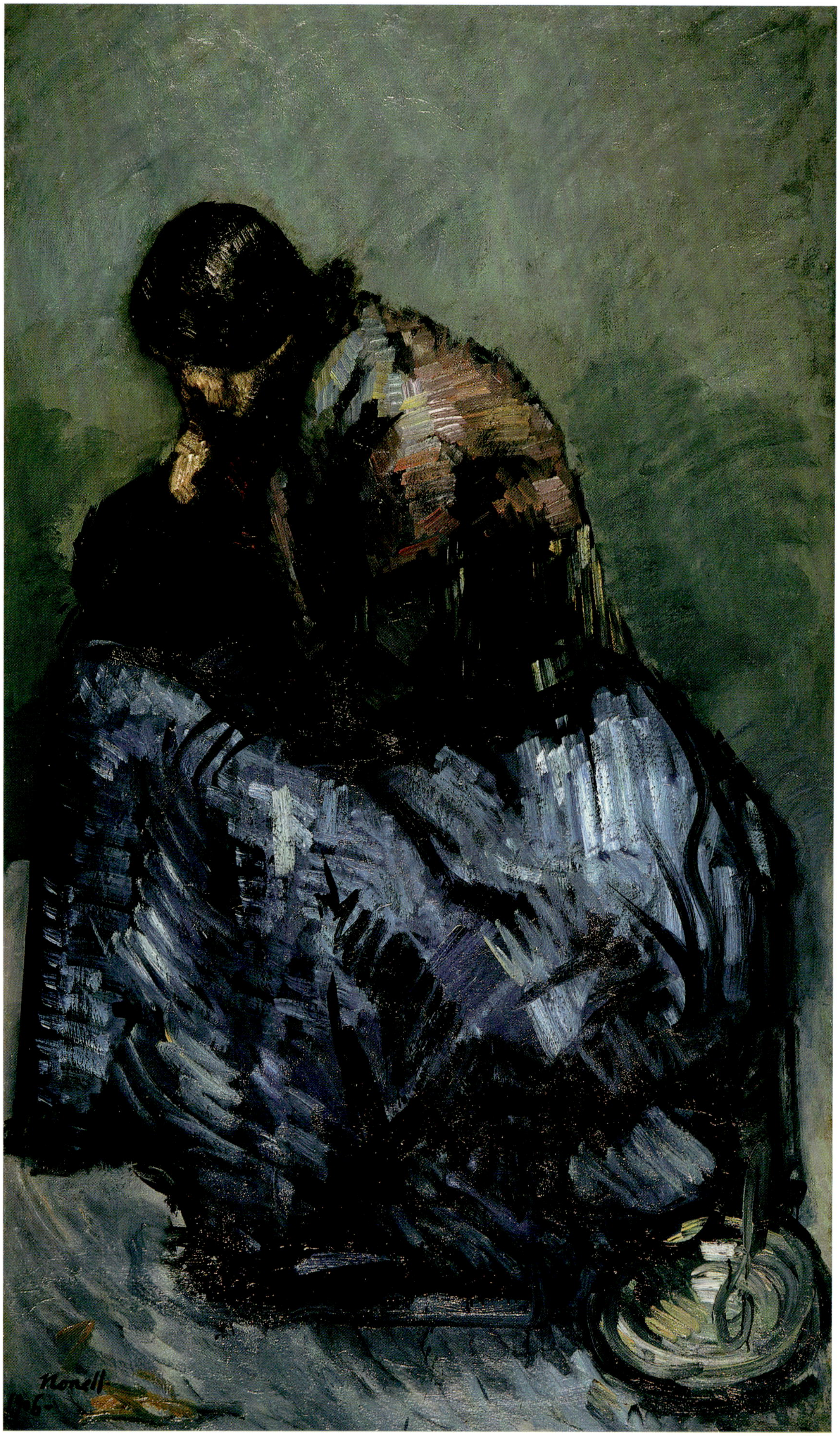

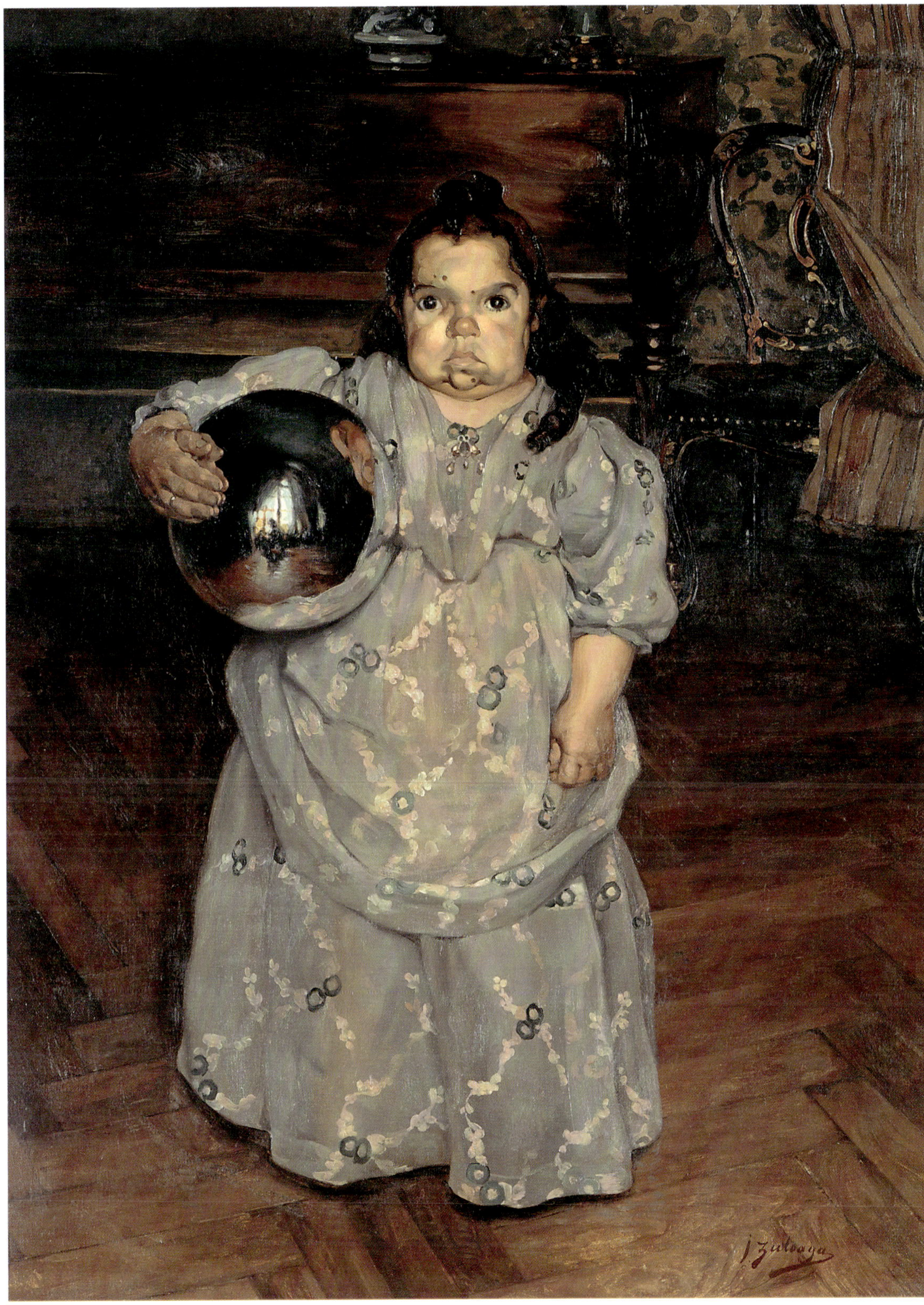

CAT. 78. Isidro Nonell. *Study of a Gypsy*, 1906. Colección Masaveu

CAT. 79. Ignacio Zuloaga. *The Dwarf Doña Mercedes*, 1899. Paris, Musée d'Orsay [RF 1977-438]

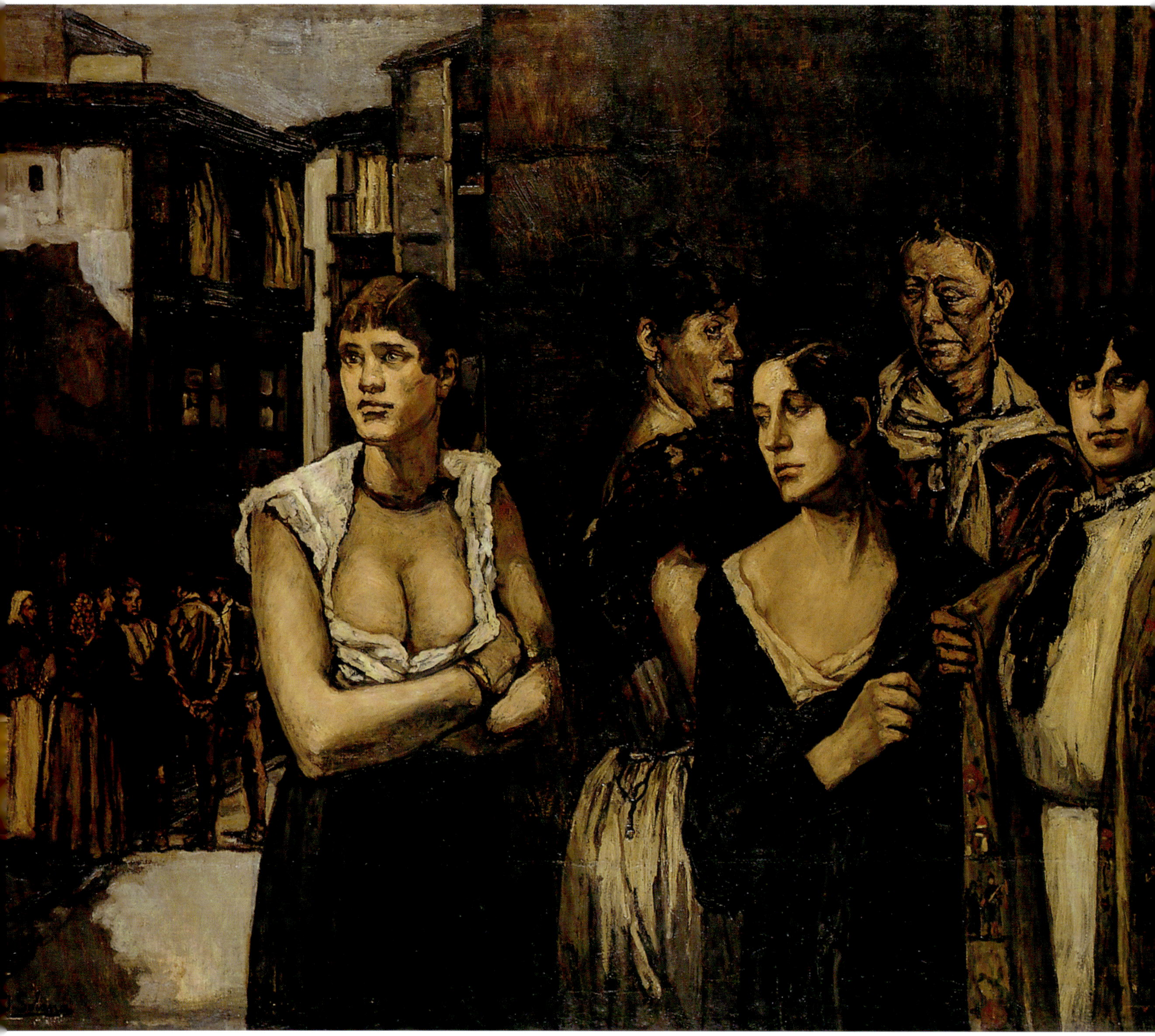

CAT. 80. José Gutiérrez Solana. *Mujeres de la vida, ca.* 1915. Bilbao, Museo de Bellas Artes [82-278]

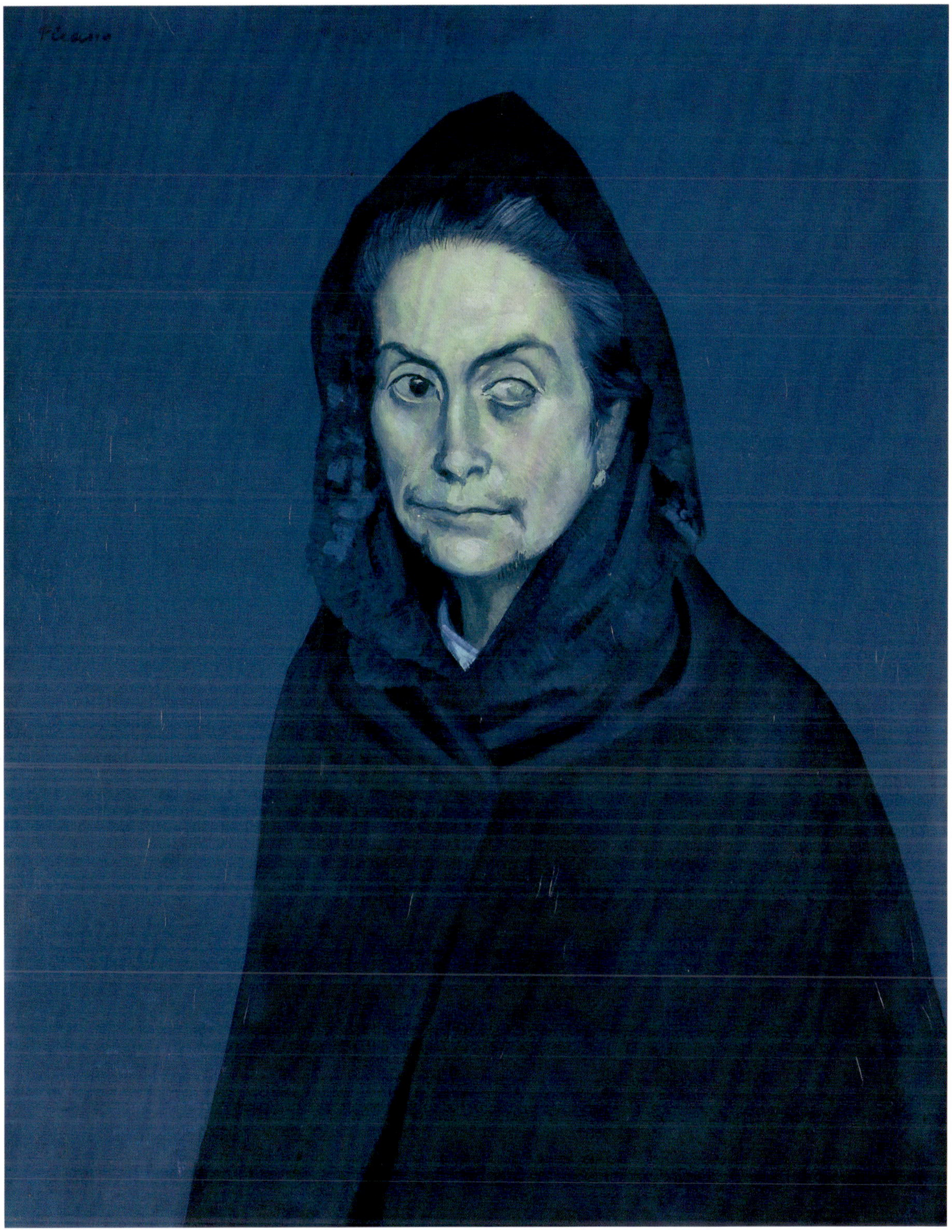

CAT. 81. Pablo Picasso. *La Celestina*, 1904. Paris, Musée Picasso [MP 1989-5]

CAT. 82. Pablo Picasso. *Self Portrait*, 1901. Paris, Musée Picasso [MP 4]

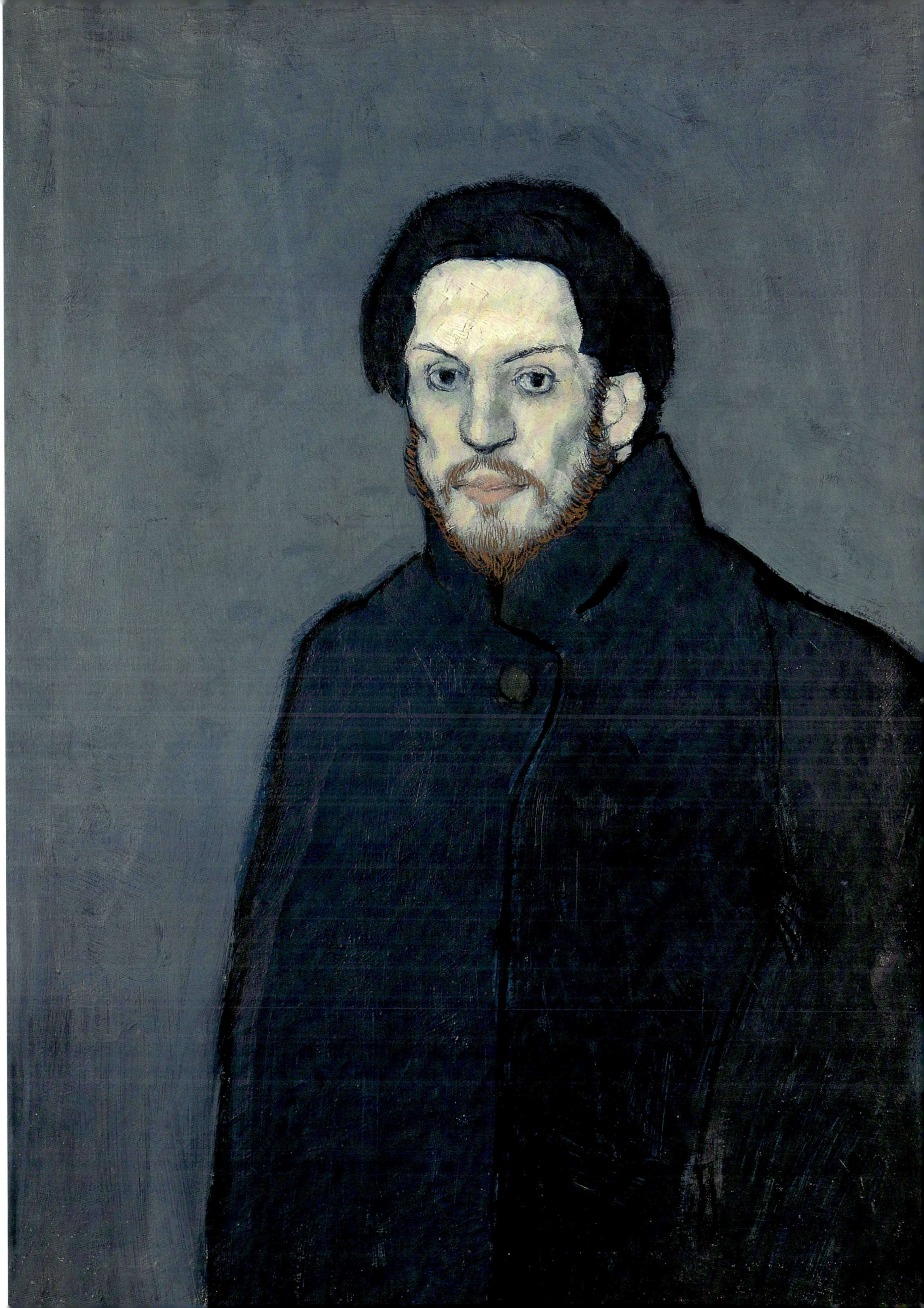

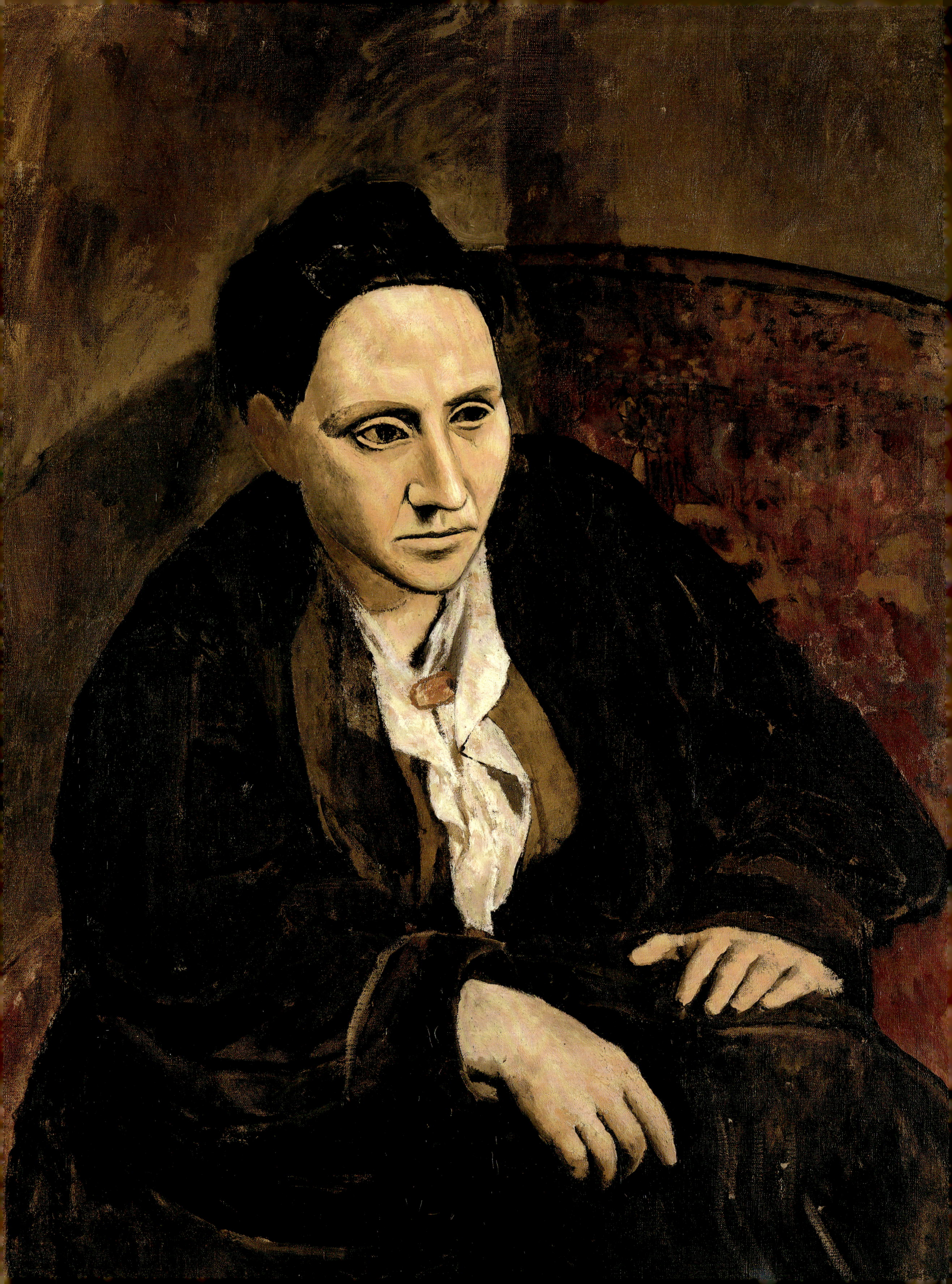

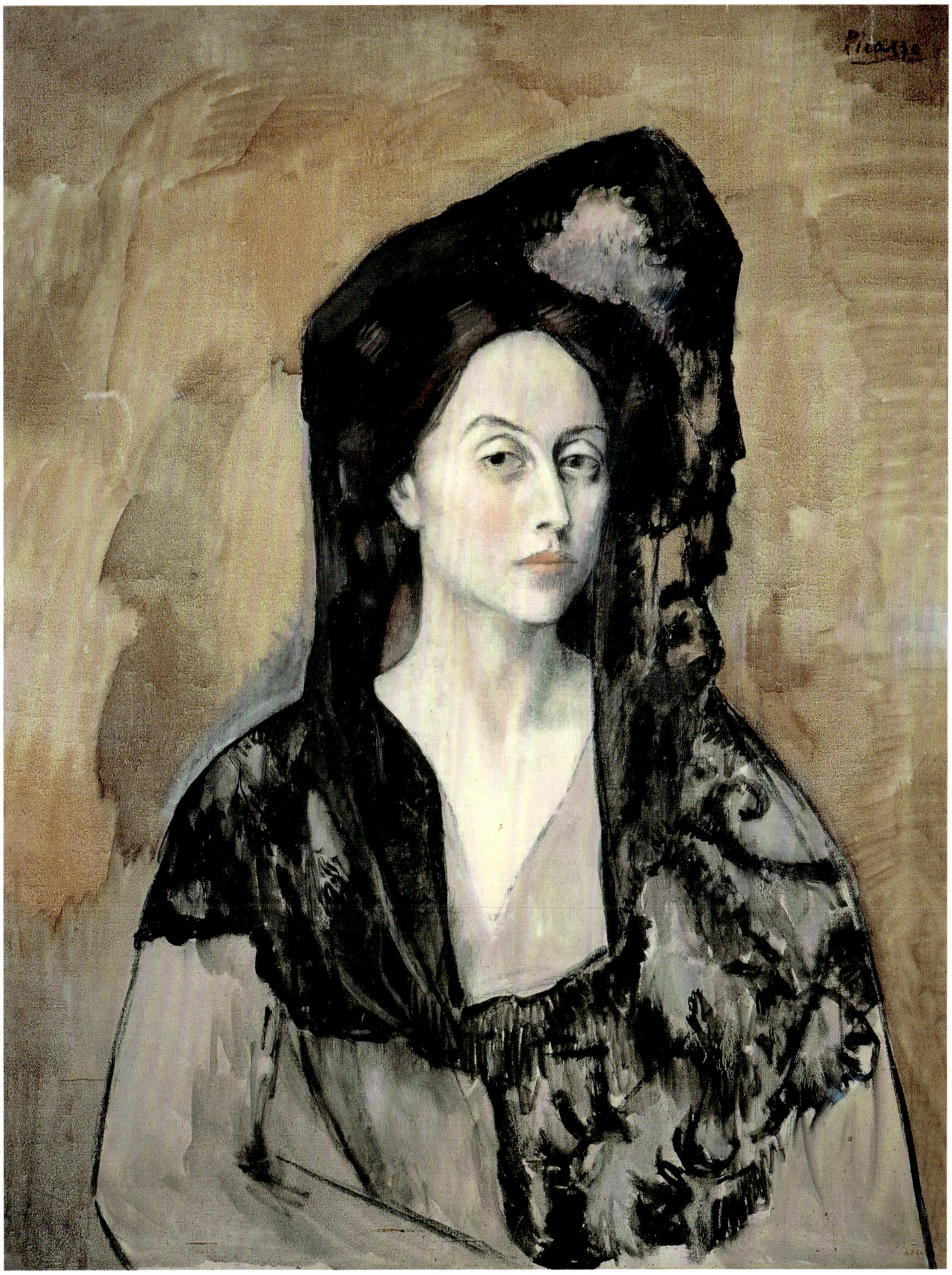

CAT. 83. Pablo Picasso. *Gertrude Stein*, 1906.
New York, The Metropolitan Museum of Art.
Bequest of Gertrude Stein, 1946 [47.106]

CAT. 84. Pablo Picasso. *Señora Canals*, 1905.
Barcelona, Museu Picasso [4266]

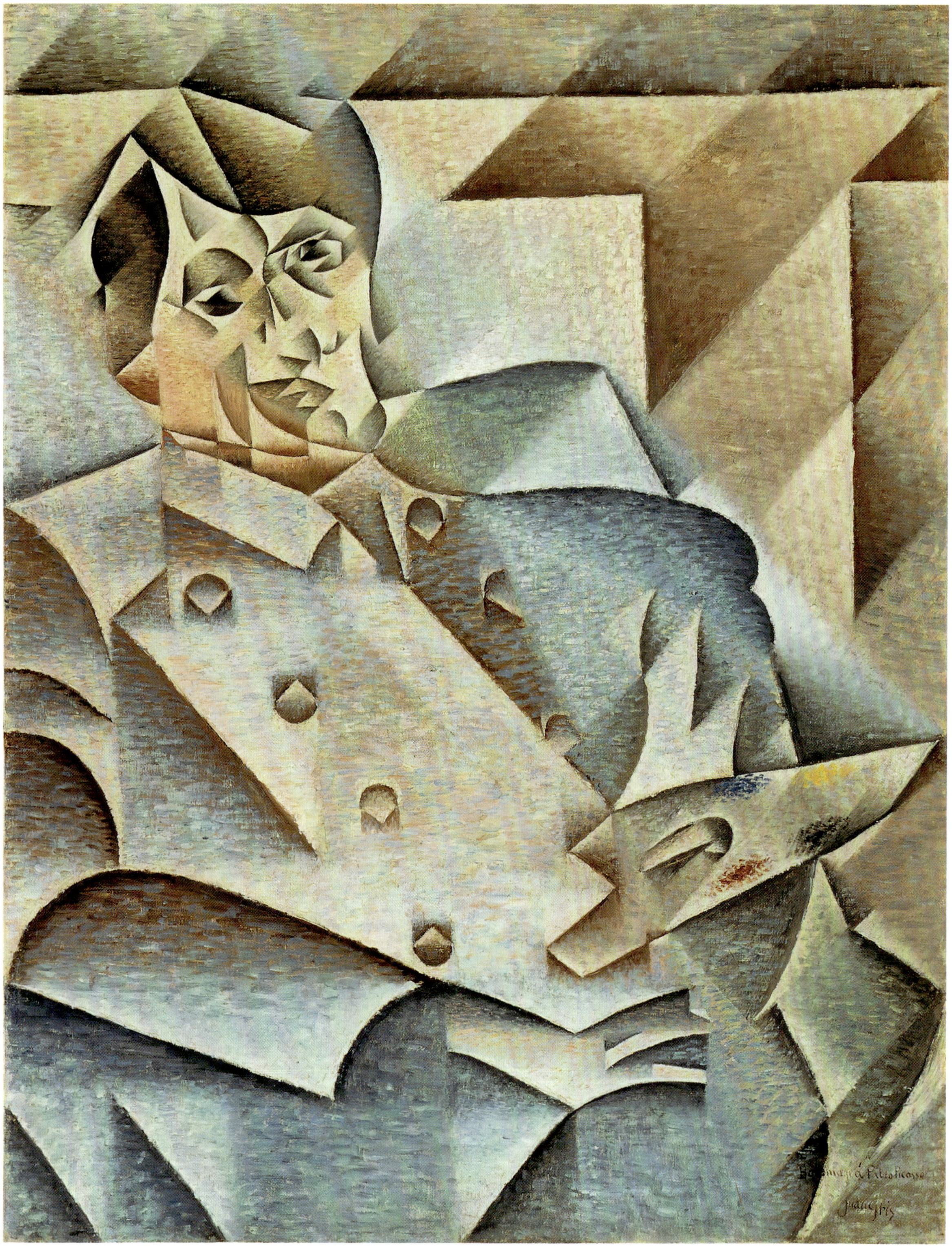

CAT. 85. Juan Gris. *Homage to Pablo Picasso*, 1912.
Chicago, The Art Institute of Chicago, Gift of Leigh B. Block [1958.525]

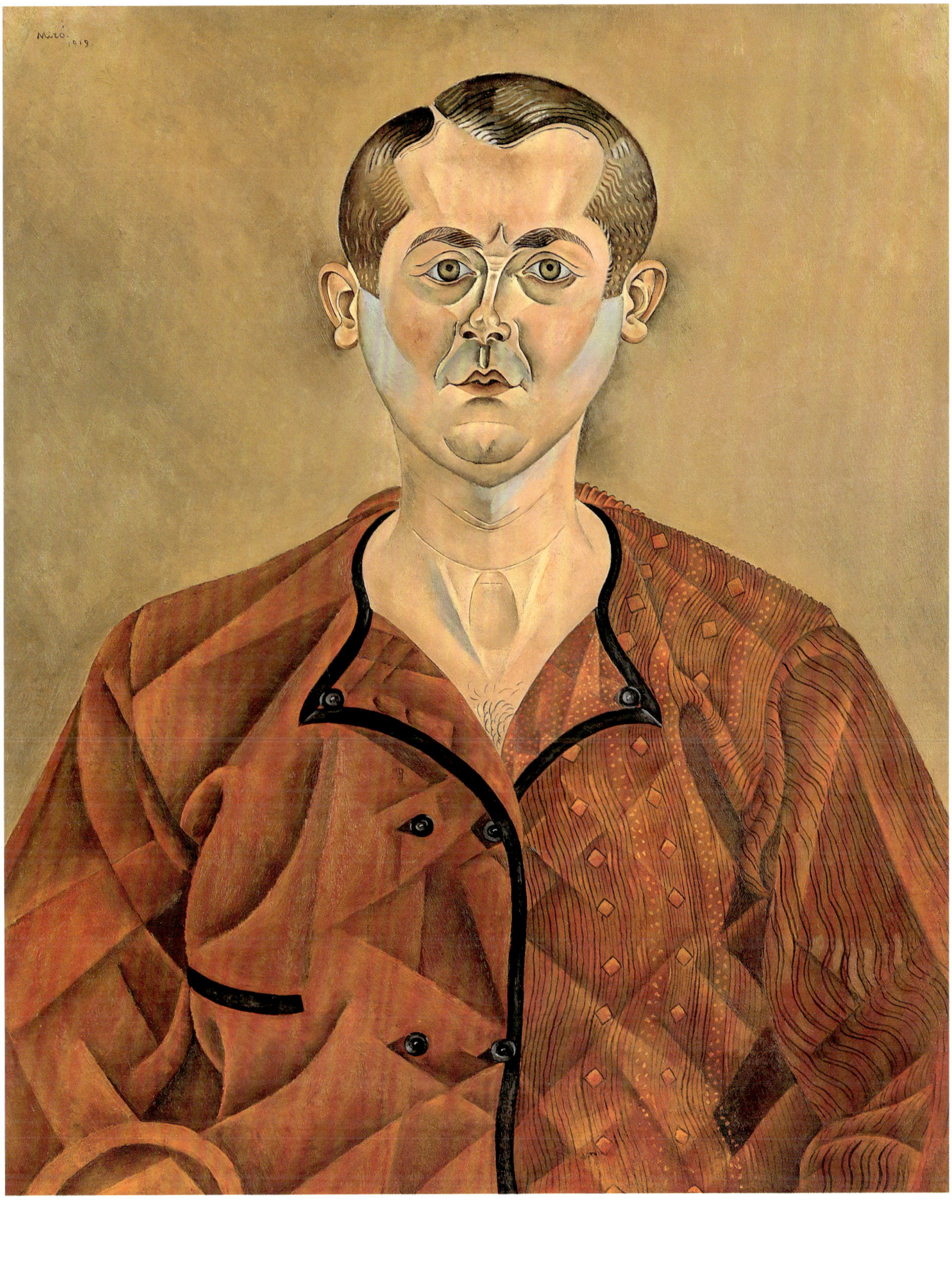

CAT. 86. Joan Miró. *Self Portrait*, 1919.
Paris, Musée Picasso [RF 1973-79]

CAT. 87. Pablo Picasso. *Self Portrait*, 1972. Private collection, courtesy of Fuji Television Gallery

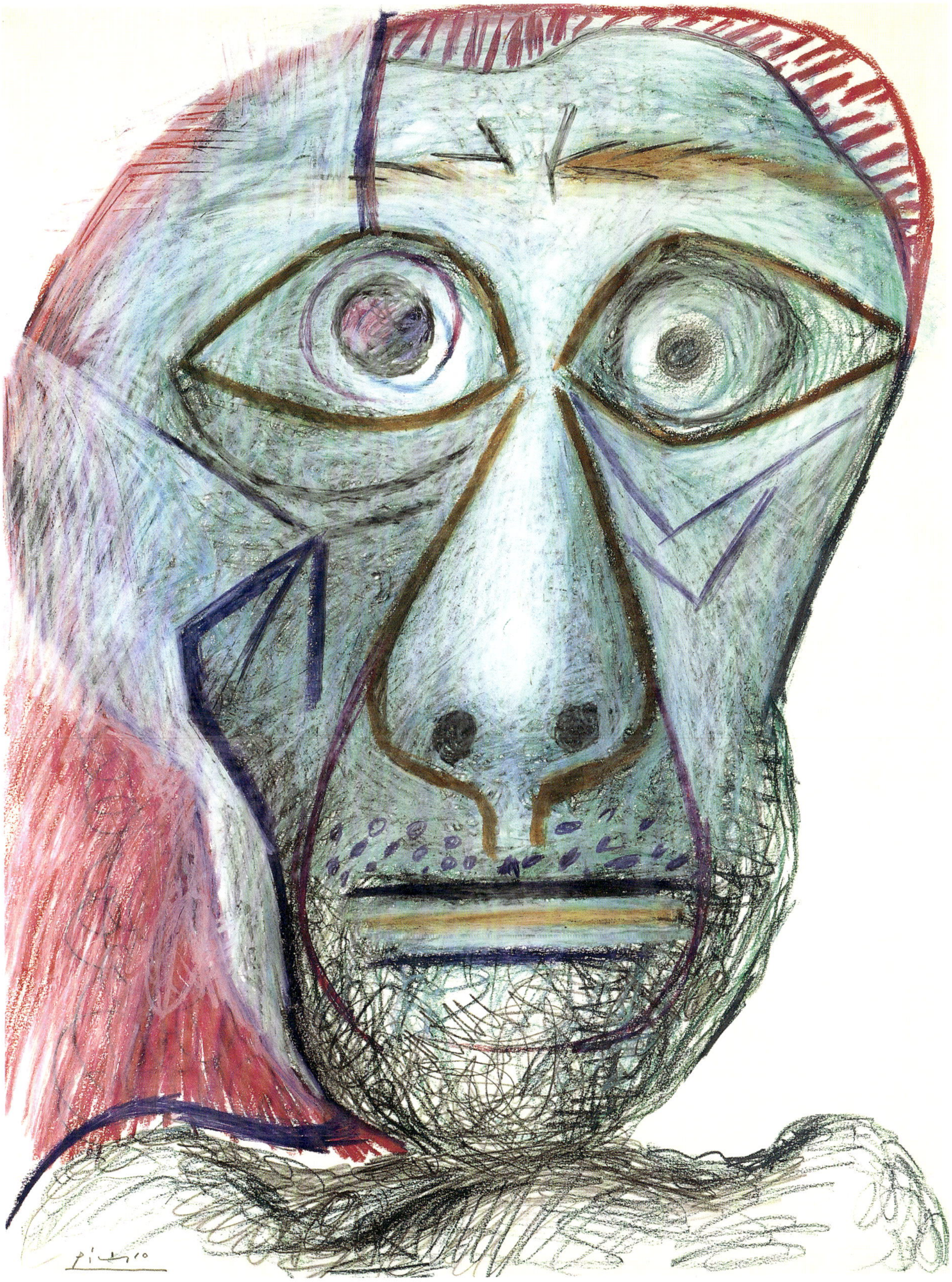

Catalogue

AEPS	Alfonso E. Pérez Sánchez
GF	Gabriele Finaldi
JAL	José Álvarez Lopera
JB	Javier Barón
JP	Javier Portús
LRG	Leticia Ruiz Gómez
MMM	Manuela B. Mena Marqués
NG	Nigel Glendinning
PSM	Pilar Silva Maroto

I The Origin of Portrait Painting in Spain

1 Bartolomé Bermejo
[doc. 1468–1501]

Saint Dominic of Silos, 1474–1477
Oil on panel, 242 x 130 cm
Madrid, Museo del Prado, P-1323

PROVENANCE
Altarpiece dedicated to Saint Dominic of Silos, in the church of the same name in Daroca (Zaragoza). Museo Arqueológico Nacional, 1869. Museo del Prado, since 1920.

ESSENTIAL BIBLIOGRAPHY
Campillo and Casamor 1875, p. 550; Serrano and Sanz 1914, pp. 455–58 and 1916, pp. 482–85; Tormo and Monzó 1926, pp. 11–87; Post V 1934 pp. 115–26; Young 1975, pp. 44–46 and 138–39; Berg-Sobré 1977, pp. 484–500; Mateo Gómez 1985, pp. 4–13; Berg-Sobré 1997, pp. 45–64 and 192–96; Lacarra Ducay 2003, pp. 170–79, no. 9; Berg-Sobré 2003, pp. 20–22, Alcolea 2003, pp. 444–47, no. 66.

Bartolomé Bermejo was commissioned to paint the altarpiece for the church of Saint Dominic of Silos in Daroca, in the province of Zaragoza, on 5 September 1474; he undertook to complete the work by Christmas 1475 and to do it all by his own hand. The central panel showing Saint Dominic enthroned must already have been finished when Bermejo moved to the city of Zaragoza in 1477. Despite being bound by a contract that allowed for his excommunication (and publication of the fact that it had been put into effect) if he left Daroca before completing the altarpiece, he did indeed leave for Zaragoza without having done so.

There, in the capital of Aragon, on 28 September 1477 the patrons of the altarpiece for the church in Daroca signed another contract, with the painter Martín Bernat, in which the latter agreed that, should Bermejo fail to complete the altarpiece, he would do so himself.

On 17 November a further contract was signed, with Bermejo present, which gave him until May 1479 to finish the work and whereby he undertook to paint the predella himself. As for the panels for the body of the altarpiece, which were yet to be done, Bermejo undertook to paint only the two principal figures and the nudes and faces – that is, the flesh.

The subject matter of the central panel, showing Saint Dominic of Silos, prevents it from being classified as a portrait. In Aragon, in the same way as it was in Castile for Pedro Berruguete, if a painter wished to avoid the wrath of the Inquisition he could not represent a holy figure – in this case the Benedictine saint – using the features of a known person. Nevertheless, because of Bermejo's naturalistic depiction of features, and above all the strong characterisation he imprints on all his figures, his paintings of this kind are rather like 'concealed portraits'. Furthermore, in the case of Bermejo we can see the difference between such images (in which similar features, those favoured by the artist, are repeated) and the three surviving portraits of known individuals – shown in religious works in their capacity as donors – that bear his signature. The earliest of these, on a panel painted in 1468 for the parish church in Tous, is a portrait of Antonio Juan, who is depicted kneeling in front of Saint Michael triumphant over the Devil (London, The National Gallery, NG 1468), in profile and on a smaller scale than the saint. Also shown on a smaller scale, but much more individualised, is Francesco della Chiesa, the donor painted by Bermejo in his *Triptych of the Madonna of Montserrat* in Acqui Terme cathedral. Canon Lluís Desplá, on the other hand, is painted to the same scale as, and also shares the same space with, the Virgin, Christ and Saint Jerome in Bermejo's *Pietà* of 1490 now in the museum in Barcelona Cathedral – without doubt the best-known portrait by any Spanish painter of the fifteenth century. In this work, Bermejo flaunts his mastery of Flemish techniques, which enabled him to capture the qualities of objects and to differentiate between materials.

Whether in the Low Countries themselves, as has so often been said, or without ever leaving the kingdom of Aragon where he worked all his life, in Valencia in the studio of the Alimbrots, Bartolomé Bermejo must have had access to the secrets of Flemish art. Certainly his knowledge of oil painting techniques – far greater than that of other Spanish-Flemish painters – is the ultimate reason for his naturalism, as can be verified in the panel of *Saint Dominic of Silos* in the Museo del Prado. Although Bermejo followed the instructions of the committee responsible for supervising the execution of this altarpiece by representing the saint dressed as a bishop, instead of as the Benedictine abbot that he was, and by painting the seven virtues he had been asked to include, he did not comply with the requirement for Saint Dominic to be shown 'seated on a chair in pontifical robes encrusted with gold'. If Bermejo had heeded the committee's demands – as did all the painters who worked in Aragon and also in Catalonia during this period – and adorned with gold the rich chasuble worn by the saint, the final effect would have been very different. Gold in relief interferes with the visual impact of an image in such a way that if Bermejo had used it as required, rather than simulating the three dimensions with his brush on the flat surface, the air of strength, of monumentality, in the figure of Saint Dominic – deep in thought and with his body and head facing forward – would have been lost, since the decorative elements would have dominated the picture. [PSM]

2 Pedro Berruguete
[*ca.* 1445/1450–1503]

Hezekiah, *ca.* 1490
Oil on panel, 94 x 65 cm
Paredes de Nava,
Museo Parroquial de Santa Eulalia

PROVENANCE
Paredes de Nava (Palencia), altarpiece over the high altar in the church of Saint Eulalia. It is preserved in the same place for which it was painted. See text.

ESSENTIAL BIBLIOGRAPHY
Martí and Monsó 1898–1901; Laínez Alcalá 1935, pp. 39–40; Angulo Íñiguez 1946; Post IX 1947, pp. 84–89; Angulo Íñiguez 1964, pp. 76–77; Angulo Íñiguez 1965, pp. 5–12; Cabrera Garrido and Garrido Pérez 1982, pp. 152–57; Zalama Rodríguez 1988, pp. 366–69, 373 and 375; Reynaud and Réssort 1991, pp. 108 and 110; Silva Maroto 1998, pp. 183–92; Silva Maroto 2000b, pp. 292–93; Silva Maroto 2003, pp. 144–61.

The painting forms part of the predella of the altarpiece in the church of Saint Eulalia in Paredes de Nava (Palencia), the painter's birthplace, which remains *in situ*. Although this altarpiece, made around 1490, is not documented, there is a record of its author in a later document published by Miguel Ángel Zalama in 1988. When the name of the church was changed in the middle of the sixteenth century and it was rededicated to Saint Eulalia, the parishioners planned to replace the old altarpiece above the high altar, painted by Pedro Berruguete, with a new sculpted one to be commissioned from Inocencio Berruguete, a relative of Pedro. Fortunately for us, since the parishioners did not have the 3,000 *ducados* it would have cost, the Bishop of Palencia, Pedro de la Gasca, ordered a much cheaper one to be made, which he finally commissioned from the sculptor Esteban Jordán on 15 December 1559. The new altarpiece was to incorporate the panels from the old one dedicated to the Virgin: on the predella 'the painted panels of the prophets, which are six, that are by Berruguete the elder' (as Pedro Berruguete was known in the sixteenth century, to distinguish him from his son Alonso); in the main tier 'it is to have three painted panels on each side [of the centre panel] which are also by Berruguete the elder'.

In an article published in 1964, Angulo refers to the fact that the presence of a wart (*verruga* in Spanish) in works by Pedro Berruguete, an allusion to his surname, was a kind of signature that helped identify his hand, much like Van Dyck's oak leaves. Berruguete was not, in fact, the only painter of this period to give his figures warts, but Hezekiah clearly has one on his face. Because of it, and because he is the only one of the six prophet kings on this predella not to carry a sceptre, it has been suggested that this might be a self-portrait of the artist. As indicated above, it is inconceivable that Berruguete would have dared put his own face, or that of any person well known to his fellow-countrymen, on a figure from the Holy Scriptures on the high altar, since this would have had him flung into prison by the Inquisition. There is, however, no reason to dismiss the possibility (although we do not think this was Berruguete's customary way of working) that the features of Hezekiah were taken from someone the painter had met on his numerous travels, both in Italy and Castile, whom he had sketched in order to use the face later in a place where it would not be recognised. Indications that this could have been the case are to be found in the frequent changes Berruguete made in his compositions, right from the stage of the underdrawing (as with the face of Hezekiah, to which he made several alterations, affecting particularly the positioning of the eyes – initially drawn lower down but later rectified) to the extent of completely transforming the final expression of the figure.

Whether or not Berruguete made use of such a sketch for his *Hezekiah* in the church in Paredes de Nava (and in our opinion he most likely did not) he was hovering on the boundary between portraiture and fiction, not only in his realistic execution of the features but also in his way of representing both this figure and the other five prophet kings on the predella – certainly one of the artist's masterpieces, which in 1946 was considered by Angulo to show the first portraits in Spanish painting. The way in which he arranges the figures, with their ample, monumental forms, their elegant gestures, attitudes and poses, leaves no doubt that their author was inspired by Italian art, although their calm gestures and naturalness are far from any attempt at copying. It is not surprising that these kings became one of the principal arguments for supporting Berruguete's intervention in the 'portraits of illustrious men' in Federico de Montefeltro's *studiolo* in Urbino.

In Paredes, Berruguete shows the Kings of Judah just over half-length, in front of a balustrade which in the composition serves the function of a windowsill. Like the Italian and Flemish painters before him, he places objects on the balustrade or makes them protrude over it, as in the case of *Hezekiah*, thus breaking through the barrier between real space and the pictorial representation of it. In addition, the fact that he has placed the kings on a golden background – as required by his patrons – makes their strongly modelled volume stand out against this bright light. Berruguete's knowledge of Flemish techniques and the very personal way in which he used them, particularly in the elaborate details on the surface of the picture, enhanced his interpretation of qualities and textures – as can be seen in the rich garments and the motifs he designed on them, such as the light-coloured fabric on which the pomegranates are drawn with the tip of the brush in his *Solomon* on the predella in Paredes, which recalls the *Seneca* in Urbino. [PSM]

3 Juan de Flandes
[doc. 1496–1519]

Portrait of an Infanta, ca. 1496
Oil on panel, 31.5 x 22 cm
Madrid, Museo Thyssen-Bornemisza, 141 (1930.36)

PROVENANCE
Joaquín Arteaga y Echagüe, Duque del Infantado, Madrid. Thyssen-Bornemisza Collection, 1930. Museo Thyssen-Bornemisza, Madrid.

ESSENTIAL BIBLIOGRAPHY
Mayer 1930, pp. 307–08; Glück 1931, pp. 315–16; Benesch 1945, pp. 75 and 152, no. 9; Haverkamp-Begemann 1952, pp. 240–41; Brans 1953, p. 28; Bermejo 1962, pp. 34 and 45–46; Vandevivere and Bermejo 1986, pp. 12 and 14; Eisler 1989, pp. 158–63; Bermejo and Portús 1990, pp. 14 and 84; Pita Andrade and Borobia Guerrero 1992, pp. 676, no. 141; Silva Maroto 2000a, p. 184, no. 7.

Ever since this panel was first known and ascribed to Juan de Flandes, it has been considered to be a portrait of one of the daughters of Ferdinand and Isabel. It was first thought to be Joanna – by Friedländer in 1930 – on account of its physical similarity to the portrait of Joanna in the Kunsthistorisches Museum in Vienna (inv. 3873), which is so large that it is difficult not to assume it is of her. Given the apparent age of the girl in the portrait – between 12 and 15 – it could indeed be of Joanna (born 7 November 1479) if she looked rather young at the time, which is not known. But one point about which there is no doubt is that Juan de Flandes could have painted a portrait of Joanna when she was not yet sixteen years old. It is most probable that he painted at least one portrait of her for her mother before 20 August 1496, when the Infanta, accompanied by Queen Isabel, embarked for Flanders to marry Philip the Fair. The Flemish painter was in Castile at that time, for the earliest record of Juan de Flandes' connection with the court of Queen Isabel is dated 12 July 1496, when he was paid 6,000 *maravedíes* in Burgos 'as a favour by Her Highness to help with his costs'.

Following Glück's suggestion of 1931 drawing attention to the flower held by the Infanta, associated with the Tudor rose, the figure has been identified with Catherine of Aragon, the youngest daughter of Ferdinand and Isabel, born in Alcalá de Henares on 16 December 1485. Although the first English delegation sent to arrange her marriage to Arthur, Prince of Wales arrived in 1489, many years were to pass before the year 1501, when Catherine married the prince, who died the following year. Nevertheless, Catherine did not return to Castile, for she became betrothed to and later married her brother-in-law, the future Henry VIII of England. It was Queen Isabel, sad at her daughter's absence, who sent her court painter Michel Sittow to England to paint her. The portrait of Catherine of Aragon attributed to Michel Sittow, now in the Kunsthistorisches Museum in Vienna (inv. 5612), shows different features from those of the Museo Thyssen-Bornemisza portrait – particularly with regard to the nose. Despite the age the Infanta seems to be in the portrait, it could be Catherine, who was not yet eleven when Juan de Flandes arrived; he would have painted her the following year. Although at that time the final arrangements were being made for her marriage into the Tudor family, we consider that, since her features do not match those of the Sittow portrait, in all probability the portrait in the Museo Thyssen-Bornemisza is not of Catherine.

If, as the features suggest, the portrait is also not of Joanna, it could perhaps be of her sister Mary, future Queen of Portugal, born 29 June 1482 and therefore aged fourteen when Juan de Flandes arrived in Castile. In addition, as Elisa Bermejo suggested in 1962, the flower held by the Infanta does not necessarily refer to the Tudor rose but may have been used as a symbol of marriage. It was precisely in 1496 that Ferdinand and Isabel were negotiating with King Manuel of Portugal for him to marry one of their daughters. Although Mary was the one designated by her parents, the monarch preferred their eldest daughter, Isabel, widow of Prince Alfonso of Portugal, whom he married the following year. It was only after the death of her sister in 1498 that Mary herself married Don Manuel, in 1500. In summary, although it is not entirely certain which of the Infantas is portrayed, Joanna or Mary, and despite the fact that the features swing the balance in favour of Joanna, it cannot be ruled out that it was Mary, in 1496 or early 1497 when Ferdinand and Isabel offered her in marriage to the King of Portugal.

The quality of this portrait – of which there is a replica in the University Art Museum in Santa Barbara, California – shows the skill of Juan de Flandes, court painter to Queen Isabel from 1496 to 1504, as a portraitist. He deliberately chose to paint just a bust of the Infanta, so that her face would become the sole focus of attention. For this reason – justified by the presumed purpose of the work as a betrothal portrait – he allows a glimpse, on the left, of just two fingers of her right hand holding a flower, an allusion to her marriage, which goes almost unnoticed in view of the impact of the face, with its large eyes – and with very little foreshortening, like the body – on which the look of self-absorption is just such as Joanna, who so loved poetry, might have had. Juan de Flandes simplifies her delicate features, captures the different qualities and textures and handles the light in masterly fashion. Such is his skill in the treatment of the light effects on her face that the sensation of defencelessness and fragility is accentuated. [PSM]

4 & 5 Pedro de Campaña
[1503–1587]

Don Diego with Don Alonso Caballero and his Son and Doña Leonor with Doña Mencía de Cabrera and her Daughters, 1555–1556
Both oil on panel,
104 x 95 cm and 105 x 95 cm
Seville, Cathedral

PROVENANCE
Seville Cathedral, altarpiece in the Chapel of the Purification. The works are preserved in the place for which they were painted. See text.

ESSENTIAL BIBLIOGRAPHY
Gestoso II 1890, pp. 365–70; Gestoso 1908, pp. 279–83; Angulo Íñiguez 1951, pp. 20–25; Serrera 1984, pp. 355 and 388–90; Valdivieso 1986, pp. 68–69; Magdaleno 1999, p. 57; Serrera and Méndez Rodríguez 1999, pp. 42–44, nos. 14–15.

The paintings form part of the predella of the altarpiece in the Chapel of the Purification in Seville Cathedral, which remains *in situ*. This chapel is also known as the Marshal's Chapel, after its founder, Marshal Diego Caballero, who on 12 January 1555 commissioned Pedro de Campaña and Antonio de Alfián to paint the altarpiece. Although both undertook to finish it by the end of August that year, they did not do so. The altarpiece was completed in 1556, since in March of that year the painters were paid the second of the three payments stipulated in their contract. Although it was not specified in the contract, Alfián was only involved in the polychrome work and all the rest of the painting was done by Campaña.

The founder of the chapel, Don Diego Caballero, made his fortune in the West Indies. As a young man he went off to Hispaniola (now Santo Domingo) and later to Peru, where he took part in the conquest of the country. On his return to Hispaniola, in payment for his services to the crown Charles V appointed him Chief Treasurer of the island, and in 1536 Marshal of the island. When he returned to Seville in 1540 he was made one of the *veinticuatro* (the members of the City Council). Engaged in trade with the West Indies, Don Diego and his brother Alonso set up an import and export company that was continued after the latter's death by his widow, Doña Mencía, and brought her great wealth.

A comparison between the portraits painted by Campaña and what was commissioned by Don Diego in the contract – published by Gestoso in 1908 – demonstrates that the initial plan for representing the patrons was modified considerably: 'in the niche of the predella between the pedestals below the said panels the portrait of the Marshal from life with his wife and in the other niche the portrait of Alonso Caballero his brother, glory be, and of his wife and with his arms on both sides.' When he drew up the contract, Don Diego had wanted depicted in the predella, together with his arms, on one side a portrait of himself and his wife, Leonor de Cabrera, and on the other a portrait of his brother Alonso (by then dead) with his widow, Doña Mencía de Cabrera, who was the sister of his wife's sister. Thus the number of portraits commissioned was four, rather than the eight actually painted. Although there is no record of Don Diego's reasons for such a radical change, it is most likely that he wanted to perpetuate, too, the memory of all his family's descendants, in the traditional manner of donors. As a result, he ordered them to be arranged by placing on one side the male members of the family – Don Diego, Don Alonso and the latter's son – and on the other side the female members – Doña Leonor and Doña Mencía de Cabrera and her three daughters. But the way in which Campaña interpreted them had nothing to do with the traditional manner of representing donors – kneeling in front of the divinity, with their hands together in prayer; instead, he shows them standing, in a meditative attitude, in keeping with the new times.

Although, when painting this altarpiece, Pedro de Campaña was more strongly influenced than ever by Raphael, when it came to doing the portraits for the predella he returned to his Flemish origins. As Serrera observed, the realistic way in which he painted the Marshal's family, in all their rawness, particularly the women – without disguising the equally ugly features of each of them – makes these portraits the forerunners of the early portraits by Velázquez, who so admired 'Maese Pedro' (as the Flemish painter was called in Seville). Without doubt, the image of Doña Mencía, the widow of Don Alonso, with her disturbing presence, was a precedent for Velázquez's *Venerable Mother Jerónima de la Fuente* [CAT. 29].

On a dark ground, Pedro de Campaña arranged the figures, three-quarter length, all with the body turned towards the centre. Of the three male portraits – on the gospel side – Don Diego Caballero with his white hair and beard stands out from the rest. Unlike his brother Alonso and his nephew, whose faces and gazes are directed upwards to the right, like their bodies, he looks to the left, towards the viewer. The heightened realism of his features must be in response to his stipulation in the contract that his portrait be the only one 'done from life', perhaps because he knew that Campaña – as Francisco Pacheco states in his *Libro de retratos* – painted his portraits without the subjects being present, but later on, 'with a few finishing touches he made in their presence, the portrait was perfect'. The five female portraits – on the epistle side – presented Campaña with a more complex problem, which he resolved by breaking the symmetry and placing the two younger daughters on the extreme left, in front of their mothers and facing each other. Although 'Maese Pedro' applied his raw Flemish realism to these five portraits, this rawness was certainly much more apparent in two of them. In the land where charm was the most precious of all gifts, he produced the least attractive portraits of young girls to be found in Seville. [PSM]

6 Domenikos Theotokopoulos, El Greco
[1541–1614]

The Adoration of the Name of Jesus (Allegory of the Holy League), *ca.* 1577–1580
Oil on canvas, 140 x 110 cm
Patrimonio Nacional, Real Monasterio de San Lorenzo de El Escorial, 10014683

ESSENTIAL BIBLIOGRAPHY

Santos 1657; Ceán 1800, V, p. 12; *Notice des Tableaux de la Galerie Espagnole...* 1838, no. 256 (version in The National Gallery, London); Poleró 1857, no. 62, p. 38; Cossío 1908, no. 45, pp. 315–32; Blunt 1939–1940; Soria 1948, p. 251; Camón Aznar 1950, pp. 219–36 and no. 262; Wethey 1962/1967, no. 117; Braham 1966, pp. 307–10; Pita Andrade 1981, p. 51 and no. 60; Jordan in Madrid/.../Dallas 1982–1983, exh. cat., no. 12; Álvarez Lopera 1993, pp. 122–23 and no. 64; Marías 1993, pp. 68–69; Constantoudaki 1995, pp. 117–18; Dillon 1995, pp. 240–43; Joannides 1995, pp. 206–07; Marías 1997a, p. 126; Goniotakis 1999; Álvarez Lopera in Madrid/Rome/Athens 1999–2000, exh. cat., no. 29; L. Ruiz Gómez, in Vienna 2001, exh. cat., no. 7; Finaldi in New York/London 2003b, exh. cat., pp. 126–27.

This enigmatic work, one of the most purely pictorial ever painted by El Greco, has been the subject of a number of highly diverse interpretations. There is no documentary evidence relating to the circumstances or date of its execution. From its stylistic features – including sumptuous colours that are truly Venetian and the presence of compositional and iconographic details of Byzantine origin that are close to those in early paintings such as the *Allegory of the Christian Knight* in the Modena triptych – and from other information such as the handwriting of the signature and what we know of El Greco's relationship with Philip II, it is generally accepted that it was painted between 1577 and 1580, very likely being one of the artist's first works in Spain. In fact, the reduced replica in the National Gallery in London is signed in Greek capital letters, as in paintings from the Roman period and the early years in Toledo. When the London picture was in the collection belonging to Don Gaspar Méndez de Haro (inventory of 1687), it was considered the pair to the other reduced replica of the *Expolio* (at present in Upton Downs). It has sometimes been noted that El Greco might have painted this work on his own initiative as a gift for Philip II, by way of making his talents known. However, there is no information to support this theory.

The first person to make reference to the painting was Padre Santos in 1657, who interpreted it as the Adoration of the Name of Christ by Host of Heaven, the Church Militant, Purgatory and Hell. At the time, he cited the source of inspiration as being Saint Paul's Epistle to the Philippians: 'Wherefore God also hath highly exalted him, and given him a name which is above every name: That at the name of Jesus every knee should bow, of *things* in heaven, and *things* in earth and *things* under the earth' (2: 9–10). At that time it hung in the chapel of the Pantheon of the Kings and was given the title of *La Gloria del Greco*, relating it to *'La Gloria'* [FIG. 41] by Titian which also hung in El Escorial. Throughout the nineteenth century the complexity of the painting (which permits several interpretations that are not mutually exclusive) caused it to be known by several titles. Ceán referred to it as 'a painting that represents a glory, and below, purgatory and hell, with many small figures'. Others continued referring to is as *La Gloria del Greco*. At the same time, the London replica (which was in Louis Philippe's Galerie Espagnole before becoming part of the Stirling-Maxwell Collection) was interpreted as either *The Last Judgement* or *Philip II adoring the Name of Christ in Heaven*. The name which gained most acceptance was, however, the one given by Poleró to the painting in El Escorial, *The Dream of Philip II*, a title that has generally been considered somewhat whimsical but which represents an obvious parallel with *The Vision of Philip II*, the name given to the London replica when listed in the 1687 inventory of the Méndez de Haro collection.

The interpretation that has enjoyed most prestige in recent decades is that formulated in 1939–1940 by Anthony Blunt, who considered the painting to be the *Allegory of the Holy League* (the alliance formed in 1571 by Spain, Venice and the Pope against the Turks) believing the figures kneeling in the foreground next to Philip II to be Pope Pius V (in front) accompanied by two cardinals, Doge Alvise Mocenigo (rear view, with yellow cloak and ermine collar) and the King's brother, Don John of Austria (seen from the front, idealised with Roman armour and his arms on the sword resting on the ground). This interpretation – which according to Blunt had already been considered by Stirling-Maxwell – was hinted at for the first time in 1838 in the *Notice des Tableaux de la Galerie Espagnole* in relation to the London replica and found further support in an engraving commemorating the Battle of Lepanto, published in Venice in 1614 and which depicted, in addition to Philip II, Pius V, Doge Mocenigo and the three generals: Don John of Austria, Marcantonio Colonna (commander of the papal forces) and Sebastiano Venier (Venetian admiral). The fact that Don John of Austria died in 1578, combined with the painting having been hung in the mid-seventeenth century in the Pantheon of El Escorial, led Blunt, on the other hand, to think that it had been painted as a funeral tribute to the King's brother.

Blunt's proposal does not exclude the possibility of this work being considered as an *Adoration of the Name of Jesus*; rather, it complements the hypothesis, enriching its allegorical significance. However, there are several weak points: there is no clear allusion to Lepanto, the central character of the painting is Philip II and not Don John of Austria (as can be seen more clearly in the London replica), and finally, it seems illogical that a painting intended to recall Don John of Austria should idealise this character to the point of making him unrecognisable. It would also appear that the other two figures cannot certainly be identified as Colonna and Venier, leaving a gap in interpretation that is difficult to fill. All this, together with the painting's visionary character, does not exclude the possibility that its theme may be simply the *Adoration of the Name of Jesus* or even the *Last Judgement*. In fact, in 1966 Allan Braham compared the painting with a *Last Judgement* by Giovanni Battista Fontana, engraved by Pieter Balten in 1578. It does not seem likely that the work by Fontana need have served as an inspiration for El Greco. In view of the imagery of the Modena Triptych and certain stereotypical iconographic features, it would be more appropriate to consider common sources. Nevertheless, the debate is not over. Recently, Fernando Marías has insisted on the 'obvious eschatological meaning' of the composition and has gone back to calling it *The Glory of Philip II*, arguing that in it – and following the precedent of Titian in his *'La Gloria'* – El Greco was portraying the monarch awaiting the Final Judgement or else contemplating his own Particular Judgement. [JAL]

2 Court Portraits in the Spanish Monarchy (1530–1660)

7 Titian

[*ca.* 1485–1576]

Philip II, 1551
Oil on canvas, 193 x 111 cm
Madrid, Museo del Prado, P-411

PROVENANCE

Royal Collection. Sent to Mary Tudor in 1553; bequeathed by her to Philip II in 1558. On the King's death in 1588 it was hanging in the Guardajoyas of the Alcázar; taken to the Palacio Real Nuevo, Madrid, following the fire of 1734, from where transferred to the Museo del Prado in 1827.

ESSENTIAL BIBLIOGRAPHY

Crowe and Cavalcaselle 1877–1878, II, pp. 204–11; Allende Salazar and Sánchez Cantón 1919, p. 58; Suida 1935, pp. 107–08; Tietze 1936, II, pp. 299; Beroqui 1946, pp. 112–18; Wethey II, 1971, pp. 126–28; Hope 1980, p. 117; Campbell 1990, p. 552; Checa 2001, pp. CLXXIV–CLXXVI; Falomir 2003, no. 34, pp. 218–19.

The first meeting between Philip II and Titian took place in 1549 in Milan, one of the cities visited by Philip on his journey around the imperial territories. This voyage stretched from 1549 to 1551, and was intended to introduce the son of Charles V and Isabel of Portugal to the principal towns of the empire. It was to prove a formative journey for the diverse artistic map of Europe. In November 1550 the prince and painter met again in Augsburg, the city where the ceremonial armour worn by the prince was made by Colman Helmschmid. This armour is conserved in the Real Armería of Madrid. For the occasion, Titian reworked the military image he had used for Charles V a couple of years earlier, of a soldier *all'antica* who is portrayed standing, dressed in half armour and holding a general's staff, next to a table on which a helmet is lying. We know of several copies of this important portrait, destroyed in the El Pardo fire, which were produced in the Spanish court, an indication of how well received this imperial iconography was and of the dynastic continuity courted by such images. For the portrait of Philip, the painter changed the position of the subject from that of his father, making him turn towards the left, as though wishing to make it a *pendant* of the emperor's image. As radiography of the canvas has shown [FIG. 46], the artist painted the portrait of Philip II not onto a new canvas but onto one which appears to be an early unfinished version of his *Charles V with Armour*, abandoned after a complex work of fitting, in which the emperor carried a sword and not a staff as he did in the final version, and had his left hand resting on the table, in a manner similar to the half-length Philip II studio portrait by Titian (Museo del Prado, P-452). For some reason, Titian finally decided to paint Charles V on another canvas, and later used the first canvas to paint this image of Philip II, following the earlier lines to a large extent; the prince's right eye is painted over that of the emperor, as is part of the beard as well as some parts of the armour and even the Golden Fleece. From the original painting he eliminated the large window and helmet sketched on the right, as well as extending and raising the table, a change that was required in order to make Philip's right hand rest on the helmet in a convincing way. The resulting image reproduces the powerful impact of the emperor's portrait, perhaps even taking it further, in the manner of the prince addressing the viewer in a haughty and distant way, and in the military authority expressed by the hand resting on the helmet, which is reinforced by other elements and features such as the presence of the column, the table and the way in which he is holding the sword.

Next to the portrait of Charles V, this *Philip II* with armour became, thanks to Titian's authority as a portraitist, a work of reference as to the way royal majesty should be depicted. However, Titian's portrait was not well received by Philip II. In a letter to his aunt, Mary of Hungary, sent on 16 May, he told her of his impression of the Italian's work: 'It can be seen that he did it in a hurry, and were there more time I would make him do it again.' The future King of Spain came to prefer the Flemish painter Anthonis Mor as portraitist, a painter respectful of the Titianesque models but whose brushwork was more concise and finished, and who in 1557 painted a second portrait of the King with armour, this time to commemorate the Battle of Saint Quentin. This painting met with the King's full approval, and is housed in the monastery of El Escorial. [LRG]

8 Anthonis Mor

[*ca.* 1519–1576]

Joanna of Austria, ca. 1559
Oil on canvas, 195 x 104 cm
Madrid, Museo del Prado, P-2112

PROVENANCE

Royal Collection. Inventory of Joanna, 1573; 1600, mentioned in the Guardajoyas of the Alcázar; 1794, possibly mentioned (no. 857) in the Palacio del Buen Retiro. In the Museo del Prado in 1854.

ESSENTIAL BIBLIOGRAPHY

Hymans 1910, pp. 115–16; Pérez Pastor 1914, II, p. 365; Marlier 1934, no. 9, p. 96; Sánchez Cantón 1956–1959, p. 229; Friedlander 1995, no. 394; Campbell 1990, no. 266; Sofonisba Anguisola e le sue sorelle 1994, p. 136; Bermejo 1990, no. 14, p. 138; Antonio 1998, no. 2, pp. 218–19; Portús 1998, no. 11, p. 204.

Joanna of Austria (1535–1573), daughter of Charles V and Isabel of Portugal, was Princess of Portugal by her marriage to her cousin,

Prince Juan Manuel, from which union was born Sebastián, posthumous son of the Portuguese heir and King between 1568 and 1578. Shortly after her son was born, Joanna left Lisbon for ever, leaving the small prince in the care of his parents-in-law. Joanna had to take charge of the regency of Spain between 1554 and 1559 in the absence of her father and brother, and she then took on the care of her nephews and nieces, first prince Carlos and later Isabel Clara Eugenia and Catalina Micaela. She was also considerably involved in the political and religious life of Spain, had close ties with the Jesuit Order and founded the Franciscan monastery of Las Descalzas Reales, a place of seclusion for the women of the dynasty for more than a century.

The princess was the most frequently painted woman in the Philippine period, and was painted by almost all the major portrait painters of the time. In fact, this image is undoubtedly the culmination of a decade in which Cristóbal de Morales and Alonso Sánchez Coello, among others, had captured all the dignity and majestic bearing that characterised the princess, whose presence aroused all the 'solemnity, maturity, severity and good sense' which could be expected of a '*hija de quien era*' (the daughter of whom she was), as Padre Carrillo put it in 1616 (Carrillo, fols 4 and 13). But it was Anthonis Mor who produced the most eloquent portrait. The sister of Philip II is depicted in a very simple way, according to the formulas which were beginning to become established at that time in portraits of the Hapsburg dynasty. Joanna is portrayed full length, life size and turning slightly to the left; she is dressed in black, to indicate her widowhood, and has her hair gathered in a bonnet which, together with the high ruff characteristic of the period, helps to frame her intense and defiant expression. The image of the princess manages to create a successful scenic distance not only by her manner and haughtiness, but also thanks to the armchair on which she is leaning. This is an element which began to be used at around this date and reflects the high status of the subject of the portrait. It also reflects her role as a woman of state, since the *frailero* armchair suggests the proximity of a table, the one from which the kingdom is administered and justice imparted. These were tasks delegated to her by her father, the Emperor, referred to by the small figure of Hercules which hangs from Joanna's *manteleta*, the small shawl that covers her shoulders. The simplicity of the representation is underlined by the spatial austerity – an imprecise background which helps to emphasise the solidity of the figure – making the princess the very epitome of royal majesty. [LRG]

9 Alonso Sánchez Coello
[1531/2–1588]

The Infantas Isabel Clara Eugenia and Catalina Micaela, 1575
Oil on canvas, 135 x 149 cm
Madrid, Museo del Prado, P-1138

PROVENANCE
Royal Collection. In 1636 in the Alcázar, Madrid; later, in the Palacio del Buen Retiro, Madrid. Listed as being in the Museo del Prado from 1819.

ESSENTIAL BIBLIOGRAPHY
Lostalot 1894, vol. II, p. 248; Roblot-Delondre 1913, p. 136; Mayer 1922, p. 225; Angulo Iñiguez 1954, p. 300; Lafuente Ferrari 1978, p. 254; Breuer-Hermann 1984, pp. 209–11, no. 11; Perlingieri 1992, p. 146; Campbell 1998 no. 186; Marías 1999b, pp. 443–56.

The two daughters of Philip II, Isabel Clara Eugenia (1566–1633) and Catalina Micaela (1567–1597), were painted by Alonso Sánchez Coello from a very early age, in a style whose characteristics differ very little from the usual court portrait, because, among other things, the approach to this type of image always went beyond the private sphere. Although such portraits reflected the healthy development of the younger members of the dynasty, they were not merely a demonstration of familial love, since matters of succession and matrimonial politics found one of their most valued instruments in the making of portraits. There is every reason to believe that Philip II had enormous affection for these girls, born from his marriage with Isabel de Valois; but also, with the passage of time, the two princesses would help establish Philip's influence in spheres as delicate for Spain as the Low Countries and the North of Italy.

In this portrait in the Prado, dated 1575, the Infantas are depicted standing, in a double portrait which places them in an indefinite interior, furnished with a table covered by a green tablecloth. The other two surviving paintings of the girls are also double portraits. The first, a work which must have been painted in 1568, the year in which their mother died, is in the monastery of Las Descalzas Reales in Madrid; the other dates to 1571 (London, Buckingham Palace). In these versions, the figures are arranged in a similar way, as a juxtaposition on the same plane of two isolated figures arranged according to the established conventions for portraits of adults. The distancing, severe look and statuesque impassivity, and the richness of the clothing, repeat their full meaning. What we have here is not so much a double portrait of children as a portrait of the daughters of the King, as their characterisation had to correspond with that of the whole family.

The link between the two figures is established very simply, through both of them stretching their arms towards the central point of the composition, a crown of flowers. This arrangement is very similar to the English version of 1571, although now a relationship of dependence can be perceived: the younger of the girls, the shy Catalina Micaela, turns slightly towards Isabel Clara Eugenia, who gazes openly at the viewer. Recently, Lorne Campbell has suggested about this arrangement that Sánchez Coello might have had in mind the compositional arrangement of the *Portrait of Giovanni Arnolfini and his Wife ('the Arnolfini Marriage')* by Jan van Eyck, then in the collection of Philip II and now in the National Gallery, London. [LRG]

10 Juan Pantoja de la Cruz
[1553–1608]

Philip II, *ca.* 1590
Oil on canvas, 181 x 95 cm
Patrimonio Nacional,
Real Monasterio de San Lorenzo de El Escorial, 10034484

PROVENANCE
Royal Collection. Painted for the library of the Royal Monastery of El Escorial. Transferred to the convent of El Rosario in 1809 to form part of the Museo Josefino. Returned to El Escorial in 1814.

ESSENTIAL BIBLIOGRAPHY
Beruete 1911, pp. 101–05; Sánchez Cantón 1916, p. 128; Sánchez Cantón 1947, p. 114; Checa 1992, p. 445; Mulcahy 1996, pp. 517–21; Bouza 2000, p. 66; García-Frias 2001, pp. 407–08; Kusche 2003, pp. 473–83.

In the early 1580s, the image of the King as an old man was consolidated as part of the established imagery of Philip II. Alonso

Sánchez Coello and Juan Pantoja de la Cruz were primarily responsible for disseminating this late likeness of Philip II, although only copies or studio versions of their paintings remain, other than the work in Florence (Galleria Palatina), a painting dated 1587 only recently discovered. The popularity of these portraits can be traced from the paintings now in the Real Maestranza de Ronda (Royal Cavalry Order of Ronda), the one from the Museo del Prado deposited in the Spanish Embassy in France (P-6181) and the one in a private collection in Madrid (Kusche 2003, plate 434, p. 482). These all appear to relate to a very similar model which culminated in the portrait in El Escorial – very probably the portrait in which Philip II is seen at his oldest. The King is shown on foot, dressed strictly in black, the colour he adopted permanently after the death of his third wife, Queen Isabel de Valois of France, and the only sign he wears identifying him as a Hapsburg is the Golden Fleece. One hand is resting on the hilt of his sword and the other on the *frailero* armchair, which indicates by established convention his dual role as defender and governor of the realm. The pose of the monarch, the way in which he is addressing the viewer, the very dimensions of the canvas, serve to remind us of the value of the portrait as a substitute – an invitation to imagine that we are standing before the very person of the King, during one of his rare appearances in the halls of the Alcázar. This is made clear by the curtains which reveal and frame Philip II, and the column on a high plinth in the background, an architectural element introduced by Titian in some of his portraits of Charles V, which made the connection between the emperor and the legend of Hercules.

In the opinion of Checa Cremades, we have before us the image which best represents the final days of the hidden King, a perfect depiction of the idea of royal majesty, 'essentially based on seclusion, which was becoming the emblem of the Hapsburg dynasty'.

This was the first of a small series of dynastic portraits destined for the library of El Escorial, a project dating from 1585, which began to be fulfilled in 1589 with the commissioning of the furniture for the library. In addition to Philip II there were portraits of Charles V, Philip III and Philip IV, the first two painted around 1608; they were hung according to the order set out by Juan Pantoja de la Cruz shortly before he died. To this disciple of Sánchez Coello we owe the portraits of Charles V, a copy of an original by Titian [FIG. 45] and the one of Philip III. Pantoja is also believed to be the painter of this portrait of *Philip II*, evidence for which comes from its late date of production, the relationship of the Valladolid painter with this series, and its early attribution to Pantoja in an anonymous list from the Biblioteca de Ajuda in Lisbon dating to 1650. Another feature pointing to to Pantoja is its theatrical sense of light, which in this case highlights a 'spectral' quality, an adjective used by Sánchez Cantón to describe this painting. María Kusche, however, argues against this attribution and considers Sánchez Coello as the more likely painter of the portrait. Among other reasons, this expert on the genre points out the lack of a signature, stylistic concerns and, most notably, the existence of a bust portrait of Philip II as an old man that appears as a miniature in a letter patent of nobility dated 1588 (Madrid, Fundación Casa de Alba) and is based, according to Kusche, on the work in El Escorial, which would indicate that the El Escorial *Philip II* was painted before Coello's death. Nevertheless, and as we have pointed out, during the final ten years of the King's life there were various models depicting the King as white-haired and old, and it cannot be conclusively determined whether or not the miniature was based on the painting in El Escorial. [LRG]

11 Diego Velázquez
[1599–1660]

Philip IV, 1623–1627
Oil on canvas, 198 x 101.5 cm
Madrid, Museo del Prado, P-1182

PROVENANCE

Royal Collection. Possibly from the Real Alcázar, it may be the one listed as the portrait 'in the early style of Velázquez' in the inventory of the Palacio del Buen Retiro of 1701. Listed in the same location until 1794. Passed to the Palacio Real until 1816, when transferred to the Real Academia de San Fernando. Entered the Museo del Prado in 1827.

ESSENTIAL BIBLIOGRAPHY

Curtis 1883, no. 105; Mayer 1936, no. 205; López Rey 1963, no. 241, Gudiol 1973, no. 39; Brown 1986, p. 47; Gállego 1990, no. 18, pp. 132–37; Brown and Garrido 1998, no. 2, pp. 27–30.

Philip IV (1605–1665) came to the throne in 1621, at the age of sixteen and with little preparation to take on the governance of the most powerful country of the time (but which was then entering its decline). On the other hand, the King had received a refined artistic education which had developed in him a particular sensitivity for music, theatre and painting, interests to which he dedicated a considerable part of his life, delegating the affairs of state for twenty-one years to the Count-Duke of Olivares (1587–1645).

Shortly after the beginning of Philip IV's reign, Velázquez, close in age to the King, settled at the court, where he was to construct the image of the King for almost forty years. In the early years of his career, the court portrait as created in the reign of Philip II maintained its force, albeit revitalised now by the new monarch, who saw in the figure of his grandfather a personal reference and a stimulus for his own reign.

In this work in the Prado, Velázquez created the first full-length portrait of Philip IV, a work painted using a very limited chromatic range, in browns and greys, with tight and concise brushstrokes, reflecting the images of Philip II in his mature years. Philip IV is depicted standing, dressed in black, close to a table and holding a piece of paper in one hand while the other grasps the sword – three elements which the viewer of the period would immediately have identified with the three fundamental tasks of the sovereign: justice, government and the defence of the realm. To allude to his status, the monarch has only to show himself, impassive and stern, with the Golden Fleece as his sole dynastic emblem. The plain collar worn by the King, fruit of the decree imposed by him in 1623, helps to date the painting, which was retouched at a later stage to correct the position of the legs, the tall hat standing on the table and the swirl of the cape, changes which are visible to the naked eye. Radiographic evidence has also revealed changes made to the hands and face, in the latter case to soften the King's features. It is thought that these alterations were made about four years later, after various versions or copies of the work were made in 1623 (among others, those in the Metropolitan Museum of Art, New York, and the Museum of Fine Arts, Boston). The reason for these changes is not clear, although their result is greater elegance in the position of the legs and a more graceful and slender figure, placed in a slightly oblique position which changed both the figure's spatial composition and his proximity to the table. [LRG]

12 Diego Velázquez
[1599–1660]

Philip IV, ca. 1653
Oil on canvas, 69 x 56 cm
Madrid, Museo del Prado, P-1185

PROVENANCE
Royal Collection. 1816, in store at the Real Academia de San Fernando. Entered the Museo del Prado in 1827.

ESSENTIAL BIBLIOGRAPHY
Curtis 1883, no. 128; Mayer 1936, no. 246; López Rey 1963, no. 266, Gudiol 1973, 146; Brown, 1986, pp. 221–22; Gállego 1990, no. 78, pp. 446–49; Gállego (1972) 1984, p. 276.

In the 1550s, the natural biological decline of Philip IV was aggravated by the personal and political upheavals that King and kingdom had been suffering since the end of the previous decade. In addition to the serious social and political conflicts the country was undergoing, Philip IV had lost his first wife and his son Baltasar Carlos, as well as the architect of his once happy Madrid court, the Count-Duke of Olivares. The 'planet king' (Brown and Elliot 1980, ch. II), who had shone with refinement and elegance for almost thirty years, was now a dejected and defeated man immersed in feelings of sin and guilt, who sought in religion a refuge from and atonement for his misfortunes.

During this period Velázquez's portraits of the King are fewer but intensely intimate, as can be seen in this bust portrait, painted with an economy as notable as the essence it captures of the persona of Philip IV; in this stark portrayal the features of the face become the focus of our very perception of the portrait, no other resources being available to inform us of the social category or lineage of the subject. Velázquez has not even depicted the Golden Fleece which appears in the somewhat later version in London (National Gallery, NG 745). Here, the King's features are imbued with the full level of representation of the Hapsburg dynasty since Titian outlined in the face of Charles V, with its similarly pronounced jaw and drooping eyes, the dynastic model that was to become the very expression of regal dignity, as described by Julián Gállego: 'These long faces, these drooping nostrils, these projecting lower jaws, these thick lips, this type of physiognomy which some people in our times see as a condemnation of the decadence of a dynasty and of a particular family, the Hapsburgs, were in the sixteenth century the embodiment of the idea of majesty in a human face' (Gállego (1972) 1984, p. 276). But, at the same time, the heavy burden of humanity on the face of the King, and the pictorial sobriety with which Velázquez paints him – seen by some as close to collapse, by others as wearing a distant and somewhat sleepy expression, indifferent to what is going on – is far removed from the conventions of the court portrait.

The portrait was not completed until after 1653, when the King wrote to the nun Sister Luisa Magdalena de Jesús about the time that had passed since Velázquez painted him: 'It is nine years since any has been done and I am not inclined to subject myself to the temperament of Velázquez so as not to see myself growing old.' In 1657, the engraver Pedro de Villafranca produced an illustration taken from the slightly later version in London, for the frontispiece of the book *Descripción breve del monasterio de San Lorenzo el Real del Escorial.* [LRG]

13 Diego Velázquez
[1599–1660]

Queen Mariana of Austria, ca. 1652–1653
Oil on canvas, 234 x 131.5 cm
Madrid, Museo del Prado, P-1191

PROVENANCE
Royal Collection. Inventories of the Royal Monastery of El Escorial, 1700, 1764, 1771, 1794, 1838 and 1843. In the Museo del Prado from 1845.

ESSENTIAL BIBLIOGRAPHY
Curtis 1883, no. 237; Mayer 1936, no. 484; López-Rey 1963, no. 355; Brown 1986, pp. 221 and 222; Gállego (1972) 1984, p. 23; Gállego 1990, no. 71; Brown and Garrido 1998, no. 27, pp. 174–80; Brown 1999, no. 9, pp. 140–43.

Mariana of Austria (1634–1696) was the daughter of Emperor Ferdinand III and Maria of Hungary, who was the sister of Philip IV. Mariana married her uncle in 1649 – when she was not yet fifteen – to alleviate the family setbacks that had taken place between 1644 and 1646, when Isabel of France and Prince Baltasar Carlos died. The Queen produced a male heir for the Spanish throne in 1661, a child who would go on to reign as Charles II. However, he soon exhibited numerous physical problems as well as some mental deficiency, becoming a figure permanently under the protection of his mother, who took over the regency of the kingdom in 1665 on the death of Philip IV. This marked the beginning of a turbulent decade both for Spain and for Mariana herself.

This full-length portrait of her, faithful to the Hapsburg tradition of portraiture, was painted by Velázquez after his return from his second trip to Italy in June 1651 in response to a request from Emperor Ferdinand, who wanted a portrait of his daughter – although he was finally sent a studio version (Vienna, Kunsthistorisches Museum). The artist had to concern himself with painting an adolescent who was at the time in a delicate state of health following the birth of Princess Margarita, her first child. The Queen, enveloped in an ostentatious black dress with a *guardainfantes* (a huge hoop skirt) decorated with rich silver *passementerie*, shows the statuesque demeanour of her public appearances (Gállego (1972) 1984, p. 231). Resting her right hand on a *frailero* armchair, signifying her high status, and holding in the other a large handkerchief of white linen, Mariana's distant and impassive appearance is similar to all the images of the women of the dynasty. Also true to tradition is the inclusion of the drapery, in Gállego's opinion rather more than a sign of nobility, 'an extremely useful feature for creating alternatives of light and shade', an effect which is somewhat impaired by the section added at the top of the painting. More innovative is the presence of the tower clock standing on a table in the background, which may be an allusion to moderation and prudence as virtues of the ruler, and by extension, in this case, to her family.

The aim of this type of image can also be glimpsed in the colour treatment, 'limited' to a harmonious combination of blacks, whites, greys and crimsons – the latter enlivening Queen Mariana's fragile face. The overall effect is achieved with the characteristic pictorial technique of Velázquez in his last period, loose and varied, with small brushstrokes applied onto broad areas of colour, creating an extraordinary effect that enables us to understand the different qualities and textures. One interesting detail is the portrayal of the serious, circumspect and not particularly pretty face of the young Queen, painted, as the radiograph has allowed us to discover, on a canvas on which the head of Philip IV had been sketched. The painter sought on this occasion to mitigate these rather unattractive features by emphasising the regal apparel, notably the dress and hairstyle, as splendid as they are harmonious in formal and chromatic terms. Velázquez prefers on this occasion to 'dignify' the Queen by overshadowing her face with the admirable beauty of his painting; in the opinion of Professor Julián Gállego, 'Velázquez, with his usual discretion, conserving the traditional approach to the portrait of the Hapsburg dynasty, is destroying the very principle of the portrait'.

In 1700 the work is listed in the monastery of El Escorial as one of a pair with the portrait of *Philip IV, with Armour and a Lion at his Feet* (Madrid, Museo del Prado, P-1219), a studio painting of a larger size, which led to this portrait of the Queen being extended by an addition of some twenty-eight centimetres to its height – a solution that has inevitably detracted from the look of the painting. [LRG]

14 Diego Velázquez
[1599–1660]

The Infanta Margarita in Blue, ca. 1659–1660
Oil on canvas, 127 x 107 cm
Vienna, Kunsthistorisches Museum, Gemäldegalerie, 2130

PROVENANCE
Sent to Vienna, probably in 1659, it was destined for the palaces of Hofburg and Stallburg; in the latter it was cut out in the eighteenth century.

ESSENTIAL BIBLIOGRAPHY
Mayer 1936, no. 534; López-Rey 1963, no. 406; Bardi 1969, no. 123; Gudiol 1973, no. 157; Brown 1986, p. 229; Palomino 1986 (ed.), p. 190.

The first offspring of the marriage between Philip IV and Mariana of Austria, the Infanta Margarita was born in 1651. The chronicles describe her as a pretty and extraordinarily vivacious child. She was engaged at a very young age to her cousin Leopoldo, future Emperor of Austria, and they married in December 1666. Margarita died just seven years later, in March 1673. In addition to her maternal family's interest in marking her development, the engagement of the Infanta is the reason for three portraits of Margarita being sent to the Imperial Court between 1654 and 1659. In them it is possible to appreciate the progressive freedom with which the painter approached the traditional portrait, not only in the immense height of the pictorial values which each one possesses, but also in his very conception of the model, a suggestive combination of family dignity and individualisation of character.

This Vienna portrait is the last of the images of the Infanta to come from the brush of Velázquez. For the occasion, the protagonist of *Las Meninas* [CAT. 43] is wearing a shiny dress of blue silk, with trimming in metallic *passementerie* that emphasises the splendour of her voluminous *guardainfantes* – the characteristic garment of the female profile in the Spanish court, and a feature that led to the open spread of the arms, creating a solid pyramidal figure which reinforced the impression of sculptural stillness in the female subjects of Velázquez's portraits. The outline of the dress relates the portrait of Margarita to the one Velázquez painted of her mother, Queen Mariana of Austria, shortly after his return from Italy [CAT. 13], and, as in that painting, the chromatic approach is of a careful austerity, even more limited in this particular case. Blues, browns and ivories are lit up by the golden glimmers of the dress and the child's shining hair. To highlight her pale face, Velázquez has painted some greyish bows placed strategically close to her cheeks and on one of her temples. The handkerchief that was held in the Queen's left hand is replaced here with a fur muff, an extremely unusual garment in this type of portrait, and one which may be a reference to a gift from the Austrian court. In the background, which is seriously damaged as a result of poor conservation, a high-legged console table is sketched, against a wall on which one can just make out a picture or mirror. On the table are an ebony clock and at least one small bronze lion, elements that emphasise the courtly setting in which the future empress is portrayed, as well as her high position. The portrait was described by Palomino as a work 'most excellently painted, and with the majesty and beauty of its original' (Palomino (ed.) 1986, p. 190). [LRG]

3 The Portraits of El Greco

15 Domenikos Theotokopoulos, El Greco
[1541–1614]

A Nobleman with his Hand on his Chest, ca. 1577–1580
Oil on canvas 81 x 66 cm
Madrid, Museo del Prado, P-809

PROVENANCE
Royal Collections, Madrid, Quinta del Duque del Arco (1794); Royal Palace, Madrid (1814); first recorded at the Prado in 1834 in the *Inventario General de los cuadros de S. M. existentes en la Galería del Real Museo* among the paintings in the 'Large store. Italian School'.

ESSENTIAL BIBLIOGRAPHY
Baroja 1900; Cossío 1908, pp. 398–400 and no. 72; *'La mano al pecho'* 1926; Willumsen 1927; Cassou 1931, pp. 59–61; Camón 1950, pp. 1.087–1.093 and no. 723; Angulo 1956; Márquez Villanueva 1959; Wethey 1962 and 1967, no. 145; Gudiol 1971, p. 54 and no. 32; Gómez-Menor 1982, p. 52; Bouza 1994a; F. Checa in Barcelona 1996–1997, exh. cat., no. 3; Carr 2001, p. 49; L. Ruiz Gómez in Vienna 2001, exh. cat., no. 19; Álvarez Lopera 2003, pp. 179–81, 186–87, 199–200 and 204–06; Davies 2003a.

A Nobleman with his Hand on his Chest, certainly painted between 1577 and 1580, is probably the earliest of El Greco's portraits of Spanish noblemen. In it the artist begins to establish the portrait model that he was to use in the years that followed, with a half- or bust-length figure emerging from a neutral background and with the light and expressiveness concentrated on the face and hands. The technique is clearly Venetian in origin, and the handling smooth and unified, as is usual in works of these years. At the same time, however, El Greco reveals his exceptional faculties in the treatment of textures, and in spite of the frontal view of the face he makes subtle use of asymmetry and linear distortion.

There is no information on the identity of the sitter, in relation to which different theories have been put forward. Ricardo Baroja and Willumsen, interpreting the gesture of the hand as one of self-assertion, thought that it was a self-portrait. This idea, although extremely unlikely, was also proposed, at least as a possibility, by Jean Cassou (who saw similarities between the face of this nobleman and that in the supposed self-portrait in New York) and by Camón (who in turn related it to the possible self-portrait of the aged El Greco that appears in the *Pentecost* in the Prado). Another idea, lacking in credibility but which has circulated unofficially – that the subject was Miguel de Cervantes – arose from Angulo's theory that the sitter's left arm had been amputated, perhaps as the result of a battle. For his part, the Marquis de Lozoya put forward the idea that it could be Antonio Pérez, secretary to Philip II, stating that 'there is an obvious similarity with the portraits of the famous personality'. More recently, Gómez-Menor has suggested – again with no sound basis – that it could be a nobleman of the Conde de Mora's family, from whose collection he supposes, without any grounds whatsoever, that all El Greco's portraits in the Quinta del Duque del Arco were sold. After being included in the museum's catalogue, the identity that has found the most favour has been that put forward, apparently verbally, by the Marquis de Hermosilla and Moreno Guerra, who interpreted the nobleman's gesture as one of swearing an oath and suggested that he could be Don Juan de Silva, a knight of the Order of Santiago, Marqués de Montemayor and chief notary of Toledo. However, there is no known portrait of the Marqués de Montemayor that could be used as a comparison, and no other evidence to support this proposition.

Recently, Angulo's old theory that the nobleman had lost an arm (a theory that some believe to have been confirmed by the restoration carried out in 1996, which emphasised the dropped shoulder on that side) and the publication in 1995 of a biography of Don Juan de Silva, Conde de Portalegre, in which its author, Fernando Bouza, revealed that the latter had lost his left arm as a result of injuries suffered in the battle of Alcazarquivir (1578), have given rise to an extraordinary degree of confusion, with some historians believing that these two factors constituted, if not confirmation, at least a further indication that the portrait was that of Don Juan de Silva, chief notary of Toledo.

However, it should be noted that, although similar and both from Toledo, they are two different people: Don Juan de Silva Ribera, a knight of the Order of Santiago, Marqués de Montemayor and chief notary of Toledo (but who did not lose an arm, as far as is known) and Don Juan de Silva Silveira, knight of the Order of Calatrava and Count of Portalegre (whose arm was rendered useless after Alcazarquivir). This Don Juan de Silva owned a *Saint Francis* by El Greco in 1597 but, as Bouza himself has pointed out, he is an unlikely candidate since in 1578 (the earliest date that could be ascribed to the portrait) he would have been around 45 years old, considerably older than the nobleman in the painting.

There is no certainty, either, with regard to the significance of the nobleman's gesture. The hand on the chest has given rise to a great diversity of readings (self-assertion, testifying to something, a sign of repentance, a simple gesture intended to signify distinction…) and consequently these have in turn led to different theories. Márquez Villanueva, supported by a series of texts taken from the *Viaje de Turquía* by Pedro de Urdemalas and *Los baños de Argel* and *La Gitanilla* by Cervantes, attempted to demonstrate that the nobleman is shown in the act of swearing on his honour, according to a formula used by Spanish noblemen at that time, and which 'among unbelievers enjoyed more credit than that sworn in the name of religious beliefs'. From this and the prominence of the sword, it has been suggested that the subject could be a knight belonging to a military order, whose insignia appear half-hidden among his robes, at the moment of taking the oath in that way. However, Márquez Villanueva has accepted that the gesture of the hand on the chest is simply a pose of affected elegance (some lines by Lope de Vega from his play *Santiago el Verde* have been quoted as evidence, although these refer to portraits of women). Whether it is a fashionable gesture or has some other meaning understood only by those initiated into the world of rhetoric, as suggested by Checa, it is anyway surprising that this gesture was not used by other painters of the time.

Finally, it should be noted that the open hand on the chest, with the middle and third fingers touching, was an expressive device used repeatedly by El Greco in religious paintings as a gesture of acceptance of the divine will or awareness of spiritual revelation (see, for example, the *Saint Mary Magdalene* in the Budapest Museum of Fine Art, the figure of Christ in the *Expolio*, or his various full-length representations of *Saint Francis* either alone or paired with another saint). In the only other two portraits in which it appears – that of the gentleman praying in the *Christ Crucified* in the Louvre and the portrait of *García Ibañez Múgica de Bracamonte*, which is not an autograph work – there is also an association of a religious nature. [JAL]

16 Domenikos Theotokopoulos, El Greco

[1541–1614]

Jerónimo de Cevallos, 1613
Oil on canvas 64 x 54 cm
Madrid, Museo del Prado, P-812

PROVENANCE

Royal Collections, Madrid, Quinta del Duque del Arco (1794); first recorded at the Prado in 1834 in the *Inventario General de los cuadros de S. M. existentes en la Galeria del Real Museo* among the paintings in the 'Large store. Italian School'.

ESSENTIAL BIBLIOGRAPHY

Cossío 1908, pp. 429–30 and no. 79; Meier-Graefe 1910/1926, p. 104; Allende Salazar and Sánchez Cantón 1919, pp. 175–78; Camón 1950, pp. 1.117 and 1.122 and no. 741; Wethey 1962 and 1967, no. 133; Gómez-Menor 1966; Gudiol 1971, p. 283 and no. 242; Pita 1981, pp. 136–37 and no. 275; Gómez-Menor 1974; Roteta 1985, pp. 16–17; Rodríguez de Gracia 1988; Aranda Pérez 2001; Álvarez Lopera 2003, pp. 179–81, 186–87 and 212–15.

This portrait is probably the last in the series of gentlemen painted by El Greco as a head and shoulders in three-quarter view against a neutral background. Wearing a large ruff on a greenish outfit, Cevallos appears to be concentrating and alert, and although facing the spectator he is diverting his gaze to create an almost imperceptible – but at the same time highly effective – sense of instant movement. His penetrating attitude and pose, completely lacking in haughtiness, are befitting of the shrewd politician he appears to have been. As seems appropriate for his last years, El Greco used a light and summary technique. The fair beard and the ears are merely hinted at in a few master strokes. The paint is fluid and sparsely applied, revealing the ground beneath the brushstrokes that define the ruff. Cossío related this work to two other portraits, also originating from the Quinta del Duque del Arco (Museo del Prado, P-810 and P-811), and, comparing them with those from his early Toledan period, pointed out that 'it can be observed…how his technique has become lighter and how the painter has gained control, with increasing mastery, of the difficult secrets of simplicity in art'.

Identification of the subject was made by Allende Salazar and Sánchez Cantón, who noticed the extraordinary similarity of the sitter to the portrait of Cevallos contained in his book *Tractatus de cognitione per viam violentiae in causis Ecclesiasticis* (Toledo, 1618), engraved by Pedro Ángel. Indirect documentary confirmation can be found in some genealogical notes on the Cevallos family, information that was also known by the above-mentioned authors, stating that the politician had been painted by El Greco in 1618 (probably an error for 1608). Subsequently, Ana Maria Roteta has rejected the identification on the sole basis of facial variations and differences in expression which she believes she can see between the subject of the painting and the image of Cevallos in the engraving by Pedro Ángel. However, her position is not shared by other specialists. Although in fact Cevallos was aged fifty-three at the time, on the engraving by Pedro Ángel is the inscription 'AETATIS SUAE 51, / 1613'; this is certainly the date of El Greco's painting. The number 368, in yellow in the lower left-hand corner, indicates its origin as being the Quinta del Duque del Arco, where it was recorded in the inventory of 1789–1794 as being in the 'twelfth room' together with other portraits by El Greco under the number 366 (368 related to the *Nobleman with his Hand on his Chest*, but the numbers were doubtless confused).

Cevallos was born in the town of Escalona in 1560 and baptised on 4 October of that year. Of a noble family in straitened economic circumstances, he was the son of Melchor de Cevallos and grandson of Diego de Cevallos, bailiff to the Marqués de Villena. His father had been granted a patent of nobility by the High Court of Appeals in Valladolid in 1572. He studied law in Valladolid and Salamanca and graduated from the University of Sigüenza in 1589. (Nicolás Antonio's statement, afterwards repeated by all, that he was a private tutor in the college of the bishop, Don Álvaro de Mendoza, in Avila is not correct; nor did he teach at the Colegio Mayor de San Bartolomé, University of Salamanca.) He settled in Toledo in 1590, where he married María de Herrera that same year; he practised for a time as a lawyer, and then, in 1596–1597, as a public notary. In 1605 he was appointed alderman on the city council on the noblemen's bench. In addition to his activities as an alderman he frequently attended the literary meetings that were held in the house of Don Francisco Rojas y Guzmán, Conde de Mora and nephew of Cardinal Sandoval y Rojas, writing numerous treatises in Spanish and Latin. In addition to the *Tractatus de cognitione* he wrote the *Communes contra communes* (published in three separate books, *Speculum practicarum*, *Speculum Opinionum* and *Speculum aureum*, between 1600 and 1613), the work entitled *Ruina de la Monarquía* (dated 1620 and now lost) and the *Arte Real para el buen govierno...dirigido a la Católica Magestad del Rey Don Felipe IIII* (1623). In the latter, which was to confirm his reputation, he criticised the large number of members of religious orders in Spain and advised the monarch to cease having favourites. After leaving the post as alderman, which he passed on to his grandson in 1621, and being widowed in 1623, he became a priest. In 1626 he was appointed chaplain of the Capilla de Reyes Nuevos in Toledo Cathedral and in 1631 became a member of the Governing Council of the Archbishopric of Toledo, taking over the presidency of the Council in August 1639. He died on 22 July 1644. There is no documentary information linking him with El Greco, whom he must have known well. In 1625 he signed a petition by Jorge Manuel addressed to the Governing Council of the Archbishopric in relation to work on the altarpieces in the Hospital de Afuera, and when he died he owned a 'San Francisco del Dominico'. Also among his possessions was an unattributed *Portrait of the Lawyer, Dr Cevallos when he was Married*, which is perhaps the Prado picture. [JAL]

17 Domenikos Theotokopoulos, El Greco

[1541–1614]

Portrait of a Painter (Jorge Manuel Theotocopouli), *ca.* 1603
Oil on canvas. 74 x 51.5 cm
Seville, Museo de Bellas Artes, E.97.P

PROVENANCE

Bought from Serafín García de la Huerta, Madrid, by Baron Taylor for King Louis-Philippe of Orléans; Paris, Galerie Espagnole of King Louis-Philippe in the Louvre (1838–1848); London, heirs of King Louis-Philippe (1850–1853); sale of Louis-Philippe's Gallery in London, Christie's, 1853, bought by Colnaghi; Seville, Duke of Montpensier's collection, San Telmo Palace; given to the Seville Museum by the Infanta María Luisa Fernanda, Dowager Duchess of Montpensier, in 1897.

ESSENTIAL BIBLIOGRAPHY

Notice des tableaux de la Galerie Espagnole..., 1838, no. 260; *Catalogue of the Spanish Gallery of...King Louis-Philippe*, 1853; Sanpere i Miquel 1900, pp. 396–98; Cossío 1908, pp. 430–32 and no. 14; Camón 1950, p. 1.132 and no. 749; Wethey 1962 and 1967, no. 158; Gudiol 1971, p. 214 and no. 179; Baticle and Marinas 1981, no. 269, pp. 174–75; Pita 1981, p. 136 and no. 271; Moreno Mendoza *et al.* 1991, p. 76; Álvarez Lopera 1993, no. 256; T. de Antonio in Barcelona 1996/1997, exh. cat., pp. 112–13, no. 4; Álvarez Lopera in Madrid/Rome/Athens 1999–2000, exh. cat., pp. 405–06, no. 67; Carr 2001, p. 49; Muñoz Rubio 2003.

The *Portrait of a Painter* in the Seville Museum was published for the first time in the catalogue of the Galerie Espagnole of Louis-Philippe, having previously belonged to the restorer and art dealer Serafín García de la Huerta. It was believed at that time to be a self-portrait by El Greco, and considered as such throughout the nineteenth century. In 1900, Sanpere rejected the idea that it could be a self-portrait, on the basis of the signature ('one cannot understand,' he wrote, 'why he himself should say of his portrait *done by Domenikos Theotokópoulos*'), and expressed his conviction that it was a portrait of Jorge Manuel. The basis of Sanpere's argument was very weak and rested mainly on the similarity he believed he could see between the subject's features and those of the *Lady in a Fur Wrap* [FIG. 56], whom he believed to be El Greco's wife. However, and although Cossío did not accept this identification and catalogued the painting as *Portrait of a Painter*, Sanpere's view found wide and immediate acceptance.

Nowadays, although not absolutely secure, the identification appears to be firmly established on the basis of the following evidence: (a) the date of the canvas, which is certainly after June 1600 (the date on which Philip III authorised the wearing of 'ruffs of one-eighth of a *vara* and starched') and, for reasons of style, before 1605; (b) the consistency between the age of the sitter and that of Jorge Manuel at that time; and (c) the similarity between this painter and one of the gentlemen shown in the painting of *The Virgin of Charity* in Illescas, in which we know that El Greco painted his son (in one of the documents relating to El Greco's legal action against the Hospital de la Caridad, the latter's representative, Antonio Suárez, presented as one of the 'imperfections and errors' of the altarpiece the fact that the artist 'had painted a portrait of his nephew [here the term is used to designate an illegitimate son] Jorge Manuel wearing a very large ruff').

Jorge Manuel, the illegitimate son of El Greco and Jerónima de las Cuevas, was born in 1578. As a reaffirmation of his roots, the painter gave him the names of his father and brother. There is no doubt that he had real affection for him. In *The Burial of the Count of Orgaz* [FIG. 17]he portrays him as the page who is gesturing towards the count, with his date of birth marked on the handkerchief that is emerging from his pocket. Later on, he painted him (as already stated) in the *Virgin of Charity* as well as in this portrait, which is one of the most lively El Greco ever executed. Almost half-length, Jorge Manuel elegantly poses against a greenish background and wears a black doublet and a large pointed ruff, in the fashion of the time. The palette and paint-brushes he displays allude to his occupation, but his air of distinction is that of a nobleman. In showing him thus idealised and distinguished, El Greco depicts his son displaying qualities he certainly would not have possessed, but which he doubtless would have wanted him to have. In his annotations to Barbaro's edition of Vitruvius, the artist complained about the decadence of architecture, stating that this 'most noble occupation has become so despicable that no good father would place his son in any similar art'. However, Jorge Manuel shone more as an architect than as a painter, an occupation in which he was no more than a pale follower of his father – but perhaps the latter, blinded by affection, did not see that. Jorge Manuel, who already appeared to be associated with his father's studio in 1597, continued to live in his shadow throughout his youth. In 1603 he married Doña Alfonsa de los Morales but still did not leave his father's household, where he began to emerge not just as a mere assistant but as his father's partner. The ratification of the contract with the Hospital de la Caridad in Illescas, on 9 July 1603, specified that the work was entrusted to 'domingo griego and xorje manuel, painters'. The birth during the following year of Jorge Manuel's first child, Gabriel de los Morales, filled the old master's last years with joy. The painting in the Seville Museum belongs precisely to those years of the domestic and professional fulfilment of El Greco's son. [JAL]

18 Domenikos Theotokopoulos, El Greco

[1541–1614]

An Elderly Gentleman, *ca.* 1587–1596
Oil on canvas, 46 x 43 cm
Madrid, Museo del Prado, P-806

PROVENANCE

Royal Collections, Alcázar Real, Madrid (recorded in the inventories of 1666, 1686 and 1701); not recorded in any eighteenth century royal inventory; recorded in the *Inventario y nota de los cuadros, estampas, dibujos, etc. de la propiedad de S. M. que existían en el estudio del primer pintor de Cámara D. Vicente López...* and which were handed back by the latter on 12 April 1839; exhibited in the Prado from 1839.

ESSENTIAL BIBLIOGRAPHY

Cossío 1908, pp. 403–04 and no. 74; Camón 1950, pp. 1.114–1.117 and no. 738; Wethey 1962 and 1967, no. 139; Gómez-Menor 1966, pp. 77–79; Gudiol 1971, p. 166 and no. 127; Pita 1981, pp. 70–71 and no. 78; Jordan in Madrid/.../Dallas 1982–1983, exh. cat., no. 59; Álvarez Lopera 2003, pp. 177–78, 186–87, 200–03 and 209–10; Finaldi in New York/London 2003b, exh. cat., no. 76, pp. 274–75.

This painting is recorded for the first time in the Alcázar in Madrid, in the 'Room adjacent to the Galería del Cierzo that overlooks the park' in the 1666 inventory: 'Painting half a *vara* high with a white frame, portrait by the Greek'. Its origin is not known, nor the time when it became part of the Royal Collection. There is no information on the identity of the subject. Gómez-Menor put forward the suggestion that it could be Don Gaspar de la Fuente, son of the doctor, Don Rodrigo de la Fuente, and royal *aposentador* but his sole arguments for this identification are the 'physical likeness, truly remarkable' that he thought he could see between his face and that of the doctor, whose portrait is in the Prado, and the fact that both paintings were already hanging in the Alcázar in 1686 (he believed it likely that both paintings became part of the Royal Collection via Don Gaspar).

Although unusual, there is no doubt that the format is the original one. There is no evidence of the height having been reduced and the presentation is similar to that of other portraits such as that of the *Elderly Gentleman* (assumed to be a self-portrait) in the Metropolitan Museum in New York. We are led to think of this painting as an 'intimate' portrait of somebody who was close to the painter. We see this from the simplicity and openness of the portrayal, the complete absence of any details denoting the subject's position or social standing (not even by the elegance of the pose as is the case in other half-length portraits in the Prado), the closeness of the focus and the way in which emphasis is given to the head, prodigiously painted, against a grey background that creates a kind of luminous aura all around him but which scarcely produces a feeling of depth, and clothes that are surprisingly flat and lacking in detail.

The possibility of it being a portrait of someone who was not a public person, and intended for private family use, should not be excluded. This is one of the most intense and psychologically complex characters in the career of El Greco and one of the most refined from a technical point of view. Cossío linked it to the noblemen in the *Burial of the Count of Orgaz* although observing the features that are evidence of a technique that is more highly developed: 'The palette,' he wrote, 'has been lightened; there are fewer shadows, the brush-strokes are more free and independent; the carmine gradually starts to become more pronounced in the flesh tones.' Other authors have emphasised the richness of the painting's texture: in some areas the effect is so fluid and light that the weave of the canvas is highly visible; in others, such as the collar, vigorous impasto is used. The artist's prodigious technique is apparent in the execution of the head and skin, and in the subtle differentiation established between the hair of the head and the beard. The assymetries and distortions have been accentuated in comparison with previous portraits. A sinuous line that passes down via the nose, descending from the central lock of hair on the head to the point of the beard, divides the face into two assymetrical halves which, as Finaldi has observed, seem to be transmitting different expressions: the hint of an animated smile on our right side; and concentrated and pensive on the other.

There is no agreement on the date of the painting. Based on the relationships that can be established with the noblemen in the *Burial of the Count of Orgaz*, Cossío placed it between 1584 and 1594, and Wethey between 1585 and 1590. However, because of the technique used, more highly developed than that of the *Burial*, other specialists have dated it later. Mayer placed it between 1594 and 1600, Soehner between 1592 and 1596 and Camón towards 1600. It is most likely that it was painted well into the 1590s. [JAL]

19 Domenikos Theotokopoulos, El Greco
[1541–1614]

Fray Hortensio Félix Paravicino, *ca.* 1609–1613
Oil on canvas, 113 x 86.1 cm
Boston, Museum of Fine Arts, Isaac Sweetser Fund, 04.234

PROVENANCE
Duke of Arcos, Madrid (1724); probably in the monastery of San Hermenegildo (Barefoot Carmelites) in Madrid (1786); Francisco Javier de Muguiro, Madrid (late nineteenth century and early twentieth century); Durand-Ruel, Paris (1903–1904); purchased by the Boston Museum of Fine Arts in 1904 with money from the Isaac Sweetser Fund.

ESSENTIAL BIBLIOGRAPHY
Palomino 1724/1947, p. 842; Cossío 1908, pp. 439–43 and no. 278; Polentinos 1933, p. 50; Alarcos García 1937; Camón 1950, pp. 1.136–1.141 and no. 751; Wethey 1962 and 1967, no. 153; Gudiol 1971, p. 283 and no. 243; Cerdan 1978; Kagan 1982, p. 69; Jordan in Madrid/.../Dallas 1982–1983, exh. cat., no. 63; Cerdan 1994; Portús 1996, pp. 79–81; Carr 2001a, pp. 50–51; Carr 2001b in Vienna exh. cat., no. 32; Finaldi in New York/London 2003b, exh. cat., no. 81, p. 286.

Fray Hortensio Félix Paravicino y Arteaga, one of the most celebrated preachers and poets of his time, was born in Madrid on 12 October 1580. He was the natural son – his parents had married but never completed the formalities, giving him the status of an illegitimate son, which he always tried to conceal – of Mucio Paravicino, an Italian from Como, of noble stock, who was paymaster general of the Milan army between 1603 and 1613, and Doña María de Arteaga, born in Guadalajara of a family said to be noble. In 1595 he was sent to Salamanca where he studied civil and canon law, starting his novitiate in the monastery of the Barefoot Carmelite friars in 1599. He took his vows in April 1600 and after completing his studies at the University Monastery of Saint Thomas in Avila, he graduated as Master of Theology in Salamanca in January 1603. He lived there until 1606 when, shortly after being ordained as a priest, he was sent to Madrid to 'preside over and preach' in the Provincial Chapter held in April of that year. After that he settled in the Convento de la Trinidad in the Calle de Atocha (no longer extant, but in the nineteenth century it housed the National Museum of Painting) and apart from a few journeys, he lived there until his death at the age of only fifty-three, on 12 December 1633.

His brilliant and complex sermons that made extensive use of conceits, soon made him famous in Madrid (there was the saying 'Hortensio has not preached so the festivities cannot be over') and in December 1617 he was appointed Royal Preacher to Philip III. He carried out the same role for Philip IV and was admired by the Count-Duke of Olivares and other nobles of the time. Although twice appointed Superior of his monastery in Madrid and twice elected Provincial of Castile and Representative for Andalucía, it appears that the end of his life was clouded by disagreements with other members of his order. Proceedings for his appointment as Bishop of Lérida were in hand when he died.

Lope de Vega referred to 'his clarity and purity, shining adornment, solemn brilliance', and from what we know, he had aristocratic and refined tastes from which worldliness was not exempt, and a high opinion of his own worth. In the monastery he had servants to wait on him and according to records of that time, in the rooms he occupied he had assembled 'one of the richest and most abundant libraries of this court' and had hung his portrait that was 'so like the original that it seemed that art could advance no further'. There he often received important members of the nobility and some of the court's most eminent literary figures. As a marked feature of his personality, the fact should also be noted that in a Madrid that was divided into opposing literary groups of which he belonged to one – the culteranistas – he succeeded in winning the friendship and admiration of such diverse figures as Góngora, Lope de Vega and Quevedo.

Although it has been suggested that the painter and the friar became acquainted through the Paravicino family (Cerdán) or that they were introduced by the brothers Eugenio and Alonso de Narbona (Kagan), there is no known information on the time or circumstances when El Greco and Paravicino met. There is no evidence that they were friends (their meetings must have been sporadic since the friar lived in Madrid) much less, close friends. The warmth felt by El Greco for Paravicino is clearly obvious, in the portrait he painted of him and the admiration of the latter for the former in the four sonnets he dedicated to him.

Cossío has dated this portrait as having been painted in 1609 because in the sonnet he dedicated to him ('To the same Greek, in a portrait he painted of the author') Paravicino mentioned that he was twenty-nine at the time. However, the date cannot be accepted as definitive. On the one hand, as Portús has noted, account should be taken of the existence of manuscript versions of the sonnet before its publication in 1641 (eight years after the death of Paravicino and therefore in an edition that the author did not control) in which other ages are transcribed, of which one is equally likely, that of thirty-three, in which case the portrait could have been painted in 1613. It is also possible that even if the age stated in the printed version is correct (as seems most likely), the portrait could have been painted in 1611 at a time when Paravicino was certainly in Toledo, as proved by the sonnet that he dedicated to the catafalque raised by El Greco in honour of Queen Margarita (there is no record of his having been there in 1609). Although we do not know the reasons, we know that on occasions Paravicino misrepresented his date of birth, putting it back by a couple of years. In the letter he sent Philip IV on account of his celebrated dispute with Calderón de la Barca, he stated that early in 1600 he was seventeen years old (although he was already nineteen), and an account of his life written by a friar from his own monastery who lived with him, states that he was born in 1582 (see Cerdán 1978, p. 64). However remote it may seem, the possibility cannot be discounted that Fray Hortensio wrote that he was twenty-nine years old in 1611.

This portrait is, in all likelihood, the one that, according to contemporary sources, Paravicino had in his cell. The way it is arranged is highly unusual. The fact that Paravicino appears seated and is depicted down to his knees is reminiscent of the portraits of high ecclesiastical dignataries. However, the friar's frontal and unsteady pose, the sense of immediacy and movement he transmits and details such as his dishevelled hair, give the image a certain air of informality. Placed against a neutral background that avoids any distraction and forces us to focus our gaze on his face, he appears seated on a upright chair which curiously, is the same one used by the painter for the *Portrait of a Trinitarian Monk* in the Nelson Atkins Museum, Kansas City. On his knees and the arm of the chair rests a large tome that doubtless alludes to his profession as a theologian, and on it, held half-open with his middle finger, is a small octavo book related to his role as a poet. Titian used the same device (the sitter shown with a small book half-open in his hand, as if he had stopped reading in order to pose) in some of his portraits of literary figures, such as that of the supposed *Jacopo Sannazzaro* in Hampton Court Palace, or the one of *Benedetto Varchi* in the Kunsthistorisches Museum in Vienna. As in El Greco's portrait of Cardinal Niño de Guevara, the hands suggest different states. The left hand, painted very summarily, implies movement and activity; the right hand, falling elegantly and more finished, indicates rest and confidence. Finaldi has suggested that this is an allusion to the life of the friar, both active and contemplative. Technically, the painting has the same characteristics as other works in his last years. The painter is playing with different degrees of finish and uses the reddish brown ground to define the background and the shadows of his white habit. In the areas intended to attract the attention (the head, the right hand, the habit) the execution is energetic, with a speed and freedom that contrasts with the treatment of the background and the cape. The range of colour may be small but it is brought to life by the contrasting blacks and whites and the counterpoint of the red stains of the lips and the cross on his habit. [JAL]

4 Portrait and Reality: Ribalta, Zurbarán, Ribera

20 Francisco Ribalta
[1565–1628]

Saint Luke, 1625–1627
Oil on canvas, 83 x 36 cm
Valencia, Museo de Bellas Artes de Valencia, 471

PROVENANCE

Painted as part of the *retablo mayor* of the charterhouse of Porta Coeli, Bétera, Valencia; transferred to the Museo de Bellas Artes de Valencia in 1835, after the suppression of the monasteries.

ESSENTIAL BIBLIOGRAPHY

Espresati 1948, pp. 184 and 186; Kowal 1985, p. 94; *Los Ribalta y la pintura valenciana de su tiempo* (Valencia/Madrid) 1987–1988, cat. no. 47, p. 178.

According to tradition, the evangelist Luke was a physician and a painter. He is often shown painting a picture of the Virgin, or the Virgin and Child, and Ribalta's Evangelist paints a demure Virgin engrossed in her prayer book. She recalls the *Virgen de las Tocas* (the Madonna of the Veil), an iconographic type popular in eastern Spain. His painting rests on a simple wooden easel and he applies his paints from a plain rectangular palette. A small container, presumably for oil, rests on the ledge of the easel. In the left foreground an ox, the symbol of Luke, intrudes into the picture.

The painting is part of a series of evangelists painted for the lower part of the *retablo mayor* of the church of the Charterhouse of Porta Coeli in Bétera near Valencia. Ribalta received the commission in 1625 and delivered the sixteen paintings which formed the altarpiece in 1627 (only thirteen are known today). It was dismantled in the 1830s.

Saint Luke has been traditionally identified as a self-portrait of Francisco Ribalta. The particularised features, the intense gaze directed at the viewer and the absence of a halo (present in the paintings of the three other Evangelists) lend support to this idea. There are, of course, numerous precedents of artists imprinting their own features on those of the saint when they painted this subject. The German scholar August L. Mayer (1908) thought that in this work Ribalta had painted a portrait of Michelangelo in the guise of Saint Luke, but his was a lone voice; most of those who have written on this painting have accepted that it is a self-portrait. Ribalta would have been about sixty years old when he painted the picture and it would have afforded him the opportunity to meditate on a lifetime of executing religious works in the service of the Church. He was to die very shortly afterwards. [GF]

21 Francisco de Zurbarán
[1598–1664]

The Crucified Christ contemplated by a Painter, 1630s
Oil on canvas, 105 x 84 cm
Madrid, Museo del Prado, P-2594

PROVENANCE

Collection of the Infante Don Sebastián Gabriel, Pau, 1876; his son, Don Alfonso de Borbón Braganza; by descent to the wife of Don Cristóbal Colón, duque de la Veragua, Madrid; bought from him by the Prado in April 1936.

ESSENTIAL BIBLIOGRAPHY

Guinard 1960, no. 107, p. 221; Carrasco Muñoz 1973, pp. 175–76; *De Greco à Picasso. Cinq Siècles d'Art Espagnol* (Paris), 1987–1988, cat. no. 52, p. 209; *Zurbarán* (Madrid) 1988, cat. no. 95, pp. 384–85; Stoichita 1996, p. 70; Caturla/Delenda 1994, pp. 50, 53; *Zurbarán, Cuarto centenario* (Seville) 1998, cat. no. 70, p. 206.

Christ on the cross is contemplated by a painter who holds a palette and brushes in his left hand and places his right on his chest in a gesture of pious devotion. He has traditionally been identified as Saint Luke, the evangelist-painter who according to legend made a portrait of the Virgin. Although he wears an antique-style tunic and cloak, appropriate to the evangelist, he is not shown with a halo, nor indeed is there an iconographical precedent for Saint Luke painting Christ on the cross.

It has also been proposed that this is a self-portrait of Zurbarán. If the painting were dated to the 1650s, as has recently been argued (see reference in *Zurbarán, Cuarto centenario* (Seville), 1998), then the figure's elderly appearance would not *per se* be an obstacle to the identification. In fact the style and conception of the work make it more likely that it is a work of the 1630s, in which case he would be too old for the artist. If Zurbarán intended the painter as an 'allegorical' or 'conceptual' self-portrait, then he might not have been concerned with accurate rendition of age, or indeed likeness (we do not actually know what Zurbarán looked like).

More interesting perhaps are the conceptual questions raised by Stoichita (1996). Does the painting show the artist having a vision, or is he shown projecting himself, as in an Ignatian meditation, into the drama of Golgotha? He might be standing before a painting he has just completed, or he could even be contemplating a highly realistic sculpted crucifix, which, like the *Cristo de la Clemencia* made by Martínez Montañés for the Cathedral of Seville, looks down at the devout viewer as though speaking to him. Zurbarán intentionally leaves these ambiguities unresolved, but it is interesting to note that the scale of the figure of Christ is smaller than that of the painter, strengthening the notion that the painter is before an image rather than before the reality. The painting may well be making the basic point that the artist is endowed with a special ability to make an image which is able to inspire the viewer to devotion towards the prototype it represents. [GF]

22 Francisco de Zurbarán
[1598–1664]

Don Alonso Verdugo de Albornoz, 1635
Oil on canvas, 186.6 x 104.5 cm
Signed, lower right:
Franco dezurbaran. F. and inscribed: ÆTAS. 12. A[NNO]S.
Berlin, Staatliche Museen zu Berlin, Gemäldegalerie, 404C

PROVENANCE
Alphonse Oudry, Paris; his sale, Hôtel Drouot, Paris, 16–17 April 1869, no. 155, where bought by Prince Jérôme Napoléon; his sale, Christie's, London, 9–11 May 1872, no. 327, where bought by Holloway; collection of Alfred Morrison, London; acquired by the Kaiser Friedrich Museum, Berlin, in 1906.

ESSENTIAL BIBLIOGRAPHY
Saltillo 1928, pp. 33–34; Caturla 1960, p. 407; Guinard 1960, no. 585; Brown 1973, p. 108; *Zurbarán* (Paris) 1988, p. 281, cat. no. 46; Caturla/Delenda 1994, p. 127.

Alonso Verdugo de Albornoz was the son of Alonso Verdugo de la Cueva y Sotomayor, one of the *veintecuatro* (members of the City Council of Seville) and Juana de Albornoz, sister of Cardinal Gil de Albornoz, minister of Philip IV and subsequently Governor of Milan. He was baptised on 12 February 1623 in Carmona, near Seville and at five years of age he became a Knight of Alcántara. The green cross of the order is emblazoned on his breastplate and is also visible behind the coat of arms at upper right. The inscription on the portrait records that it was painted when the sitter was twelve, and it presumably marks his appointment as captain of his uncle's guard. He wears armour, baton and sash, appropriate to his military status, and he rests his left hand on the hilt of his sword. His slashed pantaloons with the enormous rosettes fixed at the knee are showy and fashionable and they are identical to those worn by the military commanders in Zurbarán's *The Defence of Cadiz* [FIG. 68] painted in Madrid in 1634.

This portrait is usually supposed to have been made in Seville, although the painter is not actually documented there (or anywhere) during 1635. Caturla speculated that it may have had some influence on Velázquez and cited the Velazquian *Portrait of Prince Baltasar Carlos* in the Kunsthistorisches Museum in Vienna, dating from about 1640, as evidence (see *Varia Velazqueña*, Madrid, 1960, I, pp. 463–70), but in fact Velázquez had already painted two earlier portraits of the prince where the young boy adopts a similar military bearing and posture (Boston, Museum of Fine Arts, 1631; London, Wallace Collection, 1632). The marked tenebrism of the portrait and the use of a dark and practically unmodulated background from which the sharply lit figure emerges, are likely to have been considered slightly old-fashioned in Madrid in 1635, and this strengthens the argument for the portrait having been executed in Seville. Zurbarán's handling of materials, texture and light are extraordinarily accomplished. The soft chamois leather of Don Alonso's shoes, the stiff fabric of his pantaloons, the thick edges of the cuffs and *golilla* collar, and the reflections of the scarlet sash on his breastplate, are superbly rendered. The boy's expression, which combines aristocratic haughtiness with a childish vulnerability, demonstrates Zurbarán's sensitivity and skill as a portrait painter. [GF]

23 Francisco de Zurbarán
[1598–1664]

Fray Francisco Zúmel, ca. 1630
Oil on canvas, 204 x 122 cm
Inscribed: M.º F. FRANCISCO / ZVMEL
Madrid, Museo de la Real Academia de Bellas Artes de San Fernando, 664

PROVENANCE
Painted for the library of the Merced Calzada in Seville; seen in the library there by Ceán Bermúdez, 1800; collection of Don Manuel Godoy, Príncipe de la Paz, Madrid, by about 1802; in 1808 passed to the Real Academia de San Fernando.

ESSENTIAL BIBLIOGRAPHY
Guinard 1960, pp. 96–97, no. 418, p. 260; *Zurbarán* (Paris), 1988, pp. 122–23; Caturla/Delenda 1994, p. 65.

The painting was part of a series of eleven portraits of distinguished Mercedarians seen by the eighteenth-century writer Ceán Bermúdez in the library on the first floor of the convent of the Merced Calzada in Seville (now the Museo de Bellas Artes). Five are in the Academia de San Fernando, two are in other collections (Pau and Seville) and four are lost. Of the five Academia paintings, four are identified by inscriptions like the one on the present picture, and they are presumed to be imaginary portraits, with the exception of that of Fray Hernando de Santiago who died in 1636 and whose portrait is inscribed VERA EFIGE (true likeness).

Francisco Zúmel had died long before Zurbarán could have painted him. Born in 1540, he became a professor at the University of Salamanca in 1570 and acquired a European reputation as a Thomist theologian, writing brilliantly on the themes of predestination and human liberty. Tirso de Molina paid tribute to his skills as a teacher saying that audiences would listen to him in silence, hanging on every word. He became General of the Mercedarian order and acted as adviser to both Philip II and Philip III. He died in 1604. Zurbarán must have selected a friar from the convent to pose as Zúmel, presumably one whose appearance, to his mind, corresponded with that of a learned ecclesiastic. Interestingly, the artist appears to have employed the same model for the portrait of *Fray Pedro Machado*, also in the Academia collection.

Zúmel is writing in an open folio volume, but his gaze is not fixed on the page. Zurbarán shows him as though concentrated on his inner thoughts; his writings are merely their external manifestation. To the right is a table on which rest a book and an academic cap, identical to those that appear in the portraits of Machado, Hernando de Santiago and Jerónimo Pérez. Zurbarán's great reputation as a painter of white draperies rests on paintings like this one. [GF]

24 Jusepe de Ribera
[1591–1652]

Portrait of a Jesuit, 1638
195.6 x 111.5 cm
Signed lower left: *Jusepe de Ribera español valenciano /, F, 1638*
Milan, Museo Poldi Pezzoli, 332-95

PROVENANCE
In the collection of Conte Carlo Castelbarco, Milan, by 1870 (probably inherited from his father); his sale, Hotel Drouot, Paris, 2, 5 and 6 May 1870, lot 30; with the Milanese dealer, G. Basilini, from whom acquired by G. G. Poldi-Pezzoli in 1881.

ESSENTIAL BIBLIOGRAPHY
Jusepe de Ribera, lo Spagnoletto, 1591–1652 (Fort Worth), pp. 186–87, cat. no. 25; Bugli and Della Valle 1982, no. 210, pp. 162–63; *Ribera, 1591–1652* (Naples), p. 232, cat. no. 1.75; Spinosa 2003, p. 174, cat. A206, p. 312.

This portrait of a priest is remarkable for its austerity and concentration and for the astounding virtuosity of handling, particularly in the head and hands and in the black of the sitter's cassock. The sitter's right hand rests on the head of a lion, more symbolic than real, which has been variously interpreted as an emblem of Christ, an allusion to the Society of Jesus, and more specifically to the order's missionary activity. The lion could equally refer to the name of the sitter, perhaps Leone, or Marco (after Saint Mark), or possibly Girolamo, since Saint Jerome is customarily accompanied by a lion. The setting and the composition are almost identical to the *Saint Augustine* which Ribera had painted two years earlier for the Augustinian nuns of the convent in Salamanca (still *in situ*) founded by the Count of Monterrey, Viceroy of Naples from 1631 to 1637, and an avid patron and collector of the works of the artist. In that painting the saint is similarly posed in a three-quarter view facing left and dressed in the black Augustinian habit; his left hand, at waist height, holds a folio volume and his right is extended in a manner similar to this painting, drawing attention to his attribute, a bishop's mitre.

When the work was sold in Paris is 1870 it was described merely as 'Un personage vêtu de noir' but in the modern literature he has always been said to be a Jesuit. The combination of black cassock, belted at the waist, and black cloak, is typical Jesuit dress and in a little-known drawing by Ribera at Chatsworth (inv. 204; see McDonald 1993, fig. 5), showing a *Scene from the Life of Saint Francis Xavier*, the Jesuits there wear identical dress. In his eighteenth-century *Life of Ribera*, Bernardo De Dominici makes reference to the Count of Monterrey's Jesuit confessor (he does not give his name) and states that he was responsible for commissioning Ribera to paint the three scenes from the life of Saint Ignatius, founder of the order, that are in the large marble altar dedicated to the saint in the church of the Gesù Nuovo in Naples (early 1640s). Felton has speculated that the Poldi Pezzoli portrait shows this unidentified Jesuit (see *Jusepe de Ribera, lo Spagnoletto, 1591–1652* (Fort Worth), pp. 187–88). [GF]

25 Jusepe de Ribera
[1591–1652]

Maddalena Ventura with her Husband ('The Bearded Woman'), 1631

Oil on canvas, 196 x 127 cm

The Lerma Bequest. Toledo, Palacio Tavera, Fundación Casa Ducal de Medinaceli

Inscribed at the top of the painting:

DE FOEMINIS ITALIAM QVE GERENS MI [?R]ANDA FIGVRA ET PVERVM LACTANS / OCVLIS MIRABILE MONSTRVM

(An Italian woman of wondrous appearance suckling a child / An astounding monster for eyes to see)

Inscribed on the blocks of stone to the right:

EN MAGNV[M] / NATVRA / MIRACVLVM / MAGDALENA VENTVRA EX- / OPPIDO ACVMVLI APVD / SAMNITES VVLGO, EL ABRVZZO, REGNI NEAPOLI-TANI ANNORVM 52 ET / QVOD INSOLENS EST CV[M] / ANNVM 37 AGERET COE / PIT PUBESCERE, EOQVE / BARBA DEMISSA AC PRO-/ LIXA EST VT POTIVS / ALICVIVS MAGISTRI BARBATI / ESSE VIDEATVR, QVAM MV- / LIERIS QVAE TRES FILIOS / ANTE AMISERIT QVOS EX / VIRO SVO FELICI DE AMICI / QVEM ADESSE VIDES HABVERAT. / IOSEPHVS DE RIBERA HISPANVS CHRISTI CRVCE / INSIGNITIVS SVI TEMPORIS ALTER APELLES / IVSSV FERDINANDI IJ / DVCIS, IIJ DE ALCALÁ / NEAPOLI PROREGIS ADVIVVM MIRE DEPINXIT. / XIIIJ KALEND. MART. / ANNO MDCXXXI.

(A Great Wonder of Nature Maddalena Ventura from the town of Accúmoli of the Samnites, in the vernacular, Abruzzo, in the Kingdom of Naples, aged 52. And what is remarkable is that at 37 she began to become hirsute and grew a beard so thick and long that it is more like that which may be seen on any bearded man than on a woman who had previously borne three children, as she had from her husband, Felice De Amici, whom you see here. Jusepe de Ribera, Spaniard, decorated with [the order of] the Cross of Christ, another Apelles in his time, painted this from the life for Fernando II, third Duke of Alcalá, Viceroy of Naples, on the 16th of February in the year 1631.)

PROVENANCE

Commissioned by the third Duke of Alcalá in 1631; by 1637 in the Casa de Pilatos in Seville; by descent to the Dukes of Medinaceli; after 1808 taken to Paris for the Musée Napoleon and returned in 1813; deposited in the Real Academia de San Fernando, Madrid, and listed in its catalogues from 1818 to 1829; returned to the Medinaceli family; deposited in the Hospital Tavera, Toledo.

ESSENTIAL BIBLIOGRAPHY

Jusepe de Ribera, lo Spagnoletto, 1591–1652 (Fort Worth), pp. 128–31, cat. no. 11; De Vito 1983, p. 43; Brown and Kagan 1987, pp. 242–43 and 251 (item V. 19); *Ribera, 1591–1652* (Madrid), pp. 228–30, cat. no. 32; Spinosa 2003, pp. 150–51, cat. A101, p. 281.

This painting depicts Maddalena Ventura from the Abruzzi who achieved notoriety at the viceregal court in Naples in 1631 due to her acute hirsutism, which, as the inscription on the stone ledge indicates, first appeared when she was thirty-seven years old. She was a guest of the viceroy, Duke of Alcalá, and at his request Ribera painted her portrait in the Royal Palace. The episode is recorded in a letter of 11 February 1631, from Marc'Antonio Padovanino, the Venetian diplomat in Naples, or *residente*, to the Venetian Senate: 'In the rooms of the Viceroy there was a very famous painter making a portrait of a married woman from Abruzzo with many children who has a totally virile face, with more than a palm's length of beautiful black beard. Her breast is all hairy, and His Excellency took pleasure in showing her to me as a marvellous thing, for truly she is so' (De Vito 1983).

It is, of course, Ribera's portrait that has ensured Maddalena Ventura's fame down the centuries. Several copies of it are known, and when Goya made a drawing of a bearded woman nursing a child in her arms (private collection, USA), he inscribed it as follows: 'This woman was portrayed by José Ribera el Españoleto around 1640.'

Ribera shows her holding a baby at the breast, but given her age, fifty-two, and the excess of male hormones she was suffering from, it is evident that this is not her child, and the inscription specifies that she had had three children by her husband, the timid, troubled Felice De Amici who lurks in the shadows on the left, before her beard grew. As Padovanino commented, her face was 'totally virile', and Ribera represents it with no trace of feminine lineaments or skin texture. Thus, the child is there as a paradoxical attribute of both her femininity and her maternity; as are her dress, cap and wedding ring, and the wool and skein on a metal spindle (emblems of female domesticity) on the stone ledge on the right.

Pérez Sánchez has commented that 'the artist's genius has transformed an abnormal and, almost repugnant medical case into a superb work of art in which beauty of painterly treatment is combined with the marked suggestion of mystery' (*Ribera, 1591–1652* (Madrid), p. 228). The painting thus demonstrates the artist's concern to provide an accurate record of this phenomenon of nature, which was certainly what the patron wanted, but also to create a work of art worthy of his fame. Fernando Afán de Ribera y Enríquez (1583–1637), third Duke of Alcalá, and Viceroy of Naples between 1629 and 1631, was a collector with academic and scientific leanings – he owned numerous scientific and mathematical instruments – and the inventory of the collection that he gathered in the Casa de Pilatos in Seville (and the list of the separate collection sold in Genoa at his death in 1637) shows that in addition to '*The Bearded Woman*' he had several portraits of dwarves and giants, and paintings of other phenomena of nature such as a three-horned bull. In the inscription Ribera proudly refers to himself as the new Apelles of his age, in reference to the mythical Greek artist; implicit in the epithet is that he was painting for a new Alexander the Great, the Duke of Alcalá, who was undoubtedly one of Ribera's most brilliant patrons. [GF]

26 Jusepe de Ribera
[1591–1652]

Democritus (?), 1630
125 x 81 cm
Signed: *Jusepe de Ribera español / F, 1630*
Madrid, Museo del Prado, P-1121

PROVENANCE
Possibly identifiable with the latter of a pair of *Philosophers* in the collection of the Duke of Alcalá, in the Casa de Pilatos, Seville, by 1637 ('Dos Philossophos el uno escriviendo y el ottro con un compaz de joseph de Rivera [...]', Brown and Kagan 1987, p. 251, VII. 9); in the Spanish Royal Collection from at least 1700 and recorded in the Monastery of El Escorial; in the Museo del Prado from 1837.

ESSENTIAL BIBLIOGRAPHY
Fitz Darby 1962; Brown and Kagan 1987, p. 243; Ferrari 1986, pp. 112 and 156; *Ribera, 1591–1652* (Madrid), pp. 222–24, cat. no. 29; Spinosa 2003, p. 146, cat. A71, p. 281.

The painting, which has been cut down on the right hand side, is Ribera's earliest dated 'ragged philosopher'. Ribera appears to have been largely responsible for the invention of the genre in the mid-1610s, and it enjoyed great success in Italy over the course of the seventeenth century. This philosopher was traditionally identified as Archimedes, the Sicilian mathematician, on account of the compass he holds. He holds a sheaf of papers with geometric designs on them and to the left are more papers and some books. Since Delphine Fitz Darby proposed in 1962, on the basis of his grin, that he should be identified as Democritus, the laughing philosopher, the painting has usually been given that title. The painting may be identifiable with a painting of a 'Philosopher with a compass' that belonged to the third Duke of Alcalá, who was Viceroy of Naples between 1629 and 1631 and Ribera's principal patron during those years. He owned several paintings of philosophers including three others by Ribera.

In painting the picture, Ribera must have posed his model before him, just as he would have done for a portrait. The individual and distinctive physiognomic traits of the model are conveyed with great fidelity: his broad nose and large mouth, the crow's feet deeply etched into his face on account of his no doubt perennial grin, and his long, bony fingers. His facial skin painted in gritty impasto has a joyous glow to it, and the halo of lighter coloured paint around his head (the visual effect of dense underpaint in the area of the head) endows him with an optimistic vivacity. Spinosa has commented eloquently on the individual and archetypal character of the representation: 'It is almost a portrait from life of some peasant from the streets of vice-regal Naples, whose ancient Greco-Levantine traits were distilled by the painter into an image of typically irrepressible Mediterranean vitality and humanity' (Spinosa 1978, no. 40, p. 99).

The painting dates from the year in which Velázquez visited Naples and while it shows no trace of the stylistic influence of Velázquez, it bears a familial relationship – as has often been pointed out – with the *Drinkers* (Madrid, Museo del Prado, P-1629). Velázquez must have remembered this, and similar paintings by Ribera, when he came to paint his philosophers [CAT. 31]. [GF]

27 Bartolomé Esteban Murillo
[1617–1682]

Four Figures on a Step, *ca.* 1655–1660
Oil on canvas, 109.9 x 143.5 cm
Fort Worth, Texas, Kimbell Art Museum, AP1984.18

PROVENANCE
Charles B. Plestow, England; Richard Abraham, London; exhibited at the American Academy of Fine Arts in New York in 1830; by 1838 in the collection of Sir Charles Henry Coote, Baronet, Ballyfin House, Ireland; then Sir Ralph Algernon Coote, Baronet, Ballyfin House; sold by him at Christie's, London, 7 May 1923, lot 284, and purchased by Kendall; A. L. Nicholson; S. F. Aram, New York; apparently on the art market in Germany in 1930; Erik Bergmann, Monroe, Michigan; C. Russell Feldmann; private collection in Greenwich, Connecticut; acquired by the Kimbell Art Museum in 1984.

ESSENTIAL BIBLIOGRAPHY
Angulo 1981, I, p. 456, II, no. 401, p. 310; Brown 1982, pp. 35–42; Perry 1990, pp. 126 and 150–51; Brown 1998, p. 228; *Murillo. Scenes of Childhood*, pp. 36–37 and cat. no. 11, p. 102; *Bartolomé Esteban Murillo (1617–1682), Paintings from American Collections*, cat. no. 31, pp. 180–83.

Three of the figures in this painting engage the viewer's gaze. The youth at the left, wearing white hose with laced breeches, a slash-sleeved jacket and a hat decorated with a scarlet bow, looks out with a knowing but natural smile, while the girl in penumbra behind him (perhaps a moral penumbra) raises her veil to reveal a wincing expression. The old woman who looks up from her task of delousing the young boy's hair wears *quevedo* spectacles, perhaps to help her in her activity. In Murillo's *Old Woman delousing a Boy* in the Alte Pinakothek in Munich, which is close in date to this work, the woman has a pair of octagonal spectacles tied to her bodice with a ribbon and tucked under her arm.

Although the painting has often been described as a family group, Cherry and Brooke (*Murillo. Scenes of Childhood*, p. 106) point out that the survey of the 'respectable' poor that was carried out in Seville by Miguel de Mañara [see CAT. 42] in 1667 mentions old widows who cared for children not necessarily of their own family. If this is a family, it is not necessarily poor, as all the members are well-dressed and the child, in spite of his torn trousers, wears hose and shoes. In 1925, when the painting was exhibited at the Ehrich

Galleries in New York, it was described as the family of the artist: 'A Family Group (Presumed to be Doña Beatriz, wife of Murillo, and their three children)' (quoted in *Bartolomé Esteban Murillo (1617–1682): Paintings from American Collections*, p. 180). This is evidently highly unlikely for several reasons. More recent interpretations of the painting as a scene of prostitution, with the old woman playing the procuress to the young female 'temptress', have focused on parallels with the extended 'family' of ruffians and prostitutes presided over by the elderly Celestina in Fernando de Rojas's *Tragicomedia de Calisto y Melibea* (1499). An interesting visual parallel has been drawn with Michiel Sweerts' *Street Scene* (Rome, Galleria dell'Accademia Nazionale di San Luca, mid-1640s), which shows a woman delousing her recumbent child while her older daughter is solicited by an elegant client. Murillo's painting, which has much in common with that work, as pointed out by Brown (1982), is also rather different: the figures are life size, and the ambiguous handling of the 'narrative' ensures that the scene eludes sure interpretation. The figures are presumably in an interior, with the step on which the boy rests and the old woman sits marking the separation from the street. Brown's speculation that the revealing tear in the seat of the boy's pants suggests an interest in prohibited sexual practices among Murillo's clients, seems wide of the mark.

The artist's skill at characterisation is clearly apparent in the three principal figures, each one responding to the viewer in a distinctive manner. He deploys the same sensitivity to individual psyche that is apparent in his portraits [see FIG. 84 and CAT. 41], and as regards the young male at the left, Murillo certainly painted the same model a second time, for the similarly cocky youngster appears as the *Laughing Boy* in the collection of Juan Abelló in Madrid. The elderly woman may be the same model as the *Old Woman delousing a Boy* in Munich. [GF]

28 Bartolomé Esteban Murillo
[1617–1682]

Boy Leaning on a Sill,
ca. 1660–1669
Oil on canvas, 52 x 38.5 cm
London, The National Gallery,
NG 74

PROVENANCE

Comtesse de Verrue, Paris; her sale, 29 April 1737, lot 66 (with pendant of a 'jeune fille tenant son voile'), M. Randon de Boisset; his sale Paris, 27 February 1777, lot 19 (with pendant), Marquis of Lansdowne; his sale, London, 20 March 1806, lot 50, where sold for £115 and 10 shillings (lot 51 was *Portrait of a Girl*, possibly the pendant from the Verrue and Randon de Boisset sales); M. M. Zachary, before 1818; given by him to The National Gallery in 1826.

ESSENTIAL BIBLIOGRAPHY

Soria 1948; MacLaren/Braham 1970, no. 74, pp. 64–65; Angulo 1981, II, no. 380, pp. 297–98; *Bartolomé Esteban Murillo* (London) 1983, cat. no. 71, p. 193; *Murillo. Scenes of Childhood*, cat. no. 19, pp. 118–19.

As is the case with other works in this exhibition, this charming image of a young boy leaning on a window sill does not readily conform to the strict definition of a portrait, but the lively rendition of the features and expression suggests that Murillo painted the picture from a model. Perhaps the same child who posed for this painting reappears as the figure on horseback in the *Moses striking the Rock* in the church of the Hospital de la Caridad in Seville (1667–1670). Here his expression shows amusement at something he can see on the other side of the sill on which he leans. The object of his interest is perhaps the girl who appears in the painting that was probably conceived as the pendant to this one, the *Young Girl lifting her Shawl* in a private collection (*Murillo. Scenes of Childhood*, cat. no. 20). She is slightly older than him and the two youngsters may be playing out an adult drama of flirtatious courtship (*ibid.*, p. 118).

The bare shoulder conveys a physical sensuality which recalls that of Caravaggio's early paintings of young males, particularly the two versions of the *Boy bitten by a Lizard* (Florence, Fondazione Longhi, and London, The National Gallery, mid-1590s). Here no moralistic reading is intended, however. A *pentimento* in the area of boy's breast and upper arm shows that Murillo decided to reveal more of his flesh than initially intended.

The handling of the paint is fluid and confident and Murillo's skill at combining passages of remarkably thin paint with denser areas of creamy impasto is also manifest. The sketchy handling, particularly visible in the hands and the ear, suggests a date slightly earlier than that which is usually proposed for the painting, the mid-1670s, by which time he was employing a smoother and more modulated manner. [GF]

5 Velázquez and the Baroque Portrait

29 Diego Velázquez
[1599–1660]

The Venerable Mother
Jerónima de la Fuente, 1620
Oil on canvas, 160 x 110 cm
Signed and dated:
'Diego Velázquez f. 1620'
Madrid, Museo del Prado, P-2873

PROVENANCE

Convent of Santa Isabel de Toledo. Acquired by the Prado in 1944.

ESSENTIAL BIBLIOGRAPHY

Mayer 1936, no. 546; Pantorba 1955, no. 18; López-Rey 1963, no. 577; Gállego 1990, no. 6; Véliz 1999, pp. 80–89.

In the upper part of the portrait are the words: 'BONUM EST PRESTOLARI CUM SILENTIO SALUTARE DEI'. In the lower part, on either side of the figure, is the following lengthy inscription: 'This is the true portrait of Mother Jerónima de la Fuente, a nun in the Convent of Santa Ysabel de los Reyes de Toledo, Founder and first Abbess of the Convent of Santa Clara de la Concepción of the first order of the City of Manila, in the Philippines. She left this foundation at the age of 66 on Tuesday, the twenty-eighth day of April in 1620. She left this convent accompanied by Mother Ana de Cristo and Mother Leonor de San Francisco, both nuns, and Sister Juana de Sanct Antonio, a novice. All of them persons of great importance for such an exalted task.'

Sister Jerónima de la Fuente Yánez, born into a noble Toledan family, was a Franciscan nun in the Convent of Santa Isabel de Toledo.

In 1620, when she was sixty-six, she travelled to Seville prior to setting sail for the Philippines to found the Convent of Santa Clara de la Concepción in Manila, of which she was the first abbess until her death in 1630.

There can be no doubt that the portrait, which shows her standing firmly grasping a crucifix in her right hand and a prayer book – or perhaps the rules of the Order – in her left, was painted in Seville during her stay in the city in June 1620, before setting off on the long voyage.

This impressive image is witness to the work of Velázquez before he moved to Madrid, immersed in the Caravaggio-inspired gloom with intense characterisation under a harsh light that emphasises all the features of the face and hands, sparing no detail.

The energy of the nun is wonderfully expressed, both in her face with its intense and penetrating gaze, and in the way she is brandishing the crucifix, holding it up almost like a weapon, as has often been remarked.

The portrait is a response to the wish of the nuns to hold on in some way to the image of their absent Mother Superior, as testified by the existence of at least two other similar versions of the portrait. Another full-length portrait similar to this one, likewise originating from the Convent of Santa Isabel in Toledo, belongs to the Fernández Araoz collection and differs only in relation to the position of the crucifix. Another, a half-length portrait, now in the Apelles collection in Santiago, Chile, shows the crucifix in the same position as in the Prado version although the technique used is somewhat harder.

The order in which the paintings were executed is not clear but the half-length portrait perhaps precedes the others, which are painted with a lighter brush.

The lengthy biographical details on the portraits, both in the Prado and the Fernández Araoz collection, are clearly an addition, but the scroll that appears in the latter with the inscription 'Satiabor dum gloria… ficatus verit', which also appears in the Prado version and was erased in the belief that it was a later addition, is – and was – indisputably authentic and gave the portrait the appearance of being a sacred image, since the virtues of Sister Jerónima were already well known in her lifetime; among her sisters in the convent and the order she had a reputation for saintliness and on her death they even considered her canonisation.

In painting her portrait, Velázquez achieves an image that is marked by truthfulness whilst creating a model of exemplary sanctity.

When this portrait was in the convent it bore an attribution to Luis Tristán. It was discovered at the time of the *Exposición Franciscana* in 1926, and following restoration Velázquez's signature and the date were revealed. [AEPS]

30 Diego Velázquez
[1599–1660]

Luis de Góngora, 1622
Oil on canvas, 50.2 x 40.6 cm
Boston, Museum of Fine Arts,
Maria Antoinette Evans Fund, 32.79

PROVENANCE

Francisco Pacheco. Probably passed to Velázquez on Pacheco's death, since a portrait of Góngora appears in the inventory of his goods made when he died in 1660. Owned by the Marqués de la Vega Inclán early in the twentieth century, it was sold to Thomas Harris in London, from whom it was purchased in 1932 by the Museum of Fine Arts, Boston, USA.

ESSENTIAL BIBLIOGRAPHY

Mayer 1936, no. 239; Pantorba 1955, no. 22; López-Rey 1963, no. 496; Gudiol 1973, no. 32; Gállego 1990, no. 12.

Luis de Góngora y Argote (1561–1627), the prodigious poet and exponent of the literary style known as *culteranismo*, was born in Córdoba, son of Francisco de Argote and Leonor de Góngora. Ordained a priest but lacking a genuine vocation, Góngora failed to complete his university course and led a dissolute life, dedicated to gambling, women and poetry. He enjoyed certain ecclesiastical privileges in Córdoba, granted by his uncle, Francisco de Góngora, but when it emerged that there had been deception in relation to the conversion to Catholicism of a great grandfather, this embittered his character, and he was always struggling with financial difficulties. His work, published posthumously, constitutes one of the most astonishing achievements in Spanish poetry. Complex, learned, laden with metaphor and hyperbaton, his defining worth was finally acknowledged in the twentieth century.

Velázquez painted Góngora's portrait in Madrid in 1622, and according to Pacheco this was doubtless in order to have a model who could be included in the latter's *Libro de verdaderos retratos* ('Book of true portraits'). Until 1921 when Mayer published this portrait, which at that time belonged to the Marqués de la Vega Inclán, it was thought that Velázquez's original was the version that hung in the Prado. The radiograph of the Boston portrait shows that a crown of laurel originally encircled his brow.

This magnificent portrait is evidence of the subtle change in Velázquez's technique after his first contact with the Spanish Court. The dark background of the portraits painted in Seville became gradually lighter, giving way to olive greys.

Painted with precise modelling and sober colouring, the portrait perfectly conveys the bitterness of the subject's character. Julián Gállego was right in remarking on the scornful gaze that is fixed on the spectator in which there is 'a mixture of obstinacy, pride and deceit'.

Sixty years of age when Velázquez painted his portrait, Góngora was at the centre of violent literary debate and was opposed by the sharpest minds in the Spanish Court, in particular Quevedo and Lope de Vega. In spite of this, his fame explains the copies or replicas that exist of this portrait. The most important and best known are those in the Prado (P-1223) and the Lázaro Galdiano Museum, Madrid, regarded as studio copies and sometimes even the work of the master himself (Gudiol). [AEPS]

31 Diego Velázquez
[1599–1660]

Aesop, *ca.* 1638
Oil on canvas, 179 x 94 cm
Madrid, Museo del Prado, P-1206

PROVENANCE

1703, Torre de la Parada, for which it was painted; 1714, Palacio de El Pardo; 1772 and 1794, Palacio Nuevo de Madrid; 1819, entered the Museo del Prado.

ESSENTIAL BIBLIOGRAPHY

Curtis 1883, no. 30; Mayer 1936, no. 73; Pantorba 1955, no. 79; Gerstenberg 1960, p. 202; López Rey 1963, no. 73; Palm 1967, pp. 207–17; Gudiol 1973, no. 109; Harris 1982, p. 132; Brown 1986, p. 163; Madrid exhibition 1990, no. 49; Rico 1991, pp. 345–47; Tromans 1996, pp. 332–36; Cruz Valdovinos 1999, pp. 141–47; New York exhibition 2003, no. 75.

Aesop and its companion, *Menippus*, are mentioned for the first time in the 1703 inventory of the Torre de la Parada, a hunting lodge in the hills round El Pardo, outside Madrid. There they were accompanied by, among others, an extensive range of mythological paintings by Rubens and his workshop, various buffoons by Velázquez, a number of portraits of members of the royal family in hunting attire, also by Velázquez, and another pair of pictures of Ancient Greek philosophers, Heraclitus and Democritus, painted by Rubens and very similar in height to the pictures by Velázquez although slightly narrower. The four are presumed to have formed a set and to have been painted at the same time, around 1638, although it is not clear why Rubens was not commissioned to produce the whole set.

Aesop (7th to 6th century BC) was one of the most famous writers of Antiquity as a result of his *Fables*, which were widely published. In the painting by Velázquez he appears with a book in his hand (presumably one of his own works) and surrounded by objects relating to his life. His shabby garments are a reference to his origins as a slave and his humble living conditions. The pail of water is an allusion to a clever answer he gave to the philosopher Xanthus, his master, who in recompense granted him his freedom. The belongings on the right are a reference to his violent death: while in Delphos, he was openly critical of the city's inflated reputation, and in return the inhabitants hid a goblet among his possessions, accused him of stealing it and threw him over a cliff.

The artist places him in an indeterminate interior, portraying his face in realistic detail and showing him in garments and shoes of the sort that would be worn by any beggar in any Spanish town. The association between philosophy and poverty, which can be seen in this painting and in its companion, had become something of a cliché in European Baroque art, and it should probably be linked to the prevailing popularity of the Stoics and their thinking. The way in which the figure is situated in the picture space is similar to that of many of Velázquez's other portraits, and although there are plenty of objects that allow for a symbolic interpretation, the artist plays above all on the boundaries between portraiture and fiction. Both the face and the full-length figure show a highly individualised expression, and this has meant that for a long time historians and critics have speculated on the possibility that the features are those of a specific person, following a procedure that was used by Velázquez and by other Spanish painters of the period, as demonstrated in this exhibition [CATS 26 and 32]. However, since Gerstenberg pointed out the similarities between this face and the one used by the famous physiognomist and writer Giacomo Dalla Porta (whose book was in the artist's library), to illustrate one of his facial types, the picture has become an example of the very blurred borders between portraiture and realistic description, and of how artists such as Velázquez were able to create an extraordinarily life-like expression in his figures from history or mythology. [JP]

32 Diego Velázquez
[1599–1660]

Democritus, 1625–1627 and 1638–1640
Oil on canvas, 101 x 81 cm
Rouen, Musée des Beaux-Arts, Collection Gabriel Lemonnier, 822.1.16

PROVENANCE
Marqués del Carpio. Pedro Rodríguez, 1692. Bureau des Finances, Rouen, 1789. Musée des Beaux-Arts, Rouen since 1889.

ESSENTIAL BIBLIOGRAPHY
Mayer 1936, no. 67; Pita Andrade 1952, p. 236; Pantorba 1955, no. 33; López-Rey 1963, no. 76; Gudiol 1973, no. 51; Brown 1986, p. 57; Gállego 1990, no. 13.

Despite the liveliness and unusual quality of the face, including such features that are so personal that it appears to be a portrait, it has been claimed that the model was the same as in *Pablo de Valladolid* [CAT. 51]. The oldest references enable us to confirm, without hesitation, that Velázquez intended to depict a philosopher from ancient times, in the style of those by Ribera, which were doubtless well known in the world of Seville. In this case it is obviously the philosopher *Democritus*, who is laughing, as described in the inventory of the estate of the Marqués del Carpio in 1692: 'a portrait of a philosopher laughing with a globe original by Diego Belázquez'; the painting was given, together with other works, to the Marqués's gardener, Pedro Rodríguez, in payment of wages he was owed.

The figure of the philosopher laughing at the world's extravagances and absurdities, in contrast with the melancholy and tearful Heraclitus, was familiar in educated circles throughout the Christian world. The two philosophers had been depicted by Rubens in 1603 in the painting that now hangs in the Valladolid Museum of Sculpture, executed for the Duke de Lerma. There they rest on an enormous globe with contrasting expressions.

This work was certainly painted during Velázquez's early years at the Spanish Court since the entire lower part, the globe and the subject's clothes, in particular the cloak or cape that stands out in the foreground, are directly related to works painted during that period and even to the subjects in *The Drinkers* [FIG. 97], probably painted in 1627–1628 and paid for in 1629. It is clear that the head, the white collar and the hand – depicted using another technique that was looser and 'bolder' – is the result of a subsequent reworking, perhaps towards 1639–1640, because of the relative similarity of the technique with that used in *The Buffoon Calabacillas* painted around that time [CAT. 33].

Velázquez obviously used a life model to paint this canvas, however it cannot be considered a portrait in the true sense of the word as the face of the subject – who is anonymous – has been used in order to portray a character from ancient times in a way that painters often did and who, in order to bring up to date and lend realism to tales from mythology, resorted to copying the most vividly contemporary reality as can be seen in the *Triunfo de Baco* ('Triumph of Bacchus'), which is the true subject of *The Drinkers*, or in *The Spinners* (Madrid, Museo del Prado, P-1173), which, interpreted for a long time as depicting a simple group of weavers, actually shows the fable of Arachne.

There are two paintings that have been considered the work of Velázquez but which his brush has certainly not touched. They depict the same character holding a slender glass of wine in his gloved left hand. They hang in the Toledo Museum (Ohio) and the Zorn de Mora Museum (Sweden). Jonathan Brown has considered these as being allegories relating to pleasure, insisting that they cannot be regarded as portraits. It is also curious to point out that in the nineteenth century, the character with whom we are concerned was believed to be a portrait of Columbus and attributed to Ribera.

The knowledge of the Carpio inventory (made known by Pita Andrade in 1952) dispenses with further discussion on all the 'identifications' that have been attempted in relation to various Palace jesters. [AEPS]

33 Diego Velázquez
[1599–1660]

The Buffoon Calabacillas, *ca.* 1635–1640
Oil on canvas, 106 x 83 cm
Madrid, the Prado, P-1205

PROVENANCE

Royal Collections. Torre de la Parada, 1700. Palace of El Pardo. Palacio Nuevo, 1772. Museo del Prado since 1819.

ESSENTIAL BIBLIOGRAPHY

Curtis 1883, p. 66; Cruzada Villaamil 1885, pp. 109–10; Moreno Villa 1939, pp. 85–87; Mayer 1936, no. 446; Angulo Íñiguez 1947, pp. 85–88; Pantorba 1955, no. 67; López-Rey 1963, p. 75, no. 424; Gudiol 1973, no. 104; Gállego 1990, no. 53; Mena 1999, pp. 297–334.

Sitting on some rocks with his legs crossed in an uncomfortable position, he raises his squinting gaze with an ambiguous smile and keeps his hands clenched on his knees holding some indeterminate object. He is wearing a dark green doublet with a large collar and cuffs of Flanders lace. In front of him is a container that appears to be a glass or small cask full of wine, and to one side a gourd that the artist painted over a pitcher with handles, which was his first idea. On the other side, a gilded water-bottle, as stated in the Prado's 1854 inventory, which was formerly interpreted as being another gourd because of the obsession with identifying the subject as the buffoon Juan Calabazas, who served the cardinal Prince Ferdinand before serving Philip IV in 1632 and died in 1639. It was doubtless thought that gourds – truly and falsely understood as being such – were an allusion to the name of the supposed buffoon.

The oldest inventories of the Royal Collection that make reference to this painting in the Torre de la Parada and in El Pardo, do not give it any name whatsoever, referring to it simply as 'portrait of a buffoon with a Flemish collar'. It is in the inventory of the Palacio Nuevo (New Royal Palace) in 1794, in the Dining Room, where for the first time it is called the *Bobo de Coria* ('Half-wit from Coria') – a title that made its fortune and with which it went to the Prado in 1819.

The identification as Juan Calabazas appears for the first time in the 1910 catalogue, where it is described 'with a gourd on either side', adding that 'this could be the so-called Calabacillas', alluding to a suggestion made by Cruzada Villaamil. The identification was reaffirmed in 1920 when some of his biographical details were published. The publication in 1939 by Moreno Villa of the date of Calabazas' death meant that the date of the portrait, previously thought to be 1646–1648, had to be brought forward ten years.

The Juan Calabazas who died in 1639 was in fact painted by Velázquez in a canvas that was catalogued in the collection of the Marquis de Leganés as follows: 'Another [painting] of Calabazas with a turban by Velázquez' and another entry recorded in the Buen Retiro inventory of 1701 reads: 'A buffoon a *vara* and one-third wide and two and a half *varas* high, of Calabacillas, carrying a portrait in one hand and a paper in the other, by Velázquez.' Attempts have been made to identify this as a painting that now hangs in the Cleveland Museum of Art but which does not exactly fit the inventory description because the subject is carrying not a piece of paper but a paper windmill, although his other hand is holding a miniature portrait. Not all critics attribute this painting to Velázquez nor does the sitter appear to be the same person we are concerned with here because apart from his squint, his facial features do not correspond and although he is a buffoon, the model is clearly much younger.

The identification of the sitter in the Prado painting is far from certain, as Manuela Mena has indicated, and the fact that it was inspired by Dürer's print of *Desesperado* as Angulo showed, overturns the conventional belief that it is a simple portrait that catches the sitter off guard. The evidence of its complex formal preparation and the non-existence of the second gourd make the traditional identification as Juan Calabazas extremely doubtful.

The views of Mena on the significance of the painting as a possible allegory or hieroglyph, based on the position of the hands that are hiding something and in the quizzical gaze of the subject, in which we see not a fool but a *pícaro* or rogue, do not prevent the power of the image striking the spectator with the intensity of something that is alive and real. Regardless of the artist's intention – which we may never succeed in discovering – the erroneously entitled *Bobo de Coria* or *Juan Calabazas* reveals to us a strong and individualistic personality. This is in keeping with Velázquez's customary way of investing subjects of allegorical or mythological content with an appearance that is so real and specific that from the nineteenth century some of his most complex paintings – for example *Las Hilanderas (The Spinners)* – as being simply representations of the most objective reality. [AEPS]

34 Diego Velázquez
[1599–1660]

El Niño de Vallecas, *ca.* 1635–1645
Oil on canvas, 107 x 83 cm
Madrid, Museo del Prado, P-1204

PROVENANCE

Royal Collections. Probably in the Torre de la Parada. In 1714 in the Palace of El Pardo from where it was moved to the Palacio Nuevo, where it is referred to in 1772 and 1794. From there it went to the Prado, where it has remained since the museum opened in 1819.

ESSENTIAL BIBLIOGRAPHY

Curtis 1883, no. 67; Mayer 1936, no. 457; Moreno Villar 1939, pp. 107–10; Pantorba 1955, no. 68; López-Rey 1963, no. 429; Camón Aznar 1967, p. 454; Gudiol 1973, no. 103; Brown 1986, p. 83; Gállego 1990, no. 52.

This is one of a set of four paintings that hung in the small palace of Torre de la Parada and which are among the painter's best and most extraordinary works and on which an abundant bibliography exists.

They are 'portraits' of people who are clearly physically and mentally handicapped – the 'dwarves' – executed with extreme delicacy and exceptional skill. There have been various attempts at identifying them but these are far from being definitive.

In relation to this work, the earliest identification is in the 1794 inventory of the Palacio Nuevo, in the *Pieza de Truecos* (Games Room), when it is called the 'Niño de Vallecas'. Surprisingly this is not cited in the Prado's first catalogue of 1819 which refers to it as 'A half-witted girl'. The 1828 catalogue lists the portrait as the *Niño de Vallecas*, but the original reason for this identification is unknown.

Research by José Moreno Villa into the Palace Archives identified him as Francisco Lezcano, a dwarf who entered the service of

Prince Baltasar Carlos in 1634. He accompanied him to Zaragoza in 1644 – where some believe the picture was painted – and died in 1649. Lazcano's name it attached to the portrait for the first time in the Prado's 1942 catalogue and has been accepted unanimously, without opposition.

It is clear that the portrait is of a particular individual, obviously suffering from mental illness or oligophrenia but there is uncertainty as to whether he can be identified as Lezcano. The meaning of these images of dwarves that were painted so brilliantly by Velázquez has not been established and, as suggested by Manuela Mena in relation to the portrait *The Buffoon Calabacillas* [CAT. 33], identification of the individuals is by no means certain. It is possible that these paintings conceal a hidden allegorical or symbolic meaning that has so far eluded us.

Although accepting that the sitter was Lezcano, Gállego recognised certain details that would enable an interpretation that was more charged with the use of conceits than that of a simple portrait of a 'palace rascal'. The scene, a cave similar to Ribera's hermit-like settings, is a place that lends itself to meditation; the object that he is holding in his hands – and which has led to many interpretations – is probably a pack of cards. It would not be very rash to consider that the meaning of the picture involves chance, meditation and human stupidity that places reliance on gambling. But aside from these possible interpretations the work is impressive for the presence of the human being in front of us. He is seen and portrayed with a deep melancholy and affectionate sympathy which softens that which could be perceived as disagreeable about the sitter. [AEPS]

35 Diego Velázquez
[1599–1660]

Portrait of a Man, 'The Pope's Barber', ca. 1650
Oil on canvas, 50.5 x 47 cm
Madrid, Museo del Prado, P-7858

PROVENANCE

Chilham Castle, Sir Edward Davis. Paris, private collection. New York, Wildenstein. Acquired for the Prado in 2003.

ESSENTIAL BIBLIOGRAPHY

Curtis 1883, no. 229; Mayer 1936, no. 463; Pantorba 1955, no. 170; Lópe-Rey 1963, no. 482; Gudiol 1973, no. 139; Gállego 1990, no. 69; Salort 2003, p. 314, no. 10.

This portrait of a head and shoulders, with the model dressed entirely in black with a simple broad white collar, black hair, moustache and goatee beard is undoubtedly a person of low social standing. The serene and somewhat melancholy gaze does not reveal anything about his personality.

Its technique is impressive and its state of preservation impeccable, with light strokes and impasto that emphasise the highlights on the white collar in a masterly fashion. The face is painted with subtle variations in tone that lend it delicacy, softness and gentleness and an exceptional feeling of life.

The portrait appeared for the first time in 1909 in the English collection of Sir Edward Davis and its attribution to Velázquez was accepted unanimously. In 1936, Mayer believed that it represented a buffoon and that it could not have been dated prior to 1647, but in 1940 it was accepted that the portrait was in fact painted during Velázquez's second Roman trip. In his report on that stay, among the portraits of sitters in the papal court Palomino refers to 'monsignor Miguel Angelo, the Pope's barber'. It has been supposed that this unusual painting could be that of Michaelangelo Augurio, and that identification has been accepted. But, as Brown has observed, there is nothing that enables this to be confirmed, and another argument against the arbitrary identification is the fact that the sitter – who according to Palomino was 'monsignor', that is to say, a priest – is not in ecclesiastical dress. More recently Salvador Salort has put forward another identity, which is more likely but which again lacks documentary support. According to this young researcher, it could be Juan de Córdoba, the closest colleague of Velázquez in the assignment that took him to Rome in order to obtain sculptures for the Alcázar.

Whatever the identity of the sitter, it is one of the painter's most intense works which, precisely because of the simplicity of its approach, devoid of all official pomp and ceremony yet rigorously finished, establishes a perfect relationship with the spectator who feels as if they are looking at a real, living and breathing person. [AEPS]

36 Diego Velázquez
[1599–1660]

Portrait of a Man, ca. 1640–1650
Oil on canvas, 76 x 64 cm
London, English Heritage
(Apsley House)

PROVENANCE

Quinta del Duke del Arco, given to Philip V in 1737. Royal Collections. Royal Palace. 1789–1794 inventory. Removed by King José I and seized by Wellington at the battle of Vitoria (1813), it was given to the Duke by Ferdinand VII.

ESSENTIAL BIBLIOGRAPHY

Curtis 1883, no. 209; Mayer 1936, no. 378; López-Rey 1963, no. 550; Gudiol 1973, no. 125; Harris 1976, pp. 304–08.

A head and shoulders portrait facing left, the sitter fixes his intense and penetrating gaze on the spectator. Dressed in black with a ruff, he radiates an incredible sensation of life and truth.

There have been many attempts to identify the subject of the portrait, from the clearly absurd, in the form of Antonio Pérez, secretary to Philip II, as appears in the Royal Palace inventory in 1794, to the no less unlikely suggestion of it being a self-portrait by Velázquez, a portrait of Alonso Cano or of Calderón de la Barca. The most likely and perhaps the definitive identity is that proposed in 1976 by Enriqueta Harris, who sees in the magnificent painting a portrait of José Nieto Velázquez, a Palace courtier who appears in the background of *Las Meninas* [CAT. 43] silhouetted on the lighted staircase. He was the Queen's *Aposentador* and competed with Velázquez for the position of King's *Aposentador*, a post to which the painter was finally appointed.

There is a clear physical similarity between the subject of the portrait and the head that appears in *Las Meninas*, despite the fact that due to his position in the background of the picture it is out of focus. As Harris points out, the pronounced geometric nature of the nose, the hairstyle, the moustache and beard, as well as the suit, ruff and pose, makes it almost certain that it is the same person.

José Nieto Velázquez, who was probably born during the first decade of the seventeenth century and who died in 1684, would have been very well known to Velázquez as both were courtiers and belonged to the circle of Don Juan de Fonseca, cannon of Seville and *Sumiller de cortina* to Philip IV. Fonseca was Velázquez's patron and Velázquez and the wife of José Nieto were responsible for valuing his estate after his death in 1627.

The age of the subject – around forty – when he was painted, would place the portrait between 1640 and 1645. As Harris warns, it is very difficult to put an accurate date on it using stylistic criteria. This portrait has been dated to after that of the *Duke of Modena* (1638) (Modena, Galleria e Museo Estense) and before those painted in Rome (1650), a period which is appropriate for the style and estimated age of the sitter. *Las Meninas* (1656) is doubtless a somewhat later work.

The individual's social importance is evidenced by the number of copies of this portrait that have survived. Harris has traced five, of which one was believed to be a self-portrait by Mazo (Museo de San Carlos, Mexico) and others, portraits by Alonso Cano, but which are clearly copies of this painting. [AEPS]

37 Juan Bautista Martínez del Mazo
[1605–1667]

The Infanta Margarita de Austria, ca. 1665
Oil on canvas, 212 x 147 cm
Madrid, Museo del Prado, P-1192

PROVENANCE
Until 1734, in the Alcázar of Madrid; inventories dated 1747, 1772 and 1794, in the Palacio Real Nuevo; entered the Museo del Prado in 1819.

ESSENTIAL BIBLIOGRAPHY
Curtis 1883, no. 246; Mayer 1936, no. 537; López-Rey 1963, no. 409; Gállego 1990, no. 79; Garrido Pérez, 2004, pp. 22–23.

The critics have considered this work as the last painting of Velázquez, although some thought that Mazo might have completed it after the master's death. The fact that a similar portrait of the Infanta, dressed in blue, appears on the easel in *The Family of the Painter*, by Mazo [CAT. 44], supported the hypothesis that it was by Velázquez. But there are insufficient reasons to consider this to be his work, not even that, unfinished, it may have been completed by his assistant and disciple. The Infanta Margarita, born in July 1651, seems older, taller and more mature here than the age of nine that she should have been for Velázquez to have painted her before his death in July 1660. A comparison with the blue portrait in Vienna by Velázquez, dated to 1659 [CAT. 14], leaves no room for doubts on this important aspect, since in that painting the girl is obviously younger than she is in this one.

Although changes in fashion were slow, the girl's coiffure, with the large puffed-out red ribbon, which falls to one side of her face, the shorter and more natural hair than in other portraits, as well as other details of the sleeves, are closer to the more over-elaborate attire subsequent to 1660, well-known from portraits of women by Carreño and others. The existence of a version of this painting in the Kunsthistorisches Museum in Vienna, of excellent quality, if not superior to that of the Prado, also makes it difficult to accept that this work was by Velázquez, in spite of its undoubted beauty. Indeed, the composition would not have been difficult for Mazo, since all he did was to adapt, with some minor changes, other portraits by Velázquez: the one of her older sister, María Teresa, dated 1656 (Vienna, Kunsthistorisches Museum), similar in the position of the figure and holding the handkerchief in a like manner with her left hand; as well as the portrait of her mother, Mariana of Austria, from around 1653, with the large drapery on the left [CAT. 13]. Even the portrait of the young Felipe Próspero, who stands out dressed in red against the reds of curtains, armchair and carpet [CAT. 54] could have been an inspiration for Mazo's image. However, the simplicity of Velázquez and the austere elegance of his works are lost in this portrait of the Infanta through an excessive accumulation of details, such as the exaggerated development of the drapery and the heavy decoration of the carpet on top of which the dress of the young girl cannot stand out in all its geometric beauty.

Contrasting with a certain hardness of the face, evident in the way the eyes are painted or the curl of hair on her forehead, we have the gleaming sparkles of the silver of the dress, viewed always by those championing the idea that Velázquez was the painter as the leading proof of his authorship. However, Velázquez never needed such an accumulation of brushstrokes, sometimes muddled up one of top of the other, to achieve the desired effects. In spite of the overloading of material, the author of this work has not managed to clearly define the forms, which always remain blurred and lacking in volume: such as the hand holding the roses, the contours of the dress, the white handkerchief or, above all, the jewel on the decoration on the breast, which indicate a different hand to the one that painted the same effects on the Infanta Margarita in *Las Meninas* [CAT. 43]. The undoubtedly successful physical likeness in this portrait makes us forget the poetic charm she had in the portraits that Velázquez painted of her, here her superficial smile replacing the melancholic intensity of the last portrait by Mazo's master in Vienna, dressed in blue. [MMM]

38 Diego Velázquez
[1599–1660]

Portrait of a girl, ca. 1640–1642
Oil on canvas, 51.5 x 41 cm
New York, The Hispanic Society of America, A108

PROVENANCE
London, 1885. Sir William W. Knighton, Edinburgh. A. Sanderson, 1897, Paris. Rudolph Kann, Paris. Wildenstein & Co. New York. Duveen Brothers, 1907. Acquired by The Hispanic Society of America in 1908.

ESSENTIAL BIBLIOGRAPHY
Mayer 1936, no. 569; Trapier 1944, pp. 45–48; Trapier 1948, p. 286; López-Rey 1963, no. 608; Gudiol 1973, no. 120, p. 209.

The painting is executed in an incredibly summary technique, with delicate brushstrokes to suggest the dress, which is doubtless unfinished, but with a volume that is perfectly executed. The head is more defined, her great black eyes fixed and her thin lips rendered with a light touch of carmine.

The dark chestnut hair falls either side of the face. A very narrow range of colour is used with a golden-brown tone dominating; the rosy tones of the little girl's smooth cheeks and neck are extremely delicate.

The portrait has an air of intimacy and immediacy, far removed from any official emphasis, which has led critics to believe that the sitter was a member of the painter's family, perhaps his granddaughter Inés, born in January 1635 to his daughter Francisca and his son-in-law, the painter Juan Bautista Martínez del Mazo.

As the girl in the portrait appears to be between five and seven years old, this would place the date between 1640 and 1642, which corresponds perfectly with his technique.

In addition, it has been noted that the inventory of the property of Velázquez at the time of his death in 1660 mentions 'another portrait of a little girl', which could well be this one, although its early provenance is unknown. In 1885 it appeared at a public sale in London as a portrait of the Infanta Margarita, an identification which is clearly erroneous. [AEPS]

39 Claudio Coello
[1642–1693]

Doña Nicolasa Manrique, ca. 1690–1692
Oil on canvas, 82 x 61 cm
Madrid, Instituto Valencia de Don Juan

PROVENANCE
Owned by the family since it was painted.

ESSENTIAL BIBLIOGRAPHY
Sánchez Cantón 1923, p. 137; Gaya Nuño 1957, pp. 23 and 38, engraving 43; Barettini 1972, p. 163; Pérez Sánchez 1986, p. 302, no. 136; Sullivan 1989, no. P.88.

According to an extensive inscription on the back of the portrait, the sitter is Doña Nicolasa Manrique de Mendoza, Condesa de Valencia de Don Juan, Duchess of Nájera, wife of Don Beltrán Vélez de Guevara, who was born in 1672 and declared by her contemporary, the genealogist Salazar y Castro, to be 'one of the greatest heiresses of our time'. Sánchez Cantón enumerated the long list of her titles 'in expressive truth of her importance', and relates the dramatic story of her later years.

On Monday, 6 June 1687 Doña Nicolasa married Don Beltrán Vélez de Guevara, commander of the ships of Montiel of the Order of Santiago, commander-in-chief of the Sicilian galleons and then of those of Naples and later those of Spain. He was also the brother of the tenth Count of Oñate. The wedding took place in happy circumstances and the couple's only child, a daughter, Doña Ana Sinforosa was born in 1698.

On the death of Charles II, Don Beltrán took the side of the Archduke Charles rather than Philip V and under the pretext of letters from the duchess to her husband having been intercepted, Doña Nicolasa and her daughter were imprisoned on the orders of Philip V and in 1708 shut away in the fortress in Segovia, in addition to their estates being seized. The couple were never reunited. The hardships she suffered severely affected Doña Nicolasa, who wrote her will in prison and died there in 1710. Don Beltrán died in Barcelona in 1713 and their daughter, after regaining her freedom, still had years to wait before being able to recover her estates which were returned to her by Royal Warrant signed in the Buen Retiro Palace on 9 March 1715.

The portrait is extraordinarily precise, both in terms of the drawing and the technique – which achieves admirable definition in relation to the lace dress and the flowers and jewellery – and the psychological treatment of the subject, whose delicate and sensitive femininity is expressed by means of her not especially attractive face with its rather large nose, although with a warm smile.

Her apparent age – between eighteen and twenty – dates the portrait between 1690 and 1692. It is therefore one of the master's last works, since he is known to have died in April 1693.

Its extraordinary warmth makes us regret that we do not have more examples of Coello's work as a portrait painter, particularly in relation to bust portraits of this kind that are more direct and intimate than full-length official court portraits with all their pomp and ceremony. Palomino often makes reference to the portraits of Coello and it should not be forgotten that his masterpiece, *The Adoration of the Eucharistic Host of Gorkum* in El Escorial [FIG. 25] is essentially a magnificent gallery of portraits.

The work was incorrectly ascribed by Barettini Fernández to Carreño, an attribution that was clearly wrong and never accepted. [AEPS]

40 Juan Carreño de Miranda
[1614–1685]

The Duke of Pastrana, ca. 1666
Oil on canvas, 217 x 155 cm
Madrid, Museo del Prado, P-650

PROVENANCE
Presumably painted for the family. In 1896 it was sold in the sale of the Duke and Duchess of Osuna's collection and was purchased for the Prado.

ESSENTIAL BIBLIOGRAPHY
Allende Salazar-Sánchez Cantón 1919, pp. 242–44; Berjano Escobar S.A., p. 146; Trapier 1957, p. 269; Marzolf 1961, pp. 179–180; Barettini 1972, p. 23; Pérez Sánchez 1985, pp. 68–69, plates 59 and 60; Pérez Sánchez 1986, no. 30.

The portrait depicts Don Gregorio de Silva y Mendoza (1640–1693), Duke of Pastrana and Estremera, Prince of Mélito and Eboli and Count of Saldaña; he is dressed in black with a *golilla* collar and wears the scallop shell of the Order of Santiago, which he was awarded in 1666. In 1693, the year of his death, he attained the Golden Fleece. He was a person of importance and political influence in the court of Charles II.

In this portrait he appears to be between the ages of twenty-five and thirty. If we consider that he was twenty-six when he gained the Order of Santiago, we may also assume that he was painted immediately after receiving it.

The subject, with his ostentatious and offhand bearing, is depicted standing looking straight ahead with a riding crop in his right hand and the left hand resting on his hip near the striking sword hilt. A page or servant half-kneeling next to him appears to be adjusting the spur on his right foot. Behind, a groom is preparing a white horse, elaborately decorated with blue ribbons and bows in its mane.

The severe figure of the Duke, his head in a frontal view, is enveloped by a kind of encircling movement made up of colouristic and dynamic elements that lend the painting an unequivocally baroque character. The richness of tone, from the gold trimming on the tunic of the kneeling servant to the white form of the horse and the delicate transparency of the landscape – once again borrowed from the Venetian tradition – make this painting one of the most sumptuous as well as the most elegant in Spanish painting of the period.

Nothing like this is to be seen in any of the portraits painted by Velázquez, indubitably more severe, including those featuring hunters, which are set in the open air, away from the seriousness of the palace interiors. On this occasion, Carreño has been inspired by Van Dyck's English portraits, particularly those of Charles I as a hunter with servants, horses and grooms in a forest clearing or garden. The Spanish painter has perfectly assimilated Van Dyck's refined if rather affected elegance.

The portrait's identity, now fully accepted, was put forward in 1919 by Allende Salazar and Sánchez Cantón. Until then it had been known simply as the 'Knight of Santiago'.

There are other portraits of the subject. Carreño himself painted him later in a bust portrait now in a private collection in Madrid (Pérez Sánchez 1985, plate 93) and he also features in the *Auto da Fé in the Plaza Mayor in Madrid* by Francisco Rizi (Museo del Prado, Madrid, P-1126) and in the *Adoration of the Eucharistic Host of Gorkum* by Claudio Coello in the sacristy of El Escorial [FIG. 25]. [AEPS]

41 Bartolomé Esteban Murillo
[1617–1682]

Don Justino de Neve, 1665
Oil on canvas, 206 x 129.5 cm
Inscribed: ETATIS SVÆ. 40 / Bartholome Murillo Romulensis / Præcirca Obsequium desiderio pingebat, / A.M. [D] C.L.X.V.
(His age 40. Bartolomé Murillo of Seville painted this with the intention of making a gift of it in the year 1665).
London, The National Gallery, NG 6448

PROVENANCE

Painted for Don Justino de Neve; from 1685 in the Hospital de los Venerables Sacerdotes, Seville; removed to the Alcázar by the French authorities in Seville in 1810 with a view to including it in Joseph Bonaparte's museum of Spanish painting; taken to England by Delahante and sold to George Watson Taylor, M.P., before 1818; in his sale at Erlestoke Park on 24 July 1823, no. 77, where acquired by Lord Lansdowne for 480 guineas; in the Lansdowne collection at Bowood until acquired by The National Gallery in 1979.

ESSENTIAL BIBLIOGRAPHY

Fray Miguel de Pineda, *Oración fúnebre en las honras, que en la Santa Metropolitana [...] Iglesia de Sevilla se hizieron el sabado 7 de julio deste año de 1685 a la buena memoria del señor D. Justino de Neve y Chaves canonigo en dicha santa iglesia [...]*, Sevilla, 1685; Gabriel de Aranda, Vida del V. P. Fernando de Contreras, Sevilla, 1692, pp. 459–66; Palomino 1715–1723, III, p. 432; Ponz 1772–1794, IX, 1780, p. 123; Arana de Varflora (1791) 1996, pp. 59 and 69–70; Ceán Bermúdez 1800, IV, p. 60; Braham 1980; El Greco to Goya, cat. no. 44, pp. 86–87; Angulo 1981, I, pp. 463–65, II, no. 415, p. 325; Xanthe Brooke in Murillo. Scenes of Childhood, p. 52.

Justino de Neve was born in Seville in 1625, the son of Juan de Neve, who was of Flemish origin, and Sebastiana de Chaves y Castilla of Málaga. The coat of arms in the painting, which, like the inscription, appears to have been added to the portrait at an early date (and perhaps not by Murillo), is composed of the arms of the Neve family on the left and the Chaves family on the right (described in Angulo 1981, II, p. 325). Don Justino was a canon and prebendary of Seville Cathedral and was renowned for his devotion, eloquence and learning. Gabriel de Aranda describes him as 'a charitable and exemplary churchman, beloved in this city, his homeland [...] highly esteemed by the Chapter [of the Cathedral] for the skill, activity and zeal which he brought to bear on the most serious matters for over forty years in the service of his diocese'. He died on 14 June 1685, aged 60, and was buried in the Cathedral.

Justino de Neve was a patron and close friend of Murillo, obtaining for him the commission for a series of canvases for the church of Santa María la Blanca in Seville (1662–1665) – 'the focus of his devotion' (*blanco de su devoción*) according to Aranda, another series of nine paintings for the chapter house of Seville Cathedral (1667–1669), and commissioning paintings from him for the foundation he established for poor and retired priests in Seville, the Hospital de los Venerables Sacerdotes, notably the so-called *Inmaculada Soult* of about 1678 in the Museo del Prado. His collection of paintings comprised 165 works, of which eighteen were by or attributed to Murillo, and in his will he bequeathed this portrait to the Venerables Sacerdotes, requesting that it be hung where the priests could see it so that they 'might remember to pray to God our merciful Lord for my soul'. The personal closeness of the two men is confirmed by Murillo's naming Don Justino as one of the executors of his will.

The painting is one of a relatively small group of portraits by Murillo. Don Justino, dressed in ecclesiastical black, both austere and sumptuous, engages the viewer directly with an expression of intelligent intensity. He is seated on a wooden chair in a room which opens on to a terrace with a landscape beyond. Murillo adopts the portrait convention of showing his sitter as if momentarily distracted from his activity: he holds a small book marking a page with his index finger, suggesting that he is at prayer. On the table is an elegant clock (the inventory of his goods lists at least eight), which marks the time as ten to four (close to the liturgical time of nones), a larger book and a silver bell, an object that appears in several Roman ecclesiastical portraits, notably Raphael's *Pope Leo X with Cardinals Giulio de' Medici and Luigi de' Rossi* (1518; Florence, Uffizi). Similarities have been drawn with Titian's *Eleonora Gonzaga, Duchess of Urbino* (*ca.* 1536–1537; Florence, Uffizi), in which the Duchess sits by a table on which are a clock and a recumbent lapdog, with a landscape visible through an open window (Braham), but in fact Murillo's conception owes more to the tradition of papal portraits from Raphael to Velázquez, and to portraits of cardinals by Italian painters, such as Guido Reni's *Cardinal Roberto Ubaldini* (1625; Los Angeles County Museum). Compositionally, there is very little by way of precedent in Spanish portraiture, but the portrait of Don Justino retains a distinctively Spanish reticence and *gravitas*. The English lapdog (*perrilla inglesa*) with scarlet ribbon and bells on its collar that gazes up faithfully at its master was commented on by Palomino for its lifelike quality: its appearance was so convincing that it set real dogs snarling and barking.

The date on the portrait and the inscription suggest that Murillo painted it in gratitude to Don Justino for his support in obtaining the important commission of Santa María la Blanca, completed in 1665. Don Justino may be shown among the pilgrims that appear in the lower part of the painting of the *Infant Jesus distributing Bread to Pilgrims*, a painting commissioned from Murillo in 1678 for the Hospital de los Venerables and now in the Museum of Fine Arts in Budapest. [GF]

42 Juan Valdés Leal
[1622–1690]

Don Miguel de Mañara, 1681
Oil on canvas, 196 x 225 cm
On the right, on a crumpled sheet of paper that has fallen to the ground, is written: 'To Don Miguel de Mañara y Vicentelo de Leca, knight of the Order of Calatrava and of God, Provincial of the Brotherhood, and Chief Brother of the Santa Caridad of Our Lord Jesus Christ, Seville.' On the left of the picture is the inscription: 'Completed in the year 1681'
Seville, Hermandad de la Santa Caridad

PROVENANCE

The Hospital de la Santa Caridad, Seville.

ESSENTIAL BIBLIOGRAPHY
Beruete 1911, pp. 81–85; Gestoso 1916, pp. 162–65; Trapier 1960, pp. 65–67; Kinkead, 1978, pp. 287–89 and 448–50; Valdivieso-Serrera 1980, pp. 91–92; Valdivieso 1988, pp. 196 and 271, no. 230.

Miguel de Mañara y Vicentelo de Leca was born in Seville in 1627, the ninth child of Tomás de Mañara and Jerónima Anfriamo. A knight of the Order of Calatrava from 1635, in 1638 he lost his father and had to take care of the family. He married in 1651 and became one of the senior aldermen of the city. The death of his wife in 1661 had a profound effect on him. In 1662 he was admitted to the brotherhood of the Santa Caridad; in 1663 he was elected Chief Brother of the Brotherhood and undertook the reform of the confraternity, in relation to both its statutes and regulations and the renewal of the hospital and adjacent church. His *Discurso de la Verdad* (1671) was a learned dissertation on the road to salvation, disregard for worldliness and the carrying out of charitable works. He died in the brotherhood's own hospital in 1679.

In this portrait, seated at a table covered in a rich velvet cloth fringed with gold, he gazes out at the viewer while making an expressive gesture of the right hand towards a painting hanging on the wall in the background, which presents an allegory of the Mountain of God, alluded to by Mañara in his rules for the Santa Caridad, portraying the ascent of the soul from earth to heaven, practising charity.

On the table there is a small lectern with a book – the Rules of the Order – which he is no doubt explaining, a crucifix on a flaming heart, two wooden urns used for casting votes, and several books, one of them the *Discurso de la Verdad*, his most important work. On the left of the composition, sitting on a low seat, is a boy wearing the uniform of a nurse of the Brotherhood and with a book on his knee, gesturing silence with a finger on his lips, exhorting the spectator to listen to what Mañara is saying. Behind him in the middle ground and in shadow is a cabinet, and on it a sand clock, some books, a skull and a vase of tulips, obvious allusions to the fleeting nature of life, the ephemeralness of beauty and knowledge, and the inexorable march of death – that is, all the ingredients of a typical baroque *vanitas*.

The painting, completed in 1681 and therefore a posthumous portrait, is a magnificent example of a speaking image, charged with meaning that goes beyond the mere portrayal of the subject.

If the representation of the space in depth, the complexity of the additional details and the presence of the boy create direct communication with the spectator, and thereby define the work as clearly baroque, conceptually the richness of the meaning makes it a veritable moral sermon. Not only does it provide us with the image of the sitter, it also illustrates his way of thinking, his activities, his attitude to the vagaries of the world and his exemplary devotion.

However, in the portrait Valdés makes much of the black vestments of the red cross of Calatrava which sets him apart and distinguishes him, trumpeting his nobility and distinction. The inscription he had carved on his tomb on the threshold of the church also speaks volumes about his vainglory and his affected humility: 'Here lies the world's greatest sinner.' [AEPS]

6 Goya, a Free 'Disciple' of Velázquez

43 Diego Velázquez
[1599–1660]

Las Meninas, *ca.* 1656
Oil on canvas, 318 x 276 cm
Madrid, Museo del Prado, P-1174

PROVENANCE
1666, in the Alcázar in Madrid, in the king's study; inventories dated 1696 and 1700, in the same location; inventories dated 1772, 1794 and 1814, in the Palacio Nuevo; entered the Museo del Prado in 1819.

ESSENTIAL BIBLIOGRAPHY
Palomino (1724) 1986, pp. 181–83; Curtis 1883, no. 21; Mayer 1936, no. 166; López-Rey 1963, no. 229; Gállego 1990, no. 73; Marías (ed.) 1995; López-Rey and Delenda 1996, no. 124, Mena Marqués 1997, pp. 135–61.

The biography of Velázquez in *El museo pictórico y escala óptica* (1724), by the painter and theoretician Antonio Palomino, is the traditional source for dating this painting and identifying the place shown and the figures that appear in it. Completed, according to Palomino, in 1656 – a date that would seem to be borne out by the age of the Infanta, born in 1651 – the portrait is set in the chamber of Prince Baltasar Carlos, in which hung, according to the inventories of the Alcázar, the two paintings that can be seen in the background. These are copies by Juan Bautista Martínez del Mazo of originals by Rubens and Jordaens in the Torre de la Parada: *Minerva punishing Arachne* and *Apollo and Pan*. Two *meninas*, or maids of honour, Isabel de Velasco, kneeling on the left, and María Agustina Sarmiento, standing on the right, are attending the child, the first offering her a small red clay pitcher of water. In the foreground, on the right, we see the dwarf Maribárbola and the dwarf Nicolás Pertusato, who is teasing a sleepy mastiff. Behind them are Marcela de Ulloa, chaperone to the queen's ladies-in-waiting, and an unidentified gentleman chaperon. In the background, on the well-lit staircase, is the queen's chamberlain, José Nieto Velázquez. Finally, on the left, standing before his easel with his palette and brushes, is Velázquez himself. Reflected in the mirror at the back are the images of the Infanta's parents, Philip IV and his wife, Mariana of Austria.

Palomino tells us that once the picture was finished, it was the king himself who painted the cross of Knight of Saint James which the painter wears on his chest, but as this honour was not bestowed on him until November 1659, this observation falls within the realm of artists' legends. Radiographs of the picture reveal one essential change in this important area, which is the presence of another figure, a young gentleman who is not Velázquez, with a vandyke collar instead of a Spanish ruff, under the figure of the painter and in a different position, advancing towards the Infanta. This figure indicates a fundamental change to the composition, suggesting that the artist was not initially included in the scene. His inclusion in a portrait centred on the Infanta Margarita has caused some surprise and has been interpreted in a number of ways: from a purely naturalistic depiction of an everyday scene, in which the artist portrays himself painting the royal family, to an allegory of the art of painting, at a time when Velázquez, like other Spanish artists, was fighting for greater recognition of his work in society. Other changes in the composition, such as that to the Infanta's right hand – originally raised, as can clearly be seen on the painting's surface – now concealed by the red pitcher, nevertheless seem to suggest an earlier and different version of the scene, with which the figure of the gentleman under Velázquez would also correspond. Without the painter's presence before his easel, the picture would no longer be an allegory on painting. Its meaning would have to be sought within the official portraiture of the king's family and, in this case, the highlighting of the Infanta, who, at around that time, when no male heir existed, would have been seen as possible successor to the throne (as would her sister María Teresa, who was, however, promised to Louis XIV of France).

This work became famous as soon as it was painted, and it had an immediate influence on Spanish painting, and later on, on the work of other painters from Spain and abroad, such as Luca Giordano and Goya. It is, of course, considered one of the most emblematic paintings in the history of Spanish art. [MMM]

44 Juan Bautista Martínez del Mazo

[1605–1667]

The Family of the Painter, 1664–1665
Oil on canvas, 148 x 174.5 cm
Vienna, Kunsthistorisches Museum, Gemäldegalerie, 320

PROVENANCE

1800, purchased in Italy for the imperial collections.

ESSENTIAL BIBLIOGRAPHY

Justi 1902, t. II, p. 333; Gaya Nuño 1960, t. I, pp. 474 and 479; Buschbeck 1960, p. 367; *Kunsthistorisches Museum*, 1965, t. I, no. 593; *Pintura española de los siglos xvi al xviii*, 1981–1982, no. 22.

This painting was identified by Justi, at the end of the nineteenth century, as representing the family of the painter Juan Bautista Martínez del Mazo, son-in-law and disciple of Velázquez, by means of the artist's coat of arms: the armoured arm holding a *mazo* (mace). Influenced by *Las Meninas*, it shares with that painting the sense of space in the background, which probably reflects the interior of the Alcázar in Madrid, perhaps the Casa del Tesoro, which was the studio of Velázquez, in his final years, and of Mazo too. On the wall hangs a portrait, then at the Royal Collection, of Philip IV in black, by Velázquez, which corresponds to the 1658 version (London, The National Gallery), and on the table stands the bust of a Roman woman, now considered a portrait of the Empress Faustina la Mayor, identifiable by the damage to the left ear, from which a small piece is missing, which was in the Alcázar at the time, and now in the Prado. The delicate roses on the desk, beneath the portrait of Philip IV, appear to be a homage to the king – the patron of Velázquez and Mazo – who died in 1664, but may still have been alive when the picture was painted.

The space of the background has a certain mystery. Separated from the scene at the front by the green drapery, the scale of the figures increases the sense of distance between the group in the foreground and that of the painter, with his back to us before his canvas. He is painting a portrait of the Infanta Margarita, as a woman approaches him with a small girl, who is holding out her arms. Identified by some as Mazo himself, others see this painter as Velázquez, since the slim black silhouette is reminiscent of his self-portrait in *Las Meninas*.

Mazo, married to Francisca, one of Velázquez's daughters, who gave him nine children. He became a widower in 1654, and married again between 1656 and 1657, this time to Francisca de la Vega, who in turn died in 1665, with whom he had four more children. Some see in this scene a portrait of his second wife, seated on the right, with the children of their marriage, José Antonio, Luis, Francisco and Fernando Felipe, this last son born in 1663. The older children, from the first marriage, Velázquez's grandchildren, would be those on the left: Gaspar, born between 1636 and 1637, Melchor, in 1652, Baltasar, in 1654, and María Teresa, born in 1648, who married in 1666. Others have identified her with his sister Inés, born in 1638, married in 1654, and again in 1661, although the age of the young woman depicted here is nearer the sixteen years of María Teresa than the twenty-six of Inés.

The traditional identification of the figures is not entirely convincing. The youngest boy, identified as Fernando Felipe, the child born in 1663, with his mother's arms around his shoulders, is in fact a girl judging from the dress and the pearl earrings and coral bracelet, characteristic of female attire. Perhaps the painting, since it is about Mazo's family, might have another explanation. The painter's second daughter, Inés, had married in 1654, and then again in 1661, and it may be that she is the mother seated on the right, although the lack of information on her marriage and children makes it impossible to be certain of this theory. The painting would then be a homage to Velázquez, in the figures of his grandchildren and great-grandchildren, who continued the family's distinguished lineage, linked with that of Mazo. [MMM]

45 Francisco de Goya

[1747–1828]

The Family of the Infante Don Luis, 1783
Oil on canvas, 248 x 330 cm
Parma, Fondazione Magnani-Rocca

PROVENANCE

1783, Palace of the Infante Don Luis in Arenas de San Pedro (Ávila); from 1820, in all the inventories of the palace of his descendants in Boadilla del Monte (Madrid); from 1904, in the palace in Florence of the Italian branch of the family, the Prince and Princess of Ruspoli; 1974, acquisition by the Fondazione Magnani-Rocca, Parma.

ESSENTIAL BIBLIOGRAPHY

Gassier and Wilson 1970 (1974), no. 208; Gudiol 1970, no. 152; Mena Marqués 2000, no. 9.

The picture of the Infante Don Luis with his family and servants was painted by Goya in the summer of 1783, in the Palace at Arenas de San Pedro (Ávila) where Charles III's elder brother lived a life exiled from the court. Don Luis of Bourbon, son of Philip V and Isabel Farnese, was born in 1727. Destined for the Church and made a cardinal in 1735, he was appointed Archbishop of Toledo and, in 1739, Archbishop of Seville. Having no religious vocation and, on the contrary, very much inclined towards women, Don Luis renounced his ecclesiastical position at the age of twenty-three and lived at court during the reigns of his step-brother Ferdinand VI and his brother Charles III. The latter refused to authorise his marriage to a lady of royal blood since this would have meant that his children, as Spaniards, would have taken precedence in line to the throne over those of Charles, all of whom were born in Naples. Only when Don Luis's love life began to verge on the scandalous did the King give permission for his marriage, but to a lady of low birth. Moreover, he published the Pragmatic Sanction ten days before the wedding, and therefore the forced morganatic marriage of Don Luis invalidated the right of his children to use the paternal surname and, consequently, to succeed to the throne. The young lady chosen, Doña María Teresa de Vallabriga, daughter of a cavalry captain from the lower ranks of the Aragonese nobility, was thirty-two years younger than her husband. She gave him four children, of whom only the three shown in the painting survived: Don Luis, the firstborn, Doña María Teresa Josefa, the future Countess of Chinchón, and Doña María Luisa Fernanda. The three were sent to Toledo on their father's death in 1785 and were separated from their mother. The eldest son, destined for a religious career, became, like his father, Archbishop of Toledo; the girls entered a convent, presumably with the idea of preventing them from marrying and having children, thus assuring for Charles III the dynastic line descending from him and his children.

In the summer of 1783, Goya was invited to the palace in Arenas de San Pedro. Don Luis was a cultured man, fond of music and art, and his small court was dominated by his young wife, around whom palace life and its intrigues revolved. Goya was well received in the court at the start of his career; He was a friend of Francisco del Campo, one of Don Luis's secretaries, and went hunting with the Infante. Goya painted a number of portraits of Don Luis during his first and second visits (a year apart), that pleased him very much. The large family portrait, in which Goya portrayed himself painting at his easel, consists of Don Luis, his wife and children, ladies-in-waiting and other servants, such as the hairdresser. It has not been possible to identify all the sitters with any certainty, but they may have included the musician Luigi Boccherini, who might be the young man in profile in the foreground, and also perhaps Goya's friend Francisco del Campo. María Teresa de Vallabriga is the central figure in the scene, highlighted by the strong lighting that is reflected on her shawl. Don Luis has paused in his card game at the table and is looking straight ahead at the group of courtesans or servants, in a severe profile that is associated with royal effigies on coins. The scene is lit from the candle in the centre, a device that Goya borrowed from the Venetian masters, particularly Bassano, while the general arrangement recalls the basic format of *Las Meninas* [CAT. 43], with the self-portrait of Goya in front of his easel. In this example of a group portrait – seldom found in Spanish painting, and one of the most spectacular of the entire eighteenth century – the artist combined the idea of the intimate portrait, such as the English 'conversation pieces', generally small in size, with the monumental portrait of palatial proportions, in a painting in which Don Luis most likely wished to present his family in a manner he considered it deserved. Goya skilfully created this complex scene, in which fourteen persons appear. By then, his talent for composition – albeit not so noticeable in portraits – had been more than proved in his frescoes, religious pictures and tapestry cartoons. Here, however, he also showed his great flair for portraiture, with the wide variety of faces of different type and character, from young to old, from the candour of the children to the tiredness and bitterness of some of the adults, producing portraits of great psychological depth and also surprising naturalness. [MMM]

46 Francisco de Goya
[1747–1828]

The Family of Charles IV, 1800
Oil on canvas, 280 x 336 cm
Madrid, Museo del Prado, P-726

PROVENANCE
1814, stored in the passage to the galleries in the Palacio Real Nuevo, Madrid; 1834, in the Gabinete de Descanso de los Reyes (Royal Rest Room) at the Museo del Prado.

ESSENTIAL BIBLIOGRAPHY
Gassier and Wilson 1974, no. 783; Gudiol 1973 and 1970, no. 434; Tomlinson 1992 (1993), pp. 79–97; Mena Marqués 2002, pp. 67–195.

The large painting of *The Family of Charles IV* is well documented through Queen María Luisa's correspondence with Manuel Godoy and through Goya's bills for materials. It was painted in Madrid between June and December 1800, after the artist returned from Aranjuez, where he had made studies from life of the various royal persons to save them having to spend long hours posing. All the members of the family appear in the painting, although the scene is centred on the figure of Queen María Luisa, who is holding the hand of the young Infante Don Francisco de Paula, who in turn holds his father's hand. The Queen has her arm round the shoulder of the Infanta Doña María Isabel, still a young girl, and to the left of her is the heir to the throne, Ferdinand, Prince of Asturias, and behind him his brother, the Infante Don Carlos. On the right-hand side, the Infanta María Luisa, with her husband, Don Luis of Bourbon, Prince of Parma, holds her firstborn, the Infante Carlos Luis. The King's brother and sister occupy the back of the scene: on the left the Infanta Doña María Josefa, and on the right the Infante Don Antonio Pascual. Beside him is a lady in profile, identified as his wife and niece, the Infanta Doña María Amalia, who had died two years earlier, and was also a daughter of the King and Queen. Behind the crown prince, an elegant young lady is shown in profile, looking up at the pictures in the Royal Collection. Goya used this device to represent the future Princess of Asturias, who had not yet been selected by the King and Queen from among the possible European candidates. Finally, following Velázquez's idea in *Las Meninas* [CAT. 43], the artist included himself in front of a large canvas on his easel, at the left of the picture, and the composition of that historic painting is also reflected in the two pictures hanging in the background.

The family portrait was most likely painted for one of the principal chambers of the Royal Palace, which was being redecorated that year. It is therefore of a dynastic nature, emphasising the monarchy and its succession and also transmitting a reassuring message in times of upheaval, when Spain was being affected by French revolutionary ideas and under threat from Napoleon. The portrayal of the Queen as a prolific mother and of the King as a good, peaceful man, and the inclusion in the scene of the future Princess of Asturias – thus helping to assure the continuation of the line – as well as the other Infantes, even the one who had died, and their spouses, indicate the painting's fundamental message. Goya used all the resources of his art and his knowledge to represent the sovereign and his family, to depict the dignity of royalty and the Bourbon dynasty's links with the earlier Hapsburg monarchs, through the visual references taken from *Las Meninas*. At certain historical moments, in France in the nineteenth century and in Spain in the early twentieth century, the painting has been considered as a criticism of the monarchy and the Old Regime. This was most probably not Goya's aim, for he tried to serve his patrons in the best possible way. With respect to other contemporary representations of the King and Queen, here Goya is sympathetic to the sitters, and where signs of weakness or pride have wrongly been observed, as in the case of the Queen, the artist was in fact following the conventions for poses and gestures used at the time in the portrayal of royalty.

The picture is technically prodigious, in its freedom, in its calculated pursuit of effects and in the representation of matter, and also in what is most important of all: the psychological depth with which he has captured each member of the royal family and their relationships amongst themselves. [MMM]

47 Diego Velázquez

[1599–1660]

Philip IV on Horseback, *ca.* 1635–1636
Oil on canvas, 301 x 314 cm
Madrid, Museo del Prado, P-1178

PROVENANCE

Between 1637 and 1791, in the Salón de Reinos of the Buen Retiro Palace in Madrid; inventories of 1734, 1772, 1794 and 1814, Palacio Real Nuevo, Madrid; entered the Museo del Prado in 1819.

ESSENTIAL BIBLIOGRAPHY

Curtis 1883 no. 97; Mayer 1936, no. 185; Pantorba 1955, no. 60, López-Rey 1963, no. 187; Gudiol 1973, no. 78; Brown 1986, pp. 111–14; Gállego 1990, no. 38; Garrido Pérez 1992, pp. 366–83; López-Rey and Delenda 1996 no. 74; Baticle 1999, pp. 57–69.

Velázquez painted an initial equestrian portrait of Philip IV in 1625, on his second and final trip to Madrid. This work, now lost, hung in the Alcázar until another one by Rubens, painted in Madrid in 1628, replaced it. There is no record of what that first painting by Velázquez was like, in which the king may perhaps have been presented in a more relaxed pose, with the horse walking slowly, similar to the existing examples of equestrian portraits of Philip II. The more lively models by Rubens no doubt inspired Velázquez to opt for a more graceful and warlike position for the horse when he came to paint the king on horseback for the series of equestrian portraits for the Salón de Reinos of the Buen Retiro Palace: Philip III and his wife, Margarita of Austria, the reigning monarch Philip IV and his first wife, Isabel of Bourbon, and his heir, Prince Baltasar Carlos. The resumption of hostilities with France in 1636 and the Thirty Years War, may be the explanation for this determined attitude of the king, with his horse in a daring curvet, which shows him in his full warlike splendour, with the sash of pink silk and the army field marshal staff of command, capable of taking his country to victory.

The model chosen also coincides with the one supplied from Madrid, undoubtedly by Velázquez, to the Florentine sculptor Pietro Tacca, who in 1635 was making the bronze statue of the king, today situated in Plaza de Oriente, in which Philip IV and his horse appear in a similar pose, with the sash of the field marshal also similarly arranged, which, in parallel with the horse and rider, enhances the sense of the king's movement. The changes made by Velázquez can be clearly seen on the canvas: in the field marshal's sash itself, which initially appeared behind the shoulder of the monarch, moved by the wind; in the upper part of his back, as well as in the horse's hind legs, the position of which was changed slightly. The king, born in 1605, and around thirty at the time of this portrait, is wearing very simple armour of damascened steel, and is riding like the perfect horseman, as he was indeed described by contemporary sources, with absolute control over the powerful animal. A small tug on the reins, held in his left hand, has caused the horse to rise up in this momentary *levade*, without however perturbing the impassive monarch. The face of Philip IV, characteristic in its whiteness, with the prominent jaw of the Hapsburgs, is captured by Velázquez in strict profile, as on a coin, a rather unusual approach for this type of portrait, conferring on him the sense of distance and elegance peculiar to this image.

Intended to be hung to the left of one of the entrance doors to the Salón de Reinos, above it and on the other side would have hung the portraits of his son and heir and of his beloved queen, Isabel of Bourbon, towards whom the king appears to direct his gaze. Behind him, a splendid tree encloses the composition and leads the eye towards the broad landscape, which recreates in a naturalistic way the landscape around Madrid, perhaps the area of El Pardo, or possibly of El Escorial. Velázquez marked his authorship of the painting with the white piece of paper left on a stone, a device he used in some of the portraits of the Salón de Reinos, in *The Surrender of Breda*, and in the portrait of the Count-Duke of Olivares on horseback [FIG. 75]. [MMM]

48 Francisco de Goya

[1747–1828]

Charles IV on Horseback, 1799–1800
Oil on canvas, 336 x 282 cm
Madrid, Museo del Prado, P-719

PROVENANCE

1814, stored in the passage to the galleries in the Palacio Real Nuevo, Madrid; 1819, entered the Museo del Prado.

ESSENTIAL BIBLIOGRAPHY

Gassier and Wilson 1970, no. 776; Gudiol 1970, no. 422; Glendinning (1977) 1982, pp. 260–61; Camón 1980–1982, vol. III, p. 118; Moreno 1997, no. 88; Mena Marqués 2002, pp. 96–101.

The painting formed a pair with the equestrian portrait of Queen María Luisa (Madrid, Museo del Prado, P-1184), documented through her correspondence with Manuel Godoy in September and October 1799. This one of the King, which was perhaps begun at the same time, must have not been completed until the following year, according to Goya's bill for materials in 1801. The head is most certainly taken from the same study from life used for the portrait of Charles IV as a hunter, which indicates that the two paintings are close to each other in date. The King is wearing the dress uniform of a colonel of the Royal Guards, regulated by decree in 1795, with all the decorations he held, from the ribbon of the Order of Charles III, the red Order of the Golden Fleece, which also hangs from its ribbon on his chest, to the Order of Saint Esprit and the crosses of the four orders of chivalry: Santiago, Calatrava, Alcántara and Montesa.

Here, Goya abandoned the heroic pose of earlier equestrian portraits of sovereigns, with the horse prancing, and showed the King, who had never been in combat, as a kindly, peaceful man. His horse is facing forwards, as in the portrait of Queen Margarita of Austria by Velázquez (Madrid, Museo del Prado, P-720), thus giving a predominant feeling of calm and temperance rather than any military air. In this Goya must have followed the recommendations of the King himself, who wanted a peaceful reign that would improve the country's prosperity. The sovereign's courage and spirit, however, are emphasised by his tranquillity, alone in the dark landscape, at dusk, in stormy weather, symbolising perhaps the difficulties inherent in the exercising of royal power. The horse, a large and powerful animal, as noble and handsome as the horses in the portraits by Velázquez of the Hapsburg sovereigns, is entirely under the control of the King. That attitude emphasises his dignity in a natural way, his firm hand holding on the reins being a metaphor for how affairs of state should be handled. Goya's virtuosity and precision is evident in the detailing of the uniform and its textures. [MMM]

49 Francisco de Goya
[1747–1828]

Charles III as a Hunter, ca. 1788
Oil on canvas, 214 x 136 cm
Inscription on dog's collar:
Rey N.º S.º
('The King, our Sovereign')
Madrid, Museo del Prado, P-737

PROVENANCE
Probably painted for the New Palace; Palacio del Buen Retiro; 1847, transferred to the Museo del Prado; 1915, removed to the Museo de Lérida; 1929, removed to the Museo Municipal de Madrid; 1942, returned to the Museo del Prado.

ESSENTIAL BIBLIOGRAPHY
Gassier and Wilson 1970, no. 776; Gudiol 1970, no. 230; Moreno 1997, no. 50.

This portrait of Charles III, probably painted the year he died, shows the King in hunting costume. It is reminiscent of Velázquez's portrait, *Philip IV as a Hunter* (Madrid, Museo del Prado, P-1184), which had hung in the royal hunting lodge, La Torre de la Parada, in the hills outside the Palace of El Pardo. Charles III was born in Madrid in 1716, the son of Philip V and Isabel Farnese. Heir to the Duchy of Parma through his mother, he was King of Naples from 1734 until 1759, when he succeeded his childless brother Ferdinand VI as King of Spain. His wife, Maria Amalia of Saxony, died in 1761, and the grief-stricken monarch never remarried. After her death, the King – always a keen hunter – spent much of his time hunting in the hills around his favourite palace, El Pardo. The palace itself was tastefully decorated, and boasted a beautiful set of tapestries for which Goya had painted the cartoons. In this portrait, the King's tanned features show no sign that his life was almost at an end; he died in late 1788.

Very little is known about the commissioning of the portrait. Another excellent version, bearing the inscription 'Goya did it', was perhaps commissioned by the seventh Count of Fernán Núñez, in whose family collection it remains. Indeed, it is generally considered to be the first of a series of copies, of which the Prado one – originally in the Royal Collection – is one of the best in terms of quality. It has been suggested that Goya based his portrait on prints rather than sittings; yet this seems unlikely, given the psychological insight and the precision with which the King's features are captured, in both the Prado version and the first version in the Fernán Núñez collection. Goya was appointed Court Painter in the summer of 1786, and by 1788 had produced some of his finest portraits of the time, clearly demonstrating his mastery of the genre. This is undoubtedly among the best portraits of Charles III, exceeding those painted by Mengs more than twenty years earlier. The painting was probably intended for the New Royal Palace in Madrid, to be placed beside the portraits of Philip IV as a hunter, his brother the Infante Don Fernando and his son Prince Baltasar Carlos [CAT. 50] by Velazquez, which at that time hung in the King's Chamber. Although he is dressed for hunting, the King's attire suggests an official portrait; he wears the blue sash of the Order of Charles III, the red sash and insignia of the Order of the Golden Fleece, and the dark blue ribbon of the French Ordre du Saint Esprit.

Here, Goya made full use of his familiarity with the works of Velázquez in the Royal Collection. Although both the posture and the background landscape of this picture – evocative of the Pardo hills at the foot of the Sierra de Guadarrama – owe much to Velázquez's portraits of members of the Hapsburg dynasty in hunting costume, the positioning of the King also recalls another Velázquez work, the portrait of *The Buffoon 'Don Juan de Austria'* (Madrid, Museo del Prado, P-1200). [MMM]

50 Diego Velázquez
[1599–1660]

Prince Baltasar Carlos as a Hunter,
1635–1636
Oil on canvas, 191 x 103 cm
Inscribed: ANNO ÆTATIS SUÆ VI
Madrid, Museo del Prado, P-1189

PROVENANCE
Inventory dated 1701, in the Torre de la Parada (Madrid); from the mid-eighteenth century, in the Palacio Real Nuevo; inventories dated 1772 and 1794, Palacio Real Nuevo; 1819, Museo del Prado.

ESSENTIAL BIBLIOGRAPHY
Curtis 1883 no. 137; Mayer 1936, no. 271; Gudiol 1973, no. 199; López-Rey 1963, no. 304; Gállego 1990, no. 45; López-Rey and Delenda 1996, no. 77; Mena Marqués 2000, pp. 116–23.

Prince Baltasar Carlos as a Hunter was part of a series of portraits painted by Velázquez for the Torre de la Parada, the hunting lodge of the kings of Spain in the hills of El Pardo, refurbished by Philip IV in the 1630s. Next to the portrait of the prince were those of the king and of his brother, the Infante Ferdinand, also portrayed as hunters. According to the inscription, the child was six, which fits in with the age he would then have been, since he was born in 1629. This is one of the first paintings for this exceptional lodge, which was completed around 1640 with the rich group of mythological paintings by Rubens and his studio.

The hunting of large game, which was the sole preserve of the nobility and royalty, was exercised as part of the prince's education, to harden him and to accustom him to the greater dangers of war. Diego Saavedra Fajardo in his *Idea de un príncipe politíco-christiano*, of 1635, recommended hunting because 'in it youth develops, gains strength and lightness, the military arts are practised, the lie of the land is understood [...] the sight of the spilled blood of wild beasts, and their grotesque movements in death, purges the emotions, fortifies the soul, and creates generous spirits which constantly scorn the shadows of fear'. According to Philip IV's master of the hounds, Juan Mateos, in his *Origen y dignidad de la caza*, from an early age the prince speared wild boar with a skill that was admired by all. In 1642 the book entitled *Serenissimi hispaniarum principis Baltasaris Caroli Venatio* was published in Brussels, in which the hunting activity of the small heir to the crown was illustrated in prints.

Various copies contemporary to this painting in the Prado are known, which reflects the success enjoyed by this image. Thanks to them it is known that the original arrangement of the scene, now cut down on the right side to a width of 103 cm instead of the 136 cm of the king's portrait, included two hounds, instead of the single one seen now. They are, without doubt, the animals sent from Lombardy as a gift to the child from his uncle, Ferdinand of Austria. The serene, determined and majestic attitude of the prince already reveals the benefits of hunting on his education, and Velázquez produced with his gracious model, one of the finest portraits of any of the family of the king until the one of the Infanta Margarita twenty years later. The background of the painting with the Monte del Pardo, on which the Torre de la Parada stood, and the mountains of Guadarrama in the distance, is one of the most naturalistic and modern landscapes the painter produced, in which he again uses the powerful resource of the tree, on the right, a symbol of the power of kings in the Bible. [MMM]

51 Diego Velázquez
[1599–1660]

Pablo de Valladolid, *ca.* 1635
Oil on canvas, 209 x 123 cm
Madrid, Museo del Prado, P-1198

PROVENANCE
Inventory dated 1701, in the Buen Retiro palace, for which it was undoubtedly painted; inventories dated 1772, 1794 and 1814, Palacio Real Nuevo; 1816–1827, deposited at the Real Academia de Bellas Artes de San Fernando; entered the Museo del Prado in 1827.

ESSENTIAL BIBLIOGRAPHY
Curtis 1883, no. 71; Mayer 1936, no. 449; López-Rey 1963, no. 433; Gudiol 1973, no. 107; Brown and Elliott 1980, pp. 132–33 and 254–55; Gállego 1990, no. 57; López-Rey and Delenda 1996, no. 82.

The painting is described for the first time in the inventory of the Royal Collection of 1701 in the Buen Retiro palace, as a 'portrait of a jester with ruff called Pablillos de Valladolid'. Indeed this Pablo de Valladolid appears in the documents of the Alcázar, with 'two stipends' (*dos raciones*), which his children, Pablo and Isabel, inherited on his death in 1648. He was a 'buffoon' (*hombre de placer*) or perhaps court actor, but from 1633 onwards he did not live in the Alcázar, like the jesters and dwarves, but was given instead an *aposento*, a room outside it. In his will he appointed as executor the painter Juan Carreño de Miranda, who lived in the same house as him. He was probably born around 1600, judging from the age of thirty or thirty-five that he appears to be in the picture, painted, like the rest of the series of jesters for the Buen Retiro palace before 1634, when extra payments were made to Velázquez for paintings produced for this purpose.

Pablo de Valladolid is not dressed as a jester in the portrait, with the peculiar garments of the court 'locos' such as 'Barbarroja' or 'Don Juan de Austria' (both in Madrid, Museo del Prado), but his attire, a black velvet suit and cape of the same colour, of good cloth, ruff and fashionable coiffure, give him more the air of a gentleman. It is thought by many that the destination of the paintings of jesters, including *Pablo de Valladolid*, was to be part of the decoration of the queen's room in the Buen Retiro palace, from a reference in 1661 which mentioned in its rooms a *sala de los bufones* or jester's hall. It is possible that the large paintings by Velázquez with life-size figures depicting actors, jesters and other court servants were part of the decoration of this palace, in which theatre was one of the most important activities. The style of the painting, which in the 1701 inventory is described as being in the painter's 'early style', coincides in any case with a date in the early 1630s, since the treatment of the light is still similar, in its intensity, to the figures of *Vulcan's Forge* (Madrid, Museo del Prado) and *Joseph's Coat* (El Escorial, Real Monasterio), painted by Velázquez during his first trip to Italy.

The portrait is one of the most spectacular and unusual by Velázquez in the arrangement of the figure in space, since the artist does not follow the traditional rules of perspective, in which the space is represented by means of geometry, with the support of the ground and its intersection with the walls in the background. Here the figure is in an ambiguous space, very well lit, in which Velázquez has set him perfectly by means of the spreading of his legs and his shadow on the ground, the extended right arm and the expressive profile of his clothing, standing out in the light on the right. He thus suggests the movement of the actor on the stage, an unreal space, and his half-open lips intimate that the action is about to begin. The painting's modernity is the reason for the subsequent esteem in which it was held, for example by Goya, in the eighteenth century, or Manet in the nineteenth. [MMM]

52 Francisco de Goya
[1747–1828]

Francisco Cabarrús, 1788
Oil on canvas, 210 x 127 cm
Madrid, Banco de España Collection

PROVENANCE
1788, Banco de San Carlos, later Banco de España.

ESSENTIAL BIBLIOGRAPHY
Gassier and Wilson 1970, no. 228; Gudiol 1970, no. 249; Moreno 1988–1989, no. 15, pp. 165–67; Baticle (1992) 1995, pp. 90, 95 and 102–15; Ansón Navarro 1995; Symmons 1998.

The portrait of Cabarrús was commissioned in 1788 by the Banco de San Carlos, through the noted scholar and print collector Agustín Ceán Bermúdez, who had been Chief Secretary to the bank since 1785. At the same time, Goya was commissioned to paint portraits of several other founders of the national bank, although this was the largest and most impressive of the set.

Francisco Cabarrús, a key figure in the Spanish Enlightenment, was Minister of Finance from 1783 to 1790. He was born in 1752 in Bayonne, the son of a French merchant, and came to Spain in 1768 to work in Juan Zafras' trading company at the Zaragoza wholesale market. He was a member of the Aragon Economic Society of Friends of the Country, where he met a number of leading local figures, including Juan Martín de Goicoechea and Martín Zapater, both friends of Goya. In Spain, he married Maria Antonia Galabert, the daughter of a Valencia merchant, and in 1777 moved to Madrid, probably armed with letters of recommendation for Floridablanca, the newly-appointed Minister of State, to whom it is thought he lost no time in proposing the founding of a national bank, the Banco de San Carlos. The Spanish National Library holds a handwritten copy of the bank's foundation plan, dated 22 October 1781 and entitled: *Report presented to His Majesty by Don Francisco Cabarrús, for the Foundation of a National Bank by his Excellency the Count of Floridablanca*; the scheme met with some initial opposition from more conservative figures, and the final revised plan was not signed until 2 June 1782. Cabarrús also founded, in 1785, the Philippines Trading Company, to trade with the East; the first director was one of his assistants, Bernardo de Iriarte, and Cabarrús himself carried through a number of brilliant though risky financial deals with France. He is an outstanding example of the rise to power of a new class, the highly-trained and enterprising bourgeoisie, who were to hold key posts in the Administration. Cabarrús ventured beyond the boundaries of his family background in trade, to become a shrewd and intelligent financier as well as a liberal-minded politician with considerable public influence; he was made Count of Cabarrús in 1789.

Goya's portrait, painted in 1788 – the year in which Cabarrús attained his greatest power and influence – captures both his human qualities and his drive. Indeed, this is a true psychological portrait of Cabarrús, whom Jovellanos described as frank, lively, passionate and decisive. A man of enlightened views that were shared by his friend Jovellanos, he supported a single common education system for all 'children of the same fatherland', and favoured divorce and the creation of licensed brothels to put an end to street prostitution; even more boldly, perhaps, he advocated the abolition of the hereditary nobility and the system of primogeniture, arguing that current members of the aristocracy should be allowed the title but no other privileges. It was in part these progressive ideas, which Cabarrús flaunted openly in a speech entitled 'In Praise of Charles III' (*Elogio a Carlos III*) delivered at the Society of Friends of the Country in July 1789, that led to his downfall. On the death of Charles III, a new political situation arose; Cabarrús's supporters fell from power, and the slander of his enemies – who accused him of embezzlement and of being in contact with revolutionary France – led to his own dismissal. He spent two years in prison (1790–1792), was investigated by the Inquisition, and subsequently failed in his attempt to flee to France. Later, however, he regained his position and returned under Joseph Bonaparte to his old post of Minister of Finance, which he held until his death in Seville in 1810.

Goya was paid 4,500 *reales* for the portrait on 21 April 1788, suggesting that it may have been painted that winter, a hypothesis supported by the sitter's fur-lined frock coat. Cabarrús probably sat for the portrait in February on his return from Paris, where he had attended the wedding of his daughter Thérèse, who was later to become a *muse* of the French Revolution. Goya chose to dress him in a light green frock coat, whose glinting golden sheen almost envelops the wearer; this visual simile perfectly conveys the financier's remarkable and widely renowned ability to generate wealth. Goya made use of Velázquez's portrait of *Pablo de Valladolid* [CAT. 51] in capturing Cabarrús's dynamic, decisive posture; he seems to be turning within the space, his right hand outstretched, in a movement that stresses his advance from the shadowy background. Like Velázquez, Goya has placed his subject in an ambiguous, undefined space; the overall effect is that of a 'positive' reflection of the dark figure of Velázquez's actor, who by contrast is set against a well-lit background. Ceán Bermúdez, in *A Memoir of the Life of Jovellanos* (*Memoria para la vida de Jovellanos*), published in 1814, described Cabarrús with a literary image which reflects Goya's visual achievement: his main failing, apparently, was that he 'acted with no knowledge of the terrain'. [MMM]

53 Francisco de Goya
[1747–1828]

Manuel Osorio Manrique de Zúñiga, 1788
Oil on canvas, 110 x 80 cm
Signed, on the calling card:
Dn Franco Goya
Inscribed: EL S.R D.N MANUEL OSORIO MANRRIQUE DE ZUÑIGA S.R DE GINES NACIO EN ABR. A 11 DE 1784
(Don Manuel Osorio Manrique de Zuñiga, Lord of Gines, born 2 April 1784)
New York, The Metropolitan Museum of Art, The Jules Bache Collection, 1949 (49.7.41)

PROVENANCE
Madrid, Altamira collection; 30 March 1878, sold to Hotel Drouot, Paris; Paris, Bernstein collection; Paris, E. Jonas, New York, Duveen; New York, Jules Bache collection; 1949, donated to the Metropolitan Museum of Art by Jules Bache.

ESSENTIAL BIBLIOGRAPHY
Gassier and Wilson 1970, no. 233; Gudiol 1974, no. 251/262; Glendinning 1987, p. 239; Tomlinson 1994, pp. 64–65.

Don Manuel Osorio Manrique de Zúñiga was the younger son of the Count of Altamira. In around 1787–1788, Goya had painted a portrait of his father Don Vicente Osorio de Moscoso, as part of a set of portraits of the founders of the Banco de San Carlos. The Count was presumably pleased with his own portrait, which was something of a challenge given that he was an extremely small man; Lord Holland described him as 'the shortest man I have seen in Society, shorter than the dwarves they show at fairs'. Goya also painted the Countess, María Ignacia Álvarez of Toledo, holding her baby daughter (New York, Metropolitan Museum). At around this time, Goya painted portraits of a number of children, among them those of the Duke of Osuna (now lost but mentioned in the family records) and the large family portrait in the Museo del Prado [FIG. 21].

Like the Duke of Osuna's sons, Manuel Osorio, aged three, wears a light, loose-fitting suit. As befitted the Age of Enlightenment, the children of the nobility were no longer reared with such formal etiquette, and tight, stiff clothes were no longer worn; similarly, the boy is portrayed with unadorned hair, instead of the powdered hair or wig of earlier generations. Games had become fashionable, and looser clothes allowed greater freedom of movement. This portrayal of the little boy as a keen naturalist reflected – with interesting variations – an approach that expressed the educational views of the Enlightenment. Children were shown studying and experimenting in geography, botany or the natural sciences, the main areas of education in the eighteenth century. The cage full of finches, difficult to breed in captivity, and the pet magpie on a string in the foreground, may simply indicate the boy's early interest in the sciences, mixed at this age with his love of playing; however, the portrait is open to other, more metaphorical, readings.

In the foreground, the magpie on a lead – a tame bird if reared as a pet – holds the painter's calling card in its beak. Goya may be referring to a real event that took place in the child's home, involving a tame bird taught to pick things up. Magpies, of course, are known to steal shiny, precious objects; here, the precious object is the painter's card, complete with palette, canvas and brushes. The three cats lurking wide-eyed in the background are a clear threat both to the magpie and to the finches. But the boy has them all under control; the cats leave the magpie alone, and the finches are safe in their cage. Goya is offering us a neat metaphor for the education of youth: the patience and discipline with which the child has tamed his magpie are also to be applied by his parents in his own upbringing. The frail little boy is dressed in red, a symbol of his lively, untrained nature that echoes the red heads of the little wild finches; he is watched over and protected, like the birds in their cage. Only in his father's home is he safe from the natural dangers of childhood, symbolised by the threatening cats that loom in the background. [MMM]

54 Diego Velázquez
[1599–1660]

Prince Felipe Próspero, ca. 1659
Oil on canvas, 128.5 x 99.5 cm
Vienna, Kunsthistorisches Museum, Gemäldegalerie, 319

PROVENANCE
1659, sent to Vienna by Philip IV to his nephew the Emperor Leopold I of Austria; in the Treasury Room of Graz Palace; 1765, in the Imperial Palace of Vienna; from 1816, in the gallery of paintings of the Belvedere Palace (Vienna), until transferred to the Kunsthistorisches Museum.

ESSENTIAL BIBLIOGRAPHY
Curtis 1883, no. 147; Mayer 1936, no. 304; López-Rey 1963, no. 334; Gudiol 1973, no. 158.

Born in Madrid on 20 November 1657, Felipe Próspero eventually became heir to the throne, because, following the death of Baltasar Carlos in 1649, the king had no further male descendants. The child had a stepsister, the Infanta María Teresa, daughter of Philip IV's first wife, Isabel of Bourbon, promised in marriage to Louis XIV of France, whom she married in 1660; and a sister, the Infanta Margarita of Austria, the central subject of *Las Meninas*, like him, child of the king's second marriage, to his niece Mariana of Austria. The birth of the child brought great joy to the king and the nation, which had viewed the lack of a male heir as a bad omen for the Crown, since it presaged an uncertain future for the dynasty and the possible fall of Spain into the hands of foreign monarchs. His arrival was celebrated with parties, religious and secular, plays, bullfights and fireworks, but the hopes placed in the child soon vanished, as he died in 1661 aged four, after anaemia and epileptic fits made his weakness evident. Velázquez painted him here, in 1659, when he was only two, in a type of portrait which is generally reminiscent of the one of his brother, *Prince Baltasar Carlos with a Dwarf* (Boston, Museum of Fine Arts). Doubtless the idea was to make a parallel with that healthy and attractive prince, but Felipe Próspero, son of an uncle and niece, both of whom themselves carried impoverished blood as a result of the many intermarriages of the Hapsburgs for dynastic reasons, showed the degeneration of the family. His brother Carlos, who reigned as Carlos II, was born in November 1661, a few months after his death, and he was to be the last monarch of the Hapsburg dynasty in Spain.

Felipe Próspero, who bore as his first name that of several illustrious ancestors of his family, and that of Próspero as a good omen for his reign, here appears still dressed in his infant clothing: the dress with skirts worn by both boys and girls, in red, a colour appropriate for children, and protected by an apron of fine transparent cloth. On this are numerous protective amulets and the bells and tassels that alerted people to his movements. The prince's surroundings reflect his high lineage: the red drapery on the left, symbol of the king, whose heir he was, as well as the footstool, on which his bonnet rests, like a crown. The child is standing on a rich carpet, which also reflects his royal status, although the portrait must have been painted in winter, when the floors of the Alcázar would still have been covered with carpets. He is resting his right hand on the red velvet chair, in the traditional manner of so many portraits of kings and princes of the sixteenth and seventeenth centuries, from Titian to Sánchez Coello and Pantoja de la Cruz, or Velázquez himself, but in his own way. A small white dog is sitting on it gazing at the spectator. The loyalty and faithfulness symbolised by dogs, which had accompanied his predecessors on the throne, from the emperor Charles V to Philip IV and the Infanta Margarita in *Las Meninas* [CAT. 43], reappears here in the form of this tiny lapdog, to match the age of the prince, and is one of the finest moments of painting by Velázquez, in a portrait *per se* of these pet animals, which became an independent genre in painting in the seventeenth and eighteenth centuries. The austerity of the old Alcázar can again be seen in the background which, with the half-open and well-lit door, is reminiscent of the space in *Las Meninas*, but here, in spite of its undoubted grandeur, it is oppressive, gloomy and melancholic, without the vigour of life and hope expressed in his former masterpiece. [MMM]

7 The Spanish Portrait in the Eighteenth Century

55 Antón Rafael Mengs
[1728–1779]

Self Portrait, 1774
Oil on canvas, 134 x 96 cm
Madrid, Fundación Casa de Alba

PROVENANCE
1817, purchased by Carlos Miguel Fitzjames-Stuart, 14th Duke of Alba, in Florence; in the Alba Collection up to the present time.

ESSENTIAL BIBLIOGRAPHY
Sánchez Cantón 1929a, no. 16: *Antonio Rafael Mengs*, 1980, no. 1, p. 16; *L'art en les col·leccions*, 1987, p. 114; Roettgen 1999, vol. I, no. 282, p. 350.

Mengs painted self-portraits on a fairly regular basis throughout his career, initially, it seems, in response to the demands of patrons and admirers. The inscription on the back of the one now in the Walker Art Gallery in Liverpool gives a good indication of how such commissions came about: 'Portrait of Anton Raphael Mengs painted by himself for George Clavering Nassau, Lord Fordwich and Earl of Cowper at Florence in 1774' (*Ritratto d'Antonio Raffaelo Mengs fatto da lui medesimo per Lord Nassau Conte di Cowper in Firenze l'anno 1774*). In this instance, Mengs depicts himself with the sketch for one of his works on the easel in front of him, probably a preliminary study for his *Perseus and Andromeda*, a painting completed in 1779 for the Hermitage at St Petersburg in Russia (Roettgen 1993, no. 1, p. 46). The unfinished *Self Portrait* in the Prado, painted slightly earlier to judge from the relative smoothness of the virtually unfurrowed cheeks, shows him with his brushes in his right hand. And although the brushes are a clear sign of the artist's profession, there is no specific work in progress to show his quality. In the first catalogue of Mengs's work made by his friend José Nicolás de Azara, there is a reference to his inclination to paint 'less than half-length' self-portraits (Mengs 1780, pp. XLIX–L), and this inevitably suggests that his face was the main object of his study. The public also wanted first and foremost to know what the artist looked like. Certainly the self-portrait given by the artist to Bernardo de Iriarte – who was building up a collection of self-portraits with his brothers – concentrated on his facial features and made no reference at all to his profession. This was the image which subsequently circulated widely in an engraving by Mengs's son-in-law Manuel Salvador Carmona, which is found opposite the title-page in the edition of Mengs's *Obras* published in Madrid in 1780.

Mengs focuses on the more expressive and sensitive elements in his facial features, and on his sharply perceptive gaze, which is fairly standard in self-portraits. He seems to have painted these works quite quickly. In February 1775, according to Frederick Robinson, the brother of the British Ambassador in Madrid, he took only two days to make a self-portrait destined for some unknown patron in Denmark (Bedford County Record Office, Wrest Park Papers, L 30/17/2/105). But we also know, of course, that he could polish off a fairly finished likeness in a mere two hours, as he did in the case of his Swedish friend, Count Franz-Xaver Orsini-Rosenberg, in Rome in 1756 (*Anton Raphael Mengs 1728–1779*, 1993, no. 12, p. 70).

The self-portrait from the Alba Foundation, bought in Florence in 1817, seems a relatively early work by Mengs: larger in scale than the generality of later paintings of this kind, showing him at three-quarter length as opposed to half or bust length, and painted on canvas instead of panel. His figure is lit from the right – the direction in which he is looking – and the light falls on his face, the sensitive and slender fingers of his right hand, and the left-hand side of his body. The housecoat he wears, with its fur edging, his shirt and waistcoat, are all painted with considerable freedom, and no effort has been made to elaborate the chiaroscuro effects in the folds. Despite the fact that the painter is holding a port crayon in his right hand, and curls the fingers of the left over the edge of a large portfolio of prints and drawings – leaning it slightly away from him, as if he were about to open it or lay it down flat –this is not a conventional portrait of the artist at work. The canvas, rather, shows us the artist in contemplative mood, thinking about his subject or imagining the possibilities of a scene, or even working out some synthesis of details taken from Nature, which Mengs believed was the way to idealise reality to turn it into a work of art. As he himself said in his letter to Ponz, 'the subjects which an artist wants to depict must be selected, like those of the poet, from amongst the realities that Nature provides' (Mengs, 1780, p. 203). It seems that Mengs may have set out to record himself following such a selective process. [NG]

56 Luis Meléndez
[1716–1780]

Self Portrait, 1746
Oil on canvas, 98 x 81 cm
Inscription: 'Luis Melendez fac[ieb]a.t año de 1746'
Paris, Musée du Louvre, Bequest of Paul Cosson, 1926, R.F.2537

PROVENANCE
Collection of the Infante don Sebastián Gabriel de Borbón; passing by inheritance to the Duchess of Marchena; in the Paul Mantz sale, 10–11 May 1895, no. 56; left to the Louvre by Paul Cosson in 1926.

ESSENTIAL BIBLIOGRAPHY
Rouches 1927, p. 252; Sánchez Cantón 1929b, pp. 197–98; Tufts 1971, pp. 193–94; *El arte europeo* 1980, no. 37, p. 90; Tufts 1985, no. 1; Gerard Powell and Ressort 2002, pp. 320–22; Cherry 2004, pp. 15–16.

The artist advertises his various skills in this *Self Portrait*, made when he was 30 years old. The drawing he holds up for us to admire provides evidence of his knowledge of both ancient sculpture and life study. It shows that he can depict a man running, and we can deduce from it his potential as a painter of mythological and historical subjects, and dramatic scenes of all kinds. His skill as a portrait painter is also evident. His own face is carefully drawn, and he has chosen to depict different kinds of material in his clothes, in order to display his abilities in that field. His coat seems to be made of some sort of silk and this enables him to emphasise his mastery of folds and the way light illuminates different surfaces. The cloak on which he rests his right hand, gripping a port crayon, appears to be of blue velvet. In painting it, Meléndez shows once more his facility for capturing different materials and colour tonalities, and his skill with the play of light and shadow. The ingeniousness of the painting does not stop there. Meléndez naturally presents a frontal view of himself, but the naked figure in his drawing is shown from the back (no doubt in part for reasons of modesty). The light in the painting as a whole comes from the left, from the spectator's point of view, but the drawing is lit from the right. Meléndez conveys a sense of the moment of time admirably by varying the position of his hands. He holds the drawing with the fingers of his left hand, grouped close together, and carries the port crayon in his right, gripping the instrument with two fingers together and two more spaced apart and extended.

It is a pity that Meléndez's obvious aptitude for painting works in the major genres failed to earn him commissions, perhaps because of his father's expulsion from the Academy in 1747, which led to his own exclusion. His extraordinary inventive powers, however, and his taste for subtle and varied contrasts – plain to be seen in this self-portrait – are abundantly evident in his admirable still-life paintings. [NG]

57 Luis Paret y Alcázar
[1746–1799]

María de las Nieves Micaela Fourdinier, Wife of the Painter, ca. 1780
Oil on copperplate, 37 x 28 cm
Inscribed (in Greek): 'Luis Paret to his beloved wife, wanting to paint her in colours, did so in the year 1.78...'
Madrid, Museo del Prado, P-3250

PROVENANCE
In the collection of Antonio Chicharro Papiri; acquired from this collector in 1975 for the Museo del Prado.

ESSENTIAL BIBLIOGRAPHY
Salas 1978, p. 29; *Luis Paret y Alcázar 1746–1799*, 1991, no. 10, pp. 203–05; Morales Marín 1997, no. 41; Blanco Mozo 1998, pp. 299–316.

Paret's wife, to whom the artist was already married in 1775 when court painter to the Infante don Luis – shortly before Charles III banished Paret to Puerto Rico on suspicion of his being involved in the Infante's sexual adventures – was from Hubersent in north-western France, between Boulogne and Montreuil. Her great uncle, Robert, and her grandfather, Miguel, had settled in Madrid in 1724 and set up in business as upholsterers and furniture manufacturers. They also provided living accommodation and all kinds of furnishings for 'those coming to the capital from outside Madrid and others who needed such things' (Blanco Mozo 1998, p. 301). Their business flourished and the brothers were soon admitted to the upholstery and furnishing department of the Royal Palaces, where Miguel Fourdinier became a supernumerary craftsman on 23 December 1735, and was placed on the permanent staff from 1761. Michaela's mother died in 1767, and subsequently Paret's wife and her brothers and sisters divided the inheritance between them. He father, in the meantime, had taken over the direction of the family firm and was able to provide material help for Michaela and Paret later, when he returned from Puerto Rico.

The materially comfortable background of Michaela and the fact that she had relatives in France who knew about the latest international fashions – probably as easy to acquire in Bilbao, in fact, as in Madrid – explain the elegant clothes that she wears in this portrait, and the refinement of her hairstyling and headwear. Her hair and the graceful bonnet recall the style displayed by Marie Antoinette in the engraving made by François Jurinet three or four years previously, in 1777, or that of the Duchess of Osuna, in the portrait painted by Agustín Esteve around 1780, or shown off by the Marquesa de San Andrés, in another portrait by Esteve. However, the style of Paret's portrait is very different from these, in which luxury is an adjunct of power and status, and there is no indication of the personal interests or private life of the sitters. Paret, in contrast, shows Michaela sitting on an armchair on a balcony or gallery in her house, half way between the domestic world of the interior and that of Nature outside. It looks as if the young lady is teaching a canary to sing, turning the handle of her 'serinette', an instrument designed for that purpose. Another intimate aspect of the portrait is revealed by the painter's viewpoint. We look at her from outside, and from a certain distance, between the pillars supporting the roof of the gallery or balcony. Since she is not returning the observer's gaze, it seems that the artist has surprised her when she was absorbed in her own work. [NG]

58 Luis Paret y Alcázar
[1746–1799]

Self Portrait, 1786
Oil on canvas, 39.8 x 31.8 cm
Inscribed on the side of the plinth with two classical busts on it:
L. PARET
Madrid, Museo del Prado, P-7701

PROVENANCE
Félix Boix's collection; with Apolinar Sánchez, an antique dealer, in Madrid; subsequently in a private collection in the Basque country; given to the Prado Museum.

ESSENTIAL BIBLIOGRAPHY
Delgado 1957, pp. 251–52; *Luis Paret y Alcázar 1746–1799*, 1991, no. 26, pp. 267–69; Calvo Serraller 1996, pp. 13–42; Morales Marín 1997, no. 56.

In the centre of the picture an unfinished oval-shaped canvas stands on the artist's easel, but its subject remains a mystery. It is not a known work by Paret, and this, together with doubts about the characteristics of the artist's face, led scholars at one time to question whether the picture was a self-portrait at all. But the fact that a similar vessel to the one in the painting on the easel (flying the flag of the Port of Bilbao) appears in the portrait of a naval officer by Paret suggests that the artist knew of the loss of a specific ship: the *San Pedro de Alcántara*. So it is likely that this disaster is the subject of the oval painting in the self-portrait, and not impossible that Paret did indeed make – or at least sketch – such a picture, perhaps with a potential commission in mind.

The shipwreck in question took place 'in the natural harbour of Papoa' according to the information available at present, which is near Peniche, to the north-west of Lisbon and west of Obidos, in an area with dangerous rocks on the Portuguese coast (*Luis Paret y Alcázar 1746–1799*, 1991, no. 25, pp. 204–05). Paret no doubt had to document himself about the site and he is known to have made a drawing for a print of the recovery of the sunken vessel. This would explain the presence of a map on the table at the artist's side, which seems to depict Cape Carvoeiro. The general lie of the land and the line of the coast on this map, on which Paret rests his elbow, could certainly be identified with the Papoa peninsular, between Peniche and Remédios, and the adjoining area.

Perhaps the whole painting depicts the evolution of a work of this kind, underlining the combination of research, imagination and intuition needed to bring this kind of shipwreck to life on canvas, representing the terrible end of a vessel that had probably just crossed the Atlantic Ocean. Near the artist, there are antique Greek heads on the floor, books on the table and the floor too, and a portfolio with a single preliminary drawing in red chalk or sanguine wash, at Paret's feet, next to the palette which has temporarily been put on one side. The details emphasise the study and thought that the artist has to bring to the handling of a subject like this, in order to make a work of art out of it. Paret is thinking, or musing, not painting. He apparently draws inspiration as much from epic poetry as from real life and concrete facts, such as those provided by the map. One of the two busts is a blind man and probably Homer, in whose *Odyssey* there are detailed and moving descriptions of storm and shipwreck in Books V and XII. At all events, light falls strongly on the bust that seems to be Homer, and draws attention to the fact that he has lost his sight, while the second bust is in an area of shadow.

So far as clothing is concerned, the artist seems to be richly attired: wearing a red waistcoat and a jacket lined with material of the same colour. This reminds one of the regional dress of the period, or that of *majos* who apparently wore short satin jackets, velvet caps and hairnets. The tactile pleasure of the clothing Paret is wearing – together with the silken handkerchief the artist is touching with his fingers – may have given the artist a feeling of well-being that encouraged creativity, much as the German composer, Richard Wagner, later experienced, when he surrounded himself with silk for inspiration.

This image of the artist is very different from Paret's earlier self-portrait, made when he was in exile in Puerto Rico, dressed as a *gíbaro*, carrying a load of bananas on his shoulders, and a large knife in his left hand to cut the bunches of fruit from the trees. (The term *gíbaro* means hunchback and was presumably applied to those who carried loads on their shoulders.) Paret apparently made the earlier painting with the intention of sending a copy of it to Charles III, to encourage the latter to grant him a pardon. This second self-portrait, made under far less adverse circumstances involving banishment from Madrid, underlines his status as a philosophical painter, erudite and serious, and ready to undertake any kind of artistic commission. [NG]

59 Francisco de Goya y Lucientes
[1747–1828]

Self Portrait while Painting, *ca.* 1799
Oil on canvas, 42 x 28 cm
Madrid, Museo de la Real Academia de Bellas Artes de San Fernando

PROVENANCE
Unknown before entering the collection of the Conde de Villagonzalo some time in the nineteenth century; acquired in 1982 for the San Fernando Academy.

ESSENTIAL BIBLIOGRAPHY
Goya en las colecciones madileñas, 1983, no. 22, p. 156; Gállego 1983, pp. 46–47; Harris 1983, pp. 511–12; Morales Marín 1994, no. 102 (dated 1781–1782), p. 165; *Goya. El capricho y la invención*, 1994, no. 62 (dated 1794–1795 and also 1794–1797), pp. 256–58.

Variety is one of Goya's objectives in his self-portraits as it is in other genres. He presents the right-hand side of his face more particularly in eight works of this kind, and the left-hand side likewise in eight; in another one he faces the front. Usually the light falls more strongly on the side which he has chosen to accentuate, but this is not always the case. When he portrays himself presenting a sketch to Count Floridablanca, for instance [FIG. 106], or painting the family of the Infante don Luis, or that of Charles IV [CATS 45 and 46], he inevitably puts his own face in a zone of shadow so as not to distract attention from the major players in these scenes. Strangely enough, he also puts his face in shadow in the Academy's *Self Portrait while Painting*. He depicts himself against the luminous background of the vast window, so to speak *contre jour*, as photographers call it. And in this case, the result is to increase the mystery of the artist's features and force us to study his face still harder.

There is not only variety in the poses of Goya's self-portraits, but also in the dimensions and objectives of these works. With respect to the major traditions of self-portraiture – the artist at work and the artist as an individual with his own personality and no references at all to his career – there are five self-portraits of Goya as a painter or painting (and three of these are the already mentioned group portraits), and twelve which give no explicit indication that the man portrayed is an artist. So far as dimensions are concerned, nine are more or less life-size (heads, busts or half-length depictions), and eight are small or very small. It seems fairly evident that Goya is increasingly interested in himself as an individual, scrutinising the changing nature of his features, rather than contemplating his career development. He seems to have needed to record his features on a fairly regular basis between 1771 and 1800: thirteen times in all. With the new century, from 1801 onwards, he either made fewer records of his appearance, or fewer of those he made have survived. It seems as if Goya does what many human beings do: look in the mirror less as the years go by, with less concern for the image we project and greater awareness of the reality of decline.

The *Self Portrait while Painting* is a work full of ironies or mysteries. It is a small-scale picture in which the artist is painting a canvas that is much larger than he is: a canvas that could perhaps be *The Family of Charles IV*, for instance, in which Goya's head, curiously enough, appears in a similar pose, and also in shadow, though without a hat. Light falls on the upper part of his right foot, and the back of his left leg sheathed in his trousers: long trousers which are tight fitting and all of a piece, in the style that began to be introduced at the end of the 1780s and during the 1790s in eighteenth-century Europe (*The Pictorial Encyclopaedia of Fashion*, 1958, figs 322 and 353). Goya himself depicts people wearing such trousers in some of his satirical drawings: *Mascaras crueles* and *Humildad contra soberbia*, for instance (Gassier and Wilson, nos 415 and 433). As it happens, the trousers in the first of these are worn with a fairly short jacket, though not as short as that worn by Goya in this self-portrait. Normally, in fact, a fairly long coat was worn with trousers of this type. Goya's hat is not for street wear, of course, but for use in his studio: to improve his ability to see rather than to be seen. Small tubes or candle-holders are fixed round the crown of the hat so that special lighting can be created when he is working. According to Goya's son Javier, the artist wore this when giving the final touches to a painting by artificial light. This is, of course, yet another strange element in this small composition. It is as if the artist needed to display his skill at stimulating the spectator's imagination, with a minimum of light (apart from the window) and colour. Nearly the whole picture is made up of whites, ochres, earth tones, greys and blacks, with only occasionally slightly stronger notes in the dull red touches on the jacket, and the pale blues on some objects on the table, which add to the interest of the picture in the immediate vicinity of the artist's head. All these muted tones make the work the antithesis of Goya's *Family of Charles IV*, with its variety of colours, multitude of gleaming objects, and large dimensions.

The hat with lights on it – lights which Goya did not need for this self-portrait – is emblematic of the artist's inventiveness and his wish to capture chiaroscuro effects to the best of his ability. Apparently there was a distinguished precedent for these special lighting effects in Michelangelo. According to Vasari, the latter used a similar contraption when working with the chisel. He made a helmet out of cardboard, 'fixing an oil-lamp on top in the middle, to light up whatever he was working on', enabling him to work without interruption by leaving both his hands free. In France, one of Goya's contemporaries, Girodet, appears to have used a similar device, and hats with candles on them still had their devotees decades later. Van Gogh is said to have made use of an apparatus of this sort to finish his pictures (Harris 1983, p. 512). [NG]

60 Francisco de Goya y Lucientes [1747–1828]

Sebastián Martínez, 1792
Oil on canvas, 93 x 67.6 cm
Inscribed (on the paper the sitter is holding): *D. Sebastian / Martinez / Por su Amigo / Goya / 1792*
New York, The Metropolitan Museum of Art, Rogers Fund, 1906, 06.289

PROVENANCE
Listed, after Martínez's death, among property inherited by his daughter Catalina, who was married to Francisco Viola (Archivo Provincial de Cádiz, Potocolos de Cayetano Rodríguez Villanueva y Morán, 1805, II. Leg. 5738, f. 1311v). The Conde de Maule claimed that the Violas soon sold their paintings to English purchasers, but no details of such sales are currently known. The portrait was later in the Salcedo collection in Madrid; the Galerie Trotti, Paris; and entered the collection of The Metropolitan Museum of Art, New York, in 1906 with support from the Rogers Foundation.

ESSENTIAL BIBLIOGRAPHY
Cruz Bahamonde 1813, pp. 339 and others; Trapier 1964, pp. 8–9; Pemán 1978, pp. 53–62; Morales Marín 1994, no. 213, pp. 221–22.

The portrait is dated 1792 and must have been painted in Madrid between May and about July of that year. Martínez said he was on the point of leaving Cadiz on 20 April 1792, and he took his leave of Pedro González de Sepúlveda in Madrid on 27 July, presenting him with some tracings of Raphael heads made by Mengs in Rome (Biblioteca Nacional, MS 12628 f. 142v).

Martínez was forty-four years old when Goya painted him. He had been born on 25 November 1747 in Treguajantes, a village near Soto in the province of Logroño, the son of Diego Felipe Martínez and Inés Pérez. His father came from Hornillos, and the family lived there much of the time. But Sebastián moved to Cadiz around 1760 – with his father according to some sources – and in 1771 he was admitted to work in the South American trade with the right to 'trade and sail to our South American Kingdoms'. Three years later he married María Errecarte y Odobraque, and thanks to his wife's family he came to have relatives in the South American trade, and a friend of the family, Juan Bautista de Oxangoiti (a cousin of the writer José Cadalso), who seem to have provided some financial support for Martínez's business. He soon grew rich and began to build up a remarkable collection of paintings and an impressive library: fairly typical signs of prosperity and status amongst merchants in Cadiz. His art gallery was not the largest in the city in the 1780s, when the Inquisition complained of some of the prints and paintings in his possession and commissioned drawings of some of the pictures to make a case against him. But by the early 1790s the quality of the collection was widely known, and Antonio Ponz, a friend of Martínez, gave details of some of more important holdings in his *Viage de Espana* (Ponz 1947, pp. 1587–88). The Conde de Maule provides additional information in notes he wrote at the end of the century, which were eventually published in 1813 (Cruz Bahamonde (1813) 1997, p. 227). The count more particularly praised 'the very good portrait of Martínez painted by Goya' and noted that Don Sebastián also had 'three caprices or overdoors' by the same artist. These last-mentioned works by Goya are usually identified with the fine picture of a girl sleeping (Dublin, National Gallery of Ireland), and two canvases of similar dimensions, *A Girl asleep* (Madrid, private collection), and *Two Young Ladies in Conversation* (Hartford, Connecticut, Wadsworth Atheneum). Each of these is in some sense mildly erotic.

Martínez's aesthetic taste was eclectic. He bought prints, books, paintings and objects relating to classical antiquity: bronze statues of Hercules and Neptune, found in Santiponce, very near Cadiz; Piranesi's *Vedute di Roma* and *Antiquità romane*; *Antigüedades de Hercolaneo* with commentaries; books by Winckelmann, Du Bos, Milizia and Mengs. And his neoclassical inclinations are similarly reflected in his acquisition of paintings by Mengs, and his appetite for pictures of ruins, which were typical of his period. But he was also attracted by the naturalistic style of Velázquez and Murillo, and had many paintings of popular pastimes by artists from the Low Countries and Italy. Moralising scenes from everyday life were not absent from his collection either, and he had among his many prints the 'paintings of Horgat [*sic*] valued at 75 Reales', according to documents dividing his property between his heirs, drawn up in Madrid in 1803 and Cadiz in 1805. These were evidently prints made by William Hogarth, from one of the eighteenth-century editions.

It is also interesting to observe echoes of the new taste for the Sublime in Martínez's collections, in prints of waterfalls, storms, fires, shipwrecks and the death of soldiers in war.

An analysis of the books in his house in Cadiz inventoried after his death in 1800 found 22.9% in the areas of Geography and History, 19.6% in the fine arts and 16.3% in literature (García-Baquero 1988). The novels he owned are also interesting: Swift's *Gulliver's Travels*, Fielding's *Tom Jones* and Richardson's *Clarissa* amongst them. The world of the imagination seems to have attracted him as much as the deductions to be drawn from calculations. Goya would no doubt have looked at his books as well as his prints, drawings and paintings when he was living in Martínez's spacious house in Cadiz in 1793, recovering from the illness that drove him deaf. His collections were undoubtedly exceptional in Cadiz, and as Ceán Bermúdez said, it was unlike those elsewhere in Spain too, 'owing to the money laid out on drawings, rare prints, models and Fine Arts books' (Ceán Bermúdez 1800, vol. I, p. XXI, note 10).

His extraordinary taste is also visible in his clothes. In Goya's portrait of him he wears a striped silk jacket, and there were several silk frock coats and breeches of the same material in the posthumous inventory of his belongings. He seems to be wearing clothes of the latest European fashion, the 'unbelievable' style (*incroyable*) that was all the rage in France. The paper in his hand, blue to match his coat, may be either a letter or a drawing. But presumably Martínez himself, with his refined aesthetic sensibilities, would have encouraged Goya in these colour harmonies. He probably also approved of Goya's use of Velázquez's impressionistic techniques to capture the effect of the silk in his striped jacket, by clever brushwork for the stripes themselves and ingenious use of the background tonality. The world of commerce seems far away from this, and there is, in fact, no reference at all to the sitter's career.

In early 1797, Martínez moved permanently to Madrid to take up his appointment as Treasurer General and Councillor to the King. But he was forced to retire in the middle of 1800 for reasons of serious ill health, and died on 24 November that year. [NG]

61 & 62 Francisco de Goya
[1747–1828]

The Duchess of Alba, 1795
Oil on canvas, 194 x 130 cm
Inscribed (on the ground):
A la Duquesa de Alba
Fr.co de Goya 1795
Madrid, Fundación Casa de Alba

The Duchess of Alba, 1797
Oil on canvas, 210.3 x 149.3 cm
Inscribed and dated: *Solo Goya*
('Only Goya', these words inverted so as to face the Duchess); *1797*
New York, The Hispanic Society of America, A102

PROVENANCE

The 1795 portrait has always belonged to the Dukes of Alba. The 1797 portrait has a more complicated history. The Duchess herself may well have had it in the first instance, and her heirs may have returned it to Goya after her death in 1802. It appears in the 1812 inventory made in the artist's house (with the number X. 14), and becomes the property of Javier Goya at that point. Javier sold it to Baron Taylor for Louis Philippe's collection in 1836. Von Loga (1903) believes that P. Sohège had it in Paris and then Iruereta Goyena in Seville at the end of the nineteenth century. It passed to Archer P. Huntington and then the Hispanic Society via Gimpel & Wildenstein.

ESSENTIAL BIBLIOGRAPHY

For a summary of material on the Alba portrait, see Morales Marín 1994, no. 257, p. 241; Symmons 2002, pp. 49–62. For the Hispanic Society portrait, see Trapier 1964, no. 25, pp. 13–14; Baticle and Marinas 1981, no. 107, pp. 88–89; Morales Marín 1994, no. 263, pp. 243–44.

The first of these two great Goya portraits of the Duchess depicts her at the age of thirty-three. The picture may have been intended as a pair for the portrait of her husband, which has similar dimensions, but the backgrounds are very different: the Duke leaning on his piano in a drawing room; the Duchess, out in the country, perhaps near Sanlúcar in Andalusia, with her dog.

The personality of the Duchess remains hard to define. All the sources – both the factual ones and those inclined to mythologise her – agree about her beauty. She is Venus herself; there is not a hair on her head that fails to arouse desire, everyone stares at her in the street and is impelled to follow her (Ezquerra del Bayo 1959, pp. 154–66). But when attempts are made to define her character, opinions divide. Some feel that she always showed great sensitivity and generosity to friends and also to people of the lower orders; others think she never grew up, and that she was spendthrift, wilful and had little common sense and even fewer morals (cf. March 1961, pp. 153–243). She was an only child and her father died before she was seven; she married when only twelve, and inherited the Alba titles and estates, various palaces and a huge income from her grandfather when fourteen. She was bound to have been spoilt and slightly out of control. And when she was sixteen people already thought that she would come to a bad end (letter from Frederick Robinson to his brother Lord Grantham, 29-X-1778, Bedford County Record Office, L 30/14/333.135).

Because she was wealthy and attractive, people around her were obsessed by her changes of hairstyle, the jewels she wore and her general behaviour. She was 'prettily but fantastically dressed' in December 1778, at a dinner given by her mother, according to the slightly critical but fascinated Lord Grantham, the British Ambassador, who was a guest. Grantham noted in April the following year that there were chains of pearls on her gown between rows of diamonds, and diamond flower patterns in the middle of each link in the chain. In May 1779 she caught the same gentleman's eye riding a horse gypsy fashion, or astride, with her hair combed back and a bunch of ribbons over her left ear (*ibid.*, letters from Lord Grantham of 21-XII-1778 and 2-IV-1779, L 30/15/54/108 and L 30.17/4/245). In March the same year she was going about with the future Duchess of Osuna (then Marquesa de Peñafiel), and both were wearing ribands with Viva Keppel on them, only a month after Admiral Keppel had defended himself honourably, against unjust charges that he had misdirected a naval battle against the French, which had led to popular riots in his support against the Admiralty in London (*ibid.*, letter from Grantham to his brother, 27-III-1779, L 30/15/54.127). A year later the British dramatist and covert diplomat in Madrid Richard Cumberland reported that the Duchess had caused a great scandal by riding postilion on her own coach, while her friend the Marquesa de Torremanzanal took the reins and various male friends dressed in the Alba livery rode at the back as lackeys. (Cumberland 1807, vol. II, pp. 144–45).

The Duchess's dynamism and spontaneity attracted more favourable comment on other occasions. The poet Quintana praised her generosity in adopting a little black girl, on whom she lavished attention. Quintana was also impressed by her concern for the inhabitants of the towns and villages on the Alba estates, under the more or less feudal system that still existed. Various poets and painters enjoyed her protection, and she seems to have been genuinely interested in recent cultural developments. She was, furthermore, surrounded by masterpieces belonging to her family, for instance Velázquez's *Venus and Cupid* (now in The National Gallery, London), a *Reclining Venus*, which counterbalanced the Velázquez, then attributed to Titian; *The School of Love* by Correggio; a series of tapestries based on Raphael cartoons, and some excellent portraits. The Duchess was evidently interested in the arts and drew herself. Lord Grantham reported in March 1779, that a gilder had brought him a magnificent frame for a not very good drawing of a ship the Duchess had given him (*ibid.*, letter from Grantham, 5-III-1779, L 30/15/54/123). She was particularly keen on opera and commissioned copies of music scores of the works she liked (March 1961, p. 216). She subscribed, separately from her husband, to Tomás de Iriarte's *Collected Works* (1787), and – later than Goya – to the Spanish edition, in eleven volumes, of Samuel Richardson's *Clarissa* (1794).

The two full-length, life-size portraits of the Duchess painted by Goya register different aspects of her personality and also reflect changes in her situation. The first of the two was made while her husband was still alive, and the second after his death. It is not surprising that the earlier of the two shows her with a great head of curly hair, since this was the fashion of the period. The initial letters of her own and her husband's surnames are intertwined in a monogram on the broad bracelet on her left arm (ST, standing for Silva/Toledo) and she is smartly attired in a white dress, set off with a band of red silk round her waist and a rich necklace of red coral round her neck. In the second portrait, on the other hand, she is dressed soberly in black, although she wears gold bangles and another red sash of a slightly less lustrous silk. In the first, the dog adds a note of jollity beside the duchess: trotting along, apparently, and matching its mistress with its combination of red and white – red ribbon on one leg and coat of long white hair – a model accessory, painted with marvellous freedom. There is no dog to enliven the second portrait – and perhaps it, too, had died, since Goya started an etching about an ill or injured animal, surrounded by weeping women, at that time. In the Hispanic Society's portrait the background seems more clearly to capture the landscape around Sanlúcar than that of the Alba Foundation. But the imperious arm gesture of the duchess in the latter would go well with the idea of her as an aristocratic estate owner, and the scene is not totally unlike some not very wooded parts near the river at Sanlúcar.

There is less bustle, less jewellery and more tranquillity in the Hispanic Society portrait of the duchess in *maja* dress. It looks as if she has just stopped walking and turns her head to look at the artist (or the spectator). Her attire is no longer the international fashion but a black, Spanish national dress, richly embroidered. She wears no necklace, bracelet or arm band, but has two rings on her fingers, of a kind apparently found in Spain at the time, each bearing a name: Alba and Goya, presumably as a sign of friendship or affection (Muller 1972, p. 177). In this portrait her hand points to the ground, at an inscription reading 'Only Goya', which seems to indicate a closer commitment than mere friendship. The portrait probably must have been painted between November 1796, when the duchess moved to Sanlúcar from Seville with some friends, and April 1797, when Goya returned from Andalusia to Madrid. [NG]

63 Francisco de Goya y Lucientes
[1747–1828]

Don Gaspar Melchor de Jovellanos, 1798
Oil on canvas, 205 x 133 cm
Inscribed: *JoveLlanos / por / Goya*
Madrid, Museo del Prado, P-3236

PROVENANCE
Left by Jovellanos to his friend and financial adviser Arias Saavedra; by family inheritance to Antonio Botija; with Mariano Santamaría in 1877; the Duchess of Torres in 1961; the Viscountess of Irueste subsequently; acquired for the Museo del Prado in 1974.

ESSENTIAL BIBLIOGRAPHY
Helman 1983, pp. 97–140; González Santos 1994; Moreno 1997, pp. 220–22.

Both the portraits of his friend and patron Jovellanos (or Jove Llanos) by Goya contain references to the sitter's Asturian backgound, his concern for the fortunes of his home province, and also his commitment to the economic, social and political development of Spain in the second half of the eighteenth century. The earlier of the two, painted *ca.* 1783 (Oviedo, Museo de Bellas Artes de Asturias), places him squarely in the region of Gijón, where he was born on 5 January 1744, and refers indirectly to the plans to improve port facilities in his home town, envisaging their expansion in the Arenas de San Lorenzo area, which is in the background of the portrait. Jovellanos himself presented these plans to the Municipal Authorities on 30 August 1782. In relation to the sitter's role on the broader Spanish stage, it can be noted that he wears the insignia of the Order of Alcántara, which he had joined in 1780 – a year in which he was also appointed to the Royal Council of Military Orders, and became an academician of the Royal Academies of History and Fine Arts (San Fernando). The fact that the sitter's gaze is not directed towards the viewer, suggests that he is thinking of the future of his province and his country.

If this first portrait emphasised Jovellanos's Asturian background and his involvement in local developments, more than his participation in Spanish reforms and Enlightenment policies, the second reflects a shift in his priorities or change in his destiny. This time he is depicted in his ministerial office in Madrid late in 1797, after his appointment as Secretary of State for Grace and Justice, deeply immersed in his work. He is sitting at his table, with the bundles of official documents and proposals he has to deal with tied up with the regulation pink string, and the image is primarily that of a minister who ponders and analyses the problems he has to solve. Beyond his desk area stands a statue of Minerva, presiding over his labours. She is the goddess of wisdom in the first place, and a suitable guide for any politician's conduct. But she also presided over the arts and crafts, whose development in Spain was a constant preoccupation of Jovellanos and his contemporaries. Recently attention has been drawn to the shield which is part of this sculpted figure, and the coat of arms has been shown to be that of the Royal Asturian Institute, founded in Gijón in 1794, with support from Jovellanos, his family and friends, to encourage technical, scientific and nautical training together with the study of foreign languages, in order to stimulate the economic development of the region. It seems clear that Jovellanos asked Goya to include this detail to show that progress in Asturias – which in any case had official backing in Madrid too – was as important to the politician as national goals and Enlightenment policies.

There is, of course, an aesthetic or artistic image in these portraits. In the first of the two, Goya's stylistic aims (and probably those of Jovellanos also) stemmed jointly from the examples of Mengs and Velázquez. The careful draughtsmanship in the elaboration of the sitter's face and slight idealisation seems Mengsian, while the handling of his jacket, long waistcoat and breeches, the shore and the sea behind him, are painted with much freer brushwork, in Velázquez's manner. The style of the second is more unified and distinctly Velázquez-like in the brushstrokes used for the features of the face and the hair. Fashions in clothing have also moved on. The waistcoat is now short, and the minister has abandoned his wig. He seems to be wearing winter clothing, with velvet breeches, and a heavy coat with ermine trimmings. [NG]

64 Francisco de Goya y Lucientes
[1747–1828]

La Condesa de Chinchón, 1800
Oil on canvas, 226 x 144 cm
Madrid, Museo del Prado, P-7767

PROVENANCE
To descendants of the sitter, down to the present Dukes of Sueca; acquired in 2002 for the Prado.

ESSENTIAL BIBLIOGRAPHY
Pereyra undated; Trapier 1964, pp. 1–3; Jarne 1992, no. 37, p. 104; Artola 2002, pp. 197–211.

Goya painted María Teresa de Borbón y Vallabriga's portrait on several occasions. She was the daughter of the Infante Don Luis and his wife María Teresa de Vallabriga y Stuard, and so a first cousin of Charles IV. He first painted her when she was two years and nine months old, against a landscape background, accompanied by a white dog. Then, the same year, in the group portrait of *The Family of the Infante Don Luis* [CAT. 45]. Later he painted her more than once when she was married to Godoy, the all-powerful royal favourite. Her life was far from easy. She was born on 26 November 1780 and her father died in 1785. At that time, when she was not yet five, she was separated from her mother and moved from the comfortable and cultured environment in which she passed her early years to the harsh austerity of a convent in Toledo. Twelve years later, however, she left this isolated existence to marry Godoy and become Princess of the Peace and Duchess of Alcudia. And this brought her back to the court from which Charles III had banished her father, with the possibility that she might restore her family's fortunes. Despite the fact that she is usually called the Countess of Chinchón in relation to the portrait, she did not have that title when it was painted, and probably did not obtain it until her brother died in 1823. The subject of the portrait should properly be called in Spanish 'La princesa de la Paz y duquesa de Alcudia'.

When María Teresa married she probably did not realise that her all powerful husband would continue his relationships with other women, and more particularly with his great love, Josefa Tudó, nor that she would have to suffer the embarrassment caused by the public nature of his affair. But at least she shared with Godoy a fondness for the arts, and could once more live in a palace that was full of paintings and fine furniture. Her father had formed an extensive collection of prints and paintings: works of the great artists of the past – Spanish, Italian and Flemish – and of promising contemporaries also, such as Maella, Francisco Bayeu, Joaquín Inza and the Italian Francesco Sasso. Amongst the younger Spanish artists the Infante had put Paret and Gregorio Fierro on his payroll, and commissioned important work from Goya. The Infante had also been keen on architecture and was interested in the decorative style and furnishings of his residences. Godoy was equally passionate about such things, and, like the Infante, he commissioned major paintings from Goya. But, unlike the Infante, he did this when Goya was already the leading court painter rather than at the start of his career.

Godoy naturally assumed that his marriage to a Bourbon would bring new opportunities to extend his power and fortunes, once María Teresa was fully accepted at court. No doubt he was anxious to start a new branch of the Bourbon family, and his correspondence with Charles IV and María Luisa reveals that his wife was three months pregnant in September 1799. She had apparently had an earlier miscarriage, according to a letter from the Queen dated 24 March 1800, and had the misfortune to lose this second child too. But by the time the letter just mentioned was written María Teresa was pregnant again, and she finally gave birth safely to her daughter, Carlota, on 7 October 1800.

Goya was asked to paint the present portrait of María Teresa in April 1800 when she was just twenty-one. This was to be an image of her looking hopefully to the future, presumably, since she was still in the early stages of pregnancy and had yet to be received at court. Goya was to paint her again later the same year, standing rather than sitting, wearing the sash of the Order of Noble Ladies of María Luisa, with a different hairstyle, looking more beautiful, and wearing a rich bracelet designed by the Queen's jeweller for presentation to ladies-in-waiting when they had their first child (Florence, Uffizi). This second portrait must have been painted in the middle of December 1800. The sitter had been awarded the Queen's Order on 10 October, and was due to be received formally by Charles IV and María Luisa early in December. A portrait made at that stage would celebrate these developments, and the self-confident expression in María Teresa's eyes showed that she now felt more secure about the future.

It is instructive to contrast these two portraits. The first of the two makes María Teresa look slightly apprehensive and insecure, no doubt because she has failed to bring two earlier pregnancies to term. She does not look directly at us, and her blue eyes seem to reflect her timidity. The ring on her finger contains a miniature portrait of a person wearing the Order of Charles III, presumably Godoy. Imitation ears of corn which she wears at the front of her bonnet, on the top of her head, may be a fertility symbol associated with her desire to have children. The later portrait depicts a much more self-assured princess, who looks straight at us, shows off the sash of the Order of María Luisa, which is a sign of her acceptance at court, together with other members of her family. This last prize, which may have seemed difficult to achieve earlier in the year, to judge from the first portrait, is clearly already hers in the second. [NG]

65 Francisco de Goya y Lucientes
[1747–1828]

Self Portrait, ca. 1816
Oil on canvas, 40 x 32 cm
Inscribed (not in Goya's hand):
Fr.co Goya / Aragones / por si mismo
Madrid, Museo del Prado, P-723

PROVENANCE

In 1849 in the hands of Goya's son Javier, in whose house it was apparently seen that year; acquired from the latter by Román de la Huerta; purchased by Royal Order of 5 April 1866 from Huerta for the Trinity Museum in Madrid, transferred to the storage deposits of the Prado Museum in 1872.

ESSENTIAL BIBLIOGRAPHY

Yriarte 1867, p. 133; Beruete 1916, p. 168, no. 6; Gassier and Wilson 1974, no. 1552; Gállego 1978, p. 16; Camón Aznar 1980–1982, vol. IV, p. 34; Moreno 1977, pp. 296–98.

The Prado's self-portrait dates from a period of greater personal insecurity in Goya's life. Both his self-portrait on panel of the San Fernando Academy, signed and dated in 1815 and the one under discussion seem to reflect the harsh circumstances the painter had to endure during the oppressive period of absolute rule by Ferdinand VII after the Peninsular War (or War of Independence as the Spanish call it). The face of the artist in the Academy painting has a resolute and still energetic look, and his gaze is still piercing, despite his age, the furrows on his brow and his thinning hair. In the Prado self-portrait, on the other hand, while his expression still carries resolve, his eyes have a slightly more apprehensive look about them, and the pout of his mouth is more resentful. In the Prado version, the artist's head does not seem to lean towards us so much as it does in the 1815 Academy picture, which slopes more to the left. But the Prado picture is, nevertheless, extremely powerful and has more tragic overtones. The fact that it is painted on canvas rather than panel is an advantage from the spectator's point of view. Canvas allows the artist to achieve subtler effects and less abrupt tonal transitions. Goya's brushwork seems bolder on canvas.

The painting seems to have been in Javier Goya's house at the Calle de las Aguas, 9, in 1849. William Stirling-Maxwell, the Scottish scholar, distinguished historian of Spanish art and collector, saw it there at that period, noting that Goya's son had two self-portraits by his father. The better of the two was life-size and full face, painted when the artist was seventy, according to his notes (Brigstocke 1999, p. 13). The only other autograph self-portrait painted by Goya at that age was the one dated 1815 which was already in the Academy when Stirling paid Javier Goya a visit, since it had entered the collection of that institution in 1829.

Over the years there has been some doubt about the authenticity of this painting, but it is universally accepted at the present time, and is often preferred to the 1815 Academy *Self Portrait* as a compelling image of the aging artist. [NG]

66 Francisco de Goya y Lucientes
[1747–1828]

Self Portrait with Doctor Arrieta, 1820
Oil on canvas, 115 x 79 cm
Inscribed: *Goya agradecido à su amigo Arrieta, por el acierto y esmero con q.ᵉ le salvó la vida en su aguda / y peligrosa enfermedad, padecida à fines del año 1819, a los setenta y tres de su edad. Lo pintó en 1820*
('Goya out of gratitude to his friend Arrieta for the skill and care with which he saved his life on the occasion of his acute and dangerous illness late in 1819, at the age of 73. He painted it in 1820')
Minneapolis Institute of Arts, the Ethel Morrison van Derlip Fund, 5214

PROVENANCE
Collection of Eduardo García Arrieta; Martínez; Ajuria Temple, Paris; E. Lucas-Moreno, Paris; Seligman, New York; Koedler & Co., New York; 1953, Minneapolis Institute of Art.

ESSENTIAL BIBLIOGRAPHY
Royo Villanova 1917, vol IV, pp. 969–92; *Goya*, 1928, pp. 91–92, unnumbered entry by Enrique Lafuente Ferrari; Trapier 1964, pp. 42–43; Ciofalo 2001, pp. 101–10.

Goya's self-portrait with his doctor friend Arrieta, and three neighbours or helpers, is in some ways a history painting: a genre much in vogue in Europe in the eighteenth century. The artist has had to select a critical moment in the episode depicted, using the poses and gestures of both primary and secondary characters to explain the nature and significance of the crisis. In this kind of picture, people play moral and emotional roles. But in this case Goya takes a present-day situation and centres it on his own experience. In part the picture documents in graphic terms a health crisis the artist went through in old age. And from this point of view the painting seems closer to what would later be called a genre painting in Spain, rather than an historical picture: a scene from everyday life. But this kind of painting was not common in Spain in Goya's day, and develops more clearly after 1830. In reality there was no obvious genre into which Goya could fit his personal experience. Twenty-six years earlier, when recovering from the serious illness he had in late 1792 and early 1793, it had not occurred to Goya to depict the reality of his own life. He had rather sought out typical subjects of disaster and tragedy into which he could channel his own fears and anxieties. It seems likely that, in so doing, he was inspired by new genres introduced into the Spanish theatre at that time, and he may, more especially, have been interested in the sentimental comedy or *comédie larmoyante*, a style of play which his friend and patron Jovellanos had recently exploited in *El delincuente honrado* ('The honourable delinquent'). The point of the new genre was to show the middle and lower classes in tragic or conflictive situations, which neoclassic norms had previously restricted to princes and kings in the theatre. Goya certainly puts middle and lower class individuals in critical situations in the series of small paintings on tinplate he painted after his illness in 1793 and 1794. He depicted imaginary events with tragic overtones in *The Fire at Night*, *The Shipwreck* and *The Picador gored by the Bull*. In these pictures Goya wants to disturb and move us. People in one or other of these scenes help one another, pray or make gestures of despair, and die. Later Goya followed a similar line when depicting real life tragedies (or ones that are definitely historical rather than imaginary), involving ordinary people in his *Disasters of War* etchings, and the great scenes of the 2nd and 3rd of May 1808. In these last cases ordinary people not only suffer and die but overcome their enemies and act heroically.

The *Self Portrait with Doctor Arrieta* cannot be fitted directly into this series of paintings and etchings, which are *comédies larmoyantes* transferred to tinplate, canvas or paper. The work is too personal, taking a step in the direction of self-confession and revelation in art, which is more characteristic of Romanticism. But the presence of assistants or visitors adds an unusual and not obviously personal note to the picture. Goya does not give us an egocentric view of his crisis. Arrieta is as important as Goya himself, of course, and they are friends. Yet Goya does not isolate them from the world around them. The subsidiary figures help to generalise the idea of suffering and the need for succour. The weakness of Goya – breathing with difficulty and fingering restlessly the sheet or blanket which is wrapped around him –is contrasted with the persistent and successful efforts of Arrieta, who helps the sick man to sit up and drink the water or medicine he raises to his lips. The secondary figures add further contrasts. A woman on the left seems to be offering to help, and a relative or neighbour on the right expresses concern.

Does the painting have a moral, or is it simply concerned with the facts of Goya's crisis and the emotions they raise? It is not easy to say. The only positive information we have about the reality of Goya's illness has to be deduced from the fact that he was recommended to take the waters at Plombières in France, which were usually prescribed for cases of rheumatism or paralysis, and a summary of Arrieta's diagnosis apparently based on the notes the doctor took at the time. According to the latter, the 1819 episode was not a recurrence of the 'Madrid colic' of 1792–1793: food poisoning caused by food or drink contaminated with lead or some other dangerous metal. It was rather some kind of typhoid infection. Fevers of the latter kind were common in periods of war and famine, and were difficult to eliminate. It would not be surprising if such a fever continued to cause trouble in Madrid for several years after the acute famine of 1812 and the War of Independence. The fever symptoms alone were treatable in Goya's time: bringing down the temperature of the patient and administering tranquillisers to reduce pain. But the painting cannot be explained by such details, regardless of whether they are accurate and relevant or not. [NG]

67 Francisco de Goya y Lucientes
[1747–1828]

Juan de Muguiro, 1827
Oil on canvas, 103 x 85 cm
Inscribed: *D.ⁿ Juan de Muguiro, por / su amigo Goya, á los / 81. años, en / Burdeos / Mayo de 1827*
Madrid, Museo del Prado, P-2898

PROVENANCE
From the sitter to the descendants of his youngest brother, Simón Muguiro; left to the Museo del Prado in 1946.

ESSENTIAL BIBLIOGRAPHY
Morales Marín 1994, no. 524, pp. 359–60; Moreno 1997, no. 123. On the sitter Núñez de Arenas 1963, pp. 226–27; Fauqué y Villanueva Etcheverría 1982, pp. 96, 98, 118, 164 and 166; Alberdi (undated).

Goya describes himself in the inscription on the table as a friend of the sitter, as he does in some eleven portraits in his career. The friendship in this instance was the result of the artist's connections with his daughter-in-law's family. When Javier Goya married Gumersinda Goicoechea, his father came into contact with an important group of bankers and businessmen in Madrid. The younger brother of the sitter, José Francisco de Muguiro, had married one of Gumersinda's younger sisters, Manuela, thus joining together the interests of the Muguiro and Iribarren families with those of the Galarzas and the Goicoecheas.

Spanish bankers at the end of the eighteenth century and the beginning of the nineteenth followed principles of commercial endogamy, not dissimilar to those of aristocratic endogamy, when arranging marriages for their heirs and descendants. The Galarzas were particularly powerful (Gumersinda's mother was one of this clan), and they also had connections with another branch of the Goicoechea family in Zaragoza, with which Goya had earlier had contacts. León de Galarza, who was involved with various Goicoecheas in the firm of Galarza and Goicoechea, specialising in ironmongery and allied products, with a shop in the Bajada de Santa Cruz in Madrid, was also on the board of the Bank of St Charles – forerunner of the Bank of Spain – in 1799 and 1800, and again in 1803 and 1804, subsequently becoming a managing director in 1805 and 1807 (Tedde 1988, pp. 290–92). An uncle of the Muguiro brothers, Juan Bautista Iribarren, was also a prosperous banker. He was one of the early shareholders of the Bank of St Charles; was on the board in 1794 and again in 1796–1797; and became managing director in 1794 and again from 1798 to 1803 (*ibid.*).

Juan de Muguiro and his brother José Francisco – both born in Aldaz in the Larrón valley in Navarra – joined their Iribarren uncle in a firm called Iribarren and Nephews (Juan Bautista Iribarren y sobrinos). Their firm had commercial contacts with French businessmen in 1805 (Madrid, Archivo Histórico de Protocolos, Po. 22863, ff 508, 1267 and 1270). These foreign connections no doubt proved useful when the brothers moved to France during the early years of the second phase of Absolutist rule under Ferdinand VII, after the brief period of constitutional government from 1820 to 1823. In Bordeaux, Juan de Muguiro stayed at the same hotel as the Goicoechea family, called Les Quatre Parties du Monde (The Four Corners of the Earth), and it is likely that Goya's contacts with them would have become closer at this period, a few years before the portrait was painted (Fauqué and Villanueva Etcheverría 1982, pp. 96, 98, etc.).

In spite of their friendship, Goya's portrait of Juan de Muguiro is fairly formal. The sitter is not depicted relaxing or pursuing some pastime or other, but as a businessman at work, reading a letter in a chair next to his desk, with paper and inkstand to hand for his rapid response. He wears a dark suit with a frock coat that seems fairly short, waistcoat, and fashionable long trousers. His gaze is a little cold, the lines of his mouth somewhat hard, and it seems unlikely that he smiled often. On the other hand his broad forehead signals considerable intellectual and mental powers, and his short fingers, all much the same length, are doubtless a sign of practical gifts and administrative ability. Two light brushstrokes indicate the presence of hair above his upper lip and old photographs of the painting raise the possibility that the portrait might once have shown him with a moustache (Von Loga 1903, p. 84 of the illustrations). A moustache might have suited him in fact, and would certainly have been quite fashionable at the period. But it is not at present possible to determine whether the brushstrokes in question were once darker and more substantial than they are now.

So far as the brushwork of the portrait in general is concerned, 'the style and freedom with which the whole is painted' is admirable, as Ceán Bermúdez declared of a portrait Goya painted some seven years earlier (Madrid, Biblioteca Nacional, MSS 21458/1, p. 113). There might be some doubt, at first sight, as to whether such a formal and straight-laced businessman as Muguiro would have approved of such freedom in the brushstrokes and so much spontaneity. But these may well have appealed to him, and there can be no doubt that Juan de Muguiro admired the artist's work. He is known to have intended to purchase *The Milkmaid of Bordeaux* (Madrid, Museo del Prado), which is equally bold in its brushwork, from Leocadia Weiss (who lived with her children, together with Goya, in Bordeaux) after the artist's death, and he did, indeed, acquire it. His heirs also inherited from him two of the miniatures on ivory which Goya painted in Bordeaux, more in the style of Velázquez than Mengs, as the artist himself said, and with a highly original mixture of satire and comedy in their approach to scenes of everyday life. In the inventory drawn up after Muguiro's death in Madrid in 1846, at the age of sixty-two, two other paintings by Goya are listed: a portrait of a lady which cannot be identified, and a Masked Ball or 'Dancers wearing Masks' (Glendinning 1994, p. 110). The inventory also included 'A small picture on white paper depicting Goya ill in bed, with a golden frame', which may in fact be F. de la Torre's lithograph of Goya on his deathbed, or a preliminary drawing, which Goya's son gave to his father's friends.

How old was Don Juan when Goya painted his portrait? The answer is probably forty-three, although some French sources of information suggest he may have been younger. Unfortunately the documents in question are not wholly reliable, and some conclusions, and some inferences drawn from other sources seem untrustworthy. The sitter has been referred to constantly, for example, as Juan Bautista Muguiro rather than plain Juan, in publications from the late nineteenth century to the present. Yet the evidence suggests that the Muguiro in the portrait was named after the Evangelist rather than the Baptist, unlike his uncle. After the period in Bordeaux, he continued as a banker in Madrid, and he was one of a group of influential businessmen who backed the Bank of San Fernando when it was set up to replace the Bank of St Charles in 1929 (Tedde 1999, p. 69). Subsequently he was a member of the Spanish parliament (Cortes); Vice-President of that body from 1836 to 1837, and Senator for Madrid from 1837 to 1845. [NG]

68 Vicente López Portaña

[1772–1850]

Félix Antonio Máximo López, 1820
Oil on canvas, 101 x 75 cm
Inscribed (on the piano case, above the keyboard): *A D. Felix Maximo Lopez / primer Organista de la R.l Capilla de S.M.C y en loor de su / elevado mérito y noble profesion, el amor filial* ('Dedicated by his loving children to D. Felix Maximo Lopez, senior organist of His Majesty's Royal Chapel, to praise his high merit and noble profession')
Madrid, Museo del Prado, P-4405

PROVENANCE

Madrid, collection of Don Pedro Bosch; purchased from this owner by Royal Order of 29 June 1879 for the Prado Museum.

ESSENTIAL BIBLIOGRAPHY

Puente 1985, no. 4405, pp. 131–32 (with errors in the date of birth of the sitter and one of his appointments); Morales Marín 1980, no. 81, p. 78; Díez 1999, vol. II, no. P-624, pp. 154–55.

The sitter was a notable organist and composer, born in 1742, who rose to become senior organist of the Chapel Royal in 1785, at the age of forty-three. He continued in this post under Joseph Bonaparte, and underwent the process of political purification after the Peninsular War, when the tribunal found in his favour and confirmed him in his post. A label fixed to the back of the painting confirms its date and explains that the composer's eldest son, Ambrosio López, paid for it to be painted. As the inscription in the portrait (ingeniously placed above the keyboard, where the plate with the maker's name is usually found) shows, the portrait is an expression of filial affection. In part, the portrait is formal in character, underlining the high rank of the sitter by portraying him in his red and blue palace uniform, with two stripes around the cuffs of his frock coat to indicate his rank in the hierarchy of palace appointments. The slightly dishevelled appearance of the uniform and the expression on the face of the elderly organist – he was seventy-eight when the portrait was painted – suggest that there is no room for idealisation in the artist's handling of his subject. But the way the sitter is lit within the painting is, unlike the majority of Vicente López's portraits, from above rather than directly in front. It falls on the broad forehead of Don Félix, the bent fingers of his left hand and the score he holds in his right, which seems to introduce a spiritual quality into the painting, and potentially hints at divine inspiration for his work as instrumentalist and composer. The stick that rests on his right arm is hardly a walking stick. It seems more like the implement used by directors of choirs and orchestras to keep time when conducting: banging the stick on the floor to give the beat, as was often the practice in the eighteenth century before the baton was introduced.

It is useful to compare this portrait with those of musicians – professional or amateur – painted by Goya. So far as the musical notation is concerned, López draws the details of the score which the sitter holds in his right hand with far greater detail and precision than Goya in his portrait of *The Duchess of Abrantes* (Madrid, Museo del Prado). In that painting the music is nearly legible, but it is impossible to transcribe it convincingly without guessing some of the notes and altering others to make them sound right. Even further from the neatness of Vicente López is the score, half in shadow, in the background of the outstanding portrait by Goya of his grandson Marianito, conducting an imaginary band of musicians (Madrid, collection of the Duke of Alburquerque). Goya gives us more than enough detail to identify the kind of classical piece that has to be played either *allegro* or *presto*: highly appropriate music for capturing the energetic musical dreams of the young man. But this is not a specific score so much as a sketchy indication of the rapid type of classical music that might have excited a young man in Goya's time. The style of music is recognisable but the specific notes (which are absent in any case) are untranscribable. Vicente López, on the other hand, appears to copy very carefully the opening nine bars of the score the sitter is holding, which seems to bear the title 'Obra de los locos / Primera parte / All[egr]o Moderato' (Work of madmen / First Part / Allegro Moderato). Of course, this could only be read by those able to understand texts written upside down, or who recognised the music – if it was indeed real – in López's time, before the invention of the photograph. However, in fact it is not altogether clear that the transcription is genuine. It may be an illusionistic score rather than a real one in part. Anyone with a rudimentary knowledge of music and period clefs can see that the piece is in the key of B major or G minor, and the first few bars are easy to play and make sense. But the four that follow are strange musically and not wholly legible. They are not likely to sound convincing. There is a similar problem with the depiction of the keyboard. A normal square piano in López's time would start with an F at the bottom, and not with a note apparently cut in half so that the keyboard can fit neatly into the case of the piano. It looks as if the artist was above all obsessed with the inscription and the symmetrical arrangement of the central part of the keyboard beneath it, so that the symmetry of the centre has probably led to the discrepancy at the bottom.

There are illusionistic elements in the depiction of the organist too. The embroidery on the uniform is notably impressionistic. The brushstrokes that create the embroidery on the waistcoat, running down from Don Máximo's cravat through the central part of his body, and following first his hollow chest and then his protruding stomach, are ingeniously done and capture the effect of the leaf pattern without any precise drawing at all, in the Velázquez manner. In reality there is far more drawing in the details of the piano and the features of the face and hands. There is an almost sadistic realism about the slightly twisted mouth and the furrows on the composer's cheeks. But the expressive eyes and penetrating gaze of the sitter, and the sensitive curve of his fingers, capture a power of concentration and control that seems not to have diminished with age.

Ceán Bermúdez, in some critical comments on two portraits by Vicente López that were exhibited at the San Fernando Academy in 1821, very close in date to the portrait of Máximo López, states that 'the likeness of the two portraits [to the sitters] is captured so precisely and so emphatically that they seem alive'. But Ceán finds their realism excessive and feels that insufficient attention has been given to the character and personality of the individuals portrayed (Madrid, Biblioteca Nacional MSS 21458/1, pp. 113–14). It is difficult to guess, and impossible to know, whether Ceán would have judged the undoubted power of the present portrait in a similar fashion. [NG]

8 The Spanish Portrait in the Nineteenth Century
THE TRIUMPH OF A GENRE

69 Vicente López
[1772–1850]

The Condesa Viuda de Calderón, 1846
Oil on canvas, 128 x 98 cm
Inscribed bottom right (on arm of sofa): *Vic.[te] Lopez F.[t] 1846*
and on the reverse: *Exma. S.[a] D.[a] Francisca de la Gándara Condesa de Calderón / pintado por D. Vicente López en 1846* ('Her Excellency Doña Francisca de la Gándara, Condesa de Calderón / painted by Don Vicente López in 1846')
Madrid, Museo del Prado, P-7041

PROVENANCE
Painted for the sitter; 1855, Valencia, Conde de Calderón; 27 February 1985, Sotheby's, Madrid; 3 June 1985, purchased by the State for the Museo del Prado.

ESSENTIAL BIBLIOGRAPHY
Díez 1999, v. I, p. 367 and v. II, p. 142, P-540.

Maria Francisca de la Gándara y Cardona was born in San Luis de Potosí, Nueva España (now Mexico), on 29 January 1786. There, in 1807, she married General Félix María Calleja del Rey (Medina del Campo, 1750–Valencia, 1828), brigadier and commander-in-chief of the army in Nueva España at the time of the rebellion. Years later, in 1818, in recognition of his victory at the Battle of Puente de Calderón, he was awarded the title of Conde de Calderón and promoted to Field Marshal. He held the post of Viceroy of Mexico from 1813 to 1816, and his wife was thus the last Vicereine of Nueva España to live in the palace in Mexico. In 1814 he was appointed Lieutenant General, and five years later was made Captain-General of Andalusia. His wife died in Valencia on 23 June 1855, during the cholera epidemic that ravaged the city.

From her seat, the Condesa regards the spectator with a lively expression. In her right hand she holds a breviary, the page marked as though she plans to resume her reading. She holds a lace handkerchief in her left hand. The painter had made use, in earlier portraits, of these devices for keeping the hands occupied; here, however, the foreshortening of the book conveys an immediacy intended to convince the spectator of the lady's pious habits.

The figure is somewhat monumental, an effect heightened by the rounded volumes of the wide, green velvet sofa. Hanging on the far wall, against the gold and burgundy floral design of the wallpaper, there is an illuminated engraving of Raphael's *The Madonna of the Chair*, a work that López himself had copied in oils, probably from a print, around 1826–1830 (Díez 1999, p. 101); perhaps, as Díez suggests, it was the print made by Manuel Salvador Carmona from a drawing by Ana María Mengs.

Despite the frontal position of the figure and the symmetrical arrangement of her arms, both of which stress her immobility, Vicente López manages to convey a certain sense of movement through the undulating stripes of her housecoat and the position of her hands. At the same time, the curved back of the sofa and the curving lines of her forehead breathe some life into the composition. The artist's workmanship is evident in his detailed treatment of the Spanish-lace head-covering; he subtly conveys the varying shades of white in the handkerchief and captures perfectly the shimmering effect of the watered silk.

The Condesa's expression is open and alert, yet also serene; she wears a housecoat and no jewellery at all except for a gold ring. All of this combines to provide an intimate, truthful view of the sitter, who had by then been a widow for eighteen years. In this late work, Vicente López clearly remains faithful to his own style, although one may still discern the influence of the new Romantic ideas introduced by younger artists, which he had also encountered on a trip to Paris in 1844, two years before this portrait was painted. [JB]

70 Federico de Madrazo
[1815–1894]

The Condesa de Vilches, 1853
Oil on canvas, 126 x 89 cm
Inscribed (bottom left, on edge of armchair): F. DE MADRAZO 1853
Madrid, Museo del Prado, P-2878

PROVENANCE
Painted for the Condesa de Vilches; 1874, second Conde de Vilches; 1892, bequeathed to the Museo del Prado, with the Conde de la Cimera retaining lifetime ownership; 1944, entered the Museo del Prado.

ESSENTIAL BIBLIOGRAPHY
Planche 1855, pp. 149–52; Bonnat 1856; Ezquerra-Pérez Bueno 1924, p. 189; Lafuente Ferrari 1946, p. 376; Puente 1985, p. 165; Reyero 1993, pp. 53 and 55; Díez (ed.) 1994b, no. 41, pp. 240 and 242.

In 1839 Amalia Llano Dotres (Barcelona, 1821–Madrid, 1874) married Gonzalo José de Vilches y Parga (1808–1879), on whom the title of Conde de Vilches had been conferred in 1848. Beautiful, witty and charming, a good conversationalist and an excellent horsewoman, she was a very popular figure in the social life of Madrid. She organised a theatre at her home, performing plays, sometimes translated from the French, in which she took the leading role. Two of her novels were published: the first, *Ledia*, in the fortnightly Madrid *Revista de España*, and the second, *Berta*, in the year of her death. After she died, several writers, led by Antonio Fernández Grilo, composed a collection of poems dedicated to her. The verses in her memory by Antonio Cánovas del Castillo were published in *La Ilustración Española y Americana* on 8 July 1879. Closely linked to Isabel II, the Condesa supported the restoration and her home was a meeting place for monarchists.

As the sitter was part of the painter's circle of friends, he charged 4,000 *reales* for the portrait, exactly half his usual fee. The Condesa attended gatherings held at the painter's home, where she sometimes played the piano and sang. According to the artist's diaries (Díez, p. 240), she also modelled for other portraits, such as that of her sister Matilde.

Madrazo portrayed her in the fashion of the Second Empire, wearing a very full blue satin dress with flounces, arranged in an oval in the lower part of the composition and elegantly surrounding the figure. The artist skilfully depicted the numerous folds, highlighted by the satin sheen, painting them with confident brushstrokes in the direction of the zigzag skirt edge, in the style of 1853. The rich cashmere shawl, embroidered in gold and silver and edged in gold with a glacé silk lining, is draped across the broad arm of the upholstered chair.

The generous low-cut neckline reveals the Condesa's beautiful shoulders, delicately modelled by the painter and highlighted with a subtle use of chiaroscuro. In addition to her ring, she wears only two bracelets – one of gold, the other of gold with precious stones. This discreet jewellery, a sign of great elegance at the time, emphasises the beauty of her shapely and carefully drawn arms. Through the use of light and drawing, the smooth bulk of the figure and the shiny surfaces of the jewels, the golden nails, the wood and the materials stand out from a barely defined background of semi-darkness. The hair, parted in the middle and covering the ears, and with plaits forming a diadem, accentuates the graceful oval face. The expression is charming, with its soft gaze and lips slightly parted in the hint of a smile.

The painter has attempted to portray the woman's elegance as well as her beauty, and this is evident in the positioning of the hands. The left is carelessly holding a feather fan, and the ring and little fingers of the right hand are touching her face. This pose is reminiscent of several female portraits by Ingres in which, however, the face generally rests upon the index finger, making the attitude used here by Madrazo more suitable for showing the seductive elegance of his model. Claude-Marie Dubufe, a painter with whom Madrazo was compared by French critics when he showed this work, along with thirteen others, at the Universal Exhibition in Paris in 1855, frequently used similar poses in his female portraits.

Madrazo's contributions to the exhibition were harshly attacked by Gustave Planche, in an article that led to a defamation suit whereby the critic was ordered to pay a 500-franc fine. Planche wrote of this portrait that the subject was badly posed, making it impossible to make out the shape of the right knee. Other authors, such as Théophile Gautier, appreciated the work, while About pointed out: 'This painting will be accused of being clean and smooth like an old medal after being rubbed to a shine' (Reyero, p. 53). Most of the French critics considered the portraits as a whole, stating that the artist had been more influenced by the French than the Spanish tradition.

The following year, Madrazo sent the work (under the title *Retrato de la Excma. Sra. condesa de V.*) along with five others to the 1856 Exposición Nacional de Bellas Artes. The fact that Madrazo was both an exhibitor and a jury member provoked strong criticism, particularly where the placing of the works was concerned. The coverage given to Planche's article resulted in fierce attacks on the artist from several other critics, such as Manuel Murguía. Others, including Manuel Cañete, defended him. One of those who adopted a more neutral position was Agustín Bonnat, who, in response to objections that it was impossible to distinguish the anatomy in the portrait, pointed out that the painter had depicted the gown as it was. It was simply for reasons of fashion that it hid the shape of the body. However, he did criticise the work for showing 'too much of a tendency towards prettiness, and it is well known that pretty is not beautiful...the pose is contrived; the colour unnatural, too much impasto, and one might even point out the incorrect drawing of the hands and arms.'

The work certainly sought to achieve elegance, but both the colouring and the model's peculiar pose were quite unusual for Spanish portraiture at the time, and such refinement must have been surprising. As with Ingres's portraits, the painting was drawn with great precision. The oval-shaped pattern is repeated in the face, the fan, the large, horizontally deployed skirt and the chair back, which forms a vertical frame for the figure. The oval is carried over into the format of the composition through the feigned triangular corners. There are echoes of Velázquez in the suggestion of depth of the room, where an octagonal mirror can be glimpsed on the rear wall. This portrait's balanced composition, elegant drawing and skilful use of thin paint for the soft flesh, its bright foreground illumination and misty background, make it Madrazo's masterpiece. [JB]

71 Federico de Madrazo

[1815–1894]

Carlos Luis de Ribera, 1839
Oil on canvas, 97 x 72.5 cm
Signed (bottom right):
F. de Madrazo / Paris 1839
and inscribed (top left):
CARLOS LUIS DE RIBERA
Madrid, Museo del Prado, P-7799

PROVENANCE

Juan Antonio de Ribera (the sitter's father); private collection, Madrid; 6 May 2002, acquired by the state for the Museo del Prado.

ESSENTIAL BIBLIOGRAPHY

F. de Madrazo (1838–1839) 1994; J. de Madrazo (1839, 1841) 1998, pp. 376 and 449; González López 1981, pp. 143–44, no. 51; Díez 2003, p. 68.

Carlos Luis de Ribera y Fievée (Rome, 1815–Madrid, 1891), the eldest child of the Neoclassical painter Juan Antonio de Ribera, trained in Madrid with his father and at the Academia de San Fernando, which named him an academician of merit in 1835. He collaborated on the Romantic magazine *El artista* by contributing lithograph illustrations. In 1836 he travelled to Paris, where he lived for nine years and attended Paul Delaroche's studio. Federico de Madrazo, Ribera's friend and fellow student, settled in the French capital with his wife between 1837 and 1839, and had close dealings with Ribera.

As the sons of acclaimed artists who had also been fellow students and rivals, Federico and Carlos Luis kept up a friendship which was not without rivalries of its own. Thus, on the day Federico arrived in Paris, 13 October 1837, he ended his first letter to his father with the remark: 'Carlos does not seem to have done much work.' Eight days later, he expands on this judgement: 'He works very little; it is quite plain that his father had him on a tight rein. He has come here and fallen in with greedy, whining Spaniards, and this has been more than enough for him to lose his love of study.'

Ribera was working on his painting *Rodrigo Calderón being carried to his Tomb* (Madrid, Palacio Real), which he intended to exhibit at the Salon. In view of this, Federico put renewed effort into 'exhibiting more than one thing and a rather large picture of an interesting subject. Emulation is a very good thing that gives very good results' (F. Madrazo, 6 July 1838).

The jealousy felt by Juan Antonio Ribera towards José de Madrazo, who was more successful on the contemporary artistic scene, influenced the two young men's rivalry. Consequently, José wrote to Federico: 'Thank heaven that you deal with him affectionately, but do not become too familiar with him and keep a distance where art is concerned; try to get ahead of him as much as you can' (28 July 1838). Juan Antonio's envy increased when jury and critics alike showed greater appreciation for Federico's pictures. As a result, José gave his son the following advice concerning Carlos: 'Without wishing him any ill, quite the contrary, you must hold back because one day he may be your greatest enemy' (29 June 1839).

However, Carlos's quiet temperament prevented any serious rivalry with Federico. The latter specialised in portraiture and murals, and was later court painter to Isabel II and a teacher and director of the Escuela Especial de Pintura, Escultura y Grabado de Madrid.

In Paris, the young men's relationship gradually became cordial. Together they visited the Salon and the Louvre, where they discovered and appreciated artists hitherto unknown in Spain, such as Van Eyck (27 April 1839). They frequented each other's studios, kept in close touch concerning their various activities, and exchanged opinions about the works they were preparing for the Salon. They also suffered the same worries on seeing their pictures hung and when there were omissions or delays in the reviews. Both decided to send their pictures to the exhibition at the Academy in Madrid, so as to 'form a unified front' against artists they considered unworthy (23 June 1839).

In April 1838 the two artists decided to paint portraits of each other, with the intention of showing them at the Academia de San Fernando's annual painting exhibition and then presenting them to their respective fathers (27 April 1838). On 26 June Federico set himself the target of completing the portrait between 1 and 10 August, still with the exhibition in mind, but it was then postponed by a commission: a portrait of the Marqués de Espeja. On 7 September he drew a portrait of Carlos (Museo del Prado, D-5390), which was very different from the oil painting. However, the preparation of their pictures for the 1839 Salon must have absorbed both painters.

Hence, it was not until 6 April 1839, when the event had already opened, that Federico announced that both portraits were 'quite advanced'. On 27 April he wrote: 'Today or tomorrow Carlos will finish my portrait, which I believe will please you...next week I shall finish his.' Carlos finished on 1 May, and three days later Federico was still working on his. On 11 May he was expecting to complete it the following day. Meanwhile, it had been seen by the painters Jean Alaux and J.-M. Gué, who liked it very much. The portrait must have been painted at the studio rented by Madrazo at no. 30 Rue Tour d'Auvergne, near his house. Both portraits were sent to Madrid around 1 July, along with the paintings for the Salon to be exhibited together at the Academia. When José saw them, he criticised the dry and 'Germanic' look of Ribera's portrait, saying that he much preferred the portrait of the latter by his son, because 'it has more size, more brilliance and more substance. The hair is divinely arranged and cannot be bettered' (J. Madrazo, 24 August 1839). Two years later, José wrote of this portrait: 'It stands comparison with those of Velázquez and Van Dyck' (1 March 1841).

Both pictures (Ribera's portrait of Federico is now at the Hispanic Society of New York) are important early works. The two artists, aware of the significance of this, were careful to mention the places and dates where they were painted, with the sitters' names in capitals at the top. Federico's composition is similar to a format used by Ingres and Delaroche, and previously by David in works such as *Monsieur Meyer* (Paris, Louvre), of 1795, whose classical foundations are linked to Roman sculpture (the *Agrippina Capitolina*), lending it an air of noble elegance.

The painter was obviously pleased by the pose, since he repeated it years later in the portrait of Baron Weisweiller (Bayonne, Musée Bonnat). Here he represents the subject in a pose of Romantic lassitude, highlighted by the cape that almost hides the armchair, so that the figure seems to float above this garment, its folds painted in the broad brushstrokes of Velázquez. The diagonal arrangement, much used by Ingres, avoids immobility and only a certain bulging of the chest makes the figure a little stiff. A very similar but inverted pose was adopted by Federico himself in the best-known photographic portrait of him, taken in about 1858 and now at the Biblioteca Nacional.

Ribera's head is depicted in a manner similar to other portrait drawings of 1839, such as those of Calixto Ortega and Ramón San Juan (Museo del Prado, D-5375 and D-5393), though very different from his own portrait, drawn in 1838. The work painstakingly combines blacks and browns enlivened by the glossy reflections of light. The smooth transition between the outline of the figure and the background, which brings the artist closer to Delaroche, also reveals a Romantic bias. This is reflected in the subject's fashionably long hair and elegant attire.

The portrait successfully shows Ribera's rather melancholic nature. This was mentioned by the painter Adrien Dauzats, who wrote to Federico telling him (as the latter subsequently told his friend Valentín Carderera): 'Ribera works a lot and has lost some of his shyness, so that if I take too long in going to Paris I shall not recognise him. He also says that he would seem to me to be a natural man and his father would be furious if he could see the influence that Paris has had on him' (28 June 1837).

Once there, Federico himself says of the man he affectionately calls Carluccio: 'He is very stylish, but has not managed to rid himself of that air...well...that somewhat clumsy or rascally demeanour, however you wish to understand it' (to Carderera, 6 July 1838).

Ten years later, the two artists portrayed each other once again, this time in drawings, which were used for woodcuts published by Ángel Fernández de los Ríos in his *Álbum biográfico. Museo Universal de retratos* (Madrid, *Semanario Pintoresco Español*, 1849, pp. 90 and 91). [JB]

72 Eduardo Rosales
[1836–1873]

The Condesa de Santovenia, 1871
Oil on canvas, 163 x 106 cm
Signed: *E. Rosales / 1871*
Madrid, Museo del Prado, P-6711

PROVENANCE

Painted for Francisco Serrano y Domínguez, first Duque de la Torre; 10 July 1925, given on long-term loan by María Gayangos, his widow, to the Museo de Arte Moderno, Madrid; 11 November 1932, Francisco Serrano y Domínguez, second Duque de la Torre, renewed the long-term loan until 8 August 1935; 12 November 1935, returned to the Museo de Arte Moderno; 1 December 1936, deposited in Valencia; 1946 or before, Bilbao, Félix Fernández-Valdés Izaguirre; 1977, Bilbao, Esteban Fernández-Valdés Amézola; 5 November 1979, Pedro and Estefanía Fernández-Valdés Escauriaza; 1 March 1982, donated to the Museo del Prado by the Banco de España, Caja Postal de Ahorros and Fundación Amigos del Museo del Prado.

ESSENTIAL BIBLIOGRAPHY

Tubino 1871, p. 178; Cañete 1871, p. 663; Cotarelo 1902, p. 47; Chacón 1926, pp. 151–53, 166 and 167; Lafuente Ferrari 1946, republished 1962, pp. 62–64; Salas 1982, pp. 28 and 29; Rubio Gil 2002, p. 144.

The eldest of five children born to General Serrano, Duque de la Torre (1810–1885), María de la Concepción Serrano y Domínguez was born in Havana in 1860 while her father was Captain-General of Cuba. Her beauty recalled that of her mother, Antonia Micaela Domínguez, the second Condesa de San Antonio, who greatly influenced her husband and subsequently enjoyed considerable political power in Spain. In 1880, Concepción Serrano married José María Martínez de Campos, the second Conde de Santovenia, in Paris. He was in possession of a substantial fortune, and was the son of José María Martínez de Campos, the first Conde de Santovenia, and Elena Martín de Molina, Marquesa de Castell Florite. At the same time, Concepción's brother Francisco Serrano married José María's sister Mercedes Martínez de Campos in a sumptuous ceremony organised by the Duquesa de la Torre.

The Condesa de Santovenia died in 1941 in Biarritz, her habitual residence, where her mother had passed away in 1917. According to her son, Carlos Martínez de Campos y Serrano, born in 1887 and holder of the title of third Duque de la Torre, his mother felt a special love and veneration for her father, General Serrano, and was his favourite child.

The portrait at the Prado, painted by Rosales in Madrid, shows the eleven-year-old girl in an elegant and balanced pose. By then, her father was the nation's most powerful figure: during the period from the proclamation of the new Constitution on 15 July 1869 to 2 January 1871, when Amadeo de Saboya ascended the throne, General Serrano became regent of the kingdom and was addressed as 'your Highness'. Afterwards, the king ordered him to appoint a cabinet and made him President of the Government, the position he held when the portrait was painted. The little girl's elegance, dressed in a bright pink satin dress edged with lace and a black velvet *dolman* trimmed with marten fur, reveals her prominent social position.

In 1871, shortly after the portrait was painted, it appeared under the title of *Portrait of Señorita C.S.* in the Exposición Nacional de Bellas Artes, which also included three other history paintings by Rosales. The most important, *The Death of Lucretia*, earned him a gold medal but was also criticised for its lack of background detail. This condemnation was also levelled at the portrait, where it was considered to be either a sign of weakness or, in the words of Cotarelo, 'a brilliant mistake by a great artist'. The work must have had a surprising effect, as it was a far cry from the customary Spanish portrait of the time. The artist has breathed new life into the outdoor portraits of girls often painted by Spanish painters of his own and the previous generation, giving it a spirit and monumentality that are linked to the great Spanish tradition. He captures the quality of the fabrics and the changing tones of the reflections using strong, confident brushstrokes in the style of Velázquez.

The tree on one side is a reminder of the portraits in hunting attire painted by Velázquez for the Torre de la Parada. The striking demeanour of the young lady, which recalls the *Portrait of Señorita Olea* (1870, private collection), is also reminiscent of female portraits by Goya. The pose is very similar to that of *Ferdinand VII before a Military Camp* (Museo del Prado, P-724), which had recently been moved, in May 1869, from the Escuela de Ingenieros de Caminos to the Museo de la Trinidad. The synthesis of execution has been compared by Lafuente Ferrari to the French portraits of the time, and especially those of Manet. Its elegance has been likened to that of Whistler's portrait of Miss Cecily Alexander (Chacón, p. 167), though this was a later work. However, the clearest debt emerges from an examination of Velázquez's paintings. The artificial, open background shows a quality that anticipates that of Rosales' late outdoor landscapes painted in Murcia.

A study of the head for this portrait was sold after the painter's death at an auction held in the Salas de Bosch (formerly the Platerías Martínez) in Madrid. [JB]

73 Ignacio Pinazo
[1849–1916]

Learning by Heart, 1898
Oil on canvas, 107 x 107 cm
Signed (top left corner): *I. Pinazo*
Madrid, Museo del Prado, P-4576

PROVENANCE

Purchased from the painter by the State on 8 June 1899, for the Museo Nacional de Arte Moderno.

ESSENTIAL BIBLIOGRAPHY

Mélida 1899, p. 299; Alcántara 1899; González Martí 1920, pp. 64, 65, 138, 139 and 235; Pompey 1946, p. 137; Aguilera Cerni 1982, p. 257, p. 116; Díez (ed.) 1994b, p. 220.

The subject of this portrait is the artist's youngest son, Ignacio Pinazo Martínez (Valencia, 1883–Godella, Valencia, 1970), who was to later become a sculptor. He first attended the Escuela de Bellas Artes de San Carlos, in Valencia, and in 1900 enrolled at the Escuela Especial de Pintura, Escultura y Grabado in Madrid. Having received a grant from the Valencia Provincial Council in 1903, he spent the next three years in Rome, and in 1907 spent a further year in Paris. His sculpture *The Serve*, produced in 1914 and awarded a Second Class medal in Madrid the following year, reflects his interest in Valencian folk culture. He sculpted numerous busts and public monuments, and was awarded a First Class medal in the National Fine Arts Exhibition held in Madrid in 1948.

Pinazo painted a number of watercolours and oil paintings of his son from early childhood onwards, as well as countless sketches. Ignacio is here portrayed at age fourteen or fifteen. The artist had planned this portrait some time before, and a related oil painting measuring 68 x 96 cm is in a private collection in Madrid. Work was temporarily suspended when the boy contracted typhus. In a preliminary study measuring 75 x 98 cm, now in the Museo Pinazo at Godella (Valencia), young Ignacio's features are still those of a child, and his hair is cut very short; he sits at a desk on which a book lies open. By the time he had recovered, the child had become an adolescent; on resuming the portrait, Pinazo was faced with the challenge of transforming his model. In order to do this, he first produced a study of the head (González Martí 1920, plate 53) and then returned to the painting itself. He may have produced several other versions before this one. In a photograph reproduced in Aguilera Cerni (1982), a canvas of the same size and composition, with a patchily sketched background, is visible on an easel; there are also two self-portraits on the easel, one dating from 1901. The portrait of Ignacio visible in the photograph cannot, therefore, have been the Prado version, which had been acquired two years earlier.

Although he had already been awarded a First Class medal in 1897, Pinazo submitted five paintings – including this portrait – to the General Fine Arts Exhibition held in 1899 in Madrid. At that time, it was common – and allowed by the Exhibition Rules – for a painter who had already obtained a medal to submit work to later exhibitions in the hope of being awarded a further medal by a different jury. This not only served to confirm the quality of the artist's output in general, but also dispelled any possible suspicion of bias, or fear that the first medal had been no more than a lucky break for a single painting. Moreover, it had been decided that works receiving a First Class medal would be purchased by the State at 6,000 pesetas each and placed on permanent display in the newly founded Museo de Arte Moderno. These were powerful incentives for Pinazo, who had received no payment for his prize-winning painting at the 1897 exhibition – a portrait whose owner refused to exchange it for a different work.

Though the portrait was well received at the exhibition, it was scarcely mentioned in the press, perhaps because Pinazo – who lived and worked in Valencia – was too far removed from the circles frequented by journalists and intellectuals in Madrid. The work was also difficult to classify, in that it fell somewhere between portrait and genre painting, and this may have hindered its proper appraisal. Nonetheless, two leading critics spoke highly of it: José Ramón Mélida remarked that it could 'pass for a portrait' and that 'the colours were beautiful'; Francisco Alcántara offered general praise for Pinazo's 'very fine portraits'. The portrait was unanimously awarded a First Class medal, and was purchased by the State for the Museo de Arte Moderno, at the stipulated price. It appeared, under its original title, in the Valencia Regional Exhibition of 1909 (no. 304) and in an exhibition of Spanish paintings at the Royal Academy in London in 1920 (no. 153). In 1946 it was displayed as *Portrait of the Artist's Son Ignacio* in an exhibition of 'Outstanding Portraits in Madrid Collections' (Madrid 1946, no. 69).

By the time the portrait was painted, young Ignacio had already produced some sculptures; only a year later, he won critical acclaim for a terracotta bust displayed in a shop window in Valencia. Here, the boy's slight frown and lost gaze convey the abstraction involved in learning by heart. Pinazo, who painted many portraits of children and adults, adopts an elegant approach to the difficulty of capturing a face whose physical features are rapidly changing. The boy is sitting on a folding chair, which also appears in other portraits of him, and leaning on a wooden pedestal table; he is wearing long trousers and a short grey cape of which the pink lining is visible. The range of colours, the naturalness of the pose, the sketched-in forms clearly defined by sharp outlines, and the breadth of brushstroke, all recall seventeenth-century Spanish painting. The influence of Velázquez can be clearly discerned in the long brushstrokes of the lining; but critics have also noted a debt to El Greco (González Martí 1920, p. 139), an artist Pinazo admired. [JB]

74 Joaquín Sorolla
[1863–1923]

Aureliano de Beruete, Father, 1902
Oil on canvas, 115.5 x 110.5 cm
Inscribed (bottom left):
A mi amigo A. de Beruete /
J. Sorolla y Bastida / 1902
Madrid, Museo del Prado, P-4646

PROVENANCE

1902, given by the painter to the sitter, Madrid; 1912, María Teresa Moret y Remisa, Madrid; 13 July 1922, bequeathed by the owner to the Museo de Arte Moderno, Madrid.

ESSENTIAL BIBLIOGRAPHY

Jiménez 1904, p. 24; Pantorba 1970, no. 1,059; Marín Valdés 1985, pp. 55 and 56; Puente 1985, p. 247; Marín Valdés 1988, p. 297; Santa Ana 1997, p. 174.

Aureliano de Beruete (Madrid, 1845–1912) was one of the most prominent landscape artists of his time. He came from wealthy aristocratic stock and received a sound and wide-ranging education, gaining a doctorate in law from the University of Madrid. He was a founder member of the Institución Libre de Enseñanza. In 1874 he began painting landscapes, receiving lessons from Carlos de Haes of the Escuela Especial de Pintura, Escultura y Grabado de Madrid. A connoisseur of old master painting, he published a monograph on Velázquez in Paris in 1898, which was translated into English in 1906 and German in 1908. Beruete was a close friend of Sorolla, despite being older and wealthier, and exerted a considerable influence on his work.

This painting was shown at the Exposición Nacional de Bellas Artes in 1904 and subsequently in several exhibitions dedicated to the artist's work, in Paris (Galerie Georges Petit, 1906), Berlin, Cologne and Düsseldorf (Casa Schulte, 1907) and London (Grafton Galleries, 1908). In the last of these it was seen by Archer Milton Huntington, who had not come across Sorolla's work before and wanted to buy it for his gallery of illustrious Spaniards at the Hispanic Society of New York.

Sorolla approached the owner, who refused to sell it – aware of its quality. In a letter from Madrid dated 16 May 1908 (Marín Valdés, 1985, p. 56), he wrote: 'As you know, I have set it aside, along with that of Maria Teresa, for the Museo Moderno. I know you would paint me another and that it would be *even* better, but this painting belongs to a time gone by; it has something that I doubt very much could be captured in another, even though it were better art. As you are also aware, since it became known it has reaped enormous success: it has been the envy of many. All of this means that, despite great sympathy for your interest, I am unable to help you on this occasion.'

Beruete suggested that Sorolla make a copy from the portrait in the exhibition, but the latter preferred to paint a new one from life. He did this for Huntington in 1908, and the result was very different. The 1902 work appeared in Sorolla's exhibition at the Hispanic Society in 1909. In 1912, after Beruete's death, it was placed on an easel at the great exhibition of Sorolla's work held at his studio in Madrid, 'loaned by him as an affectionate tribute to the memory of his old friend' according to the catalogue.

The poet Juan Ramón Jiménez pointed out that 'the shadow of the old masters is always with Sorolla' and said that, like those of El Greco and Goya, his portraits embodied 'the malice of deceptive surroundings'; the one of Beruete he described as 'easily as good as a Whistler'. The extraordinary chromatic quality of the narrow range of greys and blacks combines very well with the simple elegance of the sitter. A reserved person, he appears nonchalantly seated on a coat, top hat in hand, as if he has just come in from the street. Sorolla often used this almost snapshot-like pose with the model seated and in profile, head turned towards the onlooker, achieving a characteristic feeling of immediacy.

The picture follows the same arrangement as *María Teresa Moret, Señora de Beruete* (Museo del Prado, P-4655), painted a year earlier, of which this work is the companion piece; the sitter is also shown in profile on a large cloak against a chair back. Also in 1902, Sorolla painted *Aureliano de Beruete the Younger* (Museo del Prado, P-7683).

In the background, resting on a field easel, is a landscape painted by Beruete. This features the bridge of San Martín in Toledo, which he painted in several of his oils, including one sent to the Exposición Nacional de Bellas Artes in 1901 (no. 51 in the catalogue, 50 x 69 cm). Beruete felt a real fondness for Toledo and often painted there between 1875 and 1911, especially after 1903. He spent each October in the Castilian city, of which he was the most prominent painter, and was accompanied there by Sorolla during his stay in 1906. As Marín points out, the paintings of Toledo gathered at his studio in 1912 may have inspired Sorolla to return that year to paint in the city. [JB]

75 Ramón Casas
[1866–1932]

Santiago Rusiñol, 1889
Oil on canvas, 166 x 96 cm
Inscribed (bottom left):
A l'amic Santiago / R Casas
('To my friend Santiago / R Casas')
Private collection

PROVENANCE
Santiago Rusiñol; María Rusiñol Denís; Mercedes Planás Denís; private collection.

ESSENTIAL BIBLIOGRAPHY
Rahola 1889; Castillo 1958, pp. 16, 67, no. 118; Mendoza-Doñate 2001, pp. 20, 50 and 82; Coll, 2002, pp. 27–28 and 166–67, no. 98.

The painter and writer Santiago Rusiñol (Barcelona, 1861–Aranjuez, 1931) also collected antiques, especially old ironware, and was among the earliest champions of El Greco, purchasing two of his paintings in 1894. As a student under Tomás Moragas, he first exhibited in 1878. Although he was best known for his delicate, elegant garden paintings, the courtyards he painted in Sitges from 1891 onwards marked him out as an interesting painter, influenced by Symbolism. The friendship between Rusiñol and Casas dated back to 1882, when they were introduced by the sculptor Enrique Clarasó, with whom they were both to exhibit on many occasions. Rusiñol's painting *The Agreement*, showing Casas and Clarasó deep in conversation, was submitted to the Paris Salon in 1888. Early the following year Casas and Rusiñol painted portraits of each other, which were exhibited that February at the Parés Gallery in Barcelona; later, Rusiñol sent his portrait, entitled *Ramón Casas, Cyclist* (Barcelona, Banco de Sabadell) to the Paris Salon. The two artists exchanged portraits, and kept them throughout their lives. Over the years, Casas produced a number of expressive charcoal drawings which highlighted Rusiñol's strong personality.

Still in 1889, following Rusiñol's separation from his wife, the relationship between the two artists grew closer, and they even shared a studio in Calle Ample, Barcelona, where this portrait was probably painted. Good proof of their friendship is the double portrait *Rusiñol and Casas Painting each Other* (Sitges, Museo del Cau Ferrat), from 1890, in which both are shown painting outdoors. In late October 1890 they travelled to Paris together, taking lodgings at the Moulin de la Galette; there, Rusiñol came under the influence of Symbolism, which was to inform much of his later work.

The soft colouring is typical of Casas's paintings from that period, when his style closely mirrored that of Rusiñol; at the same time, however, it is reminiscent of the elegant Parisian portraits with which Casas was so familiar, having studied in 1881 and 1882 under one of the greatest portrait painters of the time, Carolus-Duran. It was in his studio that Casas was first attracted to the work of Velázquez, an artist greatly admired by Carolus-Duran. In this portrait, the pose, the restrained gesture and the expression all evoke Velázquez. At the same time, the strong influence of Manet is apparent in the relationship between the figure and the objects on the floor, particularly the cigar butts. This detail was not well received by the critics, any more than it was in Manet's work. Federico Rahola complained that 'unpleasant details, such as the rubbish on the floor and the vulgar background' detracted from the elegance of the portrait. Like Manet himself, Casas sought by this means to convey a sense of both truthfulness and immediacy.

The presence of one of Rusiñol's own works on the wall is a modern touch recalling Degas, and also Manet, whose *Portrait of Émile Zola* the artist may have seen. As in the Manet portrait, the modern painting is placed so as to partially conceal an older work. This is clearly intended as a tribute to Velázquez, for the painting underneath – only the upper part is visible – is a copy of the Infanta Margarita from *Las Meninas*, her head just visible beside the far door. The painting may have been done by Casas himself or, as Isabel Coll has suggested, by his friend the French painter Maurice Lobre, with whom in 1885 he had copied works by Velázquez in the Museo del Prado. The composition of the overlaid landscape, a panel entitled *The Road*, showing a wide road in the foreground and some trees cut off by the upper edge of the canvas, is characteristic of Rusiñol's work in 1888. Also typical are the soft, light tones, which to some extent recall the landscapes of the Olot school; Casas had painted in Olot in the autumn of 1888. The fact that the landscape virtually conceals the copy may suggest that, while imitation of the great masters is a necessary first step before representing the real world, in the end the painter should paint the world just as he sees it – as, indeed, Rusiñol did.

The portrait of Rusiñol offers a good illustration of this view. Although he is shown indoors (while Rusiñol painted Casas outdoors), and although the artist is elegantly dressed – striped tie, watch and chain, two rings on the left hand – the portrait manages to capture the sitter's real interests. A book appears to stick out of the jacket pocket, indicating Rusiñol's love of reading; he stands beside the door, his trousers tucked into his boots and his hat on, suggesting that he has just returned from a walk, or that he is just about to set off, perhaps for the country, to do some painting. The latter possibility is borne out by the parasol and the portfolio of drawings, which might also contain painting equipment. Moreover, the pose suggests a certain impatience, as though he is anxious to finish the session and be on his way. [JB]

9 The Spanish Portrait from Zuloaga to Picasso

76 Pablo Picasso
[1881–1973]

Woman in Blue, 1901
Oil on canvas, 133.5 x 101 cm
Inscribed: *P. Ruiz Picasso*
Madrid, Museo Nacional Centro de Arte Reina Sofía, AS-1618

PROVENANCE
1901, left behind by Picasso at the premises of the General Exhibition of Fine Arts in Madrid, transferred to the Museo de Arte Moderno, Madrid.

ESSENTIAL BIBLIOGRAPHY
R. Baroja (1935) 1952, pp. 39 and 40; P. Baroja 1952, p. 206; Zervos XXI 211; Daix-Boudaille 1966, III-5; Daix 1987, p. 35; Richardson 1995, p. 182.

In terms of both size and character, this is the most striking and most complete of the many portraits of courtesans painted by Picasso in 1901. The tight, dark blouse contrasts sharply with the vast white crinoline skirt, whose embroidered motifs also feature in another painting from the same period, *Spanish Woman* (Copenhagen, Ny Carlsberg Gliptotek). The triangular face tapering down to a pointed chin – a look typical of the courtesans of the day – peeps out from between a fashionable broad-brimmed hat with somewhat garish floral decoration and a huge white bow, which does not quite conceal the decorative gold necklace and matching earrings. The woman's imperious posture, gloved left hand gripping a green parasol, is echoed in her expression. The crinoline had been out of fashion for at least ten years, and its appearance here may owe something to Picasso's study of Golden Age female portraits in the Museo del Prado or to performances of Baroque plays, which prompted many Spanish painters of the day to produce portraits in this style. The butterfly bow and the huge flowers in the hat – contemporary fashions taken here to fantastic extremes – signal an open, exaggerated femininity. The curious costume, the golden glint of the jewellery and the silvery sheen of the dress combine to give this high-class courtesan something of the air of a precious icon; an effect heightened by the makeup and rouge, in which Picasso – both here and in similar works from the same period – achieves a pastel-like quality. The icon-like air is enhanced by the plain background, clearly divided into two strips; the intense, saturated violet-blue of the lower panel is quite different from that of the Blue Period, on which Picasso was to embark a few months later.

This painting was perhaps based on Picasso's own memories of Paris nightlife, or perhaps on pictures by artists such as Toulouse-Lautrec and Alexandre Steinlen. It may represent what Picasso saw as the dangerous side of femininity – a side which, personified in his friend Germaine Gargallo, had partly been the cause of Casagemas's suicide. The portrayal of the woman as a figure that haunted the imagination was not lost on those who saw the portrait, such as painter and engraver Ricardo Baroja, who in 1935 recalled 'the figure of a phantasmagorical woman. Green eyes, blue lips, an enormous black hat and a large crinoline skirt covered with the gaudiest of floral designs. Painted in dim candlelight, she was a vamp, of the sort that would now be called *femmes fatales*' (R. Baroja, pp. 39–40).

That was, indeed, how Picasso had painted her; he submitted the picture to the General Fine Arts Exhibition in Madrid, which opened on 29 April 1901, as though anxious to exorcise his obsession by presenting it to the public. At the Exhibition, the painting – under the title *A Figure* (cat. no. 963) – was hung in the worst possible place, the so-called 'Murder Hall' in the upper galleries of the Palacio del Hipódromo. Alongside it were pictures by Darío de Regoyos, who had submitted ten landscapes, and a portrait by Ricardo Baroja. Baroja's novelist brother Pío, who also had a picture at the exhibition, clearly recalled that in Madrid Picasso 'spent his time painting from memory, women with a Parisian look, with mouths as round and red as wafers' (P. Baroja 1952, p. 206); this portrait matches the description perfectly.

Unlike his submissions to the National Exhibitions of 1895 and 1897, which had received special mention, this painting went unnoticed. Picasso either forgot it, or deliberately left it behind in Madrid when he set off for Barcelona to set up the exhibition at the Vollard Gallery. The picture was unearthed many years later and – in accordance with Exhibition Rules – transferred to the Museo de Arte Moderno in Madrid. [JB]

77 Pablo Picasso
[1881–1973]

La Nana, 1901
Oil on cardboard, 104.5 x 61 cm
Signed (lower left): *Picasso*
Barcelona, Museu Picasso, 4274

PROVENANCE
Luis Plandiura, Barcelona; October 1932, Museos de Arte de Barcelona.

ESSENTIAL BIBLIOGRAPHY
Zervos I, 66; Cirici Pellicer 1946, p. 104; Boeck 1958, p. 124; Penrose 1958, p. 73; Pool 1960, pp. 387 and 388; Daix-Boudaille 1966, IV.2; Palau 1980, p. 226.

Picasso painted this work in Barcelona in the spring of 1901, before travelling to Paris for a second time. The theme links up with the habitual presence of dwarves in Golden Age Spanish painting. During a short stay in Madrid in 1895, Picasso had copied the faces of two buffoons by Velázquez, *Calabacillas* and *El niño de Vallecas* (both copies are in the Museo Picasso in Barcelona). The motif is clearly contemporaneous, since it comes from the cabarets the artist frequently visited during this period.

The composition's verticality and lack of symmetry are reminiscent of a Japanese print, but particularly of Degas, whose oblique setting it shares. The figure, captured very directly and physically in a proscenium, is also related to several by Degas, though the taste for the grotesque shows close ties with Toulouse-Lautrec. Cirici describes it as 'a *fleur du mal*, whose made-up and deformed figure is dominated by horizontals'. He describes the picture as having 'a Goyaesque audacity' which 'lends personality to the character and the pictorial technique itself' (Cirici 1946, p. 104). The use of the divided brushstroke and pure colour reveal an awareness of Post-Impressionist painting, seen during his first stay in Paris, where he had also encountered, and been considerably influenced by, the work of Toulouse-Lautrec. This amalgam of styles reveals an expressiveness that lends consistency to Picasso's work. The figure is surrounded by myriad multi-coloured brushstrokes, as in Van Gogh's paintings, boldly positioned in the proscenium, her arrogant attitude reminiscent of Goya.

The variations of highly saturated colour capture the intense reflections of artificial light, creating a strongly vibrant atmosphere. The arrangement of the figure, legs at an angle and one arm on the hip, and the shape of the face with its pointed chin, accentuate the predominant triangular pattern, whose sharp angles express aggressiveness. It has been assumed that the exhibition of Goya's work in Madrid, in 1900, may have influenced the artist in his choice of motif, and also *The Dwarf Doña Mercedes*, by Zuloaga (Pool, p. 388) [CAT. 79], though that is far removed from this painting.

This painting did not feature in the exhibition organised by Vollard in June 1901, with works by Iturrino and Picasso, but it anticipates the cabaret themes of the paintings seen there, which included several of prostitutes. The oblique angle, colour and rectangular shape of the background brushstrokes are more closely related to the grotesque *La femme aux bijoux* (Zervos VI, 389). The face bears some similarities to that of the *Woman in Stockings* (Zervos XXI, 246). However, in *La Nana* the conception of space is more complex, with a certain depth that derives from the use of the brushstroke. Furthermore, the figure has a very direct eroticism, manifested in the pose, attire and adornments, such as the black and red ribbon that graces her throat and the voluminous flowers. [JB]

78 Isidro Nonell
[1872–1911]

Study of a Gypsy, 1906
Oil on canvas, 185 x 110 cm
Inscribed (lower left corner):
Nonell / 1906.
Masaveu Collection

PROVENANCE

In 1934 it belonged to Andreu Bassas, Barcelona; 1960, owned by Blanca Bassas de Iturriagagoitia, Barcelona; later deposited in the Museo de Arte Moderno de Barcelona; in 1970 it was returned to its owner; 23 May 1989, auctioned by Edmund Peel & Asociados, Madrid, no. 1; sold to the Masaveu Collection.

ESSENTIAL BIBLIOGRAPHY

Nonell 1963, p. 221; Mendoza-Doñate 2000, p. 162.

Paintings of gypsy women were frequent in Nonell's work after he settled in Barcelona in 1900, where he stayed until 1907. Earlier he had already shown in his drawings a strong interest in depicting social outcasts. Unlike those drawings, however, there is no clear social intention in these later paintings, for the artist himself said that what fascinated him about gypsies was their expressiveness and character. In any event, his repetition of the subject, which was rejected by a large part of the Catalan artistic milieu of the time, was due to his sympathies towards that marginal, deprived world. Although he usually concealed the facial features from the viewer, and with them part of the individuality of the women he portrayed, these were paintings done from life, with models chosen by the artist.

The vertical format enabled Nonell to arrange the figures to give a certain monumentality. In this work, the narrow space left on the sides of the canvas and its almost geometrical structure accentuate this feature; the skirt has something of the form of a cube and the torso that of a pyramid, with one side formed by the right arm, on which the head is resting, which increases the figure's appearance of being hunched over itself. Nonell used this same posture, associated with the representation of melancholy, in at least two other pieces of the same year, as can be seen in *Gypsy Woman* (Barcelona, Viuda de J. Valentí Collection) and *Meditating* (Barcelona, Museo de Arte Moderno). The presence of the plate and spoon is exceptional in these paintings, where it is rare to find any other element apart from the figure, though one had appeared in *Rest* (Barcelona, Museo de Arte Moderno), painted two years earlier. The artist gave this painting the title of *Study*, which he used often during this period; that was the title under which it was shown, along with three other paintings, in the Fifth International Exhibition of Art held in 1907 in Barcelona. The fact that it was not a simple study is demonstrated by the price of 2,500 pesetas put on it by Nonell himself, the highest price given to any of his works at that time.

Like another picture with the title *Gypsy Woman* (Masaveu Collection), of the same year and which also belonged to the Bassas Collection (*Art*, no. 10, Barcelona, July 1934, p. 344), it was one of the largest formats that Nonell ever painted. The composition bears some relationship to the figure on the right in *Two Gypsy Women* (Barcelona, Viuda de Barbey Collection) of the same year. The ambitious construction is more evident in this *Study of a Gypsy Woman* not only because of its architectural solidity but also the way of composing the mass through small planes defined by parallel brushstrokes. These strokes, which are almost compacted in the head, are shorter and closer together in the upper part of the figure and longer in the lower part; in addition, on the shoulder the close, almost horizontal, strokes are superimposed on the outline of the shawl, interrupting its continuity, while further down a few wavy, very long brushstrokes emphasise the fall of the skirt. The artist, who usually did the upper part of his compositions first, thus seems to suggest, through a progressively freer execution, a diminishing density of the volumes from top to bottom.

In a similar way, the change from the black tone of the hair and the red of the shawl to the blues of the skirt, highlighted by the range of greens in the background, shows a gradation from warm to cool tones. In each colour there is a variety of tones that indicates the richness of the colouring within the narrow range of the artist's palette. The bright patches of light among the blues of the skirt add animation and vivacity to the figure, contrasting with her static pose. Although executed with very different brush strokes, they reflect Nonell's interest in El Greco, which led him in 1903 to go and see his works in Toledo after having visited the Prado.

The space in which the figure is placed is ambiguous, with a slight difference between the planes of the floor and the wall on the left achieved by using a lighter colour on the ground; on the other hand this distinction is not clear on the right-hand side of the composition. Nevertheless, the opulence of the painterly matter is such that, combined with the intricate colouring of certain parts of the picture, the painting has the air of a tapestry or wall-hanging, recalling the artist's fascination with gypsy shawls, which he liked to acquire to hang on the walls of his studio. Despite the woman's downcast attitude, the profile of the head shows no sign of the pain or anguish that could be seen in earlier works. In this painting, as in others of the same year, we can observe the beginnings of the shift in Nonell's artistic development that occurred in 1907, when he stopped using gypsy women as models. The painting thus reflects a balance between the expressive orientation of the works from the preceding years and the harmony of his later paintings. [JB]

79 Ignacio Zuloaga
[1870–1945]

The Dwarf Doña Mercedes, 1899
Oil on canvas, 130 x 95 cm
Signed (lower right): *I. Zuloaga*
Paris, Musée d'Orsay, RF 1977-438

PROVENANCE
1901, purchased from the artist by the French state for the Musée National de Luxembourg.

ESSENTIAL BIBLIOGRAPHY
Lafuente Ferrari 1950a, pp. 50 and 219, no. 94; Milhou 1981, p. 28; Barón 1999, p. 18.

The picture depicts a dwarf, Mademoiselle Bouey, from the town of Saint-Médard-en-Jalles, near Bordeaux. Marie-Louise Thierrée, second wife and widow of Albert Dethomas, owned a house and garden there, at which the painter stayed with his wife Valentine Dethomas in the summer of 1899, a few months after their wedding on 18 May of that year. The figure is shown in the drawing room of the estate, known as Le Couénic, which no longer exists.

Zuloaga had already exhibited *The Dwarf of Éibar* five years before at the Salon de la Société Nationale des Beaux-Arts, though his most famous painting of a dwarf was *Gregorio el Botero*, exhibited at the same Salon in 1908. In the same year, he also painted *Gregorio in Sepúlveda* (Pedraza, Museo Zuloaga). Unlike these last two works, a testimony to his maturity as a painter and of his proximity to Ribera, *The Dwarf Doña Mercedes*, which is equally monumental, is closer to that of Maribárbola in Velázquez's *Las Meninas*. The subject is also reminiscent of *Eugenia Martínez Vallejo, 'La Monstrua vestida'* by Juan Carreño de Miranda (Madrid, Museo del Prado, P-646). However, contrary to Golden Age portrayals of jesters, Zuloaga paints from a higher perspective, accentuating the deformity of the short, stout figure whose head appears below the level of the furniture in the background. Despite this being French, its dark tones, like those of the flooring, evoke the atmosphere of a bygone era in Spain, creating an overall impact that pleased the artist.

The crystal ball makes the dwarf look more bulky and distorted, and reflects the rest of the room – even the artist himself, seated at the easel with light coming in from his left through the large window in the background, probably one of several at the front of the house, facing the garden. Zuloaga was undoubtedly aware of the use by Van Eyck and other Flemish Renaissance artists of reflections in mirrors and convex surfaces, as well as being familiar with seventeenth-century Dutch *vanitas* paintings in which glass also reflected the artist working at the easel.

The portrayal of a dwarf with a crystal ball was used nine years earlier by Luis Menéndez Pidal in a painting inspired by Velázquez and entitled *The Jester's Mirror*. This was displayed at the 1890 Exposición Nacional de Bellas Artes in Madrid. While Zuloaga's painting bears many similarities to Velázquez, since it shows the sitter dressed in seventeenth-century style and surrounded by Castilian furniture of the time, it also shows clear differences, and is closer in expressiveness to Goya.

According to Lafuente Ferrari, this is the first personal work by Zuloaga, signalling 'the beginning of an investigation of character that is not held back by being grotesque'. Furthermore, it shows his move away from intimate sentimentality in search of transcendentalism (Lafuente Ferrari, p. 50). He liked it so much that he sent it to the seventh exhibition of *La Libre esthétique* in Brussels in 1900, and also to the Schulte Gallery in Berlin in the same year. [JB]

80 José Gutiérrez Solana
[1886–1945]

Mujeres de la vida, ca. 1915–1917
Oil on canvas, 99 x 120 cm
Signed (bottom left corner):
J. Solana
Bilbao, Museo de Bellas Artes,
82-278

PROVENANCE
August 1919, directly from the artist to the Museo de Bellas Artes, Bilbao.

ESSENTIAL BIBLIOGRAPHY
Madariaga-Valbuena 1976, p. 80; Barrio-Garay 1978, pp. 88, 107 and 123; Alonso Fernández 1979, pp. 70, 157, P. 73.

This picture, also known as *The Prostitutes* and *The Girls' Doorway*, shows a group of four prostitutes and their procuress, awaiting clients in the street. Prostitutes and chorus girls were a common theme in the work of Solana, who often frequented the brothels of Madrid and Santander. One Santander brothel was in Arrabal Street, and Solana used the street name as a generic term in the titles of some of his works, for example *Woman on Arrabal* (previously in Madrid, Emilio Fernández Peña Collection), which was painted at around the same time as this picture and features the same figure with exposed breasts. The procuress figure reappears in the various oil and pastel versions of *The House on Arrabal* painted between 1931 and 1934 (there is one in the Grupo Santander Collection and another in the Círculo de Bellas Artes, Madrid). It has been suggested (Madariaga-Valbuena) that the procuress was in fact Claudia Alonso, the madame of a Santander brothel who was well known for her strong character; Solana, who lived in Santander from 1909 to 1917, may well have met her.

Solana's compositions frequently featured a compact group of large figures. Here, they are echoed in a background group of six smaller men and women; however, while the background figures seem to be chatting, those in the foreground appear immobile, silent. As though in a family portrait, the main group consists of women of different ages. Since the Dutch Baroque, the theme of age has been associated with a moral reflection on the passing of time. This is particularly evident here; the two youngest girls are facing the same way as the procuress, as though she were foretelling their future transformation. The innocent gaze of the girl with exposed breasts and the melancholy attitude of the girl beside her contrast strongly with the dark, watchful stare of the procuress, who dominates the group by virtue of her height; her face appears to be deformed by scars which are like the sharp edges of an angular volume. The figure on the right, opening her cloak to show herself better, gazes out with a defiant expression. Despite the female clothing and the coral earrings, she still looks more like a man. It has been suggested that this was a male friend of Solana's, with whom he had quarrelled, and that Solana took his revenge by portraying his friend in this guise (Madariaga-Valbuena). But the figure also resembles the photograph of a homosexual transvestite published in a book by Constancio Bernaldo de Quirós and J. María Llanas Aguilaniedo, entitled *La mala vida en Madrid* ('Low Life in Madrid') (Madrid 1901, fig. 38). The procuress, too, bears some resemblance to another photograph in the book, that of a 'drunken prostitute' (*ibid.*, fig. 8); here, however, the painter takes her deformities to extremes, in order to make her as debauched and repulsive as possible (see Barrio-Garay 1978, p. 88).

The sombre tones, ranging from black to the dirty whites of the women's underwear – with their twofold connotation of immodesty and soiled innocence – emphasise the moral destitution of the setting. The background against which the prostitutes are placed (with the partial exception of the youngest, on the left of the group) is the wall of the brothel. As in other paintings by Solana, the solid, unbroken mass of the wall is highly significant. Here, it takes up the whole height of the canvas; unlike the houses to the left of the picture, the brothel wall is windowless and unlit. Its enormous visual weight looms ominously over the figures. At the far right of the canvas, however, there is a doorway with a bedspread hanging over it, a scene described by Solana himself in a section about 'Brothels' in the final chapter of his book *La España negra* ('Black Spain'), published in Madrid in 1920. Solana greatly admired art that, like his own, addressed the concerns of the common man – an art which had its roots in Goya's wild streak – and wrote about some of the artists who had produced it, such as Leonardo Alenza, Francisco Javier Ortego and Ignacio Zuloaga.

This painting was one of three (the others were by Gauguin and Anglada Camarasa) purchased at the First International Exhibition of Painting and Sculpture held in 1919 in Bilbao, to which Solana had submitted three paintings. Years later, around 1932–1933, he produced an etching with the same subject matter (Alonso Fernández 1979, p. 345, AG. 12), perhaps using a photograph of the painting. The only, albeit significant, difference is that in the etching the procuress has been removed from the group of women. [JB]

81 Pablo Picasso
[1881–1973]

La Celestina, 1904
Oil on canvas, 70 x 56 cm
Signed (upper left): *Picasso*
Paris, Musée Picasso, MP 1989-5

PROVENANCE
ca. 1938, acquired from the artist by Max Pellequer; Paris, Georges Pellequer; December 1987, Didier Imbert; June 1988, Fredrik Roos; 1989, donated to the Musée Picasso, Paris.

ESSENTIAL BIBLIOGRAPHY
Zervos I, 183; Daix-Boudaille 1964, IX-26; Leymarie 1971, p. 4; Palau 1980, pp. 366–68; Daix 1988, throughout; Richardson 1995, pp. 288 and 290.

This half-length portrait clearly shows the influence of El Greco. The work is inspired by a real model whose name and address were on the back of the canvas (but have now been covered): Carlota Valdivia / calle conde Asalto, 12 /4.º, 1.ª escalera interior, marzo 1904. Although it has been maintained that the work was painted in 1903, this inscription suggests a more likely dating of March 1904, the beginning of the late Blue Period (Daix 1988). According to Palau, the address is that of the Edén Concert, a bar in Barcelona frequented by the artist. The woman lived off the inner stairway. Picasso must have met her in 1904 and decided she would make a suitable subject, painting her at the end of his stay in Barcelona before settling in Paris.

Like many figures of the time, including the *Self Portrait* of 1901 [CAT. 82], the woman is wrapped in a shawl which hides her arms and she wears a hood-shaped headscarf. It is believed that this bears some relation to the cap worn by prostitutes suffering from syphilis, seen by Picasso in 1901 at the Saint-Lazare women's hospital and used in several works. The use of a hood, wimple, shawl, mantilla or headscarf lent the woman an air of devotion, but was also often used by procuresses to hide their faces. This occurs especially in the works of Goya, whose *Caprichos* Picasso knew well, since he had copied one of them, no. 17, in 1898 (drawing at the Museo Picasso in Barcelona). It is also seen in a wide range of nineteenth-century paintings and drawings, including works by Leonardo Alenza and Eugenio Lucas, both followers of Goya. It was used by Joaquín Sorolla in his 1894 *White Slavery* (Madrid, Museo Sorolla), where the procuress is not dissimilar to Picasso's.

The blind eye is related to pictures of beggars which he painted during this period; although many beggars were blind, the artist also had a particular fear of loss of sight, and there may also be a reference to the idea of turning a blind eye to moral turpitude. However, the face is neither crudely evil nor even old, but rather, as Daix (1988, p. 36) points out, marked by profound human experience.

Before painting the figure in oils, Picasso depicted her in several drawings. In the one known as *Celestina acting as a Go-Between* (Zervos I, 191), the woman's pose is the same as in the oil painting. In another, she appears in a café with Picasso and his friend Sebastián Junyer-Vidal (Zervos VI, 480). In a third, Picasso depicts himself standing before the canvas painting her (Zervos XXII, 54). These drawings, and especially the last one, show that the figure of this woman obsessed him and many years later he remembered her perfectly.

Picasso was familiar with the great works of Golden Age literature. The one that interested him most was Fernando de Rojas' *La Tragicomedia de Calixto y Melibea* (1499), as can be seen in this painting. He possessed several editions of the work, some of them very old. Many years later, in 1967 and 1968, he returned to this motif in a series of drawings and engravings, the latter known as *Suite 347*, which were illustrations for his own version of the tragicomedy. One of his last etchings, dated 21 May 1971, returns to the theme yet again.

The most recent cleaning of the work has revealed the loosely painted lace lining of the hood, which is toned down by the contrast of the dark blue cape and hood against the brighter background. The white in the hair, earring and shirt collar, and the rosy cheeks, create a chromatic variety that lends volume to the head, making it stand out against the flat surfaces of the shawl and background, all highlighting the differences between this and other works from the height of the Blue Period. [JB]

82 Pablo Picasso
[1881–1973]

Self Portrait, 1901
Oil on canvas, 81 x 60 cm
Paris, Musée Picasso, MP 4

PROVENANCE
The artist's collection; Musée Picasso, Paris.

ESSENTIAL BIBLIOGRAPHY
Zervos I, 91; Barr 1946, p. 22; Berger 1973, p. 50; Daix-Boudaille 1966, V-1; Palau 1980, p. 285; Daix 1987, pp. 41 and 420; Varnedoe 1996, pp. 124 and 125.

Painted in Paris at the end of 1901, this picture bears profound testimony to the crisis suffered by the painter after the suicide of his friend Casagemas. According to Daix, this was the real reason behind the haggard face. The cheeks, hollowed out by blue shadows and the left cheek by the outline itself, reveal an expression of anguish that has also been related to hunger, cold and disillusionment (Barr, p. 22), to the loneliness of the foreigner in Paris and to the sense of rootlessness in the big city (Berger, p. 50). This is how he had also painted his friend Jaime Sabartés (Moscow, Pushkin Museum), who understood that Picasso had reflected the spectre of his own loneliness in the picture.

The only clear part of the picture is the face, framed by the dark mass of hair, as compact as a helmet, and the neck rising from the overcoat as though for protection from the cold. The effect, the direct transition between head and shoulders, has been linked (Varnedoe, p. 124) with Rodin's *Balzac*, which Picasso had seen the previous year. The incorporation of a large flat silhouette, an effect highlighted by the fact that the figure is cut by the edge of the canvas; the use of an almost monochrome background, and the way in which the overcoat has been defined with a few confident lines, evoke the posters of Toulouse-Lautrec and, to a certain extent, the synthesism of Gauguin. The expressive intensity of the face is reminiscent of Van Gogh's self-portraits, but here the feeling of profound melancholy is made more intense by the use of blue. The composition of the half-length figure gazing directly at the observer against a monochrome background, and the dissymmetry between the shoulders, also seen in other works, are related to portraits by El Greco. The striking originality of this image, painted by Picasso at the age of twenty, lies in its use of stark simplification.

One very important feature of the work is the subject's gaze. Unlike other self-portraits by Picasso in which it is very intense, here it is almost glazed, denoting not only sadness but also a psychic weakness. This has been linked to a possible feeling of failure at a time when he was about to break off relations with his first dealer, Pere Mañach, who disapproved of the turn that Picasso's work had begun to take at the beginning of his Blue Period.

Yet there is no commiseration or sentimentality in this painting. Picasso kept it for himself, since more than any other piece it reminded him of the sufferings he had undergone as a result of being faithful to his own creation. He appears to have painted it as an intense testament to his crisis, a kind of exorcism or catharsis that would help him to rid himself of it. Yet instead of using a more expressionist style, as he had done in previous self-portraits, he painted it with extraordinary smoothness as if the brushes had caressed the surface, thus capturing the profoundly symbolist melancholy. [JB]

83 Pablo Picasso
[1881–1973]

Gertrude Stein, 1906
Oil on canvas, 100 x 81.5 cm
New York, The Metropolitan Museum of Art, Bequest of Gertrude Stein, 1946, 47.106

PROVENANCE
Gift by the artist to Gertrude Stein, Paris, 1946, bequeathed to The Metropolitan Museum of Art, New York.

ESSENTIAL BIBLIOGRAPHY
Zervos I, 352; Stein 1943, pp. 30 and 31; Penrose 1958, pp. 115 and 116; Daix-Boudaille 1966, XVI-10; Stein 1967, pp. 64, 66, 74, 79, 87 and 159; Palau 1980, pp. 436 and 469; Richardson 1995, pp. 404 and 410; Werth 1997, pp. 283 and 284.

Gertrude Stein (Allegheny, Pennsylvania, 1874–Neuilly-sur-Seine, Paris, 1946) came from a wealthy Jewish family of Austrian extraction and lived in Vienna and Paris as a child. In 1903, she abandoned her medical studies at Johns Hopkins University in Baltimore and travelled throughout Europe with her brother Leo, with whom she settled in Paris.

The two acquired numerous works of art by Daumier, Manet, Cézanne and Gauguin, followed from 1905 onwards by works by Derain, Vlaminck and Matisse and then by Picasso and Gris, who were Gertrude's two favourite painters.

Although an outstanding writer of intense vitality, Stein was at first little appreciated. Her Parisian home was a meeting place for many of the leading artistic personalities of the time, including Apollinaire, Cocteau, Satie, Eliot, Rousseau, Matisse, Gris and Delaunay. During the first world war, she worked for the American ambulance service. In the 1920s she was the central figure of a group of American writers including Hemingway and Scott Fitzgerald, and in 1933 her *Autobiography of Alice B. Toklas* brought her world renown. By the time she died, she had amassed a highly important art collection which included thirty-eight works by Picasso.

Picasso met Stein in Clovis Sagot's gallery in the autumn of 1905 and asked her to pose for him. She sat in a broken armchair at his studio on Rue Raviganan in Montmartre for more than eighty sessions. Eventually, the dissatisfied artist wiped out the head and abandoned the portrait. In her memoirs (Stein 1967), she recalls how Picasso sat very close to the canvas and used a very small palette with a single colour midway between light brown and grey. This was an appropriate choice for the light brown corduroy skirt suit that Stein usually wore, according to Picasso's lover Fernande Olivier, who read La Fontaine's fables during the sessions. The sitter appears to be absent-mindedly reflective, an unusual feature in female portraits by Picasso. In fact, she was pondering her book *Three Lives*, which she finished soon afterwards; one of the characters was inspired by Fernande.

Having spent the summer in Gósol with Fernande, Picasso finished the portrait in the late summer or autumn of 1906. Stein writes: 'He said that he could not see me any more and left for Spain; it was his first journey after the Blue Period. On his return, he painted the head without having seen me and gave me the picture. I was, and still am, pleased with my portrait. For me, it is me. It is the only picture of myself in which I am still me' (Stein 1943, p. 31, translated from the French).

These words are relevant, given criticisms of the portrait's mask-like appearance, which might not seem to bear much resemblance to that of the model. However, as Picasso had anticipated, it was eventually considered that he had achieved an admirable likeness (Penrose, p. 116).

Picasso had painted several portraits of the elderly Josep Fontdevila, the owner of the guest house where he stayed during his visit to Gósol, and some commentators believe these influenced the rapidly painted final version of the image. The roundness of the skull was superimposed like a mask onto the memory of Gertrude. This produces a certain hardness in the portrait, accentuated by the clarity of the outline. Gertrude Stein pointed out that at the time her portrait was done, Picasso's drawing had become firmer and that the painter was no longer a youth, but a man. She was implying that contact with her had been the catalyst to this change of style. She wondered why Picasso needed a model at all, and concluded: 'The Spanish spirit re-emerged in him, and I was American. To a certain extent America and Spain have many things in common' (Stein 1943, p. 30, translated from the French).

It is more likely that Gertrude Stein's physical peculiarities interested Picasso as a model. He was powerfully attracted by her figure, described by Fernande Olivier as 'huge, short, massive', by her high forehead and limpidly intelligent gaze. Moreover, her androgynous look and plain style of dress lent her an air of essentiality, which was appropriate to Picasso's quest for objectivity at the time. The portrait, which is closely related to the *Self Portrait with Palette* (Philadelphia Museum of Art), signalled a decisive step towards the beginning of Cubism. [JB]

84 Pablo Picasso

[1881–1973]

Señora Canals, 1905
Oil on canvas, 88 x 68 cm
Signed (top right): *Picasso*
Barcelona, Museu Picasso, 4266

PROVENANCE
Collection of Ricardo Canals, Barcelona; acquired by Luis Plandiura, Barcelona, before Canals' death in 1931; October 1932, Museos de Arte de Barcelona.

ESSENTIAL BIBLIOGRAPHY
Zervos I, 263; Daix-Boudaille 1966, XIII-9, pp. 82 and 84; Palau 1980, p. 424; Richardson 1995, p. 290.

This painting is of the Italian model Benedetta Bianco Coletta (Cervaro, Italia, 1870/71–Barcelona, 1958), the future wife of the painter Ricardo Canals (1876–1931). Canals was a good friend of Picasso's, and lived in Paris at the same time as him, in 1905. A former model for Degas, Benedetta had also posed for the *Monument to the Dead* by the sculptor Paul-Albert Bartolomé (1848–1928), now at the Père-Lachaise cemetery in Paris. Canals met her in 1900 and married her in 1906, the year that he returned to Barcelona. A woman of great beauty and a cheerful, passionate and strong personality, she also posed for numerous works by her husband.

Fernande Olivier, who refers to Benedetta as 'la belle romaine', lived with her and Canals at the Bateau-Lavoir, the artists' colony in Montmartre. She recounts in her *Picasso et ses amis* that Benedetta went to considerable trouble to prepare food, usually macaroni, for all the mostly Spanish friends who called in to Canals' studio. She appears to have been the dominant partner, pushing her husband to work harder and allowing him only one cigarette at each break. Occasionally, Fernande and Benedetta reclined on the divan while the artists, mostly Spaniards, discussed painting and admired their beauty.

Canals painted both women in his 1902 work *A Box at the Bullfight*, for the banker Ivo Bosch. Benedetta was blamed for exerting considerable influence over Canals to paint in a style that would be pleasing to the middle classes, but which distanced him from the artistic renewal of his early works.

Canals had met Picasso during the period when the latter was frequenting the café 'Els Quatre Gats' in Barcelona. In Paris, he was a neighbour and friend to Picasso and also helped him perfect his etching technique. Further testament to the close relationship between the two artists at the time comes in Picasso's three sketches of Canals' eldest son Octavio, and his photographic portrait of Canals himself, probably taken with Canals' camera. In the latter, he includes himself in the mirror taking the photograph. Beside him is a photographic portrait of Benedetta. The painting itself was done for Canals, and was eventually acquired, after much insistence, by the Catalan collector Luis Plandiura.

Picasso appears to have been attracted by the balance and purity of the model's features, and the head recalls the elegance of Ingres. He has made her quite Spanish with the black mantilla, which frames her head and neckline. The influence of Goya is evident in the sketchy treatment of the ochre dress. The almost monochrome tone, the only colourful note being the mauve adorning the head, was a distinguishing feature of portrait painting in Spain in Picasso's formative years, and also during the Golden Age. The bright face stands out in contrast to the darkly coloured mantilla. The expressive restraint, painstaking drawing and solid form of the head evoke the works of the Renaissance, though a relationship with Velázquez's *Lady with a Fan* [FIG. 77] has also been pointed out. This portrait was painted during Picasso's Rose Period, but at a time when he was rethinking his work. It has a timeless quality, and not surprisingly it was succeeded by paintings that are strongly classical or Mediterranean in style. [JB]

85 Juan Gris

[1887–1927]

Homage to Pablo Picasso, 1912
Oil on canvas, 93 x 74 cm
Inscribed and signed (lower right): *Hommage à Pablo Picasso / Juan Gris*
Chicago, The Art Institute of Chicago, Gift of Leigh B. Block, 1958.525

PROVENANCE
Before 1921, Daniel-Henry Kahnweiler, Paris; 13–14 June 1921, first sale of the Kahnweiler Collection, Hôtel Drouot: sold to Grassot for Kahnweiler; 5 May 1949, sold by Kahnweiler (Galerie Simon and Galerie Louise) to Curt Valentin; Mary and Leigh B. Block, Chicago, by 3 January 1956; 1958, donated to The Art Institute of Chicago.

ESSENTIAL BIBLIOGRAPHY
Apollinaire (1912) 1991, II, pp. 430–31; Kahnweiler 1971, p. 220; Gaya Nuño 1974, p. 78; Cooper 1977, p. 26, no. 13; Rosenthal 1983, p. 24; Green 1992, pp. 14–15.

José Victoriano González, known as Juan Gris, travelled to Paris in the autumn of 1906. In the winter or the following spring, the painter Daniel Vázquez Díaz, whom he had met in Madrid in 1903, introduced him to Picasso. The latter obtained a studio for him in the cellar of the same building at the artists' colony of Bateau-Lavoir in Montmartre where he had his own studio. Gris then met Guillaume Apollinaire, André Salmon and Max Jacob. In 1907, Picasso introduced him to Georges Braque and to Maurice Raynal, whose portrait he painted in 1911. During these years he witnessed the birth of Cubism.

Juan Gris painted this work in January and February of 1912 and exhibited it with two other canvases at the Salon des Indépendants. Apollinaire reviewed the exhibition on 25 March in *L'Intransigeant*, writing that these pictures could be described as 'integral Cubism' and describing how a Czech painter (who turned out to be Bohumil Kubista) had remained for a long time meditating on this work until the exhibition hall was due to close.

Picasso is depicted as Gris essentially saw him: a painter, palette in hand. The monumentality of the figure, the great breadth of the torso and the military-style stiff coat and buttons are constructed on a limited number of planes using lines that are often broken and almost form right angles. These give the figure a strong personality in accordance with his leading role in Cubism. However, the head is composed of multiple planes meeting at much sharper angles, especially in the eyes, nose and mouth, suggesting the artist's huge versatility and creative ingenuity.

This is not a figure study but a genuine portrait showing the sitter's personal features, despite the fragmented planes. Rosenthal has pointed out its compositional similarity to Picasso's portrait of Gertrude Stein. Both paintings pay homage to their subject. This is made explicit in the inscription, and Gris might well have been influenced, perhaps unconsciously, by this very familiar image.

Cooper points out that Gris's drawings between 1909 and 1911 show the distinctive nature of his relationship with Cubism. As well as bearing the mark of Cézanne, they are very clearly influenced by Picasso's analytical Cubism, as evidenced by the inscription. Other artists, such as Jean Metzinger and Henri Le Fauconnier, had also worked in the preceding years with figures fragmented into angles, but in Gris the composition is unified through the use of light, which plays a fundamental role. Moreover, the use of the lattice structure enables him to create the 'flat, coloured architecture' advocated years later in his text *Posibilidades de la pintura*.

In a review in January 1912, André Salmon had saluted Gris as 'Picasso's disciple'. However, Picasso was disturbed by descriptions of Gris as a Cubist, and was unfair to him on more than one occasion, as Gertrude Stein reminded him. Fernande Olivier herself stated that Gris, who was received as a friend by Picasso in his studio, 'studied the tricks of Cubism and used them quite intelligently but without art' (Olivier, 1932, p. 159). This insult suggests distrust on the part of Picasso, who was secretly amazed at his fellow countryman's lucid artistic explorations. After Gris's death, he told Kahnweiler, who had been dealer and friend to both artists: 'It is beautiful, a painter who knew what he was doing' (Kahnweiler, p. 325). [JB]

* I am grateful to Dr Stephanie D'Alessandro, Associate Curator of The Art Institute of Chicago, for clarification of the provenance, based on documents relating to Kahnweiler in the Institute's archives.

86 Joan Miró
[1893–1983]

Self Portrait, 1919
Oil on canvas, 73 x 60 cm
Signed and dated (upper left corner): *Miró / 1919.*
Paris, Musée Picasso, RF 1973-79, Picasso donation 1973–1978

PROVENANCE
Prior to July 1919, from the artist to Josep Dalmau; prior to April 1921, gifted by Dalmau to Pablo Picasso, Paris; 1973, French State; September 1985, Musée Picasso, Paris.

ESSENTIAL BIBLIOGRAPHY
Pérez-Jorba 1920; Pérez-Jorba 1921; Rowell 1986, p. 62; Lubar 1989, pp. 157, 158 and 313; Weelen 1989, pp. 37 and 39; Combalía 1990, pp. 62, 126 and ff.; Lanchner 1993, p. 368, no. 14; Dupin 1993, pp. 67, 68 and 70; Seckel-Klein 1998, pp. 180–183, no. 56.

This self-portrait, the second one produced by the artist, after the first in 1917 (New York, Edward A. Bragaline Collection), forms part of what are known as his *détailliste* paintings, executed with great precision in minute detail. Unlike other earlier portraits, which include a number of decorative elements, this one has a neutral background. Because of this and its frontal composition, its somewhat ingenuous appearance and the dominance and firmness of the drawing, it can be related to another early work, the *Portrait of a Young Girl* (Barcelona, Fundació Joan Miró). However, the volumes are much more solid here, particularly in the head and neck, with their carefully modelled light effects that make them stand out clearly against the two-dimensional background. The treatment of the clothes – the red Garibaldi shirt edged in black – shows a subtle deconstruction into planes of Cubist inspiration.

The eyes, fixed on the viewer, have something of a look of puzzlement about them. For this reason, and because of its mysterious static nature and the solid volumes, the work has been linked with the Magic Realism that triumphed in Europe after the Great War. Nevertheless, the painting – executed with, as Dupin describes it, 'the delicacy of a miniature', as is clearly evident in the treatment of the hair – is inspired by the great Romanesque frescoes of Catalonia and by the paintings of the primitives, represented in the Barcelona museums which the artist had known since his childhood. Although this influence of the Catalan Romanesque has been considered a possible sign of nationalism in Miró's art, other factors should also be taken into account, such as Picasso's ascendancy, and in particular the need that the artist felt at this time to capture faithfully the profound structure of reality through his mastery of drawing.

The picture was painted in Barcelona during the winter and spring of 1919. Miró considered sending it to the International Exhibition of Art being organised by the City Council in May that year. However, he did not finish it until afterwards, as we know from a letter he wrote to his friend Enric Ricart on 9 July 1919 (Rowell 1986, p. 73). He exhibited it later, along with another work, at the 1920 Salon d'Automne in Paris, where it stood out from the rest of the Catalan section. The painting was handed over to his dealer, Josep Dalmau, who, in order to gain favour with Picasso, who had liked it, offered it to him without Miró being informed or receiving any money at all before April 1921. On that date Miró held an exhibition at the Galerie La Licorne, in which the self-portrait was included and described as being the property of Picasso. Miró had heard a great deal about Picasso, as their families were acquainted; he had seen Picasso's ballet *Parade* when it was performed in Barcelona in November 1917, and knew his work even before his visit in 1919 to María Picasso's home in Barcelona. When he arrived in Paris at the end of February 1920 he went to see Picasso, and from then on, despite a certain initial reserve, their relationship was a close one. Picasso's return to the clarity of the figure, in his so-called neoclassical period, was an important starting point for Miró, who regarded it as a kind of benchmark.

In Paris, the painting was acclaimed by a number of critics, particularly the writer Juan Pérez-Jorba, who noted the concentrated intensity of the work, which, 'with the force of an intimate flame, almost a fire, is severe, austere, noble, strong' (Pérez-Jorba 1920, included in Combalía 1990, p. 128). Miró always retained an interest in his *Self Portrait*, as shown by his correspondence with Picasso (published by Rowell), advising against it being lent for one exhibition but asking for it for another, such as the 1954 Venice Biennale, and arguing that it was an important piece in his artistic output. [JB]

87 Pablo Picasso

[1881–1973]

Self Portrait, 1972
Wax crayon on paper, 657 x 505 mm
Signed (lower left): *Picasso*
Tokyo, private collection,
courtesy of Fuji Television Gallery

PROVENANCE

1972, Galerie Louise Leiris; 1974, acquired by Fuji Television Gallery, Tokyo

ESSENTIAL BIBLIOGRAPHY

Zervos XXXIII, 435; Daix 1987, pp. 403 and 404; Sylvester 1988, p. 146; Varnedoe 1996, pp. 170, 172 and 173.

This work, undertaken on 30 June 1972, is the artist's penultimate self-portrait, the last being a less individualistic drawing done two days later (Zervos XXXIII, p. 436). Picasso showed it to Pierre Daix the day after he drew it, telling him: 'I think I've come up with something...it doesn't look like anything I've done before' (Daix, p. 403). The almond-shaped eyes are reminiscent of those in his 1907 *Self Portrait*, but the shape of the head evokes a skull.

The highly pictorial use of crayons was common during the return to expressionist painting in the international art of the late 1970s and early 1980s. These late works by Picasso were clear forerunners of the trend. The artist uses very limited means (crayons and paper) in this self-portrait, which signals an intensification of the already exaggeratedly baroque expressiveness of his late period. The thick outline clearly defines the shape, but is interrupted at the top left and elsewhere, and appears to fade into the background. The red of the shadow-like backdrop also appears in the pupil, giving it a wounded look which lacks the incisive clarity of most of Picasso's self-portraits. Its fuzzy appearance makes him seem to be looking within himself, an impression emphasised by the spirals around the pupil. On the other hand, the bluish-mauve colour is reminiscent of the saturnine melancholy often ascribed to painters. The loosely scribbled graphics around the chin and torso contrast with the cleanly defined lines surrounding the eyes and nose.

The deeply sunken shape of the lower third of the head is even more pronounced in another self-portrait drawn at around the same time (Zervos XXXIII, p. 436), which shows the shape of the emaciated skull. The expression in the eyes is intense and stunned. The mouth is merely suggested by three parallel lines, making the figure even more disturbing. The dominating presence of eyes and nose in this strongly frontal sketch is emphasised by the unbroken line framing the nose and mouth.

The softness of the nose, with the nostrils clearly visible, has been likened to that of a monkey (Varnedoe, p. 173), a caricature of the painter. In this sense, the fearful expression has a more pronounced physical nature. Moreover, although the essential lines are clearly marked out, other parts of the composition are more blurred. The confident solidity normally associated with Picasso seems almost to be dissolving into a liquid state. According to Sylvester, this could be a reflection of his failing eyesight, but it could also be a premonition of death.

The monumentality of the head, highlighted by an absence of space on both sides, accentuates its weight in relation to the visible narrow band of the torso. The fact that the head is cut off by the upper edge of the paper also seems to push it downwards, an effect made all the more pronounced by the missing neck, so that it appears to be balanced on a precarious support. This is an image of extreme old age, immediately before death. Few artists, perhaps none at such an advanced age, had so far approached the end of life with such truthfulness in their work. Picasso did not like talking about death, and for many years he had taken refuge in silence whenever one of his friends died. This would surprise and sometimes even disturb the family of the deceased – as was the case with Matisse. When Picasso showed this drawing to Pierre Daix the day after he did it, he held it next to his own face, as if to make it clear that the fear reflected in the portrait was mere invention. Three months later, Daix saw the artist again and noted: 'He had hardened the smoke-coloured strokes and maroon-mauve lines in the upper part of the bluish-green cranium.' These colours reminded Daix of Picasso's painting after the death of Julio González. Here we see the cathartic projection of the artist's feelings in the face of his own demise. [JB]

Bibliography

Abril 1935. M. Abril, *De la Naturaleza al Espíritu. Ensayo crítico de pintura contemporánea desde Sorolla a Picasso*, Madrid, 1935.

Águeda 1982. M. Águeda, 'La colección de pinturas del infante don Sebastián Gabriel', *Boletín del Museo del Prado*, III, no. 8, 1982, pp. 102–17.

Águeda 1991. M. Águeda, 'La influencia de Velázquez y el arte de su tiempo en la obra de Goya', in *Velázquez y el arte de su tiempo*, Madrid, 1991, pp. 427–34.

Águeda and Salas (eds) 1982. M. Águeda and X. de Salas (eds), *Francisco de Goya. Cartas a Martín Zapater*, Madrid, 1982 (2nd edn, 2003).

Aguilera Cerni 1982. V. Aguilera Cerni, *I. Pinazo*, Valencia, 1982.

Aguirre 1793. S. Aguirre, *Prontuario alfabético y cronológico por orden de matterias de las instrucciones, ordenanzas, reglamentos, pragmáticas y demás reales provisiones no recopiladas, expedidas hasta el año de 1792*, Madrid, 1793.

Agulló 1978. M. Agulló, *Noticias sobre pintores madrileños de los siglos XVI y XVII*, Granada, 1978.

Agulló 1981. M. Agulló, *Más noticias sobre pintores madrileños de los siglos XVI al XVIII*, Madrid, 1981.

Agulló 1994. M. Agulló, *Documentos para la historia de la pintura española. I*, Madrid, 1994.

Agulló 1998. M. Agulló, 'Una familia de pintores: los Arellano', exh. cat., *Juan de Arellano 1614–1676*, Madrid, 1998.

Alarcos García 1937. E. Alarcos García, 'Los sermones de Paravicino', *Revista de Filología Española*, XXIV, 1937, pp. 162–97 and 249–319.

Albiac Blanco 1998. M.ª D. Albiac Blanco, *El conde de Aranda. Los laberintos del poder*, Zaragoza, 1998.

Alcántara 1899. F. Alcántara, 'Exposición de Bellas Artes', *El Imparcial*, Madrid, 8 May 1899.

Alfonso X 1985. Alfonso X, *Leyes de Alfonso X. I. Espéculo*, ed. G. Martínez Díez, Ávila, 1985.

Alonso Fernández 1979. L. Alonso Fernández, *José Gutiérrez Solana*, Madrid, 1979.

Alonso Fernández 1979. L. Alonso Fernández, *J. Solana. Estudio y catalogación de su obra*, Madrid, 1979.

***Alonso Sánchez Coello* 1990.** *Alonso Sánchez Coello y el retrato en la corte de Felipe II*, exh. cat., Madrid, 1990.

Allende-Salazar and Sánchez Cantón 1919. J. Allende-Salazar and F. J. Sánchez Cantón, *Retratos del Museo del Prado. Identificación y rectificaciones*, Madrid, 1919.

Álvarez 2003. M. T. Álvarez, 'Jan Gossaert. "Portrait of a Grand Commander of the Order of Santiago"', in *The Renaissance, The Triumph of Flemish Manuscript Painting in Europe*, exh. cat., Los Angeles, 2003.

Álvarez Lopera 1987. J. Álvarez Lopera, *De Ceán a Cossío: La fortuna crítica del Greco en el siglo XIX*, Madrid, 1987.

Álvarez Lopera 1993. J. Álvarez Lopera, *El Greco. La obra esencial*, Madrid, 1993.

Álvarez Lopera 1999. J. Álvarez Lopera, entries 29 and 67 in *El Greco. Identidad y transformación. Creta, Italia, España*, exh. cat., Madrid–Rome–Athens, 1999.

Álvarez Lopera 2003. J. Álvarez Lopera, 'El Greco en las colecciones reales. Los retratos del Museo del Prado', in *El Greco*, Barcelona–Madrid, 2003, pp. 175–215.

Amezúa 1949. A. G. Amezúa Mayo, *Isabel de Valois, reina de España*, Madrid, 1949.

Angulo 1946. D. Angulo Íñiguez, *Pedro Berruguete en Paredes de Nava*, Barcelona, 1946.

Angulo 1947. D. Angulo Íñiguez, *Velázquez. Cómo compuso sus principales cuadros*, Seville, 1947.

Angulo 1951. D. Angulo Íñiguez, *Pedro de Campaña*, Seville, 1951.

Angulo 1954a. D. Angulo Íñiguez, *Pintura del Renacimiento* (Ars Hispaniae XII), Madrid, 1954.

Angulo 1954b. D. Angulo Íñiguez, *Juan de Borgoña*, Madrid, 1954.

Angulo 1956. D. Angulo Íñiguez, 'El caballero de la mano al pecho', *Goya*, no. 11, 1956, pp. 290–91.

Angulo 1964. D. Angulo Íñiguez, 'Las verrugas de Berruguete y las hojas de roble de Van Dyck', *Archivo Español de Arte*, 1964, pp. 76–77.

Angulo 1965. D. Angulo Íñiguez, 'Las pinturas de Pedro Berruguete del retablo mayor de Santa Eulalia de Paredes de Nava', *Informes y trabajos del Instituto de Conservación y de Restauración*, IV, 1965, pp. 5–12.

Angulo 1981. D. Angulo Íñiguez, *Murillo*, 3 vols, Madrid, 1981.

Angulo and Pérez Sánchez 1969. D. Angulo and A. E. Pérez Sánchez, *Pintura madrileña del primer tercio del siglo XVI*, Madrid, 1969.

Ansón Navarro 1995. A. Ansón Navarro, *Goya y Aragón: familia, amistades y encargos artísticos*, Zaragoza, 1995.

***Anton Raphael Mengs* 1993.** *Anton Raphael Mengs. 1728–1779*, exh. cat., London, 1993.

Antonio 1996. T. de Antonio, entry no. 4, in *El Greco y su revalorización por el Modernismo catalán*, exh. cat., Barcelona, 1996.

Antonio 1998. T. de Antonio, 'Antonio Moro, "Doña Juana de Austria"', in *Las sociedades ibéricas y el mar*, exh. cat., Lisbon, Madrid, 1998, pp. 218–20.

***Antonio Rafael Mengs* 1980.** *Antonio Rafael Mengs, 1728–1779*, exh. cat., Madrid, 1980.

Apollinaire (1912) 1991. G. Apollinaire, 'Le Salon des Indépendants. Suite de la promenade à travers les salles', *L'Intransigeant*, Paris, 25 March 1912; collected in Apollinaire, *Oeuvres en prose complètes. II*, Paris, 1991.

Arana de Varflora (1791) 1996. F. Arana de Varflora, *Hijos de Sevilla. Ilustres en santidad, letras, armas, artes o dignidad* (1791), Facsimile edn with an introduction by A. García Baquero González, Seville, 1996.

Aranda 2001. F. J. Aranda Pérez, *Jerónimo de Ceballos: un hombre grave para la República. Vida y obra de un hidalgo del saber en la España del Siglo de Oro*, Córdoba, 2001.

Aranda 1692. G. de Aranda, *Vida del V. P. Fernando de Contreras*, Seville, 1692.

Aretino 1916. P. Aretino, *Il secondo libro delle lettere. Parte Prima*, ed. de F. Nicoloni, Bari, 1916.

Arias de Cossío 1978. A. M. Arias de Cossío, *José Gutiérrez de la Vega. Pintor romántico sevillano*, Madrid, 1978.

Armas 1981. F. A. Armas, 'Pintura y poesía: la presencia de Apeles en el teatro de Lope de Vega', in M. Criado del Val (ed.), *Lope de Vega y los orígenes del teatro español*, Madrid, 1981, pp. 730 *et seq.*

Arnaiz 1981. J. M. Arnaiz, *Eugenio Lucas. Su vida y su obra*, Madrid, 1981.

***Art en las Col·leccions* 1987.** *L'art en las colleccions de la casa de Alba*, exh. cat., Barcelona, 1987.

***Arte Europeo* 1980.** *El arte europeo en la corte de España durante el siglo XVIII*, exh. cat., Madrid, 1980.

***Artistas Pintados* 1997.** *Artistas pintados. Retratos de pintores y escultores del siglo XIX en el Museo del Prado*, exh. cat., Barcelona, 1997.

Artola 2002. M. Artola, 'La condesa de Chinchón', in *Goya*, Barcelona–Madrid, 2002, pp. 197–211.

Aterido 1994. Á. Aterido, 'El verdadero asunto del "Homenaje a Velázquez"', *Archivo Español de Arte*, 268, 1994, pp. 369–99.

Augé (ed.) 1989. J. L. Augé (ed.), *Les élèves espagnols de David*, exh. cat., Castres, 1989.

Ayala 1666. J. de Ayala, *Sarao de Aranjuez, de varios versos y novelas*, Madrid, 1666.

Azara 1846. J. N. de Azara, *El espíritu de José Nicolás de Azara, descubierto en su correspondencia epistolar con don Manuel de Roda*, 3 vols, Madrid, 1846.

Azcárate 1982. J. M.ª de Azcárate, *Colección de documentos para la historia del arte en España*, vol. 2, Zaragoza–Madrid, 1982.

Azorín (1913) 1954. Azorín, 'Lo del Van der Goes', *La Vanguardia*, Barcelona, 1 April 1913, collected in Azorín, *Pintar como querer*, Madrid, 1954.

Azorín 1970. Azorín, 'La España de un pintor', in Azorín, *Tiempos y cosas*, Madrid, 1970.

Baetjer 1981. K. Baetjer, 'El Greco', *The Metropolitan Museum of Art Bulletin*, XXXIX, no. 1, 1981 (monographic issue), pp. 4–48.

Baldassari 1997. A. Baldassari, *Le Miroir noir. Picasso, sources photographiques 1900–1928*, Paris, 1997.

Balsinde and Portús 1997. I. Balsinde and J. Portús, 'El retrato del escritor en el libro español del siglo XVII', *Reales Sitios*, XXXIV, no. 131, 1997, pp. 41–57.

Barcia 1901. Á. M. Barcia, *Catálogo de los retratos de los personajes españoles que se conservan en la sección de Estampas y Bellas Artes de la Biblioteca Nacional*, Madrid, 1901.

Bardi 1969. P. M. Bardi, *Tout l'œuvre peint de Velázquez*, Paris, 1969.

Barettini 1972. J. Barettini Fernández, *Juan Carreño. Pintor de cámara de Carlos II*, Madrid, 1972.

Baroja 1900. P. Baroja, 'Cuadros del Greco. I: Los retratos del Museo del Prado', *El Globo*, Madrid, 26 June 1900.

Baroja 1952. P. Baroja, *Desde la última vuelta del camino. Memorias. Galería de tipos de la época*, Madrid, 1952.

Baroja (1935) 1952. R. Baroja, *Gente del 98* (1935), Barcelona, 1952.

Barón 1999. J. Barón Thaidigsmann, 'La mujer en la pintura de Iturrino y Zuloaga', in *Iturrino. Zuloaga. La mujer: inteligencia emocional*, Madrid, 1999, pp. 13–21.

Barr 1946. A. H. Barr Jr., *Picasso. Fifty Years of his Art*, New York, 1946.

Barrio-Garay 1978. J. L. Barrio-Garay, *José Gutiérrez Solana, Paintings and Writings*, Lewisburg–London, 1978.

Barrio Moya 1995. J. L. Barrio Mora, 'El inventario de los bienes del hidalgo leonés don Andrés González de Bricianos, contador de los gastos secretos de Carlos II y Felipe V (1708)', *Tierras de León*, XXXV, no. 99, 1995, pp. 29–55.

***Bartolomé Esteban Murillo* 1983.** *Bartolomé Esteban Murillo*, exh. cat., London, 1983.

Bartolomé Esteban Murillo 2002. *Bartolomé Esteban Murillo (1617–1682) Paintings from American Collections*, exh. cat., ed. S. Stratton-Pruitt, Fort Worth (Texas), 2002.

Bass 2000a. L. Bass, 'A su imagen y semejanza: La Naturaleza como retrato en "El pintor de su deshonra"', in P. Calderón de la Barca, *El pintor de su deshonra (Auto sacramental)*, Madrid, 2000.

Bass 2000b. L. Bass, *The Portrait in the Play: Subjectivity and Representation on the Seventeenth-Century Spanish Stage* (PhD thesis), Princeton, 2000.

Baticle 1984. J. Baticle, 'À propos du Greco portraitiste: Identification de la "Dame à la fourrure"', in J. Brown and J. M. Pita Andrade (eds), *El Greco: Italy and Spain*, Washington, D.C., 1984, pp. 11–21.

Baticle 1988. J. Baticle, 'Goya et son temps', in *Goya*, (La Bibliothèque des Expositions), Paris, 1988.

Baticle 1990. J. Baticle, *Velázquez. Pintor hidalgo*, Madrid, 1990.

Baticle (1992) 1995. J. Baticle, *Goya*, Barcelona, 1995 (French edn, Paris, 1992).

Baticle 1999. J. Baticle, 'El retrato ecuestre del rey Felipe IV', in *Velázquez*, Barcelona–Madrid, 1999.

Baticle and Marinas 1981. J. Baticle and C. Marinas, *La Galerie Espagnole de Louis Philippe au Louvre. 1838–1848*, Paris, 1981.

Beamud 1985. A. M. Beamud, *The Invisible Icon: Poetry about portraiture in the Spanish Golden Age*, Ann Arbor, 1985.

Benesch 1945. O. Benesch, *The Art of the Renaissance in Northern Europe*, Cambridge (Mass.), 1945.

Benito 1994. F. Benito, 'El retrato moralizado en España: Contrarreforma e influencia del retrato como género', in *El retrato en el Museo del Prado*, Madrid, 1994, pp. 183–92.

Berg-Sobré 1977. J. Berg-Sobré, 'Bartolomé de Cárdenas, the Pietà of Johan de Loperuelo and Painting in Daroca (Aragón)', *The Art Bulletin*, LIX, 1977, pp. 484–500.

Berg-Sobré 1997. J. Berg-Sobré, *Bartolomé de Cárdenas, 'el Bermejo': pintor errante en la corona de Aragón*, San Francisco–London–Bethseda, 1997.

Berg-Sobré 1989. J. Berg-Sobré, *Behind the Altar Table. The Development of the Painted Retable in Spain, 1350–1500*, Columbia, 1989.

Berg-Sobré 2003. J. Berg-Sobré, 'Sobre Bartolomé Bermejo', en *La pintura gótica hispano-flamenca. Bartolomé Bermejo y su época*, exh. cat., Barcelona–Bilbao, 2003.

Berger 1973. J. Berger, *Ascensión y caída de Picasso*, Madrid, 1973.

Bergmann 1979. E. Bergmann, *Art Inscribed: Essays on Ekphrasis in Spanish Golden Age Poetry*, Cambridge (Mass.), 1979.

Berjano [1925]. D. Berjano Escobar, *El pintor Juan Carreño de Miranda (1614–1685). Su vida y sus obras*, Madrid, undated [1925].

Bermejo 1962. E. Bermejo, *Juan de Flandes*, Madrid, 1962.

Bermejo and Portús 1990. E. Bermejo and J. Portús, *Juan de Flandes*, Madrid, 1990.

Beroqui [1927]. P. Beroqui, 'Una biografía de Goya escrita por su hijo', *Archivo Español de Arte*, III, 7 [1927].

Beroqui 1946. P. Beroqui, *Tiziano en el Museo del Prado*, Madrid, 1946.

Beruete [1903] 1926. A. de Beruete Moret, *La pintura española en el siglo XIX. Elementos nacionales y extranjeros que han influido en ella* [1903], Madrid, 1926.

Beruete 1911. A. de Beruete Moret, *Valdés Leal. Estudio crítico*, Madrid, 1911.

Beruete [1914]. A. de Beruete Moret, *El Greco, pintor de retratos*, Madrid, [1914].

Beruete 1916. A. de Beruete Moret, *Goya, pintor de retratos*, Madrid, 1916.

Blanco Mozo 1998. J. L. Blanco Mozo, 'Varia Paretiana: I La familia Fourdinier. II Paret en el país vasco: su relación con algunos miembros de la Real Sociedad Bascongada de los Amigos del País', *International Congress 'Pintura española. Siglo XVIII'*, Marbella-Paracuellos de Jarama, 1998, pp. 299–316.

Blunt 1939–1940. A. Blunt, 'El Greco's "Dream of Philipp II": An allegory of the Holy League', *Journal of the Warburg and Courtauld Institutes*, III, 1939–1940, pp. 58–69.

Bodar 1990. A. Bodar, 'Erasmus en het Geleerdenportrey', *Nederlandese Portretten. Bijdragen over de portretkunst in de Nederlanden uit de Zestiende, Zeventiende en Achttiende Eeuw*, The Hague, 1990, pp. 17–68.

Bodart 1998. D. Bodart, *Tiziano e Federico II Gonzaga. Storia di un rapporto de commitenza*, Rome, 1998.

Boeck 1958. W. Boeck, *Picasso. Con un estudio preliminar por Jaime Sabartés*, Barcelona, 1958.

Bonnat 1856. A. Bonnat, 'Exposición de Bellas Artes. Artículo quinto', *Las Novedades*, Madrid, 18 June 1856.

Bonnefoy 1994. Y. Bonnefoy, *Rome, 1630: L'horizon du premier baroque*, Paris, 1994.

Bottari 1822–1825. G. G. Bottari, *Raccolta di lettere sulla pittura, scultura ed architettura scritte da' più celebri personagi dei secoli XV, XVI y XVII, pubblicata da M. Gio. Bottari, e continuata fino Ana Ioannovna nostri giorni da Stefano Ticozzi*, 8 vols, Milan, 1822–1825.

Bottineau 1986. Y. Bottineau, *El arte cortesano en la España de Felipe V (1700–1746)*, Madrid, 1986.

Bouza 1991. F. Bouza, *Locos, enanos y hombres de placer en la corte de los Austrias*, Madrid, 1991.

Bouza 1994a. F. Bouza Álvarez, 'Corte es decepción. Don Juan de Silva, conde de Portoalegre', in J. Martínez Millán (ed.), *La corte de Felipe II*, Madrid, 1994, pp. 451–502.

Bouza 1994b. F. Bouza Álvarez, 'La majestad de Felipe II. Construcción del mito real', in J. Martínez Millán (ed.), *La corte de Felipe II*, Madrid, 1994.

Bouza 1998. F. Bouza, *Imagen y propaganda. Capítulos de historia cultural del reinado de Felipe II*, Madrid, 1998.

Bouza 1999. F. Bouza, 'Entre la realidad y la memoria: los retratos en el siglo de Velázquez', in *En torno a Velázquez*, Seville, 1999, pp. 51–72.

Bouza 2000. F. Bouza, 'Pinturas y pintores en San Lorenzo El Real antes de la intervención de Velazquez. Una "Descripción" escurialense en la Biblioteca de Ajuda de Lisboa (h. 1650)', *Reales Sitios*, no. 143, 2000.

Bracons Clapes 1989. J. Bracons Clapes, 'Operibus monumentorum quae fieri facere ordinamus. L'escultura al servei de Pere el Ceremoniós', in *Pere el Ceremoniós i la seua època*, Barcelona, 1989.

Braham 1966. A. Braham, 'Two Notes on El Greco and Michelangelo', *The Burlington Magazine*, CVIII, no. 759, 1966.

Braham 1980. A. Braham, 'Murillo's portrait of Don Justino de Neve', *The Burlington Magazine*, CXXII, no. 924, 1980, pp. 192–94.

Brandi (1937) 1993. K. Brandi, *Carlos V. Vida y fortuna de una personalidad y de un imperio mundial* (1937), Mexico City, 1993.

Brans 1953. J. V. L. Brans, 'Juan de Flandes. Pintor de la reina y de Castilla', *Clavileño*, IV, 1953, p. 28.

Bravo Lozano 1981. J. Bravo Lozano 'Pintura y mentalidades en Madrid a finales del XVII', *Anales del Instituto de Estudios Madrileños*, XVIII, 1981.

Breuer 1984. S. Breuer, *Alonso Sánchez Coello* (PhD thesis), Munich, 1984.

Brigstocke 1999. H. Brigstocke, 'El descubrimiento del arte español en Gran Bretaña', in *En torno a Velázquez: The Apelles Collection*, Oviedo, 1999.

Brihuega 1981. J. Brihuega, *Las vanguardias artísticas en España. 1909–1936*, Madrid, 1981.

Brilliant 1991. R. Brilliant, *Portraiture*, London, 1991.

Brooke 2001. X. Brooke, 'Seville and Beyond: The Taste for Murillo's Genre Painting across Europe', in *Murillo, Scenes of Childhood*, exh. cat., London, 2001, pp. 51–79.

Brown 1973. J. Brown, *Francisco de Zurbarán*, New York, 1973.

Brown 1980. J. Brown, *Imágenes e ideas en la pintura española del siglo XVII*, Madrid, 1980.

Brown 1982. J. Brown, 'Murillo, Pintor de temas eróticos. Una faceta inadvertida de su obra', *Goya*, nos 169–71, 1982, pp. 35–43.

Brown 1986. J. Brown, *Velázquez. Pintor y cortesano*, Madrid, 1986 (English edn, New Haven–London, 1986).

Brown 1988. J. Brown, 'Enemies of Flattery: Velázquez's Portraits of Philip IV', in R. J. Rotberg and T. K. Rabb, *Art and History. Images and their Meaning*, Cambridge (Mass.), 1988, pp. 137–54.

Brown 1994. J. Brown, 'La monarquía española y el retrato de aparato de 1500 a 1800', in *El retrato en el Museo del Prado*, Madrid, 1994, pp. 135–60.

Brown 1998. J. Brown, *Painting in Spain 1500–1700*, New Haven–London, 1998.

Brown 1999. J. Brown, *Velázquez, Rubens y Van Dyck*, exh. cat., Madrid, 1999.

Brown (ed.) 1999. J. Brown (ed.), *Picasso y la tradición española*, Hondarribia, 1999.

Brown and Carr (1982) 1984. J. Brown and D. A. Carr Jonathan, 'El "Retrato de un cardenal": símbolo o simulacro?', in J. Brown *et al.*, *Visiones del pensamiento. El Greco como intérprete de la historia, la tradición y las ideas*, Madrid, 1984, pp. 57–73 (English edn, 'Portrait of a Cardinal: Niño de Guevara or Sandoval y Rojas', in J. Brown (ed.), *Figures of Thought. El Greco as interpreter of History, Tradition and Ideas*, Washington, D.C., 1982, pp. 33–42).

Brown and Elliott 1981. J. Brown and J. H. Elliott, *Un palacio para el rey: El buen Retiro y la corte de Felipe IV*, Madrid, 1981.

Brown, Elliott and Garrido 1999. J. Brown, with J. Elliott and C. Garrido, '"Las meninas" como obra maestra', in *Velázquez*, Barcelona–Madrid, 1999, pp. 85–124.

Brown and Garrido 1998. J. Brown and C. Garrido, *Velázquez: la técnica del genio*, Madrid, 1998 (English edn, New Haven–London, 1998).

Brown and Kagan 1987. J. Brown and R. Kagan, 'The Duke of Alcalá: His collection and its evolution', *The Art Bulletin*, LXIX, 1987, pp. 231–55.

Bugli and Della Valle 1982. M. Bugli and A. Della Valle, *Dipinti. Museo Poldi Pezzoli*, Milan, 1982.

Burke and Cherry 1997. M. B. Burke and P. Cherry, *Spanish Inventories*. I: *Collections of Paintings in Madrid, 1601–1755*, 2 vols, Los Angeles, 1997.

Bury 1989. J. B. Bury, 'Francisco de Holanda's Treatise on Portraiture', *IV Simposio Luso-Espanhol de história da arte. Portugal e Espanha entre a Europa e além-mar*, Coimbra, 1989.

Buschbeck 1960. H. Buschbeck, 'Quelques observations sur la vision de l'enfant chez Velázquez et ses disciples', in *Varia Velazqueña*, 2 vols, Madrid, 1960.

Cabrera and Garrido 1982. M. Cabrera Garrido and C. Garrido Pérez, 'El dibujo subyacente de las predelas del retablo mayor de la iglesia de Santa Eulalia de Paredes de Nava (Palencia) y del retablo mayor de la catedral de Ávila', in *Colloque IV sur le dessin sous-jacent dans la peinture. Le problème de l'auteur de l'œuvre de peinture. Contribution de l'étude du dessin sous-jacent à la question des attributions*, Louvain-la-Neuve, 1981, Proceedings, 1982.

Calderón 1945. P. Calderón de la Barca, *Comedias de Pedro Calderón de la Barca*, Madrid, 1945.

Caliena Corbero and Iranzo Munio 1991. C. Caliena Corbero and M. T. Iranzo Munio, 'Las exequias de Alfonso V en las ciudades aragonesas. Ideología real y rituales públicos', *Aragón de la Edad Media*, IX, 1991.

Calvert and Gasquoine 1907. A. F. Calvert and C. Gasquoine, *The Prado. A description of the principal pictures in Madrid Gallery*, London, 1907.

Calvete de Estrella (1552) 1930. J. C. Calvete de Estrella, *El felicísimo viaje del muy alto y muy poderoso príncipe don Felipe* (1552), Madrid, 1930.

Calvo Ruata (ed.) 1996. J. I. Calvo Ruata (ed.), *Cartas de fray Manuel Bayeu a Martín Zapater*, Zaragoza–Madrid, 1996.

Calvo Serraller 1981. F. Calvo Serraller, *Teoría de la pintura del Siglo de Oro*, Madrid, 1981.

Calvo Serraller 1995. F. Calvo Serraller, *Las meninas*, Madrid, 1995.

Calvo Serraller 1996. F. Calvo Serraller, 'Un retrato melancólico', in *Luis Paret y Alcázar, Autorretrato en el estudio*, Madrid, 1996, pp. 13–42.

Calvo Serraller 1998. F. Calvo Serraller, *Paisajes de luz y muerte. La pintura española del 98*, Barcelona, 1998.

Camón 1950. J. Camón Aznar, *Dominico Greco*, 2 vols, Madrid, 1950.

Camón 1980–1982. J. Camón Aznar, *Francisco de Goya*, 4 vols, Zaragoza, 1980–1982.

Campbell 1990. L. Campbell, *Renaissance Portraits. European Portrait Painting in the 14th, 15th and 16th Centuries*, New Haven–London, 1990.

Campillo Casamor 1875. T. de Campillo Casamor, 'Santo Domingo de Silos, pintura en tabla, procedente de su advocación en Daroca y hoy colocado en el Museo Arqueológico Nacional', *Museo Español de Antigüedades*, IV, 1875, pp. 447–71.

Canellas (ed.) 1981. Á. Canellas (ed.), *Francisco de Goya. Diplomatario*, 1981.

Cano (1777–1778) 1988. J. Cano Olmedilla, *Colección de trajes de España tanto antiguos como modernos* (1777–1788), ed. Valeriano Bozal, Madrid, 1988.

Carderera 1855–1864. V. de Carderera, *Iconografía española*, 2 vols, Madrid, 1855–1864.

Carducho (1633) 1979. V. Carducho, *Diálogos de la pintura. Su defensa, origen, esencia, definición, modos y diferencias* (1633), ed. Francisco Calvo Serraller, Madrid, 1979.

Carmona 1991. E. Carmona, *Picasso, Miró y Dalí y los orígenes del arte contemporáneo en España*, Madrid, 1991.

Caro Baroja 1986. J. Caro Baroja, *Género biográfico y conocimiento antropológico*, Madrid, 1986.

***Carolus* 2000.** *Carolus*, exh. cat., Madrid, 2000.

Carr 2001a. D. W. Carr, 'Regarding El Greco's Portraits', in *El Greco*, exh. cat., Vienna, 2001, English edn, pp. 47–52.

Carr 2001b. D. W. Carr, 'Fray Hortensio Félix Paravicino', in *El Greco*, exh. cat. Vienna, 2001.

Carrasco Muñoz 1973. J. M. Carrasco Muñoz, *Francisco de Zurbarán*, Madrid, 1973.

Carreño, Rizi, Herrera 1986. *Carreño, Rizi, Herrera y la pintura madrileña de su tiempo*, exh. cat., ed. A. E. Pérez Sánchez, Madrid, 1986.

Carrillo 1616. J. Carrillo, *Relación de la Real Fundación del Monasterio de las Descalzas de Santa Clara de la villa de Madrid*, Madrid, 1616.

Casanova 1924–1935. G. Casanova de Seingalt, *Mémoires écrites par lui-même*, 12 vols, Paris, 1924–1935.

Caso González undated. J. M. Caso González, *Vida y obra de Jovellanos*, Madrid, undated.

Cassou 1931. J. Cassou, *Le Greco*, Paris, 1931.

Castelnuovo 1973. E. Castelnuovo, 'Il significato del rittrato pittorico nella società', *Storia d'Italia, V: I documenti*, Turin, 1973.

Castelnuovo 2002. E. Castelnuovo, '*Propter Quid Images Faciei Faciut*. Aspetti del ritratto pittorico nel Trecento', in *Le metamorfosi del ritratto*, Renzo Zorzi (ed.), Venice, 2002.

Castigos e documentos del Rey don Sancho (1292) 1952. *Castigos e documentos del rey don Sancho* (1292), Madrid, 1952.

Castillo 1958. A. del Castillo, *Exposición Ramón Casas, conmemorativa del XXV aniversario de la muerte del artista. Catálogo*, Barcelona, 1958.

***Catálogo de las estampas de Goya* 1996.** *Catálogo de las estampas de Goya en la Biblioteca Nacional*, Madrid, 1996.

***Catalogue... Spanish Gallery* 1853.** *Catalogue of the Pictures forming the celebrated Spanish Gallery of His Majesty the Late King Louis Philippe, which will be Sold by Auction by Messrs, Christie & Manson...*, London, 1853.

Caturla 1960. M. L. Caturla, 'Velázquez y Zurbarán', in *Varia Velazqueña*, I, Madrid, 1960, pp. 463–70.

Caturla 1982. M. L. Caturla, *Antonio de Puga, pintor gallego*, La Coruña, 1982.

Caturla and Delenda 1994. M. L. Caturla and O. Delenda (ed.), *Francisco de Zurbarán*, Paris, 1994.

Cea 2004. A. Cea, 'El concepto de verdadero retrato en las imágenes grabadas de la Virgen', *Revista de Dialectología y Tradiciones Populares*, LIX-2, 2004 (in press).

Ceán Bermúdez (1800) 1965. J. A. Ceán Bermúdez, *Diccionario histórico de los más ilustres profesores de las Bellas Artes en España*, Madrid, 1800 (Facsimile edn), Madrid, 1965.

Ceán Bermúdez 1821. J. A. Ceán Bermúdez, 'Manifestación en la Academia de San Fernando de las obras pertenecientes a las Bellas Artes, executadas en este año de 1821', en *Ocios sobre Bellas Artes*, Madrid, Biblioteca Nacional, MS 21.458/1.

Ceñate 1871. M. Ceñate, 'La Exposición de Bellas Artes de 1871. Artículo III', *La Ilustración Española y Americana*, XV, no. 23, 1871.

Cennini 1988. C. Cennini, *El libro del arte*, ed. Franco Brunello, Madrid, 1988.

Cerdán 1978. F. Cerdán, 'Elementos para la biografía de fray Hortensio Félix Paravicino y Arteaga', *Criticón* (Toulouse), no. 4, 1978, pp. 37–74.

Cerdán 1994. F. Cerdán, *Paravicino y su familia según el expediente C.7720/1 del Palacio Real de Madrid y otros documentos*, Toulouse, 1994.

Cetina 1990. G. de Cetina, *Sonetos y madrigales completos*, ed. B. López, Madrid, 1990.

Chacón 1926. J. Chacón Enríquez, *Eduardo Rosales*, Madrid, 1926 (reissued 1962).

Checa 1987a. F. Checa Cremades, *Carlos V y la imagen del héroe en el Renacimiento*, Madrid, 1987.

Checa 1987b. F. Checa Cremades, 'La imagen impresa en el Renacimiento y el Manierismo', *El grabado en España (siglos XV al XVIII)*, Summa Artis, XXXI, Madrid, 1987.

Checa 1992. F. Checa Cremades, *Felipe II, mecenas de las artes*, Madrid, 1992.

Checa 1996. F. Checa Cremades, Entry no. 3, in *El Greco y su revalorización por el Modernismo catalán*, exh. cat., Barcelona, 1996.

Checa 1998. F. Checa Cremades, 'El príncipe Felipe con armadura', in *Felipe II. Un monarca y su época. Un príncipe del Renacimiento*, exh. cat., Madrid, 1998.

Checa 1999. F. Checa Cremades, *Carlos V, la imagen del poder en el Renacimiento*, Madrid, 1999.

Cherry 1993. P. Cherry, 'Nuevos datos sobre Bartolomé González', *Archivo Español de Arte*, no. 263, 1993, pp. 1–9.

Cherry 2004. P. Cherry, 'Luis Meléndez and the fruits of a frustrated career', en *Luis Meléndez. Still Lifes*, exh. cat., Dublin, 2004.

***Chronique Catalane* 1941.** *Chronique catalane de Pierre IV d'Aragon, III de Catalogne*, ed. Amédée Pagès, Toulouse, 1941.

Ciofalo 2001. J. J. Ciofalo, *The Self-Portraits of Francisco Goya*, Cambridge, 2001.

Cirici Pellicer 1946. A. Cirici Pellicer, *Picasso antes de Picasso*, Barcelona, 1946.

Civil 1991. P. Civil, 'De l'image au texte: portrait de l'auteur dans le livre espagnol des XVIe et XVIIe siècles', *Le livre et l'édition dans le monde hispanique, XVIe–XXe siècles: Pratiques et discours paratextuels. Actes de Colloque International CERHIUS*, Grenoble, 1991, pp. 45–62.

Civil 1999. P. Civil, 'Retrato y poder en el teatro de principios del siglo XVII: "Las grandezas de Alejandro" de Lope de Vega', in M. G. Profeti and A. Redondo (eds), *Représentation, écriture et pouvoir en Espagne à l'époque de Philippe III (1598–1621)*, Paris, 1999.

Clair 2004. J. Clair, 'Parade and Palingenesis. Of the Circus of Picasso and Others', in *The Great Parade. Portrait of the Artist as Clown*, New Haven–London, 2004.

Cloulas 1967. A. Cloulas, 'Documents concernant Titien conservés aux Archives de Simancas', *Mélanges de la Casa de Velázquez*, III, 1967, pp. 197–288.

Coll 2002. I. Coll, *Una vida dedicada al arte. Ramón Casas 1866–1932. Catálogo razonado*, Murcia, 2002.

Coll Mirabent 1986. I. Coll Mirabent, *Santiago Rusiñol*, Barcelona, 1986.

Coll Mirabent 1999. I. Coll Mirabent, *Ramón Casas: Una vida dedicada a l'art*, Barcelona, 1999.

Collar de Cáceres 1983. F. Collar de Cáceres, 'En torno al "Libro de retratos de los reyes" de Hernando de Ávila', *Boletín del Museo del Prado*, IV, no. 10, 1983, pp. 5–36.

Collar de Cáceres 1995. F. Collar de Cáceres, *Libro de retratos, letreros e insignias reales de los reyes de Oviedo, León y Castilla*, Madrid, 1995.

Colomer 1999. J. L. Colomer, 'Roma 1630. "La túnica de José" y el estudio de las pasiones', *Reales Sitios*, XXXVI, no. 141, 1999, pp. 39–49.

Combalía 1990. V. Combalía, *El descubrimiento de Miró. Miró y sus críticos*, Barcelona, 1990.

Condorelli 1965. A. Condorelli, 'Un ritratto firmatto: opus Johannes Burgundi', *Commentari*, XVI, 1965, pp. 77–84.

Constantoudaki 1995. M. Constantoudaki-Kitromilides, 'Italian Influences in El Greco's Early Work. Some new Observations', in N. Hadjinicolaou (ed.), *El Greco of Crete*, Heraklion, 1995, pp. 97–118.

Cooper 1977. D. Cooper, *Juan Gris. Catalogue raisonné de l'œuvre peint établi avec la collaboration de Margaret Potter*, Paris, 1977.

Cossío 1908. M. B. Cossío, *El Greco*, Madrid, 1908.

Cotarelo 1902. A. Cotarelo y Valledor, *La Exposición Rosales. Artículos publicados en 'El Imparcial'*, Madrid, 1902.

Covarrubias (1611) 1987. S. de Covarrubias, *Tesoro de la lengua castellana* (1611), ed. M. de Riquer, Barcelona, 1987.

Crowe and Cavalcaselle 1877–1878. J. A. Crowe and G. B. Cavalcaselle, *Titian: His Life and Times, with Some Account of His Family*, 2 vols, London, 1877–1878.

Cruz Bahamonde 1813. N. de la Cruz Bahamonde, conde de Maule, *Viaje de España, Francia e Italia*, XIII, Madrid, 1813.

Cruz Valdovinos 1999. J. M. Cruz Valdovinos, 'Menipo y Esopo en la Torre de la Parada', in *Velázquez*, Madrid–Barcelona, 1999.

Cruzada Villaamil 1885. G. Cruzada Villaamil, *Anales de la vida y la obra de Diego de Silva Velázquez*, Madrid, 1885.

Cumberland 1807. R. Cumberland, *Memoirs Written by Himself Containing an Account of his Life and Writings...*, II, London, 1807.

Curtis 1883. Ch. B. Curtis, *Velázquez and Murillo. A Descriptive and Historical Catalogue*, London, 1883.

Daix 1987. P. Daix, *Picasso creador. La vida íntima y su obra*, Buenos Aires, 1987.

Daix 1988. P. Daix, 'La Célestine' et ses retours dans l'œuvre de Picasso', en *Picasso. La Célestine*, Paris, 1988.

Daix 1995. P. Daix, *Dictionnaire Picasso*, Paris, 1995.

Daix y Boudaille 1966. P. Daix y G. Boudaille, *Picasso 1900–1906. Catalogue raisonné de l'œuvre peint*, Neuchâtel, 1966.

Davies 1998. D. Davies, 'The Anatomy of Spanish Habsburg Portraits', in *1648. War and Peace in Europe*, exh. cat., Münster–Osnabrück, 1998.

Davies 2003a. D. Davies, 'El "Caballero de la mano en el pecho"', in *El Greco*, Barcelona–Madrid, 2003, pp. 231–51.

Davies 2003b. D. Davies, 'El Greco's Portraits: The Body Natural and the Body Politic', in *El Greco*, exh. cat., New York–London, 2003, pp. 250–83.

Davies 1975. G. A. Davies, '*Pintura*: Background and Sketch of a Spanish Seventeenth Century Court-Genre', *Journal of the Warburg and Courtauld Institutes*, XXXVIII, 1975, pp. 288–313.

De Greco à Picasso 1987. *De Greco à Picasso. Cinq Siècles d'Art Espagnol*, exh. cat., Paris, 1987.

De Vito 1983. G. de Vito, 'Ribera e la svolta degli anni '30', in *Ricerche sul '600 napoletano*, Milan, 1983, pp. 39–55.

Delenda 2004. O. Delenda, *Zurbarán en la sacristía de Guadalupe*, Madrid, 2004.

Delgado 1957. O. Delgado, *Paret y Alcázar*, Madrid, 1957.

***Diario de Madrid* 1797.** *Diario de Madrid*, 10 March 1797.

Díaz Padrón 1982. M. Díaz Padrón, 'Influencia y legado del retrato flamenco del siglo XVII en la España de los Austrias', *Archivo Español de Arte*, LV, 218, 1982, pp. 129–42.

Díez 1991. J. L. Díez García, 'Retratos privados en la pintura española del siglo XIX', in C. Reyero (ed.), *Tesoros de las colecciones particulares madrileñas: Pinturas españolas del Romanticismo al Modernismo*, exh. cat., Madrid, 1991, pp. 45–61.

Díez 1992a. J. L. Díez García, *Pintura española del siglo XIX. Del Neoclasicismo al Modernismo*, exh. cat., Madrid, 1992.

Díez 1992b. J. L. Díez García, *La pintura de historia del siglo XIX en España*, exh. cat., Madrid, 1992.

Díez 1994a. J. L. Díez García, 'El retrato español del siglo XIX', in *El retrato en el Museo del Prado*, Madrid, 1994, pp. 323–50.

Díez 1994b. J. L. Díez García, 'Federico de Madrazo. El inventario de sus pinturas', in J. L. Díez (ed.), *Federico de Madrazo y Kuntz (1815–1894)*, exh. cat., Madrid, 1994, pp. 435–71.

Díez (ed.) 1994a. J. L. Díez García (ed.), *Federico de Madrazo y Kuntz (1815–1894)*, exh. cat., Madrid, 1994.

Díez (ed.) 1994b. J. L. Díez García (ed.), *El mundo literario en la pintura del siglo XIX del Museo del Prado*, exh. cat., Madrid, 1994.

Díez 1997. J. L. Díez García, 'La imagen del artista en la pintura española del siglo XIX', in *Artistas pintados. Retratos de pintores y escultores del siglo XIX en el Museo del Prado*, exh. cat., Barcelona, 1997.

Díez (ed.) 1998. J. L. Díez García (ed.), *José de Madrazo (1781–1859)*, exh. cat., Santander, 1998.

Díez 1999. J. L. Díez García, *Vicente López (1772–1850)*, 2 vols, Madrid, 1999.

Díez 2003. J. L. Díez García, 'Retrato del pintor Carlos Luis de Ribera', in *Museo Nacional del Prado. Memoria de Actividades 2002*, Madrid, 2003, p. 68.

Dillon 1995. G. Dillon, 'El Greco e l'incisione veneta. Precisazioni e novità', in N. Hadjinicolaou (ed.), *El Greco of Crete*, Heraklion, 1995, pp. 229–49.

D'Olwer 1933. N. d'Olwer, 'L'Art dans la vie sociale d'après les romans du XVe siècle', in *La Peinture catalane à la fin du Moyen-Âge*, Paris, 1933.

Domínguez Casas 1993. R. Domínguez Casas, *Arte y etiqueta de los Reyes Católicos. Artistas, residencias, jardines y bosques*, Madrid, 1993.

***Dos Opúsculos Isabelinos* 1979.** *Dos opúsculos isabelinos*, ed. Keith Whinnom, Exeter Hispanic Texts XXII, Exeter, 1979.

Duby 1991. G. Duby, *La época de las catedrales. Arte y sociedad, 980–1420*, Madrid, 1991.

Dupin 1993. J. Dupin, *Miró*, Paris, 1993.

Durán Sanpere 1960. A. Durán i Sanpere, *Per a la història de l'art a Barcelona. Gloses a documents dispersos*, Barcelona, 1960.

Edgerton Jr. 1985. S. Y. Edgerton, *Pictures and Punishment. Art and Criminal Prosecution during the Florentine Renaissance*, Ithaca–London, 1985.

Egido 1983. A. Egido, *'Retratos de los reyes de Aragón' de Andrés Uztárroz y otros poemas de Academia*, Zaragoza, 1983.

Eichberger and Beaven 1995. D. Eichberger and L. Beaven, 'Family Members and Political Allies: The Portrait Collection of Margaret of Austria', *Art Bulletin*, LXXVII, 2, 1995, pp. 225–47.

Eisler 1989. C. Eisler, *The Thyssen-Bornemisza Collection. Early Netherlandish Painting*, London, 1989.

***El Documento Pintado* 2000.** *El documento pintado*, exh. cat., Madrid, 2000.

***El Greco* 2001.** *El Greco*, exh. cat., Vienna, 2001.

***El Greco* 2003.** *El Greco*, exh. cat., New York–London, 2003.

El Greco de Toledo 1982. *El Greco de Toledo*, exh. cat., Madrid, Washington, DC, Toledo (Ohio), Dallas (Texas), 1982–1983; Madrid, 1982 (English edn, *El Greco of Toledo*, Boston, 1982).

***El Greco. Identidad y transformación* 1999.** *El Greco. Identidad y transformación. Creta, Italia, España*, exh. cat., Madrid–Rome–Athens, 1999.

***El Greco in Italy & Italian art* 1994.** *El Greco in Italy and Italian Art*, exh. cat., Athens, 1994.

***El Greco to Goya* 1981.** *El Greco to Goya. The Taste for Spanish Paintings in Britain and Ireland*, exh. cat., London, 1981.

***El Greco y su revalorización* 1996.** El Greco y su revalorización por el Modernismo catalán, exh. cat., Barcelona, 1996.

***El Linaje del Emperador* 2000.** *El linaje del Emperador*, exh. cat., Cáceres, 2000.

***El Mundo Literario* 1994.** *El mundo literario en la pintura del siglo XIX del Museo del Prado*, exh. cat., Madrid, 1994.

***Elegantes de 1900* 2000.** *Elegantes de 1900*, exh. cat., Granada, 2000.

Encina 1924. J. de la Encina, *Crítica al margen (Primera serie)*, Madrid, 1924.

***Es un Voto* 1997.** *Es un voto. Exvotos pictóricos en La Rioja*, exh. cat., Logroño, 1997.

Espí Valdés 1975. A. Espí Valdés, *El pintor Emilio Sala y su obra*, Valencia, 1975.

Espresati 1948. C. Espresati, *Ribalta*, Barcelona, 1948.

***Estatutos* 1757.** *Estatutos de la Real Academia de San Fernando*, Madrid, 1757.

Eusebi 1828. L. Eusebi, *Noticia de los cuadros que se hayan colocados en la galería del museo del rey, nuestro señor, sito en el Prado de esta corte*, Madrid, 1928.

***Exposición de Retratos y Dibujos Antiguos y Modernos* 1910.** *Exposición de retratos y dibujos antiguos y modernos*, exh. cat., Barcelona, 1910.

***Exposición Nacional de Retratos* 1902.** *Exposición nacional de retratos*, exh. cat., Madrid, 1902.

Ezquerra del Bayo 1934. J. Ezquerra del Bayo, *Retratos de la familia Téllez-Girón, novenos duques de Osuna*, Madrid, 1934.

Ezquerra del Bayo 1959. J. Ezquerra del Bayo, *La duquesa de Alba y Goya. Estudio biográfico y artístico*, Madrid, 1959.

Ezquerra del Bayo and Pérez Bueno 1924. J. Ezquerra del Bayo and L. Pérez Bueno, *Retratos de mujeres españolas del siglo XIX*, Madrid, 1924.

Falomir 1994. M. Falomir Faus, *La pintura y los pintores en la Valencia del Renacimiento*, Valencia, 1994.

Falomir 1996a. M. Falomir Faus, 'Sobre los orígenes del retrato y la aparición del "pintor de corte" en la España bajomedieval', *Boletín de Arte*, 17, 1996, pp. 177–95.

Falomir 1996b. M. Falomir Faus, *Arte en Valencia, 1472–1522*, Valencia, 1996.

Falomir 1998. M. Falomir Faus, 'Imágenes del poder y evocación de la memoria. Usos y funciones del retrato en la corte de Felipe II', in *Felipe II. Un monarca y su época. Un príncipe del renacimiento*, exh. cat., Madrid, 1998, pp. 203–27.

Falomir 1998–1999. M. Falomir Faus, 'Imágenes de una santidad frustrada: el culto a Francisco Jerónimo Simón, 1612–1619', *Locus Amœnus*, 4, 1998–1999, pp. 171–81.

Falomir 1999. M. Falomir Faus, 'De la cámara a la galería. Usos y funciones del retrato en la corte de Felipe II', in *Doña María de Portugal. Princesa de Parma (1565–1577) e o suo tempo. As relaçoes culturais entre Portugal e Italia na segunda metade de Quinientos*, Oporto, 1999.

Falomir 2000a. M. Falomir Faus, 'Imágenes e ideas para una monarquía compleja', in *El linaje del Emperador*, exh. cat., Cáceres; Madrid, 2000.

Falomir 2000b. M. Falomir Faus, 'La internacionalización del gusto de la nobleza española', in *Carolus*, exh. cat., Toledo; Madrid, 2000, pp. 375–405.

Falomir 2001. M. Falomir Faus, 'Tiziano, el Aretino y "las alas de la hipérbole". Adulación y alegoría en el retrato real de los siglos XVI y XVII', in *La restauración de 'El emperador Carlos V a caballo en Mühlberg' de Tiziano*, exh. cat., Madrid, 2001, pp. 71–86.

Falomir 2003a. M. Falomir Faus, 'Tiziano: réplicas', in *Tiziano*, exh. cat., Madrid, 2003, pp. 77–91.

Falomir 2003b. M. Falomir Faus, 'Felipe II', in *Tiziano*, exh. cat., Madrid, 2003.

Fauqué and Villanueva 1982. J. Fauqué and R. Villanueva Etcheverría, *Goya y Burdeos, 1824–1828*, Zaragoza, 1982.

***Federico de Madrazo* 1995.** *Federico de Madrazo y Kuntz (1815–1894)*, exh. cat., Madrid, 1995

***Felipe II. Un Monarca* 1998.** *Felipe II. Un monarca y su época. Un príncipe del Renacimiento*, exh. cat., Madrid, 1998.

Felton 1982. C. Felton, Entry no. 24, in *Jusepe de Ribera, Lo Spagnoletto, 1591–1652*, exh. cat., ed. C. Felton and W. B. Jordan, Fort Worth (Texas), 1982.

Ferino-Pagden 2000. S. Ferino-Pagden, 'La imagen ideal y "natural" del poder: los retratos de Carlos V por Tiziano', in *Carolus*, exh. cat., Toledo; Madrid, 2000.

Ferino-Pagden and Kusche 1995. S. Ferino-Pagden and M. Kusche, *Sofonisba Anguissola. A Renaissance Woman*, exh. cat., Washington, 1995.

Fernández de Oviedo [1550–1552]. G. Fernández de Oviedo, *Batallas y quinquágenas, Batalla segunda, quinquágena segunda, diálogo XXXVII*, [1550–1552], Biblioteca Universitaria de Salamanca, Ms. 359.

Fernández de Oviedo 2000. G. Fernández de Oviedo, *Batallas y Qinquágenas*, Madrid, 2000.

Fernández Gracia 2002. R. Fernández Gracia, *Iconografía de don Juan de Palafox. Imágenes para un hombre de Estado y de Iglesia*, Pamplona, 2002.

Feros 2002. A. Feros, '"Sacred and Terrifying gazes": Languages and Images of Power in Early Modern Spain', S. Stratton (ed.), *The Cambridge Companion to Velázquez*, Cambridge, 2002.

Ferrari 1986. O. Ferrari, 'L'iconografia dei filosofi antichi nella pittura del sec. XVII in Italia', *Storia dell'Arte*, 57, 1986, pp. 103–81.

Ferrari and Scavizzi 1992. O. Ferrari and G. Scavizzi, *Luca Giordano, L'opera completa*, 2 vols, Naples, 1992.

Ferrarino 1975. L. Ferrarino, *Tiziano e la Corte di Spagna nei documenti dell'Archivio Generale di Simancas*, Madrid, 1975.

Ferrer 1934. San Vicente Ferrer, *Sermons*, ed. J. Sanchis Sivera, Barcelona, 1934.

Finaldi 2002. G. Finaldi, 'La familia del conde de Santisteban. Homenaje a Velázquez', in *Luca Giordano y España*, exh. cat., Madrid, 2002, no. 26, pp. 152–58.

Finaldi 2003a. G. Finaldi, 'Ribera, the Viceroys of Naples and the King. Some Observations on their Relations', in J. L. Colomer (ed.) *Arte y diplomacia de la Monarquía Hispánica en el siglo XVII*, Madrid, 2003, pp. 379–87.

Finaldi 2003b. G. Finaldi, Entries 76 and 81, in *El Greco*, exh. cat., New York–London, 2003.

Fitz Darby 1962. D. Fitz Darby, 'Ribera and the Wise Men', *The Art Bulletin*, 44, 1962, pp. 279–307.

Fletcher 2003. J. Fletcher, 'Tiziano retratista', in *Tiziano*, exh. cat., Madrid, 2003, pp. 63–75.

Fontán and Axer 1994. A. Fontán and J. Axer, *Españoles y polacos en la corte de Carlos V*, Madrid, 1994.

Fontbona 1975. F. Fontbona, *La crisi del Modernisme artístic*, Barcelona, 1975.

Francastel 1978. G. P. Francastel, *El retrato*, Madrid, 1978.

***Francisco Sabatini* 1993.** *Francisco Sabatini 1721–1797. La arquitectura como metáfora del poder*, exh. cat., Madrid–Aranjuez, 1993.

Freedberg 1992. D. Freedberg, *El poder de las imágenes. Estudios sobre la historia y la teoría de la respuesta*, Madrid, 1992.

Freedman 1995. L. Freedman, *Titian's Portraits Through Aretino's Lens*, University Park (PA), 1995.

Frerichs 1947. L. J. Frerichs, *Antonio Moro*, Amsterdam, 1947

Friedländer (1936) 1975. M.J. Friedländer, *Early Netherlandish Painting. XIII. Anthonis. Mor and his Contemporaries*, Leyden–Brussels, 1936 (2nd edn, New York–Washington, 1975).

Furió Querol 1993. F. Furió Querol, *El Concejo y consejeros del príncipe*, ed. Henry Méchoulan, Madrid, 1993.

***Gaceta de Madrid* 1778.** *Gaceta de Madrid*, 28 July 1778.

Gachard 1984. L. P. Gachard, *Don Carlos y Felipe II*, San Lorenzo del Escorial, 1984.

Gállego 1972. J. Gállego, *Visión y símbolos en la pintura española del Siglo de Oro*, Madrid, 1972 (1st French edn, Paris, 1968).

Gállego 1978. J. Gállego, *Autorretratos de Goya*, Zaragoza, 1978.

Gállego 1983. J. Gállego, 'Los retratos de Goya', in *Goya en las colecciones madrileñas*, exh. cat., Madrid, 1983.

Gállego 1984. J. Gállego, *Visión y símbolos en la pintura española del Siglo de Oro*, Madrid, 1984 (1st Spanish edn, Madrid, 1972).

Gállego 1990. J. Gállego, *Velázquez*, exh. cat., New York–Madrid, 1990.

Gallwitz 1971. K. Gallwitz, *Picasso laureautus, son œuvre depuis 1945*, Paris–Lausana, 1971.

Galofre 1851. J. Galofre, *El artista en Italia y demás países de Europa*, Madrid, 1851.

García 1867. J. García, *Las Bellas Artes en España 1866*, Madrid, 1867.

García-Baquero 1988. A. García-Baquero González, *Libro y cultura burguesa en Cádiz: la biblioteca de Sebastián Martínez*, Cádiz, 1988.

García-Frías 2001. C. García-Frías, 'La retratística de la casa de Austria en el monasterio del Escorial', in *El monasterio del Escorial y la pintura*. Proceedings of the Symposium held at San Lorenzo del Escorial, 1–5 September 2001, pp. 397–419.

García Sanz and Ruiz Gómez 2000. A. García Sanz and L. Ruiz Gómez, 'Linaje regio y monacal: la galería de retratos de las Descalzas Reales', in *El linaje del Emperador*, exh. cat., Cáceres, 2000; Madrid, pp. 135–58.

Garnelo 1914. J. Garnelo, 'Caracteres de la obra pictórica del Greco', *La Ilustración Española y Americana*, LVIII, no. 13, 1914, pp. 222–25.

Garrido 1992. C. Garrido Pérez, *Velázquez, técnica y evolución*, Madrid, 1992.

Garrido 2003. C. Garrido Pérez, 'Aproximaciones a la técnica pictórica de Tiziano', in *Tiziano*, exh. cat., Madrid, 2003, pp. 93–109.

Garrido 2004. C. Garrido Pérez, 'Puntualizaciones sobre algunos retratos de Velázquez', *Goya*, no. 298, 2004.

Gassier and Wilson (1970) 1974. P. Gassier and J. Wilson, *Vida y obra de Francisco de Goya* (1970), Barcelona, 1974.

Gaya Nuño 1950. J. A. Gaya Nuño, *Autorretratos*, Barcelona, 1950.

Gaya Nuño 1957. J. A. Gaya Nuño, *Claudio Coello*, Madrid, 1957.

Gaya Nuño 1960. J. A. Gaya Nuño, *Pintura española fuera de España*, Madrid, 1960.

Gaya Nuño 1974. J. A. Gaya Nuño, *Juan Gris*, Barcelona, 1974.

Gerard Powell and Ressort 2002. V. Gerard Powell and C. Ressort, Musée du Louvre, Département des Peintures. *Catalogue écoles espagnoles et portugaise*, Paris, 2002.

Gerstenberg 1960. K. Gerstenberg, 'Velázquez als Humanist', in *Varia Velazqueña*, 2 vols, Madrid, 1960, I, pp. 207–16.

Gestoso 1889. J. Gestoso y Pérez, *Sevilla monumental y artística*, 2 vols, Seville, 1889.

Gestoso 1899–1900. J. Gestoso y Pérez, *Ensayo de un diccionario de los artífices que florecieron en Sevilla desde el siglo XIII al XVIII inclusive*, 3 vols, Seville, 1899–1900.

Gestoso 1908. J. Gestoso y Pérez, *Ensayo de un diccionario de los artífices que florecieron en Sevilla desde el siglo XIII al XVIII inclusive*, Seville, 1908.

Gestoso 1916. J. Gestoso y Pérez, *Biografía del pintor sevillano Juan Valdés Leal*, Seville, 1916.

Giesey 1960. R. E. Giesey, *Le rey ne meurt jamais. Les obsèques royales dans la France de la Renaissance*, Paris, 1960.

Giovio (1546) 1999. P. Giovio, *Ritratti degli uomini illustri* (1546) ed. C. Caruso, Palermo, 1999.

Glendinning 1963. N. Glendinning, 'Notas biográficas de los retratados', in *Goya and His Times*, exh. cat., London, 1963.

Glendinning (1977) 1982. N. Glendinning, *Goya y sus críticos*, Madrid, 1982 (English edn, New Haven–London, 1977).

Glendinning 1981. N. Glendinning, 'Goya's Patrons', *Apollo*, CXIV, 1981, pp. 236–47.

Glendinning 1982. N. Glendinning, 'Ideas políticas y religiosas de Cadalso', *Cuadernos Hispanoamericanos*, no. 389, 1982, pp. 1–16.

Glendinning 1984. N. Glendinning, 'Cambios en el concepto de la opinión pública a fines del siglo XVIII', *Nueva Revista de Filología Hispánica*, XXXIII, 1984, pp. 157–64.

Glendinning 1989. N. Glendinning, 'Nineteenth-Century Editions of Goya's Etchings. New details of their sales statistics', *Print Quarterly*, 1989.

Glendinning 1992. N. Glendinning, *Goya: La década de los Caprichos. Retratos 1792–1804*, exh. cat. Madrid, 1992.

Glendinning 1994. N. Glendinning, 'Spanish Inventory References to Paintings by Goya, 1800–1850: originals, copies and valuations', *The Burlington Magazine*, CXXXVI, no. 1.091, 1994.

Glendinning 1999. N. Glendinning, 'Cambios en los géneros pictóricos en tiempos de Goya', in *Ideas en sus paisajes. Homenaje al profesor Russell P. Sebold*, Alicante, 1999.

Glendinning 2000. N. Glendinning, 'Goya y el espíritu de Velázquez', in J. Vega (ed.), *Estudiar a los maestros: Velázquez y Goya*, Zaragoza, 2000.

Glendinning 2002. N. Glendinning, 'El retrato en España en el siglo XVIII', in *Siglo XVIII. España. El sueño de la razón*, exh. cat., Rio de Janeiro, 2002, pp. 304–29.

Glendinning, Harris and Russell 1999. N. Glendinning, E. Harris and F. Russell, 'Lord Granham and the Taste for Velázquez: "The Electrical Eel of the Day"', *The Burlington Magazine*, CXLI, 1999, pp. 598–605.

Glück 1931. G. Glück, 'Bildnisse von Juan de Flandes', *Pantheon*, VIII, 1931, pp. 315–16.

Gómez de la Serna (1918) 1986. R. Gómez de la Serna, *Pombo* (1918), Madrid, 1986.

Gómez de la Serna 1972. R. Gómez de la Serna, *Solana*, Madrid, 1972.

Gómez-Menor 1966. J. C. Gómez-Menor, 'En torno a algunos retratos del Greco', *Boletín de Arte Toledano*, Toledo, I, no. 2, 1966, pp. 77–88.

Gómez-Menor 1967. J. C. Gómez-Menor, 'Ávila de Vera', *Boletín de Arte Toledano*, I, no. 3, 1967, p. 129.

Gómez-Menor 1974. J. C. Gómez-Menor, 'Nuevos datos biográficos sobre el licenciado Jerónimo de Cevallos', *Anales Toledanos*, X, 1974, pp. 185–93.

Gómez-Menor 1982. J. C. Gómez-Menor, *Vida y obra del Greco*, Toledo, 1982.

Gómez-Moreno [1943]. M. Gómez-Moreno, *El Greco (Domenico Theotocopuli)*, Barcelona, undated [1943].

Goniotakis 1999. I. Goniotakis, 'A Source for El Greco's "Allegory of the Holy League"', in N. Hadjinicolaou (ed.), *El Greco in Italy and Italian Art, Proceedings of the International Symposium*, Rethymno (Crete), 1999, pp. 177–84.

González García 2004. J. L. González García, 'Imágenes empáticas y diálogos pintados: arte y devoción en el reinado de Isabel la Católica', in *Isabel la Católica. La magnificencia de un reinado*, exh. cat., Valladolid, 2004.

González López 1981. C. González López, *Federico de Madrazo y Kuntz*, Barcelona, 1981.

González Martí 1920. M. González Martí, *Pinazo, su vida y su obra (1849 a 1916)*, Valencia, 1920 (2nd edn, 1971).

González Santos 1994a. J. González Santos, *Jovellanos aficionado y coleccionista*, exh. cat., Gijón, 1994.

González Santos 1994b. J. González Santos, 'Jovellanos por Goya. Precisiones históricas e iconográficas sobre dos conocidos retratos', *Boletín del Museo del Prado*, no. 31, 1994.

González de Zárate 1987. J. M. González de Zárate, 'El retrato en el Barroco y la emblemática: Velázquez y "La lección de equitación del príncipe Baltasar Carlos"', *Boletín del Museo e Instituto Camón Aznar*, 1987, pp. 27–38.

Goodman 2000. E. Goodman, *The Portraits of Madame de Pompadour. Celebrating the Femme Savante*, Berkeley–Los Angeles–London, 2000.

***Goya. 250 aniversario* 1996.** *Goya. 250 aniversario*, exh. cat., Madrid, 1996.

***Goya. El capricho y la invención* 1994.** *Goya. El capricho y la invención*, exh. cat., Madrid, 1994.

***Goya en las colecciones madrileñas* 1983.** *Goya en las colecciones madrileñas*, exh. cat., Madrid, 1983.

***Goya und Velázquez* 1991.** *Goya und Velázquez. Das königliche Portrait*, exh. cat., Frankfurt, 1991.

Green 1992. Ch. Green, *Juan Gris*, London, 1992.

Greub 2001. T. Greub, *'Las Meninas' in Spiegel der Deutungen: eine Einführungen die Methoden der Kunstgeschichte*, Berlin, 2001.

Gudiol 1922. J. Gudiol i Cunill, *La pintura mig-eval catalana II. Els Trescentistes*, Barcelona, 1922.

Gudiol 1927. J. Gudiol i Cunill, *Els Primitius, I (La pintura mig-eval catalana)*, Barcelona, 1927.

Gudiol 1971. J. Gudiol Ricart, *El Greco, 1541–1614*, Barcelona, 1971.

Gudiol 1973. J. Gudiol Ricart, *Velázquez, 1599–1660. Historia de su vida; catálogo de su obra; estudio de la evolución de su técnica*, Barcelona, 1973.

Guevara 1788. F. de Guevara, *Comentarios de la pintura*, Madrid, 1788.

Guinard 1960. P. Guinard, *Zurbarán et les peintres espagnols de la vie monastique*, Paris, 1960.

Gutiérrez Burón 1987. J. Gutiérrez Burón, *Exposiciones nacionales de pintura en España en el siglo XIX*, Madrid, 1987.

Gutiérrez Solana 1975. J. Gutiérrez Solana, *La España negra*, Barcelona, 1975.

Hadjinicolaou 1993. N. Hadjinicolaou, 'Inequalities in the Work of El Greco and their Interpretation', *Ariadne*, Rethymno, VI, 1993, pp. 175–212.

Haraszti-Takács 1983. M. Haraszti-Takács, *Spanish Genre Painting in the Seventeenth Century*, Budapest, 1983.

Harbison 1967. C. S. Harbison, 'Counter-reformation iconography in Titian's Gloria', *Art Bulletin*, XLIX, 3, 1967.

Harris 1976a. E. Harris, 'Velázquez's Portrait of Prince Baltasar Carlos in the Riding School', *The Burlington Magazine*, CXVIII, 871, 1976, pp. 266–75.

Harris 1976b. E. Harris, 'Velázquez's Apsley House portrait: An Identification', *The Burlington Magazine*, 1976.

Harris 1982. E. Harris, *Velázquez*, Oxford, 1982.

Harris 1983. E. Harris, 'Goya in Madrid', *The Burlington Magazine*, CXXV, no. 965, 1983, pp. 511–12.

Harris 1970. H. Harris, 'Casiano dal Pozzo on Diego Velázquez', *The Burlington Magazine*, 112, 1970.

Haverkamp-Begemann 1952. E. Haverkamp-Begemann, 'Juan de Flandes y los Reyes Católicos', *Archivo Español de Arte*, XXV, 1952, pp. 237–47.

Hellwig 1999. K. Hellwig, *La literatura artística española del siglo XVII*, Madrid, 1999.

Helman (1963) 1983. E. Helman, *Trasmundo de Goya* (1963), Madrid, 1983.

Helman 1970. E. Helman, *Jovellanos y Goya*, Madrid, 1970.

Herrero García 1936. M. Herrero García, 'Un dictamen pericial de Velázquez y una escena de Lope', *Revista Española de Arte*, XIII, 1936, pp. 66–68.

Herrero García 1943. M. Herrero García, *Contribución de la literatura a la historia del arte*, Madrid, 1943.

Hidalgo Ogáyar 1997. J. Hidalgo Ogáyar, 'Doña Mencía de Mendoza, marquesa del Zenete, condesa de Nassau y duquesa de Calabria, ejemplo de mujer culta en el siglo XVI', in *La mujer en el arte español*, Madrid, 1997, pp. 83–102.

Holanda (1548) 1921. F. de Holanda, *De la pintura antigua* (1548), trans. M. Denis, Madrid, 1921.

Hope 1980. Ch. Hope, *Titian*, London, 1980.

Hope 1988. Ch. Hope, 'La produzione pittorica di Tiziano per gli Asburgo', in *Venecia e la Spagna*, Milan, 1988.

Horn 1989. H. J. Horn, *Jan Cornelisz. Vermeyen. Painter of Charles V and his Conquest of Tunis*, Davaco, 1989.

Hurtado de Mendoza 1990. D. Hurtado de Mendoza, *Poesía*, ed. L. F. Díaz Larios and O. Gete Carpio, Madrid, 1990.

Hymans 1910. H. Hymans, *Antonio Moro*, Brussels, 1910.

Jarne 1992. R. R. Jarne, Entry 37, in *Goya*, exh. cat., Zaragoza, 1992, p. 104.

Jenkins 1977. M. Jenkins, *Il ritratto di stato*, Rome, 1977.

Jiménez 1904. J. R. Jiménez, 'Joaquín Sorolla y sus retratos', *Forma*, Barcelona, 1904, pp. 21–26.

Jiménez 1960. J. R. Jiménez, *Españoles de tres mundos*, Madrid, 1960.

***Joan de Joanes* 2000.** *Joan de Joanes. Una nueva visión del artista y su obra*, exh. cat., Valencia, 2000.

Joannides 1995. P. Joannides, 'El Greco and Michelangelo', en N. Hadjinicolaou (ed.), *El Greco of Crete*, Heraklion, 1995, pp. 199–214.

Jordan 1982. W. B. Jordan, Entries 12, 59 and 63, in *El Greco de Toledo*, exh. cat., Madrid, 1982.

Jordan 1994. A. Jordan, *Retrato de Corte em Portugal. O legado de António Moro (1552–1572)*, Lisbon, 1994, pp. 179–82.

Jovellanos [1781]. G. M. de Jovellanos, *Oración pronunciada en la Junta Pública que celebró la Real Academia de San Fernando el día 14 de julio de 1781*, Madrid [1781].

Junoy 1934. J. M. Junoy, 'Isidre Nonell', *Art*, I, no. 10, 1934.

Junta de Iconografía Nacional 1914. *Junta de Iconografía Nacional. Retratos de personajes españoles. Índice ilustrado*, Madrid, 1914.

Juretschke and Kleinmann (eds) 1987. H. Juretschke and H.-O. Kleinmann (eds), *Berichte der diplomatischen Vertreter des Wiener Hofes aus Spanien in der Regierungszeit Karls III. (1759–1788)*, 18 vols, XII, Madrid, CSIC, 1987.

***Jusepe de Ribera, lo Spagnoletto* 1982.** *Jusepe de Ribera, Lo Spagnoletto, 1591–1652*, exh. cat., C. Felton and W. B. Jordan (eds), Fort Worth, 1982.

***Jusepe de Ribera. Prints and Drawings* 1973.** *Jusepe de Ribera. Prints and Drawings*, exh. cat., J. Brown (ed.), Princeton University, 1973.

Justi (1888) 1903. C. Justi, *Diego Velázquez und sein Jahrhundert* (1888), Bonn, 1903.

Kagan 1982. R. L. Kagan, 'La Toledo de El Greco', in *El Greco de Toledo*, exh. cat., Madrid, 1982.

Kagan 2003. R. L. Kagan, 'El Greco y su entorno humano en Toledo', in *El Greco*, Barcelona–Madrid, 2003, pp. 99–115.

Kahnweiler 1971. D.-H. Kahnweiler, *Juan Gris. Vida y pintura*, Madrid, 1971.

Kantorowicz 1957. E. H. Kantorowicz, *The King's two Bodies; a Study in Medieval Political Theology*, Princeton, 1957 (1st Spanish edn, Madrid, 1985).

Kantorowicz 1965. E. H. Kantorowicz, *Selected Studies*, Locus Valley, 1965.

Kantorowicz (1957) 1989. E. H. Kantorowicz, *Los dos cuerpos del rey. Un estudio de la teología política medieval* (1985), Madrid, 1989.

Kinkead 1978. D. T. Kinkead, *Juan de Valdés Leal (1622–1690). His Life and Work*, New York–London, 1978.

Kowal 1985. D. M. Kowal, *Ribalta y los ribaltescos. La evolución del estilo barroco en Valencia*, Valencia, 1985.

Kusche 1991. M. Kusche, 'La antigua galería de retratos del Pardo: su reconstrucción arquitectónica y el orden de colocación de los cuadros', *Archivo Español de Arte*, CLIII, 1991, pp. 1–28.

Kusche 1999. M. Kusche, 'Rolán de Moys, más allá de Aragón', in *El arte en las cortes de Carlos V y Felipe II*, Madrid, 1999.

Kusche 2003. M. Kusche, *Retratos y retratadores. Alonso Sánchez Coello y sus competidores Sofonisba Anguissola, Jorge de la Rúa y Rolán Moys*, Madrid, 2003.

***La Catedral de Toledo* 1999.** *La catedral de Toledo. 1549. Según el Dr. Blas Ortiz*, Toledo, 1999.

***La Miniatura Retrato en España* 1916.** *La miniatura retrato en España*, exh. cat., Madrid, 1916.

Labrot 1992. G. Labrot, with A. Delfino, *Italian Inventories I, Collections of Paintings in Naples, 1600–1780 (Documents for the History of Collecting)*, The Provenance Index of the Getty Art History Information Program, Munich, 1992.

Lacarra Ducay 2003. M. C. Lacarra Ducay, 'Encuentro de santo Domingo de Silos con el rey Fernando I de Castilla de Bartolomé Bermejo y Martín Bernat', in *La pintura gótica hispanoflamenca. Bartolomé Bermejo y su época*, exh. cat., Barcelona–Bilbao, 2003.

Lafuente Ferrari 1928. E. Lafuente Ferrari, *Goya*, exh. cat., Madrid, 1928, pp. 91–92.

Lafuente Ferrari 1935. E. Lafuente Ferrari, *Los retratos de Lope de Vega*, Madrid, 1935.

Lafuente Ferrari 1941. E. Lafuente Ferrari, 'La inspección de los retratos reales en el siglo XVII', *Correo Erudito*, 1941.

Lafuente Ferrari 1942. E. Lafuente Ferrari, Introduction, in W. Weisbach, *El barroco como arte de la Contrarreforma*, Madrid, 1942.

Lafuente Ferrari 1946. E. Lafuente Ferrari, *Breve historia de la pintura española*, Madrid, 1946 (reissued 1962).

Lafuente Ferrari 1950a. E. Lafuente Ferrari, *La vida y el arte de Ignacio Zuloaga*, San Sebastián, 1950.

Lafuente Ferrari 1950b. E. Lafuente Ferrari, 'Los retratos de Zuloaga', *Príncipe de Viana*, XI, nos 18 and 19, Pamplona, 1950, pp. 3–35.

Lafuente Ferrari 1962. E. Lafuente Ferrari, *De Trajano a Picasso*, Barcelona, 1962.

Lafuente Ferrari 1978. E, Lafuente Ferrari, *El Prado. Pintura española de los siglos XVII y XVIII*, Madrid, 1978.

Laínez (1935) 2003. R. Laínez Alcalá, *Pedro Berruguete, pintor de Castilla* (1935), Madrid, 2003 (Facsimile edn).

Lanchner 1993. C. Lanchner, *Joan Miró*, New York, 1993.

***Las Cortes del Barroco* 2003.** *Las cortes del Barroco: De Bernini y Velázquez a Luca Giordano*, exh. cat., Madrid, 2003.

Lassalle 1981. Ch. Lassalle, 'Felipe de Liaño: el pequeño Tiziano', *Boletín del Museo e Instituto Camón Aznar*, 2–3, 1981, pp. 51–84.

Leal, Ocaña, Cerverau *et al.* 2003. B. Leal, M. T. Ocaña, L. Cerverau *et al.*, *Picasso. De la caricatura a las metamorfosis de estilo*, Barcelona, 2003.

Lecercle 1987. F. Lecercle, *Le Chimère de Zeuxis. Potrait poétique et portrait peint en France et en Italie à la Renaissance*, Tubingen, 1987.

Lee 1977. R. W. Lee, *Names on Trees: Ariosto into Art*, Princeton, 1977.

Leroy 1986. B. Leroy, 'La Cour des rois de Navarre dans la deuxieme moitié du XIVe siècle et au debut du XVe siècle, une recontre de techniciens', *Anuario de Estudios Medievales*, 16, 1986.

Leroy 1988. B. Leroy, 'La Cour des rois Charles II et Charles III de Navarre (vers 1350–1425), lieu de rencontre, milieu de gouvernement', in A. Rucquoi (coord.), *Realidad e imágenes de poder. España a fines de la Edad Media*, Valladolid, 1988.

Levey 1976. M. Levey, *Painting at Court*, New York, 1976.

Leymarie (1971) 1985. J. Leymarie, *Picasso. Métamorphoses et unité, Paris*, 1985 (1st edn, Geneva, 1971).

Liedtke 1989. W. Liedtke, *The Royal Horse and Rider. Painting, Sculpture and Horsemanship, 1500–1800*, New York, 1989.

Ligo 1970. L. L. Ligo, 'Two Seventeenth-Century Poems which link Ruben's Equestrian Portrait of Philip IV to Titian's Equestrian Portrait of Charles V', *Gazette des Beaux-Arts*, LXXV, 1970, pp. 345–54.

Lisón 1992. C. Lisón Tolosana, *La imagen del rey (Monarquía, realeza y poder ritual en la casa de los Austrias)*, Madrid, 1992.

Llompart 1973. G. Llompart, 'Aspectos folclóricos en la pintura gótica de Jaume Huguet y los Vergos', *Revista de Dialectología y Tradiciones Populares*, XXXIX, 1973, pp. 397–403.

Llorens 1986. T. Llorens, *Julio González en las colecciones del IVAM*, Valencia, 1986.

Longhi 1914. R. Longhi, 'Il soggiorno romano del Greco', *L'Arte*, XVII, fasc. 4, 1914, pp. 301–303.

López de Prado 1999. C. López de Prado, 'La imagen de la mujer', in *La mirada complacida y la mirada inquieta. La pintura finisecular entre la tradición y la modernidad*, La Coruña, 1999, pp. 176–96.

López Fernández 2003. M. López Fernández, 'Mujeres pintadas: la imagen femenina en el arte español de fin de siglo (1890–1914)', in *Mujeres pintadas. La imagen de la mujer en España 1890/ 1914*, Madrid, 2003, pp. 14–57.

López Navío 1962. J. López Navío, *La gran colección de pinturas del marqués de Leganés*, Madrid, 1962 (separate issue of *Analecta Calansanctiana* no. 8, pp. 262–330).

López-Rey 1963. J. López-Rey, *Velázquez. A Catalogue Raisonné of his Oeuvre*, London, 1963.

López-Rey 1971. J. López-Rey, 'Zurbarán as Portrait-Painter', *Apollo*, 1971, pp. 120–25.

López-Rey 1996. J. López-Rey, *Velázquez*, 2 vols, Cologne–London, 1996.

López-Rey 1999. J. López-Rey, *Velázquez*, Cologne, 1999.

***Los Austrias* 1993.** *Los Austrias. Grabados en la Biblioteca Nacional*, exh. cat., Madrid, 1993.

***Los Ribalta y la pintura valenciana de su tiempo* 1987.** *Los Ribalta y la pintura valenciana de su tiempo*, exh. cat., ed. F. Benito Doménech, Valencia–Madrid, 1987.

Lostalot 1894. A. Lostalot, 'Le Musée du Prado. L'École espagnole', *Gazette des Beaux-Arts*, 3rd season, XI, 1894, pp. 232–50.

Lozoya (ed.) 1975. M. de Lozoya (ed.), *Sotomayor*, exh. cat., Madrid, 1975.

Lubar 1989. R. S. Lubar, *Joan Miró before 'The Farm', 1915–1922: Catalan Nationalism and the Avant-garde*, New York, 1989.

Lubar 1999. R. S. Lubar, 'Narrar la narración: Picasso y el mito del Greco', in J. Brown (ed.), *Picasso y la tradición española*, Hondarribia, 1999, pp. 39–72.

***Luis Paret y Alcázar* 1991.** *Luis Paret y Alcázar 1746–1799*, exh. cat., Vitoria–Gasteiz, 1991.

Luna 1975. J. J. Luna, 'Algunos retratos franceses del XVIII en colecciones españolas', *Archivo Español de Arte*, XLVIII, 1975, pp. 365–84.

Luxemberg 1997. A. Luxemberg, 'Jean Ranc: *Carlos III as a Child*', in R. Kasl and S. L. Stratton (eds), *Painting in Spain in the Age of the Enlightenment. Goya and His Contemporaries*, exh. cat., Indianapolis, 1997, pp. 136–37.

Luxemberg 2001. A. Luxemberg, 'Retrato emblemático e identidad. *Carlos III, niño* de Jean Ranc', *Boletín del Museo del Prado*, Madrid, XIX, no. 37, 2001, pp. 72–78.

Maclaren/Braham 1970. N. Maclaren, revised and edited by A. Braham, *National Gallery Catalogues. The Spanish School*, London, 1970.

Madariaga and Valbuena 1976. B. Madariaga de la Campa and C. Valbuena de Madariaga, *Cara y máscara de José Gutiérrez Solana*, Santander, 1976.

Madrazo 1994a. F. de Madrazo, *Epistolario (1838–1839)*, ed. J. L. Díez, Madrid, 1994.

Madrazo 1994b. F. de Madrazo, 'Recuerdos de mi vida', in *Federico de Madrazo (1815–1894)*, exh. cat., Madrid, 1994.

Madrazo 1998. J. de Madrazo, *Epistolario (1839–1841)*, ed. J. L. Díez, Santander, 1998.

Madurell Marimón 1952. J. M. Madurell Marimón, 'El pintor Lluís Borrassá. Su vida, su tiempo, sus seguidores y sus obras', *Anales y Boletín de los Museos de Arte de Barcelona*, X, 1952.

***Maestros Valencianos* 1997.** *Maestros valencianos de la pintura valenciana del siglo XIX*, exh. cat., Madrid, 1997.

Magdaleno 1999. R. Magdaleno, 'Intervención en los retratos de la familia Caballero', *Boletín del Instituto Andaluz de Patrimonio Histórico*, no. 27, 1999.

Mancini 2000. M. Mancini, 'La elaboración de nuevos modelos en la retratística carolina: La relación priviligiada entre el emperador y Tiziano', in *Carlos V y las artes. Promoción artística y familia imperial*, Valladolid, 2000, pp. 221–34.

***Manet/Velázquez* 2003.** *Manet/Velázquez. The French Taste for Spanish Painting*, exh. cat., New York, 2003.

Mann 1998. N. Mann, 'Petrarch and Portraits', in N. Mann and L. Syson (eds), *The Image of the Individual. Portraits in the Renaissance*, London, 1998.

Mano 2002. J. M. de la Mano, *Trazos de las luces. Dibujos españoles del siglo XVIII*, Madrid, 2002.

'La mano en el pecho' 1926. 'La mano al pecho', *Archivo Español de Arte y Arqueología*, II, no. 6, 1926, p. 292.

March 1941. P. J. M. March, S. J., *Infancia y Juventud de Felipe II*, Madrid, 1941.

March 1948. P. J. M. March, S. J., 'Tres tablas del Palau de Barcelona atribuibles a Mabuse', *Boletín de la Sociedad Española de Excursiones*, LII, 1948.

March 1961. P. J. M. March, S. J., 'Los XII duques de Alba vistos desde Barcelona', *Boletín de la Real Academia de la Historia*, CXLIX, 1961, pp. 153–243.

Marcos Villalón 2003. E. Marcos Villalón, *Luis Bagaría. Entre el arte y la política* (PhD thesis), Universidad Complutense de Madrid, 2003.

Marías 1993. F. Marías, 'Reflexiones sobre una colección de pinturas del Greco y la "Gloria de Felipe II"', *Anuario del Departamento de Historia y Teoría del Arte*, Unviersidad Autónoma de Madrid, V, 1993, pp. 59–70.

Marías 1995. F. Marías, 'El género de *Las meninas*: los servicios de la familia', in F. Marías (ed.), *Otras meninas*, Madrid, 1995.

Marías (ed.) 1995. F. Marías (ed.), *Otras meninas*, Madrid, 1995.

Marías 1997a. F. Marías, *El Greco. Biografía de un pintor extravagante*, Madrid, 1997.

Marías 1997b. F. Marías, 'Juan Pantoja de la Cruz: El arte cortesano de la imagen, las devociones femeninas', in *La mujer en el arte español*, VIII Jornadas de Arte del Departamento de Historia del Arte Diego Velázquez, Madrid, 1997, pp. 103–16.

Marías 1999a. F. Marías, *Las meninas*, Madrid, 1999.

Marías 1999b. F. Marías, '¿Un rey solo? Felipe II, sus mujeres y las artes', en *Felipe II y el arte de su tiempo. Debates sobre arte*, VIII, Madrid, 1999.

Marías and Bustamante 1981. F. Marías and A. Bustamante, *Las ideas artísticas del Greco (Comentarios a un texto inédito)*, Madrid, 1981.

Marin 1981. L. Marin, *Le Portrait du Roi*, Paris, 1981.

Marín Valdés 1985. F. A. Marín Valdés, 'Aureliano de Beruete: cartas a Joaquín Sorolla', *Liño*, V, no. 5, 1985, pp. 7–98.

Marín Valdés 1988. F. A. Marín Valdés, 'Aureliano de Beruete y la ciudad de Toledo', *Anales Toledanos*, XXV, Toledo, 1988, pp. 285–325.

Mariño 1990. B. Mariño, *Contribución a la iconografía del trabajo urbano en el arte medieval hispánico (siglos XI al XIII)* (PhD thesis), Santiago de Compostela, 1990.

Marlier 1934. G. Marlier, *Antonio Moro*, Brussels, 1934.

Márquez Villanueva 1959. F. Márquez Villanueva, 'En torno al "Caballero de la mano al pecho" (textos literarios coetáneos)', *Archivo Español de Arte*, XXXII, 1959, pp. 193–97.

Martí Monsó 1898–1901. J. Martí y Monsó, *Estudios histórico-artísticos relativos a Valladolid*, Valladolid, 1898–1901.

Martín Morales 1986. F. Martín Morales, 'Aproximación al estudio del mercado de cuadros en la Sevilla barroca (1600–1670)', *Archivo Hispalense*, no. 210, 1986.

Martindale 1988. A. Martindale, *Heroes, Ancestors, Relatives and the Birth of the Portrait*, Groningen, 1988.

Martínez 1788. F. Martínez, *Introducción al conocimiento de las bellas artes, o diccionario manual de pintura, escultura, arquitectura, grabado, etc. Con la descripción de sus más principales asuntos*, Madrid, 1788.

Martínez (*ca.* 1673) 1950. J. Martínez, *Discursos practicables del nobilísimo arte de la pintura* (*ca.* 1673), ed. J. Gállego, Barcelona, 1950.

Martínez (*ca.* 1675) 1988. J. Martínez, *Discursos practicables del nobilísimo arte de la pintura* (*ca.* 1675), ed. J. Gállego, Madrid, 1988.

Martorell 1983. J. Martorell, *Tirant lo Blanch*, ed. Martín de Riquer, Barcelona, 1983.

Marzolf 1961. R. M. Marzolf, *The Life and Work of Juan Carreño de Miranda (1614–1685)*, Ann Arbor, 1961.

Mateo Gómez 1985. I. Mateo Gómez, 'Reflexiones sobre aspectos iconográficos en el "Santo Domingo de Silos", de Bermejo', *Boletín del Museo del Prado*, no. 16, 1985, pp. 4–13.

Matilla 2000. J. M. Matilla, 'El grabado y la casa de Austria: la imagen del rey, la difusión de la idea dinástica y la memoria de los hechos imperiales', in *El linaje del Emperador*, exh. cat., Cáceres, 2000, pp. 79–98.

Matthews 2001. P. G. Matthews, 'Jacob Seisenegger's Portrait of Charles V, 1530–32', *The Burlington Magazine*, CXLIII, 2001.

Maurer 2002. G. Maurer, '"La familia de Carlos IV" de Francisco de Goya. Del Palacio Real al Museo del Prado', in M. Mena Marqués (ed.), *Goya. La familia de Carlos IV*, Madrid, 2002, pp. 195–270.

Mayans y Siscar (1776) 1996. G. Mayans y Siscar, *Arte de pintar* (1776), ed. A. León, Madrid, 1996.

Mayer 1916. A. L. Mayer, 'Paintings by el Greco in America. Part One', *Art in America*, IV, no. V, 1916, pp. 245–57.

Mayer 1922. A. L. Mayer, *Meisterwerke der Gemäldesammlung des Prado in Madrid*, Munich, 1922.

Mayer 1930. A. L. Mayer, 'Die Ausstellung der Sammlumng Schloss Rohoncz in München', *Pantheon*, VI, 1930, pp. 307–08.

Mayer 1936. A. L. Mayer, *Velázquez. A Catalogue Raisonné of the Pictures and Drawings*, London, 1936.

McDonald 1993. M. P. McDonald, 'Some Drawings by Jusepe de Ribera', *Storia dell'Arte*, 78, 1993, pp. 156–61.

Meier-Graefe (1910) 1926. J. Meier-Graefe, *Spanische Reise*, Berlin, 1910 (English edn, *The Spanish Journey*, London, 1926).

Mélida 1899. J. R. Mélida, 'La Exposición Nacional de Bellas Artes. Artículo segundo', *La Ilustración Española y Americana*, XLIII, no. 19, Madrid, 23 May 1899.

***Memoria Histórica* 1988.** *Memoria histórica del Siglo de las Luces: Retratos de los españoles ilustres*, Madrid, 1988.

Mena 1989. J. de Mena, *Obras completas*, Barcelona, 1989.

Mena Marqués 1997. M. Mena Marqués, 'El encaje en la manga de la enana Maribárbola', in *El Museo del Prado. Fragmentos y detalles*, Madrid, 1997.

Mena Marqués 1999. M. Mena Marqués, '¿El bufón Calabacillas?', in *Velázquez*, Barcelona–Madrid, 1999.

Mena Marqués 2000. M. Mena Marqués, 'Velázquez y la Torre de la Parada', in *Velázquez y Calderón. Dos genios de Europa (IV Centenario, 1599–1600–1999–2000)*, Madrid, 2000, pp. 101–55.

Mena Marqués 2002. M. Mena Marqués, '1800. La familia de Carlos IV', in M. Mena Marqués (ed.), *Goya. La familia de Carlos IV*, Madrid, 2002, pp. 67–193.

Mena Marqués (ed.) 2002. M. Mena Marqués (ed.), *Goya. La familia de Carlos IV*, Madrid, 2002.

Méndez Casal 1936. A. Méndez Casal, 'La pintura antigua española en Escandinavia', *Arte Español*, Madrid, XIII, 1936, pp. 2–10.

Mendoza and Doñate (eds) 2000. C. Mendoza and M. Doñate (eds), *Isidre Nonell, 1872–1911*, exh. cat., Barcelona and Madrid, 2000.

Mendoza and Doñate (eds) 2001. C. Mendoza and M. Doñate (eds), *Ramón Casas, el pintor del Modernismo*, exh. cat., Barcelona–Madrid, 2001.

Mengs 1780. A. R. Mengs, *Obras de D. Antonio Rafael Mengs…, publicadas por don José Nicolás de Azara*, Madrid, 1780.

Menjot 1988. D. Menjot, 'Un Chrétien qui meurt toujours. Les funérailles royalles en Castille à la fin du Moyen-Âge', in *La idea y el sentimiento de la muerte en la historia y en el arte de la Edad Media*, Santiago de Compostela, 1988, pp. 127–38.

Miguel Egea 1981. P. de Miguel Egea, *Carlos Luis de Ribera. Pintor romántico madrileño*, Madrid, 1981.

Miguel Egea 1983. P. de Miguel Egea, 'Juan Antonio de Ribera, "Pintor neoclásico"', *Academia*, 1983, pp. 185–212.

Milhou 1981. M. Milhou, *Ignacio Zuloaga et la France*, Bordeaux, 1981.

Mínguez 1991. V. Mínguez, 'El espejo de los antepasados y el retrato de Carlos II en el Museo Lázaro Galdiano', *Boletín del Museo e Instituto Camón Aznar*, XLV, 1991, pp. 71–81.

Miralles 1988. M. Miralles, *Dietari del capella d'Alfons el Magnànim*, ed. V.-J. Escartí, Valencia, 1988.

Moffitt 1981–1982. J. F. Moffitt, 'Goya y los demonios: el autorretrato con el doctor Arrieta y la tradición del *ars moriendi*', *Goya*, no. 163, 1981–1982, pp. 2–13.

Moffitt 1991. J. F. Moffitt, 'La lección ecuestre del príncipe Baltasar Carlos', in J. F. Moffitt, *Velázquez, Práctica e idea: estudios dispersos*, Málaga, 1991, pp. 195–212.

Molina 1999. J. Molina, *Arte, devoción y poder en la pintura tardogótica catalana*, Murcia, 1999.

***Monstruos, enanos y bufones* 1986.** *Monstruos, enanos y bufones en la corte de los Austrias*, exh. cat., Madrid, 1986.

Morales Marín 1979. J. L. Morales Marín, *Los Bayeu*, Zaragoza, 1979.

Morales Marín 1980. J. L. Morales Marín, *Vicente López*, Zaragoza, 1980.

Morales Marín 1994. J. L. Morales Marín, *Goya. Catálogo de la pintura*, Torrejón de Ardoz, 1994.

Morales Marín 1997. J. L. Morales Marín, *Luis Paret. Vida y obra*, Zaragoza, 1997.

Morán 1990. M. Morán Turina, *La imagen del rey. Felipe V y el arte*, Madrid, 1990.

Morán 2003. M. Morán Turina, 'Reinterpretando a Velázquez: Carreño y el retrato de corte', in *Las cortes del Barroco: De Bernini y Velázquez a Luca Giordano*, exh. cat., Madrid, 2003, pp. 63–72.

Morán and Checa 1985. M. Morán Turina and F. Checa Cremades, *El coleccionismo en España*, Madrid, 1985.

Moreno Carbonero 1898. J. Moreno Carbonero, *Discursos leídos ante la Real Academia de Bellas Artes de San Fernando en la recepción pública de D. José Moreno Carbonero el día 27 de noviembre de 1898*, Madrid, 1898.

Moreno de las Heras 1989. M. Moreno de las Heras, 'Francisco de Cabarrús', in *Goya y el espíritu de la Ilustración*, exh. cat., Madrid–Boston–New York, 1989.

Moreno de las Heras 1996. M. Moreno de las Heras, Entry no. 147, in *Goya. 250 aniversario*, exh. cat., Madrid, 1996, no. 147, p. 41.

Moreno de las Heras 1997. M. Moreno de las Heras, *Goya. Pinturas del Museo del Prado*, Madrid, 1997.

Moreno Garrido 1976. A. Moreno Garrido, 'El grabado en Granada durante el siglo XVII. I. La calcografía', *Cuadernos de Arte de la Universidad de Granada*, XIII, 1976, pp. 61 *et seq*.

Moreno Mendoza *et al.* 1991. A. Moreno Mendoza, E. Pareja López, M. J. Sanz Serrano and E. Valdivieso González, *Museo de Bellas Artes de Sevilla*, 2 vols, Seville, 1991.

Moreno Villa 1939. J. Moreno Villa, *Locos, enanos, negros y niños palaciegos*, Mexico City, 1939.

Moreno Villa 1944. J. Moreno Villa, *Vida en claro*, Mexico City, 1944.

Moreno Villa 1951. J. Moreno Villa, *Los autores como actores*, Mexico City, 1951.

Morte 1990–1991. C. Morte, 'Pintura y política en la época de los Austrias: los retratos de los reyes de Sobrarbe, condes antiguos y reyes de Aragón para la diputación de Zaragoza (1586) y las copias para el Buen Retiro de Madrid', *Boletín del Museo del Prado*, XI, no. 29, 1990, pp. 19–35; and XII, no. 30, 1991, pp. 19–33.

Morte 1999. C. Morte, 'Roland Moys, el retrato cortesano en Aragón y la sala de linajes de los duques de Villahermosa', in *El arte en las cortes de Carlos V y Felipe II*, exh. cat., Madrid, 1999, pp. 445–68.

Mulcahy 1996. R. Mulcahy, 'Alonso Sánchez Coello and the Grand Duke Ferdinando I de'Medici', *The Burlington Magazine*, CXXXVIII, 1996, pp. 517–21.

Mulcahy 2000. R. Mulcahy, 'La imagen real o la real imagen. Imágenes y percepciones de Felipe II', in L. Ribot (ed.), *La monarquía de Felipe II a debate*, Madrid, 2000, pp. 473–96.

Muller 1972. P. E. Muller, *Jewels in Spain, 1500–1800*, New York, 1972.

Muñoz 1554. A. Muñoz, *Sumaria y verdadera relación del buen viaje que el invictíssimo Príncipe de las Españas don Felipe hizo a Inglaterra, y recebemiento en Vicenstra donde casó, y salió para London*, Nájera, 1554.

Muñoz Rubio 2003. M. del V. Muñoz Rubio, 'Piezas singulares. El Greco. Retrato de su hijo Jorge Manuel Theotocopuli', *Mus-A*, Seville, 1, no. 1, 2003, pp. 54–57.

***Murillo. Scenes of Childhood* 2001.** *Murillo. Scenes of Childhood*, exh. cat., ed. X. Brooke and P. Cherry, London, 2001.

Nelken 1917. M. Nelken, *Glosario (obras y artistas)*, Madrid, 1917.

Nolhac 1884. P. de Nolhac, 'Una Galerie de peinture au XVIe siècle: Les collections de Fulvio Orsini', *Gazette des Beaux-Arts*, XXIX, 1884, pp. 427–36.

Nonell 1963. C. Nonell, Carolina, *Isidro Nonell, su vida y su obra*, Madrid, 1963.

Nordau undated. M. Nordau, *Los grandes del arte español*, Barcelona, undated.

***Notice des tableaux* 1838.** *Notice des tableaux de la Galerie Espagnole exposés dans les salles du Musée Royal au Louvre*, Paris, 1838.

***Noticia de los Cuadros* 1828.** *Noticia de los cuadros que se hallan colocados en la Galería del Museo del Rey, nuestro señor, sito en el Prado de esta corte*, Madrid, 1828.

Núñez 2000. B. Núñez, *Zacarías González Velázquez (1763–1834)*, Madrid, 2000.

Núñez de Arenas 1963. M. Núñez de Arenas, *L'Espagne des Lumières au Romantisme*, Paris, 1963.

Olaechea 1969. R. Olaechea, *El conde de Aranda y el 'partido aragonés'*, Zaragoza, 1969.

Olivier 1933. F. Olivier, *Picasso et ses amis*, Paris, 1933.

Olivier 1990. F. Olivier, *Recuerdos íntimos*, Barcelona, 1990.

Orozco 1977. E. Orozco, 'Lo profano y lo divino en el retrato del Manierismo y del Barroco', in E. Orozco, *Mística, plástica y Barroco*, Barcelona, 1977.

Pacheco (1599) 1985. F. Pacheco, *Libro de descripción de verdaderos retratos de ilustres y memorables varones*, (1599), ed. M. Piñero and R. Reyes, Seville, 1985.

Pacheco (1638) 1956. F. Pacheco, *Arte de la pintura*, (1638), ed. F. J. Sánchez Cantón, Madrid, 1956.

Pacheco (1638) 1990. F. Pacheco, *Arte de la pintura* (1638), ed. B. Bassegoda, Madrid, 1990.

Palau 1980. J. Palau i Fabre, *Picasso vivo (1881–1907)*, Barcelona, 1980.

Palluchini 1966. A. Palluchini, 'Il Greco e Venezia', in A. Pertusi (ed.), *Venezia e l'Oriente fra Tardo Medioevo e Rinascimento*, Florence, 1966, pp. 351–71.

Palm 1968. E. W. Palm, 'Diego Velázquez: Äesop und Menipp', *Lebende Antike Symposium für Rudolf Sühnel*, Berlin, 1968.

Palomino (1715–1724) 1944. A. Palomino de Castro, *El museo pictórico y escala óptica* (1715–1724), 2 vols, Buenos Aires, 1944.

Palomino (1715–1724) 1947. A. Palomino de Castro, *El museo pictórico y escala óptica* (1715–1724), 3 vols, Madrid, Aguilar, 1947.

Palomino (1724) 1986. A. Palomino de Castro, *Vidas* (1724), ed. N. Ayala, Madrid, 1986.

Panofsky 1951. E. Panofsky, *Gothic Architecture and Scholasticism*, Latrobe, 1951 (Spanish edn, 1986).

Panofsky 1968. E. Panofsky, *Problems in Titian Mostly Iconographic*, London–New York, 1968.

Pantorba 1955. B. de Pantorba, *La vida y la obra de Velázquez. Estudio biográfico y crítico*, Madrid, 1955.

Pardo 1908. L. Pardo, *De arte y por el arte*, Madrid, 1908.

Parker 1999. G. Parker, 'Prólogo', in Pedro Navascués (ed.), *Carolus V Imperator*, Barcelona, 1999.

Parmelin 1968. H. Parmelin, *Habla Picasso…*, Barcelona, 1968.

Pawlowski undated. Pawlowsky, 'Chrétien, Gilles-Louis', in *La Grande Encyclopédie. Inventaire raisonnée des sciences, des lettres et des arts par une société de savants et de gens de lettres*, Paris, XI, undated.

Pemán 1978. M. Pemán, 'La colección artística de don Sebastián Martínez, amigo de Goya, en Cádiz', *Archivo Español de Arte*, LI, no. 201, 1978, pp. 53–62.

Penrose 1958. R. Penrose, *Picasso: His Life and Work*, London, 1958.

Pereyra undated. C. Pereyra, *Cartas confidenciales de la reina María Luisa y de don Manuel Godoy, con otras tomadas del Archivo Reservado de Fernando VII, del Histórico Nacional y del de Indias*, Madrid, undated.

Pérez de Montalbán 1636. J. Pérez de Montalbán, *Fama póstuma de … Lope de Vega*, Madrid, 1636.

Pérez y Morandeira 1971. R. Pérez y Morandeira, *Vicente Palmaroli*, Madrid, 1971.

Pérez Pastor 1914. C. Pérez Pastor, *Noticias y documentos relativos a la historia y literatura españolas*, Madrid, 1914.

Pérez Rojas 2000. F. J. Pérez Rojas, *El retrato elegante*, exh. cat., Madrid, 2000.

Pérez Rojas 2003. F. J. Pérez Rojas, 'Dos historias casi paralelas. "Vividoras del amor" y "Les demoiselles d'Avignon"', in *Julio Romero de Torres. Símbolo, materia y obsesión*, Córdoba, 2003.

Pérez Sánchez 1981. A. E. Pérez Sánchez, 'El "San Lucas pintando a la Virgen" de Ribera', in *Ars Auro Prior, studia Ioannis Bialostocki sexagenario dicata*, Warsaw, 1981, pp. 403–06.

Pérez Sánchez 1985. A. E. Pérez Sánchez, *Juan Carreño de Miranda (1614–1685)*, Avilés–Madrid, 1985.

Pérez Sánchez 1986. A. E. Pérez Sánchez, *Carreño, Rizi, Herrera y la pintura madrileña de su tiempo, 1650–1700*, Madrid, 1986.

Pérez Sánchez 1988. A. E. Pérez Sánchez, 'Pintura de los siglos XVI al XVIII en la colección del Banco de España', in J. M. Viñuela (ed.), *Colección del Banco de España*, Madrid, 1988.

Pérez Sánchez 1992. A. E. Pérez Sánchez, 'Ribera y España', in *Ribera, 1591–1652*, exh. cat., A. E. Pérez Sánchez and N. Spinosa (eds), Madrid, 1992, pp. 79–105.

Pérez Sánchez 1994. A. E. Pérez Sánchez, 'El retrato clásico español', in *El retrato en el Museo del Prado*, Madrid, 1994.

Pérez Sánchez 2003. A. E. Pérez Sánchez, *Catálogo de la Colección de Dibujos del Instituto Jovellanos de Gijón*, 2nd edn, Gijón, 2003.

Pérez-Jorba 1920. J. Pérez-Jorba, 'Los artistas catalanes en el Salón de Otoño', *Las Noticias*, Barcelona, 26 October 1920.

Pérez-Jorba 1921. J. Pérez-Jorba, 'Crónica de Paris. Joan Miró y su pintura en El Unicornio', *El Día Gráfico*, Barcelona, 6 May 1921.

Perlingieri 1992. I. S. Perlingieri, *Sofonisba Anguissola. The First Great Woman Artist of the Renaissance*, New York, 1992.

Perry 1990. M. E. Perry, *Gender and Disorder in Spain in Early Modern Seville*, Princeton, 1990.

Peyton 1962. M. A. Peyton, 'The Retrato as Motif and evice in Lope de Vega', *Romance Notes*, IV, 1962, pp. 51–57.

Pineda 1685. Fray M. de Pineda, *Oración funebre en las honras, que en la Santa Metropolitana […] Iglesia de Sevilla se hizieron el sábado 7 de julio deste año de 1685 a la buena memoria del señor D. Justino de Neve y Chaves cánonigo en sicha Santa Iglesia […]*, Seville, 1685.

***Pintura Española de los Siglos XVI al XVIII* 1981.** *Pintura española de los siglos XVI al XVIII en las colecciones centroeuropeas*, exh. cat., Madrid, 1981.

Pita 1952. J. M. Pita Andrade, 'Los cuadros de Velázquez y Mazo que poseyó el séptimo marqués del Carpio', *Archivo Español de Arte*, 1952.

Pita 1981. J. M. Pita Andrade, with J. Álvarez Lopera, *El Greco*, Milan, 1981.

Pita and Borobia 1992. J. M. Pita Andrade and M. M.ª Borobia Guerrero, *Maestros antiguos del Museo Thyssen-Bornemisza*, Madrid, 1992.

Planche 1855. G. Planche, 'Exposition des Beaux-Arts. Écoles diverses. Espagne, Belgique et Hollande', *Revue des Deux Mondes*, Paris, 1 October 1855.

***Poetas Líricos* 1966.** *Poetas líricos de los siglos XVI y XVII*, I, ed. A. Castro, Madrid, 1966.

Polentinos 1933. C. de Polentinos, 'El convento de San Hermenegildo, Madrid', *Boletín de la Sociedad Española de Excursiones*, XLI, 1933, pp. 36–61.

Poleró 1857. V. Poleró Toledo, *Catálogo de los cuadros del Monasterio de San Lorenzo llamado de El Escorial, en el que se comprenden los del Real Palacio, Casino del Príncipe y Capilla de la Fresneda*, Madrid, 1857.

Polignano 1989. F. Polignano, 'Ritratto e biografia: due insiemi a confronto, dalla parte dell'iconologia', in A. Gentili (ed.), *Il ritratto e la memoria*, Rome, 1989.

Pommier 1998. É. Pommier, *Théories du portrait. De la Renaissance aux Lumières*, Paris, 1998.

Pompey 1946. F. Pompey, *Museo de Arte Moderno. Guía gráfica y espiritual*, Madrid, 1946.

Pons-Sorolla 2001. B. Pons-Sorolla, *Joaquín Sorolla. Vida y obra*, Madrid, 2001.

Ponz (1772–1794) 1947. A. Ponz, *Viaje de España, en que se da noticia de las cosas apreciables y dignas de saberse que hay en ella* (1772–1794), Madrid–Seville, 1947.

Pool 1960. Ph. Pool, 'The Picasso Exhibition: the Most Important four Rooms', *The Burlington Magazine*, CII, no. 690, London, 1960, pp. 386–92.

Pope-Hennessy 1966. J. Pope-Hennessy, *The Portrait in the Renaissance*, London–New York, 1966.

***Portrait Espagnol* 1970.** *Le Portrait espagnol: du XIV au XIX siècles*, exh. cat., Brussels, 1970.

Portús 1996. J. Portús, 'Fray Hortensio Paravicino: La Academia de San Lucas, las pinturas lascivas y el arte de mirar', *Espacio, Tiempo y Forma*, UNED, Madrid, series VII, vol. IX, 9, 1996, pp. 77–105.

Portús 1997. J. Portús, 'Entre el divino artista y el retratista alcahuete: el pintor en la escena barroca española', in M. Morán y J. Portús, *El arte de mirar: La pintura y su público en la España de Velázquez*, Madrid, 1997, pp. 131–56.

Portús 1998. J. Portús, 'Doña Juana de Portugal', in *Felipe II. Un monarca y su época. Las tierras y los hombres del rey*, exh. cat., Valladolid; Madrid, 1998, p. 204.

Portús 1999a. J. Portús, 'Retrato, humildad y santidad en el Siglo de Oro', *Revista de Dialectología y Tradiciones Populares*, LIV, 1999.

Portús 1999b. J. Portús, *Pintura y pensamiento en la España de Lope de Vega*, Hondarribia, 1999.

Portús 2000a. J. Portús, 'Temas artísticos en el auto "El pintor de su deshonra"', in Pedro Calderón, *El pintor de su deshonra (Auto sacramental)*, Madrid, 2000, pp. 29–58.

Portús 2000b. J. Portús, '"Soy tu hechura". Un ensayo sobre las fronteras del retrato cortesano en España', in *Carlos V. Retratos de familia*, Madrid, 2000, pp. 181–219.

Portús 2000c. J. Portús, 'El retrato cortesano en la España de los primeros Austrias: Imagen, propaganda, identidad', in *El linaje del Emperador*, exh. cat., Cáceres, 2000, pp. 17–40.

Portús 2000d. J. Portús, 'Tres miradas ilustradas a Velázquez: Mengs, Jovellanos y Ceán', in J. Vega (ed.), *Estudiar a los maestros: Velázquez y Goya*, Zaragoza, 2000, pp. 97–113.

Portús 2002. J. Portús, 'Orden y concierto: Escenas familiares en la pintura española del Renacimiento a Goya', in *Ternura y melodrama. Pintura de escenas familiares en tiempos de Sorolla*, exh. cat., Valencia, 2002, pp. 19–68.

Post 1934. Ch. R. Post, *The Hispano-Flemish Style in Andalusia (A History of Spanish Painting, V)*, Cambridge (Mass.), 1934.

Post 1947. Ch. R. Post, *The Beginning of the Renaissance in Castille and Leon (A History of Spanish Painting*, IX), 2 vols, Cambridge (Mass.), 1947.

Puente 1985. J. de la Puente, *Museo del Prado. Casón del Buen Retiro. Catálogo de las pinturas del siglo XIX*, Madrid, 1985.

Quondam 1989. A. Quondam, 'Il naso di Laura', in *Il ritratto e la memoria. Materiali, I*, Rome, 1989.

R[ahola] 1889. F. R[ahola], 'Exposición Parés', *La Vanguardia*, Barcelona, 24 Feburary 1889.

Ramos Gómez 1996. F. J. Ramos Gómez, 'Nuevos datos documentales sobre el pintor Hernando Rincón de Figueroa', *Boletín del Museo e Instituto 'Camón Aznar'*, LXVI, 1996, pp. 80–83.

Raquejo 1981–1982. M. A. Raquejo, 'El donante en la pintura española del siglo XVI', *Goya*, nos 164–65, 1981–1982, pp. 76–87.

***Retratos de Mujeres* 1918.** *Retratos de mujeres por artistas españoles anteriores a 1850*, Madrid, 1918.

***Retratos de niño en España* 1925.** *Retratos de niño en España*, Madrid, 1925.

Reyero 1993. C. Reyero, *Paris y la crisis de la pintura española, 1799–1889. Del Museo del Louvre a la torre Eiffel*, Madrid, 1993.

Reyero 2004. C. Reyero, 'Pintar a Isabel II: en busca de una imagen para la reina', in J. S. Pérez Garzón (ed.), *Isabel II. Los espejos de la reina*, Madrid, 2004, pp. 231–46.

***Reyes y Mecenas* 1992.** *Reyes y mecenas. Los Reyes Católicos, Maximiliano I y los inicios de la casa de Austria*, exh. cat., Toledo, 1992.

Reynaud and Réssort 1991. N. Reynaud and C. Réssort, 'Les Portraits d'hommes illustres du Studiolo d'Urbino au Louvre par Juste de Gand et Pedro Berruguete', *Revue du Louvre*, XLI, 1991, pp. 82–114.

***Ribera 1591–1652* (Madrid) 1992.** *Ribera 1591–1652*, ed. A. E. Pérez Sánchez and N. Spinosa, exh. cat. Madrid–Naples; Madrid, 1992.

***Ribera 1591–1652* (Naples) 1992.** *Ribera 1591–1652*, ed. A. E. Pérez Sánchez and N. Spinosa, exh. cat. Madrid–Naples; Naples, 1992.

Richardson 1988. J. Richardson, 'L'Époque Jacqueline', in *Late Picasso: Paintings, Sculptures, Drawings, Prints 1953–1972*, London, 1988, pp. 17–47.

Richardson 1995. J. Richardson, *Picasso. Una biografía. I, 1881–1906*, Madrid, 1995.

Rico 1991. F. Rico, 'Los filósofos de Velázquez o "El Gran Teatro del Mundo"', in *El Siglo de Oro de la pintura española*, Madrid, 1991.

Roblot-Delonde 1913. L. Roblot-Delonde, *Portraits d'enfants. XVI siècle. Étude iconographique*, Paris–Brussels, 1913.

Rodríguez de Gracia 1988. H. Rodríguez de Gracia, 'El inventario post mortem del licenciado Gerónimo de Ceballos', *Toletum*, LXXI, no. 22, 1988, pp. 149–64.

Rodríguez G. de Ceballos 2000. A. Rodríguez G. de Ceballos, 'Retrato de estado y propaganda política: Carlos II', *Anuario del Departamento de Historia y Teoría del Arte*, XII, 2000.

Roettgen 1999. S. Roettgen, *Anton Raphael Mengs, 1728–1779. Das malerisches und zeichnerische Werk*, Munich, 1999.

Ronchini 1865. A. Ronchini, 'Giulio Clovio', in *Atti e memorie delle RR. Deputazione di storia patria per le provincie modenensi et parmensi*, III, Módena, 1865, pp. 259–70.

Rose- de Viejo 1981. I. Rose- de Viejo, 'Un proyecto dieciochesco malogrado: el plan de reproducir en grabados los cuadros principales existentes en las colecciones reales españolas', *Academia. Boletín de la Real Academia de Bellas Artes de San Fernando*, 1981, pp. 173–81.

Rose- de Viejo (ed.) 2001. I. Rose- de Viejo (ed.), *La imagen de Manuel Godoy*, exh. cat., Badajoz, 2001.

Rosenblum 1976. R. Rosenblum, *Cubism and Twentieth-Century Art*, New York, 1976.

Rosenthal 1971. E. Rosenthal, 'Plus Ultra. Non Plus Ultra, and the Columnar Device of Emperor Charles V', *Journal of the Warburg and Courtauld Institutes*, no. 34, 1971.

Rosenthal 1983. M. Rosenthal, *Juan Gris*, Berkeley, 1983.

Rossi 1974. P. Rossi, *Tintoretto. I ritratti*, Milan, 1974.

Roteta 1985. A. M.ª Roteta de la Maza, *La ilustración del libro en la España de la Contrarreforma. Grabados de Pedro Ángel y Diego de Astor (1588–1637)*, Toledo, 1985.

Rouchès 1927. G. Rouchès, 'Un Tableau espagnol récemment entré au Louvre: le portrait de Luis Meléndez par lui-meme', *Revue de l'art*, 1927.

Rowell (ed.) 1986. M. Rowell (ed.), *Joan Miró. Selected Writings and Interviews*, Boston, 1986.

Royo Villanueva 1917. R. Royo Villanova, 'Goya y la medicina' (lección inaugural del curso de patalogía y clínica médicas de 1917–1918), *Universidad*, Zaragoza, IV, no. 4, 1977, pp. 969–92.

Rubin 1988. W. Rubin, 'La génesis de "Les demoiselles d'Avignon"', in *Les demoiselles d'Avignon*, Barcelona, 1988, pp. 368–487.

Rubin 1991. W. Rubin, *Picasso y Braque. La invención del Cubismo*, Barcelona, 1991.

Rubin 1996. W. Rubin, 'Reflections on Picasso and Portraiture', in W. Rubin (ed.), *Picasso and Portraiture. Representation and Transformation*, New York, 1996, pp. 12–109.

Rubio 2000. L. Rubio Gil, 'Introducción a la vida y obra de Eduardo Rosales', in *Eduardo Rosales en las colecciones privadas*, exh. cat., Zaragoza, 2000, pp. 11–114.

Rubio 2002. L. Rubio Gil, *Eduardo Rosales*, Barcelona, 2002.

Rubio Lluch 1908–1921. A. Rubio Lluch, *Documents per l'historia de la cultura catalana mig-eval*, vol. I, Barcelona, 1908, and vol. II, Barcelona, 1921.

Ruiz García 1991. P. Ruiz García, 'Tadea Arias de Enríquez, un personaje de Goya', *A Distancia*, 1991.

Ruiz Gómez 2001. L. Ruiz Gómez, entries 7 and 19 in *El Greco*, exh. cat., Vienna, 2001.

Rusiñol undated. S. Rusiñol, *Impresiones de arte*, Barcelona, undated.

Sabartés 1946. J. Sabartés, *Picasso. Portraits et souvenirs*, Paris, 1946.

Salas 1960. X. de Salas, 'Some Notes on a Letter of Picasso', *The Burlington Magazine*, CII, no. 692, 1960, pp. 482–84.

Salas 1967. X. de Salas, *Miguel Ángel y El Greco (discurso leído en el acto de su recepción pública)*, Madrid, Real Academia de Bellas Artes de San Fernando, 1967.

Salas (ed.) 1973. X. de Salas (ed.), *Exposición de la obra de Eduardo Rosales, 1836–1873*, Madrid, 1973.

Salas 1978. X. de Salas, *Museo del Prado. Adquisiciones de 1969 a 1977*, Madrid, 1978.

Salas 1982. X. de Salas, 'Semblanza de Eduardo Rosales', in *Retrato de la condesa de Santovenia. Eduardo Rosales*, Madrid, 1982, pp. 21–29.

Salort 2002. S. Salort Pons, *Velázquez en Italia*, Madrid, 2002.

Saltillo 1928. M. del Saltillo, 'Un retrato del museo del emperador Federico, de Berlín, por Zurbarán: datos para su identificación', *Investigación y Progreso*, Madrid, 1 May 1928.

Saltillo 1944. M. del Saltillo, 'Un pintor desconocido del siglo XVII: Domingo Guerra Coronel', *Arte Español*, XV, 1944, pp. 43–48.

San Esteban 1662. J. de San Esteban, *Vida y virtudes del venerable hermano fray Juan de la Magdalena, religioso lego de la orden de nuestro padre San Agustín de los Descalços*, Seville, 1662.

San Román 1927. F. de B. San Román Fernández, 'De la vida del Greco. Nueva serie de documentos inéditos', *Archivo Español de Arte y Arqueología*, III, 1927, pp. 139–95 and 175–330.

Sánchez Cantón 1916. F. J. Sanchez Cantón, *Los retratos de los reyes de España*, Madrid, 1916.

Sánchez Cantón 1923a. F. J. Sánchez Cantón, *Catálogo de las pinturas del Instituto de Valencia de Don Juan*, Madrid, 1923.

Sánchez Cantón 1923b. F. J. Sánchez Cantón, *Fuentes literarias para la historia del arte español*, I, Madrid, 1923.

Sánchez Cantón 1929a. F. J. Sánchez Cantón, *Antonio Rafael Mengs. 1728–1779. Noticia de su vida y de sus obras, con el catálogo de la exposición celebrada en mayo de 1929*, Madrid, 1929.

Sánchez Cantón 1929b. F. J. Sánchez Cantón, 'El autorretrato de Luis Meléndez en el Museo del Louvre', *Archivo Español de Arte y Arqueología*, 1929.

Sánchez Cantón 1941. F. J. Sánchez Cantón, *Fuentes literarias para la historia del arte español*, V, Madrid, 1941.

Sánchez Cantón 1942. F. J. Sánchez Cantón, *La mujer en los cuadros del Greco (lecture)*, [Barcelona], 1942.

Sánchez Cantón 1947. F. J. Sánchez Cantón, 'Sobre la vida y obras de Juan Pantoja de la Cruz', *Archivo Español de Arte y Arqueología*, 1947.

Sánchez Cantón 1948. F. J. Sánchez Cantón, *Los retratos de los reyes de España*, Madrid, 1948.

Sánchez Cantón (ed.) 1956–1959. F. J. Sánchez Cantón, *Inventarios Reales. Bienes muebles que pertenecieron a Felipe II*, 2 vols, (*Archivo Documental Español, X–XII)*, Madrid, 1956–1959.

Sanpere Miquel 1900. S. Sanpere Miquel, 'Domenikos Theotokopoulos', *Revista de la Asociación Artístico-Arqueológica Barcelonesa*, IV, no. 18, 1900, pp. 369–98.

Santa Ana 1997. F. Santa Ana, 'Joaquín Sorolla y Bastida, "El pintor Aureliano de Beruete"', in J. L. Díez (ed.), *Artistas pintados. Retratos de pintores y escultores del siglo XIX en el Museo del Prado*, exh. cat., Madrid, 1997, p. 174.

Santa Ana 1999. F. de Santa Ana, 'La perdurabilidad de Velázquez en la pintura española del siglo XIX: Sorolla', in *Velázquez y el arte de su tiempo*, Madrid, 1999, pp. 435–40.

Santiago 1990. E. Santiago, *Miguel Jacinto Meléndez*, Madrid, 1990.

Santos (1657) 1984. F. de los Santos, *Descripción breve del Monasterio de San Lorenzo el Real del Escorial. Única maravilla del mundo* (1654), Madrid, 1984 (Facsimile edn).

Sebastián 1991–1992. S. Sebastián, 'La emblematización del retrato de Carlos II por Carreño de Miranda', *Goya*, no. 226, 1991–1992.

Seckel-Klein 1998. H. Seckel-Klein, *Picasso collectionneur*, Paris, 1998.

Serra Desfilis 2002–2003. A. Serra Desfilis, 'La historia de la dinastía en imágenes: Martín el Humano y el rollo genealógico de la Corona de Aragón', *Locus Amoenus*, 6, 2002–2003, pp. 57–74.

Serrano y Sanz 1914. M. Serrano y Sanz, 'Documentos relativos a la pintura en Aragón durante el siglo XV', *Revista de Archivos, Bibliotecas y Museos*, no. 31, 1914, pp. 455–58.

Serrano y Sanz 1916. M. Serrano y Sanz, 'Documentos relativos a la pintura en Aragón durante el siglo XV', *Revista de Archivos, Bibliotecas y Museos*, no. 34, 1916, pp. 482–85.

Serrera 1984. J. M. Serrera, 'Pinturas y pintores del siglo XVI en la catedral de Sevilla', in *La catedral de Sevilla*, Seville, 1984, pp. 353–404.

Serrera 1990. J. M. Serrera, 'Alonso Sánchez Coello y la mecánica del retrato de corte', in *Alonso Sánchez Coello*, exh. cat., Madrid, 1990, pp. 38–63.

Serrera 1999. J. M. Serrera, '"La Adoración de los Reyes Magos", un retrato casi de familia', in *Velázquez*, Barcelona–Madrid, 1999, pp. 351–65.

Serrera and Méndez Rodríguez 1999. J. M. Serrera and L. Méndez Rodríguez, '"Retratos de la familia Caballero"', in *Velázquez y Sevilla*, exh. cat., Seville, 1999, pp. 42–44.

Silva Maroto 1998. P. Silva Maroto, *Pedro Berruguete*, Salamanca, 1998 (1st edn, reissued 2001).

Silva Maroto 2000a. P. Silva Maroto, 'Juan de Flandes. "Supuesto retrato de Catalina de Aragón"', in *Carolus*, exh. cat., Toledo, 2000.

Silva Maroto 2000b. P. Silva Maroto, 'Pedro Berruguete en Italia', in *Sixto IV. Le arti a Roma nel primo Rinascimento. Atti del Convegno Internazionali di Studi, ottobre 1997*, Rome, 2000, pp. 289–303.

Silva Maroto 2003. P. Silva Maroto, 'Retablo de la vida de la Virgen. Santa Eulalia de Paredes de Nava', in *Pedro Berruguete, el primer pintor renacentista de la corona de Castilla*, exh. cat., Paredes de Nava (Palencia); Valladolid, 2003, pp. 144–61.

Silva Maroto 2004. P. Silva Maroto, 'La colección de pinturas de Isabel la Católica', in *Isabel la Católica. La magnificencia de un reinado*, exh. cat., Valladolid; Madrid, 2004.

***Sofonisba Anguissola* 1994.** *Sofonisba Anguissola e le sue sorelle*, exh. cat., Cremona–Vienna–Washington, 1994.

Soria 1948. M. Soria, 'Murillo's Boy and Girl Companion Pictures', *The Burlington Magazine*, XC, 1948, pp. 22–25.

Soria 1948. M. S. Soria, 'Some Flemish Sources of Baroque Painting in Spain', *The Art Bulletin*, XXX, no. 4, 1948, pp. 249–59.

Soria 1957. M. S. Soria, *Agustín Esteve y Goya*, Valencia, 1957.

Soria Ortega 1981. A. Soria Ortega, 'Sobre biografismo de la época clásica: Francisco Pacheco y Paulo Jovio', *1616. Sociedad Española de Literatura General y Comparada*, IV, 1981, pp. 123–43.

Spinosa 1978. N. Spinosa, *L'opera completa del Ribera*, Milan, 1978.

Spinosa 2003. N. Spinosa, *Ribera*, Naples, 2003.

Starobinski 1970. J. Starobinski, *Portrait de l'artiste en saltimbanque*, Geneva, 1970.

Stein (1938) 1943. G. Stein, *Picasso* (1938), Buenos Aires, 1943.

Stein 1967. G. Stein, *Autobiografía de Alice B. Toklas*, Madrid, 1967.

Stoichita 1996. V. Stoichita, *El ojo místico. Pintura y visión religiosa en el Siglo de Oro español*, Madrid, 1996.

Suida 1935. W. Suida, *Le Titien*, Paris, 1935.

Sullivan 1986. E. J. Sullivan, *Baroque Painting in Madrid. The Contribution of Claudio Coello, with a Catalogue Raisonné of his Works*, Columbia, 1986 (Spanish edn, *Claudio Coello y la pintura barroca madrileña*, Madrid, 1989).

Sullivan 1989. E. J. Sullivan, *Claudio Coello y la pintura barroca madrileña*, Madrid, 1989.

Sylvester 1988. D. Sylvester, 'End Game', in *Late Picasso. Paintings, Sculpture, Drawings, Prints 1953–1972*, London, 1988, pp. 136–48.

Symmons 1998. S. Symmons, *Goya*, London, 1998.

Symmons 2002. S. Symmons, 'La mujer vestida de blanco: el primer retrato de la duquesa de Alba', in *Goya*, Barcelona–Madrid, 2002, pp. 49–62.

Tedde de Lorca 1988. P. Tedde de Lorca, *El Banco de San Carlos (1782–1829)*, Madrid, 1988.

***The Genius of Venice* 1983.** *The Genius of Venice*, exh. cat., London, 1983.

Tietze 1936. H. Títese, *Tizian*, Vienna, 1936.

Tobar 2004. M. L. Tobar, 'Un documento del año 1783 sobre la jubilación de actores conservado en el Archivo Histórico Nacional', in Patrizia Garelli and Giovanni Marchetti (eds), *Un 'Hombre de Bien'. Saggi di lingue e letterature iberiche in onore di Rinaldo Froldi*, Alessandria, 2004, pp. 617–33.

Tomlinson (1992) 1993. J. A. Tomlinson, *Goya en el crepúsculo del Siglo de las Luces*, Madrid, 1993 (English edn, *Goya in the Twilight of Enlightenment*, New Haven–London, 1992).

Tomlinson 1994. J. A. Tomlinson, *Francisco de Goya y Lucientes, 1746–1828*, London, 1994.

Tormo 1916. E. Tormo Monzó, *Las viejas series icónicas de los reyes de España*, Madrid, 1916.

Tormo 1926. E. Tormo Monzó, 'Bartolomé Bermejo, el más recio de los primitivos españoles', *Archivo Español de Arte y Arqueología*, II, 1926, pp. 11–87.

Tormo 1927. E. Tormo Monzó, *Las viejas series icónicas de los reyes de España*, Madrid, 1927.

Tormo 1944. E. Tormo Monzó, *En las Descalzas Reales de Madrid. Treinta y tres retratos*, Madrid, 1944.

Torre 1961. A. de la Torre, 'Maestre Antonio Ynglés, pintor', in *V Congreso de Historia de la Corona de Aragón: Fernando el Católico y la cultura de su tiempo*, Zaragoza, 1961, pp. 167–72.

Tramoyers 1891. L. Tramoyers, *Pinturas murales del Salón de Cortes de Valencia*, Valencia, 1891.

Trapier 1944. E. du Gué Trapier, 'Velázquez. New Data on a Group of Portraits', *Notes Hispanic*, 1944.

Trapier 1948. E. du Gué Trapier, *Velázquez*, New York, 1948.

Trapier 1957. E. du Gué Trapier, 'The School of Madrid and Van Dyck', *The Burlington Magazine*, no. 653, 1957, pp. 265–73.

Trapier 1958. E. du Gué Trapier, *El Greco. Early Years in Toledo. 1576–1586*, New York, 1958.

Trapier 1960. E. du Gué Trapier, *Valdés Leal. Spanish Baroque Painter*, New York, 1960.

Trapier 1964. E. du Gué Trapier, *Goya and His Sitters. A Study of his Style as a Portraitist*, New York, 1964.

Trapp 2001. J. B. Trapp, 'Petrarch's Laura. The Portraiture of an Imaginary Beloved', *Journal of the Warburg and Courtauld Institutes*, LXIV, 2001, pp. 55–192.

Tromans 1996. N. Tromans, 'The Iconography of Velázquez's Aesop', *Journal of the Warburg and Courtauld Institutes*, LIX, 1996.

Tubino 1871. F. M. Tubino, *El arte y los artistas contemporáneos en la Península*, Madrid, 1871.

Tufts 1971. E. M. Tufts, *A Stylistic Study of the Paintings of Luis Meléndez*, New York, 1971.

Tufts 1985. E. M. Tufts, *Luis Meléndez. Eighteenth-Century Master of the Spanish Still Life with a Catalogue Raisonné*, Columbia, 1985.

Úbeda 2002. A. Úbeda, 'Felipe V y el retrato de corte', in *El arte en la corte de Felipe V*, exh. cat., Madrid, 2002, pp. 89–140.

***Un mecenas póstumo* 1993.** *Un mecenas póstumo. El legado Villaescusa. Adquisiciones 1992–1993*, exh. cat., Madrid, 1993.

Unamuno [1920]. M. de Unamuno, '[Zuloaga]', in *Ignacio Zuloaga*, Madrid, undated [1920], pp. 16–24.

Urrea 1994. J. Urrea, 'La corte como observatorio de retratos', in *El retrato en el Museo del Prado*, Madrid, 1994, pp. 303–21.

Utrillo 1907. M. Utrillo, 'Zuloaga', *Forma*, II, 1907.

Valdés 1996. A. de Valdés, *Obra completa*, ed. A. Alcalá, Madrid, 1996.

Valdivieso 1981. E. Valdivieso, *Pintura sevillana del siglo XIX*, Seville, 1981.

Valdivieso 1986. E. Valdivieso, *Historia de la pintura sevillana. Siglos XIII al XX*, Seville, 1986.

Valdivieso 1988. E. Valdivieso, *Juan de Valdés Leal*, Seville, 1988.

Valdivieso and Serrera 1980. E. Valdivieso and J. M. Serrera, *El hospital de la Caridad de Sevilla*, Seville, 1980.

Van der Velden 1998. H. van der Velden, 'Medici Votive Images and the Scope and Limits of Likeness', in N. Mann and L. Syson (eds), *The Image of the Individual. Portraits in the Renaissance*, London, 1998, pp. 126–36.

Vandevivere and Bermejo 1986. I. Vandevivere and E. Bermejo, *Juan de Flandes*, exh. cat., Madrid, Museo del Prado, 1986.

Vardenoe 1996. K. Vardenoe, 'Picasso's Self-Portraits', in *Picasso and Portraiture*, exh. cat., New York, 1996, pp. 111–79.

Varela 2000. L. Varela, 'El rey fuera de palacio: la repercusión social del retrato regio en el Renacimiento español', in *El linaje del Emperador*, exh. cat., Cáceres, 2000; Madrid, pp. 99–134.

***Varia Velazqueña* 1960.** *Varia velazqueña*, 2 vols, Madrid, 1960.

Vega 2000. J. Vega, 'Pinturas de Velázquez grabadas por Francisco de Goya, pintor', in J. Vega (dir.), *Estudiar a los maestros: Velázquez y Goya*, Zaragoza, 2000.

Vega Carpio 1963–1972. F. Lope de Vega Carpio, *Obras de Lope de Vega*, ed. M. Menéndez Pelayo, Madrid, 1963–1972.

Vegué y Goldoni 1928. Á. Vegué y Goldoni, 'El cardenal Quiroga, retratado por el Greco', *Archivo Español de Arte y Arqueología*, IV, 1928, pp. 135–37.

Velázquez 1963. M. del C. Velázquez, *La España de Carlos III. De 1764 a 1776. Según los embajadores austríacos. Documentos*, Mexico City, 1963.

***Velázquez* 1990.** *Velázquez*, exh. cat., Madrid, 1990.

***Velázquez, Rubens y Van Dyck* 1999.** *Velázquez, Rubens y Van Dyck, pintores cortesanos del siglo XVII*, exh. cat., Madrid, 1999.

Véliz 1999. Z. Véliz, '"La venerable madre Jerónima de la Fuente"', in *En torno a Velázquez. Pintura española del siglo de Oro*, exh. cat. Oviedo; London, 1999.

Venturi 1929. A. Venturi, *Storia dell'arte italiana*, IX: *La pittura del Cinquecento*, Milan, 1929.

Vincent 2002. C. Vincent, 'Les saintes vierges et martyres de Francisco de Zurbarán', *Cauces*, 3, 2002, pp. 17–30.

***Visages du Grand Siècle* 1997.** *Visages du Grand Siècle. Le portrait français sous le règne de Louis XIV 1660–1715*, exh. cat., Nantes, 1997.

Von Loga 1903. V. von Loga, *Francisco de Goya*, Berlin, 1903.

Warnke 1993. M. Warnke, *The Court Artist: on the Ancestry of the Modern Artist*, Cambridge, 1993.

Waterhouse 1930. E. K. Waterhouse, 'El Greco's Italian Period', *Art Studies*, VIII, 1930, pp. 61–88.

Weelen 1989. G. Weelen, *Joan Miró* (1984), New York, 1989.

Weiss 2004. J. Weiss, 'Fleeting and Fixed: Picasso's Fernandes', in *Picasso. The Cubist Portraits of Fernande Olivier*, Washington–Princeton–Oxford, 2004, pp. 1–48.

Werth 1997. M. Werth, 'Representing the Body in *1906*', in M. McCully (ed.), *Picasso. The Early Years, 1892–1906*, Washington, 1997, pp. 277–87.

Wethey 1962. H. E. Wethey, 'Portraits du Greco en France'. *Revue du Louvre*, XII, no. 6, 1962, pp. 273–80.

Wethey (1962) 1967. H. E. Wethey, *El Greco y su escuela*, 2 vols, Madrid, 1967 (English edn, *El Greco and his School*, 2 vols, Princeton, 1962).

Wethey 1971. H. E. Wethey, *The Paintings of Titian, II: The Portraits*, London, 1971.

Wethey 1984. H. E. Wethey, 'El Greco in Rome and the Portrait of Vincenzo Anastagi', in J. Brown and J. M. Pita Andrade (eds), *El Greco: Italy and Spain*. Washington, D.C., 1984, pp. 171–78.

Willumsen 1927. J. F. Willumsen, *La Jeunesse du peintre El Greco*, Paris, 1927.

Wilson-Bareau 2003. J. Wilson-Bareau, 'Goya and France', in *Manet/Velázquez. The French Taste for Spanish Paintings*, exh. cat., New York, 2003, pp. 139–59.

Woodall 1990a. J. Woodall, 'Honour and Profit. Antonis Mor and the Status of Portraiture', in *Nederlandese Portretten. Bijdragen over de portretkunst in de Nederlanden uit de Zestiende, Zeventiende en Achttiende Eeuw*, The Hague, 1990, pp. 69–89.

Woodall 1990b. J. Woodall, *The Portraiture of Moro*, 1990.

Woodall 1992. J. Woodall, 'Visualizando la identidad: retrato de Felipe II de España, realizado por Antonio Moro', *Urtekaria. Anuario*, Museo de Bellas Artes de Bilbao, no number, 1992.

Woodall 1995a. J. Woodall, 'His Majesty's Most Majestic Room. The Division of Sovereign identity in Philip II of Spain's Lost Portrait Gallery at El Pardo', *Image and Self-Image in Netherlandish Art, 1550–1750. Netherlands Yearbook for History of Art*, no. 46, 1995.

Wright 2000. A. Wright, 'The Memory of Faces: Representational Choices in Fifteenth-Century Florentine Portraiture', in G. Capelli and P. L. Rubyn (eds), *Art, Memory and Family in Renaissance Florence*, Cambridge, 2000.

Yarza 1994. J. Yarza, 'El retrato medieval: la presencia del donante', in *El retrato en el Museo del Prado*, Madrid, 1994, pp. 67–98.

Young 1975. E. Young, *Bartolomé Bermejo, the Great Hispano-Flemish Painter*, London, 1975.

Yriarte 1867. Ch. Yriarte, *Goya. Sa biographie, les fresques, les toiles, les tapisseries, les eaux-fortes et le catalogue de l'œuvre*, Paris, 1867.

Zalama 1988. M. A. Zalama Rodríguez, 'El retablo mayor de la iglesia de Santa Eulalia en Paredes de Nava (Palencia)', *Boletín del Seminario de Arte y Arqueología de la Universidad de Valladolid*, LIV, 1988, pp. 361–75.

Zamora Vicente (ed.) 1976. A. Zamora Vicente (ed.), *La novela picaresca española*, Barcelona, 1976.

Zappella 1988. G. Zappella, *Il ritratto nel libro italiano del Cinquecento*, Milan, 1988.

Zarco 1931. Zarco Cuevas, *Pintores españoles en San Lorenzo el Real de El Escorial*, Madrid, 1931.

Zayas 1662. A. de Zayas, *Vida y virtudes del venerable siervo de Dios... el doctor Martín de Zayas, natural de la ciudad de Toledo*, Madrid, 1662.

Zervos 1932–1978. Ch. Zervos, *Pablo Picasso*, 33 vols, Paris, 1932–1978.

***Zurbarán* (Madrid) 1988.** *Zurbarán*, exh. cat., J. M. Serrera (ed.), Madrid, 1988.

***Zurbarán* (Paris) 1988.** *Zurbarán*, exh. cat., J. Baticle (ed.), Paris, 1988.

***Zurbarán, Cuarto centenario* 1998.** *Zurbarán, Cuarto centenario*, exh. cat., Enrique Valdieso (ed.), Seville, 1998.

Index of Illustrations

PHOTOGRAPHIC CREDITS

Barcelona, Arxiu Fotogràfic de Museus, Ajuntament de Barcelona: CAT. 77, 84 ■ Barcelona, Gassull fotografia: CAT. 75 ■ Barcelona, Ramon Manent: FIG. 33 ■ Barcelona, Museu Nacional d'Art de Catalunya (Calveras, Mérida, Sagristà): FIG. 28, 30, 32, 125 ■ Berlin, Bildarchiv Preussicher Kulturbesitz (Jörg P. Anders): CAT. 22 ■ Bilbao, Museo de Bellas Artes de Bilbao: CAT. 80; FIG. 42, 48, 83 ■ Boston, Museum of Fine Arts: CAT. 19, 30 ■ Buenos Aires, César Calderella: FIG. 124 ■ Bordeaux, Musée des Beaux-Arts (Lysiane Gauthier): FIG. 86 ■ Burgos, Museo de Burgos: FIG. 81 ■ Chicago, The Art Institute of Chicago: CAT. 85; FIG. 131 ■ Copenhagen, Hans Petersen: FIG. 54, 89 ■ Dallas, SMU, Meadows Museum: FIG. 70 ■ Dublin, National Gallery of Ireland: FIG. 102, 110 ■ Figueras, Fundación Gala y Salvador Dalí: FIG. 134 ■ Florence, Serge Domingie and Marco Rabatti: FIG. 51 ■ Florence, Scala: FIG. 37, 53 ■ Fort Worth, Kimbell Art Museum (Michael Bodycomb): CAT. 27; FIG. 65 ■ Glasgow, Glasgow Museums, Pollok House: FIG. 56 ■ Kansas City, The Nelson-Atkins Museum of Art: FIG. 58 ■ Lexington, University of Kentucky Art Museum: FIG. 67 ■ London, The Bridgeman Art Library: FIG. 69 ■ London, English Heritage Photo Library (Nigel Corrie): CAT. 36 ■ London, The National Gallery: CAT. 28, 41; FIG. 1, 36, 66, 74 ■ London, The Wallace Collection: FIG. 77 ■ Los Angeles, The J. Paul Getty Museum: FIG. 35 ■ Madrid, Biblioteca Nacional: FIG. 15, 90–94 ■ Madrid, Colección Banco de España: CAT. 52, 106 ■ Madrid, Carmen Thyssen-Bornemisza Collection, on deposit in the Museo Thyssen-Bornemisza: FIG. 126 ■ Madrid, courtesy of Christie's: FIG. 82 ■ Madrid, courtesy of José Luis Díez: FIG. 113, 115, 117, 118 ■ Madrid, Joaquín Cortés: FIG. 116 ■ Madrid, Fundación Lázaro Galdiano: FIG. 12, 14, 114 ■ Madrid, Cuauhtli Gutiérrez: CAT. 10, 55, 61; FIG. 80, 104 ■ Madrid, Instituto de Valencia de Don Juan: CAT. 39 ■ Madrid, José de la Mano Galería de Arte: FIG. 109 ■ Madrid, Museo Nacional Centro de Arte Reina Sofía: CAT. 76; FIG. 128, 133, 135 ■ Madrid, Museo Nacional del Prado (J. Baztán and A. Otero): CAT. 1, 7–9, 11–13, 15, 16, 18, 21, 26, 29, 31, 33–35, 37, 40, 43, 46–51, 57, 58, 63–65, 67–74; FIG. 4, 5, 7, 8, 19–21, 23, 26, 27, 34, 38, 40, 41, 43–47, 49, 50, 52, 59, 68, 75, 84, 87, 88, 96–101, 105, 107, 112, 120 ■ Madrid, Museo Thyssen-Bornemisza: CAT. 3 ■ Madrid, Oronoz: FIG. 85 ■ Madrid, Patrimonio Nacional: CAT. 6; FIG. 25, 71, 95, 119 ■ Madrid, courtesy of Javier Portús: FIG. 3 ■ Madrid, Real Academia de Bellas Artes de San Fernando: CAT. 23, 59; FIG. 103, 108 ■ Madrid, Gonzalo de la Serna: CAT. 78; FIG. 122, 123 ■ Madrid, courtesy of Sotheby's: FIG. 6 ■ Milan, Museo Poldi Pezzoli: CAT. 24 ■ Minneapolis, The Minneapolis Institute of Arts: CAT. 66 ■ New York, The Frick Collection: FIG. 55, 64 ■ New York, The Hispanic Society of America: CAT. 38, 62; FIG. 79 ■ New York, The Metropolitan Museum of Art: CAT. 53, 60, 83; FIG. 60, 63, 76, 111 ■ New York, The Museum of Modern Art/ Scala, Florence: FIG. 129, 130 ■ Palencia, Javier Marín: CAT. 2 ■ Paris, Réunion des Musées Nationaux: CAT. 81; Hervé Lewandowski: CAT. 56, 79; FIG. 62; B. Hatala: CAT. 82; J. G. Berizzi: CAT. 86; R. G. Ojeda: FIG. 57; Gérard Blot: FIG. 72 ■ Parma, Fondazione Magnani-Rocca: CAT. 45 ■ Rome, Galleria Doria Pamphilj: FIG. 9 ■ Rouen, Catherine Lancien: CAT. 32 ■ Santander, Colección Santander Central Hispano: FIG. 127 ■ Santo Domingo de la Calzada, Domingo Contreras: FIG. 22 ■ Sarasota, The Ringling Museum of Art: FIG. 73 ■ Schloss Rohrau, Graf Harrach'sche Familiensammlung: FIG. 11, 24 ■ Seville, Luis Arenas: CAT. 4, 5, 42 ■ Seville, Pedro Feria: CAT. 17 ■ Seville, Fundación Casa Ducal de Medinaceli: CAT. 25 ■ Sitges, Consorci del Patrimoni de Sitges: FIG. 121 ■ Tokyo, courtesy of Fuji Television Gallery: CAT. 87 ■ Toledo, Antonio Pareja: FIG. 31 ■ Valencia, Francisco Alcántara: CAT. 20; FIG. 13, 78 ■ Vienna, Kunsthistorisches Museum: CAT. 14, 44, 54; FIG. 2, 39 ■ Washington, The National Gallery of Art: FIG. 16, 29

CATÁLOGUE (SPANISH EDITION)

PUBLISHER
Museo Nacional del Prado

COORDINATOR
Raquel González Escribano

EDITING AND PRODUCTION
Ediciones El Viso
Santiago Saavedra
Lola Gómez de Aranda
Isla Aguilar
Ignacio Fernández del Amo

DESIGN
Francisco J. Rocha

BIBLIOGRAPHY AND INDEX OF ILLUSTRATIONS
Isabel Morán García

TYPESETTING
Cromotex

COLOUR ORIGINATION
Lucam

PRINTING
Brizzolis

BINDING
Ramos

EXHIBITION

CURATOR
Javier Portús

COORDINATOR
Lucía Villarreal Gato

DESIGN AND INSTALLATION MANAGEMENT
Jesús Moreno & Asociados

INSTALLATION
Empty S.L.

INSURANCE
STAI
Garantía del Estado

TRANSPORT
SIT Transportes Internacionales, S.A.